W9-AOM-164

ALSO BY WRIGHT MORRIS

Novels

Plains Song (1980)
The Fork River Space Project (1977)
A Life (1973)
War Games (1972)
Fire Sermon (1971)
In Orbit (1967)
One Day (1965)
Cause for Wonder (1963)
What a Way to Go (1962)
Ceremony in Lone Tree (1960)
Love Among the Cannibals (1957)
The Field of Vision (1956)
The Huge Season (1954)
The Deep Sleep (1953)
The Works of Love (1952)
Man and Boy (1951)
The World in the Attic (1949)
The Man Who Was There (1945)
My Uncle Dudley (1942)

Photo-Text

Photographs & Words (1982)
Love Affair: A Venetian Journal (1972)
God's Country and My People (1968)
The Home Place (1948)
The Inhabitants (1946)

Essays

Earthly Delights, Unearthly Adornments (1978)
About Fiction (1975)
A Bill of Rites, A Bill of Wrongs, A Bill of Goods (1968)
The Territory Ahead (1958)

Anthology

Wright Morris: A Reader (1970)

Short Stories

Collected Stories 1948–1986 (1986)
Real Losses, Imaginary Gains (1976)
The Cat's Meow (1975)
Here Is Einbaum (1973)
Green Grass, Blue Sky, White House (1970)

Memoirs

A Cloak of Light: Writing My Life (1985)
Solo (1983)
Will's Boy (1981)

writing MY

WRITING LIFE MY li

gmy LIFE MY li

riting W

my LIF

W

Writing

MY

Life

W

Writingmylife

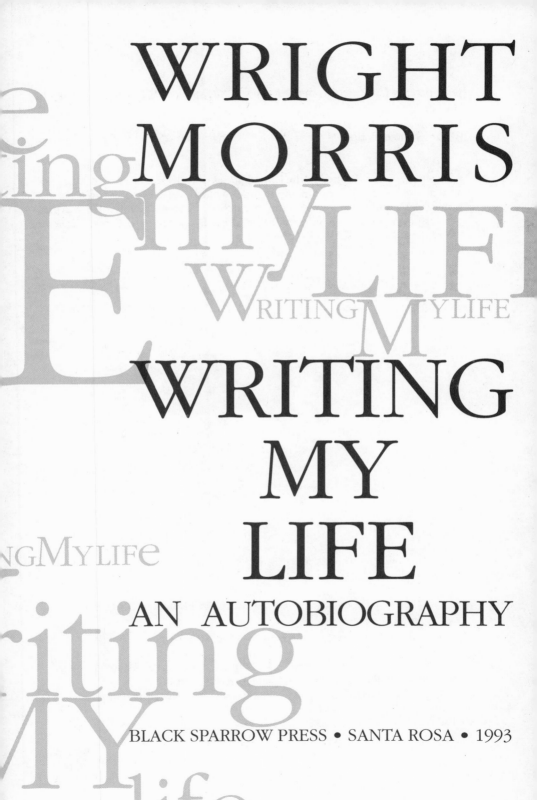

WRIGHT MORRIS

WRITING MY LIFE

AN AUTOBIOGRAPHY

BLACK SPARROW PRESS • SANTA ROSA • 1993

WRITING MY LIFE: AN AUTOBIOGRAPHY. Copyright © 1981, 1983 and 1985 by Wright Morris.

Author's introduction "To the Reader" Copyright © 1993 by Wright Morris.

All rights reserved. Printed in the United States of America. No part of this book may be used or reproduced in any manner whatsoever without written permission from the publisher except in the case of brief quotations embodied in critical articles and reviews. For information address Black Sparrow Press, 24 Tenth Street, Santa Rosa, CA 95401.

Black Sparrow Press books are printed on acid-free paper.

LIBRARY OF CONGRESS CATALOGING-IN-PUBLICATION DATA
Morris, Wright, 1910–
    Writing my life : an autobiography / Wright Morris.
       p.   cm.
    ISBN 0-87685-909-0 (cloth) : $25.00. — ISBN 0-87685-908-2 (paper) : $15.00. — ISBN 0-87685-910-4 (signed cloth) : $35.00
    1. Morris, Wright, 1910–   —Biography. 2. Novelists, American—20th century—Biography. I. Title.
PS3525.07475Z478   1993
813'.52—dc20
[B]   93-13802
                                             CIP

THIRTY YEARS INTO MY NEW LIFE, BY THEN A settled part of my old one, the poet Vaclav Havel, President of Czechoslovakia, speaking to the assembled members of the American Congress, let it drop—almost casually, not to fluster his listeners—*that consciousness preceded being.*

These few words alerted me, in my eightieth year, as to why I had stopped *Writing My Life* prematurely. Both my early buried life, and my late one, resisted the intrusion of consciousness. However it suited the characters in my novels, why should the author, so late in life, risk this awakening? In his personal life, for one thing, he lacked the novelist's authority. That once imagined pond in *Will's Boy,* on which the raindrops were falling that lapped and overlapped as they expanded, was surely the appropriate image of a consciousness still in the process of becoming. If I had once thought of revising *Will's Boy*—for the easy way he accommodated intractable losses—I could now start paying on the arrears, of both gains and losses, that would prove to be inexhaustible.

Wright Morris
Mill Valley, 1992

TABLE OF CONTENTS

WRITING MY LIFE

An Autobiography

WILL'S BOY

A Memoir

For Buz Wyeth

To the Reader:

Few things are so wondrous as our assurance that we are each at the center of a cosmos. Nor does learning we are not long disturb us. In the early thralldom of this feeling we accumulate the indelible impressions we will ceaselessly ponder but never question, pebbles that we fondle in the mind's secret pockets. One center and one only lies within us, as clearly perceived in a dream of Joseph, told by Thomas Mann.

For lo, the world hath many centers, one for each created being, and about each one it lieth in its own circle.

Since first reading those words my mind has sought an image that is commensurate with my wonder. One I find congenial is that of a vast tranquil pond on which a light rain is falling. Each drop that falls is the center of a circle that is soon overlapped by other circles. The apparent obliteration of the circle does not eliminate the radiating vibrations. This image of endlessly renewed and expanding circles is my own ponderable cosmos.

The first of my childhood impressions is that of lampglow and shadows on a low ceiling. But under my steadfast gaze it dissolves like tissue. It resists both fixing and enlargement. What I am left with is the ache of a nameless longing. On my child's soul lampglow and shadows have left radiating circles that a lifetime drizzle, of lapping and overlapping, have not washed away.

I WAS BORN ON THE SIXTH OF JANUARY, 1910, IN the Platte Valley of Nebraska, just south of the 41st parallel, just west of the 98th meridian, just to the north, or south, or a bit to the east of where it sometimes rained, but more than likely it didn't, less than a mile from what had once been the Lone Tree station of the Pony Express on the Overland Trail

My father had come west from Ohio to begin a new life with the Union Pacific Railroad in Chapman, Nebraska. My mother had been born on the bluffs south of the Platte in a house with the cupola facing the view to the west. They met in the barber shop of Eddie Cahow, who had come up from Texas on the Chisholm Trail, but found that he preferred barbering to a life in the saddle. The open range had been closed by strips of barbed wire, and the plow, for both better and worse, had replaced the six-shooter and the man on horseback, a change predicted when the town called Lone Tree at its founding was changed to Central City before I was born. Early settlers felt, and with reason, that a Lone Tree might encourage maverick, wandering males, but discourage most marriageable females. My childhood impressions were not of the big sky, and the endless vistas, but of the blaze of light where the trees ended, the sheltered grove from where I peered at the wagons of the gypsies camped at its edge.

Six days after my birth my mother died. Having stated this bald fact, I ponder its meaning. In the wings of my mind I hear voices, I am attentive to the presence of invisible relations, I see the ghosts of people without faces. Almost twenty years will pass before I set knowing eyes on my mother's people. Her father, a farmer and preacher of the Seventh-Day Adventist gospel, shortly after her death would gather up his family and move to a new Adventist settlement near Boise, Idaho. My life begins, and will have its ending, in this abiding chronicle of real losses and imaginary gains.

My father, William Henry Morris, born on a farm near Zanesville, Ohio, was one of fourteen children, all of whom grew to maturity. In the early 1890s, with his older brother, Harry, he came west to the treeless plains of Nebraska. To my knowledge no one ever referred to my father as Bill. Both friends and relations called him Will. The housekeeper, Anna, brought up from Aurora to take care of a house, a widower, and a motherless child, pronounced this word as in

15

whippoorwilllll, the sound tailing off like the bird's song, greatly enhancing my impression of the man who often took his meals with his hat on. He was a busy father; the bicycle he rode to and from his work often lay on its side, the front wheel still spinning.

On weekends in Chapman, the farmers parked their buggies at the hitch bar in front of Cahow's barber shop. This provided free bleacher seat views, for those in the buggies, of the man being clipped or shaved in the chair. If the chair was pumped up, and the occupant erect rather than horizontal, he was able to exchange glances with those peering over the half curtain. In this manner, according to Eddie Cahow, my father first set eyes on my mother, leaping from the chair, the cloth dangling from his collar, to help her down from the buggy. That is the story, and who am I to change it? She was the youngest, and most favored, of the four Osborn girls. Her name was Grace. Her sisters, Winona, Violet and Marion. Grace Osborn and Will Morris were soon married, and used his recently acquired railroad pass to spend their honeymoon in San Francisco, from where he wired the bank to send him another fifty dollars. A son, Fayette Mitchell, born in 1904, lived for only a few days. Six years will pass before I am born, and a few days later Grace Osborn Morris is dead, having given her life that I might live.

On her death a debate arose as to who should raise me, my father or my mother's married sister, Violet. More than sixty years later my Aunt Winona wrote me:

> When your mother died my sister Violet wanted to take you, but your father would not consent to it. He said, "He is all I have left of Grace." O dear boy, you were the center of so much suffering, so many losses you will never realize, know or feel . . .

This decision would be crucial to the child who played no part in it. Much of my life would be spent in an effort to recover the losses I never knew, realized or felt, the past that shaped, yet continued to elude me. Had Grace Osborn lived, my compass would have been set on a different course, and my sails full of more than the winds of fiction. Am I to register that as a child's loss, or a man's gain?

The small creatures of this world, and not a few of the large ones, are only at their ease under something. The cat crawls under the culvert, the infant under the table, screened off by the cloth that hangs like a curtain . . . in the Platte Valley of Nebraska, street culverts, piano boxes, the seats of wagons and buggies, railroad trestles, low bridges, the dark caves under front porches were all favored places of

16

concealment. With Br'er Fox I shared the instinct to lie low. Seated in dust as fine as talcum, my lap and hands overlaid with a pattern of shadows, I peered out at the world through the holes between the slats. (Earthly Delights, Unearthly Adornments, 1978)

In a room of lampglow, where the shadows waver on a low ceiling, I lie full of longing at the side of a woman whose bosom heaves, but she is faceless. Would this be my father's second wife, in a marriage soon ended? Not knowing the nature of the longing I felt, would it persist and reappear as a poignant yearning for what it is in the past that eludes me?

I have another memory of lampglow and shadow. A figure looms above me, swaying like smoke, and against the flickering lamplight I see her fingers unbraid her hair. I hear the lisp of the comb, and the rasp of the brush. This will prove to be Anna, a friend of my mother's sisters, who has been hired to take care of me. Heavily, her arms resting on the bed, she kneels to pray. Her hushed whispering voice fills me with awe. To test the height of the wick's flame she stretches one of her gray hairs across the top of the chimney. Did I see it glow, like the filament of a light bulb, or is that something I have imagined, a luminous fiber in my mind, rather than the lamp? My child's soul is enlarged by this nightly ceremony of light and shadow, and the voice of prayer. It is appropriate to this emotion that the details are vague. Later, gripping her hand in the church pew, I feel the throb of her voice before I hear it, and share her passion with fear and trembling.

One reason I see it all so clearly is that I have so often put it into writing. Perhaps it is the writing I remember, the vibrant image I have made of the memory impression. A memory for just such details is thought to be characteristic of the writer, but the fiction is already at work in what he remembers. No deception is intended, but he wants to see clearly what is invariably, intrinsically vague. So he imagines. Image-making is indivisibly a part of remembering. (Earthly Delights, Unearthly Adornments)

In this same house, in my sleepers with the "feet," I hurry to stand on the hot-air floor radiator while I am dressed. In the kitchen my eyes are below the level of the table where raw sugar cookies are being rolled for baking. I reach and clutch some of the dough: I love its sweet, raw taste.

In the large room at the front, where I lie with pneumonia, the

17

panels of colored glass in the window make a bright pattern on the bedclothes. With my warm breath, and the sleeve of my elbow, I rub a hole in the frosted window and peer out. The world is white. I am able to see the white birches in the yard against the black, twisted buggy lanes in the road. Gifts are placed on the bed. The flames of candles glitter on the Christmas tree tinsel. A huge bearlike man, with a booming voice, comes in with the winter trapped in his coat. He is Dr. Brown. I am puzzled why the fur of his coat is on the inside. For reasons that are not clear he comes to see me only when I am sick.

If I attempt to distinguish between fiction and memory, and press my nose to memory's glass to see more clearly, the remembered image grows more illusive, like the details in a Pointillist painting. I recognize it, more than I see it. This recognition is a fabric of emotion as immaterial as music. In this defect of memory do we have the emergence of imagination? . . . Precisely where memory is frail and emotion is strong, imagination takes fire. (Earthly Delights, Unearthly Adornments)

Mr. and Mrs. Riddlemosher live in the house on the corner, facing the railroad tracks. It sits flat on the ground. Spears of grass grow between the loose boards on the front porch. In the barrel under the rain spout bugs skitter on the water and polliwogs cast shadows on the slimy bottom. The white hairs of a mare's tail, put into the barrel, will turn to garter snakes.

I sit on the side porch of the house building an airplane with rubber bands and matches. Mrs. Riddlemosher, wearing a sunbonnet, picks gooseberries in her garden. The tinfoil I collect from gum and candy wrappers I sell to Mr. Riddlemosher for seven cents a pound. In the summer dusk, from the dark of the alley, I watch my father in the porch off the kitchen crumble cornbread into a tall glass, pour Carnation milk from a can on it, and squish it up and down with the handle of his spoon before he eats it.

I see my father, against the wind-rocked streetlight, standing in his underwear at the open front window. Bells are ringing, whistles are blowing. My father scratches himself as he listens. Thinking it must be the end of the world, I wait for it to end.

I am given a drum for Christmas, and I am aware as I beat it of the power that it gives me to annoy others.

At school I sit in a circle of chairs with my classmates. When my turn comes I go to the blackboard and spell out a word that is my name. I write this word on a piece of lined paper and bring it home—a gift of myself to Anna, who is full of praise. Although largely unobserved, I instinctively take shelter beneath a buggy, a culvert, a porch or a table, from where I peer out.

When did I thieve and strike a box of kitchen matches, sucking the charcoal tips for the flavor of the sulphur? I hear the abrasive scratch of the match, but it does not light up the darkness around me.

Gerald Cole and Dean Cole are my friends. Dean Cole is small and thin-faced, like a witch, but Gerald Cole is big and round-faced, like a pumpkin, or Happy Hooligan without a can on his head. We run shrieking across the pasture to where the airplane that has done the loop-the-loops limps along like a crippled bird.

So much for my impressions of my friends—what of theirs of me? Was I a sniveler, a tattletale, a crybaby? A snot-nosed little fart, or a slack-jawed snorfler? In all my childhood no mirror or window returns a reflection I remember.

Is it a fact that Gerald Cole, with my collaboration, dipped my head into a barrel of soft roofing tar, then clipped the curls from my head with his father's sheep shears? That is written somewhere. Is it the writing I remember? Sixty-five years later, in a photograph of children gathered in the open for their picture, I recognize myself as the plump-faced open-mouthed child with the adenoids in the first row. My scalp gleams where my hair is parted. On my right, surely, is the witch-faced, apprehensive Dean Cole, wetting his pants. On my left, a bow in her hair, the girl who hid the eggs in our yard at Easter. Not a child in this assembly smiles at the birdie. We are sober, worried expectant and fearful. Such incidents as I remember are uniformly free of the impression, if any, I made on my companions. I am a camera, but who it is who clicks the shutter I do not know.

The long, long thoughts of childhood approximate dreaming in the way they hover between waking and sleeping. The voice the child attends to is the one that speaks without the need of an answer—the voice of fire, of thunder, of wind, rain and silence.

If I had had faculties of a different order—what my father would have called the brains I was born with—the changing pitch of the mail train's whistle as it approached from the west, then receded, would have given my dreaming mind something to ponder, but I preferred the shimmering fragment of suspended time that I saw through the porch slats where the train had just been, but was no more.

Neither the bitter cold of winter, nor the heat of summer, nor rolling balls of fire caused by lightning, nor straw driven through the planks of a barn left on me the indelible impression of a fuzzless caterpillar, green as quicklime and spotted with bull's-eyes, seen in the fresh manure in the dark of the stable. Nor did my father's horse, his tail sweeping the buckboard, lead me to marvel as I did at the time seen on my new dollar watch. The even tenor of this time was occasionally broken by the spring Chautauqua, in the weeds behind the water tower, or the Hagenbeck and Wallace circus, the train pulled on the siding beyond the cattle loader where the caged animals howled at the edge of darkness. Found weeping at the carnival, where I had lost fifteen cents in the sawdust, the voice that comforted me said, "You're Will's boy, aren't you?" And so I proved to be.

My memory of the caterpillar is still green as money, but I see nothing whatsoever of the food on my plate, if my feet are shod or bare, if my face is freckled, is my nose is runny, if I wear knee-length britches or bulging rompers, or if the glass ball on the doily on the sewing machine snows like a winter blizzard when it is shaken.

*She would come up with her lamp, the wick swimming in oil, and cross the room like the figures in his dreams, without taking steps. Holding the lamp close to his face, she would see that he was asleep. He would feel the heat of the lamp on his forehead, catch a whiff of the oil. She would first open the damper, then turn with the lamp so that the room darkened behind her, but her snow white hair seemed to trap the light. During the day it would be piled high on her head, but when she came up with the lamp it would be in braids. With a silver handled comb that rattled when she used it, she would comb out the tangled ends of the braids. Out would come, like the burrs in a dog's tail, the knotted hairs. When all the hairs stood up straight, like a brush, she would pass the ends over the flame in the chimney, where they would curl at the tips and crackle with a frying sound. The smell was like that when she singed a chicken over a hole in the kitchen range, turning the bird slowly in the flame of a cob dipped in kerosene. (*The Field of Vision, *1956)*

On Hallowe'en, big, rough, loud-mouthed boys came out of hiding and carted privies into the square on flat farm wagons. On the one with the cushioned seats I read the words NO MAN'S LAND, the wickedness of which did not escape me.

I sang and whistled "Over There" and "It's a Long Way to Tipperary" without concern as to where it was.

A movie, *The Beast of Berlin,* was shown at Donaldson's theater, to which I gained admission by distributing leaflets. When the Kaiser Devil appeared on the silver screen we pelted him with tomatoes and rotten eggs.

In the lot beside the tracks, where the cow was pastured, boxes and cartons were piled as high as the telephone wires, on top of which

20

a scarecrow figure with a funnel hat was thrown to be burned. In this way the Kaiser Devil was burned in effigy. When the fire cooled, Gerald Cole and I retrieved the blackened funnel and returned it to his mother.

I was cautioned not to bother my father at his work in the station, or risk being killed by crossing the tracks. In the long summer dusk, if I looked to the east, I might see the smoking fires of hoboes behind the piles of track ties, or the covered wagons of the gypsies near the switch tower, their hobbled horses munching the ditch grass. To the west, if the lights were on, I would see my father's pale face, green in the shadow cast by his visor. If the window stood open I might hear the cricket chirp of the telegraph key. The light would glitter on the metal strips for sealing freight cars, hanging like keys from a loop of wire, or the polished knobs of the rubber stamps that had to be stamped to be read. If I waited long enough I would see the semaphore, west of the cattle loader, switch from red to green.

The summer I was old enough to roller skate, a short stretch of concrete paving was put into the street just behind the depot. What shift in continental gravity dictated that when this piece of paving was extended it would go to the east, not to the west? I reflected this same shift in allegiance in my preference, on the station platform, for the wide diner windows of the eastbound trains when they stopped for water. From the platform I observed the white-jacketed, black-faced porters pour water into the gleaming crystal glasses. I exchanged glances with smiling faces. I cared little about where these people were from, but I was captivated by where they were going. On the map on the wall in the station lobby all of the railroad lines converged on Chicago, the home of Montgomery Ward and Sears and Roebuck. It did not interest me that some lines continued to other places. Chicago was where the trains went and the roads ended. I do not recall hearing my father speak of a place called New York.

Once it had entered town from the east, the Lincoln Highway made a dog-leg turn at the "square," an open space where five streets converged, in order that the main street would exit parallel to the Union Pacific Railroad as it followed the curve of the Platte Valley. This confusion of streets impinging on the square left me both perplexed and enlarged. I was living not in one town only, but two towns, each of which had its own railroad. The Burlington, that came up from Aurora one day, and went down to it several days later, had a locomotive with a funnel-shaped smokestack and a cowcatcher that actually caught cows. On the brick station platform where it came to a stop the pistons hissed warm steam on my bare feet and legs. Down this track to the south, on a rusty spur, was the sandpit rumored to be bottomless with sinks of quicksand at its edges. From the raft on its surface I could peer into its depths, or gaze at the shimmering foreshortened image of myself. On one occasion, with Anna, I had traveled to Aurora with butterflies that flew in and out of the coach windows. Where these tracks crossed the Union Pacific a switch tower had been erected, square as a blockhouse, with the windows at the top so wide I could watch the man in the tower seize and grapple with the switch levers. If there were freight cars on the spur to the cattle loader I might climb to the top of the cars to munch my nut Hershey, or chew the whips of licorice and spit juice on the rails. I was never long free—once I was conscious of it—of my impression of time as a liquid in which all things were suspended, a space measured by the flights of sparrows and pigeons.

One Sunday I am driven, by horse and buggy, past the cemetery where my mother lies buried. A man with a scythe cut the grass between the stones. I was saddened but comforted by the thought that my mother, in heaven, had her eyes on me.

In a room flooded with light I lie on a table and have my adenoids out. Afterward, to quench my thirst, I am given bottles of grape juice and put in the rear of the buggy where I can whoop it up. After whooping it up, I can drink more of it. Down the road the sun smokes, the sky blazes with light that spreads on the plain, splashing on objects. It shames me to know that my mother's eyes are on me, my own burning with tears.

Through the vines was Bickel's General Store and a brown dog drinking at the fountain. Sparrows dropped from the trees to the wires and then from the wires to the ditch grass. A pigeon dropped from the belfry to the roof of the barn. He went along the tin roof to the hole, dropped inside. Jewel's Tea Wagon passed and the dust came up and went by. More sparrows dropped from the wires, stirred the grass near the road. Mrs. Riddlemosher stopped picking currants and turned with her pan. Mrs. Willard came and stood at the screen. Behind the feed store Mr. Cole's mare whinnied and Mr. Bickel smoothed his apron, stopped shooing flies. Tipping her sunbonnet back, Mrs. Riddlemosher looked toward the square where the dust came marching down the road with the rain. (The Inhabitants, 1946)

Clearly, from a low point of elevation, I see the street, with its crisp afternoon shadows, the corner where the main street dog-legs to the left, the barber shop and its pole, the blazing window of the hardware store, the fringe-topped buggy held up at the crossing gates

22

until the eastbound flier thunders past. Few images, after more than sixty years, are more indelible. What explains it? I was seated in Dr. Brown's office on a high wire-handled potty, waiting for the final verdict in my long battle with a tapeworm.

An hour or so before, on Dr. Brown's orders, I drank a glass of amber liquid guaranteed to finish off whatever ailed me. It looked and tasted like tobacco juice. I would sit on the potty until the verdict was rendered. Time passes, and this serene tableau, like those I observed through the side slats of the porch, will join the select views that grow brighter rather than dimmer. The train that rumbles past does so in silence. A cloud of dust sparkles over the empty crossing. I hear the subdued voice of Anna as she speaks to Dr. Brown, as if muttering a prayer. Unaccountably, he chuckles. He has never had a tapeworm, or sat for hours on a potty at an open window.

That winter we had a blizzard that left the snow drifted as high as the second-floor windows, darkening the house. I could open a window, push through my sled, and glide through the bushlike trees of the neighbor's orchard. A small mound of dirty snow, hard as a salt cake, was still in the yard in June.

One night I woke to see the flare of lights in the yard and hear the cough of a gasoline motor. An automobile was in the yard, the motor still running, because my father didn't know how to turn it off. He had bought it in Columbus, on his way back from Omaha, and driven it to Central City in second gear rather than shift. With him he had a young woman, dark hair framing her face, her teeth white between her smiling red lips. I could smell her perfume. My father said, "Son, come and kiss your new mother!" and I am led forward to face her. She says, "You're not going to kiss me?" Why am I so reluctant? Her hands beckon me toward her, but I am bewildered. I stand my ground between the old and the new mother. Her name was Gertrude, and with her arrival my childhood world expands.

MY NEW MOTHER WAS NEARER TO MY AGE THAN my father's, and we got along fine. She had kid brothers like me, with whom she wrestled, but my old mother, Anna, did not like her so much. In her opinion Gertrude was old enough to take care of herself. It was agreeable to me to have two mothers, but Anna preferred to live in Aurora, with her own people, where I could come and visit her when I wanted. If my father was too busy to drive me down in his new car, I would go on the Burlington local with the butterflies in the coaches. The conductor knew me, and would see that I got off in the right town.

In 1918 my father was in his mid-thirties, a jovial good-natured man with wavy brown hair, his head on the pedestal of a high stiff collar. He liked to josh people. He was friendly, but too busy for friends. His sleeves were usually rolled. I see him crossing the tracks on a trot. I see his head wag, his teeth-clenched smile, as he turns, hearing his name called. His name is Will. I like to hear people call him Will. Level on his head he wore a rolled-brim Stetson that he might forget to take off at mealtime. Anna would say, "Will, your hat," and he would take it off. Gertrude didn't seem to mind. The men she knew not only wore hats, they smoked cigars.

It was my father's idea, once he had a new wife, to supply the Union Pacific dining car service with day-old Leghorn eggs. To do that he would first have to raise the chickens from eggs hatched in incubators. To do that he would need a farm with nothing on it but thousands of chickens. The man in charge of the Union Pacific commissary in Omaha felt that my father was the man. T. P. Luckett liked me, and I liked him. He was not the first man to rest his hand on my head, mussing up my hair, but he is the first that I remember. I liked that. It was something my father had never done.

T. P. Luckett's office was in Omaha, but he could ride the railroad free any time he wanted as far as Cheyenne, Wyoming, or Ogden, Utah. The eastbound flier stopped in Central City just to let him off. He told my father, and my father told Gertrude, there was a great future with the dining car service in fresh day-old Leghorn eggs.

Without Anna to feed and care for me, we had most of our meals in local cafés. On weekends my father would drive us to Grand Island, where we would eat in a Japanese restaurant that served black bread.

24

In a glass case at the front of the restaurant, if the proper coin was inserted, a wax hand holding a bow played a violin. I was given the coins to insert. Gerald Cole told me that the music was made by a midget violinist concealed in the box. I kept this information to myself, fearing my father would no longer supply me with coins if he knew that.

In Central City we had our meals in the café on Main Street with tables for ladies. People seated in their buggies parked at the front could peer over the half curtain at the front and watch us eat. Some of the older, bigger boys might stop and make faces. When we came out in the street they would hoot and whistle. This amused me and Gertrude, but angered my father. I had never before heard him use words I had first heard from Gertrude. She had learned them from her older brothers and her father, who was a "dirty-minded old bastard." That didn't mean she didn't like him. It wasn't at all clear to me what it was she meant. On the side of a freight car near the station I saw the name MORRIS printed under a drawing that I knew to be dirty but did not know why. The shame I felt kept me from talking about it.

Was it perhaps the local gossip that led my father to move us first to Kearney and then to Schuyler? My new mother and his pretty wife, accustomed to life in a big city, sat all day in a rented house with the green shades drawn against the heat and light. She had no lady friends. There were no radios. All she had was me to talk to, and to fight with over the flavors in the box of Whitman chocolates. I wound the Victrola for her and played her favorite record, "When You Wore a Tulip, a Bright Yellow Tulip, and I Wore a Red, Red Rose." I had some boys to play with, in the willows along the river, until we all went to eat and then to a movie. Gertrude liked mushy movies. I liked William S. Hart, Tom Mix, Hoot Gibson and Harry Carey. We both liked Charlie Chaplin. Watching Charlie Chaplin, I got the hiccups so bad I often had to leave my seat and go for a drink in the lobby.

On the Fourth of July we were living in Schuyler, where I spent all day in a piano box with three other boys smoking firecracker punk and corn silk rolled up in toilet paper. One or the other made me so sick I just lay there in the box until my father found me.

On a cold, sunless day I walked with my classmates to where a railroad coach had been parked on a siding. Inside the coach it was dark, but the shining steel blades of swords and bayonets reflected the dim light. The coach was full of war gear and weapons taken from the "enemy" on the western front. I had heard about the western front, but I did not know where it was. There were shells and shell casings, helmets with spears on the top, helmets shaped like buckets, leather puttees and belts, a pistol in a holster, a uniform with a bullet hole through the chest pocket. Some of us saw it and giggled. In a war with BB guns, my eye at a knothole in a privy, I was hit just below the eyeball by a BB that just stuck there. When it fell out it left a big freckle. I had been warned not to shoot a gun at anybody. I left the coach before the others and ran back to the station to get away from the smells and the unwelcome impressions. The station lobby was warm, there was a scale near the door, and as I weighed myself without a penny I heard the chirp of the telegraph key through the grill at the ticket window.

In Kearney and Schuyler my father first spoke to us as "you two." "What have you two been up to?" or "What would you two like to do?" We were usually of one opinion. We wanted to eat, then go to a movie. We had similar tastes in ice cream and sundaes, but I liked Black Jack gum better than Juicy Fruit or Spearmint. We both liked popcorn better than Cracker Jacks. When I came home from school we might play checkers or caroms, or she would dress me up in her clothes and we would have a party. In the mirror, standing on the bed, I saw myself wearing her shoes and hats. If we wrestled and I started to win, she would tickle me or bite.

If we met other people, my father referred to us as "they" or "them." "They don't like that"; or "I've got them to consider." In arguments we took the same side—it was *us* against *him*. I often felt sorry for Anna but in league with Gertrude, whose tastes and opinions I shared. She especially hated Schuyler. She made my father drive up clear to Columbus to eat.

Late in the fall he drove us back to Central City to a farm he had bought a mile north of town. The house had been repainted, had a pump in the kitchen, and mice in the walls we could hear scrambling at night. Behind the house were the new sheds with incubators to hatch the eggs that would soon be Leghorn chickens.

Because we were living out of town and had no place to eat, my father was able to persuade Anna to come from Aurora and take care of us. We lived in the front bedroom upstairs, with a pipe that came up from the stove in the kitchen, and if I turned down the damper it filled the rest of the house with smoke. If we didn't turn it down we almost froze. My father lived downstairs, in a room off the yard, where he could keep an eye on the incubators that had to run all night. The farm had ten acres, planted with beans for the war effort, when my father bought it. On the east, high on an embankment, the Burlington local went north on one day, and came back south on the next. We knew when it was coming back because it always whistled approaching Central City.

26

More could happen to a chicken, my father found, than could happen to an egg. While they were still pullets, too young to lay eggs, some of them acted strangely and took sick. They huddled off by themselves, their eyes lidded. In a few days most of them were dead. They began to die so fast my father had to hire help to bury them. A big pit was dug in the yard, the dead chickens thrown in, then covered with quicklime. The smell was so bad we kept the windows closed and the shades drawn at the back of the house. Before the last pullets died, my father put them into crates and sent them to his brother Harry in Norfolk, who left them uncalled for on the station platform out of fear of infecting his Plymouth Rocks.

The chickens that didn't die wandered around in the bean field until it snowed, and we could no longer see them. My father's clothes were so filthy and he smelled so bad, Anna brought us our food to our room, where we had an oil-burning heater to warm us. We huddled around it playing caroms, which was the one game Gertrude was good at. On the weekends people who had heard about the chickens would drive out in their buggies to see what was happening. It pleased my father that they couldn't see the Leghorns after it snowed. If they parked their buggies near the house Gertrude would stand at the window, thumbing her nose at them. I'd never seen a woman do that. To see it thrilled and pleased me more than it shamed me.

In the second week the bigger pullets were dead before he picked them up. It was not necessary to cut their throats or wring their necks. They were stiff, yet they seemed very light when he scooped them up on the shovel, as if dying had taken a load off of them. During the third week three experts arrived, at his expense, from Chicago, and took most of one day to tell him there was nothing to be done. Then they went off, after carefully washing their hands.

Sometimes he stopped long enough to look out at the road, and the rows of buggies, where the women and the kids sat breathing through their handkerchiefs. That was something they had picked up during the war. When the flu came along, everyone had run around trying to breathe through a handkerchief. In spite of the smell they all liked to sit where they could keep their eyes on the house, and the upstairs room where the boy and girl were in quarantine. He had more or less ordered them to stay inside. Now and then he caught sight of the boy with his head at the window, peering at him, and one evening he thought he heard, blown to him, the music of their phonograph. Something about a lover who went away and did not come back.

Nothing that he did, or paid to have done, seemed to help. The hens he shipped off to Harry died on the railroad platform. They were left in their crates and shipped back to him for burial. He was advised to keep his sick chickens to himself.

And then it stopped—for no more apparent reason than it had begun. It left him with one hundred and twenty-seven pullets still alive. He sat around waiting for them to die, but somehow they went on living, they even grew fatter, and early every morning the three young roosters crowed. It was something like the first, and the last, sound that he had ever heard. When he heard them crow he would come to the window, facing the cold morning sky, and look at the trees he had planted at the edge of the yard. They were wired to the ground, which kept them, it was said, from blowing away. (The Works of Love, 1952)

In April we opened the windows and let the fresh air into the house. The stink of the quicklime was gone. In the corners of the bean field, packed around the fence posts, you could still see the bodies of some chickens, white as snow.

Coming back from town, where we had gone to eat, and had put Anna on the train for Aurora, the way the sun blazed on the upstairs windows the house looked on fire.

"It looks on fire!" I said.

Gertrude said, "I wish to Christ it was!"

We were still in the car, parked beside the house, when my father asked us, "Where would you two like to live?"

We both said Omaha. We had often talked it over, and that was it.

On our way to Omaha a few days later, the fields on both sides of the road were green as grass. "Look at the grass!" Gertrude cried.

"It's not grass," my father said, "it's winter wheat."

I didn't know what it was, but when Gertrude laughed to learn it was winter wheat, I laughed along with her. It was us against him.

UNTIL MY FATHER FOUND A HOUSE FOR US, WE lived in a hotel near 18th and Farnam. From the fourth-floor window, my legs held by Gertrude, I peered to see the buglike people in the street. During the day, while my father was at his business, Gertrude and I sat in the lobby. Between the plants growing in wooden tubs at the front there were oak rockers facing the window. All day long streetcars passed and automobiles I didn't know the names of. My father's car, a Willys Knight touring, might be parked at the curb. I was free to walk to the corner in either direction, or sit in the car and watch the people passing. In April all the kids my age were in school, and I saw only grownups.

Most people thought Gertrude was my sister. The man who worked at the desk would ask me, "And how is your sister?" and I would say fine. Behind the desk were rows of pigeonholes for keys and mail, and to the left of the desk was the cigar case. A pad of green cloth sat on top of the case, along with a leather cup for rolling dice. If you rolled the dice and won, the glass top of the case would slide back so you could help yourself to one of the cigars. If you didn't roll the dice the girl behind the counter would reach for the cigar herself and hand it to you.

What I liked was the sound of the dice in the leather cup. It puzzled me why Gertrude had given up playing and rolling the dice to marry my father, who did not even smoke. If I was on the fourth floor and leaned over the stair rail, or listened at the gate to the elevator, I could hear the dice rattle in the cup and the sound they made spilling out on the pad. I liked the tile floor of the lobby, the swinging doors, and the men's room I could go to all by myself, now that I had pants that buttoned at the front. When my father found a house we were both disappointed: we didn't want to leave.

The house was near a big park at the end of the streetcar line, the night sky lighting up when the conductor reversed the trolley. I had a bedroom to myself, and with the window open I could hear the slam-bang as he walked through the car turning back the seats. I walked through the park to get to the school, but I played hookey most of the time to hunt for lost golf balls. Five days a week the park was empty, and I wondered why they cut the grass the way they did in parts of it, but on weekends there were clumps of men wearing

29

knickers, carrying their bags of clubs. I watched them tee off. I watched
them look for the balls in the uncut grass. The balls were easy to find
if I took off my shoes and walked around in the tall grass barefoot.
If the balls were not dented I sold them back to the players. With this
money I bought pop, candy and marbles, which I told Gertrude I had
won playing "keeps." Gertrude's family lived in Omaha, but they were
not people she liked to visit. Her older sister, Evelyn, worked at the
cigar counter at the Paxton Hotel, on 14th Street, and went to movie
matinees with me and Gertrude on Saturday afternoons. After the
movie we might go to a drugstore for a cherry Coke.

My father's place of business, on 11th Street, was a low
dilapidated frame building with an office at the front. In the large room
at the back he fed and fattened chickens, killed and plucked them,
and candled eggs. Empty egg cases filled with flats and fillers were
piled along the walls. The plank floor of the room was smeared with
chicken blood, feathers and the laying mash he fed the chickens. My
father killed chickens by clamping the birds between his knees, slicing their necks with the blade of a razor, snapping their necks, then
tossing them to flap their wings and bleed in the center of the room.
Sometimes they got up and walked around, like they were tipsy, and
had to be cut again. When they were bled, my father dipped them
into a boiler of steaming water, hung them on a hook, plucked off
their feathers. My father was so good at it he could pluck two or three
chickens a minute if he didn't stop for the pin feathers. It took me
three or four minutes a chicken, and the smell of the wet feathers didn't
help any. I preferred to candle eggs.

My father's candling room was like a dark, narrow pantry, the
only light coming from the two holes in the candler, a Karo syrup
pail with a light bulb in it. If eggs were held to the holes and given
a twist, you could see the orange yolks twirl and the dark or light
spots on them. You could also see the shrinkage at the end of the egg
and tell if it was fresh or out of cold storage. The creameries that sent
my father their eggs always tried to mix cold storage eggs in with the
fresh ones, and that was why they had to be sorted. I got so I could
tell a really bad egg by just picking it up.

My father could candle six eggs at a time, three in each hand,
and sort them into three grades of size and freshness. He could candle two cases of eggs while I candled one. On Saturday mornings, when
I came along to help him, he would pay me ten cents a case for the
eggs I candled, and five cents for each plucked chicken.

I hated picking chickens, but I liked to be with my father in the
candling room. He worked with his coat off, his Stetson hat on, his

30

sleeves turned back on his forearms, a sliver from one of the egg cases wagging at the corner of his mouth. While he candled eggs he would whistle or hum snatches of tunes. Right after breakfast he might talk to me about his plans to make a deal with all the state's creameries to send him their eggs. He planned to expand, with a store in Fremont, and maybe another one in Columbus. He planned to get his own truck so he wouldn't have to use the back seat of the Willys Knight for deliveries. If he got worked up he would pause in his candling to chip the dung off one of the eggs with his thumbnail. To candle eggs you lean your front against one of the cases and get excelsior and splinters in your vest and pants front. My father bought a pair of coveralls to avoid this, but they were hard to pull on over his pants, and even harder to pull off. They were also hot to wear in muggy summer weather. What we both disliked about candling was having to break the cracked and the not-so-good eggs into a big tin pail we sold to the bakeries. Some of these eggs were so rotten I had to hold my breath while I fished them out of the pail. A really bad egg gives off heat, which you can feel in your fingers, and might explode in your hand if you aren't careful with it. I buried these eggs in a hole I dug at the rear of the shop.

I was so reluctant to work for my father I might pretend to be sick. One reason was I would rather not work at all on Saturdays, when baseball games were played in the park, and the other reason was that his contracts were not binding. Having promised me ten cents a case, he wouldn't happen to have the change in his pocket, and would *owe* it to me. It soon got so he owed me so much neither of us liked to bring it up.

In the candling room, smelling of cracked eggs and excelsior, the scorched smell given off by the candler, my father was a ponderable presence, more than a voice, more than a father. The light flashed on, then off, his face. I heard the eggs drop into the fillers. In the intense beams of light from the candler the air was thick as water. Many things swam in it. Inside the egg the yolk twirled, there was an eye like a hatpin, there was a lumpish cloud soon to be a chicken, there was a visible shrinkage, indicating age, all revealed in the light beam. I was not well paid, but I was well schooled, and would not soon forget what I had learned.

Saturday afternoons, given my freedom, I would go over to Douglas Street and make my way from pawnshop to pawnshop, appraising and comparing the watches. The choice was wide. Silver watches, wound with a key, so large they would not squeeze into my watch pocket. Gold watches with engraved cases, the lid flipping open

31

when the stem was pressed. Watches with seven jewels, with seventeen jewels, with twenty-one jewels and five adjustments. If the lid of the case was unscrewed, one could look at the ticking movement. I had gone that far. I had asked to look at the works. The ultimate in watches, worn by conductors to determine a train's arrival and departure, might have twenty-three jewels, five adjustments and the minutes as well as the hours printed on the dials. A railroad watch. Pending a purchase, I was wearing a dollar Ingersoll.

On the north side of 14th and Douglas began the movies and girlie shows. I liked to look at the buxom ladies in black tights, but I had been cautioned that inside, in the dark, anything might happen. There were men who picked up boys. What then happened? My fear was greater than my curiosity. I tipped the scales at seventy-four pounds, and was known to bleed easily when hit.

The Moon, a movie house that featured Westerns, was both cheaper and not so dangerous. Along with Tom Mix, Bill Hart or Hoot Gibson I might see the latest installment of Pearl White, last seen trapped in the pit with the octopus.

I might watch the serial twice, then have an Eskimo Pie before I went to sit in the lobby of the Paxton and wait for Gertrude and my father. Sometimes my father might be there at the cigar counter talking with Gertrude's sister Evelyn while he waited for us. Gertrude was a very pretty girl that boys and men whistled at, but Evelyn was a woman. When she leaned over to give me gum or candy, I would smell her perfume and the Sen Sen on her breath. I had seen women like her in the movies Gertrude liked better than I did. She was dark, like Pola Negri, and smoked cubebs when she wasn't working. My father said it was the smoking that made her voice so low and hoarse.

In her apartment on Dodge Street, which I had visited with Gertrude, Evelyn had a piano draped with a shawl, lamps fringed with beaded tassels, and the smell of incense. She liked it dark, and wore a wide-brimmed hat that concealed most of her face but not her lips. If she gave me money I would carry it around in my watch pocket, reluctant to spend it.

One day in the summer I came back from the park to find the kitchen floor strewn with broken dishes and glasses, one of the side windows broken where pots and pans had been thrown into the yard. In their upstairs bedroom the bureau drawers had been emptied, some of her clothes ripped and torn, the bedsheets slashed, face powder and talcum spilled over the rugs, trash and towels stuffed in the bowl of the toilet. I didn't want to be home when my father returned, so I hid under the bleacher seats in the park. I thought the night would never end. When the last trolley went back into town, I crawled into the sandbox and slept with the lid down. In the early dawn light I took a walk through the woods on the west bluffs of the Missouri, from where I could see the sunrise on the muddy waters. To have seen the force of a woman's rage filled me with awe and pleasurable apprehension. With my father I was learning about eggs. All by myself I was learning about life.

On top of the papers, perhaps to keep them from blowing, was a heavy glass ball with a castle inside, and when he took this ball and shook it, the castle would disappear. Quite a bit the way a farmhouse on the plains would disappear in a storm. He liked to sit there, holding this ball, until the storm had passed, the sky would clear, and he would see that the fairy castle with the waving red flags was still there. (The Works of Love)

My father was not a religious man, but he accepted as a law that a sinner would one day get his comeuppance, and he got his. It might have been worse. One room upstairs and three rooms downstairs had been left untouched.

We were soon back in the Maxwell Hotel on Farnam Street, where I still knew some of the people in the lobby. When they asked me about my sister I said that she had gone to work. My father had learned quite a bit about the egg and chicken business, so we took our meals in cafés that gave us meal tickets for chickens and eggs. We had meal tickets for all parts of Omaha except downtown. In one my father called the "greasy spoon" we always ate baked heart and dressing, a specialty. I liked to eat with my father and listen to him talk to the cook behind the counter or the man seated beside him. It flattered most strangers to receive his attention. He did not look like a man who picked his own chickens and candled eggs. The coats of his Hart, Schaffner & Marx suits had received less wear than the pants. His head high on the pedestal of his stiff collar, he looked a lot taller than he proved to be when he stood up. I don't know for how long my father had been a talker, only about when it was I became a listener. That was when it was just the two of us, and I could listen to him talking to someone else more than to me. He was not a reader, so I don't know where it was he got his ear for words. It was the words he used that got him the listeners, along with the easy way he joshed them. "I see here . . ." he would say, with nothing in his hands to look at, as if he was reading what he said out of the paper. That usually caught their attention the way it did mine. He had a good vocabulary, but in the butter and egg business he didn't use it much.

In the middle of life, with his best years before him, he seemed to have a firm grip on all serious matters. . . . In the morning there was usually ice in the pail where the dung-spotted eggs were floating, and he could see his breath, as if he were smoking, in the candling room. If he seemed to spend a good deal of time every day looking at one egg and scratching another, perhaps it was the price one had to pay for being a man of caliber. One whose life was still before him, but so much of it already behind him that it seemed that several lives—if that was the word for them—had already been lived. Had already gone into the limbo, as some men said.

There were evenings that he sat at the desk in his office, the Dun & Bradstreet open before him, and there were other evenings that he spent in the candling room. He would take a seat on one of his egg cases, using a thick excelsior pad as a cushion, and the light from the candler would fall on the book he held in his hands. Dun & Bradstreet? No, this book was called A Journey to the Moon, *written by a foreigner who seemed to have been there. His son had read this book, then given it to his father to return to the library. One day he had wondered what it was that the boy liked to read. So he had opened the book and read four or five pages . . . after reading a few more pages he had seated himself on an egg case, adjusted the light. The candling room had turned cold before he closed the book, and when he stepped into the office it was dark outside.* (The Works of Love)

My father always introduced me to strangers as his "only son." I understood this to be a compliment, but I did not know why until I learned from a teacher that I was half an orphan. That was only half as good as a whole orphan, but I knew this to be a point in my favor. I made a favorable impression on the grownups in the lobby, having been raised to respect my elders. "Yes sir," I would say, or "Yes ma'am," with a bow of my head. I was a small plump-faced boy with a sunny nature (I think) and a chipped front tooth. My ears, like the handles to a pan, led me to favor caps with ear-muffs, or high crowns that I could lap at a rakish angle over one ear. In this brief period of my father's bachelorhood we were almost companionable. In a suit designed for boys a year or two older, one that required extensive alterations, I was shown off at breakfast in the Harney Cafeteria and to the ladies at the Christian Science Church on Sundays. We were Methodists in Central City, but my father felt the Christian Science ladies offered better pickings as wives and mothers. It gratified me to be described as "quite a little man," considering that I was half an orphan.

In his talk with these ladies I learned from my father that he was anxious to get me off the streets and back into school. I was not anxious, since I had all day to look at the trains and games in Brandeis' toy department or ride the escalator in Burgess & Nash. A man or woman might ask me to deliver a note, for a quarter. If the place was all right, and the hall wasn't dark, I would slide the note under the door and run. If I got cold feet, I would just keep the money. In McCrory's dime store on 16th Street I swiped a roll of tire tape I had no use for, not having a bike.

One day I saw my father driving west on Harney with a woman at his side, but he didn't see me. She was not so young as Gertrude, but dark, with a hat on. I had just assumed my father was down at his business, candling eggs and picking chickens. He had hired a man to help him who slept on a cot in the back, kept a low fire going, and made deliveries. He was not much of a chicken picker or candler, since he had lost one arm in the Spanish-American War. He could prove that by just rolling back his sleeve on the blue stump.

The day before Hallowe'en we moved from the hotel to an apartment near 32nd and Dewey, about two blocks west of Farnam School. My father walked me to the school, where I met the principal and Mrs. Partridge, the fourth-grade teacher, who was saddened to hear that I was a boy without a mother. From my appearance and behavior she thought he had raised me very well. I was put in one of the smaller seats at the front, on the right side of the room near the door and the gramophone. Right beside me was a girl named Elizabeth, and right behind me a boy named Joseph Mulligan, the first boy I had met who wore a bar pin on the wings of his collar to support his tie.

Until I entered Farnam School I had never seen a colored boy close up. I had seen colored janitors in public buildings and colored women and children on the streetcars, but in Mrs. Partridge's class James Smith often stood right beside me in the spelldowns. His big feet were bare, the bottoms pink as watermelon when it rained. He had holes in his pants and lacked buttons on his shirts. His skin was black as the underside of a stove lid. I looked as strange to him as he did to me, and in the cloakroom we often laughed at each other. He was so fun-loving and friendly I may have felt that wearing rags sort of pleased him.

Edward Dorsey sat at the back of the class in a desk high enough to get his long legs under. He was a lean, copper-colored young man with orange hair on his peanut-shaped head. He liked to chase white boys. When he caught one he swore a stream of crackling curses, then let him go. Mike Smith, no relation to James, was a boy so sooty black I feared to touch him, feeling it might rub off. He never said a word unless called on. His implacable hatred was so intense it included

35

everybody, including James Smith. I feared to pass him on the stairs or be alone with him in the cloakroom, but his contempt was so great I don't believe he ever saw me. He sat and walked alone. In the class photograph only his eyes and white shirt are visible. If there were any black girls in the class I have no memory of them.

In the morning we pledged allegiance to the flag, and exercised to the music of "The Clockstore," played on the gramophone. During the exercises, Joey Mulligan, the boy seated behind me, often became confused. He would bend at the knees when he should have stood erect, or hop up and down when he should have raised his arms. When Mrs. Partridge asked him what in the world was the trouble, he said that when I exercised, one of my ears wiggled. Watching my ear wiggle was such a distraction he became confused.

I was at first humiliated by this declaration, but I grew to take pride in it. No other boy in this class, black or white, proved to have this power. Nor had I known about it myself until the excitement and exhilaration of exercising. On Mrs. Partridge's suggestion I exchanged seats with Joey, whose ears were not affected by what he was doing. The fuzz was like a white nap on his pink cheeks and through his brushcut hairdo I could see his pink scalp. Everything about Joey Mulligan was crisp and scrubbed. His white shirts were starched, the wings of his collars pointed, the lines in his black stockings were straight up and down, the box toes of his hook-and-eye shoes were polished. My shoes were new enough, but they were scuffed, and the knees of my pants were soiled and puffed where I gripped them to hoist them on my thin legs. No one had seemed to notice that the dirt on my shirt collars came from my neck. Joey Mulligan was also bright as a whip on fractions, long division and the capitals of the states. When he waved his hand to attract attention he half rose out of his seat. To avoid scuffing up his shoes he did not play in the cinder-covered yard at recess. Nor did he stop and play marbles until he got home and changed his clothes.

It is spring in Omaha, Nebraska, and we stand in the cinder-covered school yard, facing the members of Mrs. Partridge's fifth-grade class. The class is gathered at the side of the building, at the edge of the red brick walk, between two small trees that are wired to the ground. The pupils are visibly arranged according to size and sex, but certain invisible forces have also been at work. The boys pair, the girls group, and the Negro boys stand in a choir—except for the happenstance that their faces cannot be seen. Their white shirts are as if in suspension against the dark wall. The eyes of Mike Smith are wide open and

36

like bolt holes in a stove, but those of Edward Dorsey were lidded just as the shutter snapped. So were the eyes of Mrs. Partridge, who had turned to speak to Stella Fry, as she often closed her eyes when she had to raise her voice. (The Man Who Was There, 1945)

ONE DRIZZLY DAY IN THE SPRING JOEY ASKED ME to come home with him and meet his mother. The mention of his mother flattered and impressed me. I had never been asked to meet a boy's mother. That spring in 1921 we were eye to eye, but with my short neck I felt Joey looked taller. Under my plump chin the wings of my collar curled to touch my cheeks. The fold of my pants at the knee concealed a hole in my stocking. He treated me to a Tootsie Roll at the bakery, then we walked north on 27th Street to the foot of the hill on Capitol Avenue. Smack in the middle of the hill was a building the color of milk chocolate left in the sun. Joey's mother was waiting for us in the swing on the porch.

Capitol Hill was so steep that when the asphalt got hot it sagged in ripples we could see in the streetlight. The Cadillac dealers on Farnam Street used the hill to test their cars on, winter and summer. Over the winter, people with bobsleds coasted so far to the west they got tired walking back. The Mulligan house was flat, with an upstairs and a downstairs, and room beneath the porch at the front to store scooters, sleds and stuff like that. Mrs. Mulligan was waiting for us in the swing. She sat in it sideways, gripping the chain, with one foot dangling so she could push off.

"So you're Joey's best friend," she said, and hugged me. When she stood up we were all about the same height, but not so thick. Joey had told her that I was half an orphan, and how he was willing to share his mother with me. Did that please me? I said that it did. If I wondered why the shades were drawn at the front windows, it was because Mr. Mulligan, a newspaper pressman, had to work most of the night and do his sleeping in the daytime. She led us down a dark hallway, where gas hissed, to a large kitchen with a half curtain at the window. She could stand there and look out, but neighbors could not look in. While she was making us cocoa I could hear water drip in the pan under the icebox.

Just two years before, Mrs. Mulligan told me, they had come from Salt Lake City to Omaha. In Salt Lake Joey's little brother Louie had died of smallpox in the pesthouse. I was shown a picture of Joey and Louie wearing boxing gloves, ready to fight each other. Mr. Mulligan had once boxed professionally in Minneapolis, Minnesota, where Mrs. Mulligan had first met him. "The one in the light tan shoes for me," she said, and that was him. What was it my father did? I said that he had once worked for the Union Pacific Railroad but that he was now in the produce business for himself. I needn't say any more, Mrs. Mulligan said, since she had heard from Joey that my mother was dead and that I was half an orphan. Saying this brought tears to her eyes. She drew me to her and hugged me. I had never before experienced the gain from such a terrible loss. Mrs. Mulligan said that if I so desired, Joey would be like a real brother to me, and she would be like a mother. I so desired it, but the lump in my throat blocked my speech. Joey began to cry, putting his arms around me, and Mrs. Mulligan drew us both to her. My eyes burned with tears, and I buried my face in her lap. I couldn't remember ever crying so hard, and feeling so good about it. When we had stopped sniffling Mrs. Mulligan cut me a slice of devil's food cake to take to my father, and Joey walked me back to Farnam Street without either of us speaking. I had a new brother whose box-toed shoes squeaked as he walked.

Knowing that I was half an orphan, Mrs. Mulligan wrote my father a letter that I personally delivered. If I would like to come and live with them, she wrote, she would be a real mother to me. The sum of five dollars a week, in her opinion, would care for the food I ate and such things as my laundry. No boy should grow up without a brother, and if I came to live with Joey we both would have one.

My father agreed I could live with Joey if some of our furniture went along with me. We had this parlor suite he no longer had use for, along with an Axminster rug and two hand-painted oil paintings. The parlor suite had a sofa that turned into a double daybed at night. The outside half, where I would sleep, curved one way, and the inside half, where Joey would sleep, curved the other. There was also an oak rocker with a seat so high Mrs. Mulligan's legs were too short to rock it. The Axminster rug was put into the bedroom, where it made the noise less when we crossed it in the morning. Gertrude's walnut Victrola was put in the front room corner where the afternoon sun wouldn't shine on it. Some of Gertrude's friends had almost ruined the Harry Lauder records by not troubling to change the needle. In the dim glow of the gas jet, which hissed softly all night, I could see the oil painting with the snow-capped mountains and the Indians who lived beside the lake in their wigwams. I sometimes felt I was in hiding, spying on them, the sunset sky behind the mountains as red and sticky-looking at Dentyne gum.

Around the house Mrs. Mulligan wore old stockings that kept the kitchen linoleum shiny, only putting on her shoes when she hung out the laundry. In the early morning she might sit in the porch swing

39

until the lamplighter turned off the streetlamps. Even the milkman would think she had just got up and was one of those early risers, like he was. He carried so many bottles they tinkled like glass chimes when he ran between the houses.

If Mr. Mulligan had not been asked by one of his friends to have a beer with him, which he couldn't refuse, he would come down the hill just about daylight, walking in the grass to ease his feet. If he was thirsty he might have an eggnog, or if he was tired a fresh cup of coffee, then he would come to the crack between the folding doors to see how we were sleeping. He didn't like us to sleep with our hands under the covers. He said a boy never knew what his hands might be doing while he was asleep. I usually had my hands out where he could see them, but Joey had a really crazy way of sleeping. He put his head down low, as if he was trying to hide or crawl into a hole, with his bottom up high. There was no way in the world to tell where his hands were. Mr. Mulligan would tiptoe in, not to wake him, then give him such a whack across the butt Joey would almost put his head through the end of the daybed. Lucky for him, that part of it was padded. The last sound I would hear from Mr. Mulligan he was winding his watch. He left it on the dresser, which made the tick so loud I seemed to hear it right in my pillow. If I opened my eyes and then stared hard at the Victor dog in the horn of the Victrola, it seemed to me the ticking sound we were both hearing was his Master's voice.

Until I had a place at Mrs. Mulligan's table I had known very little about food. At the greasy spoon near my father's place of business I usually ate baked heart and dressing. My favorite meal at the Harney Cafeteria on Sunday was macaroni and cheese with a piece of fresh rhubarb pie. In Salt Lake City Mr. Mulligan had run his own ice cream parlor, where he sold his own sherbet and hand-cranked ice cream. You could always tell his ice cream from the way it left wax on the roof of your mouth. On Sundays we had either chocolate or strawberry ice cream, devil's food cake, hot rolls or biscuits, roast pork or roast beef with gravy and creamy mashed potatoes, vegetables I didn't eat, and sometimes a big slice of runny lemon or butterscotch pie. Even back in Minneapolis Mr. Mulligan had always liked plenty to eat. He made his own beer in a crock in the pantry which sometimes exploded when he put it into bottles. Joey showed me the glass that sparkled like gems in the ceiling of the stairs that led down to the basement. Most of Mr. Mulligan's pay went for groceries at Bickel's, or for malt and hops at Weinstein's Delicatessen, but Mrs. Mulligan said that a man who worked nights had little else to do but eat.

40

I was catching for our team and Joey Mulligan was pitching a lopsided baseball with a lot of tire tape wound around it, when the batter tipped it and I caught it right on the jaw. It didn't hurt so much, but I couldn't talk. My jaw wouldn't move. I dropped my catcher's glove in the grass and just took off and ran. I ran about three blocks, the last block down the alley and across the yard into the Mulligan kitchen. When Mrs. Mulligan saw me, my jaw hanging slack, she gave me a hard whack across the back and it popped into place. I was sore behind the ears for about two weeks but I didn't mention it to my father. He wouldn't let me play any game he considered to be dangerous.

In the fall Mrs. Partridge bought us a new league baseball and brought it to the diamond where we were playing. "Throw it! Throw it!" we yelled when she held it up for us to see it, but she had never thrown a ball, so what she did was just roll it. That was so surprising we just looked at her, and she looked at us. Edward Dorsey grabbed the ball and rolled it toward second, and another player rolled it toward first. We ran around like crazy, rolling the ball until it was scuffed and dirty like an old one. Something else had to have happened, but I don't remember what it was, and I don't want to.

One Saturday Mr. Mulligan did not come home. At ten o'clock Mrs. Mulligan called the Omaha *Bee,* who said that he had left with his friend Mr. Ahearn. Since they sometimes stopped at Mr. Ahearn's, on 25th and Dodge Street, Joey and I went over to look for him. Right there coming down Dodge Street were two cars, with Mr. Mulligan at the wheel of the one being pushed by a Butternut Bakery wagon. They made the turn at 26th Street, then went along so slow and easy we went right along with them. Mr. Mulligan looked great. We had no idea he knew how to drive a car. Over on Capitol he didn't need to be pushed, and he was all on his own as he took it down the alley, which hadn't been paved. Joey and I went ahead of him, picking up bottles and cans, to where he could let it coast into the Mulligan yard, right up to the rear porch. There he squeezed the rubber horn on the driver's side and Mrs. Mulligan came out to look at it. It was just a Ford, not a Willys Knight or a Pierce Arrow with lights in the fenders, but there were leather straps holding down the hood, with a crank in the leather sling at the front. Why didn't he crank it? It wasn't quite ready yet to be cranked. The great thing about the car, which was seven years old, was that all it had done for six years was just sit, so that the tires, the leather cushions and the engine were just like new. We could see that. All it really needed was tuning up. Like any fine piece of machinery that had sat without running—like a good watch or Joey's bicycle—what it needed before it ran at all was to be taken apart and oiled. That would take a little doing, but Mr. Mulligan would have the help of Mrs. Mulligan's brother, visiting from Minneapolis, a man so big he slept crosswise on his bed and wore size eleven shoes. If they were just sitting there empty on the floor, we could step right into them with our own shoes on.

Mr. Lindstrom was a plumber, not a mechanic, but he knew that what you took apart had to be put back together in the same order. To make sure they didn't make a foolish mistake they put a number on every part they took off, along with the nuts and bolts, if there were any. They hung the parts in the tool shed as they came off, so all they had to do was reverse the order. After ten days, which was three days longer than he had meant to stay in the first place, Mr. Lindstrom had to get back to Minneapolis, but Mr. Mulligan still had his afternoons and weekends until the time came to pave the alley. Putting the car back together was not the same as taking it apart. He never had the piece he seemed to need when he was under the car. Once he thought he had it almost put together till he found some bolts that had to go somewhere. When the time came to fill the yard with sand he still had a dishpan full of loose parts. He could get the car to cough a little when he cranked it, but not kick back. He didn't seem to mind when the sand trucks appeared and dumped the sand all around it almost up to the hubcaps. Mrs. Mulligan thought it looked like a lawn swing, and in some respects she liked it even better. With the side curtains up, Joey and I could sleep in it.

All that sand in the yard meant that Mrs. Mulligan had to hang her washing in the kitchen, with the floor covered with newspapers to catch the drip. Somewhere in the sand pile Joey lost his St. Christopher medal and I lost two chameleons, both for good, that I had bought at the Hagenbeck and Wallace circus. They were there just plain as day one minute, then they were gone. On the good side, the sand stopped Leonard Seidel and his little bother from using the back yard as a shortcut, whooshing beneath Mr. Mulligan's window before he got up. On the good side, too, was that the sand was there when Mr. Mulligan threw Joey through the pantry window. Working nights the way he did, and sleeping days, made him subject to fits of temper. Joey would often forget just what time it was when he was fighting with me, which was pretty often, his voice being louder and hoarser than mine was. The time it happened Mr. Mulligan didn't say a word, either before or after. He came out of the bedroom silent as a ghost and got Joey cornered before he could run, gripped him by the collar and the seat of his pants and threw him right through the screen at the pantry window. It didn't hurt him any, but it tore all the buttons off his shirt.

NEXT DOOR TO THE MULLIGANS, UP THE HILL, lived Mr. and Mrs. Goodman and their twelve children, nine of them girls. Mr. Goodman, a short, broad-shouldered man with a huge head, appeared to have only stumps for legs, like a man walking on his knees. He worked in the streetcar barns and rode the streetcars free. Mrs. Goodman spoke no English, but she sat in the swing on the front porch shouting orders to her daughters in Yiddish. The oldest boy, Davy Goodman, had a full round face with big dark eyes, but very spindly legs. When I came to live on the hill he was having a feud with Joey Mulligan. From his uphill position, at the front of his house, he would shout at Joey, using the secret curses of the Yiddish language, which were pretty good. What Joey understood was bad enough, but what he didn't understand enraged him. His face flushed to purple. The veins stood out in his neck. If Davy Goodman would come down on Joey Mulligan's level, Joey would break every bone in his yellow Jewish body. Joey had as loud a voice—or louder— as anybody, but he didn't have Davy Goodman's vocabulary. I took Joey's side, standing close by with my arms crossed on my chest, my legs straddled. My jaw was set, but my ears were open. I had never heard or seen in a boy so small such fluent, venomous, wonderful curses. He also had the scathing looks and gestures. Atop the four-foot wall, as he was, neither did he look so small as he would have down on our level.

Naturally, I was Joey's loyal friend, but I was also confused by so much talent. It shamed me to admit it, but I admired Davy Goodman. In his fury he would spit, then grind his heel on it, rolling his sleeves high on his spidery arms. I could have outwrestled him in a jiffy, but if I didn't grab him he would give me a nose bleed, being quick with his fists.

Davy and his smaller sisters went to a grade school five blocks to the east, near Central High School, from where they had been sent home when the visiting nurse found lice in their hair. Mrs. Mulligan had been stunned to hear it, but not surprised. Mrs. Ahearn, who had been in the Goodman house, reported that it lacked rugs and furniture. Strong odors blew out of the kitchen. The two older Goodman girls, Esther and Ruth, fought over the boys who came to see them. On hot summer nights Esther might be seen dousing herself with the sprinkler, naked as a baby. When Kopfer called the police they came in a squad car and parked at the front of the house to watch her. In her loud, hoarse Jewish voice Esther shouted curses at them until they went away.

The windows open, the draft through the house would bring the smell of the iron, of the sprinkled clothes, of the scorched smell of the starch, to where he lay on the daybed in the living room. The creak of the ironing board would sometimes put him to sleep, sometimes keep him awake. Mrs. Mulligan liked to iron in her slip, the bottom pinned up so the draft would blow cool on her legs, her hair piled up high like a turban so it would also blow on her neck. She did not trust ironing to the laundry. His shirts were an especial problem due to the shortness of his neck, which flattened the collars and made the points curl up. Pins to support the tie did not help. Mrs. Mulligan took pride in his appearance and never let him wear a shirt more than three times, and straightened the lines in his stockings before he left the house. The paper lining was also left in his new caps. Boys who wore their caps over one ear were only fit to be with the Western Union, as they flew past him, furiously pumping, their butts wagging high on the saddles, racing off to some forbidden pleasure with waitresses. (One Day, 1965)

A pair of unalike twins, Burgess and Byron Minter, the only boys in class smaller than I was, played music on Friday afternoons, Byron the violin, Burgess the piano. In order to reach the pedals, only part of Burgess rested on the bench. They were often accompanied by Betty Zabriskie, owl-faced, moon-faced, red-lipped, with her long doughnut curls dangling down to rest on the cello. To brush against Betty Zabriskie in the cloakroom, or exchange a greeting on the stairs, stirred me in a way I had not experienced with other girls. She wore half socks, exposing the plump knees straddling her cello. I was responsive to music, as well as to Betty Zabriskie, and my experience with Gertrude stood me in good stead when I would wind the Victrola, put on the records and change the needles. "The Clockstore," my first favorite music, gave way to "Humoresque" and Liszt's Hungarian Rhapsody No. 2, selections that were featured in the Music Memory Contest. While the music played, Mrs. Partridge stood at the back of the room looking out the window, or over the floor register where the heat puffed out her skirts. I longed to give her something but scorned the apples given to her by girls. She suffered from headaches caused by chalk dust, and during recess would often lie down on the cot in the nurse's room off the annex. Her bone hairpins were often on the pillow, and the smell of her galoshes in the closet.

45

In the dead of the winter, during and after Christmas vacation, anybody with a sled came from all over to Capitol Hill. The steep grade leveled off at 27th Street, with a long clear coast to 28th. If the track was hard and icy some sledders might go around the corner to Davenport. The early sledders were usually the duffers, who packed down the snow and cleared a trail so we could walk up the hill. The best sleds were Flexible Flyer Junior Racers, which were low to the snow and tapered down at the back. With a second rider to give the sled a good push, then crouch down between the legs of the steerer, by the time you hit the level at the bottom of the hill you were flying. It hurt to breathe. Your cheeks would be numb and your eyes watered. The long walk back gave you time to recover and watch the other sledders whoosh by you. Where the ice was worn thin on the bumps the runners gave off sparks.

In January the bobsleds would come from somewhere and rumble down the hill like runaway trucks, as many as fifteen kids squeezed tight on the seat. Cross traffic would be stopped on 27th Street when the bobs came down the hill. It all ended the winter that something went wrong and the driver couldn't steer. The bob jumped the curb at the bottom and plowed through the basement wall of a house, killing three kids. One of the girls we knew was all broken up. It took us a while to get back to sledding and come in with our cheeks cracked, our lips chapped and sore, our toes itchy with frostbite, but our blood hot with the fever of excitement. The week I had a bad felon and couldn't go out and slide I thought I would die.

I gave up sledding for ice skating on the frozen pond of Turner Park. Billy Worthington, a freshman in high school, was the first boy I knew who was good at everything. He wore fur gloves that reached to his elbows and nobody could catch him when we played "I Got It." Billy Worthington had it, as well as hockey shoe skates with tube blades. Getting my skates sharpened took all of my spending money, but ice skating was the first sport I excelled in. Billy Worthington said so. "You're pretty good, kid," he said, and I really was.

In the spring and summer daylight we usually numbered five to seven, but at night under the streetlight we would double that number, including most of the girls but not Davy Goodman's sisters. We played games of pursuit, the darkness heightening the excitement, the climax full of shrieks and frenzied screaming. Racing across the back yards crossed with sagging clotheslines, we hung ourselves by the chin and set the wires to strumming. The night was full of cries, and not all of them friendly. In those houses without children what was it like?

On Hallowe'en we soaped windows, rang doorbells, threw strings of cans and pails onto porches, reversed garbage pails so the lid sat on the bottom, howled like cats, barked like dogs, put toads and mice into mailboxes. An enraged neighbor, hoarsely panting, having cunningly set a trap for me, chased me for blocks between and around houses, tripping and falling, muttering curses, until he groaned to collapse in the same empty lot where I was hiding in the weeds. I could hear him talking to himself, moaning. Did he live to remember the little fiend he chased but did not catch?

On the Fourth of July, up with the clop of the milk horse and the rattle of the bottles, Joey and I would shoot off our little hoard of firecrackers before breakfast. The long, long day would be spent walking along the curbs looking for firecrackers that had not gone off. At a risk, these still might be lit, or cracked in half and the black powder heaped in a pile and ignited. In this way I burned the fuzz off my cheeks, the lashes from my eyes, and singed my eyebrows. They would grow back. I was advised not to do it again.

In the late afternoon on a Fourth of July hazy with heat and the smoke of burning powder, Mr. Mulligan appeared at the top of the hill with his pressmate, Mr. Ahearn. They carried large paper bags from which Roman candles and skyrockets protruded. They sang as they approached, which brought Mrs. Mulligan from her ironing to stand at the screen. We were called inside; the front and the rear doors were locked. From the upstairs bathroom Joey and I had a bird's-eye view of the proceedings. Neighbors had gathered on the porches of nearby houses. They began with pinwheels, fastened to the porch posts, but not very spectacular in the daylight. The sparklers threw off sparks like a knife sharpener's grindstone, and we could hear most of the people laughing. Small as he was, foolish as he was, with his shirt off and his pants cuffs turned up, there was something about Mr. Mulligan like a big firecracker lying in the gutter that hadn't gone off. He gave the skyrockets to Mr. Ahearn, and selected the Roman candles for himself. They weren't much to see, light as it was, but nobody knew where they might come down. He shot some at the Goodmans, clearing them all off the porch, then he shot them at the second-floor windows of the house right below us. Some of the windows were open, the curtains drawn back to stir up a breeze. We couldn't see too well from our angle what happened, but we could hear the shouting and yelling. Lillian's father, Mr. Kovack, who had the day off from his Railway Express truck, ran into the yard waving his arms, until Mr. Mulligan aimed a candle at him and he took off. When he ran out of Roman candles he helped Mr. Ahearn with the skyrockets. They

47

smoked going up, then they smoked even more when they came down on somebody's roof.

When the big car with the side curtains came down the hill, we could see the two men in the front seat peering out through the windshield. They waited until Mr. Mulligan had run out of rockets, then one of the men opened the door and called to him. There was a big nightworks display out in Fontenelle Park, he said, and the mayor had sent him to ask if he and his friend would be part of it. He did it so nice, his tone so respectful, Mr. Mulligan sat down on the steps to think it over. He was pretty tired, and one of his hands was burned, but we could see that it appealed to him. Mr. Ahearn had no say in the matter and just stood waiting for him to make up his mind. So did everybody else.

It was hard for me and Joey to believe that two grown men would be taken in by the cops with a story like that, but they were. They both put back on their shirts and jackets—Mr. Mulligan wore sweaters with four front pockets—then they leaned on each other to keep from falling down when they crossed the yard. This little plainclothes cop got out of the car and made a big bow when he opened the rear door and pushed them both in. It shamed me so much to see it, it made my ears burn, and he was not even my father. When they left, Joey locked himself in the bathroom and bawled. All the neighbors, of course, laughed till they were sick, with the exception of Mrs. Kovack, who had had her curtains scorched by a Roman candle.

Mrs. Mulligan vowed she would not let him in when the cops brought him back, which they actually didn't, and the first we saw of either of them was when they came down the hill two mornings later with the milk wagon. Finding the door locked, he sat quietly in the porch swing until Mrs. Mulligan felt sorry for him and let him in.

The first thing he did, before he went to bed, was put his seven-jewel watch, with its chain, out on the dresser, where it ticked so loudly we could all hear it. The first sign of him being up and about was the sound of his shoes being polished, the cloth snapping like a whip at the end of the stroke, the smell of the wax strong in the kitchen. Until he had shaved at the kitchen window, where just his lathered face showed above the half curtain, he wore his snug whipcord pants with the straps of his braces dangling, his underwear unbuttoned to expose the crinkly hair on his chest. Nothing could have been more commonplace, but it left on the boy a lasting impression. No ordinary mortal rose so late in the day and walked around as he did, wearing harness, as if unhitched from the work he had accomplished while asleep. (One Day)

A glorious day in October, my father took Mr. Mulligan, Joey and me to the Omaha Western League ball park to see Babe Ruth and Bob Meusel, of the Yankees, on a barnstorming tour. My father had bought us box seats along the first-base line, where we were out in the open and could catch foul balls. Early in the game Babe Ruth hit one which Mr. Mulligan stood up and caught in his bare hands. Late in the game, with Bob Meusel pitching, Babe Ruth hit a home run so high it went over the flagpole in center field. Nobody saw it come down. As the Babe trotted around the bases, Mr. Mulligan slipped me the foul ball he had caught and said, "Go get him, kid!" At that point Babe Ruth was just rounding second, and in the confusion, with everybody yelling, I cut across the diamond between first base and third and caught him coming toward the plate. Maybe there were already a gang of kids behind me with the same idea. In any case, Babe Ruth wheeled around and headed for the dugout, but not before I had got a grip on the rear pocket of his pants. I suppose other kids got a grip on me, and in the tussle that followed I lost the foul ball, but I still had the pocket to his Yankee pants. A flannel pocket was of no use to Mr. Mulligan, but I used it to kneel on in wet weather, or rest my knuckles on when I played marbles. It brought me luck until I lost it. It disappeared with the cigar box full of my marbles when I hid it so well somewhere I forgot where it was.

I lived with Joey Mulligan, but I had some other friends. Douglas Fudge was my friend, older and bigger than I was, with an airgun that he let me shoot at birds with. Orville Browning, whose father was an Indian, was a wizard with magnetos, electric buzzers, and made his own crystal sets out of oatmeal cartons. The craziest friend I ever had was Shelley, whose last name I forget or maybe I never knew it.

One day I was playing pocket billiards with him on a man-size table in his grandmother's attic. Never before had I played real billiards. My game was really marbles, but on the previous day Shelley had won all of them, including my shooters. We had played in the soft dust under the porch because the yard was covered with an April snow. Snow glare had blazed at the holes between the porch slats. What marbles I didn't lose to Shelley I lost in the dust. He gave me some of them back so we could go on playing, but it wasn't the same, and he felt it.

"You're no good at marbles," he said, "let's play billiards." At the back of the lunchroom across from school hooded lamps hung over the tables, sucking up the smoke. On the wires overhead there were counters that the players pushed around with their cues.

Just above his right knee Shelley had holes in his britches where he reached down to pull up his stocking.He crouched with one knee cocked when he was shooting, holding the pocket to keep the marbles from spilling. The way his pockets bulged at his knees he looked pretty silly if he wasn't playing marbles.

In a serious discussion he would twist his cap around so the bill was at the back, like a racing driver. On his shooting hand his knuckles were always chapped and sore. He was a shark. No matter what he played, he played for keeps.

Aside from how he looked, he never wore a coat, as if he didn't have one. He would look right at me with his teeth chattering and say he wasn't cold. My opinion is he didn't feel it, which might help account for his unusual behavior. Almost anything might strike him as funny, like a person's name. When he learned what my name was he almost broke up. Without knowing whether I could play marbles or not, he was dumbfounded to learn that I could. "*You* play marbles?" he said. I thought he'd laugh himself sick. He just took it for granted that whatever game he played, he played best. His manner of laughing was to turn away and lean on his knees, like he might be sick, or walk around in a circle with his head on one side, his teeth clenched. He stood still so seldom I don't really know if he was smaller than me, or only looked it, but my impression was he was short and underfed.

Shelley slept in a flat on Dodge Street with his father, but he lived with his grandmother. Since she didn't play billiards, he had this big man-size table all to himself. We each had our own chalk, but we had to take turns with the only cue that had a tip. Owing to the fact that the attic was so narrow, we had to do all of our shooting from the two ends, lying out on the table to make the side shots. Balls that fell into the pockets were sometimes never seen again. They rolled around in the alleys under the table, or collected in one pocket until it was stuffed. Shelley's arms were so thin he could work them into the pockets until they were up tight under his armpits. Sometimes he would do that and then scream for help, as if he couldn't get them out.

On our way to the attic we would stop in the kitchen and look for something to play keeps for. In a sugar bowl his grandmother kept Necco wafers she liked to suck on while she was ironing. Gingersnaps, if they had any, were stored in a crock in the pantry. To make them soft and chewy, the way he liked them, Shelley would put one to soak on the roof of his mouth. If it soaked too long he would have to use a finger to pry it loose. It didn't surprise me much when he said, "You're no good at billiards, let's play poker."

Poker was played by men in the backs of saloons and I felt

corrupted just to hear about it. But I had to do something. If I didn't do something it would be too late.

"I'm not a cardplayer," I said. "I'm a runner."

He had gingersnap dough caked around his teeth, and his tongue worked at it as he looked at me. "You're a *what*?" he said. He had never seen me run, but my best running was done in and out of streetlights, where it was hard to see me. Just to take off and run in broad daylight was new to us both.

I did my best running at about twenty yards, but I was pretty good up to fifty if I was being chased. I guess my best short type of run was in Shelley's back yard. He was so close at my side I could see his head twisted, with his teeth clamped hard like they pained him. Right when he was just about even with me he let out a wild hoot and sprawled on his face. His grandmother came out of the house to lift him up and brush him off. She made some ice-cold lemonade for us and we sat on the stoop sucking the ice and eating cookies as if nothing special had happened. We didn't discuss the race at all, or who had won. One thing I do know is, from the looks he gave me, that he saw it all differently than I did, but I could never imagine what he might be like if he ever grew up.

Several months might pass before I saw my father, or received one of his letters enclosing a check for Mrs. Mulligan, a dollar bill for me. The check endorsed, I would offer it in payment on one of the weekly bills at Bickel's grocery.

One day Mr. Bickel returned this check to me because the bank would not cash it. The shame I felt walking home with this check may have exceeded all my previous torments. With little or no cause, I had stored up and nourished considerable pride. That my father was lowered in the Mulligan's opinion also lowered me. Joey and I were so evenly matched we each sought an advantage over the other, which he now had. The first bad check was soon followed by another. My dread of these checks was soon greater than my shame at their absence. With the bad check I would make the long trip to my father's place of business, which I often found locked. If he was there, he would write me a new check, which I feared to bring back with me. What good were they if Bickel's refused to accept them? My pride and shame led me to think that I might support myself. Davy Goodman sold newspapers on 24th and Farnam, and when Floyd Collins was trapped in the cave he made almost five dollars selling extras.

I began to sell papers on 24th and Farnam, and made as much as forty cents a night. I learned that more money was made on delivery routes, and got a route downtown, between Douglas and the post office. I liked the excitement of so many different people and the dark hallways of the boarding houses. I made as much as four or five dollars a week, and gave three and a half to Mrs. Mulligan. It hurt her pride to accept it, and gave me back some of the advantage I had lost. Making real money like that restored my self-esteem. If my father's infrequent letter enclosed a check, I tore it up. To restore my father in Mrs. Mulligan's eyes, as well as to give myself something I badly wanted, I presented myself a watch at Christmas I had bought in a pawnshop, but said my father gave me. It looked small in its wrapping, so I devised the stratagem of wrapping it in a series of boxes, each one larger, till I had a package big enough for a train set. I was so pleased with what I had done I have no idea how it impressed Mrs. Mulligan.

In the seventh grade at the Farnam School my teacher was Miss Healy, a big reddish-haired woman who wore mascara on her eyelashes. She scandalized the PTA meetings, sitting on a corner of her desk with one tapering silk-clad ankle dangling. If she spoke to me my heart pounded. She knew about men and boys. In conferences concerned with my selection to speak to the fourth grade about Honor or the sixth grade about Hookey, or the duties—soon to be mine—of a crossing guard at 29th and Farnam, I experienced emotions that dried my lips. She selected me and not Helen Tylor, who starred in the plays and recited poems, to give the speech of acceptance and thanks to the Daughters of the American Revolution on the gift of a scroll about which I have forgotten. I muffed the speech. My disgrace brought tears to my eyes. It also rewarded me with the weight of her arm around my shoulders, and a womanly glance from her mascaraed eyes. Orville Browning told dirty stories about her I wanted to believe.

How did the fight start? If there is room for speculation, it lies in how to end it. Neither the white boy nor the black boy gives it further thought. They stand, braced off, in the cinder-covered school yard, in the shadow of the darkened red brick building. Eight or ten smaller boys circle the fighters, forming sides. A small white boy observes the fight upside down as he hangs by the knees from a rail in the fence. A black girl pasting cutouts of pumpkins in the windows of the annex seems unconcerned. Fights are not so unusual. Hallowe'en and pumpkins come but once a year. ("A Fight Between a White Boy and a Black Boy in the Dusk of a Fall Afternoon in Omaha, Nebraska," 1970)

One winter day I saw my father's car parked in front of the café where he was eating. I sat in the car until he came out and found me.

He looked pretty good. He was chewing on a toothpick, the way he liked to, and started the motor just to show me how the warm air came out of a heater under the dashboard. What was he doing? What he was *doing* was trying to find a new mother for me. He did not want me living forever with a family like the Mulligans. He did not say so, but I knew he was thinking that we were superior sort of people. That pleased and puzzled me since he was not a good provider, as Mrs. Mulligan never tired of saying, and I knew he ran around with loose women even as he talked about a new mother for me.

We drove around for a while, then he parked the car near 32nd and Dewey where we could sit and talk. That was new. He had always been too busy a father, when he saw me, to give me anything but money. I had come up in his eyes, even as he had fallen in mine. He told me that he had found a real new mother for me, but working it out would still take a little time. She had her own nice home, where I would have a room in the basement, and a daughter who was crazy to have a younger brother. We would both go to the same high school, to which my father would drive us on his way to work. Never before had my father given me a five-dollar bill. I kept it in my watch pocket, afraid to spend it, fearing the person I gave it to would ask me where I got it, or say it was counterfeit. These days I was having so many adventures I looked forward to telling somebody about them, but when the time came I didn't, I don't know why.

In the lobby of the Gaiety Theatre on Harney, I saw a poster advertising a hula dancer. She had flowers in her hair and wore a hula skirt, but there was no mistaking Gertrude. Without her clothes she looked plumper than with them on. I was not too surprised to see her dancing, since she had often danced the hula for me. I would applaud and the dog, Shep, would bark.

At the Gaiety she was accompanied by two Hawaiians who played guitars. A day or two later, at the World Herald Building on 15th and Farnam, I came out of the alley with my bundle of papers to see my father standing on the corner. If I spoke to him he would give me some money, but I didn't need money. Seeing him just standing there alone on the corner, I felt a little sorry for him. His pants looked newer than the coat. His heels were so run-down you could see it when he walked away. I could have run to him and given him a paper, since I always carried two or three extras, but I just stood there looking at him as if he was some other boy's father. Did he sometimes think I might be some other father's son?

53

W HAT SORT OF THIRTEEN-YEAR-OLD BOY WAS I?
I got in the movies for six cents and looked about ten. Measured on
the door of the Mulligan pantry, I had lost a full inch to Joey in height,
but on the scale in the nurse's annex I weighed exactly what a boy
like me was supposed to weigh, 78½ pounds.

My father felt that what I needed was two or three weeks of fresh
air in the country. His brother Harry had a farm near Norfolk. In
turning down the crates of Leghorn chickens he had sent him, my father
felt that Harry might feel some obligation to him. He explained that
I was now a growing able-bodied boy, and there were many chores
I could do around a farm. I knew how to sort eggs, and I could pick
chickens. It would surely do me a world of good to get away from
the city for a vacation on a real farm.

Near the end of July Harry's wife, Clara, wrote me to say that
I could come, if I had to, but with all she had to do I would have
to pretty much look after myself. That was all right with me, since
I'd been doing that for some time. I would take the train from Omaha
to Columbus, then up from Columbus on the local with the gasoline
motor to Warnerville, where Uncle Harry would meet me. One of
the things I would learn was that Warnerville had been named after
one of my cousins by marriage, who had been born and raised in the
house that sat in the grove of trees near the tracks.

When I got off the train in the late summer twilight, I had a fiber
mailing carton with a change of clothes washed and ironed by Mrs.
Mulligan. I was wearing city clothes to travel in, my cap still stiff with
the paper lining, on my feet a new pair of green leather shoes with
a dark patch of leather on the ankles and toes. The soles were also
green and resisted bending, pulling away from my heels with each step
I took. They were so new I'd only worn them up and down the aisle
of the train.

Uncle Harry was not there to meet me when I arrived. I watched
the taillights of the coach go over the horizon, and when the throbbing of the gas motor died, a noise settled around me like it was trapped
in my ears. I had never heard anything like it. On both sides of the
dirt road that led to the east the weeds were almost as high as my
head. Fireflies rose from the dark fields to hover like a cloud of
sparklers. The night air was heavy and sweet with the smell of hay.

As the fields around me darkened, the bowl of the sky above me seemed to brighten. My stiff-soled shoes flicked the sand of the road to fall into the heels of my shoes. In the overall drone of the sounds around me I was able to distinguish the cadence of the locusts. It began slowly, built to a climax, then tailed off into silence. At the rim of the eastern sky I could see stars. When I stopped in the road to look around me I experienced a pleasurable apprehension. Big bugs and millers flew into my face. I sucked in small insects when I inhaled. Far down the road, in which I stood at the center, two small flickering lights came toward me. The putter of the motor rose and fell as the road tilted upward or declined. As the car approached me a cloud of insects obscured the lights. I had to move from the road to let the car pass me and proceed to a point where the driver was able to turn it around. Coming back toward me, it went ahead a few yards before it stopped. In the dusky light I saw an erect dark figure gripping with both hands the vibrating steering wheel. No feature of his face was visible.

"So you made it," he said to me, then spit into the weeds to the left of the road. What I said to him, if anything, I have forgotten. "Climb in, boy," he added, and I did as I was told.

The summer I met him, my Uncle Harry was a heavy, dour, silent man with his family, but given to deadpan joshing with his neighbors, his puckered lips sealed and stained with tobacco juice. After spitting, if his hands were free, he would pinch his pursed lips between his thumb and forefinger, then give a twist as if tightening a cap on a bottle. His wife, Clara, was a tall, lath-flat woman with a high-pitched voice, who liked to work. Her daughter, Mae, away at school that summer, planned to teach school. Her son, Will, had attended the aggie college in Lincoln and farmed the adjoining acres. His house could be seen through the stand of catalpa trees along the drive-in from the road. Just the year before, Will had married a black-haired young woman from Missouri. While I was on the farm she would bring over her baby and let it crawl around the floor while she helped Clara with the canning.

Harry and Clara's house was square, without gables, a lightning rod with a blue ball on it at the roof's peak, the windows of the upstairs bedrooms almost flush to the floor. I could lie stretched out on the floor and look out. I had Will's old room, with clothes stored in the dresser, the curtained and screened window facing the drive-in between the two houses. In the pulsing flashes of heat lightning I would see the intricate pattern of the glass curtain, the screen behind it alive with crawling, clicking, fluttering insects. The cats howled and the owls hooted. About dawn I would hear the gagging sound of the pump, and then the splash into the pail as Harry pumped up the water. As he approached the house, carrying two pails, I'd hear the occasional slurp of the water and the rub of the denim between his thighs. Up the stairwell from the kitchen would rise the smell of the kerosene spilled on the cobs. The flames would whoosh and roar in the chimney, then settle back to a steady crackle. The new day had begun, but I would pretend to sleep until Clara's shrill voice cried, "Wright, you coming?" Since I was always coming, I never really knew if she would call me twice.

She wiped the table with the dish rag then leaned there, propped on her spread arms. A few leaves rattled in the yard. Some dirty Leghorns clucked and waited at the screen. She left the rag on the table and emptied the pan toward the leaky shade. She stood there awhile, her hands pressed into the small of her back. Turning, she looked down the trail bright now with copper leaves at an old man's knees, white in the sun. She watched his brown hands lift Monkey Ward's, tear out a page. She watched him read both sides, very slowly, then tip his head. As he rose his overalls came up with a sigh and one strap hung swinging between his legs. She watched him step into the sun and hook it up. From his hat he took a feather and passed it through the stem of his pipe, then turned to strike the match on the door. (The Inhabitants)

Clara baked biscuits, fried eggs and cooked oatmeal for breakfast. The eggs were fried hard, in bacon fat, the oatmeal thick and chewy as taffy. After sitting all night, the separated cream had to be spooned out of the pitcher. My Uncle Harry would spread it on a hot biscuit like jam.

My daily chores were to fetch water and baskets of cobs. The cobs could be seen pressing against the windows of the first small house they had built on the farm. When I stooped to scoop them into the basket I might hear mice rustle the tassels. Sometimes I carried a mouse into the house. I would see it later, its whiskers twitching, spying on me over the rim of the basket. Clara set traps for mice in her cupboards, but if I heard them go off I knew she hadn't caught one. She had little respect for a boy as old as I was who couldn't set a trap.

Clara kept about thirty-eight Plymouth Rock chickens, and Harry milked about twenty Jersey cows. The cow pasture was at the far north end of the farm, down a lane of cottonwoods that Harry himself had planted. Nothing I had ever seen grew so close to the sky. Some nights the cows would come into the barn, and other nights I would have

56

to go after them. There was always one cow, when she saw me coming, that would go to the farthest corner of the pasture, where the weeds were high. In the knee-high weeds near the barn I had seen both garter snakes and sand vipers. What to do? What I had learned to do was run. Once I got behind the last cow I would hoot and holler like I was crazy, and once you get an old cow riled up she likes to run with her tail up, like a whip in a stock, her udder swinging. I'd let up running and walk once I reached the tree lane, but some of the cows would still be mooing when they reached the barn. What was it they'd seen? Uncle Harry asked me. He was also puzzled why his cows, with such good pasture, were giving so little milk. In my first week on the farm the one thing I had learned was to keep my own counsel, and my mouth shut. The cows didn't much like me in the stable either, mooing and milling around when I came near them, so I would just stand around the stable door watching Harry squirt milk right from the teat at a row of cats. To make sure they didn't miss any, they would rise up and let it splash on their fronts, then lick it off.

In the yard are the remains of a croquet set—four of the wire wickets, a striped ball, a club, and one bird-spattered end post. On the barn the hayloft window is clear and in the window are several cats—but the roof of the barn and other details are left out. On the harrow the metal seat is drawn as if copied from a photograph, but the seat itself is in suspension and not joined to the frame. The corn crib is blocked in very roughly and under the lean-to roof is a treadle grindstone. The drip can suspends over the stone as the harrow seat over the harrow, and how the treadle mechanism operates is a little obscure. Beneath the stone, in a nest of dirty feathers, is a chill white egg. The hedge is cut flat at the top and extends the length of the driveway, with a break for the trail to the privy. There is a heavy undergrowth, and it happens that all we can see of the privy is the tin on the door and the curling leaves of a catalogue. . . . The whole sketch is like a peeling fresco, or even more like a jigsaw puzzle from which the key pieces have been removed. One of the hardest pieces to fit has been the pump. It has twice been put in—and once erased out—for either the barn is much too close or the pump is much too far away. This may have more to do with the weight of a full pail of water—fetched water— than it has with the actual location of the pump. The only solution was to draw both pumps in, reconsider the matter, and then take one pump out. This he did, but the pump that he left was where no sensible pump would be. And the one he took out was the pump in which he couldn't believe. (The Man Who Was There)

When I didn't have my chores to do I liked to sit in the sun, my back against the warm boards of the barn. I wanted to look like a farmboy, my face and arms tan, when I got back to Omaha. Compared to the noise at night, the day seemed to me as quiet as a church. Here and there I saw a butterfly zigzagging, or grass stems waggle when a grasshopper jumped. Cloud shadows passed over the scarecrow in Clara's garden, the straw sticking out of one of Harry's coat sleeves. It scared the crows, but the shiny blackbirds, with eyes like hatpins, perched on his shoulders. If I listened hard I could hear Uncle Harry "gee" and "haw" his team at the end of each furrow. He plowed with horses although his son, Will, had told him there was no place for a horse on a farm. Harry had sent Will to the aggie college in Lincoln, then refused to believe anything he had learned. He scoffed at everything Will did or said. Will was not so tall, but he took after Clara, with her big adam's apple, her high-pitched voice and unblinking eyes. The way his adam's apple pumped when he swallowed made it look like he had a bend in his neck. With Will's .22 rifle I shot my first jackrabbit, but when I picked him up, his big eyes wide open, I dropped him and ran.

The Sunday before I left, the Morris and Warner families had a big reunion at their grove in Warnerville. People came from as far as Lincoln, where my father's sister May had married a Warner who sorted mail in one of the Union Pacific mail cars. May was my father's favorite sister, and the happiest grown-up person I had ever met. She laughed all the time and liked everybody. All the women at the reunion brought along whatever it was they cooked best. We had chicken and hams, potato salad and cole slaw, with everything else in a white sauce. Clara had made berry pies the week before and stored them in the storm cave until the reunion, wiping off the mold with a cloth dampened with vinegar. It didn't work for pies with meringue toppings, but it worked for hers. All I did was chase my cousins in and out of the house until we were eaten up by mosquitoes and had to sit inside. Two of my cousins from Lincoln had run around barefoot and cut the skin between their toes on the sharp sickle grass. Not having lived on a farm, or brought in cows from the pasture, they didn't know about sickle grass or very much else.

When it was time for me to leave I was tanned on my arms and had freckles on my nose. In a pillbox I had found in the cobhouse I had the forked tongue of a sandpiper, along with three copper shell casings from the bullets I had shot at the rabbit. At the Warnerville station Harry asked me who my father was married to now. I said I didn't know. He didn't ask me to come again, or wait to see if the train came and stopped for me, but got his Ford turned around, bucking in forward, then drove off in a cloud of dust. There was no wind at all to move it. When it finally settled there was nothing to see.

I WAS EAGER TO SHOW JOEY MY TAN AND TELL
Mrs. Mulligan all that had happened, but my father met me at the
station and drove me back to his apartment on Harney. While I was
on the farm one of his brothers, from Zanesville, Ohio, had come to
pay him a visit. My Uncle Verne was a plump, red-faced man who
had been gassed in the war and lived on a pension. His eyes might
roll back so that they showed all whites, but it was something he
couldn't help. At no time did he like his bald head uncovered, and
he slept on the daybed sitting up, with his hat on. He nodded his head
to what my father said, but he didn't talk himself. In the pocket of
his vest he kept gold coins of all sizes that he liked to try and balance
on their edges when we sat at café counters. If the counter was flat
and smooth he could do it. While my father talked to him about the
egg and chicken business Verne would try to balance the coins on the
counter. He had a tremor in his head that made it hard for him to
sip coffee or light his cigar, but his right hand was so steady he could
stand the dime-size gold coin on its edge. I couldn't do it myself. It
made me nervous just to try.

It was my father's idea that his brother Verne should be his partner in the egg business. He didn't have much experience, but he had
a little capital. That way he would keep it in the family. There wasn't
much to the business to show anybody, and my father found it hard
to drive and talk business at the same time. Once we were out of
Omaha, away from the cops and the traffic, he would let me drive
while he and Verne sat in the back seat and talked. That suited me
fine. West of Omaha there were stretches of road that went up and
down like a roller coaster. If I got up to forty-five miles an hour I could
feel it in the seat. If I looked in the rearview mirror I could see that
Verne liked it, rolling his eyes when we topped a good rise. We drove
all over five or six counties visiting the local egg dealers and creameries.
While my father talked with the creamery man, Verne and me would
would have a piece of pie in a café or sit on a bench in the park, if
they had one. I liked him better as I got to know him, and he liked
me better than eggs and chickens. We had some good times. If he sat
in a café with a marble counter he would stand one of his gold coins
on its edge. There were people who hadn't even seen a real gold coin.
After talking all day with the egg and creamery people my father didn't

talk the egg business to Verne on the way home. He might sit in the rear seat, behind the side curtains, while Verne would sit in the front seat with me, his hat flapping in the wind. What he liked more than anything else was the wind in his face. My father cared so little who was driving he might forget to ask me to change places with him, and I would drive in the dark to Harney Cafeteria, where we could eat all we wanted for thirty-five cents, including desert. After a long day's drive, both Verne and me got our money's worth.

With his lips chapped and his face windburned, it was all right with my father if Verne and me went riding on our own. We might go to Council Bluffs, just to cross the bridge and look at the muddy Missouri. Verne liked Iowa towns because they had more trees and benches in their parks. When we got home in the evening there would always be grass in the cuffs of his pants. Now that I was driving a car, I thought it was about time I was wearing long pants, just in case one of the cops or somebody stopped me. I wouldn't have much going for me if he looked in and saw I was wearing knee pants.

In late August, just before school, Verne and me were driving north of Douglas Street when he waved me over to the curb. That's what he did when he wanted to buy a newspaper. He got out of the car, then he leaned back in, said, "Here, kid," and put some coins in my hand. I didn't see that they were gold until he turned and went off. I couldn't do much, with the car to think of, and watched him hurry away into the Brandeis store entrance, one hand holding his hat. I drove around and around the block, but he didn't come out. I knew that he didn't like eggs or chickens, and to tell the truth he didn't much like my father or the women my father introduced him to. What he liked most of all was a roller-coaster road with the wind in his face, and then he liked me.

I had all this money but I knew better than to mention it to my father, who would try to persuade me to invest it in the egg and chicken business. I didn't know much, but at least I knew better than that.

With Verne gone, my father turned his attention to Mrs. Van Meer, the new mother he had in mind for me. She had been away for part of the summer, visiting her people in Wisconsin, leaving her daughter, Claudine, in charge of the house. Raising Claudine, who had been something of a tomboy, had been a trial for Mrs. Van Meer, and given her a strong dislike of children, especially boys. My father had explained to her that I was no longer a child. To emphasize that point we went to Browning and King's and bought me a suit with two pairs of long pants.

We didn't want to surprise Mrs. Van Meer at supper, so we put off arriving until almost dark. She was in the chain swing on the porch, behind the basket of ferns. My father didn't seem to notice the sprinkler was running until he had walked right through it. "Jesuschrist!" he said, one of his favorite expressions.

"Is that setting your son a good example?" Mrs. Van Meer said.

My father said, "Come and meet your new mother," and I walked around the sprinkler to the porch, my new crepe-soled shoes squeaking. She stayed in the swing, the streetlight dappling her face. I liked the way her braids of hair went around her head, but her round moonface and wide lipless mouth made me think of Happy Hooligan in the comics. My father said, "He's grown since I last saw him. He'll soon be the biggest one in the family!"

"I wish I thought so," Mrs. Van Meer replied, and looked through the open window to the back of the house. A short fat girl and a tall young man were in the kitchen, washing and drying dishes. I could hear the girl laugh like she was being tickled, and I liked her laugh. My father said the way I was growing up it would be good for me to have an older sister. While my father talked Mrs. Van Meer looked at me. The wire basket of ferns that hung between the posts had just been watered, and dripped on the porch rail. My father took off his coat, folding it across his lap so the lining and the label were on the outside. When he stopped talking we could hear Claudine giggle and laugh.

I would have Claudine's old room in the basement, with the door at the back I would have to keep locked. To get to my room, Mrs. Van Meer explained, I wouldn't come in the front door and walk through the house, but go around the house to the door at the rear. My father would show me where my room was. The grass at the side of the house had also been sprinkled, and we got our shoes wet walking through it. The basement was small, but had a smooth cement floor and was clean as a gym. Claudine's old room was large enough, but the only window was at the back, up too high to look out of. On the wall she had pictures of dogs and movie stars, and a map of a camp she went to in Wisconsin. She had an almost new girl's bicycle with a basket strapped to the handlebars. There was also a sink and a toilet in the basement so I wouldn't have to run up and down the stairs.

I was about ready for bed when Claudine came down to meet me and saw how tanned my feet and arms were. She wet her finger at her lips and rubbed it on my arm to see if the tan rubbed off. Claudine was a fat girl, with a face like a kewpie, and I could tell she liked to fool around.

62

"Why can't we sleep together," she said, "since we're brother and sister?" She took my hand in her fat one, said, "You like my mother? I don't like her. I don't blame your father for marrying her for her money." She gave me a quick peck on the lips, said, "I've always wanted a brother. Are you going to protect me?" I couldn't tell if she was joking or meant it. She felt my bicep muscle, said, "You're strong, aren't you?" Was it my new long pants? From the top of the stairs her mother called, "Oh, Claudine!"

"She thinks we're down here doing something dirty. You want to?"

My lips dry, I shook my head. No, I didn't want to. I was also at a loss as to how we might do it. On the stairs we could hear her mother's steps, and we just stood there, almost but not quite touching, until she came to the door and saw us. With a big squeal Claudine gave me a push and I fell on the bed.

In the morning, washing dishes, Mrs. Van Meer asked me what I thought of my father's business. Against her better judgment she had been persuaded to invest some of Mr. Van Meer's savings in it. My father made a very good impression on some people, and was plainly smarter than most of them, but Mrs. Van Meer was troubled about his business transactions. He had *been* in business. Why should he need help from her?

Only with Gertrude had I been talked to as a person who might know something worth knowing. Mrs. Van Meer didn't seem to feel that my age handicapped me. He was my father. I had known him all of fifteen years. We were eye to eye, cleaning up after breakfast, and we put all the dishes back into the cupboard, the silver back into the drawer. I was pleased to be asked my opinion, but troubled as to what it should be. In the egg and chicken business my father did not seem to prosper, smart as he was. Just recently he had found it hard to pay my board of five dollars a week. How could I recommend him? Whose side was I on? Mrs. Van Meer was a short, plump woman of the sort my father described as dumpy, but she was now my new mother. She wore a net over her hair and a bathrobe that she held gripped at her throat. While talking to me she moved around the kitchen wiping off the counters with a damp rag. Mr. Van Meer had been dead for seven years. Living with Claudine, she had grown accustomed to talking with people not much older than I was. Claudine had encouraged her to marry my father. "You better do it while you can, Mom," she told her. Mrs. Van Meer had not personally felt any need to do it one way or the other. My father had insisted. She had not known what to do. And for a year now Claudine had been going with this young man who worked at the soda fountain in the Blackstone

Hotel. His name was Max Cohn. He was of Jewish extraction. He made a salary of twelve dollars a week. If Claudine married him, as she planned, when she was old enough in November, the next thing she knew she would bring him home to live in the house.

Mrs. Van Meer liked to walk around as she talked. I sat at the table in the kitchen. Her voice would come to me from the bathroom, or from the hallway where she was dusting. Did it occur to me that in marrying my father she had hoped to head off Claudine marrying Max Cohn? I recognized that she faced bewildering decisions. If the advice I gave her was not what she wanted to hear she would just not come back from where she had walked off to. At first I thought she had gone to the bathroom, but that wasn't it.

At a gym class in the high school I stood in a long line waiting to have my throat looked at and my heart tested, when I saw Joey Mulligan in the line ahead of me. He had grown at least an inch taller than I was, but he was still wearing knee pants and high-top hook-and-eye shoes. I wanted to speak to him, but it confused me to have a new mother, a new home and a sister, with a life so different than my old one. I watched him exercise for the heart test, and saw his neck and ears get red just the way they used to. There were things he had of mine that I still wanted, like the cigar box of marbles including agates and puries, and my Flexible Flyer Junior Racer under his porch. I missed the nights under the streetlight, but if Lillian knew I was wearing long pants when we played "Run Sheep Run" it wouldn't be the same.

During Christmas vacation I was in the Brandeis store trying to make up my mind what I wanted for Christmas, when I saw Gertrude, followed by my father, come out of an elevator. Her arms were full of packages. My father was smiling, his head wagging from side to side with what he was thinking, and he held her arm as they walked toward the door, the unbuckled tops of her galoshes flapping. For just as long as I stood there I hardly knew just who, or where, I was.

In January we had a blizzard so bad Max Cohn couldn't get his Ford to start, and I went to school with Claudine on the streetcar. On the way home I would take a transfer and go down to 11th Street to help my father. I might candle some eggs, or address postcards to the egg and chicken dealers all over the state. Sometimes my father wouldn't be there, the front door locked, and I would walk up Harney Street to the Y and play Ping-Pong until time for supper. My father had become so uncertain about his meals, Mrs. Van Meer had suggested he should eat in restaurants. Sometimes I saw him in the café on 24th Street where we both used the same meal ticket. I learned from Claudine that there were nights he didn't come home at all. I got to like Max Cohn during the evenings we worked together on the superheterodyne radio he was building. The tubes alone cost him five dollars apiece. At school I had gone out for the wrestling team because it was something I was pretty good at. I made the team in the ninety-five-pound class. With my skinny legs I looked so little like a wrestler the coach said it proved to be to my advantage. My opponent, sizing me up in tights, got overconfident. I won all my matches up through January, when I didn't feel so good in the regional finals. Three or four minutes after the bout had started the referee stopped it and called over the coach. I was wearing black tights, but on my arms and chest I was speckled with red splotches. My forehead was hot, and back in the locker room a doctor told me I had chicken pox. He gave me a ride home in his car, and I was in bed when Claudine came downstairs and found me. I guess I looked pretty funny, the way she laughed. The five or six days I was in bed I read *Silas Marner, The Count of Monte Cristo* and almost all of *The Three Musketeers,* and wrote a report. I hadn't seen my father for more than a week. When I was able to get around I went to his place of business, which was locked up tight, with a sheriff's notice on the door. Someone had come to take away the chickens, but otherwise everything was pretty much as usual. One of my father's ledgers was open on the desk, with a package of gingersnaps. The coveralls he wore when he was picking chickens were on a hook on the wall.

Thanks to my Uncle Verne, I had plenty of money, but if I tried to spent it, it would make people suspicious. I might have spent the night in the lobby of the YMCA, behind one of the big chairs or couches, but when I thought about where I would feel safe I could only think of Miss Healy's classroom, on the second floor. When I cleaned the erasers on the fire escape I sometimes left the fire escape window unlatched. That way I could come back later and sit at her desk. It was the empty room that pleased me: the rows of shiny-topped desks, the high bare windows, the shadows of the trees moving on the ceiling. I often weighed myself on the scales in the nurse's annex, or sat on the sheet-covered couch.

Never before had I seen the room at night. The lights of the passing cars skipped from window to window and lit up the rack of maps, the writing on the blackboards. I could see the white dog in the horn of the Victrola. I could have it all to myself, but the window was locked. Just a few months before, I had been anxious to get out of grade school and into high school, but now I longed to be back in my seat at the front, so close to Miss Healy I could smell her perfume when she walked up and down. Across the aisle from me sat Pauline Myers, her eyes like a goldfish when she wore her glasses. In the dark under the stairs of Helen Minor's house I had kissed her when we played spin the milk bottle. Where had Betty Zabriskie gone with her cello? Or LaRue Gator, who drew galloping horses ridden by cowboys and Indians? Or Victor Musselman's sister, Glavina, who read from *Current Events* on Tuesdays. I had given up reading when confronted with the word "catastrophe." Alone in the cloakroom with Miss Healy, she would tell me what she expected of me, the smell of Sen Sen on her breath.

Between the passing cars the room went dark, as if erased from the blackboard. I had shamelessly bawled to please Mrs. Mulligan when she grieved for her son who had died in a pesthouse, but it shamed me to cry real, smarting tears for myself. On my tear-filmed eyes the approaching car lights exploded like stars. I thought I might go to Turner Park and crawl under the porch of the skate house, where whoever found me, even Mrs. Van Meer, might feel sorry for me. I had become more of a whole orphan than a half one, and I huddled with my back to the brick wall that glowed faintly with the chalk dust where I slapped the erasers. I still had the key to Mrs. Van Meer's basement, warm with the heat from the furnace, and I could pretend, if she asked me, that I didn't know what had happened to my father. I ran most of the way to keep warm. Down the street from her house, under the lamp on the corner, I could see that Max Cohn's Ford was parked at the front. That could only mean that Max and Claudine had moved into my room. I was there on the corner, wondering what to do next, when a touring car with side curtains pulled to the curb and honked at me. I didn't recognize the car, a Big Six Studebaker, but the man at the wheel was my father. When I got in he said, "How do you like it, kid?"

We drove back into town to a café on Farnam where we could eat on one of his meal tickets. It was so late we both had breakfast. To the cook my father said that Omaha was proving to be something of a disappointment, and that he was now looking for greener pastures. And where is that? said the cook. My father didn't say, but he later explained that it was none of the cook's business. He knew where they were, and that's where we were going as soon as he could settle a few accounts. We drove around for a while, just waiting for daylight, then he let me drive just to get the feel of it. I drove to Capitol Avenue, where I shifted to second before we came down it, the front blinds drawn at the Mulligan windows and the gas jet glowing in the hallway.

66

I wanted to honk, but I didn't. My father had rented a room on South 16th Street in a building where I had once delivered papers, which I thought was interesting, but I didn't bring it up.

My father thought I was going to school, but what I did most of the time was play hookey. I walked around the streets, the aisles of the stores, or played Ping-Pong at the Y when it was open. I probably played Ping-Pong better than I did anything else. In baseball I could catch, even when the batter swung at the ball, but I could only bounce it to second base. I could wrestle, but I didn't really like to, and I hated to box. I could run like a rabbit for about twenty yards, then the runners behind would catch up and go by me. I was also good at pull-ups, which I did for twelve times in Miss Healy's seventh-grade class, but what I looked forward to was running the mile in college. I had read about that in a book by Ralph Henry Barbour.

I'd meet my father at the Harney Cafeteria for supper, if he was not busy with the Holly Sisters. They were not really sisters, or much alike, but in public they had to be seen together. I could see them, if I wanted to, on the posters in the Shubert lobby, or in the alley behind the Shubert when their matinee performance was over. My father liked one better than the other, but he had to go around with both of them. Which one it was my father liked I never really knew.

In McCrory's dime store, on 16th Street, I swiped a roll of black tape without any use for it, just to swipe it, and with money to pay for it in my pocket. I was out in the street when this big fellow grabbed me by the neck, like I was a rabbit, and walked me back through the store with my feet hardly touching the floor. When he went through my pockets he found I had money and gold coins. Why had I swiped the tape? I didn't know. Where did I get the gold coins? He didn't believe me. He asked me again, then gave me a hard slap with the palm of his hand. My eyes smarted, but what hurt me worse was the shame I felt when I began to bawl. He marched me up the alley to 17th Street, then to the corner of Farnam, where he found a policeman, who walked me across the street to the courthouse and up the stairs to juvenile hall. Several boys and a girl sat in the waiting room, but I was led into the office of an elderly woman. She smiled kindly at me. What was the trouble? The policeman explained what I had done, and that my pockets were full of the money I had stolen. She asked me to show her the money I had, and I did. Where had I got the gold coins? I told her my Uncle Verne had given them to me. Did I live with him? No, I lived with my father. And where was that? I wouldn't tell her. If I told her the police would find him. Where was it I lived? she asked me, but I couldn't tell her about the Van Meers, and I was too ashamed to mention the Mulligans. I could see she was puzzled why a boy like me would refuse to say where I lived. I did tell her I was half an orphan, but hearing what I said so filled me with pity for myself I began to sniffle. She used her handkerchief to wipe my eyes and nose. I liked her. She had the friendly, motherly face of my civics teacher. You must tell me where you live, she said, or I will have to put you in the reformatory until your father or your uncle inquires about you. I couldn't speak. What I wanted to do was put my head in her lap and bawl. I think she thought I would talk more when I stopped snuffling, but feeling sorry for myself was very absorbing. When she called Miss Healy, whose name I would give her, and learned how highly she thought of me, she would be surprised. Before I told her, however, I was taken, with the three other boys, and driven to a big house on the bluffs overlooking the Missouri. A high fence went around it, and there were sheds and barns at the back. My money was taken from me, along with my watch and knife, and I was given a pair of coveralls to wear instead of my clothes. At supper I sat beside a boy who was smaller than me, but older, his head too big for his shoulders. He gulped his food, then sat with his hands in his pockets blowing on a train wheel at the front of his mouth. He followed me around but I couldn't get him to talk.

We all slept, maybe about thirty of us, in a big room with a high ceiling where an overhead light burned all night long. The boy in the bed next to me cried out in his sleep. The moment we got out in the yard after breakfast, one of the boys wanted to fight me. We walked clear to the back, behind the barn, where manure was piled for fertilizer, and after he'd hit me hard a few times I got mad and wrestled him to the ground. Another boy jumped me from behind, and they both rubbed manure on my face and my hair. Then they let me up and ran off together, maybe eight or ten of them, laughing like hyenas. It made me wonder if where they had put me was some sort of farm for kids who were crazy. I didn't let them catch me alone again and acted like I was pals with the one with the train wheel. He liked to play horseshoes, which we could do at one side of the house. What if my father didn't come for me? I wondered. After all, nobody knew where I was. I thought of telling them about the Mulligans, but I was too ashamed to have stolen something. Clear at the back of the farm, where the bluffs dropped off, there was a hole in the fence that one boy had crawled through. But what would I do if I did? I had the blue coveralls we all had to wear, and they had taken all of my money. The nights were cold. Every morning the ground was white with frost.

Then my father came for me in the Big Six Studie I could see at the front parked in the driveway, and I could hear his booming voice in the hall. He took me in his arms when he saw me, and the cold air puffed out of his coat the way it did when I had pneumonia and Dr. Brown came to see me. After I got my own clothes, we went to Brandeis and bought me a new mackinaw and a cap with ear muffs. However long I was there, it was really winter by the time I got out. My father never spoke to me about why I was there, and I never brought it up.

When I asked him where we were going he replied, "Chicago, kid." I don't know why, but the older and bigger I got the more he called me kid. We had two chicken-fried steaks at the greasy spoon where he still had a good meal ticket, then we drove across the river into Iowa. Since it's when you cross state lines you get into trouble with the cops, I let him drive.

If they ever got married, Max and Claudine probably did it in Council Bluffs, since being sixteen years of age was old enough in Iowa. I first really had the feeling of putting things behind me when we were out on the bridge, over the flowing muddy water, and up ahead was Chicago, where my father and I would begin a new life.

IN 1925 THE CITY STREETS WERE PAVED, BUT THE country roads were dirt or gravel. The dirt soon turned to mud when it rained, with the ruts as deep as a car's axles. If you got out of the ruts the car would skid into the ditch, like it was ice. To get out of the ditch you had to walk to a farm and hire a farmer to hitch up his horses and pull you out. On the other hand, if the road had just been graveled it would soon chew up the old tires. I didn't know at the time how far it was to Chicago, but it took us about a week. Once we crossed the Mississippi into Illinois we made pretty good time.

If a tire went flat, or you found it flat in the morning, you had to jack up the car and pound the rim and the tire off the wheel. Some rims were rusted on, and had never been off. To get the tire from the rim, in case you got it off, you had to have tire tools, which were parts of old springs, along with a hammer, screw drivers or anything else handy. Even then you might have to bounce it, pound it and jump on it to get the rim to break so you could pry the tire off. Inside the tire, if it wasn't chewed to pieces, was a tube with a slow or fast leak in it. A fast leak was better, because you could hear it, but to see a slow leak you had to have a pan of water so the leak would blow some bubbles. The spot with the leak had to be scraped with a piece of tin like a coconut shredder before you put the patch on it. The smell of the rubber cement you put on the patch made it almost worth the trouble, but not quite. Then you had to put it all back together again and pump it up, which might take half an hour. I didn't weigh enough to be good with a pump. My father weighed enough, but he was not good at it, and it left him winded and cursing. He would have to take his coat off, unbutton his collar, and loosen his belt. Then his fingers would be so swollen and dirty he couldn't rebutton his collar. My own knuckles were so bloody after using the tire irons I could hardly put my hands in my pockets. I don't mean to say it wasn't worth all the trouble, because arriving in Chicago, driving through the lights, and finally coming out on Michigan Boulevard, along the lakefront, a street so wide I was afraid to cross it, was like nothing that had ever happened to me. I was driving. My father was asleep behind the side curtains in the back seat. Only someone who has done it the way I did it, driving from Omaha and coming in after midnight, going north on Michigan toward the Wrigley Tower, the waterworks building and the Drake Hotel, will understand what it was like to reach Lincoln Park and know the lake was there and not be able to see it, just hear the boats honk.

On one of the dead-end streets we slept in the car until the morning light burned on the windshield, and when I raised my head I saw for myself the world was round. The ore boat I was watching on the far horizon dropped right behind it, leaving nothing but smoke.

All morning, as we drove around, I felt my father's elation. We had breakfast in a Raklios restaurant with grapefruit and oranges piled high in the window. We watched a drawbridge go up like a street leading into the sky. This was a city like the one I had seen on the covers of Sears, Roebuck catalogues, with great steamers arriving, trains departing, the streets thronging with cars and people, and I could feel it pulsing around me like a great locomotive taking on water, the pistons faintly hissing, the boiler throbbing with power. The white building with the clock in the tower belonged to William Wrigley, the chewing gum king.

Dear Son—
Have moved. Have nice little place of our own now, two-plate gas. Warm sun in windows every morning, nice view of park. Plan to get new console radio soon now, let you pick it out. Plan to pick up car so we can drive out in country, get out in air. Turning over in my mind plan to send you to Harvard, send you to Yale. Saw robin in park this morning. Saw him catch worm. (The Works of Love)

We took a room in a rooming house near the Dearborn railroad station. We got a room at the front so we could look out the window and keep an eye on the car. If the out-of-state people saw our Nebraska license they would stop and start a conversation with me or my father. Very few of them came from as far away as Omaha. I met a house painter from Grand Island, Nebraska, who said he had a boy my age he wanted me to meet. He took me to his room over a store, but it had nothing in it but a bed. He sat on the bed talking to me, and I walked over to look out the open window. "There's my father," I said. "I guess he's looking for me," and took off down the stairs. My father wasn't there, but it was something I could say to get out of a fix I'd got myself into. Once I walked right through the Loop, clear to Michigan Boulevard where I could look across the street at the art museum, but most of the time I sat on the benches or walked around in the Dearborn station. All day long the train callers called out the stations. High on the wall were the big posters showing scenes of the far west: the Garden of the Gods in Colorado, the Grand Canyon in Arizona and Catalina Island off the coast of California. If my father asked me what was on my mind, it was usually Catalina Island but it might be the Royal Gorge.

When my father found a position with the Northwestern Railroad, we moved from the room on State Street to an apartment on Menominee Street, just a block from Lincoln Park. If I leaned out the window I could see the bare trees and the streetcars passing on Clark Street. At night we could hear the rumble of the ice cracking up on the lake. The apartment was so big we had rooms to rent out if we could find someone who wanted to share the kitchen. The delicatessen store on the floor below stayed open until eleven o'clock on weekends, but the trouble with that was that the door slammed hard when people went in and out. The newer buildings on the street, all painted the same color, were garages for the cars of people who lived over on the Gold Coast. From the window I could watch the chauffeurs wash and polish their limousines. Two of these cars were so elegant they had the headlights in the fenders, and the chauffeur had to ride where the rain fell on him. Except for riding out in the open, I thought the life of a chauffeur was pretty soft.

To get to Menominee Street in Chicago you take a Clark streetcar in the Loop and ride north, twenty minutes or so, to Lincoln Park. If you want to get the feel of the city, or if you like to see where it is you're going, you can stand at the front of the car with the motorman. On certain days you might find Will Brady standing there. Not that he cared where he was going, but he liked the look of the street, the clang of the bell, and the smell of the crushed track sand that came up through the floor. He liked to stand with his hands grasping the rail at the motorman's back. At certain intersections he liked to turn and look—when the door at the front stood open—down the streets to the east where the world seemed to end. It didn't, of course, but perhaps he liked to think it might. On up the street he could see the park, and in the winter, when the trees were bare, he could make out the giant brooding figure of Abraham Lincoln. Soft green, like the color of cheap Christmas jewelry, or the fine copper gutters on the homes of the rich. (The Works of Love)

If I walked straight east through the park I came out on the breakwater along the lake. A cinder bridle path, shaded by trees, went along Michigan Boulevard as far as Oak Street, where the sandy beach began. From Oak Street I could read the time on the Wrigley clock.

Some of the people who had cars on Menominee Street also had horses they rode on the bridle path on Sunday mornings.

If I walked down Sedgwick Street, across North Avenue, I would be in the slums of Little Sicily, full of Italian boys as dark as Arabs, but if I walked up Clark Street to the north it was like Omaha around 24th Street. At night, on the lids of my eyes, I could see the flash of light when the trolleys on Clark Street slipped the wires. I had first seen that in Omaha, before Gertrude had left my father, but in Chicago I thought of her whenever I saw a vaudeville show. Every time I saw a hula dancer, which was often, I thought it might be her.

I seemed to like the city better than my father, who no longer enjoyed working for a railroad. To start a new chicken and egg business what he needed and didn't have was collateral. Anyone in Chicago who needed anything at all ran a want ad for it in the *Sunday Tribune,* where my father, before he put his shirt on, looked for people who were looking for him. My father wrote to them on the stationery of the Barclay Hotel, on Clark Street, suggesting that they meet him in the lobby. I first learned he had in mind sending me to Yale when he said so to a man who himself had a son in Princeton. These men had collateral, all right, but they did not seem to see a great future in eggs.

Until I would go back to school in the fall, my father worried about my idleness. At my age, back in the Platte Valley, he was doing a man's work and filling a man's shoes. Idleness was like an illness, he said, in that it got worse before it got better. That was something my father read in the *Sunday Tribune* once he had put aside the want ad section. He liked to read, and might write down on a card words or sayings that appealed to him. In the want ads, where he ran his own, big Chicago companies advertised for boys. A boy like myself could get a job making twelve to fifteen dollars a week, which was almost double what my father had made at my age. Boys like me, now working at these jobs, would one day be president of the company. They knew the business. They had learned it from the ground up. My father did not question my qualifications, but he was of uncertain mind, as I was, which business I would one day head. Commonwealth Edison appealed to him, more than it did me. Samuel Insull, a little wrinkled old man whose picture I had seen in the paper, was president of Commonwealth Edison and had his office in the Loop, right there in Chicago. When we passed it on a streetcar my father pointed it out. To get the feel of the business I would sometimes eat pie in the Raklios restaurant on the first floor.

The company that had more appeal for me was Montgomery

Ward, with whom I had had personal connections. Part of the time I had spent on my Uncle Harry's farm had been inside mail-order catalogues, and the section of watches that appealed to me most had been in the Monkey Ward catalogue. Both the retail store and the wholesale warehouse were on Chicago Avenue, where it crossed the canal, just east of the freight yards where my father worked. Every Sunday they ran an ad that they would pay boys up to eighteen dollars a week. I didn't believe everything I read, or that my father told me, but if I had to choose a company I wouldn't mind being president of, it was Montgomery Ward. My father said to me, and not for the first time, "Kid, it's your own life."

They paid me fifteen dollars a week to do what I'd have done for nothing, if they had asked me, since I loved to roller skate. My job was to fill mail orders for shoes by skating around in the mail-order shoe department. By early afternoon my fingers were so swollen I could hardly make a fist. My feet were light when I took the skates off, but I felt so peculiar I could hardly walk. I had to walk most evenings because the Larrabee streetcars were so crowded I couldn't get on. That first night my fingers and feet tingled so much I couldn't sleep. After three or four days the tingling stopped, and I'd skate up and down the aisles just because I enjoyed it, but by evening I'd be so tired I'd have slept in the stockroom if they had let me. On Sundays even my father noticed how different I looked. My legs were skinnier than ever. I could wear collars without the wings curling. I had the money to eat all I wanted, including chocolate malts, but I couldn't eat enough to keep from losing weight. Before I went to bed, which I did pretty early, practicing my harmonica under the covers, I would drink a pint of chocolate milk and eat half a carton of Lorna Doones. But it didn't help. I learned from the supervisor, who was from Pisgah, Iowa, and not too far from Omaha, that small boys had more of a problem because the skates were so heavy.

The supervisor switched me to the wrapping counter on the mail-order chute, where everything came down from the catalogue department that was small enough for people to carry and had to be wrapped. In just a few days my fingers were cut and sore from the heavy wrapping twine. From there, where the time went fast, I was switched to a counter in the retail store where it seemed hours and hours until lunch. There were times all I had to do was think. I worked with a girl who would have been pretty except for her teeth. Right at the front, where you couldn't miss it, she had one that was like mother-of-pearl, and one that was black. I liked to joke with girls, as I did with Claudine, but if something struck her as funny she would put her hand to her mouth, concealing her teeth. But I agreed with her that if she let the dentist pull them it would be worse.

If the weather was good I would walk up Larrabee to Sam's Café near Blackhawk Street. Death's Corner, which I learned about later, was right there on the corner of Larrabee and Blackhawk. As I walked up Larrabee I could see the flashing lights of the elevated trains, near North Avenue. Right across the street from Sam's Café was the Larrabee Y. Through the big windows at the front I could see the Italian kids playing Ping-Pong, and hear the click of billiard balls when the lobby door opened. But the way these boys hollered and yelled scared me. They were all black-haired, mostly with dark complexions, and I didn't understand what they yelled at each other. Some looked smaller than me, but they were all tougher. If I entered the door to the men's lobby, where there were chairs to sit on and papers to read, I could hear balls bounce and billiard cues crack when they got into fights. The Y secretary spent most of his time vaulting over the counter to break up a fight, or chase someone out the door. As a member of the Omaha YMCA in good standing, I had privileges at YMCAs elsewhere, but what good were they if I was afraid to use them? What I wanted to do most was play some Ping-Pong, then have a long hot shower.

A cold day in November, just a few yards from the Y, I saw this man stretched out on his face on the sidewalk. I figured he was drunk. In the dark I could just make out the holes, like buttons, across the back of his coat. He was sprawled his length right in front of a window with a row of small holes in the splintered glass, about chest high. Light from a passing streetcar was enough for me to see that the holes across the man's back were not buttons.

In the Y lobby a husky sandy-haired man, with a whistle dangling from his neck, was behind the counter. He knew he hadn't seen me before, and in a friendly way he asked me what it was I wanted. I said there was a man lying on the sidewalk out in front. He asked me where, and I told him. He asked me if I had seen anything else, or if anyone had seen me, and I said I didn't know. Cars had passed. He vaulted over the counter and took me by the arm to lead me to the stairs at the back of the hall, where the warm draft of air smelled of swimming pool chlorine. We went down the stairs to the locker room, through the locked door into the shelves of lockers, then clear to the back where the dirty towels were piled into a cart. He emptied out about half the towels, told me to climb in, then piled the towels on top of me. Like we were playing a game, he said, "Now you just lie quiet here, you hear me?" I lay there for half an hour or more, maybe an hour. I could hear the splashing in the swimming pool, and

75

hear the drumming of the showers. When he finally came for me my clothes were pretty damp, so I had to take them off and spread them on a radiator. He gave me a towel so I could take a shower, and follow it up with a swim if I cared to. I took a long hot shower but I didn't feel like a swim. I stayed down in the locker room until the boys' section closed, the lobby lights went off, and the man came down to get me. His name was Al Cox. I told him my name, and where I lived on Menominee Street. We had a hot chocolate together, on North Avenue, where he explained that the man had been shot by gangsters, and it was just our good luck that nobody had seen me. It was not lost on me that he had said *our*. I was a member of the Y, but I knew that he meant to be saying more than that. He walked me up North Avenue to Sedgwick Street, where we agreed that I would see him tomorrow, then I made it pretty quick to Menominee, where the delicatessen was still open. Although I didn't really like it, I had a cake of Fleischmann's yeast with my pint of milk.

The next day I played Ping-Pong with Al Cox in the lobby and beat him. I also beat the others I played with, including Emmanuel Guagliardo, a boy so hoarse-voiced he just grunted. After losing to me three times he stepped on the Ping-Pong ball and broke the handle off the paddle. When Al Cox tried to catch him, he ran out of the door hooting. But later he came back. While I played Ping-Pong with one of the others he sat in the window watching. He was not so bad-looking when he was quiet, except for his harelip. Just before the lobby closed I played him again, and when I beat him he ran off hooting, but he didn't break the paddle or step on the ball. I walked with Al Cox to the elevated station, where he asked me how long I had been in Chicago and where I was from. We shared a nut Hershey while he waited for his train, and he said that most of the boys in the lobby were real Eye-talians, from the old country, who didn't speak English unless they had to, and they were not accustomed to a boy from the west, like me. While I had a good time for myself in the lobby, I could also be doing good for others by the way I talked, the way I played Ping-Pong, and the way I didn't step on the ball or break the handle off the paddles. We shook hands. He said I should call him Al, not Mr. Cox.

I wouldn't be president of the company right away, but with the money I was making I could afford to wait. Not having to wait for my father to give me money on Sunday, I had all day to myself. "Kid," he would say, "where are you off to?"

"The Bible Sunday Club," I would reply. He couldn't object to

76

my interest in the Bible, after all that had happened to me. The Bible Club met Sunday mornings at the Y, in one of the rooms on the men's side where they showed movies. The boys' lobby was closed on Sundays, but members of the Bible Club in good standing could play cuero-quet or Ping-Pong for half an hour or so after the meeting.

I liked to play Ping-Pong at the Y so much I would grab some cupcakes in the delicatessen and eat them in the Y lobby in order to save time. On Saturdays I could play all day, with time for a shower and a swim in the evening, but on weekdays I had to hustle to get in a couple hours. There were more and more kids who wanted to play when they saw what the game was really like. Emmanuel Guagliardo stopped breaking paddles when he got it through his head that that kept him from playing. He learned fast, if he could keep his mouth shut, and when he played with me he was a different person. Mr. Ward Shults, the Y secretary, took me back to his office so we could discuss it. Until I came to the Y, Guagliardo had been the terror of the lobby, throwing balls, breaking cues, cursing and starting fights. He had stopped all of that when it got through his head that it kept him from being with me, and playing Ping-Pong. It was as simple as that. Mr. Shults didn't want to make too much of it, but my being in the lobby, and the way I played Ping-Pong, had made it possible for many of the boys, not just Guagliardo, to see the light. Boys did not learn from rules, but from examples, and it was part of my example that Guagliardo could not beat me at Ping-Pong. The other part was that they had no idea what made me tick. They'd never before seen a white-faced boy like me who didn't raid slot machines, curse, use dirty language, or swipe the bar soap in the shower room. In his three years at Larrabee Y—Mr. Shults had come from the Y in Oberlin, Ohio—he had never seen the lobby so peaceful as it was with Guagliardo quiet. Something about me seemed to awe him. If I would come to the Y three evenings a week, plus Saturday afternoon and the Bible Club on Sunday, Mr. Shults would pay me five dollars a week with the promise of quick advancement in Y work. In that regard he wanted to advise me to get on with my schooling. A boy without a high school education would soon find himself handicapped wherever he turned. Al Cox, whom I knew and admired, had delayed his own advancement several years by postponing his college education. He was now in his last year at the Y college on the South Side. A young man like myself, fresh from the west, should avail myself of the best that a city like Chicago provided. In that regard, my work at Montgomery Ward, good as it was, was not enough. The Y was fortunate in having a group of young men, all from Lakeview High School, who came down from the North Side on Thursday evening, played basket-ball, had a swim, then met for a club meeting with Mr. Shults. They were boys like me, my own age. They were clean-cut American boys like those I would have known in Omaha.

I wanted to meet those boys, but if I went back to school I would lose my new independence. I had put a deposit on a pair of shoe skates I saw in a pawnshop window and planned to give to myself for Christmas. If I stopped making money I would be back looking for it in my father's pockets. I had time to think about it since the new school semester did not begin until January, and once the weather turned really cold the lobby filled with kids who were not Y members. They saw the lights, and came in off the streets to get out of the cold.

One of these boys was Frankie Scire, who had stunted his growth by smoking cigarettes. He was small and thin, with eyes like saucers in his pale face. He spoke in a voice so low and hoarse I'd have to sit with him in the men's cloakroom to hear him. He told me he went to California in the winters and sold newspapers in Long Beach. He rode out in freight cars. I didn't believe him, but that's what he said. Frankie Scire was a year or so older than I was, and weighed about eighty pounds with his clothes on. I weighed him. I never saw him with his clothes off. I liked to sit in the cloakroom and talk with him while he leaned against the radiator. I can't explain it. He was like a hoarse-voiced little girl. He never seemed to lack for money, which he told me he got raiding slot machines in elevated stations. Coins weighted the pockets of his coat. He inhaled his cigarettes so deep smoke kept coming from his lips as he talked. I got so I liked Frankie Scire, and he didn't seem to mind my trying to reform him. He called me Morse. He couldn't believe anybody had a name like Wright. He didn't seem to care for Ping-Pong, billiards or checkers, and once he'd got himself warm he would just take off, I never knew where.

Two weeks before Christmas I was moved from the retail store wrapping counter to work for Santa Claus in the toy department. My job was to sit under the throne he sat on and blow up the balloons he passed out to the kids sitting on his lap. Who would think blowing up balloons would be such hard work? It was hot under his throne, and blowing all the time made me dizzy. I would still be warm and sweaty inside my clothes when I left the store.

A few days before Christmas, while I was standing in the lobby, Mr. Shults asked me how I was feeling. I wasn't feeling so good. He took my temperature back in his office, then said he thought I should spend the night at the Y. They had a room I could sleep in in the dormitory. It pleased me to be really living in the Y in a nice room near the gymnasium, where I could hear the yelling and the thump of the basketball on the backboard. Al Cox brought me a bowl of soup in the evening, and the next thing I remember was Mr. Shults wishing me a happy New Year. I'd been sick with the flu for more than a week. My father had stopped by to see me but I remembered nothing about it. I stayed in bed two or three days more, coming down on the Sunday after New Year's to help Mr. Shults with the Bible Sunday Club. When he called on me to pray, I stood up and prayed. I had never prayed in public before, but it seemed to come easy to me. I thanked the Lord for saving my life, and for the new friends I had, for the beautiful winter day, and for other blessings. Nobody had known I knew how to pray so well. Where had I learned? All I remembered was kneeling and praying as a child. Anna had been there combing her hair, and I prayed for both her and my father, not forgetting to ask the Lord to take my soul if I died in my sleep. Praying the way I did was a surprise to me as well as Mr. Shults.

Inside the room was a small gas plate on a marble-topped washstand, a cracked china bowl, a table, two chairs, a chest of drawers, an armless rocker, an imitation fireplace, and an iron frame bed. Over the fireplace was a mirror showing the head of the bed and the yellow folding doors. The bed was in the shape of a shallow pan with a pouring spout at one side, and beneath this spout, as if poured there, a frazzled hole in the rug. (The Works of Love)

My unexpected talent for prayer may have changed my life. I was sixteen years of age that January, and Mr. Shults felt that a young man of my talents should not be wasting them in the employ of Montgomery Ward. He could not match their salary for the time being, but he could assure me more rapid advancement and time to resume my high school education. The high school for me to go to would be Lakeview, where I would be with the young men I would have met if I hadn't taken sick just before Christmas. Three of them came to see me at the Y, Maurie Johnson, Gene Logsdon and Orville Clark. Maurie Johnson's father owned the Johnson Dairy on Ashland Avenue, just south of Lakeview High School. Orville Clark was majoring in engineering and planned to go to Purdue, where his brother was a student. Gene Logsdon was young enough to be in the boys' department, but I had often seen him in the men's side of the lobby reading the magazines and playing billiards with the men. If he had been married it wouldn't have surprised me. He dressed like a man, and brought his gym clothes to the Y in a satchel with the Northwestern University insignia. His father was a doctor, and he came to the Y in one of his father's cars. That didn't give him a big head or anything, even though he was the captain of the Lakeview swim team. They came to see me at the Y just to persuade me to go to Lakeview with them. The only stickler was, as Mr. Shults pointed out, that I didn't live anywhere close to the Lakeview area. My area was Waller High School, one of the lousiest in the whole city. It was possible, however, in such a big city, and having friends who lived so close to Lakeview High School, that I could go ahead and enroll in the school, giving Orville Clark's or Maurie Johnson's address. Mrs. Clark knew people at the school, and if they called her up she would say that I lived with Orville. If worse came to worst, which it probably wouldn't, I could live with Maurie Johnson and his brothers until the enrollment business was settled. They had rooms at the top of their house nobody had ever used. Mr. Shults did not want to conceal the fact that this was somewhat unethical behavior, but he felt it justified in terms of my future and the need we all felt to be together. Was I agreeable? Mr. Shults felt I should first discuss it with my father, who had impressed him as a reasonable man with my interests at heart.

It pretty much bowled me over to have so many fine people interested in my future. I said I'd discuss it with my father and let them know, but the truth was I didn't even mention it to him, fearing he might come up with something against it. I'd just tell him I was going back to school, and that would be it.

Orville Clark planned to be an engineer, Gene Logsdon a doctor, like his father, Maurie Johnson would be an accountant keeping the books for his father's dairy. What did I plan to do? I had no idea. Mr. Shults saw a future for me in the YMCA. As soon as I had high school behind me I would enroll in the Y college, and hold a position on the side, like Al Cox. In talks with Mr. Shults he had explained that the YMCA was a branch of Christian service, to which many were called but few were chosen. His feeling was that I was chosen. Boys just naturally looked up to me, even those who didn't like me. Their dislike for me was envy of my Christian character. They brought me money they had swiped to divvy up among them, knowing that I wouldn't take a cut, but I had later heard them howling with laughter because they thought me such a fool. When I prayed I could hear them snickering.

Until I knew better what I planned to be, the thing for me to do was take the cinch courses, like the history of art. These afternoon courses counted for double credit, and the time was passed fooling

80

around and looking at lantern slides. Mrs. Josephare taught this course, a shawl wrapped about her shoulders as she stood at the window, not troubling to turn and look at us while she talked. Her pince-nez glasses (was the pince for pinch?) dangled on a silken cord at her front and left a deep purple bruise on the bridge of her nose. When she asked for a boy to run the magic lantern, I raised my hand. I had learned how to run the one at the Y, showing pictures of the Holy Land on Sundays. Being in charge of the slides, as well as the lantern, I might stay after class to put things away. Mrs. Josephare liked to relax a moment in the empty room. On one side the windows glared with light, but on the others the walls were hung with pictures of Greece and Rome. Plaster busts were on pedestals near the door, with one of Rodin's *Hands* on her desk. She had met Rodin in Paris, where, to her dismay, his interest had proved to be in more than marble, but she thought him an artist of genius. It may have been the first time I heard the name pronounced.

After school I took the North Side elevated train to the Larrabee Y. On the twenty-minute ride I usually read my next assignment in the big thick book, *Literature and Life.* We began with Beowulf and Sir Thomas Malory. I understood little of what I read, but I was captivated by *Sir Gawain and the Green Knight,* and memorized passages while I was working in the cloakroom. I only saw my new friends in the halls at school, or on the Thursday evenings they came to the Y for a club meeting. Every day of the week I played Ping-Pong with Guagliardo. Nothing baffled him more than my going back to school. He had thought me peculiar from the first, but going back to school proved I was crazy. He was not at a loss for words in Italian, and I was not at a loss for what he was saying. Not that he didn't like me. He was also growing faster than I was and had a part-time job on a pie truck. When he had a shower and slicked his hair back, you could see how much he looked like Rudolph Valentino. The problem I had on my hands, busy as I was, was that I couldn't let him beat me at Ping-Pong. I knew that if he beat me my rule would be over. Sooner or later he would beat me, because he was good, and he had me to teach him all the fine points. When we were playing he wanted to win so bad I didn't think it was the Christian thing to beat him. So why did I do it? The day he beat me I would know if I was really cut out for Y work.

My friends at the Y had names like Domiano, Trombatore, Cavaretta, Scire, Giusi and LaMonica. The LaMonica brothers were pretty well off, and came to the Y wearing ties and rubbers on their shoes. Vito LaMonica had a birthmark on his face, but his skin was

81

so dark it hardly mattered. His older brother Johnny was working hard to be like me, Al Cox and Mr. Shults. He came to the Bible Study Club every Sunday, acted as treasurer and secretary, and helped put away the folding chairs. Sometimes he prayed aloud without being asked. Guagliardo hated Johnny LaMonica so much he snarled when he saw him, curling his lip back.

One Sunday in March I had a bad toothache and stayed home. In the rotogravure section of the *Sunday Tribune* I saw this drawing of a wolf with his fangs showing. I had never seen anything finer. Using paper I had bought for my art history notebook, I sat down and made a copy of it, using one of my father's indelible pencils. What I had done impressed both my father and me. The next day at school I showed it to Mrs. Josephare, who said, "Well, well, what have we here!" After school I showed it to Mr. Shults, who said he had no idea I had such talents. The Y lobby needed posters. Why didn't I plan to do them? He would supply me with the paper, the poster colors, the brushes, and give me seventy-five cents for each finished poster.

On the front page of the *Daily News* I saw this cartoon drawing of Calvin Coolidge. The likeness was not a copy, but it was wonderful. How was it done? In such a way I fell under the spell of art. Little it mattered that I showed little talent for it. This fever, which did not abate, persuaded me that I was destined to be an artist, with my drawings on the front pages of newspapers. I made drawings in my classes, in the study periods, on my way to and from school, in the cloakroom at the Y on Saturday nights. I filled my notebooks with sketches of my classmates. A great commitment fueled my purpose. In the basement of the Newberry Library on Clark Street I found back issues of newspapers and magazines. My fingers were black with India ink, the sleeves of my coat embedded with art gum. A pen and ink drawing of mine of Abraham Lincoln appeared in the high school paper on his birthday. The lobby of the Y hung with posters promoting moral virtues. Just in time to plan for the future it seemed obvious that I was an artist—among other things. Mr. Shults saw no conflict between this talent and the Christian work to which I was called. Quite the contrary. Guagliardo's admiration, noticeably weakening, had been restored. The Bible Sunday Club attendance, always diminished in the spring, was steady. At school Mrs. Josephare referred me to Miss Roth, head of the art department, as a student at that point in his career when special guidance would be most fruitful. With Miss Roth's permission and encouragement, I would major in art.

To get from the stove to the sink it was better to drop the leaf on

82

the table and then lean forward over the back of the rocking chair.
On the shelf over the sink were four plates, three cups and one saucer,
a glass sugar bowl, two metal forks, and one bone-handled spoon.
On the mantelpiece was a shaving mug with the word SWEETHEART
in silver, blue, chipped red, and gold. In the mug were three buttons,
a roller-skate key, a needle with a burned point for opening pimples,
an Omaha streetcar token, and a medal for buying Buster Brown shoes.
At the back of the room were folding doors that would not quite close.
(*The Works of Love*)

Over the summer I worked all day at the Y, except for the month I spent at the boys' summer camp in Michigan. I had fifteen Larrabee boys, only one of whom, Peter Deutsch, had ever seen a cow or been out in the country. There were no cows where we were. It was all woods that came right down to the edge of the lake, a mist rising off the water when we took our dips in the morning. None of them had ever heard an owl hooting at night, and they were frightened by the darkness. I would have to beam a flashlight on the ceiling and tell them stories until they fell asleep. Two of the boys wet their beds every night. Back on Larrabee Street, however, they all said they had had the time of their lives, and most of them, including me, had ringworm. Ringworm starts like a little pimple, then grows in a circle and takes weeks to cure. I had it in my right eyebrow, which made it harder to see, but it also took longer to cure. The two Scarlatti boys brought the ringworm home to their five brothers and sisters, and some relations living with them, so they still had it around at Christmas. It was silly to tell them not to use the same towel, and stuff like that.

I felt I'd lost so much time over the summer I signed up for a correspondence course in drawing in order to get the free drawing kit they would sent me. To save time between lessons, I delivered my drawings to the school on South Wabash Avenue. It was not much of a school. Three or four people sat around a big table, and I could tell they were surprised to see me. One of them explained to me that a correspondence course was by correspondence. In less than a month I went through what was supposed to have been a six-month course.

One Sunday in Lincoln Park I had been at the zoo drawing polar bears. On my way home I saw this small crowd of people gathered around the statue of Lincoln. A woman wearing a veil, with several elderly men, was placing a wreath of flowers at the foot of the statue. Some Boy Scouts with flags stood in the court at the front, and to watch what was happening I joined them. After she had placed the wreath she turned to the row of Boy Scouts and gave each of them a kiss, including me. Not until I saw the picture in the rotogravure did I know that I had been kissed by Queen Marie of Rumania. Nothing like that would have ever happened to me in Omaha.

My father didn't expect me to be home on Sundays, since I was either at the Y or off somewhere drawing. One Sunday Maurie Johnson, with his father's new Buick, brought his brothers to the Bible Sunday Club so we could all go to a movie in the Loop later. On the way we stopped by where I lived, so I could change my clothes. I ran up the stairs into the bedroom at the front, to see my father, his back to me, seated on a chair with a girl in his lap. Her name was Hilda. She worked in the German restaurant on Sedgwick Street. Her unblinking eyes, her head bobbing, stared into mine over my father's shoulder. Her head continued to bob, my father hoarsely breathing, as if unable to stop the machine he had started. I ran back down the stairs, got into the car, and we all drove around in Maurie's father's new Buick until it was time for the first matinee. If we liked the vaudeville, which we usually did, we would stay and see it twice.

I knew from experience about men and women, but from the air I breathed I had acquired my own standards. Mr. Mulligan had been the first to instruct me in morals. On a spring day in Omaha, seated in the Mulligan yard, he had spelled out the distinction between pure women, like Mrs. Mulligan, and the loose women on lower Douglas Street, who lured men and Western Union messenger boys into evil. The air around crackled with these revelations. Later Joey and I walked together, hand in hand, up Capitol Avenue and north to Creighton, until the fever of our initiation had cooled. Joey's eyes sparkled. The blond fuzz stood clear on his burning cheeks. Eggnogs were waiting for us on our return, but we gulped them in silence, easy on the nutmeg, brimming over with the awe and wonder we felt for Mrs. Mulligan. Corseted and queenly, a flush at her throat, she sat erect on the daybed, her short legs extended toward us, the gas hissing in the mantle as we waited for the spell to pass.

My father's practice deepened what was prudish in my nature, a vein that ran deep. I was shocked by the use of words I knew well, and embarrassed by the talk among my friends of things I knew better than they did. Under the racket of the elevated trains I had witnessed gang shags on YMCA mats. Whatever else I was, or might be, I was not one of them. This had the effect among the boys at the Y of enhancing my baffling character and reputation. I often watched, after the Bible Club meeting, the crap games held on the steps of the Y, but my role was that of an umpire. They would give me money they feared to be caught with.

84

In the lobby, however, where I had to keep order, if I grabbed the wrong kid because I didn't know better—a Trombatore or a Domiano—a gang of older boys might be back later and break most of the windows at the front of the building. Or they would march through the lobby to the locker room and empty all of the lockers into the pool. There was nothing to do but clean out the pool, and try not to grab the wrong kid in the lobby.

Well, that was how it was, and if it sometimes seemed strange it was hardly any stranger than anything else, and not so strange as the fact that he only felt at home in hotel lobbies. . . . He liked to sit in a big armchair at the front—in a leather-covered chair, if they happened to have one—and under a leafy potted palm, in case they had that. He liked a good view of the cigar counter, and the desk. He liked the sound of the keys when they dropped on the counter, the sound of the mail dropping into the slots, and the sound of the dice—though he never gambled—in the leather cup. God knows why, but there was something he liked about it. Hearing that sound, he immediately felt at home. (The Works of Love)

In the fall I saw more of my new school friends, Bill Miller, Orville Clark, Gene Logsdon, and the Johnson brothers, and in the big Johnson house, behind their dairy on Ashland, there were always three or four bottles of milk and boxes of cornflakes on the kitchen table. One of the few English words Mrs. Johnson knew, and liked to use, was *eat.* "Eat! Eat!" she would say to me, pointing at the table, since in her opinion I was too skinny. Maurie's younger brother, Clarey, had legs like stilts, but he was short in the waist. He had dropped out of school, which he didn't like, and helped his mother in the house and with the cooking. Maurie's older brother, Andy, should have been a girl: when he put on a woman's hat he looked like the movie star Anna Q. Nilsson. Mr. Johnson let Maurie drive his new Buick because the city traffic made him nervous. He had injured his hand in the bottling machinery and often had trouble in trying to work the gearshift. On Sundays if Maurie had use of the car we would all drive to a show where the audience sang along with the organ. There were so many good songs to sing we might take in another show in the evening. Back at Maurie's house, if his parents were in bed, we would call up one of their nearby neighbors and say that the Light and Power people were calling. Would they go to the window and see if the lights were on in the street? When Mr. Steiger, or his wife, came to the window we would be laughing so hard we could hardly stand it. Only Bill Miller could keep from laughing when he put through a call; the rest of us would be stretched out on the floor, a pillow over our heads to keep from snorting. Right when we were getting even better ideas we stopped.

My art teacher, Miss Roth, might have been the model for the Rossetti paintings on several of our lantern slides. Her crown of golden hair often glowed like a halo. When she leaned over my shoulder, or took my pencil to make a correction, my heart pounded. Her health was frail. Wrapped up in her shawls, warming her hands at the heater, she looked like a beautiful child. She had done illustrations for art magazines, and owned a drawing by James Montgomery Flagg which we were free to study for pen technique. I was torn between my plans to be a great cartoonist and my desire to illustrate the stories in the *Saturday Evening Post.* At no time did it cross my mind to paint such pictures as I saw on the slides or collected to paste in my notebooks. They came with museums, and were created by people different than myself. My art history notebook contained almost a hundred pictures, each mounted on a sheet of colored paper. *The Man with the Golden Helmet* was my favorite painting. My favorite sculpture was Rodin's *The Kiss,* but I had more sense than to admit it. In my imagination I saw his hand move slowly up her side to her breast, but something always happened before it reached its destination. I was seventeen years of age, and fuzz was growing on my upper lip.

If the night was warm his father would walk past the mossgreen statue of Abraham Lincoln, then on across the tennis courts with their sagging nets and blurred chalk lines. There would be men with their shoes off padding around in the grass. There might be women with white arms in the shadows, fussing with their hair. Under sheets of newspaper, with what was left of the food, some child would lie asleep. If there was a moon, or a cool breeze off the lake, he would walk through the park to the water, where he would stroll along the pilings or under the trees on the bridle path. In the dusk there would be lights on the Wrigley Tower, an airplane beacon would sweep the sky, and at Oak Street beach people would be lying in the warm sand. The drinking fountain would give off a strong chlorine smell. He would wet his face at the fountain, then take his seat among those people who had come to the beach but didn't care to take off their clothes: who had been hot in their rooms, and perhaps lonely in their minds. In the dark they could speak what they had on their minds without troubling about their faces, the sound of their voices, or who their neighbor was. He was their neighbor. He sat with his coat folded in his lap, his shirtsleeves rolled. (The Works of Love)

86

Although not back on his feet in the manner he had hoped, with collateral to start up his own business, my father was sorting freight waybills at night in order to have more daytime to work for himself. I would often just be getting out of bed at the time he was ready to get into it. He would drape his pants on the seat of a chair and hang his shirt and tie on the bedpost. In Chicago he had stopped wearing the high stiff collars and wore those that came with the shirt, like I did. In a pinch I could wear his shirts if I turned back the sleeves. He ate breakfast in his underwear, his pants unbuttoned, sitting straddle-legged on the edge of his chair as he poured canned milk into his coffee. If the green holes were plugged up he would open them with one prong of a fork. The smell of the canned milk in the coffee almost made me sick. I was also getting critical of the talk about his plans for himself, and his plans for me. His plans for me always included a new mother. I didn't want a new mother, and I wasn't so sure I wanted to live in the country, or go to Yale. When he read to me the want ads for men who were wanted, none of them remotely suggested my father. Who did he think he was? He seemed to think he was whoever seemed to be wanted. He was a kind man, and I think he really liked me, but I was repelled by his ways with women. How did he ever think a man like himself would find a new mother for *me*? I experienced scorn. Did my lip curl in the manner of Guagliardo when he saw Johnny LaMonica? I was determined not to work for my father, and I looked forward to not living with him. I wanted to go my own way. I did not like the way he joshed and ogled waitresses, or turned in the street to look at passing women. I did that myself, of course, just as I was not superior to sitting in the darkened bathroom, the blind raised, to watch a shapely neighbor, in silhouette, step from the tub to dry herself with a towel, or put up her hair. With my elevated moral standards my own behavior was not a problem. No woman had yet seduced me, although my hopes were rising. I had little or no suspicion that my true feelings were precisely those that I would learn to conceal.

Most of that summer I spent in northern Michigan, at Camp Martin Johnson. Martin Johnson was an old white-haired man who lived in the woods by himself, like Thoreau. He had given all of his property to the YMCA so that city boys would know what it was like to live with nature. In my cabin I had boys who were experienced with camping, and near the end of the summer about ten of us made a long canoe trip on the Little Manistee. We had to canoe in some really fast water, and spend the nights in the open, fighting mosquitoes. When we had to portage the canoes, which was often, mosquitoes would settle in a swarm between our shoulder blades, where we couldn't reach them. I had never been in real wild woods before, or lived on nothing but fig newtons and river water. The trip was marred for me by the way my companion liked to talk about girls while he was paddling. He couldn't seem to get girls off his mind, even out there in the woods. What he wanted to do was get a girl he knew all alone in the woods, in his canoe. Suppose it was your own sister? I asked him. Who would ever go camping with his sister? he replied. At the end of the summer, when the medals were awarded, I couldn't bring myself to vote for him, but he won one anyhow.

When I came back from camp, where the air had been clean, and I had drunk the water right out of the river, I found a pair of silk stockings on the hook in the bathroom and I could smell perfume on my pillow. I put my clothes into the camp duffel bag and moved to the Y. I felt great, but it was a dumb thing to do. I had to live on ten dollars a week, including carfare and weekend movies. Mr. Shults called to my attention that the neighborhood newspaper was running a contest for the best cartoon on a political subject. The prize was twenty-five dollars, with publication in the paper. The only stipulation was that the cartoonist had to live in the local area. I submitted about two dozen cartoons that Mr. Shults considered real prizewinners. About a month later they awarded the prize to a cartoon so dumb Mr. Shults complained about it. They told him that I had been the first choice for the prize, but when they tried to get in touch with me at home they couldn't. Nobody answered the phone. They concluded that I lived somewhere else and had entered the contest illegally. What stunned me was to have been both a winner and a loser in such a whimsical manner. In spite of my experience, I had never questioned that this world was good enough as it was, if not the best possible. Could rewards for the effort be so fickle? Up to this point nothing had diminished the abundant optimism of my nature, or led me to question the confidence I brought to my enthusiasms. This did—but I lacked the time to sulk. My sense of loss was too complex to explain, and for the first time I grasped that I needed a companion I did not have. In a moment so unusual I would never forget it—thinking that I was taking a girl to the movies—my father said to me, "Kid, a good girl can be the best friend a boy ever had."

I hadn't known that. It astonished me to learn that at one time in his life my father had.

ONE SUNDAY MORNING, TO MY AMAZEMENT, my father appeared in the lobby of the Larrabee Y. His new top-coat hung open to reveal a new dark suit. He had stopped to chat with Mr. Shults at the counter, and Mr. Shults was favorably impressed. My father was a good talker, and he looked pretty good when he was dressed up. Joshingly he explained that he had come to see me, since it seemed that I lacked the time to see him. Mr. Shults apologized for me, but said that my father's loss was the Y's gain, and he was certain I had a future in Christian service. He also welcomed the chance to speak to my father about me, which he did while I played a little Ping-Pong.

My father had a few words with me privately as we sat under a lamp at the back of the lobby. When he wrote me a letter he referred to me as "son," but when he spoke to me he usually said "kid," unless I was being introduced to a woman. Personally, I liked "son," since that was what I was, and the word "kid" applied to almost everybody. On the other hand, when he called me "son" it was usually because he wanted something. "Son," he said to me, "your dad's been thinking we need a new start." I figured that meant a new woman in our lives, which would explain the new outfit he was wearing.

"I've got my work here," I said, to head him off, but he replied, "Don't jump to conclusions." We both knew what those conclusions were.

"What I plan, kid," he said, "is a new start for us in California." That surprised me. All I knew about California I had learned from the posters in the Dearborn railroad station lobby, but it had been enough. He talked some more about how much he disliked the heat of the summers, which was soon followed by the cold of the winters, and why should anybody put up with that when there was a place like California to go to? I hadn't thought much about it, but I began to. I saw myself on the glass-bottomed boat sailing to Mr. Wrigley's Catalina Island, where the Cubs did their spring training. When did he plan to go? I asked him.

That was where he wanted my opinion, and it may have been the first time he ever asked it. In the want ad section, under "Personals," he had seen travel opportunities offered by people who were driving to Califoria. The owner of the car would share expenses with the person, or persons, who went along with him. What sort of people, my father asked me, did I think I would enjoy traveling with?

I hadn't given it much thought, but it pleased me to be consulted. Even my father had learned that I was the one who knew about cars, and could change tires. On South State Street, when we arrived in Chicago, I had seen a battered old touring car with tire casings roped to the front and rear bumpers, cans for gas and oil in a rack on the running board, canvas water bags between the hood and the fenders, the cracked windshield smeared with rusty water from the radiator, and the whole car, including the dashboard, under a film of dust so thick you could write in it, which was what somebody had done. Across the rear end was fingerprinted CALIFORNIA OR BUST. If I was driving that car I would need a pair of goggles and would wear my cap backwards, with the brim at the rear.

Wouldn't it depend on the car? I said. That too was my father's opinion. The larger the car, for example, the more passengers there would be to share expenses. He regretted not knowing about this form of travel when we drove from Omaha to Chicago. How soon, he asked me, would I feel free to start?

Was I able to conceal my excitement? I imagined what it might be like to drive across real deserts, and snow-covered mountains. I would go to school later, in California! I had seen college movies of suntanned boys and girls, in a shimmer of happiness, driving around in sports cars. I was all ready to go immediately, but my father thought I should finish the semester of school I had started. We would also need time to buy a car and make the necessary arrangements. What did I think, he asked me, of this?

> *Driving Southern California.*
> *Seek congenial passengers*
> *to share expenses. Warm*
> *southern route all the way.*

I recognized the cryptic shorthand style as that of a railroad agent and telegraph operator. My father felt that he should run the ad before we bought the car. If a larger number of travelers responded, we'd want a bigger car, and have more money to buy it. He had given the project considerable thought. Each passenger would be limited to one bag, and ladies, if present, should be with their husbands. After our experience with the Studebaker he wanted my advice about the best tires. I wanted Kelly Springfields, but I knew we would get what came with the car.

90

On Sunday afternoons, in my lobby of the Barclay Hotel on Clark Street, my father would meet with the people who had responded to his ad in the "Personals" column. One of them proved to be a plainclothes policeman checking on men who used want ads to seduce women. He wanted to know where my father came from, where he lived, and where he worked. My father had to bring him back to our apartment so he could meet me. I was working on a cartoon for the high school paper, and he pulled up a chair to watch me. He couldn't figure out a shady character like my father with a boy like me. My father gave our previous address as Central City, where he had been a station agent and run a big chicken business, since any address in Omaha would show the police were looking for him. They might be looking for me, if they knew I'd been put in a reformatory for stealing something.

My father was so certain the policeman would be back we put our traveling clothes into one bag and moved into a housekeeping room on Shelby. What we would do, my father said, would be to get us a car and then pick up the passengers later. Chicago wasn't the only town that was full of people who would rather live in California. Right down the road a piece was St. Louis, and just west of St. Louis there was Kansas City, a town a lot of people would like to get away from. But my father would like to see it, just in case he liked it better than Omaha.

In a garage on North Clark Street, mostly used for storage, my father stumbled on just the car we needed. A pair of old ladies had owned it, one of whom had just died, and the garageman was selling it for the storage costs. The rubber was like new. It hadn't been out of the garage for more than two years. I liked the Essex coach to look at, with its plush upholstery, but there was only room for about four people, including us. My father said that when two people of the right class, or three people if they were smaller, saw we were driving all the way in an Essex coach they wouldn't hesitate to share the expenses. Would it run? The garageman said we were free to take it for a drive around the block. The motor turned right over when I kicked the starter. If she smoked a little, as she did, that was due to the long period of time she had just sat there and not run much. I drove about a half mile north, then came back through the park. I thought she steered a little hard on the turns, but that might have been because the tires were low. On the radiator cap a thermometer registered the temperature of the water, in case it got hot. She ran pretty smooth. I liked driving around in such a tight little box.

"Kid," my father said, "how you like it?"

I said I liked it fine.

My father signed the papers and gave the garageman $125 in cash. he gave us, gratis, five gallons of gas. With the free gas we took a spin through the park, the bare trees already looking pretty much like winter. There was ice building up on the pilings along the lakefront. "What are we waiting for!" my father said, and slapped his hands together. We still had four days of paid-up rent, but my father had lost his feeling that his future was in Chicago. In no way had it lived up to his expectations. If I thought about it, which I took time to do, it was Chicago that had given me the expectations that I was now looking up to—but it was easy for me, if given the chance, to shift them over to California. I would just feel stronger what I had been feeling all the time.

Coming back to a place you like can be nice, as I had felt coming back to Omaha from the farm, but taking off for California, with the first snow falling, is like nothing else.

As the motor warmed up and began to run a little loose, I could feel this dull knock through the gas pedal, even before I heard it. It more or less stopped when I gave it the gas, or we were pulling up a long grade. I'd heard that crooked car dealers would put sawdust in an engine to take up the slack and keep a bearing from knocking, but I hadn't heard what could be done about it.

Long drives nearly always made my father sleepy, and he dozed off before we reached Joliet. Near Springfield the road curved between farm buildings that sit so close to its edge I could see in the windows. Then we crossed a bridge, the water black beneath it, with a big tilted barn dark against the snow with a deep purple shadow beside it. Nothing special. Just something I would never forget.

In 1927 most of the highways led to the center of towns, then out again. When we stopped at the lights, in Springfield, the people standing on the corner could hear the loud knock of our motor. So could my father. "What's that, kid?" he said. I thought it might be a connecting rod. I didn't know what connecting rods connected, but I didn't want to mention the word "bearing." I knew about bearings. They called for a motor overhaul. When we stopped for oil my father asked the mechanic if he would like to buy a car.

"This one?" he asked.

We nodded. He listened to the knock.

"That bearing's burned out," he said.

My father said, "Make me an offer."

He put his head in to look at the plush upholstery. "Sixty dollars," he said.

My father said, "I paid more than that for the rubber."

He said, "Take it or leave it."

"Kid," my father said, "should we take it?"

"Sure," I replied.

We had supper in a café the mechanic recommended, where we sat on stools at the counter. We had lost sixty-five dollars on the deal, but my father had gone up in my estimation. He took a large supply of toothpicks from the glass when he paid the cashier.

We took a bus to St. Louis, where we saved money by taking a night bus to Kansas City. The first thing we did was go to the Kansas City *Star* and put in the same ad we had run in Chicago. As he looked through the want ads my father asked me what I thought of a 1921 Big Six Studebaker.

"How much?" I asked him.

"One sixty-five," he said.

"Not bad," I replied.

One thing it would do would be to take at least five passengers. At twenty-five dollars apiece that would almost pay for the car. Like the Essex coach, it sat at the back of a garage, but it hadn't been owned by two old ladies. The man who owned it had turned it in on a Maxwell Coupe. The tires were not so good for a trip to California, but it had a full set of side curtains.

"Should we risk it, kid?" my father asked me.

"Sure," I said.

I put the curtains on the car, and parked across the street from the hotel's steam-heated lobby. From our room at the front we could keep an eye on it. The first person we met, but not the first to sign up, was a one-legged Greek actor going to the Passion Play in Los Angeles. The part he was in was waiting for him to get there. He wore the empty leg of his pants pinned up, and spent most of the day in a chair in the lobby waiting to see if anybody signed up. He also felt he should go for less, since with just one leg he took up less room.

Mr. Griffin, from Akron, Ohio, was on his way to meet his wife, Nora, in Pasadena. He was a soft-shoe dancer, no taller than I was, wearing a checkered suit, a tight fitting cap and patent leather oxfords. He liked me all right, but he didn't get along with Mr. Dorfmann, a gambler from New Orleans, who sat and played cards with himself. We had a woman who would go as far as San Bernardino if she could ride up front with me, if I was driving, but besides two suitcases she had a roped army locker. If it turned out we didn't have a full car she could go along, but we had seven passengers. Three would sit in the front, and my father would sit on a suitcase between the foldaway seats in the rear. We put the bags in the racks on the running boards, or between the engine hood and the fenders. I'd got to be pretty friendly with the people in the lobby, but the hotel manager was glad to see us leave.

Kansas City is on a bluff overlooking the Missouri, with a pretty steep drop to the bridge, and to save the brakes on this grade I put the car in second gear to slow it. Halfway down the slope, without any warning, the whole gear box dropped right into the street. Between the legs of Mr. Griffin, who was sitting beside me, there was this big hole in the floor. Since we were on a grade I let it coast into a garage just off the road. Several people I don't remember at all took their bags off the car and just walked away. Those who didn't just sat in the car while my father made a deal to swap the Studebaker, just as it was, for a 1919 Buick touring with a California top. It was a smaller car, and not much to look at with its low hood and bicycle-size wheels, but it had an original-type gearshift. Sitting there in the garage, it ran like a top. The four people left crowded the seats a bit, but they all appreciated the California top. I was so preoccupied with the gearshift I hardly got more than a glance at the Missouri, which looked about the same between the banks of snow as it did in Omaha.

About two weeks later, early in January, my father and me and a young man named Don arrived in Albuquerque, New Mexico. We still had the Buick, but none of the passengers. In the railroad station, where we passed the time and discussed with Don what we might do next, there were Indians waiting for the trains to sell their blankets and pottery. If I didn't dream it up, some of the streetcars had women motormen and conductors. It had been a long journey. I had grown accustomed to seeing strange things. Back in Gallup the one-legged actor had said goodbye to me in a bus station. Out in the street the car was buried in a foot of snow. Don had been the one who helped me get it started, and having nothing else to do had driven along with us, all of us sitting in front. He happened to be passing through Gallup at the same time we were, on his way to Long Beach from Amarillo. He showed me how to cut the bead off an old tire so it would lap around the flat tire you left on the rim and made a hard rubber tire you could ride on. He almost broke my arm when we Indian wrestled. While we were waiting for the snow to melt in the mountain passes, my father passed the time in the station lobby talking about his railroad experience with the agent. When the snow began to melt Don just rode along with us, since we had the room.

In Arizona we heard of a hole in the earth, wide and deep as a canyon, made by a falling meteor, but we couldn't see it from the road.

It snowed in Flagstaff, where Don left us, and we spent the night in the warm station lobby. Near Siberia, California, or where it had once been, I didn't see the turn in the road and drove about fifty yards or more into the desert's soft sand. That's where we were, wondering what to do next, when Don came along riding a motorcycle with a sidecar. My father sat in the sidecar, and I rode on the rear of the motorcycle, holding onto Don. That's why we arrived in San Bernardino with my eyes so windburned I could hardly see it. My lips were so chapped it was painful to suck on oranges. The orange trees grew right along the roads, rows and rows of them, leading back toward the mountains, some of the oranges so close we could reach out and pick them. My father had the address of a man in Cucamonga, but he was no longer living at that number, so we went on ahead, between the orange groves, the shimmering sky and the snow-capped mountains. I don't remember saying much until Azusa, where we ran out of gas.

IN LOS ANGELES WE FOUND A ROOM OFF SEVENTH
Street, in the home of a widow who was one of Aimee Semple
McPherson's angels. When she was not in the temple, she was at home
taking long hot baths. I had most of the day to walk up and down
Main Street, looking at the watches in the pawnshop windows. On
the cold rainy days I took in the shows at the Hippodrome. Sunny
days I sat in the park on Olvera Street, where Sunset Boulevard ended
at Main Street. George Young, who was from Canada, and hardly
any older than I was, had swum from California to Catalina Island
and won $25,000 of William Wrigley's money. I saw him swim in
a big glass tank of water on the stage of Grauman's Chinese Theatre.
Back in Chicago there was snow and slush in the streets and you could
almost freeze waiting for a streetcar. Who would ever believe that I
was here in California, the sun warm on my face.

Twice a day I ate the flapjacks that were cooked in a window
near the Hippodrome. One day I saw the Greek actor with the one
leg at a lunch counter in the Pacific Electric Car terminal on Seventh
Street, but he didn't see me. My father took a position with Western
Union on the strength of his experience with the Union Pacific
Railroad. I could see him, in the office on Main Street, typing out
telegrams to be sent as night letters, his shirt sleeves turned back to
keep his cuffs clean. We planned to get a car and drive to Long Beach,
where some people lived who were my second cousins and had come
out here from Ohio. If it ever stopped raining I planned to get down
to the ocean and take the glass-bottomed boat to Catalina. Running
an errand for the widow, who paid me for it, I discovered Echo Park
on West Wilshire, where there were swans on the lake and rowboats
to be rented. Even my father didn't believe me when I told him I'd
seen real swans on a lake in February.

One afternoon in Pershing Square I saw my father in discussion
with a woman. He looked good when he was sitting and talking, with
one leg crossed, his arm along the bench back, the fingers of his right
hand hooked to his vest pocket. I didn't have to hear him to know
he was talking about raising capital for the egg business, or this boy
he had who needed a new mother. When she left he crossed the street
to the Biltmore, as if he lived there, and sat in the mezzanine arcade
chewing on toothpicks. It was easy to see that his pants no longer went

with the coat. Although I'd meant to spy on where he was going, I changed my mind. California wasn't all he'd expected either, full of people who were tight-fisted with their money, or women who were suspicious of anybody not from Cedar Rapids. My father had been to Cedar Rapids, and if there was one town that made Omaha look pretty good, that was it.

In the streets south of Main were the used car lots, and I began to read the messages printed on the windshields. One that caught my eye was a dark green Marmon with wire wheels. On the windshield it read, SWEET RUNNER/MAKE OFFER.

This Marmon had a Red Seal airplane motor, and a hood so long and high the driver's seat was like a cockpit. When I scrunched down in the seat the radiator cap was on my eye level, like a gunsight. There were two foldaway seats in the rear, with room to spare for some luggage. The salesman said he was from Des Moines, but he had been to Omaha with the American Legion, and seen the Ak-sar-ben parade. "Tell your daddy to make me an offer," he said. "She's a real sweet runner, with good rubber."

The good rubber was hard to see on such small wheels. I got the idea that maybe ninety dollars would buy it, if we didn't rile up the salesman. I took my father around for a look at it, and sat behind the wheel while they talked about it. My father couldn't even crank a car, but you couldn't tell him anything about them. "That car's a gas eater," he said, which was something he'd picked up somewhere. It was painful just to hear him talk about it, since I wanted it so bad it made me ache to look at it.

"Kid," my father said, "when he really wants to sell that car we'll be back."

Wonderful as it was in Los Angeles, compared with what it was like in Chicago, there was no lack of people who had found that California hadn't lived up to their expectations. They didn't like the natives, most of whom were from somewhere else. Others were not so keen on the climate. They missed the snow in the winter. They missed the coming of spring. We could have filled two cars with the people who wanted to leave, but not all of them could put up the money on short notice. We narrowed it down to seven, not counting the fox terrier that would ride with me in the front seat. A sailor named Red, going home to Pittsburgh, sat on one of the spares with my father. Mr. Olsen, about the size of two people, was only going as far as El Paso, where we would all have room to spare when he left. A ten-year-old boy who had an uncle in Phoenix, and was living with his aunt in Alameda at the moment, wanted to ride along with us as far as Phoenix, but experience had made my father cautious. Places on the map always looked closer than they proved to be.

No one could have asked for a sweeter-running car than that Marmon was, as far as Redlands. The sailor, Red, who was sitting on a spare, was the first to say that it sounded like valves. The hiss it made was more of a valve sound than bad plugs. Up till that moment I was inexperienced with valves, which were something an airplane motor had a lot of. When they began to seal up, as we got close to Redlands, you got a hissing effect like a calliope. We got there in time to find a garage before it was dark. The two days we were there I got to know the mechanic about as well as I did the big Red Seal motor. His name was Zeke. He wore a hat he made by folding a newspaper to keep the grease out of his hair.

To make up for the time we had lost in Redlands we drove all night through the Imperial Valley but I could see better on the map how it looked. In the moonlight the Salton Sea looked black. Near Yuma the old road lay out on the sand dunes like a picket fence blown over on its side. Just out of Yuma we blew a tire and it took Mr. Olsen to pry it off the rim. Floods had washed out the bridge on the Gila River, so we had to make a detour through Indian country. It was more of a pack trail than a road, with gullies in it so deep there was a gap between the front and rear wheels. In less than half a day's driving all the tires were flat. What we did was cut the bead off the spares and just let them wrap around the rim, the way Don had showed me, or we'd still be out there somewhere. I learned later in Tucson that the Indians we saw were Papagos.

About a mile above the town we straddled the trail. Parts of it had once been a road and there was wagon room between the boulders, but now scrubs were growing at the edge and the center was bare. The foot path was smooth and dusty with donkey manure. When we knew we should have turned back there was no place to turn. It got dark while we sat and argued what we should do. Some Indians stood off a ways and looked at us. When I said "Tucson?" one of them pointed up the trail and we all felt better and started up again. It was soon so steep I had to shift to low. At that speed our lights were dim and flickered like a fan was turning in front. I had to stop and race the motor to see ahead. Coyotes were thick as cats behind a store. Their eyes blinked at the lights and when we got by they sat and howled, the echoes nice but the real thing too near. There were gullies that almost stood us on end and bent the bumper back on the fenders, and bumps I had to squeeze around or drag the rear end. . . . The battery was running down with the lights on and I kept racing the engine like hell all the time. But she had the power to burn, even when the hood rose up like a wall. After a while I kind of liked it, kind of wanted bigger gullies, liked to give her the soup and watch her climb right out. She had enough stuff in low to climb a tree. When it got really bad Red walked up front, his white cap pinned to his behind . . . when the road eased off we rolled along in second and it felt like high, which showed how it was back where we'd just come from. (My Uncle Dudley, 1942)

After we left the Papagos trading post there was no road at all, just the downgrade slope covered with scrub and cactus, a smudge of smoke way off to the southeast that might be Tucson. Except for me at the wheel, everybody walked. Now and then I could see the mirrorlike flash of sunlight on a car windshield. We came out on the level beside an irrigation canal, with the road to Tucson on the far side of it. Everybody took a rest, soaking their feet in the water, then we had to go another ten miles to reach a crossing. I didn't mind it so much as the others, because, as my father said, I didn't know any better. And for another thing I was driving. Tucson wasn't at all what I thought it would be, but we were able to buy good secondhand tires from a man with a machine for putting them on the rims. He didn't seem surprised to see us and wasn't at all talkative while he worked.

Clear over near Deming, in New Mexico, the threads stripped on the right front wheel; when it dropped off I could see it for a moment at the rim of the lights. We had to wait till daylight to find it in the desert, then spend half the morning jacking up the front end. Crossing Texas there were days we made as much as 150 miles. It was cold driving at night, but warmed up fine during the day. Windburn alone gave me a good tan, and I often had the sun on my face in the morning. I especially liked the country around Shreveport, Louisiana, where the shacks back in the woods were like cans of Log Cabin syrup. The colored people hadn't seen many cars like ours, and most of them waved.

Just before noon we rolled into Lake Village, Arkansas. There was a lake with a pier at the foot of the street, but it was no resort. The road just ended there, facing the water, so I had to turn around and go back to the tracks. Crossing the tracks, which I did real easy, I felt this thump like the wheels had dropped off in the rear. When Red got out to check the wheels they were still there, but the rear-end transmission had dropped right on the tracks. I could tell that the two or three colored people who came closer to look at us thought we were crazy. We'd been driving all night, and with Mr. Olsen gone there was room enough to sleep in the back seat. It was so warm flies buzzed around us, but nobody moved. My father sat on one of the spares, his head resting on the back of the front seat. Red walked around to the back side of the car and peed on one of the wheels. They had a general store, and a feed store with this hand-cranked gas pump, but no garage. I was so tired I just sat there at the wheel as if waiting for a train to hit us. In the quiet I could hear the far-off pealing of bells.

"Maybe they just heard the war's ended," said Red, and guffawed.

A flat wagon, hitched to some sleepy mules, came down the street toward us, then turned at the corner. Packed tight on the tailboard, their legs dangling, were five or six colored boys, one holding a puppy. They didn't holler or wave, they just sat there. A white man, wearing an apron, came out of the general store, put two fingers in his mouth, shrilly whistled. All my life I had tried to do that, and couldn't. Both Red and me looked at him with admiration. Red said to him, "What happened?"

"Levee broke," he replied, and went back inside.

Everything he owned Red left in the duffel bag on the running board. "Let's go, kid," he said to me, and I climbed over the door, forgetting all sorts of stuff I meant to remember under the front seat. We were both good runners and caught up with the wagon, but it was moving so slow we went right by it. Up ahead of us, where the road forked, we could see people strung along carrying sacks and parcels. I could see that what I'd needed all these weeks was a good long run. We passed a lot of people, all of them friendly, to where the road ended at a pier. An excursion type boat, with a canvas awning, was taking on people. They still had room when we took off, but it seemed so calm and peaceful I didn't worry. There was hardly a ripple on the water until we got to where we could see it moiling. It was more like a lake than a river but we could see by the shore how fast we were drifting. I didn't really understand what a levee was, or what it would mean to have a break in it, until we got out of the boat near Greenville and I saw the whole city in the hollow below us, the river maybe thirty feet or more above it. Except for the queasy feeling that it gave me, it was a nice warm, balmy spring day.

Once we got across the river I could see that Red didn't want me tagging along behind him. Two people made it harder to catch a ride. He said I should look him up when I got to Pittsburgh, and gave me his home address and two dollars. I was on my own.

I spent the night in the Greenville depot, waiting for the levee to break and the river to wash us all away. The station was crowded with people looking for their friends and relations. I thought I might

100

find my father, since he felt more at home in a railroad station than anywhere else. I didn't see him, nor did I see Mr. Hansen, a big Swede I had grown to like. The fact was, except for Red and my father, I wasn't sure how many of us had arrived at the river. We had been so long crossing Texas I had lost track of both time and people.

In the early morning, on the road going north, a traveling salesman in a Maxwell coupe took me almost as far as Memphis. If I hadn't minded making all of the stops I could have ridden with him farther. He called the colored people in the cotton fields on both sides of the road a lot of niggers. He didn't mean it bad. He liked most of them. It was very exceptional, he told me, to see a white boy like me walking along the road in Mississippi. I said that I was headed for Chicago, but not that I'd come all the way from California. If I'd told him that he wouldn't have believed me. For all their traveling, the salesman I met hadn't seen as much of the world as I had.

There was a lot of flooding around Cairo, but it was easy to hitch a ride to St. Louis. Until they heard me talk, most people thought I was a victim of the flood, looking for my relations. In the St. Louis bus station, where I spent the night, I got to talking with one of the drivers. He said if I would stand on the corner he told me, he might pick me up, then again he might not. It all depended. But there was a chance he might. I was there on the spot he told me, and that's how I got a free ride from St. Louis to the Loop in Chicago, my hometown.

It was still only April, but a warm drizzle made it seem like summer, the streets slick and sticky. I just walked around and around in the Loop, feeling good to be back. I had a piece of pie at Pixley & Ehlers, where you can see people making them through the window, then I took a Clark streetcar to Menominee. It was like they all said, there's nothing like spring in Lincoln Park. A team with uniforms was holding a baseball practice on one of the diamonds that was not too muddy, and I could see the batter hit the ball before I heard the crack.

My father had arrived two days before I did, but he was still in bed catching up on his sleep. While he fried some eggs he told me of his plans to get back into the egg business. Until he raised the capital, what he would do would be to work nights for the railroad, sorting waybills. Would I like to know what he had learned? I said I would. Kid, he said, take my word, the grass isn't greener on the other side of the road.

At the Y Mr. Shults was glad to see me and offered me the job I had had in the lobby, but the truth was I no longer felt like working with kids. I did help him with the Bible Club on Sunday, where I gave them a talk about my trip to California, but seeing the world had given me ideas. I forget what they were, but almost everywhere I looked the grass looked as green as Christmas jewelry.

I took a job as office boy in the insurance department of the Commonwealth Edison Company in the Loop. My job was to air out the office in the morning, adjust all the blinds, and stamp and seal a lot of letters. I also carried checks that had to be signed to Mr. Samuel Insull's office on the floor above. He was a small, quiet man who didn't say much, and looked pretty dried up. I'd seen people like him in California. On those days there were not so many letters to stamp I got in a lot of drawing practice.

If I was offered something big with Commonwealth Edison I would stay with them, and save my money, otherwise I looked forward to being with my friends at Lakeview High School. We didn't horse around so much as we used to, but talked a lot about what we planned to do. Gene Logsdon was dating some girl named Florence, so we hardly saw him on weekends. What I planned to do, and right away, was build myself up. I had grown two inches in about five months, but I was stringy as pulled taffy. Traveling around with grown men, I took a lot of kidding I wouldn't have taken if I had had more muscle. In the window of a drugstore on LaSalle Street, I saw a man with a build like Lionel Strongfort exercising with a strip of rubber. He could make every muscle in his chest ripple with it. I didn't believe everything that I saw or read, but it was less than a dollar, with instructions, so I bought it. Just before I went to bed I exercised for half an hour, and drank a pint of milk along with a cake of Fleischmann's yeast. It took some doing to get the yeast down, but chocolate milk helped. I couldn't believe it myself when I went to the Y and saw how I looked in the locker-room mirror. I'd gained more than four pounds in about three weeks. On the strength of that I exercised in the morning for at least twenty minutes before I went to work, and I used a spring-grip exerciser when I was walking around or riding the streetcars. I drank an awful lot of milk. Eddie Kovack, the Y phys ed instructor, saw me doing exercises on the parallel bars. I could see he couldn't believe it. "What's going on here?" he said, feeling my triceps. It wasn't hard for me to keep at anything that worked. I got permission to pull the weights at the Y on Sundays, after I had finished with the Bible Club.

My boss at work, Charlie Miller, who came to work in his slippers because he had foot problems, had a talk with me about my future. He had hired me because we were both farmboys, and he felt I had a future in the department. But I let my mind wander. He could see

that from where he sat. It had pleased him to take me into the department, and he had no serious complaints about my work, but increas-
ingly he felt that I was not really there in the office with the rest of
them. Not 100 percent. So where was I? I liked Charlie Miller, but
I couldn't tell him that what I had on my mind was grass so green
I could almost eat it. I saw it everywhere I looked. I said I really didn't
know where I was, because I'd already been to so many places, like
Omaha, Kansas City, Albuquerque, Yuma, Los Angeles, El Paso,
Shreveport, Louisiana, and Lake Village, Arkansas, in the flood, but
I knew all right.

One day in May Charlie Miller held my legs at the window of
his office while I emptied all of our wastebaskets on Lindbergh, the
Lone Eagle, below on Clark Street. If there was one thing Lindbergh
knew, Charlie Miller said, it was where he was. And where he was
going.

My father agreed to pay me ten dollars a week over the summer
if I would help him sort his waybills at night. That way we would
both have most of the daytime free. I'd come to work about midnight,
when the tower room was cooler, and usually work until about
daylight. I liked being in the tower, but I hated the work. Handling
the carbon sheets of waybills blackened my fingers, and I picked up
splinters from the edge of the sorting table. I didn't like the way my
father, so he could sort the bills better, always flicked his dirty thumb
on his tongue, leaving a raw-looking pink spot. He worked in his shirt
sleeves, the cuffs turned back, but leaning over the table frayed the
material at the front of his pants. He was getting a pot, like Mr. Miller,
and after working for an hour he had to rest and get off his feet. From
the tower room we could see the traffic flowing over the drawbridge,
and watch it go up like a wall when a boat passed. High at the top
of the span the lights blinked like planets. Behind it the lights of cars
glowed like a fire at an oven door. Two or three times an hour my
father would pause to look at the clock on the Wrigley Tower.

"What time is it, kid?" he would ask me, but he never remembered
what I told him. He didn't wear his own watch because it made a bulge
in his pants where he leaned on the table. Some nights we were still
there when the sky lit up in the east.

When my father took the job, and the weather was good, he
liked to walk down Chicago Avenue to the waterworks, then along
Michigan Boulevard and the Gold Coast to Lincoln Park. But that
summer his feet were so tired after standing all night he would take
a streetcar to Clark Street and transfer. The cars ran so seldom at that
time in the morning he had time to get his breakfast at a Thompson's

restaurant between transfers. I might see him sitting in the Thompson's when I passed by. On the hot summer nights there would still be people on the beach at Oak Street sleeping on the sand. Before I reached Lincoln Park there might be lights on in the windows of the top-floor apartments and rich people with their horses on the bridle path. On a walk that long I must have done a lot of thinking, but if I did I've forgotten what it was.

If the old man who sorted waybills in the freight yards felt himself more alive there than anywhere else, it had something to do with the tower room where he worked. On one side of the room was a large bay window that faced the east. A man standing at this window— like the man on the canal who let the drawbridge up and down—felt himself in charge of the flow of traffic, of the city itself. All that he saw seemed to be in his province, under his control. He stood above the sprawling freight yards, the sluggish canal, the three or four bridges that sometimes crossed it, and he could look beyond all of these things, beyond the city itself, to the lake. He couldn't see this lake, of course, but he knew it was there. And when the window stood open he could detect the smell of it . . . In the windows along the canal the blinds were usually drawn, and behind the blinds, when the lights came on, he could see the people moving around. Nearly all of them ate at the back of the house, then moved to the front. There they would talk, or sit and play cards, or wander about from room to room until it was time, as the saying goes, to go to bed. Then the front lights would go off, other lights come on. A woman would stand facing the mirror, and a man, scratching himself, would sit on the edge of the sagging bed, holding one shoe, peering into it as if his foot was still there. Or letting it fall so that it was heard in the room below . . . In all of this there was nothing unusual—every night it happened everywhere—except that the people in these rooms were not alone. The old man in the tower room, the waybills in his hand, was there with them. He had his meals with them in the back, then wandered with all of them to the front, listened to the talk, and then saw by his watch it was time to go to bed. He sat there on the edge, looking at his feet or the hole in the rug. (The Works of Love)

In the fall I went back to school and did the cartoons for the school newspaper. I saw my old school friends on weekends, when we either took in a movie or listened to the New York Philharmonic on Mrs. Johnson's new console radio. To get it into the front room the player piano had to be moved out. We listened to Wayne King, at the Aragon Ballroom, and I first heard Johann Sebastian Bach's Air for the G String on it. I bought a ukulele, and worked especially hard on "Little White Lies."

In my English class I sat across from a girl who wore a Red Cross Life Saving pin on her sweater. I, too, was a Red Cross Life Saver; I wore the pin on the lapel of my blue serge suit. In Dorothy's excitement to answer a question, her arms waving, the bone pins often fell from her hair, which I retrieved. The bone hairpins between her teeth, her arms raised to rearrange her hair, the downward gaze of her eyes left me free to be ravished by the beauty of this gesture. In the curve of her arms a halo crowned her light brown hair. Dry-mouthed, I put a tongue to my chapped lips. I did not lack images for my condition, but an occasion for adoration. In the hallways and on the stairs I plotted ways to approach her. She usually hugged four or five books to her front, an apple perched on the top. I would appear at her side and say, "Gee, I wish I was one of those books!" I planned to do so many things I am no longer sure what it was I did. The startled glance of pleasure she gave me I remember. Strands of her light brown hair framed her face. I did not have the words, but I was at ease in a landscape appropriate to my emotions. Sir Gawain and the Green Knight were my close companions. I approached the dark tower several times daily. Soon I was carrying her books the eight or ten blocks to the elevated stop where we parted. In a swoon of emotion I returned to the Y where the facts of life were my supporting fiction. I shouted in the lobby, prayed better than ever, divvied up the loot of the slot machine raids, and exercised for at least half an hour on the parallel bars after the lobby closed. Back in the room on Menominee Street I gulped down a cake of Fleischmann's yeast, and washed fig newtons down with chocolate milk, to increase my weight. In the early morning, as the school doors opened, I was there in the hall with the pounding radiators, my homework assignments, and the plaster statue of Joan of Arc with the hole in her ear where marbles were inserted.

I might see my girl, a wild exchange of glances, when she made a brief stop at her locker to pick up a book or fuss with her hair. Under pressure my father went with me into the Loop, where I could try on hats in a men's hat store. I saw my small pale face in the large three-way mirrors. I compensated by choosing a large man-size Stetson with a rolled brim, like my father's.

"Better it's a little big," the clerk said. "Give him time to grow into it."

Had he noted that I was growing in other departments? My father's coats fit me in the chest but were long in the sleeves. To show off my new muscles I took my girl to the beach where she disliked the sand and feared the water. A towel tucked about her plump knees and wide bottom, she wore a straw hat to keep the sun off her face. She did not swim a stroke. The Red Cross Life Saving pin she had acquired, in a swap of pins, from a friend who didn't swim a stroke either. Nevertheless, I was the first person to slip my hands inside of her raincoat, and she was the first to kiss, and put cold cream on, my chapped lips. She was far and away the best friend this boy had ever had.

On Sundays I rode the streetcar for two hours to where she lived, then we rode for another two hours to the movie. Back at her place we sat in the dark of the stairs where I developed a line of talk that was more than prayer. Her father played the organ in a movie on Clark Street, where he led the singing during the intermission. I saw him only in the dark. He pretended not to see us, rattling his keys. With the taste of her face powder still on my lips I would run the four blocks to the end of the car line, where the conductor might be changing the trolley, or walking through the car to switch the seats to face the other direction. I often had the long rocking, clattering ride all to myself.

I had proved my talents for prayer at the Y. Now I learned the art of fiction and self-promotion. Tirelessly and silently she listened to my weekly adventure serial. What did I say? I remember nothing. My life and great times had filled me with impressions, and I planned to be a political cartoonist, like John T. McCutcheon of the Chicago *Tribune*. The one of his I liked the best showed a boy daydreaming in the twilight of an Indian summer day, where he thought he saw Indian wigwams where there were only shocks of corn. I, too, was given to seeing things where there was little to see, or to seeing them as other than what they were. Seeing a picture of my girl, her blue eyes tinted, a wash of color over a blur of freckles, my father turned back to brushing his hair in the mirror. "You can't go wrong with her, kid," he said, as if it had ever crossed my mind. I resented the suggestion, but occasionally wondered what it might be like.

She loved music, and was a voice in the throng in the school production of Schubert's *Rosamunde*. Her love of music had come from her father. At one time he had had his own orchestra and played the solo violin under the spotlight. But with the new sound movies, all the theaters needed was the organ playing when the movie was over. I don't think he liked me, but the only time he saw me was in the dark.

On the streetcar one Sunday night, Dorothy and I heard this loud guffawing right behind us. It was my father, with one of his men friends from the office. They were laughing at us. My father was still a pretty good-looking man when you saw him dressed up. He was wearing a hat so much like mine we probably looked like a vaudeville act or something. I didn't let on that I knew him from Adam, or the hick with him, who had a boil on his neck that was healing, but I knew that my ears were burning. It ruined the evening for me, for both of us, and when I couldn't explain what was wrong with me she said I didn't like her as much as I used to. The moment she said it I knew that I didn't, and it increased my shame. I lied and said that I really liked her better than ever, which had the effect of making me moody. On the long ride home I saw my reflection in the window, the big hat tilted on my head, and that I looked like a fool. I took the hat off, put it on the seat beside me, and left it there when I got off. It was like new, that hat, the band stamped with my initials, but I could no more wear it after what had happened than I could a dunce cap, or a nightpot. I was so full of pity for myself, my throat aching, I rode past Menominee clear to Division Street, from where, since there were no more cars running, I had to walk back.

One thing that I stuck with, because it worked, was my exercise program. After the Y lobby had closed in the evening I would get in a workout on the parallel bars. In my zeal to be Lionel Strongfort I would come over on Sunday for an extra session. Yeast, milk and fig newtons were transformed into muscles overnight. Beneath the calluses on the palm of my right hand I noticed, and ignored, a point of soreness. It did not go away. And I did not stop my workouts. Soon I was hardly able to make a fist, and the skin on the back of my hand was puffy. One Saturday morning I spoke to my father, showing him my hand. He thought it was just a bruise that would heal, but we went together into the Loop to see the railroad doctor in the station. A big gruff man with a lame walk, he asked me what I had been doing to get such calluses. I told him. I think we better take a look inside, he said, and led me to the sink. He asked my father to grip my wrist while he turned the palm up, just to look at it. Tell me where it feels a little sore, he said, touching it with a knife blade, as if all he meant to do was prick it. He was quick. I watched the ribbon of black blood ooze from the cut, thickened with the creamy cloud of pus. Just that I thought, he said, and set me on a stool so I could hold my hand in a bowl of hot water. I had to soak it forever, until it looked parboiled, then he wrapped it in a bandage saturated with a solution that would shrink the flesh. In two days I would come back and see him.

I spent Sunday with Dorothy, who showed great concern, and when the doctor saw me on Monday morning he said, "Well, that looks a little better. I guess we'll just let you keep it, not chop it off."

He joshed me, but I knew that he meant it. At night, the hand beside me on the pillow, I pondered how it must feel to have one missing. I visualized it with other missing hands, in a bucket. On a visit to a class at the Y college I had caught a glimpse of a dismembered cadaver. I lacked the nerve to think about such matters, and accepted them as unthinkable subjects. When my hand was removed from the shrinking solution it was not my hand, but like that of a mummy. If the fingers touched each other it was like an electric shock.

During this time Dorothy copied out my school assignments, and held my hand like a bird when we rode on the streetcar. It shamed me to think that my love had been so weak, and I wondered what it would be like to be married. If she was my wife, perhaps my love would grow strong again. But Dorothy planned to go to Northwestern, where she would study music, and I was working for fifteen dollars a week in the cloakroom at the Y. The Y itself had changed, with open houses on weekends, and girls using the pool and the locker rooms. As strange as it seems, the water in the pool had a different smell and taste after the girls had used it. Some of them refused to soap when they used the showers. They had dances in the gym on Saturday nights, with some of the girls smoking in the lobby, and it was no surprise to me when Mr. Shults took on a brand-new Y in Sheboygan, Wisconsin. He said he would make a place for me as soon as I had finished school. But it was Dorothy's opinion, and I suppose it was mine, that anyone as smart as I was owed it to himself to go on to college. But the only college open to me, besides the Y, was the City College of Chicago, on the South Side. I had never even heard of it until she told me about it. There was no tuition. All you had to do was supply your own books. It wasn't my idea of college, once I got a look at it, a big barn of a building, like a department store, with a basketball team nobody ever heard of. One of my friends, Bill Miller, planned to be a streetcar conductor, his father knowing people in the department; Orville Clark was going to Purdue to become an engineer; and Maurie Johnson could go to work the day school was over in his father's dairy. Emmanuel Guagliardo was already making more than I was, driving a pie truck. As talented as I was, I considered myself not very talented. What I could do was apply myself, as I did to drawing and exercising, but no amount of exercising was going to make me into Lionel Strongfort. I had gone with my drawings down to the *Daily News* and looked through the smoky office for the cartoonist, who didn't look at all like an artist when somebody pointed him out. He had his sleeves rolled and his shirttails were out of his pants. When my father looked at the want ads in the *Tribune* some of them always seemed to have him in mind, but when I looked at the ads all they ever wanted was BOYS. I was no longer a boy. What I was was not clear.

While I was pondering my future I received a parcel from a man in Texas, D. V. Osborn, who claimed to be my mother's brother and my uncle. In a hand like my father's, the point of the pencil put to his lips to wet it, he said he wanted me to read the book he had sent to me to make sure I didn't follow a religious calling, like other members of the family. The book he sent me was *Elmer Gantry,* by Sinclair Lewis. I had never read anything like it. D. V. Osborn told me that if I was strong and willing to work, he would offer me a job running a tractor on his ranch. He would pay me thirty dollars a month and my keep. If at the end of the year he had a big crop, which was not unlikely, he would pay me another 20 percent, which might come to as much as six or seven thousand dollars. With that I could do pretty much as I wanted. But I shouldn't give a thought to any of it if I didn't like to work.

I knew nothing of my mother's side of the family but her name, Ethel Grace Osborn. I had the name Wright Marion from my grandfather, but I knew nothing of D. V. Osborn. The novel he sent me opened my eyes. I liked it better than those of Alexander Dumas and Walter Scott. The thought of riding around on a tractor pleased me, but I didn't believe, as I explained it to Dorothy, that I would ever get a lot of money for it. What I would get, if I worked hard enough, would be thirty dollars a month. I wrote my uncle to thank him for the book, which I liked, and to assure him that I was not at the moment contemplating a religious calling. What puzzled me was why he should think I might be. He didn't know about the talent I had for prayer, or anything like that. Mr. Shults would have said, when he got to know me, that I was pretty much open to a religious calling, but not in the church. Christian service did seem to appeal to me in those areas where I was good at it, counseling the Friendly Indians, divvying up their swag, and talking to them at camp with the lights out. I could sure use seven thousand dollars, I wrote him, since I was about to enter college, but I couldn't afford to gamble on it while I was making thirty dollars a month. If he really was my uncle and my mother's brother I thought sure he would make me another proposition—but he didn't. He didn't answer my letter, or even send me another book.

Right at the last minute Dorothy decided she would go to City College along with me. She said she didn't feel that we should be parted, but what she really wanted to do was keep her eye on me. City College was jam-packed with girls who were a lot more forward than those at Lakeview. They were also brighter. That was also true of the boys. I had never had to compete with Jewish boys before, and they ran circles around me. Dorothy had more time to study than I did, and filled me in while we were riding on the streetcars, but I was getting Cs in the history of art, where I was smart. I tried to catch up on my sleep in the study periods. In late November, flushed with a fever and the need to write a paper on Charles Martel, I sat at a table in the library where college pamphlets were available. I leafed through several, then began to read about Pomona College, in California. I had almost been there. It had been along the route, edging the foothills, my father and I had passed through on the motorcycle. At the front of the pamphlet a photograph showed the orange groves and the snow-capped mountains. The text described the details that were missing: groves of oranges, the scent of blossoming trees, shimmering sunlight on snow-capped mountains, a land without winter where boys and girls strolled about with their books in an eternal summer, tanned by the sun.

On my fevered imagination this had the effect of a vision. After all, I had been there. I was a true believer. This word image of the cloudland on the horizon met all the requirements of my extravagant dreaming. Did I thieve this pamphlet, or just the picture? Or did I really have need of either? In the thralldom of this vision I made my way home to the bed just vacated by my father. A week passed, and I was still in it, one of the fortunate survivors of that winter's flu epidemic. In the mailbox, where my father seldom troubled to look, I found a letter, forwarded from Texas, from my mother's sister Winona, in Boise, Idaho. She wanted to tell me that they all loved me, that I was one of the family, and that my grandfather was willing to pay my expenses if I would attend one of the Seventh-Day Adventist colleges. One of these colleges was in the mountains north of San Francisco. On my way to this college, if I decided to attend it, I would stop off in Boise, Idaho, and visit with my mother's people.

Was not this an example of divine intervention?

My father thought it might be, but he felt it was long overdue. He recalled that my grandfather, before I was born, had lost a fortune in land in the Galveston flood, and later owned property in Canada. By rights I was one of his heirs. Who knew what he owned in Idaho? The thought of my inheritance spurred my father to take a fresh look at the egg business.

I hastened to write my Aunt Winona that I accepted my grandfather's offer, but I did not think it advisable to explain that I was not looking forward to a religious calling. I had never heard of the

Seventh-Day Adventists. What appealed to me, and seemed divinely inspired, was that this college was in California. In one way or another I had to get there. I would appear in Boise, Idaho, as soon as I received the railroad ticket.

With sad eyes Dorothy heard this story as she studied my reflection in the streetcar window. I was wearing one of my father's old topcoats. I was wan and pale-faced, but buoyant with optimism. She saw and feared the worst. What inspired me was *flight*.

On a fiber footlocker on loan from Orville Clark, I pasted the pennants of the Big Ten colleges and others. I returned to City College to impress my history teacher with this turn in my fortunes. She had not heard of Pacific Union College. Had I finished my paper on Charles Martel? I had worked very hard to impress this woman whose mocking smile both challenged and disturbed me. While I stood waiting to be reassured she turned from me to erase the blackboard. It did not occur to me at the time, but I think she resented losing a convert. She liked boys who were both anxious and hard to please, like me.

My last night in Chicago, Dorothy and I went to see the four Marx brothers in *The Cocoanuts*. Later she cried, and we clung together in the dark stairwell smelling of wet galoshes, but fifty years would pass before I could measure my real loss against my imaginary gain.

Two of my mother's sisters, Winona and Violet, with Violet's husband, met me at the station in Boise. It was so dark I saw little of their faces. We drove through the snow to a farm in the country where my grandfather lived with Violet and her husband. In the lamplight at the supper table I first saw their smiling ruddy faces. It was explained to the old man that I was the son of Grace. He looked at me with wonder, his pale eyes blinking. He was subject to spells of absent-minded confusion and might stay in the barn with the cattle, or attempt to hitch himself to a plow or a wagon. He drew me to him to look at me closely, his hands firmly gripping my shoulders. He remembered my mother but he seemed to have forgotten she had had a son. I could see in the looks they gave me that they all doubted my existence until they saw me, and I saw them. The sisters were agreed that I resembled my mother. That I had come to them in the Christmas season was a gift from God and a revelation. Their love and interest in me loosened my tongue. I told them about my travels and adventures, but I did not say much about my father. Why had he not kept in touch with my mother's people? Seated around the table to which four leaves had been added were the parts of my life that had proved to be missing. My impression of them all—the old man already dozing, the sisters with their open, affectionate faces, the warmth I felt to be accepted as one of their number—restored to my mind an image of the good life that I had once glimpsed and put behind me.

Later I shared a large bed with two of the men, one of them Marion's husband, and in the hushed darkness, the fire crackling, he explained that if I did not find the college what I had expected I need not feel bound to stay there. They would understand. In their interest in me, in their loving remembrance, after all these years, of my mother, they were unlike any people I had ever met. Meeting them provided me with an image of human goodness that I had been lacking, and I sensed that it need not be good for me to be good in itself.

In the morning, from Marion, I learned that my Aunt Winona had once had a beau and planned to marry, but on the ride to the train her husband told me that although Winona was a remarkable woman, no man would take the place of Jesus in her affections, unless it was me. My mother had been her favorite sister, and she had waited all these years to meet me. He doubted that my mother could love me with such purity of heart.

No one had ever spoken to me in this manner of the purity of love. My eyes brimmed with tears, knowing in my heart how unworthy of such love I was. I saw her briefly at the station, her hands in a fur muff, snow sparkling in her hair when she leaned forward to kiss me, my heart almost bursting with the knowledge of my own losses. My own mother would have spoiled me, and deep in my soul I longed to be spoiled.

On the station platform at St. Helena, California, I met Mr. Kirby, a barber from Los Angeles and a dead ringer for Calvin Coolidge. A recent convert to the Adventist faith, he was on his way to enter the college at Angwin. Kirby was short and slight, deliberate in his manner, dignified. I marveled that a grown man would be entering a college. We were taken by car into the mountains where the wooden buildings of the campus sat under towering trees on the rim of a meadow. Since we had arrived together, and had no objection, we shared the same room. Steam heat crackled in the radiator. Several inches of snow bordered the paths between the buildings. That was not my idea of California but I was told it was unusual. The winters were cool, with considerable rain, but it seldom snowed.

Friendly young men came to our door to greet us and explain the rules of the dormitory. There was a curfew at nine-thirty, when the lights were put out. In the morning at seven we came together for prayers, then proceeded to the dining hall between the men's and women's dormitories. My friend Kirby greatly impressed me with his gallant behavior with the ladies, something that he had learned as a barber. He assisted with their chairs at the table. He passed them food before serving himself. During this first meal I learned that those of Adventist faith did not eat meat. A meatlike preparation, made of nuts, carrots and raisins, remained on our plates at dinner. Kirby assured me it would take a bit of getting used to. In Los Angeles he had frequently sampled similar food in a health cafeteria. His own health good, he had not required it.

Kirby was a devoted reader of the Bible, but not in the manner that I read it. What he read he took to be a fact. The whole bit about the Ark, with the animals in pairs, and Jonah swallowed by the whale, he accepted as history. He saw Jesus walking on the water. I had heard there were people like that but until I met Kirby I had not known one. In the way he liked girls he was pretty normal. Soon enough I found out that all of the readers in our dormitory were like Kirby. It was

113

news to them that there were also readers like me. At the Y, I had become a staunch supporter of Jesus, who took on, and defeated, the forces of evil, but I was pretty skimpy in matters of doctrine. The first book I bought was a leather-bound Bible with two ribbon markers to keep my place. On the flyleaf I put my name, my high school, and after considerable thought I put my address as Chicago, Illinois, U.S.A.

Every night of the week, once the lights were out, boys gathered in our room for a discussion. Some of them brought along flashlights they beamed on the ceiling. Kirby sat on a chair, being the oldest, but the rest of us sat around on the floor. I just naturally assumed that when they all knew better they would be reading the Bible my way. First I explained how it took more than six days to create the world. In the Field Museum in Chicago I had seen fossils of creatures so huge they had become extinct, thousands of years ago. And that was nowhere near the beginning. I had also heard about mastodons preserved in Siberian ice. With my own eyes I had seen petrified trees that had grown where there was now nothing but desert. How did I know that? I had read it, and believed what I had read. They really crowed to hear me talk like that, and then assured me that what I had read had been lies. The word of God was written down in the Bible, and I could read it myself.

I didn't believe that for a moment, but night after night, as we sat and talked, and as I began to make converts, it crossed my mind that I didn't know much more than they did. We believed what we had read, and we had read different books. In the Book of Genesis were the boasts of a braggart to impress his listeners, not unlike myself. The pleasure it gave me to hold their attention was like that of a prophet peaking to his disciples. I was no prophet, but they were sure good listeners. They all carried what I had said to their classes, and I was soon advised by the Dean in a very friendly and considerate manner that my own faith was my own business, but while I was a student at the college I should not try to convert others. Kirby agreed with that, since he felt his own faith was crumbling. There were trees in California which were older than the Bible's story of creation. If God could be wrong about details like that, He had probably slipped on some others.

I gave the Dean my word of honor there would be no more discussions after the lights were out. I couldn't stop what had been started, however, and most of the time Kirby and me sat alone at our table in the dining room. Only agnostics dared to sit with us. Kirby turned for consolation to the older girls who liked to take walks in the woods on weekends, and walking around the campus by myself was how

I stumbled on the gymnasium. No one had mentioned they had a basketball court, and three almost new balls. The building was pretty dark, and on the cool side, but with a floor so waxed it looked new. I played for about an hour by myself, running up and down, shooting baskets. The next day I brought Kirby along with me, but he was not the athletic type. If I flipped the ball to him it might hit him in the face, as if he didn't see it. He liked to watch me, and chase balls for me, but I soon got tired of that. Here we had a real gym, with balls to play with, and nobody playing. I brought the matter up with some boys in our dorm who seemed to know what a basketball was. They didn't know much, but they liked to play. One of the problems was they had to play in their socks on a slippery waxed floor. It was comical to see them skidding around, but they scrambled for the ball like crazy. They hollered and yelled like girls. To make it more fun, and introduce a little order, I organized them into two teams of four players each. I'd never seen grown kids get so excited. They didn't know how to shoot baskets or really dribble, so that a high-scoring game might be about six points. But since they had no idea how awful they were, they had a lot of fun.

After three or four days we had about twenty kids, which was enough for four teams, with five on a team, but not one of them let out a peep about the rule against games. The reason the gym had been sitting there empty was that any sort of competition was forbidden. You could come in and bounce the ball around, the way I did, but you couldn't take sides and play a game to win. They kept that secret to themselves because they were out of their minds to play. Skidding around in their socks on the slippery floor, they often fell down and got a lot of floor burns. Little they cared. As the competition warmed up we began to have some fights under the basket. One boy had a finger poked into his eye. There wasn't a game we didn't have several nosebleeds. The scrapping didn't always stop in the gym but began in earnest back in the dorms. One night we had a row, with pillow feathers strewn up and down the halls. One of the smaller boys was tied up like a bandit and locked in a closet. I had nothing to do with any of this, but when the Dean looked into it my name was mentioned. I had been the one to organize them all into teams. All of that was acceptable where I had come from, but it was not acceptable at the college. The Dean was grateful for what had happened, however, since it dramatized the evils of competition. I could see that myself. When boys got excited and played to win they were soon indifferent to the pain they gave to others. Others got pleasure in striking one another. The Dean was fond of me, and I liked him, but since my arrival I had

115

brought nothing but disorder and confusion to the students in the dormitory. For the sake of the college he would have to ask me to leave. He would write to my people, however, that this was in no way a reflection on my character, but stemmed from the fact that I had lacked an Adventist upbringing. The opinions I had voiced to him and others were surely made in good faith, and my own, but they were contrary to Adventist doctrine and created an intolerable confusion. He found it hard to believe that I had been one of their students just under four weeks.

When I was asked to leave the school, I didn't want to. A budding evangelist myself, perhaps I enjoyed making converts. Here at the college my audience was captive. Their ignorance, on the average, was greater than my own. I could look forward—if left to my own persuasions—to modifying the nature of Adventist doctrine. The doctrine could also look forward, as I had told the Dean, to modifying me. There was something to be said for non-competition, and I might be the one to say it.

The Dean was pleased to hear that, and his mind was not closed to possible changes in my own doctrines, but for the time being he felt sure that I would make faster progress elsewhere. From my Aunt Winona I had a loving letter assuring me that what I had done was God's decision, and their love went with me in my intention to go to work for my Uncle Dwight in Texas. I had learned from Winona that Dwight was her favorite brother. I also wrote to him that I was on my way, and that I looked forward to word from him, and a month's advance pay, care of General Delivery, Los Angeles. I believe that my friend Kirby would have left with me, but he had become attached to a plump young woman from Glendale who waited on tables. While in Los Angeles he recommended I should visit his former barber shop, mention his name and get a cut-rate haircut.

After paying my coach fare to Los Angeles I still had about twenty dollars in cash. I felt so sure I would soon hear from my Uncle Dwight that I took a room in the YMCA on Hope Street. From the fire escape on the ninth floor I could see the lights, sparkling like stars, to the black rim of the sea at Long Beach. Nothing I had previously seen so far exceeded my expectations. Just three years before I had been in Los Angeles with my father, and I knew my way around, as well as most of the movies and pawnshops on Main Street. I rode the double-decker buses out to Echo Lake Park and watched the people feed bread to the swans and the goldfish. On those days it rained I went to a movie. I ate when I was hungry. Every day I took the long walk to the post office near Olvera Street, where I expected a letter

116

from my uncle. I got to be friendly with the General Delivery clerk, who was from Akron, Ohio, and new to the city like I was. On the weekend, with the PO closed, I rode one of the Big Red cars of the Pacific Electric Railroad out to Claremont, the home of Pomona College. I walked around on the campus like I was a student, saying hi to the suntanned boys and girls. What it all made me think of was the Garden of Eden with oranges growing on the trees of knowledge. The snow-capped mountains looked so near I could touch them. On the football field I sat in the bleachers watching the shadows rise on the foothills. Nothing more beautiful could be imagined. I was dazzled with anticipation. It also seemed implausible to me that I should be deprived of something I craved so profoundly. One thing I would do would be to write to my Aunt Winona that I had found the school that I wanted. Surely they would make it possible for me to attend it. If it had been a weekday, and the college offices open, I would have introduced myself to the Dean as a prospective student from Chicago, with relations who lived in Hereford, Texas, and Boise, Idaho.

I spent the night in one of the ivy-covered buildings with windows that framed the snow-capped mountains. With dawn I was still buoyant, mingling with the students in the hallways, and I presented myself at the office of the person in charge of admissions. Perhaps he sensed it was idle to calm me. He allowed that a young man from Chicago might have something to contribute to the college. I had read, and agreed with, sentiments carved in stone on the college gates. Still buoyant, my future determined, I took the Big Red car back to the city, where I found a postcard from my uncle in Texas. He was pleased to learn that I had left a school that taught nothing but lies and falsehoods, but he was not accustomed to paying his hired hands in advance. If I was to work for him, he urged me to arrive as soon as possible, or it would be too late. The spring plowing had started. His wife, Agnes, was now taking my place on the tractor.

I found I was short the bus fare to Texas by three dollars. The PO clerk loaned me a dollar, and I pawned the silver-plated initial buckle on my belt that I had given my father the previous Christmas but borrowed to wear to California. After all, we had the same initial. When he wore it, it was always concealed by his vest.

At the Y, where I owed a week's rent, I left an IOU on the dresser, giving my address as Hereford, Texas. I then went down the fire escape to the second floor, where the last flight of stairs was suspended above the dark alley. I did not weigh enough, even with my suitcase, to lower the stairs to the ground. When I lowered and dropped my bag I was puzzled by the silence of its fall. I then let myself hang, my legs dangling, and let go, falling silently into a mound of fresh garbage. It stuck to my hands and clothes as I groped in it for my bag. I could smell it, all right, but I couldn't see it until I got into the light at the end of the alley. Smears of grease and gravy, salad greens, chunks of Jell-O, clung to my pants. I took a streetcar to Echo Lake Park, where I sat on the boat pier, my feet in the water, while I cleaned my socks and shoes.

The bus to Hereford, Texas, which proved to be near Amarillo, went through Phoenix and Globe, in Arizona, which were places I had missed on the trip west. The bus went through without stopping, but the drivers changed. I dozed off during the day, but I was usually awake most of the night. In a country with so much to see, it helped to see just a small piece of it under streetlights.

Without the high false fronts on the stores in Hereford I might have gone right through it and not seen it. The sunset burned like a fire in the second-floor windows of the general store. All around it, in every direction, the panhandle was as boundless and bare as the sea. Having seen the sea, I could say that. It even had the sort of dip and swell that the sea has. The man in the general store knew my Uncle Dwight, but there was no way to get in touch with him. His farm was about eight miles southeast, which was a long way to walk carrying a suitcase. But if I left the suitcase with him, I could walk it. He led me into the street, which was almost dark, but the sky was so full of light I blinked to look at it. He pointed out to me the trail I should follow, and the wire poles along it looked no higher than fence posts. The road was little more than smoothed-over grass, and once it got dark it would be hard to see it. What I had to look for, once it got dark, were the lights of his house and his tractor. He kept it going day and night. If I didn't see it, I would hear the cough of the engine. The light for me to keep my eye on, of course, was the one that stayed in one place. That was the house. If I walked at a good smart clip I could do it in about two hours.

After two days and two nights on the bus it felt good to walk. At one point, where I was on a rise, I could see the lights of Amarillo, like a cluster of stars. I could hear the tractor coughing before I saw it, and it sounded like a plug was missing. Some time later, when it made a turn, the lights came toward me like a locomotive. The last thing I saw was the feeble lampglow at a window of the house. I had never asked myself what he might have as a farm. A farm to me was a big old house, with some barns, and perhaps some trees along one side as a windbreak. What I saw slowly emerging in the milky darkness was a building no larger than my Uncle Harry's cobshed, set up on

118

concrete blocks. A line of wash, like ghosts, hung to one side, where a machine of some sort was covered with a tarpaulin. Fifty or sixty yards away from the house were two sheds, and still further away was the peaked roof of a privy. The white spots in the yard were Leghorn chickens. Way, way off to the south, where the sky was darkest, the dim lights of the tractor flickered, and it made me so mournful and lonely I wanted to cry. If I had not come so far and was not so tired, I would have turned back. An eerie mauve and crimson afterglow filled the western horizon, like the earth was burning. Until I was right there in the yard, beside the sagging line of wash, the dog under the house neither saw nor heard me. When he came at me barking, he scared me out of my wits. I probably let out a yell. At the door to the house, up three steps from the yard, a woman appeared with a clothes basket. She called off the dog, then said, "You're Wright?" I said that I was. "I'm Agnes," she said. "Dwight's on the tractor."

With the light behind her I could not see her face.

"Where's your bag?"

I explained that I had left it in Hereford, since I had to walk.

"Dwight's not going to like that," she said. "It means he's got to go fetch it." When I said nothing, she added, "I suppose you're hungry," and beckoned me to come in.

In the morning I saw nothing but the food on my plate, the slit of light at the window. It was on the horizon, but it might have been attached to the blind. Dawn. Sunrise would not come for another hour. The wind blowing under the house puffed dust between the floorboards, like smoke. There was never any talk. My Uncle would slip off his coveralls, like a flight suit, and eat in his two suits of underwear: one of fine, snug-fitting wool, flecked with gray, like a pigeon; the other of heavy, nubby cotton flannel with the elbows patched with quilting, the fly-seat yawning. The outer suit would come off in the spring, but the inner suit was part of my Uncle. I once saw him, plucked like a chicken, standing in a small wash basin of water while Agnes wiped him off with a damp towel. Dust. He was dusted rather than washed. (Cause for Wonder, 1963)

Sometime before dawn, the wind rising, I was awakened by the cough of the tractor approaching the house. It went on coughing while I pulled on the clothes Agnes brought me—itchy underwear and socks, two heavy flannel shirts, coveralls still stiff from drying on the wash line, cold as ice.

Agnes had explained to me the night before that I would take over the tractor when Dwight brought it in in the morning, the engine

119

never stopping because it was so hard to start. While I gulped hot biscuits and eggs fried in pork fat I could hear my uncle cursing. What was the trouble? It was just his way of keeping warm, talking to himself. When he came into the house dust caked his face, like the men I had seen in grain elevators. He did not look pleased when he saw me sitting there eating his food. He wore a cap with ear muffs, coveralls like mine, the legs tucked into three-buckle galoshes. I wouldn't know until Sunday what he really looked like, when I would first see him without his cap on—not because it was the Lord's day of rest, but my uncle's day off. His forehead, ears and neck were white as flour, the rest of his face was dark as an Indian's. Where had I seen him before? He could have been the brother of William S. Hart. He had the same steely, watery-blue eyes and thin-lipped mouth. When he smiled I could see the dirt caked at the roots of his teeth.

He didn't say who he was, or ask who I was, but came to the table and opened up a biscuit, smeared it in the pork fat, then put it in his mouth. I understood right then that you didn't talk to him while he was trying to eat. My uncle was a lean wiry man who just naturally stood with his legs flexed, as if he meant to hop. When he burned himself with a swallow of hot coffee he made a face just like I would, with his eyes creased, then he let out a stream of curses. I followed him out in the yard, where the crack of dawn was right there on the horizon like a knife slit, then we carried between us a milk can full of kerosene to the John Deere tractor. It took both of us to lift it as high as the fuel tank, and pouring it into the funnel I got my gloves and hands soaked. He shouted at me, above the cough of the motor, if I knew how to steer a tractor? I nodded that I did. He rode along behind me, seated on one of the gang plows, letting his hand trail in the loam turned up by the plow blade. His section of land was about 1,800 acres, and I could see only a portion of it at one time. With the tractor running day and night it would take a month or more to get it plowed. On the west side, headed south, the wind in my face was so cold it made my eyes blur. Headed north, the dust raised by the plows blew over my head like a cloud of smoke. But when he saw I could manage the tractor on the turns he got off the plows and walked back toward the house, his arms raised from his sides as if he carried two pails. In that great empty expanse, the sun just rising, he looked like a bug and hardly seemed to move. When the light in the house turned off I missed it.

I'd been plowing half the morning before I noticed how the big jackrabbits moved just enough to stay clear of the plows. They would wait until the last second, then hop just enough to be clear of the blades.

120

The whole section of land I was on had never before been turned by a plow. Only cattle had grazed it, most of them the white-faced Herefords that stood along the fence to watch me pass. I didn't know at that point that I was turning topsoil that had been centuries in the making. My uncle knew it, and it was why he had gambled on planting grain where it seldom rained. If it would grow grass, he argued, it would also grow wheat. Just five years before he had leased 1,200 acres, and he and Agnes, working alone, had harvested a crop worth more than $30,000. It hadn't rained a winter since then, but he was sure that it would.

In the sky around me, maybe twenty miles away, I could see cloud masses forming and drifting. I could even see mauve sheets of rain falling somewhere. A few days of steady rain was all that was needed, then months of hot sun. I thought I would die of hunger before I saw Agnes, followed by the dog, between the plowed land and the house. She brought me my lunch in a syrup pail, with a jar of black coffee. I'd never cared much for coffee, but I got to like it fine. The dog would stay with me, watching me eat, then he would trail in the fresh furrows left by the plows. When a rabbit moved, he tried to head it off and keep it running in the plowed section. He ran like the wind, so low to the ground that a plowed furrow would send him tumbling. It was hard to see the grass-colored rabbits when he chased them, just the crazy zig-zagging patterns made by the dog, like he was chasing flies. He was a sort of spitz, mixed with collie, his fur a mat of burrs picked up from the grass. His big stunt was to run straight at the Herefords if he found them all lined up like a wall at the fence. He would go right for them like a streak, and at the last split second they would break and panic, going off with their tails up, bellowing. We both loved it. I would stop the tractor and give him some attention. He was Agnes's dog. For one reason or another he didn't like Dwight. I think it was because Dwight would often shoot toward him when the two of them did a little hunting. It was Dwight who gave him the name of Jesus, because of the way a dead-looking rabbit would spring to life when he saw him.

Two hours before dawn we had left the dark house to shoot at what I thought might be cattle rustlers. In the windless pause before my Uncle ran forward hooting like an Indian, I prepared myself to shoot it out with Billy the Kid. When Dwight ran forward, hooting, I shot into the air over his head. I heard a great flapping of wings, but very little honking. I think I managed to fire two or three times. Still dark, we came back to the house where Agnes had coffee perking and a fire going. When

121

the sky was light we went out to see if we had bagged any birds. Just
shooting blind into the rising flock we had bagged nine. So we had fresh
gamy meat for two weeks and lead shot on my plate in the evening,
some of which I kept and used over in a BB gun. (*Cause for Wonder*)

The John Deere tractor, until I got used to it, sounded like a plug
was missing and it was about to stop running. It ran on the cheapest
fuel, however, and once you got it started it was hard to stop. To
start it up, you had to give the flywheel a spin, which scared the hell
out of me because of the way it backfired. The first time it died on
me I couldn't get it restarted, and Dwight knew it right away when
the coughing stopped. He could hear that the way he could hear a
rise or fall in the wind. He had got out of bed at about seven in the
morning and walked the half mile or so to where I was stalled. That
gave me plenty of time to watch him coming, his arms high from his
sides like a winded chicken. He was so mad he hardly troubled to curse
me, and grabbed the flywheel like he meant to tear it off. He didn't
catch it just right, and the loud backfire lifted him off his feet. That
made him even madder, and less smart about it, and when he grabbed
the wheel it spun him like a top and thumped him hard against one
of the wheels. That hurt him so bad, and he was so ashamed, tears
came to his eyes. If he had had a club big enough, or an axe, I think
he would have chopped the John Deere to pieces. The reason he hated
his father the way he did, as Winona had said, was that they were
so much alike. They were both hard-driving, ambitious men who were
accustomed to putting the harness on others as well as themselves.
It almost killed him to have the tractor, right before my eyes, make
a fool of him. It frightened me like the devil just to watch him, but
when it was over I liked him better, and he was friendlier with me.
By the time we got it started we were both so worn out we just got
on it and rode it back to the house, where he went back to bed, and
I sat in the sun where it warmed the wall. It made a difference between us, not such a big one that my job got to be any softer, but
I had become a hired hand and he didn't have to watch me to know
I was working.

As a rule I rode the tractor all day, and he rode it at night. He
slept until early afternoon, then he did what needed doing around the
place. Agnes raised chickens for the eggs we lived on, and the one
she stewed or fried on Sunday. By afternoon the sun would heat up
the house, but the way the wind blew around and beneath it, it would
soon cool off in the evening. After supper we would sit around the
range in the kitchen, with the oven door open. Agnes always had her

122

mending to do, or washing, or the baking of bread she did on Mondays, and she was not a person who liked to talk while she worked. Nor had I ever before lived with a woman who didn't seem to like me. Not that she *dis*liked me, but at most she felt neutral. In the house she liked me to keep in my place. The year he made a lot of money Dwight had bought a big console radio in Kansas City that required a lot of batteries to run it. He got tired of trying to keep the batteries charged, so all it did was sit there with her sewing on it. In the space on the floor beneath there were two big cartons of Haldemann-Julius Little Blue Books. They sold for five cents each, and my uncle had bought two or three hundred of them. He was a great reader, over the winter, and read the books that he liked several times. Most of the books exposed religious hypocrisy and fakery. There were also books on geology, history and travel, so I didn't lack for something to read. I often carried one of these books in my pocket and read it when I stopped for lunch. What surprised me was how much my uncle loved to talk. On the day I had off we might sit up till almost midnight doing nothing but talking. A lot of what I said got him to laughing so hard his sides ached, and he could hardly stop. He loved to hear me talk about Pacific Union College, and the stuff they believed. I liked the way his eyes watered when he laughed, and the way they twinkled when he looked at me. The good talk we often had was no reason, however, I shouldn't be on the tractor at dawn the next morning.

That morning I heard the dawn crack like a whip. A little later I could peer out and see the wind where there was neither dust, lines of wash, nor even grass to blow. The yard was like a table, with a dull, flat gloss where the shoes buffed it toward the privy. Scoured by the wind, the cracks had been picked clean by the chickens. Out there, as nowhere else, I could see the wind. The five minutes in the morning I lay in a stupor listening to Agnes build the fire, I would face the window, the dawn like a slit at the base of a door. In the kitchen Agnes would put fresh cobs on the banked fire. Was it the sparks in the chimney, the crackle in the stove? The cats would hear it, five or six of them. With the first draw of the fire they would start from the grain sheds toward the house, a distance of about one hundred yards. Was that so far? It can be if you crawl. In the dawn light I would see only the white cats, or those that were spotted, moving toward the house like primitive or crippled reptiles. How explain it? The invisible thrust of the wind. The hard peltless yard gave them no hold. Even the chickens, a witless bird, had learned never to leave the shelter of the house at the risk of blowing away, like paper bags. A strip of chicken wire, like

123

a net, had been stretched to the windward of the yard to catch them.
They would stick like rags, or wads of cotton, till my Aunt would go
out and pick them off. The cats and hens were quick to learn that the
wind would prevail. My Aunt Agnes knew, but she preferred not to ad-
mit it. The last to learn was my Uncle Dwight. (Cause for Wonder)

The way Agnes looked after my Uncle Dwight helped me to see
why it was she seemed so neutral toward me. Dwight was hers. She
liked him so much she didn't want to share him with anybody. The
way he could talk pleased her, but the pleasure he showed when I talked
made her frown and turn to her mending. She was not a pretty woman,
her skin darkened by the weather, her hands like those of a man and
chapped at the wrists, but I knew that she was a woman my uncle
could take pride in. He had found her in Kansas, put her in a buggy
and driven southwest till they came to the Pecos River in New Mexico. There he homesteaded a claim and raised sheep. Why didn't they
have children? She would have liked kids of her own better than she
liked me. Dwight was so independent in all of this thinking, he might
not have wanted to share Agnes with them. He talked to her the way
he did to me, but he considered me a better listener. I would come
back at him. And he liked that. He said a lot of things just to rile me.
I had also read some books that he hadn't, and that pleased and shamed
him. Sometimes he would put his hands to his face and just think about
it for a moment, in silence.

My Uncle Dwight had not had, as he said, much schooling, preferring to educate himself by reading, but he talked in the assured manner of a man who could give a sermon. Words came to him easily,
and quickly. His accent was like none I had heard, as if he had lived
with strange people. I would hear nothing like it until I heard ballad
singers on records. When he listened to me, his head tilted as if for
a portrait, I felt in his gaze his admiration for his own kind. Was that
what I was? Were we both pieces chipped from the same block? It
pleased me to think that we might be, because I felt for him a secret
admiration. He was strong. His mind was sharp as the glint of his
eyes. If the great men I had heard of were gathered together around
a stalled tractor on the Texas panhandle, my uncle would prove to
be the equal or the superior to most of them. They would listen in
silence and admiration as he cursed.

On his homestead on the Pecos River, near Roswell, Dwight had
found small six-sided rocks, with one or both ends sharpened to a
point, like a pencil, around the holes of small rodents. They were locally known as Pecos diamonds. He kept a sampling of them in a Bull

Durham tobacco sack, and brought them out to confound city hicks like me. What in the world had led God, he asked me, to make something like that in a hole in the ground? Nothing pleased him more than the foolishness of God compared to the almighty mysteries of nature.

The greatest marvel of nature on which he had set eyes were the Carlsbad Caverns in southern New Mexico. Dwight wanted me to see them the way Winona wanted me to see God. We stopped plowing for three days to drive there in his Willys Knight sedan, the car he kept under the tarpaulin beside the house. It still had the original tires on it, and the tools under the seat had never been used. A film of dust made it all one color, like his face when he came in from plowing. It pleased him to sit in the back seat with Agnes and let me drive. I knew about Willys Knights, and their sleeve-valve motors, from the one my father had had in Omaha that my Uncle Verne and I would take on long rides into Iowa and Kansas. On the curves I could look back and see the blue exhaust.

Jules Verne could have used the Carlsbad Caverns when he wrote *A Journey to the Center of the Earth*. That's what the caverns were like. We went down there with a large group of people who had come from places as far as Minneapolis and Chicago. We all gathered in a huge cavernous room, near a large rock, and sang the hymn "Rock of Ages." When our names were called out we would reply where we had come from. Learning I was from Chicago, a man from Milwaukee came to me and threw his arms around me. He had lived in Chicago, and often visited Lincoln Park.

I found the caverns as fantastic as my uncle had said but not so mystifying as the Pecos diamonds. At first I figured Indians must have made them and these little rodents ran off with them. But why would an Indian spend his life doing something like that? On our way back to Hereford we made a detour to see what was left, if anything, of their homestead. The shack was still there, the color of rusted machinery, and there were signs that some bums or prospectors had lived in it. I didn't see much that sheep could have grazed on, but along the rimrock of the Pecos River we found a lot of holes made by rodents, and some with these little rocks around them. They were similar, but whoever made them got tired and quit before they were finished, leaving only one end of the rock pointed. It wasn't like a smart Indian to start something, and work hard at it, then leave it unfinished.

In an alley in Clovis—I forget why I was there—I stepped on a nail that went right through the sole of my shoe. Agnes had never shown any interest in me until I stepped on that nail. Back in Hereford the first thing she did was heat a kettle of water for me to soak my foot in. Until the soreness was gone she didn't think I should work all day on the tractor, and I agreed. Actually, until we took the trip, I had more or less forgotten how close we were to the desert. The one thing you could say for sure about a desert was that it seldom rained. The idea that it wasn't going to rain in Hereford proved to be one that I couldn't get rid of. The more I looked around, in every direction, the drier it looked. What was I doing? I was working like a horse for thirty dollars a month and board that was giving me the hives. That was what Agnes told me when I began to scratch. Hives came from eating nothing much but eggs fried in pork fat, and biscuits.

My uncle got his pork and fat from a family eighteen miles to the east that raised hogs and horses. Their name was Gudger. The big house they lived in and the barns around it had once been part of a ranch, but the overgrazed land was no longer useful to cattle. From four or five miles away I could see the branches of a dead tree, the bleached color of bones, sticking up from the plain· like antlers. There wasn't a leaf on it, the bark was peeled off, and the house and the barns were the same weathered color. The Gudger business in horses had fallen off, but they hobbled the few they had left and let them wander around. There were kids in the yard when we drove up, the smaller ones with hair that made them look like goblins. They were busy carrying buckets of hot water to a mound in the yard, under a branch of the tree. In the mound was a big wooden vat, wide and deep enough to dip a hog into. The hog my uncle had agreed to buy a part of was in a fenced-in area beside the barn. He was so big that from the rear he looked like the mound of earth over a storm cave. I had to stoop over to see his feet, no bigger than the bungs you use to plug up a barrel. I couldn't believe that anything so gross had such delicate feet. Set into his huge face, like buttons, were his little eyes and long silvery lashes. He didn't mind at all my patting his back like the rump of a horse.

On our ride to the Gudgers' I had sat in the car with Dwight's Winchester rifle across my lap. On windless days I might take it along on the tractor and take potshots at a few rabbits. In a landscape so big and empty it was hard to judge how far away I was from a rabbit. My rifle bullets would kick up the dirt maybe twenty yards in front of them. I could see the arc of the bullet as it left the barrel. The older, smarter jacks would hop off a little ways, then sit up like penguins and watch me. So far as I know, I never hit one of them.

Dwight had explained to me how to shoot a hog. You take an ear of corn, with the tassels still on it, and stick the smaller end in your open fly. The hog either sees the ear of corn or he sniffs it, and comes slowly waddling toward you. When he's about gun-barrel length away you aim right between his eyes and pull the trigger. He's so surprised, he doesn't know what hit him. The only thing that's changed is the little black hole between his eyes. He might just stand there, propped like a barrel, until you take a fence post and tilt him over. It might take two or three people to budge him. Then the one with the butcher knife slits his throat and catches the blood in the pan while his heart is still pumping. It's the blood that makes the best sausage anybody ever ate.

It never crossed my mind, listening to what he told me, that I would be the one to shoot the hog. I walked along beside him to the split rail fence, where he reached into the pen for a tassled ear of corn. "Here you are, kid," he said, handing it to me, then he held the gun while I loosened the buttons and stuck it in my fly. I didn't have the time to think as to whether I wanted to do it, before it was done. I climbed over the fence about ten yards to his left, and Dwight handed me the rifle, after he'd cocked it. There was just the three of us, my Uncle Dwight, me and the hog. The hog lumbered toward me, just the way Dwight had said, then he stopped and raised his big head to look at the corn. I had never before been so close to anything so big. I could see the long silvery lashes to his eyes. He wasn't fierce at all, just huge, making little grunts like a sow with a litter, his ears alone so big and furry they didn't look real. He gave me all the time in the world to aim, and he came in so close I could have reached out and touched him. Right between the eyes I saw the hole I had made, but I hadn't heard a sound. The two of us just stood there facing each other, like Dwight had in mind taking our picture, only he was quick to scramble over the fence and slide a post under the hog's belly. When he felt that post give him a prod, he spread his legs a little bit, which propped him like a barrel. Dwight yelled at me to give him a hand, and I put down the gun and tried to help him. The hog didn't budge. Three or four of the kids who had heard the gunshot scrambled over the fence and helped us push on him. We managed to rock him over, and with his feet in the air he gave a mighty shudder, stiffening his legs. The rest of it went just the way Dwight had described it, the blood pumping from his throat as black as oil, and before the gate to the fence was lowered Mr. Gudger was there with a team of horses. It took some hauling to drag him over to the tree, get the rope through the pulley and truss him up. Trussed up like that, hung out his full length, he looked more like an ox than a hog. The idea was to let him soak for a bit in the hot water, then hoist him out so all the little

127

Gudgers could scrape at his hide with knives and pieces of broken glass. They were expert at it, and with the bristles shaved off he was almost pink. The first part of him to go was the head, which they propped in a big bucket, and in no more time than it took me to blink it was covered with flies. Every time something was added to the pail the flies rose in a cloud, buzzing like hornets. The smell of the wet hog, the sight of the steaming guts, the way the flies rose up in a cloud, then settled, led me to sort of stand off to one side watching, but I soon felt so woozy I had to lean on the car. Every time I looked at the hog he was smaller, as Mr. Gudger and my uncle hacked away at him. Soon there was nothing much but just the huge pair of hams, turning slowly as the wind blew on them, the whole pack of little Gudgers running beneath like yapping dogs.

We were all called to the house by Mrs. Gudger to eat the pies she had baked, and drink coffee. There were no rugs in the house, just the plank floor that the dust puffed through when the wind blew. We sat at a table in the kitchen, and when I raised my eyes I could see the sky through the chinks in the shingles. It rained so little they didn't have to worry about it raining inside. If I had seen that when I first arrived I might have had second thoughts about working for my uncle, but I would have missed seeing the Carlsbad Caverns, the Pecos diamonds, and the hog I shot with my uncle watching. I liked that most of all, since he would have liked nothing better than to see me miss.

Mrs. Gudger, a worn, stooped old woman with a flour-white face, but her hair black as a stove lid, gave me a piece of her pie to take along with me, I liked it so much. She did the baking, but her oldest daughter, Georgia, did the cooking. George wore a short-sleeved shirt and a pair of khaki work pants with the legs cut off at the knees. She had taffy-colored hair, like her brothers, and a light brown tan all over. Dwight caught me looking at her. But who wouldn't look at a girl as old as she was wearing knee pants instead of a skirt? From the way she liked to ride horses, bareback, she had a shine between her legs, like leather, and I had seen so many girls in the last few months I was glad I didn't have to choose one of them.

As the boy had never looked upon the sea, nor any body of water he couldn't see over, he had no word for the landscape that he faced. The land itself seemed to roll like the floors in amusement parks. Without seeming to climb they would be on a rise with the earth gliding away before them, and in the faraway hollow there were towns a day's ride away. The wheels turned, the earth seemed to flow beneath the buggy,

128

*like dirty water, but nothing else changed and they seemed to be stand-
ing still. Here and there white-faced cattle, known as Herefords, stood
in rows along the barbed wire fence as if they had never seen a buggy,
a horse, or a small boy before. They were always still there, as if painted
on the fence when he turned and looked. Then the road itself came
to an end and they followed the wavering lines in the grass that the
wheels had made the week before, on their way out. And when they
came within sight of the farm—it seemed to recede, and they seemed
to stalk it—the boy knew that he was nearing the rim of the world.
What would he see when he peered over it? The hog. The hog would
prove to be part of it. But the bleak house, with the boarded windows, was like a caboose left on a siding, and behind this house the
world seemed to end. In the yard was a tree, but it would be wrong
to say that the house and the tree stood on the sky, or that the body
of the hog, small as it appeared, was dwarfed by it. It swung from
the tree like some strange bellied fruit. Swarming about in the yard
were large boys with knives, sharpened pieces of metal, and small boys
with long spears of broken glass. They all attacked the hog, hooting
like Indians, and used whatever they had in hand to shave the stiff
red bristles from the hog's hide. The boy could see a small hole, like
a third eye, in the center of the hog's dripping head. The mouth was
curved in a smile as if the swarm of boys scraping his hide tickled
him. . . . From one of the blood-smeared pails in the yard a black
cloud of flies rose into the air, then settled again. They made a sound
as if the roaring wind had been siphoned into a bottle, leaving the
yard empty and the flies trapped inside . . . pelting the sides like a
quick summer rain.* ("The Rites of Spring," 1952)

By the first week of April it still hadn't rained. I began to think,
while I was on the tractor, how great it was in April in Lincoln Park,
with the grass greening and the trees leafing. Along with everything
else I liked, it would rain. Even on Larrabee Street I liked the way
it smelled after a rain. Some of these days I could see it was raining
somewhere, but Texas was just too big for it to rain all over. That
would be true with or without Georgia Gudger. Another problem was
that she didn't know better, and I did.

With all day on the tractor to think about the future, it seemed
drier and drier to me in the present. All the money I would get, if and
when it rained, seemed to mean less to me than a week or two in
Chicago with my friends. It would take me that long to tell them about
my adventures, and my plan to go to Pomona College. I hoped to persuade Maurie Johnson, whose father had sold his dairy to Bordens,

129

to go along with me. He would have the money. His father had bought an interest in a North Side bank. I had all but forgotten that Maurie had told me I might get a job in the bank over the summer. Working in a bank appealed to me more than a ten-hour day on a tractor.

The thinking I did about the future led my mind to wander while I was on the tractor. I got the plows out of line, and trying to get them straight, one of them jammed in the sod and stalled the engine. I knew my uncle would soon miss the racket of the tractor, and it made me a little frantic. I just about skinned my palms trying to spin the flywheel, but she wouldn't catch. When I looked back toward the house there was Dwight, with the dog, Jesus, coming toward me. To be caught like that and humiliated was one of the worst things that had happened to me. It seemed forever before he reached me, the dog running on ahead to scare up rabbits, and I could see the way he was cursing from the way his head pumped, like he was gagging. I would have heard it all before, but I had no choice but to listen to it. But what I also needed the most at that moment was an excuse to quit, and he had given it to me. While he had his back to me, wrestling with the flywheel, I just walked off. It was such a big and risky decision my throat ached, and I almost bawled. I'd gone about two hundred yards before he yelled at me, but I didn't look back. He called my name—"Wright!" he hollered. "Oh, Wright!"—which was almost as strange as hearing my father call me "son," and filled my eyes with tears. I had my fists doubled up so hard my fingers hurt. Before I reached the house he had the tractor started and I could hear the cough blowing on the wind, but he stayed out there, plowing up the section, and was out of my sight when I glanced back.

Agnes was hanging out her wash at the side of the house while I packed my bag. I would have taken off with it, and headed for Hereford, but the only money I had was what Dwight owed me. Having to drive me into Hereford would be another thing he had against me. Agnes didn't question me as to what had happened, or where it was I thought I was going, and toward three o'clock, because he was getting hungry, Dwight came in with the tractor. When he saw my packed bag he knew what I was up to. He had to get back at me, so he said, "If you're dam-fool enough to throw away ten thousand dollars it's better I know it now than later."

First of all, it was more like seven thousand, and the problem was that I wasn't dam-fool enough. In just walking out on him the way I was doing I had an advantage that he didn't know how to handle. He changed his clothes, which was a lot of trouble, just to drive me into Hereford. There was a train at five o'clock that would take

130

me to Amarillo, where I would catch the night train to Chicago. He gave me forty dollars cash, which would cover my fare, then a twenty-dollar check on an Amarillo bank I figured might bounce. The only checks I knew about, my father's, weren't worth the paper they were written on.

We got to Hereford about two hours too early, where my uncle worked up a great story as to how I was called back to Chicago on an emergency. It was not unusual for something to get to me, like the problems I got into at Pacific Union College, but I knew it was unusual for something like me to get to my Uncle Dwight. Because his pride was bigger than mine, it hurt him worse. Mad as it made him, I could also see that it had increased his respect for me. The look he gave me was that he knew we were one of a kind. We just sat there in the store, our feet on the stoveboard, sharing the package of gingersnaps he had bought me, and by the time the local train had come over from Clovis things were pretty normal between us. I really liked him, as big a fool as I thought him to be.

As I RODE NORTH ON THE CLARK STREETCAR from the Loop, I could look up ahead to the green of Lincoln Park, or down the narrow streets to the east to the trees along the bridle path and the lake and the sky like the rim of the world. I didn't like everything I saw, but it was home. My father was still in bed, a can of Carnation milk on the windowsill, with green around the holes punched in the can. In the warm spring drizzle I walked over to Ogden Avenue, and south to the Larrabee Y. They had a stocky ex-wrestler working in the lobby with a bandage on his forehead where someone had hit him with a cue ball. The stairs to the locker room still had the smell of pool chlorine, but the locker room itself had the sweet smell of cheap perfume. That's how fast things change when your back is turned.

I took a room at the back of the Y, where I could hear the balls bounce, then I looked up my old high school friends and told them all about Texas and Pomona College. What I found was that you can't explain some things to people who have always lived in Chicago. They all had families to tie them down, and I didn't. They all knew what they were going to do, and I didn't. On Saturday nights, after we had been to a movie, I might spend the night with Maurie Johnson or Bill Miller. There were eight people in the Miller family so it was easy to make room for me at their table. In the last few years Mrs. Miller had grown so large a place had been made for her in the basement, off the kitchen, so she wouldn't have to use the stairs. Mr. Miller had bought a Hupmobile sedan, which he paid us fifty cents an hour to wax. On Sundays he parked it in the front yard so the water he used to wash it wouldn't be wasted.

Across the street from the Millers the older Baker girl had a boyfriend who went to Northwestern. On the weekends they would sit in his Scripps Booth roadster, the red and green gems glowing in the dashboard light. The Baker girl had a younger sister, Lois, who first had to help her mother with the dishes before she could come out and sit on the porch steps, hugging her knees. Her father sat there after supper in his B.V.D.s, hosing the trees so the water would drip on the grass and the walk. If her sister's boyfriend didn't come down from Northwestern, she might ask us all over to stir some fudge or sing along with her at the piano. We harmonized pretty good "How

Deep Is the Ocean," "Button up Your Overcoat" and "Little White Lies." The one that suited my voice the best was "Little White Lies."

Lois wasn't old enough as yet to have real boyfriends, but not many of the boys knew it. With her long flat feet in tennis sneakers, she was still about half an inch taller than I was. Her favorite color at the time was sky-blue-pink. Since she was not yet in her first year of high school she didn't have the interest in college that I did. I was able to help her with her charcoal drawing and the problems she was having raising Belgian hares. Some of them were mean. The male Belgian hare would eat his own litter if you didn't watch him. Lois would sit with one of the big ones in her lap while I told her about butchering the hog in Texas, or the flood I escaped from in Mississippi. Almost anything I said made her laugh like she was being tickled. The way I stared at her night after night, it's hard to explain why what I see the clearest is the back of her neck. The barber she went to always used the clippers, which was the one thing that drove her crazy. She looked forward to wearing her hair in braids that hung down to her waist.

Mrs. Baker welcomed my help with the dishes, and might invite me to go to a movie with them. I was with Lois, sitting down near the front, when we saw *All Quiet on the Western Front,* and she almost died. Mrs. Baker liked me, and it worried her to think what Lois would do while I was off in California. Already the boys her older sister brought home asked for Lois the next time they called. She was only fourteen, but none of them seemed to mind. If I planned to spend four years in California, with just June, July and August in Chicago, Mrs. Baker could feel in her bones that we were all in for a lot of surprises.

After my work at the Y, I would take the streetcar and ride the thirty minutes north to the Baker house. If Lois wasn't in the hammock on the porch, she would be in her room at the back of the house, listening to Wayne King at the Aragon. I would come in from the alley, passing her hutch of Belgian hares, and climb the posts of the screened-in porch to the roof. The screen to her window was unlatched, and I could either crawl in or she could crawl out and sit there with me. Right down the hall were her two bratty little brothers, with her older sister right next to the bathroom. For an older sister she was exceptionally broad-minded. Mr. and Mrs. Baker had the bedroom at the front where I could often hear the radio playing. I could tell from the glances Mrs. Baker often gave me that she knew pretty well what we were up to. At the time I was less informed than she was. Until I got to college, and read about it somewhere, I didn't know that what we had been up to was "bundling." The early settlers used to do it. Not

133

knowing what it was, I didn't enjoy it as much as I might have. Mrs. Baker believed that there was nothing in the world Lois would remember longer than what she was now doing and feeling. Lois about died every time she heard that, but she believed it was the truth.

The friend I talked to the most, besides Lois and her mother, was a boy at the Y named Laurie Lusk. Laurie played right tackle for Lane Tech, and he was interested in going on to college. On his graduation his father gave him a Model A Ford touring, with yellow wire wheels and a new set of Kelly Springfield tires. It was Laurie's idea, as much as it was mine, that we would drive it all the way to California, the two of us camping out and sharing the expenses. Yet if I hadn't talked so much about Pomona College, and what the winter was like in California, I might have found some excuse to stay in Chicago rather than say goodbye to Lois Baker, which took me almost a week.

And yet I hardly remember our actually leaving. It was Mrs. Baker who did most of the crying, with Lois's little brother Charlie being the biggest nuisance. I don't remember how it was with Maurie Johnson, or Bill Miller, or all my friends at the Y, or what I said to my father, or he said to me. I was so anxious to get away before something went wrong I didn't write my Aunt Winona about it, fearing that might jinx it, and I forgot the racing goggles I had bought for driving in the sun and wind with the top down. I don't remember the route we took out of Chicago, or where it was we crossed the Mississippi, or if we stopped, as we had planned, in Shenandoah, Iowa, where Shelley had gone and learned to play horseshoes, but we did get eaten up by mosquitoes the night we slept in the car near Des Moines.

In Omaha the grass was all chewed up in front of the Mulligan house. Mr. Mulligan was asleep, still being a pressman, and Mrs. Mulligan didn't feel she should wake him, but she telephoned Joey at the *Daily News,* where he worked in the pressroom during the daytime. He got excited when he saw me, just the way he used to, his scalp glowing pink beneath his short blond hair. I could tell he resented the idea of Laurie now being my best friend. It was hard for us to talk, with the presses running, but I learned he had played football for Omaha Tech and he was now engaged to Lillian Kovack, the pretty Polish girl whose hand I had held in the basement of the house when we played "Run Sheep Run." She had changed so much he wasn't sure at all I would recognize her, and worked as a clerk in McCrory's dime store. He didn't understand anybody as old and smart as I was wanting to go to school instead of working and getting married, especially so far away.

134

If we went through my hometown in Nebraska, and we pretty well had to, since it was on the Lincoln Highway, I don't remember anything about it. I may have been dozing while Laurie was driving, or I may have been thinking of California, or of college, or of making up my mind if we should head for Texas, just to see if it had rained on my uncle's farm near Hereford, or go straight through to Salt Lake via Wyoming, which was what we did. I don't remember too much about Salt Lake City either, except for the mountain water running along in the ditches, but somewhere along the way we did let the top down and were soon sunburned so bad we couldn't sleep. I do remember Needles, which was hot as fire, and I wanted to look around for the Big Six Studebaker my father and me and Don had left in a place called Siberia, but they had improved the road across that part of the desert and places like Siberia were no longer on it.

Nor was California, in September, much like the way I had described it to Laurie, the glare of light off the desert so strong we had to squint to see the hazy mountains. It wasn't the time for oranges, but in the shade of the trees we could see the way the groves swept back to the foothills, which would be mountains back where we had come from. I was looking up ahead so hard for the college that we drove right by it, and had to come back. On one side was the desert, the air like ripples in glass, except where they had sprinklers running on a golf course, and on the other this dark green oasis. I wanted to arrive the way I had the first time, coming up from the Pacific Electric station with the eucalyptus trees framing a view of the mountains. On the campus they had the sprinklers running, and at that time in the morning, with the mist rising, it was like a Maxfield Parrish painting. We didn't see any students, just the ivy on the buildings and the blackbirds with their hatpin eyes. We drove up to the foothills just to look back at it, then we came back slow to where we could read what was engraved on the college gates—INCIPIT VITA NOVA—which I explained to Laurie meant "Here begins a new life." That was how I felt about it, and I had come to believe, thanks to some people I had met, that what you feel strongly enough about might happen. I was twenty years of age, and my Uncle Dwight would say it was about time.

IN MY THIRD YEAR AT POMONA COLLEGE, ABOUT
to leave for a *Wanderjahr* in Europe, I had a long talk with a girl who
believed that boys had all the luck. She could not hitchhike, as I could,
to Chicago, nor take a freighter to Greece, nor swim the Hellespont,
nor live in an attic in Paris, nor see the world through a porthole.
I shared her sense of injustice, but it did not lead me to question my
good fortune. As a boy, I was at ease in the prevailing order. Who
was I to change it? Surely Mother Nature, over the centuries, had given
the matter considerable thought and worked it out the way we found
it. If it was puzzling, and indeed it was, why nature favored some and
not others, it nevertheless seemed natural that she should smile on
a white Anglo-Saxon Protestant ignorant boy like me. Years later,
recalling my friend's face, the way her eyes avoided mine on parting,
I sensed that her smile had seamlessly mingled womanly pity and contempt. I had been so stitched and tailored to the prevailing mode I
was at ease with her second-class status, contributing, as it did, to
all the good things that were reserved for men.

My considerable experience of the world had not as yet inspired
me to try to change it, nor did the way I perceived it depress or disturb
me. I accepted things as I found them. If one day I proved to be deserving, I firmly believed I would be rewarded. I had this assurance, below
the level of discussion, from all those people who had reared and shaped
me, their feet on the ground, even as their eyes were set on the wild
blue yonder.

The wild blue yonder of my imagination had not as yet been corrupted by an idea, nor had my spirit been dampened by disenchant-
ment. I daily renewed my great expectations experienced in the words
and music of popular songs. The optimism of Dixie, the nostalgia of
the blues, charged the air I breathed with a shared intoxication, whether
I looked to the past or the future. I could feel this about me like the
hum of a powerhouse, or the tingling silence of a city at night, my
gaze held by the lights on the rising span of a drawbridge. The *Rhapsody in Blue* confirmed what I was feeling, affirmed what I knew. If
growing up meant to abandon these sentiments, Will's boy would be
slow to grow up.

136

SOLO

AN AMERICAN DREAMER
IN EUROPE: 1933–1934

For those who may have wondered
if I ever got there

On a serene and dazzling California morning, the air fragrant with orange blossoms, the light shimmering and misty with the smoke of sprinklers, I left the sheltered halls of learning for a *Wanderjahr* in Europe. I had kissed a few girls, and had read a few books, including *The Decline of the West,* by Oswald Spengler, to whom I had written to question his assumption that the West had declined west of the Missouri River. Of east of the Missouri I hesitated to speak, but of the west I had personal experience. To this letter he had not replied, but perhaps he needed time to think it over. If and when I was in or near Munich I would look him up.

I may have felt that college life had softened me up, since I planned to hitchhike to Chicago and spend the summer working at the 1933 Century of Progress, a world's fair. A fraternity brother had offered me a job at the Schlitz Garden Café on the island. With my nest egg enlarged, I would proceed to New York and work my passage on a cattle boat to France, a hot tip I had picked up from Richard Halliburton, world traveler and author of *The Royal Road to Romance.* I also had the name of a man, with fraternity connections, last believed to be living in a garret in Paris, and the address of a woman of some mystery, thought to be at home in Mallorca. I was not without experience, of an artless sort, but I had yet to ride the rails, spend the night in a hoosegow or sit around the smoking fire in a hobo jungle, swapping yarns and the butts of cigarettes, all known to be indispensable in the education of an American writer. As the author of

> *The sun*
> *Sweats through the fog*

I was not without a show of style and substance.

One of my professors drove me as far as Provo, Utah, from where I made my way eastward toward Colorado. Clear and sparkling mountain water purled in the roadside ditches, but there was little but local eastbound traffic. I had failed to consider that late in May the snow still blocked some of the mountain passes. Just east of Vernal, I spent the long morning at the side of the road, waiting. In the glare of high noon, I stepped from the shade to watch a car slowly approach.

It passed me without raising dust from the gravel road. The two farmers seated in the front looked at me, the younger man firmly gripping the vibrating wheel. Down the road fifty yards or so, the car pulled over and stopped. When I came alongside, both men studied me through the buzz of flies traveling with them.

"Can you read?" one asked me. I said I could read. He reached to open the rear door for me, and I climbed in. We then cruised along for two or three miles in the car's second gear. "He says he can read," he said to his companion. From the brown paper bag he clutched in his lap the older man removed a bottle of Listerine. As he handed it to me, he said, "Read it out loud."

I read aloud the directions printed on the green wrapper, including the fine print. All that they heard seemed to reassure them. They glanced at each other, then the younger one said that if I wouldn't mind waiting, while they tended to a sick horse, they would give me a lift as far as the Green River, about twelve miles. I said I wouldn't mind.

A mile or so ahead, the car left the highway to follow a narrow dirt trail to the top of a barren rise. In the blazing noon light the dilapidated buildings cast deep, vibrant shadows. When the car's motor stopped I could hear the hornet-like drone of the flies. In the yard, hard and smooth as a floor, a big horse stood near the tilted barn in a cloud of flies, a fly net draped over his body. He didn't trouble to twitch his side or switch his tail. Three or four barefooted kids, the same color as the yard, sat in the shadow of the house without moving or speaking. I had never seen kids that age so quiet. The man with the bottle of mouthwash peeled off the wrapper and used the blade of his pocket knife to pry out the cork. Both men had a good sniff of it. One of them poured some of the liquid into his palm and slapped it on the rump of the horse, like shaving lotion. He did that four or five times, until the black pelt glistened, then he stepped back to wait for the horse to feel better. The sweet smell of the mouthwash seemed to increase the drone of the flies. The big horse just stood there, like a propped barrel, his head hung low as if he was asleep on his feet. It seemed to me his rear quarters looked swollen.

"What's the matter with him?" I asked.

One said, "He's been gelded, but he don't get better."

Once more the man slapped the horse with the mouthwash, then he spoke to him in a comforting manner. The horse's name was Tom. The other one picked up a piece of plank from the yard and thumped the horse across the backside with it. "He's got to move around," he said. "We got to move him." The one with the bottle went to the front

140

of the horse and gave a tug on the bridle, but nothing would budge him. Through the cloud of flies over the horse's rump the side of the barn shimmered with heat. "Get going, Tom," one yelled, and gave him another loud whack with the board.

Not feeling so good, I moved to stand in the shade of the barn. Through the window at the back of the house I could hear a woman's voice singing hymns. I noticed a brown-and-white dog lying under the car as if he was dead. I thought I might pass out if I just stood there, listening to the drone of the flies and the whack of the board, so I crossed the yard and went down the driveway without anybody speaking to me. When I got to the road I sprawled out in the ditch grass, my face in the cool dampness at its roots. I just lay there till I felt better, as hot as it was. Now and then I could hear one of the louder whacks on the horse's rump. No one called to me, and it led me to think that whatever ailed the horse might ail all of them, and that they needed more than mouthwash.

A mile or so down the road, feeling a little better, I wondered how much of what I had seen had actually been there and how much the heat and flies had led me to imagine. In either case, it was the sort of experience I valued, but I seemed to lack the stomach for it. The stomach would come, I told myself, when I had toughened up.

In the ten or twelve miles I walked to the Green River, my shadow lengthened before me, but no car passed in either direction. There was more traffic to the north, across Wyoming, and to the south, across New Mexico, but I had previously detoured around the Rockies and I was determined to pass through them. Four days later I was still in Jensen City, on the Green River, where a road crew was working on the bridge. From one of these men I heard that dinosaurs had left their tracks in the rocks to the north. Lucky for me, I was not one of those greenhorns who believed everything they heard. Not far up the river, where I could see his fire at night, a white-bearded prospector camped with his burro, eating cold beans from a can with the blade of his bowie knife. He did cook the bacon he cut from a slab, however, and shared with me the coffee he boiled in a Crisco can. I shared with him one of my Camel cigarettes.

Having once vowed not to smoke until I was twenty-one (for which I had received, and wore, a skull and crossbones medal), at twenty-three I was free of that vow but not to the extent of freely inhaling. I was saving myself. In practical terms, it added up to a lot of cigarettes.

A schoolteacher and his wife, from Pocatello, Idaho, gave me a ride over the mountains to Greeley, Colorado, with a stop along the way at Steamboat Springs, but from Greeley it took me almost two days to hitch the hundred miles or so to Sterling, a railroad town on the South Platte. I could have taken a bus from there as far as North Platte, Nebraska, where there would be more eastbound traffic, but in all my previous cross-country travel, the one thing I hadn't done was ride the rails. It scared me to think about it: but not to face up to it scared me worse.

Just at sunset, concealed like Brer Rabbit in the bushes and shrubs near the station, I saw the headlight of an eastbound freight locomotive far down the tracks, smoking like a comet. As it approached, the earth trembled. I waited till the cars were clattering in the railyard, and I could see the insignia, like coats of arms, painted on the black metal of the tank cars—the Denver & Rio Grande, the Missouri Pacific, the Chicago, Burlington & Quincy, the Atchison, Topeka & Santa Fe—the first, and lasting, exposure I had had to the open and royal road to romance. But until I ran, hooting, from the shadows, I had had no idea there were a dozen or so like me crouched there, now all running for dear life and hooting like savages. One ahead of me stumbled and fell, another came up and ran by me, although in my panic I surely ran faster than I might have, until the clamor of the freight cars, right there at my side, proved to be an adversary I could compete with. I managed to get a firm grip on a rung of a ladder and climb to the top of a car. Luckily, I had picked one with an ice hatch open, and I could see the pale faces in the gloom below me. The boy who followed me down closed the hatch and there we all were, invisible in the darkness. As the freight picked up speed, the awful racket made it impossible to talk. A few matches flickered, cigarettes glowed. Where, I wondered, were we headed? In the freightyards the cars might be shifted around and go north to South Dakota, or south to Kansas. I was hoping to go eastward along the broad Platte valley through such towns as Kearney, Grand Island and Central City. I had lived in them all. In Central City I had been born. That had meant little to me until the prospect of seeing it again from the top of a freight car, clattering through it downgrade just about sunrise. In the slanting light of sunrise I could see all the way from Central City to Chapman, from one grain elevator to another. In a tassel-fringed buggy, the horse's tail sweeping the buckboard, my father had driven me all the way to Grand Island, more than twenty-five miles, to have my adenoids out. From the tops of freight cars parked near the grain elevator I had had my first bird's-eye view of Central City, and was

142

able to fathom, for the first time, the disorderly pattern of its streets. Part of the town, *my* part, paralleled the Union Pacific, and part of it paralleled the Lincoln Highway, which entered town from the east but left it headed southwest. This resulted in a public square with a dog leg, and streets that entered and left from every point of the compass. I would see all of that again, and more, if I was seated atop a freight car and we passed through the town after daylight.

When the first light appeared at the cracks in the hatch I climbed out of the compartment to ride on the top. Where were we? I had no idea. Dawn light dimly revealed the flat Platte valley. The empty freight clattered down the grade like a runaway train. Every ten or twenty minutes we flashed through a town with its water tank and grain elevator, the cattle loader on a siding across from the station. Cinders and smoke streamed into my face from the black plume of the locomotive. I lay out flat, straining to read the names on the water tanks and grain elevators. The big town of Grand Island alerted me that Chapman was up ahead, what little there was of it, with the cemetery where my mother lay buried. East of Chapman, veiled by the smoke, and much less imposing than I remembered, a black water stack rose from a clump of trees, concealing the station where my father had been the agent. Just beyond it the crossing gates had been lowered, the clanging bell changing its pitch as we thundered past. A mile to the north, where the Burlington locomotive with its big funnel stack made its approach to the town, my father had attempted to raise leghorn chickens and sell day-old eggs to the dining car service. In an upstairs bedroom of the farmhouse, where they played records on her new Victrola, his pretty wife of one year and his nine-year-old son, recently freed of his adenoids, watched from the windows as the leghorns died and were buried in deep pits of quicklime. What did that have to do with the young man on the freight car, traveling eastward into the future? I turned to watch it all recede behind me and vanish like smoke: switch tower, grain elevator, water stack, the station where my father had sat, fingering the ticker or looking off to where the tracks blurred on the horizon. Racing into the future, I saw it all vanish, and felt only relief.

My passage through the landscape on the top of a freight car corresponded to my passage as a child, when I perceived, through shuttered chinks of time, the cloudy happenings I would one day transform into fictions. The sleeping town was in the grip of the Depression, a clump of faded green in the surrounding dust bowl, but I would not see that until a year later, when I was headed back to California. Hardly a whisper of all that had reached me between the pages of

143

Spengler and Halliburton, whose opposing views—from the top of the freight car—awaited my firsthand confirmation. For a youth from a landscape so empty it awaited settlement by figures of the imagination, the high road of romance was the one to take atop a swaying Missouri Pacific fruit car. I would note that later, on my arrival in Omaha.

I SPENT THE SUMMER, AND IT SEEMED A LONG ONE, in the Schlitz Garden Café at the Century of Progress. I rose from thirteen dollars a week, plus my food, to eighteen dollars a week by the first of October, at which time I quit. My nest egg had grown to $360, which I figured would last me a year if I managed to live on a dollar a day. I had a new gabardine suit, a pair of crepe-soled shoes, a Schick razor with a year's supply of blades in the handle, an extra shirt, a change of socks, a Parker pen, a notebook, and a Modern Library edition of Thomas Mann's *The Magic Mountain*. I had already read it, but it would seem a different book if I read it at sea, on a cattle boat.

In New York I took a room at the Sloane House YMCA, and spent a week walking the waterfront, looking for a cattle boat. No one I spoke to had ever seen cattle on a boat. It was costing me two dollars a day to live in New York, so I paid for a passage on the *Black Gull*, a freighter sailing from Weehawken to Antwerp. When I got over to Weehawken, where it was docked, the boat looked pretty small. Sol Yellig, a passenger, was there before I was, and we had all day to look the boat over. Sol was from Brooklyn, on his way to Russia, where his father had an investment in the future as an engineer. The two others in my cabin included a Swede, named Lindstrom, and Mr. Schutzel, or Schlussel (I never knew which), who had been a janitor in Des Moines and was now going home to Austria. In his twenty-eight years in Des Moines, Mr. Schutzel had not learned much English. He was a stocky man, very short in the leg, his blue serge suit as shiny as oilcloth; the pants proved to be worn so thin at the knees his underwear showed through when he was seated.

Sven Lindstrom was an artist, on his way to his home in Oslo, having overstayed his student visa. He had all his stuff in a duffel, like a sailor, but he carried his guitar in a black wooden case. Until the boat sailed, he stayed belowdecks, plucking the strings and singing Russian folk songs. There were two other cabins, one with four people, and a small cabin with two people on their honeymoon, Mr. and Mrs. Lennox from Enid, Oklahoma. We were all out on the deck, even Mr. Lindstrom, when we finally embarked and sailed down the river. As we passed the Statue of Liberty, Sol Yellig turned to me and said, "What a joke."

145

That startled me at the time, but I reasoned it might be the way that smart-alecky types from Brooklyn saw it. I had now seen the Pacific, and swum in it, and in a few hours I would be crossing the Atlantic, and in the spring, or maybe even sooner, I would gaze on the blue Mediterranean. Lord Byron might have ruined the isles of Greece for me, being a bit too romantic for my taste.

The *Black Gull* had a full cargo, and set low in the sea. I liked that when I stood along the rail or up at the bow, where the spray would drench me. At the boat's midsection, around the covered hold, there was room to walk up and down and space for a few folding chairs. The honeymoon couple usually got two of them, and Mr. Siegfried Liszt was usually in the other, since it was his custom to be up about daylight. Mr. Liszt had been a chief clerk at a bank in New York but he now planned to study medicine in Vienna, where he was from. His mother still lived there, in suburban Vienna, just across from what had been his father' wagon wheel factory, the name S. Z. LISZT still visible on the bricks in the photograph he showed me. With the rise of the automobile, of course, the wagon wheel business had not been so good.

The food was all right and there was plenty of it, but getting in and out of the small dining room across from the galley proved to be a problem. The table filled the room so tightly there was not enough space to squeeze behind the chairs when getting in and out. The smart and fast eaters soon sat near the door, with the slow and big eaters at the back. Another thing we learned to do was take the food at the door, handed across from the galley, and then pass it around the table so no one had to serve it. After dinner some of us would sit there and play cards and dominoes, while the others talked.

In the talk it turned out Mr. Liszt had once been a student of literature in Vienna, a reader of Oswald Spengler and Thomas Mann. It saddened him to hear that I was reading *The Magic Mountain,* since so much of it was lost in the translation. If I so desired it, he would restore for me much that had been lost. I so desired it, but the wind on the deck made it hard to discuss such serious matters, and if we sat inside with the others, we had trouble with Dr. Haffner. Dr. Haffner was a year younger than I was, but he already had his own practice in Milwaukee and was on his way for a year of study in Stuttgart. He was a heavy-set young man, very tight in his checkered suit, with short, pudgy fingers and a round baby face. He spent most of his time reading medical journals and helping the young married couple with their French. To show me the subtleties involved in translation, Mr. Liszt read aloud to me from his copy of Count Keyserling's *Travel*

Diary. The moment he would translate what he had read, Dr. Haffner would snort, like stifling a sneeze, or wag his head from side to side as if it pained him. On occasion he would blurt out something that I understood without the need of translation. *Dummkopf,* for example, I figured out for myself.

Mr. Liszt soon came to feel, in the privacy of his cabin, that a young scholar like myself, with my love of German literature, might find Vienna more attractive than Paris. For one thing, the living would be much cheaper, and for another, the Viennese were more *gemütlich.* And what was *gemütlich?* Dr. Haffner, on hearing this word, had blown a sound through his lips that required no translation. Mr. Liszt remained silent, his own red lips puckered, his hands smoothing the wrinkles from his napkin. After a few days in Paris, he said, I would be able to appreciation what was *gemütlich* about Vienna. The people were more friendly and easygoing. The language itself—if he might say so—would prove easier to master, for the French were particularly scornful of beginners. The young married couple, in Mr. Liszt's opinion, were due for a rude awakening. In Vienna, in contrast, I would find people eager to be helpful—especially young women. Mr. Liszt spoke respectfully of Viennese women, but not without a flush that reddened his neck and ears. He was up so early, to occupy a folding chair, his freshly shaved jowls dusted with talcum, that by early afternoon his face looked blue with a five-o'clock shadow. Until I met Mr. Liszt and Dr. Haffner, and had some long talks with Sol Yellig, I thought there had to be something special between people who spoke the same language. I found that there was. The dislike they had for each other was more refined than that for people in general.

Dr. Haffner was really a *Wunderkind,* Mr. Liszt advised me, who knew all about poison gas, bugs and germ warfare, and it had come to his attention that he sent wireless messages to Berlin and Hamburg. Had I also noticed that Dr. Haffner never missed the German broadcasts of Hitler? I had heard one myself, the hoarse voice of the *Führer* lifted and blowing on the roars of those who were listening, but the static was so bad Mr. Liszt couldn't tell me much that he had said. The message I got was not one a translation would have helped.

My cabinmate Sven Lindstrom liked to sit on his upper bunk with his bare legs dangling and sing "*Ochy Chornia.*" Sol Yellig liked to sing along with him. Anything to do with Russia he thought was wonderful. He had never been there, but he knew that Russian women were wonderful. I had had a weakness for Russia myself and might have planned to go there if it had been nearer, but after five days and nights with Sol Yellig I knew I could live without it. The likable side of Sol was apparent when you caught him at something, which wasn't at all hard, and he would smile and shrug.

I often saw the honeymoon couple up at the bow of the boat, but seldom up close. If the boat was rocking he would grip the rail so she could stand with one arm around him, the other holding the book she was reading. I was curious about what the book was, but it had a plain lending library jacket. If they were in the lounge, and I spoke to one of them, she always did the talking. She was nice, but one of those tall, gangly women it wouldn't have crossed my mind to marry. After several days at sea he began a beard, which grew in orange like the coloring that came with margarine, so he shaved it off.

Near the mid-Atlantic we had some bad weather, with seas so high they spilled into the gangway. Sol Yellig was sick, Mr. Liszt was sick, and the honeymoon couple in particular were sick, but Mr. Schutzel, Lindstrom and the *Wunderkind* didn't miss a meal. I wasn't *really* sick, but the thought of food made me stand in the gangway, the spray in my face, breathing in deeply until I felt better. What I wanted to know, and had a chance to find out, was the difference between a real storm at sea and reading about a storm in Conrad. When I came to know the difference, however, and the sea had calmed, it was Conrad's storm that I remembered.

We were anchored in the pea-soup fog of the Channel for the thirteenth and fourteenth day of our crossing, and on the sixteenth of October, at about three in the morning, we made our way up the Schelde to Antwerp. I could see, hanging out of the fog, the telephone wires, as though they were all dangling from a maypole, and in the street along the dock the cobblestones glistened like metal. Not a sound anywhere. When the gangplank was lowered, clattering like a drawbridge, every window in a building I had thought might be empty went up as if a fire alarm had sounded. Framed in the windows, in nothing but their nightshirts, were the wonderful whores Sven had been telling us about. Some were leaning out and hooting, a racket like none I had ever heard. While I was on the deck, leaning over the rail, Sven ran down the gangplank in his pajamas, then ran the full length of the street, waving and throwing kisses, as if uncertain which one of them to choose. I can describe it, but who would ever believe it? The fatter women leaned from the windows holding their breasts in their hands. Sven didn't seem to notice any more than I did the car that came out of nowhere and moved up behind him. Two big fellows picked him up, the way you would a kid, put him into the car and drove off. Some of the women continued to hoot and wave—there

148

were eight or ten of us out on the deck—but when we just stood there staring, doing nothing, they slammed down their windows and went back to bed. It was suddenly so quiet we could hear drops of water drip from the wires. If nothing else had happened to me in Europe, I would have felt that what I had seen was well worth the trouble, but when I was safely back in the cabin it shamed me to see that Sven's bunk was empty. His guitar was still there, and his bag was unpacked. It had never crossed my mind that he would have the nerve to act as good as he talked. "I'm going to get me five women," he had said, "and go to bed for a week." I would have personally settled for one *good* woman, but when the time came, and he set an example, I stood on the deck with all the other chickens. I also agreed with them all that he was either crazy or a sex maniac. At times I thought I might be both, but here I was on my first night in the old world, with a whole year of it before me, and it scared me to think that I might catch something and not be able to do anything about it. Not on a dollar a day. The fact is, since I had to miss something, I wouldn't have missed what I had just seen. That's what I told myself.

I spent the day in Antwerp avoiding Sol Yellig and the honeymoon couple, who turned up all over. On the night train to Paris I shared the compartment with two peasant women, wrapped up in their shawls like parcels, each one with a fat goose in her lap. The women dozed off, but the geese and I kept wary eyes on each other. I'd been up since three in the morning, and all day on my feet, but if I let myself sleep I might miss something.

I managed to stay awake by standing in the aisle, letting the night air blow into my face. In the early dawn light I saw the fields of France, some with rows of stubble and the big two-wheeled carts I had seen in Van Gogh's paintings. It seemed normal to me that most of what I saw far exceeded my expectations. Wasn't it for this I had come to Europe? In the Gare St. Lazare my excitement was so great I watched people eating croissants and forgot to eat myself. The people milling around were smaller than I had expected and showed no interest in me whatsoever. That was surprising. In America I would have shown real interest in them. The way the waiters stood at the front of the sidewalk cafés, flipping their cloths at the chair seats, kept me from sitting down. At a busy intersection, the air blue with the exhausts of the buses, I saw a classmate of mine I had never much liked sitting on a bench at a bus stop. He had been a senior, a class ahead of me, who always wore a coat and tie to his classes. Here in Paris he wore a topcoat, with the collar turned up, and a rolled-brim fedora like those worn by my father. So far as I knew, he didn't write, or paint, or read the sort of books that were written in Paris, but on one occasion, because he had a car, I had got him a blind date. She was a smart girl and a good dancer, but after the dance she wouldn't get back in the rumble seat with him. She rode with us in the front. Later I asked him what had gone wrong.

"What I wanted was a real woman," he told me. "What you got me was a smart-ass schoolgirl."

If he had been a year in Paris I might have learned something from him, and we might even have had some good times together, but a person like that would naturally think that I had come to Paris for the same reason he did. I already had a woman. There would be two letters from her waiting for me at the American Express.

In the doorway of a shop I saw a girl who made me think of my girl, the way she was standing, looking at me over her shoulder, but when she smiled she had this one tooth, like a black kernel of corn, right in the middle of her uppers. When I smiled at her she made a gesture with her finger that was new to me, but not hard to understand.

I could read a little French, but what I heard all around me was like a language played backward. If I asked directions I never understood what was said. In the Luxembourg Gardens I sat on a bench listening to the cries and shouts of the children. One ran to stand before me, screaming like a parrot, shouting the same words until she was hoarse. Only when she ran off, and it was relatively quiet, did I realize she had been yelling, "*Me voici! Me voici!*" just like a small kid anywhere. But whatever people say in a language you don't understand seems interesting. Anxious to know what a real French apple tasted like, I bought two from a peddler, about the size of golf balls, but both had worms in them.

A classmate of mine had given me the address of a pension, near the Place St. Germaine, but when I spoke to the concierge at the door I could hear girls speaking English while they played Ping-Pong. Most of the time the ball just bounced around on the floor.

I got a room for the night near the Sorbonne, where a bird flew in and out of the small barred window. No one had told me that the toilets did not have bowls, where you could sit, but were like urinals and you had to crouch. The next two days it drizzled and all of Paris looked to me like one big dirty puddle. I decided it wasn't the right time of year for Paris and took the night train to Vienna, where the weather couldn't be any worse and the people might be more

150

gemütlich. At the stop in Basel, the waitress in the station understood what I ordered, slipped me a second pat of butter, and wished me a *sehr glückliche Reise.* Thanks to her, that was what I was on, but at least I knew better than to try to tell her. "*Auf Wiedersehen,*" I said.

ON KÄRNTNERSTRASSE, NEAR THE STEPHANSDOM, which Mr. Liszt had pointed out to me, we sat in a *Kaffeehaus* drinking large cups of coffee topped with whipped cream. When we arrived he had asked the waiter for a newspaper and it was brought to him. There were four or five old men in the café, all of them reading newspapers, but they looked a little drab and shabby compared to Mr. Liszt. His American suit had been pressed, and I could smell his aftershave lotion. I was very glad to see him, and he was friendly, but since I had last seen him on the boat he had changed. He was no longer the clerk in a New York bank, but a professor advising one of his students. His new reversible raincoat, with the tweed lining showing, hung on a hook with his plaid muffler tucked into the sleeve. My raincoat was so light that I sat with it on, my clothes still mussed from the night I had spent on the train.

We were seated, Mr. Liszt advised me, in a very famous *Kaffeehaus,* where many celebrated people had sat and talked, but to be perfectly frank, he seldom came here because the coffee was so expensive. I could believe that. Only Mrs. Mulligan's matchless eggnogs, in my Omaha boyhood, seemed to me at all comparable. I quickly said I would be glad to pay for my own, and he replied he had been about to suggest that. In the future, when we met in this manner, we would go *dutch.* Having the appropriate word for it made it acceptable to both of us.

He read the news in the paper, most of which was bad, then he made note of the rooms for rent that he considered inexpensive and suitable. There were several not far from the university, on the Ring. They were not nearby, but while we were walking he would point out the sights of interest. Near the Votivkirche was the Bankverein, where I would go to cash my traveler's checks. We stopped to buy some stamps at one of the kiosks, which also sold tobacco. Cigarettes could be bought one at a time, and we each bought one.

The first room we looked at was up three flights of stairs, where we found three women sitting in the kitchen, near a stove. They were greatly impressed by Mr. Liszt, who gave a little speech about my background, a scholar who had come all the way from California to study German literature in Vienna. They were dumbfounded, but so bundled in shawls I saw little of their faces. The one who moved about the kitchen, and showed us the room, wore skirts so long they swept the floor. The room was right off the kitchen, with a bed, a chair and a desk with a lamp. A large white bowl and pitcher sat on a stand near the window. The room would be warm, being so close to the kitchen, but Mr. Liszt pointed out that to get in and out I would always be passing through the room where the women were gathered.

We saw another one like it, but much darker, with a wall blocking the light at the window, then we climbed four flights of wide stairs to an apartment on the top floor. A gray-haired woman with the eyes of a Gypsy, her earrings swinging, peered at us through the crack in the door. Shrilly we were welcomed, the hall floor gleaming from the sweep of her skirts. A dim bulb glowed in the dark hallway, but the room at the end of it was flooded with light. The ceiling was high, as was the bed on which she sat to show it was springy; there was a desk with pigeonholes, a cold blue-tile stove, a white bowl and pitcher on a marble-topped washstand. This room, with *Frühstück,* of *Butterbrot* and *Schokolade,* came to about sixteen dollars a month. I liked both the room and the *gnädige Frau,* who hustled about like the woman on the can of Dutch Cleanser. Her name was Frau Unger. She herself had come from Pest, across the Danube from Buda. Her son Hermann, who loved to travel, had once gone there on a river excursion. While his animated mother opened wide the casement window to wave her arms at the view and the gray roofs of Vienna, her son Hermann, dressed in the coat and pants left him by his father, an "official," stood patiently beside the stove, snapping the links of his cuffs, waiting to be introduced.

At eight in the morning Frau Unger would appear with my tray of *Butterbrot* and *Schokolade.* The thick slice of bread was dark and heavy, cut from a round loaf in the delicatessen, and sold by the weight. The butter moist and unsalted. The chocolate rich and sweet. After asking me how well I had slept, she would stand, her hands rolled up in her apron, watching me eat. It seemed to astonish her that a youth who had come from where I did knew how to do it.

Was the bed soft?

Jawohl!

Was the food good?

Jawohl!

When she heard me say *jawohl,* her eyes flashed, her head wagged with pleasure, rocking her earrings. Her lips parted expectantly on her gold-capped teeth. What a woman Herr Unger had found himself before he died in the Great War. She was tall, with wide hips, and

153

listened to me with her head cocked, like a worming robin. She contrived many ways to conceal her hands, with the knobby knuckles, but there was always something that required doing. In Vienna the beds came with a feather mattress that one slept on, and another that one slept beneath. Both of these had to be aired at the open window, where they were shaken and given a good pummeling. The high window seemed to frame most of the roofs in Vienna, but nothing in the way of a landmark. Occasionally I saw the sun shining elsewhere, but never on my window. After several years of living in Southern California, I found the fall air of Vienna cold. It was early November. In the garden directly below the window, the bushes and the shrubs were bare. Gravel paths, with crisp right angles, divided the garden into sections, each with a bench like those in a park. One morning I had seen a couple seated on a bench, the woman with her hands in a fur muff, the man with his chin resting on his cane.

While my bed and the room were being aired, I wore my raincoat as a bathrobe. After breakfast I would walk up and down conjugating German verbs until Frau Unger's son Hermann paid me a social visit. He was small and frail, not at all like his mother, except for the teeth that kept his lips from closing. Hermann's large rabbit eyes were warm and gentle, and his nostrils, like those of a girl I had known, quivered in moments of excitement. He had inherited all of his clothes from his father, in the style that was current before the war. I had never before actually known a young man who wore spats. They were mouse-colored, with pearl buttons on the side, and he had several pairs. When he came to see me, snapping the links on his cuffs as he bowed, I was part of a movie of social high life, starring Bebe Daniels and Adolphe Menjou. Hermann had been born while the Hapsburgs were still in power. He told me this as we stood at the window, the pupils of his eyes as pale as water. Hapsburg was a name that meant as much to him as Jefferson and Washington meant to me, and I noticed that in the excitement of his recitation his gums tended to bleed, staining his teeth. In the strong light at the window, his pupils narrowed like a cat's. When he extended his arm to point into the garden, I noticed that his cuffs were not part of a shirt but fastened with pins to the sleeve of his jacket. It shamed me to see these details so clearly, but that did not stop me from looking. I marveled how, with a head so small, he had such a snow of dandruff on his collar. When he smiled at me, the tip of his tongue wiped the pink stain from his teeth.

Hermann had studied English, like his father, and he now wrote business letters, in English, for a bicycle firm on Florianigasse, all of

154

which he signed, "Your Obedient Humble Servant." If I would speak English and correct his grammar, he would speak and correct my German. At my suggestion he brought in a chair, on which, after bowing, he would sit. In this way the young American in his raincoat and Hermann Unger of the Hapsburg Empire would discuss the weather or New York City (*wunderbar, fabelhaft, grossartig,* etc.) while smoking short tubes of paper into which had been stuffed something like excelsior. Hermann made them himself every morning, on a machine with a crank. When he departed he bowed, taking the chair with him, then discussed all that had been said with Frau Unger, whose laugh was shrill, her voice loud and penetrating.

If I pause here to consider what I have just written, to what extent is it true to what I remember? To what extent is what I remember true to Hermann? He stood near the door, on entering the room, until I actually beckoned him closer. He was at once very eager to talk and reluctant, as if he privately had his doubts that he was the person he appeared to be in public. I liked him. This may have been at the heart of what I liked.

I would work for an hour or more on German verbs and vocabulary, then walk down Florianigasse, a street with many zigs and zags, to the university on the Ringstrasse. The school was in operation but the halls seemed empty. I had inquired about courses in German for beginners, and been advised to join the Foreign Students Club, on Schottengasse. The club had its rooms on the second floor of a building directly across the street from the bank. One of the rooms had several chairs, a rack of newspapers, a fireplace where people without chairs could stand and talk. A large adjoining room, without a rug, had a billiard table, a rack with cues on the wall, and two smaller tables for checkers and chess. At twelve o'clock and at six, the club served meals for as little as one schilling, about twenty-five cents. If I was careful and frugal, I could live through the winter on thirty dollars a month, a sum I could afford.

All foreigners, especially those speaking English, were in demand for the exchange of conversation with both native and other foreign students. Whether the American language was English or not was one of our topics of discussion. The Finns, who proved to be pretty clannish, took over the billiard table in the morning, then let the Czechs have it in the afternoon. At least four or five young men were British, and spoke the much admired Oxford English, the vowels so broad and nasal I missed a good deal that they were saying. I was not the only American—there was a girl from Buffalo and one from Brooklyn,

155

and a graduate student from Yale who did not feel the two of us had much in common. In theory, at least, an hour's exchange conversation would give each person half an hour to listen and half an hour to talk, but in practice, as I soon found out, I spent about forty-five minutes listening. Those experienced with exchange conversations, and there were many of them, knew how to make the most out of every discussion. And how are you, Herr Morris? *Sehr gut,* says I. And then he or she tells me for most of the hour, how he or she is, in great detail.

On the plus side, it did mean that I was very popular. There was little I could say in German, but I proved to be a good listener. Five students signed up to converse with me, including a young woman physical education instructor—phys ed was very popular in Vienna—with a Swiss Fiancé in Poughkeepsie. Twice a week I met with her in the alcove of the game room, where we would sit at one of the windows. Her face was still tanned from a summer of mountain climbing, her shoulders were broad, her hands were calloused from working with gymnasium equipment. On the occasions I saw her knees, I recognized the dark bruises of mat burns. It lead me to wonder what her boyfriend must be like. Were American men all big? she asked me. I said that many were, since I knew it was what she wanted to hear. She also taught swimming, and her hair might be wet, her eyes bloodshot, when she met with me for a conversation.

Three times a week I met with Pius Michael Prutscher, a history major from Innsbruck. He was a handsome, apple-cheeked young man with full red lips and good white teeth. The teeth were unusual. In our second discussion he asked me what it was I did in Vienna for women. Pius greatly admired young men like myself, who had the strength of character to resist women, but when he found himself with a *Fräulein*—a word he pronounced like music—he could not help himself. It was as simple as that. Pius was also a very religious person, but when he saw a pretty *Fräulein* he forgot all about it.

When I saw Pius Prutscher, as I sometimes did, with one of these creatures he couldn't resist, I wondered what he would do if he saw the girls we had in California. Would he go nuts? It pleased me to be admired for my character, but there were times when I wondered about it. This good-looking American girl from Buffalo, taking courses at the university, proved to be so nearsighted that without her glasses she didn't recognize people until she spoke to them. Rather than be a girl who wore glasses, she was friendly with everybody. I liked her a lot, but I was never really sure, when she smiled at me, whom she was seeing. At meals I read the menu for her, and I kept her up to date about the news on the bulletin board. Once a month we had dances at the

156

club I would take her to, then she would lose me. Anybody who cut in on her she would dance with, since we all looked alike.

Bogislav von Lindheim, the club secretary, had spent two years at Cambridge and spoke the English language the way I would have liked to. When we had dinner together all we spoke was English, since we had so much we wanted to discuss. He liked *Death in Venice,* by Thomas Mann, but his favorite writer was Kafka. I had never heard of Kafka. When I had learned enough German he would loan me some of his books.

Seen in profile, wearing his beret, Bogislav looked more like an eagle than a person. If Catherine had been able to *see* him, she would have been crazy about him. He had more women to talk to than he could find the time for, but he made extra time for me. When he had to go somewhere around Vienna I would tag along with him, and we would talk. Wherever he went he carried a leather valise that signified he was a scholar. He thought I should have one, so people would know who I was. I found that very strange coming from a person I considered so smart. We agreed on almost everything we discussed—with the exception of my liking Spengler—but it troubled me, when we were at the club, to see the way he would click his heels and bow when he met people. If it was a woman, he would lift her hand to his lips. There was quite a bit of that sort of thing at the club, but it was not one of the things we got around to discussing, like the way he never removed his rubbers. In time I figured out for myself that that was his way of saving the shoes he had bought in England.

Karl Fisher, from Dresden, worked most of the day, so I saw him only in the late afternoon. His father was an exporter of leather and fabrics, and Karl planned to go in the spring to Buenos Aires, where he would run a branch of his father's business. He spoke excellent Spanish as well as English, but he liked to talk with me just to keep in practice. Karl wore his hair even shorter than I did, clipped at the sides and rear so that his ears, like mine, stuck out. He was stocky, very energetic, and what I would have called back home a "go-getter." He also had plans to start a branch of the business in Mexico City, and if I would learn to speak Spanish he would like me to take it over. That's how he was. I could see he was shrewdly appraising me while we sat and talked. If we could find a place to sit in the alcove, at a window overlooking Schottengasse, we would have a *Butterbrot* and *Schokolade* while we talked and watched the people passing. Vienna was not like Paris. There were very few people walking the streets, and most of them were elderly, or idlers who were quick to cluster around a peddler. These men were not so frail as Hermann but they

157

had similar rabbit-like faces and large sad eyes. It led me to recall what the German, Dr. Haffner, had said to Mr. Liszt on the freighter: "The situation in Germany is serious, but not hopeless; the situation in Austria is hopeless, but not serious."

The alcove windows of the club framed views of Schottengasse where it narrowed to enter the inner city. The sidewalk widened directly below us to make an area favored by peddlers and idlers, a sort of open stage. The peddlers wore bowlers, but most of the idlers were hatless, in dark topcoats that were too large for them. From the angle of our view at the window I could see their thin necks in their collarless shirts. Just like the unemployed back in the States, they were putting in the time, and welcomed the entertainment. One of these peddlers had a portable, collapsible table, on which he put out his wares. Two or three of the idlers, at a respectful distance, would watch him set himself up for business. There was no rush. Everything in good time. It almost seemed to come as a surprise to the peddler to note the interest he had attracted. He would greet the men before him with a tip of his hat, and they would nod. He would then hold up before them the pen he was selling, unscrew the cap, and display the point. One of the idlers would be encouraged to step forward and look at it closely. What he saw was always reassuring. Filling the pen with ink, wiping the point, making lines with the pen on a pad of paper, the pad, too, offered for examination, would require five or ten minutes and attract three or four more spectators. One of these spectators, more substantial-looking than the others, wearing a wool muffler and shiny rubbers, would ask to inspect the pen, and take the liberty of writing with it on the pad. What he saw so pleased him he would buy one. On second thought, as he counted out his money, he decided to buy another. Each came in a box. He would slip them into a pocket of his coat. One of the idlers, too, would buy one, writing out his name on the pad of paper, a pen of this sort surely being one of the things he most needed. Another would follow. Three, sometimes four or five pens would be sold.

I had watched this scene many times before I recognized the peddler's accomplice. He might sometimes wear a cap, and be burdened with parcels one of his companions would hold for him. He might begin as a scoffer, backing away until coaxed to come forward. He smiled and joked. He broke the ice. Jauntily he marched away, delighted with his purchase.

What was it about this drama that held me? The gestures were minimal and expressive. In the dusky winter light, under overcast skies, it was all black and white, like a movie. The scene arranged itself in

158

a predictable manner. On my mind's eye it overlapped other scenes that I had casually collected, like snapshots. Charlie Chaplin or Buster Keaton would have performed it to perfection. Yet it did not cross my mind to take the picture I saw with a camera. I had bought a camera—not after seeing some pictures, but after talking about photographs with Karl. The few pictures I had taken might well have come with the camera. The picture I saw from the window, consisting of many exposures, overlapping images and complex emotions, was one I had captured on the mind's eye only, and separate from the one I saw in the street.

Not far from where I lived was the Dorotheum, a huge warehouse of a pawnshop run by the city. One day I went there with Bogislav, not knowing what I might see. In one of the first rooms we entered I saw this English Raleigh bike, with a four-speed Sturmey Archer gear. The bike was like new, the tires had inner tubes, there were tools, a pump, and a lamp with a generator that was turned by the front wheel. Having seen this marvel, I had to have it. On it I would see all that there was to be seen, high countries, low countries, beginning with Italy. Over and over I would save—I told myself—whatever it would cost me.

Until the day of the auction I was apprehensive that some greedy Austrian would beat me to it. Since I could not understand the rules and words of the bidding, Bogislav agreed to go along with me. Of the two dozen or more people who appeared, all but three or four of them bid on the Raleigh. One by one, as the price went up, they dropped out. I turned a deaf ear to what was happening. After what seemed forever, the bike was mine for 240 schillings. How much was that? About sixty-five dollars. More than I had planned to spend through the winter. Bogislav perceived what he had long suspected: Americans from the Far West were crazy.

Someone had swiped the valves from the inner tubes, so the tires were flat and couldn't be pumped up. I had to carry that bike, a heavy touring model, the four long blocks to Florianigasse, then up the four long flights of stairs to my room, where Hermann let me in. He, too, thought I would have a heart attack. Little did I care, knowing the treasure was mine. I had perspired so much I had to take off my clothes and wipe myself with a towel. In the dim glow of the lamp on my desk, I lay in bed and examined the bike. I was both wildly elated and depressed. It proved to be a single, inflated emotion. I was like Pius Prutscher, who was smart and knew better, but when faced with his lust he couldn't help himself. What would he think if he knew I had blown it on a bike, and not a woman?

Hermann proved a great support and consolation, since his admiration was even greater than mine. He had never before seen a Sturmey Archer gear, only in catalogues. He had never owned a bike but he knew a lot about them since he wrote the business letters for supplies to England. When the bike was placed upside down, with the wheels in the air, the pedals could be pumped and the gears operated. Everything worked. We were both out of our minds. I fell asleep reassured that my action had been mad, but like that of a foolhardy lover, fated. I could not help myself. Had it taken me more than twenty-three years to find that out?

When I complained to Hermann about the gray sunless days, he said I had come too late for the good October weather. From now on through the winter it would be gray and cold, with snow on the roofs and ice in the streets. It made him shudder to think about it. There were four rooms to Frau Unger's apartment, but two were closed off during the winter. Frau Unger and her daughter shared a bedroom, and Hermann slept on a cot in the kitchen. He liked that, being the one who shivered the most and caught the first cold. By the light of a lamp Frau Unger had shown me the furniture in the parlor, all of it covered with sheets, and protected from the sun by drapes at the windows. Her life had once been different. She unwrapped her big hands from a wad of apron to sing to me, with gestures, "*Wien und der Wein, Wien und der Wein!*" I had thought "flashing eyes" was a literary phrase until I saw hers.

We were leaning, Hermann and I, on the bedding being aired at the window. Far off to the north, beyond the *schöne blaue Donau,* there were fleeting patches of sunlight. In the garden below the window an elderly couple, arm in arm, and stately, walked the gravel paths. I was struck by how erect and dignified they were. At the sharp right-angle turns at the corners, they pivoted in a military manner. I was amused by that, and continued to watch them as they made a full tour of the garden and returned to the door at the entrance. Just before reaching it they stopped, as if at a command. A moment passed, as if they were waiting for it to open, then the man extended his hand like a sleepwalker and approached the door. As his fingers touched it, they moved along the surface till he found the latch. The door opened inward, and they marched out.

I turned to Hermann, who said, "They can't see. It's a *blind Garten.*" He said "*blint,*" and I realized he had said it before, but I had not understood him. No one came to this garden but the blind, and that was why the paths were so symmetrical. So many steps to a turn, so many steps to a bench. The men carried canes, but they

160

seldom used them. I had been reluctant to watch them from the window, since I thought they would think I was spying, but now that this seemed unlikely, I stood at the window whenever it was open. On one occasion I saw several couples marching as if to unheard music. I was witness to a parable, I realized, with many nuances and meanings, a visual metaphor that I found exciting. What I had seen from the window would prove—over the next fifty years—to be inexhaustible each time I looked.

On my way to the club I passed a public *Badehaus*. I surely needed a bath, but even more I needed to wash the clothes that I had been wearing for weeks. I discussed the problem with Hermann, and learned the cost of a bath was a matter of time. Each person had a booth, and paid for five, ten or fifteen minutes of hot water. My strategy was one I had practiced in college. I would wear my soiled clothes into the shower, work up a good lather, then rinse off, getting two baths for the price of one. There was nothing new about this practice in Vienna, except for the fact that it was strictly forbidden. But how would they ever know if I wrung out the clothes I had washed, then put them back on, wet, beneath my suit and raincoat. I would then sprint the quarter mile up Florianigasse to my room.

I did not share this strategy with Hermann before giving it a try. I paid for only ten minutes of hot water, not to arouse suspicion, and managed to wash my hair, two shirts, shorts and socks. The water was hot and plentiful, but it switched to cold while I was still rinsing. For years I had learned to do without a cold rinse. I pulled on my suit, stuffed the socks into my pocket, then sprinted up the grade in my unlaced shoes, already squishy with water. In my room I spread my wet clothes on the cold tile oven and got into bed. As I see it, the sprint up the grade had saved my life. It got me so warm I didn't feel a thing but the warmth of the bed and my pounding heart. I was not unaware that I had been a fool, and might easily come down with double pneumonia, but it seemed unimportant in the light of the challenge, the money I had saved and the strategic triumph. I lost a day at the club while my clothes were drying. Frau Unger transferred them to the warmth of her kitchen; she liked the wildness of my just washed hair and the high quality of my socks. I felt fine.

In the cloakroom at the club, and on the stairs up from the street, I sometimes observed the furtive exchange of secret signs and greetings among certain members. Hands were raised, as in "Heil Hitler," but the words that were exchanged escaped me. There was also a clasp of the hand that involved an intertwining of the fingers. It was none of my business, but I was curious, and eager to share such a secret handclasp.

I turned to my friend Pius Prutscher, an influential young man. He often gave speeches I did not understand in the courtyard of the university. His apple-cheeked face and ears flushed red with his emotions. He mocked those who asked foolish questions. It seemed to me he was marked for greatness. If he had a problem in resisting women, the women had a bigger problem in resisting him. It pleased me, at the club, to be one of those Pius always greeted and talked to. I often heard his voice at the back of the cloakroom, or hoarsely whispering in the washroom.

On a gloomy day that felt like snow, a chill wind blowing along the Ringstrasse, I came on a cluster of students huddled on the steps of the university. The doors were blocked by the police. At the club I learned that Pius Prutscher, among others, had been taken into custody. Those who knew anything would not talk about it. On a walk with Bogislav (he wouldn't talk at the club), he told me that the Nazis were behind the trouble. Dollfuss was a decent person, but he was helpless, and the Heimwehr—the so-called home forces—were already Nazi forces. Pius and his friends were a secret organization with the purpose of overthrowing Dollfuss. What they wanted for Austria was a leader like Hitler. The slogan they exchanged in the dark of the stairs was *"Österreich über Alles, wenn wir nur wollen!"* (Austria over everything, if we only will it!)

On Kärntnerstrasse, even as we were talking, we passed a company of Austrian soldiers so nondescript and pathetic I thought they must be part of a movie. But no, they were the fatherland's soldiers. I thought this turn of events would bring us closer together, but Bogislav was so ashamed of what was happening I think he regretted telling me about it, like an illicit affair. He also felt that I was part of the new world, and that he was hopelessly part of the old one. Just seeing and talking to me made him feel worse, since I was always so damned upbeat and optimistic.

It was one thing for me to be low on money, since it was all part of my adventure, but Bogislav had only what he made teaching one course at the university. It shamed him to mention how little it was. I had also figured out that he was not from Salzburg, as he had told me. I had been to his closet-sized room. The only books he owned were in his valise. He sometimes read to me, as a joke, the advertisements for husbands in the *Neue Wiener Zeitung,* where *Fräuleins* might list a cow as part of their dowry, but he also hoped that he would find some fairy princess or countess, looking for a scholar and a poet.

He knew one countess, but she was Hungarian, and not his type.

I had met her at the club, where she was playing Ping-Pong with another Hungarian. The Hungarians were great for Ping-Pong, and spent most of their time playing with each other. It was quite an occasion when they let me play. The way I served and held the paddle was so unusual it made a stir when I beat them. The Hungarian men, when they played with the countess, were smart enough to let her beat them, but when she played with me I didn't. She took the wooden paddle and broke it like a cookie, then stormed off. The Countess Maria Szapary was also a scholar, taking her doctorate in history at the university. She was a heavy, powerful young woman with frizzly orange hair, a broad flat face with small features. Her eyes were so wide apart I looked at just one at a time. They were sort of greenish, as in "Ochy Chornia," but they sparkled like the eyes of Frau Unger, which seemed to be something special about Hungarians.

I thought I would never see the countess again, but she asked Bogislav if I would help her with her English. It was not appropriate for her to exchange conversations with a character who spoke the American language, so she would pay me four schillings an hour. That was fine with me, and we met at the club three or four times a week. The very idea of a countess seemed literary to me until I met Maria Szapary. Though she was built like a fullback, she was not unattractive. Every look she gave me was that of a woman looking at a man. In practical terms, of course, it didn't mean a thing since she was the Countess Szapary and a very Catholic Catholic. But it sure helped the time pass quickly when we talked. Her English was pretty good, for the usual sort of talk, but she was crazy to talk about religion. Did I believe in God? Why not? What was it, then, I *did* believe in? It wasn't just talk she wanted, but answers, and when she didn't get the answers she would actually curse me in Hungarian. I don't know why I liked that, but I did. I was also silenced by her emotion. I thought I could see her frizzly hair stand up from her scalp when she was in a rage. It didn't matter to her who might be listening. She was the Countess Szapary, from Abony near Pest, and everyone at the club kowtowed to her. Everybody but me. That often put her into one of her rages, but it also brought her back.

She loved American jazz, and we would drive around the city in a taxi looking for recordings of the Mills Brothers and Bing Crosby. At the dances I taught her how to Balboa. She took me to watch her play tennis at a club, where she served and volleyed like a cannon. She either double faulted or served an ace. For almost three weeks I did little else but talk with the countess, or sit and wonder about

163

her, until she took off for a ski lodge in Switzerland. Bogislav told me she skied the way she did everything else.

We had our first snow, and my room was so cold I could see my breath like smoke in the morning. I bought a flannel bathrobe I could wear in my room or as the lining of my raincoat when I went to the club. The lint from the robe would come off on my coat sleeves, and I would have to stand in the dark of the cloakroom and pick it off. I would stay at the club until it closed, about ten, then take off on the double for my room, where I would get in bed with most of my clothes on until I warmed up.

Another problem I was having was with the *Butterbrot* and *Schokolade*. As hungry as I was, I found it hard to eat it. The thought of California orange juice drove me wild. I didn't look so good either, as my friend Karl Fisher told me; I had lost so much weight my clothes hung loose on me. There was a mirror high on the wall behind my washstand, where I could clearly see the room around me reflected, but not my own face. There was a face of sorts, more sallow than pale, the leaden whiteness like that of tallow, that I sometimes caught a glimpse of in shopwindows where I stood looking at something. I don't think I thought of it as my *self*. It couldn't be me, but I saw it in passing, and I still see it fifty years later, gray as the drizzle that concealed everything around me.

What I needed, Karl told me, was exercise. He rented a bike one Sunday, so we could ride out to the Wiener Wald together. There were many hikers in the woods, but few cyclists. The trees had lost their leaves, and I felt the melancholy of hikers and woods just before winter, both frail and vulnerable looking. If I looked sharp, I could often see lovers partially concealed in piles of leaves. Pius Prutscher had advised me it was not for him; he much preferred a bed.

Karl was amazed to see that I could pump up hills, weak as I was, that he would have to get off his bike and walk. I let him ride mine, and he wanted to buy it. He played a lot of soccer, and with his powerful legs he could pump up most grades without rising from the seat. We had our supper at an inn at the edge of the woods, where I drank quite a bit of what they called May wine, and joined in lustily with the singing of the "*schöne blaue Donau*" and other songs of that type. Karl said all I needed to make a good German was to eat more. The way I was feeling, it occurred to me that with winter coming, and the countess away skiing, I should take off for Greece or sunny Italy, but Karl had been to Italy, all the way to Naples and across the bay to the isle of Capri, and what impressed him more than anything else was how cold it had been

164

in March! And here it was just December, with the coldest months still ahead.

Because I didn't look so good, and badly needed a change of diet, Karl suggested I go with him to visit a Frenchman who lived in a castle about a two-hour train ride up the Danube from Vienna. Monsieur Deleglise liked to meet young people, especially Americans. He had lived and traveled in the Far West, and the Hopi Indians had made him a chief. Karl thought I should meet such an unusual man. In the first war, he had fled from France to Canada to evade the draft. That cost him his French citizenship and he could not return after the war and live in France. He had first brought his family to Vienna, where his wife was a prima donna in the opera, but he had lost most of his money in the American stock market crash and moved his family to this castle in the Wachau. At Schloss Ranna, they lived pretty much as people did in the Middle Ages. It wasn't much for comfort, without heat or plumbing, but the food was unusually good and Karl doubted I would ever see anything like it. Schloss Ranna was there when Richard the Lion-Hearted came along the Danube on his way back to England after the Crusades. He may have stopped for the night. There was a crypt that dated from the eleventh century.

I would have liked an old castle at a warmer time of year, but I had recently seen the movie about a Connecticut Yankee in the court of King Arthur, and it led me to wonder what the Middle Ages were really like. The night before we took the train, we had our first real snow. In the morning my high window blazed with light from the white roofs, and snow concealed the gravel paths in the *blind Garten*. On my way to meet Karl I passed a plump beggar, barefoot in the snow, with a big shawl-wrapped woman holding a fat baby. The man stood with his palms pressed together, as if praying, with a slit at the top where coins might be inserted. The two of them sang carols in piercing, off-key voices. Frau Unger had warned me many times about well-fed beggars, who rented foundling babies and were all better fed than Hermann, but on more than one occasion I had observed her slipping coins between a beggar's pressed palms. She saw right through the performance, but whatever she saw, she thought it better to observe the custom. As I did. Watching the man shift from foot to bare foot in the snow, I could feel the chill at the roots of my teeth.

The train we took, a wood-burning locomotive with a big funnel stack, like the Burlington locals of my boyhood, had fresh-cut logs piled high on the tender instead of coal. It went along the north shore of the Danube, and on the wide curves I could see the cloud of smoke

165

pouring from the stack. The one coach had three or four benches, like a streetcar, but there were only a few passengers. North and west of Vienna, where the valley opened, the river spread itself wide as a lake, with very little to show the current's direction. A flat-bottomed side-wheel river steamer, the paddles slapping the water, had the words BUDA-PEST painted on the fender, the hyphen between the words like the river between the two cities. In the great Mississippi flood of 1927 I had seen the river fan out wide around Cairo, and I wondered if the Marmon was still where we had left it in Lake Village, Arkansas, with my mouth organ under the front seat.

The local train made all the stops, and in the early afternoon it picked up kids on their way home from school. They either carried their books in a harness on their backs or had them bound up in long straps they could swing. They filled the coach seats, and two small boys sat on the wooden bench facing us. Both wore heavy hiking shoes with half socks, and lederhosen that exposed their pink scuffed knees. They were towheads, with almost white blond hair, and one had a shiny runner from his nose into his mouth. He had picked up right away, from the shoes I was wearing, that I was something foreign. His chubby legs were thrust toward me, showing the bottoms of his shoes, his pudgy hands were pressed to the bench seat as if he feared to slip off. The cold and excitement had flushed his face so that it glowed like a ripe cherry. I couldn't seem to stare at him enough, and he felt the same about me. Karl Fisher saw such kids all the time, and once he had been one, but there was nothing at all like this boy in Vienna and I felt very close to him. Over the long Nebraska winters my nose, too, had drained into my mouth, both nostrils sore from the drag of my mitten, and the first snapshot of myself I had seen featured the same open-mouthed, adenoidal stare. This boy was spellbound until the train stopped, then he exploded like a spring-wind toy and tried to race off in all directions. From a high, snow-covered mound near the train he turned for one more long, incredulous look at me, shouted his defiance, then took off.

On the north side of the river I saw the ruins of castles, along with some not ruined, small villages huddled at their bases. The sun was shining in Krems, a town with a big station and a wide street full of cars and shoppers. There was a bridge across the Danube where it narrowed and Karl told me that Madame Deleglise, when the weather permitted, came to Krems for her baths. Once a year she might go to Innsbruck, or as far as Salzburg, for her shopping, but she no longer went to Vienna because she believed the Viennese gossiped about her, which of course they did. The gossip was that her husband, Monsieur

166

Deleglise, kept her captive in one of the rooms at Schloss Ranna. The facts were that he didn't have to keep her captive, since there was simply no money for her to travel, or escape. Once they had traveled all over, to India, China and the Yucatán, from where Madame Deleglise had all but died on the long sea voyage to Europe.

Karl never actually said so, but the impression I got was that Monsieur Deleglise was something of an oddball, and that appealed to me. He had tried being a native in the South Seas, and being an Indian in Arizona, and since the stock market crash he had tried living in the Middle Ages.

Out the window I could see that the river had narrowed and we had left the spread of the valley behind us. When I looked back, the view was like a postcard, with the river dark between banks of snow, the sun still gleaming on the ruins of the castles. Up ahead we were entering a gorge, with the river in deep shadow. The last of the kids had left the train at Krems and we had the coach to ourselves. I sat at one window, and Karl had moved so he could sit at another. He was usually fidgety, slapping his knees and clasping his hands, but he sat there in a brown study. The sudden change from Krems, where the sun had been shining, the streets gleaming where the snow had melted, was like that of crossing an invisible boundary or rising to where the air seemed thinner and colder. A cold draft of air entered the coach when the conductor looked in on us, a ruddy-faced old man with a walrus moustache, the dangling ends stained with tobacco. When he spoke to us without removing his pipe, I saw a washer attached to the stem, green as the bit in the mouth of a horse. With it, although his teeth were parted, the pipe stayed in his mouth while he mumbled.

We left the train in Spitz, the river black in the gorge below us, the city dark and silent behind. Only one car had left its tracks in the road we followed to the west. Where this road dipped to the left, to follow the bend in the river, another forked to the right up a narrow canyon. Nothing at all had come down this road since it had snowed. On the river below us, veiled by smoke from its stack, a steamer drifted in the current, its side-wheels slapping the water, with people out on the deck who waved to us. I waved in return. All my life, from wagons, from cars and trains, from windows and elevations, or across empty spaces, from anything that seemed to be moving, I had waved at people, and they had waved at me, but only here did it occur to me how remarkable it was.

In that cold air, veiled with the smoke of our breathing, I seemed to see Richard the Lion-Hearted, on whom I had once written a term paper, cold and clammy in his suit of clanking armor, only his black eyes glinting at the visor of his helmet, weary in mind and aching in body, eaten alive by lice and gnawed with fear and suspicion, uncertain of friend and foe and whether he would ever get back to his homeland, with a large pack of vassals and hangers-on to account for, along with numerous baying dogs, thieves and beggars, pause for a moment right where we were standing, to peer down at a black, alien river he would never see again—not a great figure in history, carrying a shield, but a flesh-and-blood bully who was saddle sore and homesick. Far to the east, where the sun was still shining, the landscape was like a painting on glass through which I could see back to where I had come from, where great rivers like this one, just for starters, did not flow from the south to the north, but from the north to the south. How Richard the Lion-Hearted had felt was not strange to me.

We had an hour's walk to Muhldorf, Karl told me, then another short hike to Schloss Ranna. The brightness of the winter sky lit up the floor of the canyon, but the trees, shrubs and walls fencing us in were black. Under the snow to the left of the road I could hear water running. The air had the tang of wood smoke. Here and there on the upper slopes I could see the black stitching of grapevines.

Where the snow had blown thin on the road, a sledge had come to a stop. It was hard for me to tell which way it was headed since it was made of two saplings, on which the logs were piled, then drawn up like a bow to form a hammock. At what proved to be the rear, an old man crouched on one of the logs, smoking his pipe. "Greet God!" he said to us, and we said to him, "Greet God!"

I hadn't heard that greeting before, and I liked it. Stretched out behind him was a long branch that he used as a rudder. Was he waiting for it to snow again? What was I to think? From farther up the trail I glanced back to see him, the light glinting on the nickel cap to his pipe.

I had to stop several times to tap the caked snow out of my shoes. I was no longer cold, the climb had warmed me, but the shiny film on my eyes made everything I looked at glitter like tinsel. We were both too winded to talk, and would just stand together, wheezing like sprinters. Somewhere up ahead of us a door closed with a bang. A plume of white smoke, so close we could taste it, had drifted down the canyon from a village, and as we approached it I could see that the mill wheel was frozen in the ice. Strewn around the pond were loose barrel staves left by kids who had cleared away the snow from a small piece of the ice. We could see the scratches made by their skates. Four or five cabins, plus an inn, were set at the narrowest point in the canyon, like a cork. A small bulb burned at the porch of the inn, where a man, with his knees cocked, arched a stream of urine over

168

the porch rail into the mound of snow behind it. He moved the stream slowly from side to side, as if watering a lawn. I was amazed at how such a small man managed to pee so long.

"Greet God!" Karl greeted him, and he did the same. Another man's suit coat, a lot too big for him, hung to below his knees. Around his pants legs, like leggings, he had wrapped strips of burlap. As he buttoned up—he seemed to be in no hurry—he asked Karl where it was we were from. "Vienna," Karl replied. The man stared at us in silence, but in his white face I could see the dark hole formed by his lips.

Between two of the cabins the snow had melted on a mound of straw and manure. On the slope behind it, far back where the last of the sun's rays warmed it, a bell tower rose from a clump of buildings with conical roofs and tiny windows. In one window a light burned, like a star. Far away though it seemed, I could hear hounds baying, or just one hound repeated by echoes.

What might have been a narrow road led up from Muhldorf to pass an onion-domed church, in a cluster of trees and buildings, but Karl followed a trail that went to the north along the rim of the canyon. Everything below us was in shadow, as if we saw it in clear deep water. The houses were scattered about along the canyon bottom, and I could see a dark figure walking a lantern. The sounds of water rising in the neck of a pump, then spilling into a pail, grew louder as they rose toward us. Just to the north of the village another pond spread wide, the ice blue as skimmed milk where the kids had cleaned it. Two small boys played silently with a sled. One of them glanced upward and saw us, and I thought he would wave or holler but he didn't.

Another trail, concealed by the new snow but visible in the slanting light, crossed a field of stubble on the slope to the square blockhouse at one side of an orchard. As we stood there wheezing, catching our breath, an ear-splitting clamor sounded directly above us, the echoes rolling and colliding around us.

"Good," Karl said, calmly. "The bell is for *Jause*."

He had told me about *Jause,* an Austrian custom of getting in more food between dinner and supper, but if what I had heard was a bell, I felt the ringer must be crazy. I stood with my head down, my shoulders hunched up, in case it came again. The thought of food, however, spurred us both on and we were soon across the slope to the level of the orchard. A path had been trampled between the trees to a cluster of outbuildings in a sort of hollow. Right where we were standing, in the shadow of the blockhouse, a low rock wall ran along one side of the path that led to the entrance. I thought I saw shrubs growing behind it. I took a seat on the wall, to empty the snow from

169

my shoes, then turned to peer into a huge trench, deep and wide, in which full-grown trees were rooted. The tops of these trees I had mistaken for bushes. I was on the rim of a dry moat, at the entrance to the Middle Ages. The walls of the moat were dark, but the snow at the bottom was as wide as, or wider than, a two-lane highway. I was so flabbergasted I said nothing. The vast bulk of the castle, visible through the archway, was like that of an ocean steamer docked at a pier, the deck looming high above us. The upper part of the wall was whitewashed, luminous in the reflected snow light, but at eye level the plaster had peeled away to expose the rock foundation. The moat circling Ranna had been created by building the bulk of the structure on its own rock island.

A singsong coaxing voice, like a farmer's calling pigs, could be heard, and I saw the movement of shadows cast by a lantern. Karl stood at the low wall of the ramp, beckoning to me. In the deep shadows below us, where the snow was trampled, I could see what I thought was a pack of dogs following a man who swung a lantern. The enclosure below us was large as a farmyard, and curved away into the darkness behind the castle. As the man passed directly below us, swinging the lantern, the shadows cast on the wall of the castle had antlers. Karl called to him and he stopped and hoisted his light toward us. I could see he was hatless. His breath plumed like smoke from his mouth. In a low voice, not unlike gargling, as if he spoke with a mouthful of marbles, he said something to Karl. "And how is the Meister?" Karl asked him, but I did not understand his answer. As we turned away, I said, "Who is the Meister?"

"Monsieur Deleglise," said Karl. "They all call him the Meister."

We followed the narrowing ramp to the entrance, the huge door ajar, into a dim corridor worn to a gutter at the center. At the corridor's end I could see the sky like a piece of stained glass. On our left we entered a court, open to the sky. Stairs along the back wall mounted to a balcony landing. With a broom on the landing, Karl swept off our shoes before we entered a dark, stone-floored hallway, the floor sprinkled with snow from a slotted open window on the stairs. In the archway on our left, a wide door, with a latch. Karl rapped sharply on the door before we entered.

The room was long, with a low timbered ceiling, and a heavy table with a dozen or so high-backed chairs stood at its center. At the far end of the table a small bulb glowed in the hub of a wagon-wheel chandelier. The window in the alcove at the end of the room glowed with the winter sunset. Just in front of the alcove, a big glass tank filled with murky green water filtered the light.

170

To the right of the door we had entered, logs were piled along the wall behind a stove that was metal, not tile, and gave off heat. The sides were warm, rather than hot, so that I could stand with my backside to it, soaking up the warmth. I had got so cold on the long walk up from the river that the sudden warmth gave me the shivers, the way it used to in Omaha when, after hours of sledding or skating, I would stand on one of the floor radiators and bask in the smell of my clothes drying. How far away all of that seemed, but the smell had not changed.

Karl took a slice of bread from the basket on the table, spread it thick with butter, and shared it with me. Back in Vienna I would have said no, *danke,* but I gulped it down. When the door quietly opened at my back, the person who entered thumped into me. It startled him so much to find somebody there, he threw up his hands, knocking his hat from his head, and almost teetered over backward until Karl grabbed him. He picked up the hat he had dropped on the floor and stood honing the brim on his coat sleeve. I had never seen a uglier man. His head was loaf-shaped—he gave me time to look it over—with a crease at its center in which a few black hairs were like wires connecting his ears. His color was dark brown, like saddle leather, but there was nothing in his face to indicate his forehead or his eyebrows. Nor any chin at all, that I could determine, so that he looked like a fish seen from the front in an aquarium.

Karl took a lot of time to tell him who I was, and where I was from. At the mention of the word "America," he looked dazed. Karl was saying that Uncle James, which was what he was called, had been with Monsieur Deleglise in the United States, where, among other things, he had managed Madame Deleglise's career as an opera singer. To all this Uncle James was silent, as if his memory had failed him. Against the fading light in the alcove I could see a single long-tailed goldfish suspended as if anchored in the tank of murky water. A small, stooped figure in a fur hat pointed like a dunce cap—I first thought it might be an old woman in a turban—stood dropping into the tank small pellets of food, which fell to where the goldfish gulped them like bait. The white body of the fish was so transparent the fat sack of the belly was visible, stuffed with the pellets like a bag of shot.

Having turned to see what it was I was looking at, Karl called out a greeting, then led me back to meet Monsieur Deleglise. He gave me his small cold hand, and in a voice pitched so high it might have been a child's, he repeated phrases of greeting in English, French and German. A gray stubble concealed his face, and the soggy butt of a cigarette, stuck to his lower lip, bobbed as he talked. Karl explained to me that the fur hat he was wearing had been given to him by the

171

Hopis when they made him a chief. We came back to the table, under the chandelier, where Monsieur Deleglise placed the fur hat on the seat of his chair like a cushion, then sat on it. Doing this seemed to please him, but the smile he gave me was hard to tell from a grimace.

Karl took the place on his left, Uncle James on his right, and I took the seat to the left of Karl. A blond young man with short hair, a crisp toothbrush mustache and pale water-blue eyes sat across from me. His name was Beps. Karl explained again what a scholar I was, how much I had traveled, and how in the spring I would go to Italy, and then to Paris. Monsieur Deleglise was skeptical of Americans, but impressed. We ate bowls of potato soup served by a hefty young woman with suds drying on her plump white arms. Uncle James called her Mizi. As she leaned over me to serve the soup, I noticed her black almond eyes in a creamy white face; her breath smelled of warm milk.

We also had a fruit compote, the apples small as walnuts, then a demitasse of thick black coffee. How did I like it? I said I loved it. Uncle James advised me it was half chicory. Good coffee and tobacco were very dear in Austria. I was not asked, but later I talked about Chicago, about California, and the wonderful life I had led and was living. We all smoked a full pack of my Old Gold cigarettes and two of the smaller packets of Falk Bubies, the brand favored by Monsieur Deleglise. I liked their mildness, but they were very dry and flared up like excelsior when I lit them.

I learned from Uncle James that the suit and pants he wore, likewise the Stetson hat, were purchased in Cedar Rapids, Iowa, the scene of Madame Deleglise's greatest triumph, in *La Fanciulla del West*. I observed that Uncle James, whenever we all got to laughing, popped sugar cubes into his mouth before he took a sip of his coffee. Monsieur Deleglise ate very little, but he enjoyed the talk. He plucked the soft centers from slices of bread and rolled them into pellets the size of BBs, which he left on his plate. After the coffee we had glasses of hard cider, the same murky green color as the water in the fish tank. Without much prodding I told them about Death's Corner in Chicago, Larrabee and Blackhawk, where I had seen men shot at and found one who had been killed, with the holes across his back like a row of buttons. That got me a pop-eyed stare from Uncle James, but I could see that Beps didn't believe a word of it. At one point a husky fellow, the sleeves rolled up on his hairy arms, his shoulders so wide his head looked small, came in with a big tray and gathered up the dishes like the world's happiest busboy. He did it fast, but took the trouble to leave the pellets Monsieur Deleglise had rolled on his napkin, where they looked like rabbit turds.

172

When the time came for me to get up from the table, I preferred to just sit there. The shoes I had left to dry out beneath the stove would not go back onto my feet. I went along in my socks, carrying my shoes, Monsieur Deleglise leading with a candle up the wide stone stairs in the hall and into a long low room, like the one we had just left, the eyes glinting in the antlered trophies on the walls and all the furniture covered with sheets. In the adjoining room we could see our breath smoke, but I couldn't breathe. The stench was so intense it was like something other than air. Monsieur Deleglise walked with his candle to open wide one of the high casement windows. "Frish air!" he cried. "Frish! Frish! Frish!" If he liked a word he loved to repeat it. The room was like a loft with a high ceiling, empty of everything but two folding army cots. One was covered with a dark, coarse-haired pelt. "Moose! Moose! Moose!" Monsieur Deleglise chanted, and he shuffled about with his candle, like a dancing Indian. "He shot it in Canada," Karl explained, and Monsieur Deleglise shouted, "Bang! Bang! Bang!" I could see how the Hopis must have loved him. He wished us a *Gute Nacht,* a *Schlafen Sie wohl,* then he went off with the candle and left us standing there in the dark. But I could see the white walls, in the reflected roof light, and on the wall that I faced, fire shadows were playing. They came through the window of a room across the open court.

"Whose room is that?" I asked.

"Madame Deleglise." We reflected on that in silence. "She sleeps most of the day," he added, "but she likes to read at night."

"What's she read?" I asked him.

He replied, "French novels."

I don't know why it pleased me so much to hear that. A woman who was captive, in a castle like this, who spent her nights reading French novels. I warmed up after a while, lying under the moose hide, and noticed that the snowflakes blowing in the window were prickling my face. After the day I had had, it seemed natural to me that the old man with the sledge of logs below Muhldorf was finally going to get the snowfall he needed. I didn't need it, but I liked its cool prickle on my hot face.

BETWEEN SLEEPING AND WAKING, I SEEMED TO hear the faraway sound of ore boats honking on Lake Michigan. I was troubled when this honking faded, followed by a muffled thump. I opened my eyes on a blaze of sunlight, a cloud of sparkling snow at the open window. A hood of this snow, like a lacy nightcap, had settled on my hair. As the air at the window cleared, I could see a big fellow straddling the peaked roof across the court, a cowlick of straw-colored hair concealing his forehead, his cheeks flaming as if with a fever, his eyes popped wide, his mouth open, as if he had just shouted Hallelujah!

I had read about the legendary Till Eulenspiegel, and I thought at last I had seen him. Two or three flannel shirts, one worn over the other, opened at the collar, gave him the look of a crazy plant in flower. As I stared at him he cupped his mittened hands to his mouth and made the mournful sound of a steamboat honking. It seemed the longest time before I heard—as if it came from the river—the rolling echo. Across his lap he held a pole, with a scraper at one end, which he dipped into the blanket of roof show, then leaned his full weight on it as if he was poling a boat. The wide swatch of snow fell with a thundering *bomp* into the court. The puffing cloud of snow dust soon concealed him, but behind it I could hear him making the *bomp* sound. Really crazy. In his shoes, I might have done the same thing myself.

My friend Karl's bed was empty, the bedding turned back to air. I tapped the snow out of my shoes, managed to get them on my feet, then went out through the door we had entered, across the room with the sheet-covered furniture, and down the stairs to the floor below. Snow had blown in through the slotted window, powdering the stairs. I first knocked on the door, as Karl had done, then peered into the room, to find it empty, but several places were set at the far end of the table. No food had been left on three of the plates, but Monsieur Deleglise had plucked the soft centers from several slices of bread and rolled them into pellets. They were all on his plate, with the soggy butts of several cigarettes.

I buttered the slice of bread I found in the basket and walked to stand at the alcove window. Fresh snow had covered the millpond in the canyon. A man standing on the porch of the inn slapped his bare hands together, as if applauding.

174

There proved to be two fish in the fish tank, one like an egg that had just been dropped into boiling water, with the white oozing out. The fins of both fish were like transparent veils, but their undulating movement did not move them. The one with the shot-like pellets in his belly was like an anchored balloon.

On my legs and feet, as if a door stood open, I could feel a cold draft. It came from beneath a wide door in the left wall. I thought it must be a hallway, and peered behind it; a gloomy darkness, smelly and chill as a basement, but nothing I could see. The first match I struck blew out in the draft. I lit another, cupped it in my hands, then glanced up to see the staring eyes and gleaming teeth of a black savage. Over his head, ready to strike, he held a tomahawk. Lucky for me, the match I held flickered and went out. In the semidarkness, my heart pounding, I could make out the figure of a cigar store Indian on a pedestal. Along with his protuberant staring glass eyes, he had a partial set of human teeth. That's where I was when Karl, red-faced with cold, rushed in from the main hallway to yell at me. Had I eaten? What a fine day it was! There would be time for me to look at the Indian relics later, but right now, on such a day there was no time to lose! The Meister was ready and waiting for us in the orchard.

I followed Karl out to the landing, down the stairs, into the court, already half filled with snow pushed from the roofs. As we crossed the court Karl glanced at the sky as if he thought a piece of it might fall on him. In the dark corridor that led out to the ramp, Joseph rumbled past us pushing a wheelbarrow piled with snow. He wore a cane-sided chauffeur's cap and military breeches, but I recognized him as the smiling fellow so eager to clear away the dishes from the table. Out on the ramp, in the blinding snow glare, Karl told me that all of the snow that fell *inside* Schloss Ranna had to be shoveled up and carted out before it melted and turned to ice. There were rooms beneath the courts, and then rooms beneath them, along with a secret corridor, it was rumored, that led from Ranna to what had been a monastery in Unter Ranna. The thought of it made him excited. Snow was already melting at the edge of the pitched roofs, exposing shingles that were black as wet coal. Below us, to the south, the stubbled field sloped away to the cluster of white roofs in Muhldorf. Beyond the village, far across the valley, blue wooded ridge after ridge receded to the shimmering horizon. A zigzagging row of poles, supporting a wire like a clothesline, came up from Muhldorf to the rim of the orchard, then came up through the trees to enter the archway. From there it stretched across the moat like a sagging aerial, to a small slotted window in the white wall. Everywhere the sun shone, water was dripping. Karl scooped up a handful of the moist snow, pressed it into a ball, threw it into the blue canyon that spread behind us. A moment later we heard it fall with a plop.

Where that snowball had landed, Karl pointed out to me, there had once been a monastery. We could see the clearing, with a wall around it, that had been the garden. Kids playing on the slope across the creek had heard the snowball plot and peered up at us. Several dogs barked. I had the fleeting impression of being so high above it all that there was no connection between upper and lower Ranna, except for those who were below and looked up at it. They did not call out, or wave, or shake tiny fists at us. Their small white faces had no features. Was this how one should look if seen from heaven? It crossed my mind.

Karl had taken me by the arm to turn me around. He pointed through the archway into the orchard, where a big black-splotched creature, the size of a calf, gamboled about between the trees. He dipped his head, like a scoop, to toss up gobs of snow, which he then tried to catch, snapping his huge jaws. A small piping voice called to him. I heard clapping hands. The huge dog wanted to frisk about, like a puppy, but the footing was uncertain. Once he fell, like a structure collapsing. Monsieur Deleglise, who looked dwarfed beside him, clapped his hands above his head like a flamenco dancer. This was a game they both liked and were eager to play. The great dog reared up, a full head taller than the man, to place his paws on the man's narrow shoulders, his tongue licking his face. That knocked off his fur hat and the two of them stood there, as if grappling, the dog's long tongue stroking his face and hair until the man toppled over backward, straddled by the dog. Like two kids playing in the snow, one of them a lot bigger than the other, Deleglise lay out on his back, while the dog licked his face like a plate of gravy. He just lay there, grinning like a gargoyle, until Karl pulled the dog off him and I hoisted him to his feet. There seemed to be little to him but the clothes he was wearing, the brown mackinaw over an old army sweater. When I gave him his hat he pulled it down so that it covered his face. Why hadn't Karl told me he was crazy? With his face concealed, he looked headless.

"We walk! We walk!" he piped. "Yes?"

"Ja-jah!" Karl replied. "We walk!"

When Deleglise spoke to the dog, he went off at a loping canter, leading the way. The trail we followed led to a deep ravine full of shrubs and trees, with a creek at its bottom. As we stood there we could hear the water purling beneath the snow. At a clearing on the steep slope Deleglise crouched like a child, his legs thrust out before him, and slid on the seat of his pants to the bottom. This got the dog so excited he ran up and down the rim, baying hoarsely, until he found another way into the ravine. In the silence that followed his rumbling bark we could hear doors slamming, and the voices of women.

I refused to sit and slide in my only pair of pants, so I walked to where I could climb down, hanging on to shrubs and bushes. The village was just ahead of us, in a small clearing, with the houses set into the foot of the ridge below Ranna. Not a soul was in sight as we walked in, the dog gamboling ahead of us.

"Where's everybody?" I asked.

"It's Prince," said Karl. "They don't believe he's just a dog."

At one of the dark cabin windows I saw a face, like a goblin's, with a child's big staring eyes and a wild thatch of hair. Someone yanked him away. In the fresh fall of snow around the porch of the inn, several customers had already relieved themselves. Deleglise had shuffled ahead to a house on the left, where he paused to rap his knuckles on the door. In the silence this seemed a great racket. A dog whimpered in one of the nearby cabins. A young woman opened the door, a shawl about her shoulders, her hands rolled up in a wad of her apron. She greeted Deleglise as the Meister. For a moment their high-pitched voices were like those of two gossiping women. The Meister turned to beckon to us. "Come, come, come!" he piped, and we followed him into a dark room that seemed barren. One chair sat beside a rocking cradle. A young man had risen just as we entered, to stand beside the young woman. I thought her plump figure and round face attractive. He was much more nervous than she was. The Meister introduced me as the scholar from America. They admired me, my clothes, my shoes, and marveled that I could speak their language. The Meister stooped to look at the child, in the shadow of the crib hood, commented on its plumpness, its health, its dark hair, then took several coins from his pocket and dropped them on the crib comforter. In response to their thanks, bowing, their hands clasped, I understood him to mention that Ranna needed wood, as one might mention in passing that an ogre needed food. The huge dog stood waiting for us at the door. No one appeared in the street as we walked away and followed the stream bed up the canyon. The dog led the way.

"What a handsome couple," I said to Karl.

The Meister muttered something I did not understand.

"He wants you to know," said Karl, "that it is not his child."

I said, "How come?"

"Out here," Karl replied, "the war took all of the young men. There are many young women who will never have husbands but who are capable of having babies. If she has a healthy baby she attracts the young men. The baby, not the father, is what is important. When they saw her healthy male baby she had many proposals, some of them from as far as Spitz."

"That's hard to believe," I said, eager to believe it, and wondered who the lucky father was. Were more volunteers needed? We were walking up an incline that made it difficult to talk. My shoes slipped badly in the powdery snow. During the morning the kids had been at play on the millpond I could see from the alcove window. A road went along the east side of the canyon, rising toward open country, with fewer trees. The dog had gone ahead of us to a point on the trail to which he seemed accustomed, and sprawled waiting for us. In the large black splotch on his face his small eyes were not visible, and I missed them. How was one to guess what such a huge creature was thinking?

We all huddled together for a moment to catch our breath. Deleglise breathed hoarsely through his open mouth, a soggy butt attached to his lower lip. As he talked, it bobbled. He seemed indifferent to its being there. We stood wheezing, our breath veiling our faces, and I happened to glance back down the canyon at Schloss Ranna, the windows blazing like fire. The whole inner bulk of Ranna seemed to float on the crest of a frothy wave. Not particularly high, not in the usual cloudland of fairy castles, but at a remove that a small boy, looking upward, could appreciate. A remove with a connection. An actual Meister who occasionally made house calls, with a monster that was neither a hippogriff nor a dog, but something in between.

"It's out of this world!" I said.

"Out of! Out of!" the Meister echoed. In the deep shadows at Ranna's base the village appeared to be under water. Ribbons of wood smoke curled to fray on the sky. "Yes, yes," he repeated. "It is out of!" What I had said seemed to reassure him. He gazed at me soberly, the soggy butt at his lips wagging, the cold air filming his gray eyes. "You like—yes?"

"I've never seen anything like it," I replied.

He turned from me to speak to Karl, his head wagging. The fur hat tilted forward to conceal his eyes.

"He wants to know," Karl asked me, "if you would like to extend your visit. You are welcome to stay for a week if you would care to."

I turned to look at the Meister, his mother-of-pearl teeth set in a grin-like grimace, or a grimace-like grin. He looked cold, and frail as a medieval beggar.

"You stay, you stay—yes?"

I was eager to stay, but I was also convinced that Monsieur Deleglise, the Meister, was mad as a hatter. "Yes, yes!" I said.

From the chest pocket of his jacket he took a packet of cigarettes, offered me one, took one himself. Karl was not a smoker. He watched us light up and blow smoke at each other. Back down the trail we had come up, at the edge of the millpond, I could see several dogs waiting and watching; just behind the dogs, a cluster of furtive children. When we made a move toward them, both dogs and children scattered. The trail followed the creek bed back through the village, passing beneath the encircling outer walls of Ranna, then cutting through the ruins of the monastery. The dog galloped ahead of us to where the trail forked to the left, rising steeply up the bank to the slope below Ranna. From the rim of the canyon he peered down at us like a gargoyle. Above and behind him, the clatter of the bell seemed to come from the sky. In the clear dazzle of light it seemed louder, and more manic, than when I had heard it the previous evening, an ear-splitting, shrieking clamor. The air appeared to vibrate with it. The dog bayed.

"What madman is that?" I asked Karl.

"Antone," he replied, "the bell ringer."

On my mind's eye I could see him straddling the roof peak, his red cheeks blazing, red-mittened hands cupped to his mouth.

"He's a big fellow?" I asked. "Yellow hair, red mittens?" I could see his thick hams tight in his overalls, straddling the roof.

"You've met him?"

"I've seen him."

Karl gave me a sly smile, said, "He's very popular with the ladies."

"I can believe that," I replied.

"He makes babies. He's the baby-maker."

"That makes him the real father of his country," I said, but that was lost on Karl, who said, "I'm famished!" and led off up the trail. As frail and weak as the Meister looked, he had the wind and endurance of a climber. Tortoise-like, if we passed him he came shuffling along and went by us. Crossing the slope beneath Ranna, I could hear myself wheezing. By the time we reached the landing at the top of the stairs my ears buzzed like magnetos. The Meister swept us all off, with a broom, then removed his own three-buckle galoshes, and I saw that all he was wearing was wool socks pulled over the feet of his flannel pajamas, like those I had worn as a child. He looked like a child, as he stood before us, his dunce hat tilted back on his head, a child whom a loving and indulgent father had draped with his own coat to keep from freezing. "Eat! Eat!" he piped, his eyes creased in a grin, and walked ahead of us into the warm dining *Saal,* where an aging bulldog, with clouded eyes, wearing a soiled and slobbered-on turtleneck sweater, lay curled up but shivering in a wicker basket beside the stove.

"Madame has come to dinner," Karl said to me, and there she was.

Back under the chandelier, a strong nasal declared, "Who is Merkun? Is from See-tar Rabids?" She sat at the table, her large protuberant eyes shining with expectation. Whatever they had told her, I knew she was doomed to disappointment. Her dark, lined face resembled that of the dog in the wicker basket. She was seated on a pillow, to get the proper elevation, her small broad hands like those of a farm child. Uncle James had risen, his napkin dangling from his collar, to make a formal and lengthy introduction. Several times he repeated the word *diva.* I understood little else. She gave me one of her hands, the plump, stubby fingers cluttered with rings. Her sad eyes searched my face for what she knew to be missing. Only a child had looked at me so boldly. At the part in her glossy black hair, the roots were whiter than her scalp.

As if none of this fuss concerned him, the Meister sat at his place, reading a newspaper. Uncle James proposed a toast, then made a toast, repeating the names of the cities where she had triumphed: "Venice, Palermo, Buenos Aires, Mexico City, Vancouver and See-tar Rabids!"

"Hear! Hear!" Karl cried, raising his glass of cider. Madame Deleglise was not flustered by this praise. It was part of her continuing performance. The glimpses I had of her profile reminded me of Mussolini. Her voice, like his, was big, but fuzzy with hoarseness, as if she had a bad cold. In the large bowl of soup she had been served was the skull of a dog-like head, the sharp teeth still set in the jaws. To get at bits of meat around the teeth and eye sockets she used a metal nut pick. Her spirits were high. She laughed "Ho-ho-*ho!*" like one of the seven dwarfs.

Uncle James wore a dinner jacket, with tails, a black bow tie on his yellow wing collar. Sugar syrup glistened on his lips. His role was that of host, a master of ceremony. When had I last been in See-tar Rabids? He was careful to mimic her pronunciation. Madame spoke little English, but she understood it, and laughed hoarsely at my comments. At these moments I noticed the glances she gave her husband. Animal. One that turns from its food to growl at a rival. I could imagine her shrieking, her black eyes flashing, before the gawking, upturned faces of See-tar Rabids. To light her cigarette Uncle James swept the napkin that dangled from his neck over the table. She exhaled slowly, enjoying its fragrance.

"Tell him," she said to Karl, "I have sons in Switzerland. One is big and stronk as he is."

Karl told me.

"Will they be home from Christmas?" I asked her.

"How would I know!" she bellowed. "He tells me nothing!"

"They write to you," he replied, calmly. "They do not write to me."

"They tell me nothing! They write I want, I want, I want!"

"Jacques wants skis," the Meister replied, matter-of-factly.

"To keel himself? Bah! Marcel wants fur gloves, for skating, a Cossack hat of chinchilla."

The Meister turned back to his paper. When speaking to his wife he showed no anger, but his face seemed to be cast in a different mold, no crazy wrinkles of mirth around his eyes.

Sensing that Madame was about to leave, Uncle James rose quickly and hurried to stand at the back of her chair. As she slid from the cushion he drew the chair aside, and there she stood, hardly higher than when she had been seated. Had she been seen as a precocious child? A miniature prima donna? She had put aside scraps of food for the dog, which she carried back to the door with her. The dog whimpered and slobbered, hearing her approach. "Dolly! Dolly!" she cried, stooping to feed her the scraps. We could hear the clop-clop of the loose jowls. For a moment Madame stood with her backside to the stove, her short legs concealed by a pair of galoshes, worn to keep her feet warm while she was dining.

"*Une grande plaisir a faire votre connaissance,*" she called to me, at which point I arose and bowed. To Karl she said, "*Ciao!*"

"*Ciao,*" he replied.

Uncle James opened the door, then turned to pick up the basket with the old dog. He followed her out in the hall, drew the door closed, and we heard their voices as they went up the stairs.

The Meister said, "He is an artist. He is an actor. Molière could not have done better."

Very simply, Karl said, "He loves her."

"I also," replied the Meister, "but I am no actor."

Karl avoided the glance I gave him, said, "I've got to pack my bag. It's a long walk to Spitz." He got up to leave, then turned and said, "You're sure you're staying?"

I was no longer so sure. I envied him his leaving. I thought of my life in Vienna with pleasure. To sleep in a real bed seemed dreamy. But

181

neither did I want to hurt the Meister's feelings. His shadowed face, with the light on his wispy white hair, was like that of a child. Did I like him? Or did I just feel sorry for him?

"Go! Go!" he cried shrilly. "Go if you like!"

Which was why I stayed. It's as simple as that.

"I'm staying," I said to Karl. "I'll see you soon."

"Sure," Karl said. "Anything I can send you?"

"I've got a card you can mail," I replied, as an excuse to leave the room with him. As we mounted the stairs to the second floor we could see the fire reflections behind Madame's door, and hear the wood crackle. Uncle James was laughing and talking.

"He *is* an actor," Karl said. "When she comes to dinner he gives a performance."

Although the window to our room stood open, the stench was still in the air, like that of wet paint. "I'll leave you this," Karl said, handing me his tube of toothpaste. "If you want to shave, ask Mizi for hot water."

"What's this *Meister* stuff about?" I asked.

He seemed reluctant to tell me. "Why bother?" he said. "For you he's Monsieur Deleglise."

"It's not a bother," I said. "I think I sort of like it."

"That's what they call him. That's the way they feel about him. Unter Ranna, Ober Ranna—it's all of a piece, or pieces." He waved his arms at the window. "Whoever lives at Ranna becomes the Meister."

"And he's got this crazy dog," I said. "Right?"

"Out of this world!" Karl replied, and laughed. I agreed. "It's surely out of yours, isn't it?" he added.

If at the back of my mind I had a Connecticut Yankee eager to rummage about in his own Middle Ages, was Ranna really as out of my world as I first thought? Hadn't I just agreed to lie freezing in this room, breathing the stench, waking to find a honeycomb of ice in my hair? The sound of water dripping into the court gave me a chill.

"I've got to run," said Karl, and off he went, swinging his backpack. I followed on his heels, down the way we had come up, passing the door where Madame's fire was crackling, then across the inner court, cleaned of most of its snow, and we both glanced skyward as we hugged the wall. Out on the ramp he gripped my hand, wished me a happy adventure, then marched under the archway and down through the orchard. Wood smoke had spread a soft blue veil over Muhldorf. I hadn't noticed, till that moment, the large church, with the onion dome, at the east rim of the plateau. A few houses huddled around it. Mountains rose behind it. I watched Karl, swinging his rucksack like a schoolboy, go along, with his crisp shadow beside him. If I was out of this world, what world was I in? I thought of Hans Castorp, up on his Magic Mountain, where the living would be better than it was at Ranna, but it seemed doubtful to me that his colleagues were stranger than Uncle James, the Meister, the dog Prince, and Antone, the father of his country. To keep the chill air off my chipped front tooth, I had to close my lips.

SO BEGAN THE WINTER I SPENT OUT OF THIS WORLD.
I lived at Schloss Ranna from early December until the first week of March, sawing wood, carrying water, shoveling snow, avoiding the Meister, helping Uncle James with his stamp collection, carrying the dog Dolly, in her foul-smelling basket, into the orchard where she would do her business, reading Madame's French novels, growing a moustache, spying on Mizi and the father of his country, and ceaselessly wondering what it was that made the Meister tick.

From the big alcove window, the winter sky gray as drizzle, the barren trees black, the snow without glare, like chalk on a blackboard, the mill wheel locked fast in the pond ice, it seemed to me that time, as I used to live it, had stopped. That what I saw before me was a snippet of time, cut from the moving reel, a specimen with more of a past than a future, a crack in time's door that I had my eye to, where no bird flew, no snow fell, no child played on the pond ice and no dog barked. To be out of this world was to be out of time. One day I liked it. The next day I thought I might go nuts.

A few days after Karl's return to Vienna, I was in the alcove, dropping pellets of bread dough to be gulped by the transparent goldfish. Feeling a chill draft blowing on my legs, I glanced up to see this fellow standing in the doorway. How describe him? He was like a living winter scarecrow. A mat of straw-colored hair, no hat. A broad flat face with eyes so small the light from the window didn't glint on them. He wore a sort of brindle homespun, or it might have been burlap, that hung about him like a loose nightshirt, with strips of the same material wrapped about his legs below the knees. I had seen his like before in paintings. He dragged the sleeve of one arm across his face, spreading the shine of his nose drool like the track of a snail.

"Yes?" I said. That startled him. His brows went up, opening his eyes, and I saw his resemblance to Harry Lauder. He muttered something, but I didn't catch it. He turned away from me to lift a log from the pile, show me the sawed, powdery end. That was a pretty smart thing for him to do, and that was how we did most of our talking.

I was never clear what his name proved to be. I called him Holz. I followed him through the kitchen, where we passed Mizi stooped

184

over a tub, her backside broad as a chair back, down the stairs into the rear court, where a load of logs had just been dumped. The woodshed was right there to the left of the stairs, and in a clearing at the front they had this sawhorse. Holz took a crossbuck saw from a hook on the wall, and after a bit of bucking, on our first log, as to who was going to push and who was going to pull, we did all right. I was the better pusher. It was Holz's nature to pull. Two or three times a week he would come for me, and we would usually saw for about an hour. Holz didn't have a watch, or read the time on mine, but he had a sure sense of fifty-five minutes, and I think he would have loved a time clock.

My other chore with Holz was to carry a tub of water from the well to the kitchen. This tub was big enough for several kids to take a bath in, and full of water weighed—well, it weighed a lot. Two of the wooden staves were higher than the others, with a hole near the top through which a pipe could be inserted. Holz would be at one end, I would be at the other, with this tub full of water between us, slurping about as we carried it. In the old days, as I had seen it in paintings, the water had been cranked up in a moss-covered bucket, then carried about in jars on the heads of maidens, but the two of us worked a long-handled pump that first spilled the water into a length of rain gutter, from where it would run into our tub. Over the winter, to keep the pipe from freezing, they wrapped burlap and packed straw around it, and when we pumped the handle, bits and pieces of straw would fall into the rain gutter, then wash into the tub. Holz loved to pump, but with the first flow of the water he would stop to watch it spill into the tub. My feeling was he wanted proof that the pump was really working, but that wasn't it. One day I stood there with him, watching the pieces of yellow straw swim around in the water. Putting his big, chapped moon face toward me, he said, "Little fish maker!" and grinned like a pumpkin. It wasn't really clear to me if he was a bit of a poet or he thought they were fish. I often saw Mizi give Holz chunks of potatoes which he would gnaw on, like a carrot. She would sometimes wipe his runny nose with a wad of her apron, and if he happened to be stretched out asleep beside the stove she might stoop and stroke his matted hair, as she would a dog. These potatoes Holz gnawed were really for planting, not eating, with long green-tipped sprouts growing at the eyes, and if I had been a little bit surer of my German I would have told Mizi how I had once planted just such potato cuttings in Nebraska. But the word for potato, in German, is *Kartoffel,* which was exactly how I felt to pronounce it—Godawful.

However, I did have to ask her for some things. "*Gibt's heisses Wasser?*" I asked her.

185

She seemed to consider. "How hot?" she asked me.

"For shaving," I replied. Too late I saw that she had tricked me. Looking closely at my chin, she said, "Warm is enough!" and tested it with her finger. By the time I got the small pitcher of tepid water to my room, and some of it on my face, it was cold. That's the facts behind why I decided to grow a beard.

At the front of Schloss Ranna a long corridor connected the Meister's room on the east with the high-ceilinged music room on the west, warmed by the sun on those days we had any. The floor of this corridor tilted and dipped like those in amusement parks. Along it, at one point, was the water closet that everybody used over the winter. I tried to take a deep breath when I stepped into it, and do without breathing while I was there. On windy days a cold draft blew up it that puffed out my shirt and almost froze my bare bottom. Both Uncle James and the Meister used big flowered night pots that I had seen Mizi empty into the moats. Madame Deleglise also used a night pot, and I once saw it emptied from one of her windows into the court. Another time, when I was walking the dog, I heard this splash in the *Graben* behind me, and I thought of that painting of Brueghel showing people with their bottoms hanging out the windows.

Midway along this corridor, like a tight ship's cabin, was a small narrow room with two slotted windows in the outer wall. They were like portholes, but without glass, and burned like spotlights when the sun was on them. One wall of the room was lined with Madame Deleglise's French novels, in their yellow paper covers. There were also books in German, some Tauchnitz English editions, and three novels by Upton Sinclair, two of which I read. Beside a table strewn with old magazines and newspapers was a chair with dog or cat hairs matted on the cushion. Under some of the newspapers I found a fur-trimmed stereopticon viewer, with a cracked stereo view card in the holder, but when I tried to look at the card my breath fogged the lenses. I carried the viewer with me into the music room, where the sun had warmed the air in the alcove. What I saw was an Indian, his black hair in braids, wearing a white man's dinner jacket but his own buckskin trousers and beaded moccasins, and standing beside a short woman, her face blurred by movement, who held a small child. An elegantly dressed gentleman in a black coat and striped trousers had taken off his hat for the picture. His overexposed face had no features, but there was no mistaking Uncle James. So where was the Meister? He had taken the picture, and the woman holding the child was his wife.

186

That day the air in the music room had almost been warm. The windows faced the south, and if I stood close to the glass I could feel the sun's radiation. Just by entering the room I had stirred up the air so that dust motes danced in the light beams. Except for the grand piano, on a low platform, the large room was empty. A dozen or so folding chairs were propped along one wall. The piano lid was raised, and several pieces of sheet music, curled and faded by the sun, were on the music rack. Ivories were missing from a lot of the keys, like bad teeth.

I could peer slantwise from the window into the deep blue of the *Graben,* the snow trampled by the deer, where a fellow with a head like corn in flower stroked the flank of one of the creatures he was feeding. Was this peasant and knave the father of his country? I thought it possible. How well his muscular hams filled the legs of his trousers. I sat in the warmth of the sun, thinking of California, where the new crop of oranges would be ripening, and some of the boys who were not going home for Christmas would be sneaking out of the dorms at night to fill their pillowcases with them. Real honest-to-God oranges, right there on the trees, with a skin you could peel like a banana. It was hard for me to believe that just the winter before I had done that myself. Now I was living in a castle with some pretty weird people, a herd of deer grazing in the dry moat below me. Nobody back where I had come from would believe it. I didn't believe it myself

Sometimes I stopped to have a talk with Uncle James in his "office," a narrow room on the corridor that led out to the ramp. The only light came through a high slotted window, making a beam like a movie projector. Uncle James usually sat at his rolltop desk, in a chair that both swiveled and tilted. There he answered letters, kept accounts, wrote checks, mended his clothes—I often caught him with pins in his mouth, like a tailor—but mostly he filled out the order forms to be mailed to Sears, Roebuck in Chicago. The catalogue was customarily open there on his desk. The main problem—the others were minor—was that the items he ordered were usually out of stock, or if they weren't, the prices had altered. He had three letter files of typed correspondence dealing with this problem (he found the company scrupulous in all money matters), but nothing, no, *nothing,* would persuade them to send him an up-to-date catalogue. The one on his desk was for the fall and winter of 1926.

Uncle James had his own kerosene-burning room heater, purchased in Brooklyn just before they had sailed, but after almost eight years of use the wick was so charred the flame no longer burned, and gave off a strong smell. Orders for hard candy and tobacco were lost in the mails, or the local postal people could smell them right through the wrapping. On the other hand, such staples as winter underwear, flannel shirts, bolts of cloth, nearly always came through after months of waiting. The postman in Spitz would make a special trip to Ranna on his bike in the summer, or by sledge in the winter, when he saw it was something from Sears, Roebuck. He was a friend of Uncle James, and they would have a schnapps and discuss the latest news.

One slightly warmer day I ran around taking snapshots. I climbed to the top of the tower, where Antone rang his *Jause* bell, and took shots of the courtyards, the deer in the *Graben,* and the way the walls spiraled out over the canyon, the view south toward Muhldorf, the view east toward Ober Muhldorf, and one of Uncle James standing out on the ramp waving to me. I also took a shot of Holz, holding the bucksaw, but when it was printed his face was a blank. I caught Antone by surprise, with his thumbs in his ears, wagging his big red mittens as he hooted at me. In another one he looked like Primo Carnera when he thrust his head forward for a close-up. I could see in his face it was his understanding that by taking these pictures I got even with him. He didn't resent it. He would get even with me as soon as more snow collected on the roofs.

When Mizi saw me with my camera she covered her head with her apron and ran for the kitchen, like a baby hippo running for cover.

I got the Meister out on the ramp, from the rear. He looked exactly like a small trained bear.

I caught Joseph in the courtyard, in his bloody butcher's apron, his face beaming and happy, looking exactly like Joseph.

Right when I had almost forgotten about Hermann and Frau Unger, Joseph came for me, wearing his green chauffeur's outfit, his cap with the cane sides, to ask if I would like to go to Vienna. I wasn't sure. Going back to Vienna would put in question all of my special feelings about Ranna. It might ruin the whole thing. On the other hand, I would soon have to pick up my English bike or pay Frau Unger for another month's rent. A new renter might use it or swipe it. The thought that I might lose it decided my mind.

I put on my own shoes—I had been wearing a pair of spike-soled mountain hikers, left by a guest the previous summer—and trotted along behind Joseph to where the car, the motor running, waited at the foot of the orchard. The Meister was wrapped in blankets like a package in the back seat. I took my place beside Joseph in the front. I liked the little car, an Austrian Steyr, and it was none of my business why the Meister was going to Vienna, so I didn't ask. Soon enough I would learn why he had asked me to come along.

A light dry snow was falling in the canyon below Muhldorf, but Joseph had put on the chains, and the sky to the east seemed to be clearing. We crossed the Danube at Krems, instead of following the river, and headed for the main highway between Innsbruck and Vienna. It was snowing harder when we stopped at an inn to warm up. A guest with a chauffeur made quite a commotion and the natives left the bar to stand and gawk at us. Joseph sat at a separate table with a stein of beer, while we had mugs of chocolate. The natives looked about the same to me as the people around Ranna, with wooden-soled shoes, stained dark by the slush, burlap strips for leggings, and pale chap-smeared faces. They made me think of peasants in a Russian novel. Behind the men, a woman wrapped in a shawl stood holding a child like the beggars in Vienna. The Meister put a coin into the child's hand as we left.

A steady snow was falling, and it had darkened. We had our first problem, and I did my first pushing, when we had to steer around a big cart blocking the road. I pushed at the rear until I was dizzy, but the chains dug deeper ruts in the snow. The owner of the cart had unhitched his team and walked them over the rise, which left a broad trail for Joseph to follow and bring them back. During the time he was gone I would start the motor so the heater would warm up the car a little. When I glanced at the Meister he appeared to be asleep. On the floor at his feet he had two hot bricks; he had taken off his shoes to absorb the bloom of the warmth.

By the time Joseph returned with the farmer, and his team of horses, it was dusk. One of the horses was black, but in the falling snow he was easier to see than the white one. The farmer had had experience with automobiles and he was reluctant to hitch up his team to something that might attack them. On a recent occasion that had happened. Joseph stood for a long time in the snow, talking to him.

When we did get the two chains on the car, and the horses pulled us out of the ruts, the snow was so heavy on the windshield Joseph couldn't see where he was going. We had to let the horses drag us the half mile to the farmer's house, the rippling muscles in their broad backsides gleaming with sweat in the car lights. The house was like those in Muhldorf and Unter Ranna, with a wide-open stable on one side, open to the yard. In the stable he had an ox and a cow, their eyes shining like torches when they turned to stare at us.

Because of the darkness, and the snow still falling, it was decided we would spent the night with the farmer. I carried the two hot

189

bricks, and the shoes the Meister had taken off, while Joseph carried the Meister into the house. Until he unwrapped him I think the farmer thought he was a sleeping child. While the bed was prepared for him, I sat on a bench at the table. At the back of the room, in a gable, I could see a thick covering of straw, but there was no sign of the kids I had seen in other houses. The whole room, in the dim light of the lamp, was like the dark brown chiaroscuro in Rembrandt's paintings. Joseph's shiny ruddy face was like that in a portrait, with highlights and gleaming colors, but the farmer's dark face was like a wad of soiled burlap. The lampglow added little luster to his small eyes. In the corner of the room, near the door to the stable, a woman with a shawl over her head moved pots around on the stove. It startled me to see, when she reached for a pot, her smooth plump white arm. A place was made for me to sleep on a cot near the stove, where I would be covered with one of the lap robes, and Joseph, on his own insistence, would sleep in the straw of the loft. He said that he preferred it, but nobody believed it but himself.

Until the woman brought a large bowl of soup to the table I had not seen her face. I sat there alone. No other eyes but mine beheld this heavenly vision. The shawl framed her face, her apple cheeks, the long lashes to her ice-blue eyes, and when her lips parted, I tell you, I saw the sweet vapor of her breath. Loose strands of her straw-colored hair were touched with gold.

"*Bitte, bitte . . .*" she said, like a normal creature, putting a bowl of steaming soup before me, but I could not speak. My mouth was dry. I saw the beat of the pulse at her white throat. Dazzled as I was, nevertheless I knew that this moment was fated. Here, where it was least expected, was the climax of my expectations. A creature beautiful beyond the telling of it, one I would woo (I had reserved the word for this occasion) and take back to California with me. (None of this, at the moment, presented problems, or dampened my elation.) How she would love it! How I would love her! From the window of our cottage (I had one in mind) I would lean to pick oranges and avocados.

Seated across from me, his chauffeur's hat on the table, the top of his bald head damp with perspiration, Joseph began the tale he had mastered concerning my remarkable talents and background. Was she attentive? Did she look at me, as I did her, with enthralled disbelief? Bundled up, as she was, it was hard for me to judge all of her charms, but she was no Mizi. Normal arms would easily go around her, lift her from the floor. A flesh-and-blood person, nevertheless, with chapped wrists and a blackened thumbnail on the hand that ladled the soup. On and on Joseph babbled, cleaning his bowl with a slice of bread. Later, like Hermann, he smoked a cigarette of his own manufacture, the paper glowing like a firecracker. The lamp was then taken from the table so that beds could be made up elsewhere. The Meister lay buried under bedclothes, the pants to his dark city suit placed at the foot of the bed. From where I lay I could see the glow of one cigarette, then another, then another, punctuated with his periodic snuffles. I could hear the cattle shift their feet in the deep stable muck.

Never before, to my knowledge, had I known such a delirium of emotion. Admittedly, I was short on experience. My unworthiness troubled me, but I would labor to compensate for it. Did I sleep? Joseph pulled me to my feet in the morning to drink hot milk from a mug. The girl was gone. My breath smoked the chill air. Through the door to the stable I could see the farmer forking straw to his beasts.

Joseph went to fill the radiator with hot water while the Meister sat, like a beggar, gripping the mug of milk to warm his hands. He left several silver coins on the table, then shuffled down the path Joseph had cleared, to be rewrapped in the car. The windows were fogged with the air from the heater. Joseph cleaned the windshield with the sleeve and elbow of his jacket. The sky had cleared. The snow had settled so the road could be distinguished from the fields. When I glanced back, the farmer was standing like a bear hunter at the door to his house.

We sloshed along slowly to the main highway, then, the chains clattering, were were soon in Vienna. On Schottengasse, in front of the Studenten Klub, I was let out at the curb. At that time in the morning the peddlers had not set up their stands. I would not be returning to Ranna with Joseph because I had to take my bike to Ranna on the train. Did that concern the Meister? Did it cross his mind that I might not return?

"Look! Look!" he piped, putting up his hand. I looked and he said, "You aff mon-ee?" I wasn't sure that I had heard him correctly. "For fooooot! For train—you aff mon-ee?"

I reassured him that I had money. Through the window he gave me his grimace-like smile. Off they went, the chains slapping, through the arch to the inner *Stadt*. All this time I hadn't noticed that Joseph had put on, for adornment, a pair of clamp-type fireman's red ear-muffs, the metal band concealed by his hat. They looked like carnations, and were as unexpected as the dream that had come toward me out of the shadows, with a steaming bowl of soup.

I was in Vienna, but my feet were not yet on the ground. I saw

my friend Karl at the club, had lunch with Bogislav von Lindheim, then
had a tearful parting with Frau Unger and Hermann before I carried my
bike the four flights down to the street and rode it through the slushy
snow to the station. Did it cross my mind that I just might take off
and head for Italy? No, it didn't. I had these chores to do at Ranna.
Holz and Antone would wonder where the devil I was, and there would
be wood and water to carry. It was almost dusk when the train got
to Spitz but I was able to walk the bike most of the way to Muhldorf.
I thought I might drop dead on the road approaching Ranna, where
I slipped back a step for every one I took forward, but Antone met
me at the entrance to the stable with a basket of eggs and freshly
churned butter. The way the spinning front wheel made the bike's light
glow enchanted him. He carried the bike, I carried the basket, and
walking up through the orchard toward Ranna we were both like the
figures in Brueghel's painting of winter, returning from the hunt.

I'm reasonably sure all of this took place because the films of Holz
and Antone I had asked Karl to have developed in Vienna he mailed
back to me the next weekend. And in the walkway under the gable
roof, where chinks of sky glittered between the shingles, my English
bike with the Sturmey Archer gear was as real as the stench in my
bedroom. It's hard to tell in a country with a place like Ranna
where the real ends and the unreal begins, but these were the facts.
I showed the pictures to Antone when I got them, and he laughed
himself hoarse.

As a token of her high esteem for me, and her respect for
Americans in general, Madame Deleglise—on those days when her
dog, Dolly, seemed least disposed to use the ashes in her fireplace—
trusted to me the transport of the old dog to where there was actually
dirt to be scratched under the snow in the orchard. This was quite
a little jaunt up and down the ramp. Dolly was not heavy, but she
gave off a strong, acrid smell. When I made a clearing in the snow
for her to stand in, she would just cower there, trembling, her feeble
rear legs like those of a rabbit. It was up to me to kick a hole in the
snow and turn up some real dirt. Then she had to sniff it, walk around
and around it, crouch and whimper, do another turn around it, before
she was ready to do her business. Sometimes nothing at all happened.
"Let's get going!" I would say to her, but it was no help. She would
look at me with her clouded eyes, then slobber and whimper until I
scooped her up.

Back in Madame's room she would be fussed over, stroked and patted, given bits of goodies or a bone to gnaw on, just as if she had

192

accomplished something. It wasn't my affair, so I kept what I knew to myself.

Sometimes Madame would have a fire crackling, the room so hot the windows were steamed over; other times she might be sitting up like a princess in the robes of Russian women used to wear on sleigh rides, a fur hat on her head. Once I saw her with her hair so wild she looked like a shampooed poodle. We were both so startled we just stared at each other, as if the film had stopped.

Sometimes she might give me a piece of her Swiss chocolate, wrapped in silver or gold foil, or two or three of the little apples, the size of golf balls, that were usually reserved for compote. They were spongy to squeeze, and there was nothing much to them, but the apple scent would cling for days to my fingers. I didn't wash my hands often, the water not being handy, and my fingers would take on a shine like leather. I sometimes wondered if the Meister wet his hands at all, to avoid chapping, since it was Joseph who shaved him, and the only clean-looking spots on his hands were the fingers he used to roll the bread pellets.

The week before Christmas the two Deleglise boys came from school in Switzerland for the holiday season. I went along with the Meister to pick them up, in Innsbruck, which I thought was something special for me until we started back. What the Meister wanted, and got, was someone to help Joseph push the car out of the drifts. The car was a Steyr, made in Austria, with a boxy body like an Essex coach. The Meister and his two boys, wrapped up like parcels in thick lap robes, huddled in the rear seat, their feet on sacks of hot bricks, gabbling French at each other like schoolgirls. Their big entertainment was watching me get out and push. The snow thrown up by the spinning rear wheels soon worked its way down my collar and the back of my neck. Gobs of it plastered my face and my hair. The younger boy, Marcel, blond and pretty as a girl, had a shrill nasal voice and a girlish way of giggling.

In all my life I had never been with people who wouldn't help each other, when help was really needed. The idea of helping me didn't cross their minds. When I got back into the car, my face and hair caked with snow, they were red-faced and wheezing with laughter. Slouched between the two of them, as if he was being tickled, the Meister wore his familiar grin-like grimace, his eyes tightly closed. What tickled them all out of their minds was to see me climb out, hear the wheels spin and the chains clatter, then see me climb back in looking like a snowman. Every five or ten miles, sometimes less, I would have to

193

go through that idiotic performance. I finally got so mad I yanked the rear door open and swore at them. This startled the boys so much they sat there open-mouthed, staring at me. I was prepared to let them have it. My blood was boiling, but in the winter silence, the metal pinging, the smell of the radiator alcohol like old times, I began to laugh. I had a fit of hooting laughter, leaning on the car, as if my maddening and accumulating fury was as much a part of laughter as it was of rage. When I couldn't seem to stop laughing, they laughed at me, all of them, including Joseph, who sat slapping his gloved hands on the steering wheel. If someone had come by right at that moment he would have known we were all drunk or crazy, which were the extremes of similar contradictions. Tears of laughter had given a shine to the Meister's shaved face.

I was the first to stop laughing, and as luck would have it, we got all the way to Muhldorf, on the slope below Ranna, before the wheels started spinning. At that point I got out, but instead of pushing I just took off and followed the road toward Ranna. From the archway at the entrance I looked back to see the three of them strung out behind me. The older boy, Jacques, was first, then the Meister, and lagging far behind them, Marcel, yelling at them in his shrill, complaining voice. Joseph had left the car to go to Ober Muhldorf for help. The whole crazy incident was fresh in my mind, the starts and stops along the road, the three of them hooting with laughter, but from where I was standing, at the entrance to Ranna, it no longer seemed so peculiar. I scooped a handful of snow and held it to my forehead to cool me off.

The next two or three days I was kept busy shoveling snow. I might see the blond head of Marcel at his mother's window, and hear her hoarse laughter at his witty comments. They took their meals in her room, but when a path had been cleared on the ramp they would come out and walk up and down before *Jause*. Madame always wore a black chinchilla coat, a Cossack-style fur hat, and carried a muff. Her voice in the open was crow-like and gruff, the contrary of Marcel's musical babble. He wore boots of patent leather, white fur gauntlets, with matching fur earmuffs. I saw his brother Jacques catch him in the courtyard, and dip his head into one of the snowdrifts, holding him there till he was red as a tomato. He would just stand there screaming until Mizi or Uncle James would come and lead him away.

One day I drove the car—Joseph was busy in the kitchen—towing Jacques on his new Christmas skis up the canyon to the high plateau from where we could see into Czechoslovakia. I strained to see in the landscape the characteristics I had noted in the Czech students at the club, a close-knit tribe, like the Finns, socializing only with each other. It did not cross my mind that these characteristics were in the language, not the landscape, and the great thing about having your own language was the way you could keep secrets, and remain private, before it became a way of communication.

On the way back to Ranna, most of it downhill, the Meister would yell at me to drive faster, and faster, so Jacques would have some bad spills. This gave him the same tearful exquisite pleasure I had given him pushing the car out of snowdrifts. Nothing personal. Just the pure unmitigated pleasure of seeing someone humiliated, made a fool of, squashed, but not quite demolished. I didn't like Jacques much, so I got more pleasure from his spills than his father. I didn't like his style, his dark, hostile manner, his rude, provoking way of speaking, slurring his French, and his superior, insolent, street-tough manner. He stopped being so hostile, however, the evening I beat him at Indian wrestling, where he thought he was good. Right away he was respectful and friendly with me, knowing I was his equal or better. I might have grown to almost like him, but the day after Christmas he was gone.

I was in the rear court with Holz, pumping water, when Marcel ran out of the corridor toward us, chased by Jacques. Marcel's coat flapped open: a white wool scarf, with long tassels, hung from his neck. As he ran by, he saw his beauty had impressed me, and he was pleased.

Jacques pursued him into the woodshed at the back of the court, then held him like a child as he stuffed handfuls of snow into his shirt-front and pants. Marcel shrieked and screamed but no one came to help him. When Jacques let him go he stood there howling, like a child in a tantrum, his brother standing off to one side, grinning at him. I didn't glance up to see, but I had the feeling that the Meister was at one of the upper windows, watching. Marcel was his mother's boy. It was just the sort of thing the Meister would hate to miss.

Just before Christmas, in the sunny music room, I sat reading Stendhal's *Le Rouge et le Noir*. I had looked up from the page to reflect on Julien's admission that he admired Madame de Rênal's looks but hated her for her beauty. That startled, pleased and confused me. Was it for this one read French novels? As I brooded on this dilemma, the Meister peered into the room to *psssst* at me, like a waiter. I followed him down the long corridor to his room, where he had been sorting good apples from bad. Spread out on his bed, they were all withered and spongy with a strong musty odor, but some had a russet skin and looked less wormy than others. These he put in a sack and handed to me, but he carried a small sack of potatoes himself. We then walked back to the music room, where Joseph had started a fire in the blue-tile oven. The afterglow of the winter sunset filled the room with light. On the slope below Ranna, as if deep under water, I saw a dark file of figures emerging out of the canyon, all but a few of them carrying flickering candles. Drifting snow concealed parts of the trail and they moved along so slowly they appeared to be stationary.

I watched them come up through the orchard and follow the path that had been cleared on the ramp. They were kids mostly, without caps; their thatched blond hair made them look like goblins. All of them wore leggings of burlap, one coat sleeve dangling as if an arm was missing. A tall fellow, dressed like a schoolteacher, brought up the rear. As he passed beneath the alcove window I could see his breath smoke, his face white as a snowman.

Joseph led them up through Ranna, along the dark corridor and into the music room. If they could get their hands out of the long coat sleeves they received two spongy apples, two sprouting potatoes, and several pieces of hard Christmas candy, all of it from the Meister. Gathered in a clutter around the piano, they sang "*Stille Nacht, Heilige Nacht,*" the way it was probably sung in heaven. The tall young man who had come along with them gave a short speech of thanks, bowing low as he finished, then they all filed out through the door they had entered.

Some minutes later I saw them on the slope below Ranna, with their twinkling candles. Not to waste the fire in the oven, I stood close beside it, munching one of the apples. It occurred to me—with the time to think it over—that the Meister was a lot like Stendhal's Julien in the way he managed to surprise you. Stendhal would have liked him. They had more in common than just being French.

I might find soiled plates on the table in the morning, the fire in the stove a bed of ashes since nobody had banked it. I might find the kitchen warm, with nobody in it but Antone and Holz, asleep on the floor behind the stove. I took my supper in the kitchen, sometimes alone, sometimes with Joseph, Antone and Herr Zoller, who brought the eggs, butter and milk up from the stables. He took his long-stem pipe from his mouth when he ate; otherwise it was part of his face. He smoked a shredded yellow mixture like wood shavings, frequently blowing through the stem to keep it burning. In profile Antone's face was like the Indian on the buffalo nickel. Nobody talked. The glasses of cold green cider put everybody to sleep.

Snow collected on the roofs, in the inner and outer courts, making the carrying of wood and water difficult, and it was up to me to see that Dolly got to her scratch spot in the orchard. I stopped troubling with the basket, and the smelly cushions, and carried her whimpering and slobbering in my arms. She liked that. Sometimes she howled when I put her down. What she really wanted was the food she couldn't eat, having no teeth. At night Madame played opera music on her Victrola, all yelling and shouting, which I could hear if her fireplace smoked and her window stood open; I often missed it when it was quiet.

Once a month, weather permitting, Fräulein Schlepps came all the way from Spitz to take dictation and type business letters. I might see her red stocking cap and mittens as she mushed up the road from Muhldorf. Otherwise I would hear, in the silence of Ranna, the clack-clack of Uncle James's typewriter, an army-green Oliver that made me think of the drawbridges in Chicago. Fräulein Schlepps considered herself a big-city girl. She was pretty as a Kewpie, red-lipped, bob-haired, with big ice-blue eyes and a solemn expression, but her shoulders were thin, her figure straight and narrow as a clothespin. She wore a mat-black frock without frills or cuffs, the material flecked with typewriter erasures. Was it the long, cold walk to Ranna that gave her the feverish complexion? No, that she had always, along with her slight cough. The cough was not unusual among the young people since the war. When I met her she gave me her small, doll-like hand and said she was awed to meet me. It pleased her to practice her English on me. "How you do?" she would ask. "I do O.K." I told her about New York, the Empire State Building, and the oranges that hung from the trees in California.
"*Verstehen Sie?*" Uncle James asked her. Solemnly, her small fist pressed to her lips, she would nod and cough.

As the snow accumulated, the work of restoration in the *Graben*, and on the bastille at the entrance, came to a halt. The buckets of rocks sat around humped with snow, or dangling from the ropes attached to winches. It all stopped like a clock, and would not be resumed until spring. Just as I was getting used to him, Beps went back to Krems. I watched him walk his motorcycle down the slope to Muhldorf, where I could hear the motor cough and sputter when he tried to start it. I liked him, I think, better than he did me, after I had beaten him at Indian wrestling. He couldn't accept that. He left early so we wouldn't have to say *Auf Wiedersehen*.

Sometimes the Meister would take his meals in his room and I wouldn't see him for three or four days. His room was narrow as a boat cabin, but with French doors in one wall that opened out on a view of the valley. He had a small wood-burning stove, named the Vulcan, that smoked most of the time because he wouldn't open the damper. Uncle James would often find the French doors thrown wide to air out the smoke.

The Meister's bed was attached to the wall, like a bunk, but so high off the floor he needed a stool to climb into it. Every night Mizi brought him hot bricks, wrapped in flannel, which she put between the sheets at the foot. He slept sitting up, propped by pillows, the way people do who read a lot at night. The day I was in his room he was reading an old copy of *The Nation,* and a recent copy of *Le Monde.* He didn't show me his room, but when I knew he wasn't there I had a look at it. In a wardrobe like the one in my room in Vienna he had a dark wool suit, a heavy dark overcoat, two white shirts on hangers, one tie, and a pair of oxfords with rubbers on them. What other clothes he had he was wearing.

I wrote a long letter to my sweetheart in California, who had gone to school in England and knew that people were peculiar, but after thinking it over I didn't mail it. It might lead her to think that I was the one who was crazy. Instead I sent her a postcard view of Schloss Ranna, painted in the eighteenth century, showing peasants at work and play in the orchard, and on it I wrote "Out of This World." Before I had a chance to mail it I smudged up the address and put it into one of the pockets of my suit coat.

That's how I happened to find out that I could hardly squeeze into my gabardine suit. The zipper would no longer close on the fly of the pants, and the coat that had hung loose on me would no longer button. Had six weeks of potato soup, *Butterbrot* and sawing wood done that to me? It had. All of those weeks I had been wearing some of the cast-off clothes left by guests who came out to Ranna over the summer, including sweaters and knickers I was happy to sleep in. How fat had I grown? There were no mirrors to tell me. In the glass of a bookcase I saw that my eyes were now small in my bearded face. Some of the money I had saved living at Ranna I would have to spend in Krems for clothes that would fit me, but I was pleased to look forward to a pair of the corduroy knickers I had seen on the smart young skiers in Innsbruck. Also a pair of the shoes made of one piece of leather, appropriate to a *Wandervogel* about to cycle in Italy on a four-speed English bike. With so much fat on my bones, I would save money by eating less.

198

We had a warm spell in February, with a lot of water dripping and running in the gutters. I was basking in the sun in one of the outer courts, where the Meister spotted me from a window. It pleased me to realize he had been looking for me.

"A ride! A ride!" he said. "Yes, We go for ride, I pool, yes?"

I didn't know what he had in mind, but I was game. I met him on the ramp, at the front, and we walked down through the orchard to the outbuildings that were part of Ranna, a lot of sheds and open lean-tos on a large open courtyard. I could hear pigs squealing and see chickens picking over the exposed manure in the stable. Two big, creamy oxen, with eyes like gods', watched me as if I were something special, straws sticking out of their mouths. There was also a small saddled reddish horse, and in the snow behind it a wooden-runner sled of the sort I had once had as a boy and never liked. All you could do with such a sled was haul laundry on it. There was no way to steer it, or run and belly flop with it. I watched the Meister fasten one end of the rope to his saddle, then he gave me the other, a knot looped at its end.

"You ride! You ride!" he said. "I pool!"

I got the idea. He led the horse into the open, on the road leading to Muhldorf, then stretched the rope out behind to where I stood with the sled. "You sit, I pool!" he said. To show me what he meant, he took a seat on the sled, took a grip on the rope, braced his feet on the curved runners. At that point I might have said, "*You* ride, *I* pool!" but actually I liked sleds better than horses. My last ride on a horse, I had been left on a tree branch along a gravel road between the farm and Norfolk. So I sat down on the sled, took a grip on the rope, and waited for the Meister to mount the little horse. He took a lot of time cinching the saddle. Had he done this before? Most of the way to Muhldorf we went along at a walk while I tried to get the hang of steering the sled with my feet. It was not one of the thrill rides of my life, but some of the goblin-like kids came running out of Ober Ranna to watch us go by, and run along with us.

In Muhldorf, the fellow peeing on the porch of the inn greeted me with *Grüss Gott!* In the half hour or so since I had been sun-basking, the sky had clouded over, and a powdery snow was falling, prickling my face. In the canyon below Muhldorf the incline increased and the little horse began to canter. I was a good ten or fifteen yards to the rear, but the gobs of wet snow thrown up by his hooves began to fall on me. Some of them fell in my hair, like snow pies, and others splattered on my front. I had to use both hands to grip the rope, and it was hard to duck. When I did yell out for the Meister to stop, he didn't hear me. All I had to do was let go of the rope, but in that kind of situation it's the last thing you think of, and I've got this stubborn streak that makes me stick things out. The worse it is, the longer I'll stick. My feeling is—some fifty years later—that the Meister not only knew just what he was doing, he also knew me. I was one of those nuts like his son Jacques who would hang on until hell froze over— and it came close. Flakes of big snow plastered my face and sealed my eyes. I was steering the sled by the feel of the rope. I didn't even know when we reached the Danube and followed the highway into Spitz, since the snow concealed the river and I couldn't make out the dim lights at the inn. When the horse finally stopped I just sat there with this pancake of snow topping my head, and a bushel of it col- lected in my lap. Before the Meister looked to me he took care of his horse, which I could smell and hear wheezing, then, with a lantern, he came back to look at me. Did I look like something frozen in a cake of ice? He peeled off my snow topping, scooped the snow from my front, and that was it. Helped to my feet, I was on my own. I tailed along behind the Meister into the inn, where I stood beside the stove, thawing out and steaming, while he had a *Schokolade* and read the paper. To be fair, I have to say that he did ask me if I wanted anything, and of course I said no. The three or four men in the room, with their sad, gentle faces, their collarless shirts, were like those below the window of the club in Vienna, waiting to cluster around a ped- dler. They were like my friend Hermann with his rabbit eyes and bleeding gums. Little wonder that Antone was the father of his country.

When the time came to leave, and my hair was still wet, the bar- man loaned me a cap with earmuffs that smelled like manure, but I was glad to have it. It was dark but still snowing when we set off for Muhldorf, the Meister back on the horse while I walked along beside him, the little horse being too small for the two of us to ride. Here and there I saw the glow of a lamp, and heard dogs bark. My misery and self-pity were so great I didn't feel the cold much, or know how long it was before I left the Meister and his horse in the courtyard of the stable, and waded up through the orchard alone to Ranna, a gray hulk looming in the darkness. The dim bulb usually burning in Uncle James's small window was not visible. I used the broom on the landing to sweep off my shoes and pants, then went in, to find Uncle James asleep in a chair he had pulled up to the stove. He had taken off his shoes, and the air had the strong smell of his socks. I stood there beside him, still breathing so hoarsely nobody would guess I was almost bawling, my eyes blurred with tears.

Hearing shrieks in the kitchen, the sound of chairs scraping, I opened the door, to see Joseph pursuing Mizi, watch him catch her from behind and thump at her broad bottom with his hips. It seemed to me she didn't mind it too much.

Then he backed off, wheezing and laughing, to peer down at the butchered pig's tail sticking out of his fly like a corkscrew penis. He swaggered about in the light, showing it off, pulled it from his fly and tossed it into the bucket full of pig innards and scraps. Then they both went on about their work as if nothing had happened.

I didn't think that I had seen anything I shouldn't, but felt that something had ripped the veil to the past, just as I was passing, and I had seen through it.

At the window of the music room, my eyes creased against the sun glare, I saw in the *Graben* directly below me a bright patch of sunlight where the snow had melted. Drips from the roof honeycombed the snow. The line where the sun and the shadow overlapped quivered like a flame. On the bright side of that line I saw something strange.

First it looked to me like a mask, or shield, with a sort of putty-colored surface that crinkled. There were two small spots like widely spaced eyes, and centered, near the bottom, a small round hole or mouth. When my eyes had adjusted to the light I saw the forked brown legs, like a big insect. Now and then they moved, like butterfly wings. But the putty-colored object I had taken for a mask was the nude torso of the Meister, sunning himself. The two eyes were his nipples, and the hole was his belly button. His thin left arm lay across his face. He looked crumpled, as if he might have fallen from the sky, or the roof. When the sun left the wall, inching upward, he reached a handful of snow from the shadow and rubbed it hard on his chest and belly, then he rubbed some on his face. Just for a moment, as if he had told me, I saw what it was he liked about Indians. Then he got to his feet, buttoned up his clothes, and shuffled along the *Graben* bottom like a big trained rabbit. The feelings I had for such an odd little man in such a big strange place constricted my throat. I so wanted to like him, but he made it hard. At the top of the stairs that led to the ramp he suddenly turned and looked right toward me. Did he see me, or just a reflection? If he saw me and thought that I had been spying on him it would have ruined the whole thing.

Knowing his watch does not run, I have stopped Antone to ask him the time. He lowered the barrow he was pushing, puffed like a dragon, and removed the timepiece from the bib of his overalls. Holding it to his ear, he listens, his eyes lidded. What he has heard reassures him. He considered the face, gave the stem several twists, then returned the watch to his bib. Whatever time it is, or will be, he has it safe inside the watch. In the glance he gives me I see that the joke is on me. I like Antone. His eyes tell me that I am the odd one. In the dark corridor to the music room I caught him, red-handed, gulping the spongy little apples, cores and all, snorfeling like a dog.

Forwarded from Vienna, a letter came from a fraternity brother in California. He had once asked me about Italy, and I had urged him to go there. But not with me. No one I had ever met seemed less a *Wandervogel.* He was big and shy, his hair already thinning, with a 1924 Model-T Ford coupe I used to borrow for dates. Himself, he didn't date. On spring weekends and over the summer, he helped his father grow avocados.

His letter said that if I would name the time, and the place, he would meet me in Italy in March or April. Did I want to? We hardly knew each other. What I wanted more than the Alps, or the isles of Greece, or the white plume of Vesuvius, or the view of Naples, was to peel a bagful of oranges and lie on the beach with the sun in my face.

What time was it *really?* From Uncle James I found out we were in February, three days before Lincoln's birthday. A few days later, on the slope below Ranna, I saw another time I had failed to read correctly. With a shovel, someone had cleared away the snow to make a huge Nazi swastika:

I had seen so few actual swastikas I didn't know the image was reversed. Thirty or forty feet square, it could be seen from Muhldorf if anyone was looking. A day or two later, fresh snow covered it up, but the depression in the snow revealed the pattern. Who had made it? One thing was certain, it took a shovel and a strong back.

I wrote my fraternity friend in California that it was hard for me to make plans for the future, living as I was in the Middle Ages, but I would try to be in Trieste, Italy, the second week of March, at the American Express office.

From Genoa, Italy, I had a postcard from Karl. He was soon leaving for Buenos Aires, where he invited me to pay him a visit. I would find him at his father's fabric business. He wished me a *gute Reise* in Italy, and much success as a writer. That astonished and pleased me. What ever led him to think I might be a writer? But it seemed more plausible to me now that I had a moustache. (The beard would be shaved off.) Italy called to me, Buenos Aires called, but it snowed steadily at Ranna, filling the courts and the cracks between the planks on the floor of my room.

The night Joseph woke me up, I'd been asleep for some time. His shiny bald head loomed above me like the moon lit up from the back side. A milky moonlight filled the windows.

"*Was gibt's?*" I asked.

"Excuse me!" he said. I excused him. "The hunt! The hunt!" he said, his hushed voice urgent. He was in his chauffeur's coat and riding breeches. In the crook of his arm the barrel of a gun glistened. He waved his hand to the windows, but I did not feel urgent. I was a reader, a dreamer, not a hunter. "*Schnell!*" he said, giving me a shake, and I got up.

Something to wake me would have helped, but we did not stop at the kitchen. Our shoes rang like iron on the corridor cobbles. Out on the ramp was Antone, his hams tight in his britches, and a long coat draped the figure of Holz. He might have been sleepwalking. No features showed in his face. Antone led us off, his hair up like a scarecrow, then Joseph, with the light glinting on the gun barrel. Holz shuffled in a trance of cold at the rear. A vapor hovered about us from our own breathing, like leaks from a radiator, the snow under our feet brittle as glass.

Down we went through the orchard toward Ober Muhldorf, where a dark clump of figures waited. They were beaters. I had heard about them. They preceded the hunters, yelling and hooting, stirring up the creatures crouched in the field stubble. Softly Joseph called out, "Hallo, hallo?"

Owl-like came the answer: "Hal-looooo, hal-looooo." One of the beaters, who held a lantern, waved it, the flame hardly visible in the shimmering brightness. Now we made our approach. In a hush of muttering and white vapor the beaters huddled, shuffling their feet. Among the hunters I noted a jolly fellow with knickers, a tuft of fur at his hatband, high two-buckle galoshes. We beaters strung ourselves out in a row facing the furrowed rows of stubble. The crispness of the shadows made it confusing. Everything moved. We stood silent, shifting from foot to foot, waiting for the Big Hunter to give the signal. The four hunters had skirted the open field to a position where trees grew out of the gully. There, in concealment, they would await the rabbits. Two of the hunters were from Unter Ranna. I saw that we numbered eleven beaters, with perhaps three or four yards between each of us. His mittens cupped to his beaming face, Antone honked like a river steamer. He was silenced. But even the hunters understood about Antone. At the signal, the far hoot of an owl, the beaters flailed their arms, slapped their hands on their thighs, barked, howled, and stamped their feet as they marched. That part of it I liked, and it warmed me up.

I made a good beater. I had had some experience hooting and howling like an Indian, and my lungs were strong. Hearing me, any rabbit, or anything else, would have run for its life. We all kept up this racket for the time it took to walk from the road to the edge of the gully. I had seen nothing. But the excitement and cold had filmed my eyes, and my head buzzed. Nothing had prepared me for what then happened. The explosion of the guns, a split second apart, in spite of the great clatter we were making, splintered and demolished the great globe of the sky. The echoing thunder went up, then down, the canyons, bounced off the mountains, so that I stood with my eyes closed tight, my head lowered. All of my companions ran, some of them falling, to the point where the trees began and the hunters were gathered, gesticulating. They were fighting, surely, over the slaughter of rabbits! We all formed a panting, wheezing circle around them. Joseph pointed to where the rabbit had come from, and to the spot at his feet, where he had shot it. All were agreed. All had done the same. There at his feet. A space was cleared at the center to look for the tracks, but with all the commotion, they had been obliterated. One fact was certain, though. Joseph waited for silence to make it. The rabbit had been seen, the rabbit had been shot, and then disappeared. Anyone could see that he was not there. Nor were there tracks indicating that he had escaped. None. On the wide, gleaming moonlit slope, not the single track of a rabbit. *Unglaublich. Fabelhaft. Ausserordentlich.* Out of this world. In this pregnant pause, Holz had turned from us to pee in the snow.

The hunter from Ober Muhldorf, with the fur on his hat, invited hunters and beaters to his house to celebrate the occasion, but Joseph, looking before and behind him, glancing up the slope at the walls of Ranna, and down the slope to the roofs of Muhldorf, regretted that Herr Morris, a guest in their midst, one who had come from a world where no snow fell, was surely exhausted by the night's events and eager for the shelter Ranna provided. All eyes gazed at me, but saw little. I sucked the bitter air through a muffler concealing my face. As we departed, Antone, cupping his mittens to his face, cried out, *Hallo, hallo. Radio Wien!* like the Vienna radio announcer. There was no comment. Antone was even better known for other works.

We walked single file in the tracks we had made coming down.

Deep gulps of the air burned my lungs. We paused frequently to wait for Holz. The moon shimmered like a reflection on water. No stars anywhere. To myself I said that this was what was meant by the white nights of Russia. All around us the snow glittered like Christmas tinsel.

I stopped in the dining *Saal* to thaw my cold feet, then went up the snow-sprinkled stairs to my room. Under Madame's door I saw the flicker of fire. Hearing my steps, the old dog whimpered. In the room with the trophies, their glass eyes shining, the sheet-covered furniture appeared to be concealed by mounds of snow.

If Madame Deleglise was in a bad mood she would not let Mizi carry food into her room. It would be left on a tray at the door, and that was where they would find the dirty dishes. After I had carried Dolly to her spot in the orchard, I would leave her at the door, and knock. This time, when I knocked, she called, "Gom een! Gom een!" I went in. A log smoldered on a high mound of ashes, the air was blue with smoke. I turned to leave, but she cried, "No, no—gom een!" She reclined on a bed with a yellow comforter, propped up in a nest of cushions. A ribboned nightcap, with a puffed crown, sat on her head, like the big bad wolf in "Little Red Riding Hood." "Ow you like Ranna?" she asked me.

"Very much," I replied. Too late, I saw it was a loaded question. Her dark face clouded. She muttered several hissing curses.

"You like? You know why you like? You are nod a preez-nur. I am a preez-nur!" Her chubby hands slapped the comforter, stirring up a cloud of dust. "A preez-nur! A preez-nur!" she cried. "You hear me?" We both looked about the large room. It would have been ideal for the Prisoner of Zenda. One high-gabled window, several that were slotted, the rafters in the peaked ceiling black with wood smoke. "Gom here!" she barked at me, beckoning me closer, and I obeyed. She tilted forward to see me more closely, her hands placed dramatically on her bosom. She had more of a talent than I had suspected, and remarkable eyes. Captive in her dark tower, on a bed strewn with French novels, she perceived me as straw thrown on her fire. Her fists clenched. She turned to pull on a cord that hung at her side, and I heard the bell sound in the kitchen. Did she mean to have Mizi throw me out? I thought her capable. I was out on the stairs, headed down, as she passed me going up, a smear of flour on her cheek, a lace of suds drying on her plump arms. If only her almond eyes had given me the assurance that I, too, was a *preez-nur*, but she didn't, and little she seemed to care.

Joseph had found me reading in the library annex, where I had

205

found a Baedeker of Italy and was engrossed in the maps. What Joseph had to say to me, being novel, I did not understand. He beckoned me to follow him, and we went below to the office of Uncle James. He sat at his desk soaking stamps from the envelopes of his recent correspondence. His muffler was twisted about where his neck might have been, and his lips were shiny with the syrup of a horehound drop from Cedar Rapids. He did not appreciate the interruption, Joseph explained.

"Beek peek hass leedle peex," said Uncle James.

What did that have to do with me?

"Mutter peek"—he spread wide his arms—"roll on leedle peex. You sit and watch."

"Where?" I asked. Joseph explained. The mother pig and her new litter were at home with Herr Zoller, where they should be. Joseph would show me. I lacked experience baby-sitting little peex, but Uncle James reassured me. "Iss nutting," he said, and smiled to see them all before him. "Besides, iss varm! For leedle peex haus muss be varm!"

Joseph led me off. Already spots of green were showing in the orchard where the snow had melted. Also black ruts in the road leading to Muhldorf. In the courtyard of the stable, water sat in puddles. Were mother pigs knowledgeable in such matters? Had she timed it for spring? In the shed we passed through were the oxen, their great creamy bodies like mythical beasts. A woman opened the door, a wad of the babushka that circled her head held to her mouth. The room we entered was large, lit by lamps, the stone floor strewn with straw. At the back of the room a loft, the rafters covered with straw, with several goblin-eyed small fry staring at me. I looked at them for some resemblance to Antone. In one corner of the room a great pink and white sow sprawled on her side on a bed of hay, a squirming mass of mini-piglets tugging at her teats. They were pink and hairless as baby mice, with tiny cloven feet. The sow's eyes were lidded by long thick blond lashes. She grunted softly, like a happy dreamer, stirring bits of chaff. What did I think of? I thought of Mizi. The Lord of life would have to forgive me. Here was contentment that exceeded expectations, even mine.

A three-legged stool sat at the rim of the straw, with a pole that could be used to push or pull a piglet. There I would sit. I heard but followed little the instructions Joseph gave me. Was there a problem? There was a problem when the mother sow changed her position, rolled on her bed. Not through lack of affection, nor because she was careless, but sheer bulk complicated matters. Thirteen piglets—Joseph paused to count them—keeping the count at thirteen was the problem, since one or more was inclined to scoot under or behind her. And that would be one less. Nor was it just the loss of a piglet, but in time a pig. Frau Zoller was a woman with much work to be done, and her children were too small for piglet watchers. A man was needed. Strange as I might be, I was a man.

I litter-sat for two days and one long night. Was it possible to feel tender and fraternal affections for a sow? I felt them. It also reassured *her* that I felt them. Often she would lift her head, with its purse-size ears, and gaze at me through her long blond lashes. Oink, oink, she would say to me. Oink, I said to her. Sometimes she would snort, clearing away the floor chaff, or use her snout like a nozzle to suck up food scraps. Her brood seemed to be an immaculate conception. The bolder ones came closer to sniff me over, their little hooves like the handles of pocket knives. If I grabbed a piglet it was like a moist football. How it squealed. In moments of rebellion, weary of their greedy sucking, the mother sow would labor to her feet, with half the brood dangling like pig pods. She looked to me for help, and she got it. I would use the pole to pry them off her teats, like so many huge leeches. At night I often saw mice playing in the straw, and the flick of their shadows at the edge of the litter. Both considered me another hog, but a strange one. Twice daily I was fed a soup of gruel and milk in which pieces of blood sausage floated. Pig blood. I slurped it down and smacked my lips. On the third morning a girl, as big and strapping as Mizi, but her broad face puffy and her nose chapped, took my place. I'm afraid I greeted her with some resentment. Did she think she could take *my* place in the sow's affections? Her name was Rota Dinge. Her wooden-soled shoes, soaked dark by the slush, were sniffed by the piglets while she was napping, which she did most of the time.

The snow was melting again, and I could hear it drip and gurgle at night. On what I took to be a Sunday, or a holiday, Madame Deleglise came to dinner dressed like one of the Three Musketeers, or Cyrano de Bergerac. A large hat with a plume, the brim turned up on one side, added about eight inches to her height at the table. Purple velvet pantaloons were tucked into black leather boots, gold-and silver-looking chains dangled into her lap. It had to do with some role she had sung in opera, and what it did for her spirits was remarkable. Her eyes flashed, she roared with hoarse laughter. The cloud of her perfume hovered over the table. After bowls of soup, in which dumplings were floating, Joseph entered the room with a platter that required we clear a space at the center of the table. We all shared in the excitement. Uncle James rubbed his palms together like

207

an Indian making fire. The platter was lowered to the table, and there before my eyes, steaming like a baked apple, was a roast suckling piglet! One of my piglets! Uncle James rose from his chair to do the carving with a large blade that Joseph had just sharpened. I rose with him. Perhaps only Joseph, who looked at me with surprise, was aware that I had left. From the landing on the stairs I whooped up the dumplings, and felt the weakness in my loins, a word I treasured. If Mizi had seen me I would have died. I made my way across the court to Uncle James's office, where, some hours later, he found me still resting, my eyes to the wall to avoid the look of heavenly contentment on his grease-smeared face.

After several days of spring-like weather, the air in my room was warmer but I couldn't breathe it. I asked Joseph about it, and I saw that he knew it well. Would it continue? I asked him. It would. How long? Until the pit at the foot of the latrine was emptied. And who was it that would do the emptying? We would. Joseph often found the questions that I asked him puzzling.

That was one thing. A sledgeload of freshly sawed logs dumped at the foot of the orchard was another. Why there? The problem had a history. For three or four generations, that was where the log supplier had dumped them. At the foot of the orchard. So that was where they were dumped.

The ground was too soft and mushy for a wheelbarrow, so those logs would be carried, an armful at a time, the quarter mile from the stable into the rear court, where they would then be sawed into smaller pieces. More than two cords of fragrant, wet, unseasoned, heavy wood.

So what we did was improvise a stretcher, made up of saplings, to carry four or five logs between us from the foot of the orchard to the woodshed in the court. This stretcher of logs could not be lowered, or shifted, until we reached our destination. The chapped hands of Holz, in their ragged mittens, endured this burden like hooks. After two trips my hands were blistered. I could not shape a fist, or slip them into my pockets. A day later I managed to twist my ankle. My collapse on the ramp, very dramatically timed, got me considerable attention. My arm around Joseph's shoulders, his around my waist, I hobbled to the couch in Uncle James's office. Unfortunately, I had not foreseen that snow would be applied to reduce the swelling. I thought my foot would freeze. I was still there in the morning when the mail came up from Muhldorf, with a letter from my friend in California. He was sailing from New York to Genoa, Italy. He planned to meet me, as we planned, in Trieste. Amazing how the snow had improved my ankle in just one night! I still hobbled a bit—not of much help in the carrying of logs and water—but in a few days surely, and on a bicycle with gears to smooth out the rises, and with spring, so to speak, just around the corner, or already arriving in the Bay of Naples . . . ! When I spoke to the Meister, who had lived in Italy, who had indeed hiked in the hills above Florence, and rested in the gardens of I Tatti, he advised me that I might find Italy on the cool side in March.

Uncle James was more sympathetic. Did I think he didn't know what was "eating me"? Had he not himself been young in Vienna, and for almost three weeks on Lake Como, near Bellagio? *"Ein viertel Frühling!"* he sang. *"Ein viertel Wein, ein viertel Liebe, verliebt muss man sein!"* He broke off to recall a summer night in Verona, where Madame had performed to a standing ovation. For himself, he found the *jeunes filles* on the plump side, and well chaperoned.

It was not for the girls I went to Italy, I replied, already having a not-too-plump girl friend in California, to which news he arched his hairless eyebrows, his wide mouth contracting to a kisser's moist pucker.

Antone, the father of his country, gripped and shook my hand, then left me holding his fingerless red mitten. I had meant to give him my Magic Match, a metal nail that would strike and burn, but his prank gave him much more pleasure. At the end of the corridor, framed against the winter sky, he stood with his legs spread wide like the Jolly Green Giant, a fire in his yellow hair.

Joseph asked if I would send him a postcard from California.

Holz lay asleep behind the stove, so I didn't wake him.

Uncle James asked me not to forget him, and I didn't.

Mizi was nowhere that I looked. Nowhere.

I made my getaway. I was halfway down the ramp when the Meister called to me. The French doors to his room stood open, he basked in the sun. He waved, and I could see flecks of red in his week-old beard. Mizi came out of the room at his back to thump the head of her dust mop on the wall. She had a pale-blue dustcloth pinned to her hair, and as I waved to her she put one hand to her face, covering her mouth. Did I or didn't I hear a suppressed shriek of laughter? For a moment her broad back filled the opening, then she was gone. A big cow of a girl, really, who just happened to have a creamy complexion and the slanted eyes of women from the steppes of Russia. I was leaving just in time, I told myself, before something unforeseen might happen, and whoever might prove to be the father of the country, it wouldn't be me.

I had to carry my bike all the way to Muhldorf, the road to Ranna chewed up by the tire chains. Below Muhldorf there were lanes where the snow had melted, and I could ride. Once I got on the bike I was seized with an impulse to pedal like mad. At the foot of the canyon, seeing the Danube as muddy as the Missouri at Omaha, I felt a weakness like that at losing a sweetheart.

Uncle James had assured me that the barber in Spitz would not be offended by my long dirty hair, or my scraggly soft beard. I found his shop empty; he was seated in the chair, reinforcing the buttons on his vest. He greatly admired my long silken moustache, which reminded him of Franz Josef, often seen in Spitz before the Great War. He washed my mane of hair, wrapped it in towels, and on the heel of his hand, as he shaved me, I saw the glint of copper-colored hairs in the lather. Tilted erect, and fanned by a towel, I saw in the mirror he held before me the flushed, full-jowled face of a stranger with wavy brown hair. I was able to persuade him to go easy with the clippers. Where I was going, I said, longer hair was in fashion. And where was that? I rolled my eyes. I mentioned Capri and the Bay of Naples. He looked at me with the eyes of Hermann on first beholding my Sturmey Archer gear. Would I welcome, he asked me, a suggestion? It proved to be a touch of wax to the ends of my moustache. Whose face was it? I tried to recall if Gustav Aschenbach looked a bit roguish. To this barber shave—my first and last—I owed the impression that I was a new man. How well I understood, as he whisked me off, the compliments he gave me about the view from the rear.

Bogislav von Lindheim, paler and thinner than usual, his plus-fours tucked into the tops of his unbuckled galoshes, knew that I had been away, somewhere, but he had forgotten where. As we sat in the alcove window, overlooking Schottengasse, a ragtag company of Austrian soldiers with knapsacks, canteens, and rifles with bayonets marched by in broken ranks below us. I thought it had to be a movie. Bogislav was not amused. Chancellor Dollfuss, single-handed, was trying to unite the country. An American girl from Cleveland, in a fur-trimmed tweed skirt and jacket, her Lucky Strikes in a tin of flat fifties, had taken my place as the voice of the new world. She gave parties in her Ringstrasse apartment and sometimes arrived at the club in a taxi. Had I known that Pius Michael Prutscher had been very keen on Catherine White? No, I had not known.

The night train from Vienna got me to the Italian border, high in the Alps, just at daylight. Along the way, as the train rose into the mountains, I watched the big, moth-like snowflakes falling like ashes about the hooded station lights. The long screeching climb, the starting and stopping, the clackety-clack of the wheels in the tunnels, was like the trip of Hans Castorp, rising from the flat plains into the mountains. I wore the new hiking clothes I had bought in Krems: the wide-wale plus-fours, a sweat shirt with a zipper collar, a leather jacket with tassels on the pocket zippers, and shoes made of a single piece of leather in the prison south of the Danube. There was still wax on the tips of my moustache. The three young skiers in the compartment with me studied my outfit and me with interest. Was I an *Ausländer*? I was. I would surely have no problems, they assured me, since I spoke such excellent German. They had been to Italy. The roads of Italy were used by more German *Wandervögel* than Italians. *Auf Wiedersehen!* we all said.

At the border the Italian officials were puzzled to examine my passport. Americans did not look as I did, or appear at the top of the Alps with *biciclettas*. I was taken in hand, and sat with two border guards, waiting for the border official. A small white-haired man, with beautiful manners, a black cape about his shoulders, he did not believe me for a moment, but he liked me. Had I *really* come from California? Was I an artist? He shared my excitement to be entering Italy. He, too, was an

211

artist, he had once been young, and he felt moved to be generous.

Outside the depot it snowed. The official embraced me as we parted, and I carried my bike through the slush of Tarvisio, down the narrow road beyond it, the high air burning my lungs, my eyes blurred with cold. I was low on oxygen, but high on exhilaration. I was in Italy! The air that I breathed, the snow that fell on me, the road beneath the snow, were all Italian. I plowed ahead. I seemed to have all of it to myself. The snow let up, the road tilted downward, and where the snow thawed I was able to ride. Down, down I went, the snow thinned and disappeared, the road followed a widening, boulder-strewn river, the water running white in the narrow channels, down, down I went, through villages gray as granite, through blowing wisps of cloud, through sheets of drizzle, with the air blowing warmer and warmer, down, down into a wide river basin with the smoke of factories and the racket of traffic.

I had not eaten since the day before, but I was too excited and elated to stop. The landscape opening around me was like that of California, the mountains rising abruptly, the canyons of boulders fanning out to spread on the arid wash, but I saw it all with shining eyes. I felt nothing but a buoyant elation. A hundred or more kilometers from where I had started, I came out on a plain, with stony fields and cypress trees, the bell towers rising from clumps of trees and houses, and in the outskirts of a sprawling town I pulled over to the curb to ask where I was. My ears were ringing. A large woman, dark as an Arab, looked up from sweeping the sidewalk to smile at me. Did I smile in return? Painless as a lover's swoon, I collapsed at her feet.

I had skillfully managed to faint dead away just a few yards from a hostel, and had been put to bed in a small, comfortable room. I slept through the rest of that day, the night, and until late the next afternoon. A young girl, with coppery blond hair, brought me a thick vegetable soup and hard white rolls. When I finished she brought me a second. That I could eat and talk seemed to amaze her. An Italian policeman came to check me over, and compare my face with the one in the passport. Alas, they no longer matched. This led to much laughter. Two older women were called in to discuss this problem, and one of them perceived the person behind the moustache. My moustache was stroked and pulled to verify it was real. There were no chairs in the room, so they all stood together, like people at a party, in a fever of delight, suspicion and disbelief. After my winter at Ranna, I felt right at home. Was there anything I wanted? I said I wanted to *dormire*. How it pleased them to understand me. To sleep, of course. I wanted to sleep. They left me in a hush of quiet, the room already darkening. My head was spinning with the flood of impressions, and the need to reflect on all that had happened, but the next thing I knew, light flooded the room, and I was awake. What I thought to be a brawl in an adjoining room proved to be two men greeting each other in the hall.

In one day's frenzied pedaling, most of it downhill, I had come almost two hundred kilometers. That seemed hardly possible, but I had done it. It helped to explain my swooning collapse. My motor had run out of fuel, and the machine had stopped.

I was in Italy, but the wind off the mountains, sweeping the plain toward the sea, made my ears buzz and tingle. The cold, sunless light was like the pallor of the natives. If I stopped in a square, for something to eat or drink, a pack of boys in knee britches soon surrounded me and my bike. They had never seen one like it. They had to toot the horn and work the gears. Most of them had the lean, black-haired good looks of the boys I had known at the Y in Chicago. It made me shiver to see their bare thin legs, their knees blue with cold.

With the wind at my back I made good time, but I was always getting lost. All the natives knew where they were going, and had no need of signs to tell them. Where the sea was up ahead, so close I could smell it, I stopped at an *albergo,* the space in front crowded with trucks and wagons. Inside, a lot of Italian men were eating and playing cards. I took a seat at one of the large tables, and had a meal of *polenta,* a warm slab of corn-meal mush, served without butter or syrup. I gulped it down, and drank a glass of red wine. I would have liked to sit there, absorbing the smoke and the racket, but I couldn't keep my eyes open. A little girl with long braids led me upstairs to a cell-like room, the opening at the top covered with chicken wire. When I sat on the bed to take off my shoes, my head thumped the wall. The sheets had been slept in, but not often. I could hear men coughing and snoring around me, and one who sang to himself, softly. Over and over he sang the same refrain until I fell asleep.

So close by I marveled that I hadn't heard it was the sea. There was no beach or waves to speak of, just rocks and a frothy, dirty foam, like dishwater. It was hard for me to believe this was Homer's wine-dark sea. It looked more impressive from the road approaching Trieste, cut into the sheer side of the cliff, with the sea breaking below it, but even that was nothing to compare with the cliffs at Big Sur, near Carmel, and the cypress and the sea at Point Lobos. What would the Greeks have done if they had had a coast like California?

In Trieste I went straight to American Express, where there was no mail for me, nor any message from my friend, so I came out to stand at the front with an American girl from Ann Arbor. *Tant pis,* she said to me. She was waiting for her mother to take her by car to Ljubljana. I had never heard of Ljubljana, or why a pretty girl would want to go there. If you're accustomed to a campus crowded with American girls, especially if it happens to be in California, there's so many of them you tend to forget that there is much special about them. I didn't even think to ask her her name. As she walked away it struck me—it didn't just occur to me, because I had read it somewhere—that having to settle on just one girl, considering all the girls there were, was really one hell of a problem. I only knew a dozen or so by their first names, and I was already perplexed.

As this girl walked away—she turned once to wave at me—I saw a big fellow in a rumpled blue serge suit, a beret on his head, riding toward me on a bike with the front wheel so warped it wobbled and rubbed on the fork. The seat of the bike was too low for his long legs, and riding it wasn't something that he was at ease with. One leg of his trousers was rolled up to the calf to keep it from dragging on the chain. Until he waved at me, and smiled, I didn't know it was Lorne.

I had my reservations, but I was so glad to see his big, friendly face that I went toward him and threw my arms around him. That surprised him, since we had never been close, but I'd already been six months in Europe and felt lonelier than he did. In the few years I had known him, he'd had the habit of running one hand through his hair as if he feared he might lose it, and it was already thinner than I remembered. I was so damn glad to see him I probably talked too much. It just hadn't occurred to me, until I saw him, a big American in a blue serge suit, riding a cheap Italian bike with the wheels warped, how different Italy would be without him. When he had a chance to say something, he said, "Well, I made it, but it wasn't easy." That was a pretty long speech for him, and it was one I liked.

It rained for three or four days, maybe longer. We found a warm place to sleep, with clean sheets, in a public hostel, a big whitewashed room, the beds against the walls. If we sat up in bed we faced the person in the bed across the room. There were seldom more than two or three of the beds occupied, besides our own. In the bed directly across from me, day and night, was Professor Gianelli, from Gorizia. I saw the name in a book he had loaned me, with pictures ridiculing Mussolini. Professor Gianelli came to Trieste to rest, and refresh his mind. He had brought with him a suitcase full of books, and a duffel bag of small oranges. Now and then I saw him munching a piece of bread, but he *lived* on oranges. Every time he peeled an orange the

214

sweet fragrance of the peel filled the room. He looked imposing in the bed, with his big, craggy head and topknot of white hair, but I never saw him standing up. He was a teacher all right, accustomed to lecturing, and gesticulated like an actor when he talked, the sleeves of his long yellow underwear pushed back on his bony, sallow arms. He read most of the night. If what he read got him excited, he would wake us up to talk about it. We understood little of his speech, but it was easy to guess at what he meant to say. He had this rage about Mussolini, but he would never actually mention his name. He would make a face, spreading his mouth wide with his fingers, or he would make the gesture of a knife slicing his throat, accompanied by a sound like a sheet tearing. The sound really disturbed me, like watching someone suck on a lemon.

Although he had come to Trieste to read and relax, having us to lecture to got him excited, and confused his plans. He read aloud to us the passage he might be reading, along with what he considered helpful comments. It worried me the way he heaped abuse on Il Duce, about whom I knew little or nothing, but the two other Italians, one with a kidney problem, listened with indifference or ignored him. One was a plump, moon-faced man who pressed his suit pants nightly under the mattress. That seemed to me very funny. Something that Chaplin or Keaton might do preparatory to spending the night in the gutter. He never said a word. He never looked to me to say anything.

One day we went to the city art museum, one of the places we could go to get out of the rain, where I saw a large mural-sized painting of young people listening to music in a darkened room. They were sprawled in chairs, or reclining on a couch, and one of them, a beautiful young woman, her head resting on her interlaced fingers, seemed to gaze from the painting directly into my eyes. Her auburn hair was worn in the style of the nineties, swept up from her ears and the nape of her neck, and I was filled with an aching longing to listen to the music she was hearing. Was it too late for me to learn to play the piano, the violin? What did riding a bike around in a freezing rain have to do with love, beauty and depth of feeling? As we left the museum I happened to notice the guard dozing at the door. He was the plump, moon-faced man who pressed his pants under the mattress, and the inaudible music I had found so moving had put him to sleep.

We had our big daily meal at a café frequented by laborers and miners. The miners sat together, wearing their hats with the lamps, the whites of their eyes shining in their soot-blackened faces. The woman who sliced the *polenta* did it with a piece of string tied to one finger of each hand. This cut it quicker and cleaner than a knife. Neither of us liked it too much, but it was filling.

One day one of the miners seated near our table spoke to me in English. Were we Americans? We were. While he ate, that seemed to satisfy his curiosity. Later I offered him a cigarette, which he inhaled deeply, closing his eyes. He liked American cigarettes. He had lived for several years in America. Where? I asked him. In Utah. He had worked in a silver mine in Utah. He liked American movies. He had gone to movies every Saturday night. He had been part of a crew to work in the mines, and then he had been shipped back to Trieste. He was not Italian. He was a Yugoslav. Nor did it please him to think I thought so. When I shook his hand to say goodbye, he said to me, "So long."

I hadn't troubled to study Italian, thinking I would pick it up, like lint, on my travels, but most of the time I talked English with Lorne, or German with the *Wandervögel* we met on the highway. We did learn to count, and keep track of money, and by pointing and mugging we did all right. Italians do that naturally, and just throw in the talk to be neighborly.

The first day the wind off the mountains let up, we took off for Venice. My winter at Schloss Ranna had prepared me for what I would find in Italy, lean and hungry children, people habituated to poverty. The slap of Lorne's warped wheel on the bike fork led me to ride on up ahead a ways so I wouldn't hear it. He also had a problem keeping up with me because his old bike was so hard to pedal, and the saddle too low. It turned out that the saddle was bolted to the frame, and not on a post that he could raise or lower. Did he look forward, I asked him, to a tour of Italy on an old tricycle? That night we had a talk, and I was able to persuade him to get a front wheel that wasn't warped. He did it for me. He didn't mind the slapping noise himself.

Most of the time we had the highway to ourselves. We would pick up some food in the market, then look for a place out of the wind to eat it. Cemeteries with a wall to get behind were good, especially if the sun happened to be shining. It had always seemed to me that English poets made a point of putting off dying until they were in Italy, but after checking several hundred gravestones I had to change my opinion. One of the kids who spoke to us mentioned the name of Primo Carnera. Some of the older ones knew the names of Italian baseball players, like Tony Lazzeri. These kids would fight among themselves as to where they would take us for a night's sleep.

In a town near Venice a man and his wife got out of a bed in

216

the front room so we could use it. The sheets were pretty soiled, so we slept in our clothes, stretched out on the top of it. The man's wife had a brother living in America. She brought in the neighbor's wife and her husband, along with several kids, to look at us. She kept repeating a word that I thought to be a person, but what she was saying was *Shik*-ago, for Chicago. That's where her brother was. Surely I must know him. Actually, I couldn't say for sure I didn't. I had come to know a lot of Italians. In the excitement of this occasion I left my wristwatch under the pillow (they unbuckle the watches while you're sleeping) and I had to pedal nine miles back for it. The signora had it strapped to her own wrist, which she explained was the safest place to keep it. One of her kids ran along beside me on the highway the way a stray dog will when you get a bit too friendly.

Approaching Venice, we met three husky *Wandervögel,* in shiny lederhosen, rucksacks on their backs, who had been to Sicily. They were on their way to Dubrovnik, wherever that was. From them we learned of student hostels in Rome and Naples, and I received my first offer for my English bike. The great thing about meeting up with Germans was to say *Auf Wiedersehen* like we meant it when we parted.

Nothing had prepared me for Venice.

It was gray and cold, the chill of winter trapped in the alleys, the people small and pinch-faced, the peddlers sly and greedy, the assorted smells (except for espresso!) nauseating, the slap-slap of the refuse-littered gray-green water smelling the way Mann had described it in *Death in Venice,* but even more than Ranna, it was out of this world, an ancient rotting city flooded by the sea. Small boys hooted and kicked soccer balls in the *campos.* At one point we were followed by an old man with small cages of chirping wild birds on his back. I sometimes wanted to leave, but we were lost, until a boy led us by the hand into the Piazza San Marco. Clouds of pigeons swirled around us, like schools of flying fish. There was surely music, but I didn't hear it. Throngs of people moved about, some of them feeding the pigeons that hovered in a blur above their heads. Bells rang. We sat at the base of a monument, facing the bay, where a white ship passed by, like a scene in a painting, and I was out of this world without a clue to which world I was in.

In a café with laborers who looked like statuary, their hands and faces white with marble dust, I saw a man crouched at the canal, water lapping his feet, rinsing in the filthy water a strip of soiled cloth that he then wrapped around his forehead, covering his swollen eye. With his good eye he studied me with indifference. A frail sallow boy, with large sad eyes, like those I had seen among the children at Ranna, led us to where we found a small clean bed, and shared our body heat. I have no memory of beauty. My jumbled impressions mingled the sordid, the earthly, and the unearthly, in a way that exceeded my understanding. We didn't talk about it. In the morning we were relieved to pick up our bikes and get away from the water. We both had new bites that began to itch when we worked up a sweat.

On clear windless days, one of them a Sunday, we crossed the Po valley from Padova to Bologna. The afternoon sun tanned our faces. Three or four times a day we met up with *Wandervögel,* and I talked more German than I had in Vienna. There was snow on the mountains between us and Florence, with strong, cold winds. Down in the valley the spring sun had warmed us, but we almost froze in the mountains. Near the summit—we saw the light, like a beacon, as we pushed our bikes up the grade—we found this smart café, with booths to sit in and a counter, rows of fluorescent lights in the ceiling, behind the counter the biggest electric Frigidaire I had ever seen. Just the summer before, it had arrived from Newark. The owner's two sons had brought it from Genoa on a truck. The owner and his beaming wife had daughters in Trenton, and had pictures of their grandchildren framed on the wall. Because we were American, accustomed to refrigerators, they showed us the gleaming, empty compartments. In the summer, when it was hotter, they hoped to find more use for it. The wife made us sandwiches of salami we could eat on the road. There were so many Italians in America, as I knew from personal experience, it seemed hard to account for the number that remained in Italy.

Flying down the mountains toward Florence I got so far ahead of Lorne that when I looked back for him he was gone. Nor did he show up when I stopped and waited. I had to go back up the mountain before I found him plodding along, pushing his wreck of a bike. He had blown a tire. Actually, we saw more that way, walking along together, the rocky slopes around us turning green with spring, but after a few hours of it I suggested he take off the tire and ride on the rim, since the wheel was no good in the first place. If I was in such a hurry, he said, why didn't I ride on ahead and wait for him in Florence. He rather liked walking, and if he could do without pushing a bike he might prefer it. The *Wandervögel* were free to walk, or to stop and loaf, and they were never worried about a fancy bicycle. That was a dig at me, and I answered him back, I probably hollered at him, because I knew that he was right. My bike was great to ride but it was a damn nuisance every time we stopped and I had to leave it for three or four minutes. The kids would steal the horn, the tools, the tire caps.

218

I had to keep it right beside the bed in the room we slept in. I envied the *Wandervögel,* just as Lorne did, having all their gear in a rucksack, with a bedroll on their backs.

Lorne didn't say much at all, just stood there with his flat-tired bike, gripping the handlebars with his blue hands and chapped knuckles—we both had cracked lips, windburned eyes and peeling noses—but almost all of what I said I remembered, including some comments about anybody who would come to Italy in a blue serge suit. It pretty well ruined Florence for both of us. We found a place for the night—the kids were fighting over us—just down the street from the Uffizi Gallery, but when we got up to leave in the morning the Italian wouldn't let us have our bikes. He claimed we owed him money for bike storage. He was a thick, paunchy fellow, with a bellowing voice that led people to stop in the street and stare at us. He had our bikes in the hallway, off the street, and stood in front of us blocking the door. I was all for paying him, before we got into worse trouble. As usual, Lorne said nothing. He just stepped forward and jerked the fellow's coat off his shoulders, so that it pinned his arms to his sides, then lifted him like a fat kid and signaled to me to push out our bikes, which I did. When Lorne set him down, the paunchy fellow was speechless. My big, gentle, inarticulate companion hitched his pants up a bit, the way they do it in the movies, then we walked away and left them all staring at us. We could hear the fellow shouting, but nothing happened. What it meant was that we missed seeing the Uffizi, Ghiberti's doors, and Michelangelo's David, but it sure cleared the air between us. Lorne wanted to see the Leaning Tower of Pisa, so that was where we went next.

I took some snapshots of the tower, with Lorne beside it, and he took several shots of me, standing with my bike, all of which were still in the camera when we headed south for Livorno. My idea was that we would take it nice and easy, enjoying the scenery, as I had done it the year before hiking around Carmel. I had gone along with a college friend who was crazy about Robinson Jeffers, and we spent a night on the driftwood-strewn beach where we could feel the breakers pounding. I didn't sleep a wink. The beach shuddered as it did in an earth tremor. But there was nothing much to see south of Livorno, no thundering breakers, great white beaches, or sheer cliffs rising from the sea, just this big gray expanse of water and a wind that blew in our faces. You would have thought a wind coming off the Mediterranean would have been a sort of mild one, if not warm, with pauses you could blink your eyes and breathe in. This wind was so cold it made our heads and ears ache. If I opened my mouth to speak it made a hollow sound, like a bottle. To speak to each other we had to stop and turn our backs to the wind. If Italian grass along the road was greener, if the sea and the sky were bluer, if the air was softer and sweeter than it was elsewhere, we were too cold to feel it or to give a damn about it. The big trucks went by with a whoosh that sucked at us. There was no place to hide or get away from it, and if I covered my ears I could hear them buzzing.

Then I got this idea watching several of the trucks come to a halt at a railroad crossing. If we were quick, before they picked up speed, we might come up behind them and grab on to something. Why not? I had often done it in the past. It was not even easy for me to explain it, the way the wind whipped my hair. I could tell, the way Lorne licked his chapped lips, he was not so keen on it. He had a new front tire, but an old bike, and we could see that the road was full of potholes. What if we hit one at about fifty miles an hour?

I was so cold and fed up I said he could do as he pleased, but I was going to give it a try. When a big truck slowed for the tracks, I took off after it, and found a posthole I could grab. When I glanced back and saw Lorne, I never thought he would make it, with his old bike, but he hung in there with his head down, pumping like a fool, and somehow he managed. It was such a great relief to be rolling along out of the wind, the landscape streaming along beside us, we hooted and yelled like kids. On the long slow upgrades we could relax a little, but on the downgrades it was scary. We couldn't see a foot ahead. The road itself was a blur. What I hadn't figured on was that I couldn't release the grip I had on the truck and use the hand that was gripping the handlebar. Both my hands were blue with cold and numb. If I let go for a split second, and the side wind caught me, it would whip me around like a piece of paper. I had been scared before, but never with so much reason to be scared, and for so long. Lorne hung on with his head down, his teeth clenched. I finally let go near the top of a grade at what proved to be a lull in the wind. Lorne did the same a moment later, and we just let our bikes coast until they came to a stop. Our teeth chattered, and our limbs trembled. We were both too relieved to speak. I think my relief was greater, and took longer to sink in, since it had been my impulsive idea, and it shamed me to think that it might have cost my friend his life. We both knew that. We just stood there straddling our bikes, gazing out to sea. The sun was almost setting, there were breaks in the clouds, and we could see this island off the coast to the south. It looked very beautiful at that distance, and just seeing it there calmed us. The wind had let up somewhat, and we watched a farmer, on the slope below us, exercising a big dappled stallion in the farmyard. In the dusky, slanting light we could see clearly why the horse seemed so agitated. A long, black, pendulous penis, like the tongue of a wagon, wagged about beneath him. Now and then on the wind we could hear his neigh, and the thud of his hooves. One of the farmer's sons helped his father hold the rope, and the horse cantered about them in a widening circle, tossing his mane. Behind them, dramatic as a painting, the island was silhouetted against the sunset. Just as I had felt at Ranna, seeing the luminous bodies of the oxen in the dark, odorous stable, their great unblinking eyes staring at me, the scene was like a slotted window on a world that had vanished. A veil had been lifted, and for a moment I saw it just as it had been, with the gods watching, prepared to take sides if people, predictably, screwed things up.

In Grosseto we carried our bikes up three flights of stairs on the heels of a panting signora. She led us to an attic hung with drying laundry, a mattress on the floor to sleep on. The air was warm, antiseptic with the smell of strong soap. A small boy brought us plates of *al dente* spaghetti and a half a liter of wine in a raffia bottle. The wine burned our tongues and our raw chapped lips.

In the morning the wind was still blowing, and we walked with our heads down, not speaking, sometimes lying out of the wind in the ditches. In the late afternoon we came out on a rise with a view of the sea. Army trucks were parked in front of a large *albergo,* where we could hear music playing. On a promontory just off the coast there were gray-walled buildings that looked like fortifications. How did the wind blow so hard, I wondered, and not stir up waves?

Though it was still daylight, we were so cold and tired we went to bed, not troubling to eat. For the first time we had a double bed long enough for Lorne to stretch out in. Food smells and the clatter of dishes came through the open transom. I thought the pounding on the door that woke me up was made by someone the following morning. I asked what they wanted, but got no answer. In his sweater and underwear, Lorne went to the door, opened out on a figure holding a lantern. By its light I could see a company of soldiers wearing hats with plumes, like Cyrano de Bergerac, and broad leather belts with swords in the scabbards. Their eyes were big in the light. Two of them were so startled by the sight of Lorne they almost toppled over backward. They all looked younger than we were, like boys in an opera, picked for how they would look in the costumes. One of them managed to remove a pistol from a holster and point it in our direction, shouting. Lorne closed the door. We listened to a great hubbub in the hall, and after a moment more pounding on the door, but not so loud. Lorne opened the door on the *albergo* proprietor. Behind him, forming a line on the stairs, we could see the plumed hats of the soldiers. In a friendly manner, with many gestures, the proprietor explained that the soldiers had come for us. Why? He rolled his eyes upward. We dressed, watched by the eyes at the door, then we were escorted down the stairs and out of the building, and put into one of the army trucks, covered with a tarpaulin. Fifteen or twenty soldiers climbed in with us, their scabbards rattling. A cold wind was still blowing off the sea, and we could see lights in the fortifications. There was no talk.

We were driven a mile or so to a railroad crossing, then along the tracks to a depot. Along with the soldiers, we were unloaded into a small waiting room. There was a wood stove at the center, but no fire. The soldiers huddled together for warmth on the benches along the wall. Those near me were beardless, too young to shave. The light of a lantern, placed on the stove, cast the shadows of their hat plumes on the walls. The zippers of my jacket pockets impressed them. I could sense they were both curious and apprehensive. As time passed, a few of them slept, others cleared a space on the bench to play cards. Just before midnight, down the tracks to the north, we could hear a commotion and much shouting. Several soldiers with carbines came and stood before us. They had been awakened for this special duty, and although half asleep, tried to look determined. A few moments later a southbound express train roared through, filling the air with dust and rattling the windows. This clattering racket awakened the boys who had been sleeping, and in the silence that followed they were more relaxed.

Were we Germans? they asked.

No.

Were we then English? This seemed to exhaust their alternatives. What were we, then? I said Americans. They stared at us dumbfounded, wide-eyed, their jaws slack. We were the objects of jokes and much nervous guffawing. They took fire from each other quickly, but it did not last. I was familiar with these hoarse-voiced, dark-skinned boys who looked and sounded so much tougher than they actually were. Shortly after three o'clock a small car arrived with two men dressed as civilians, their hands thrust into the pockets of their long black coats. One of them, smiling and friendly, wore a derby.

"How it go, o-kay?" he said to me, pleased with himself.

Smiling and cheerful, like a helpful porter, he padlocked my left

222

wrist to Lorne's right one, then put us into the rear seat of the little car. The two of us filled it, and it tilted to the side Lorne sat on.

"*Bicicletta!*" I cried, suddenly remembering that we had left our bikes in the *albergo* lobby.

"Is nothing!" he said, putting one hand on my arm, and gave me the wink of an accomplice. His companion wore a black hat also, but with a rim that dipped to conceal his eyes. He smoked a cigar. Bouncing along in the car, the lights flickering up ahead, it occurred to me that we were having a bizarre adventure, one of those that we would long remember. For the first time I was wearing handcuffs! "Had run-in with the *Fascisti!*" I would write on the postcards showing the Leaning Tower of Pisa. The word for this sort of thing was *lark*. We were having a lark. I had not yet read the stories of Hemingway, so I did not recognize the characters. The smaller of the two officials intrigued me. He continued to smile in a knowing, appealing manner. Something between us. I would have time to think about what it might be. Up ahead of us, the car lights played on the walls of what I recognized to be a prison.

"Where are we?" I asked.

He replied, "Grosseto."

I had never before been in an actual prison, but I had seen a lot of movies. This one was large, and impressed me. Inside the walls, inside the main structure, tier on tier of barred cells, stairways and open walkways rose toward a dark ceiling, dim as a railroad station. Our steps echoed in the silence. We all walked the length of the building to a room lit up like a lavatory. A large unshaded bulb hung on a cord from the ceiling. The man who sat at the desk, his face puffy with sleep, had just been awakened. He wore a green visor to keep the glare out of his eyes.

This glare made it hard to see the faces around us but easy to see what we took from our pockets. Our rucksacks were also emptied, the contents spread out on a large table. Our passports brought on fits of laughter. My camera was admired. With sober mockery the prison official asked me what it was I had inside it. Pictures, I replied. Of what? He ordered me to open it up so he could see them. When I refused, he opened it up himself, exposed the film to the light. He saw nothing. Did I mean to try to make a fool of him? All of the packs of film I had shot since leaving Ranna he opened and exposed in the same manner. Then he rolled each film up as he had found it, and carefully returned them to their cartons. His eyes twinkled with humor. This was a well-rehearsed joke.

When our pockets were emptied, and the contents noted, we were ordered to remove all our clothes but our socks. All three examined our bodies. We were ordered to stoop and spread our buttocks. Their pleasure in this was too intense for laughter or bantering talk. When they had looked their fill, we were given blankets and a guard marched us back down the hall. I was taken up a spiral stairway to a second tier, put into a cell with a heavy, solid door, a small trap at its center. No bars. I heard nothing through the walls. The bed was a slab that lowered from the wall on chains. What I remember is the graffiti on the brownish-green wall that I faced in the morning, the words "Il Duce" being the most recent, with appropriate illustrations. Some of the names were familiar from my years at Larrabee Y, and to them I added, with my thumbnail, my own.

Food came in through the small trap in the door, the way a baker puts loaves into an oven. With the bowl of minestrone, which I thought good, I received a wooden spoon shaped by use into a crescent. I was open to such impressions, and I was impressed. Such details were better than I had hoped for. Later that day my clothes were returned to me in a basket, but all of the pockets were empty. With my clothes back on, I began to scratch new bites.

High in the back wall a slotted open window let in a cold gray light, and occasionally I heard the wings of a bird flapping. Later, after the creaking of several doors, I stood in line with about a dozen others as we walked single file from the great hall into a small court with high walls. The armed guards on the wall did not look aggressive. First we slowly walked in a circle from left to right, then right to left, and so on. I had seen it all pictured in a Van Gogh painting, and now I could vouch for its accuracy. Nobody spoke. We were a strange and shabby lot, more like bums and hoboes than criminals. If I looked stranger to them than they did to me—and I am certain that I did— they did not let on. We could hear the scrape of other marchers in an adjoining court. At a distance I could hear the clopping of a horse, and farther still, the whistle of a locomotive. On our way back to our cells we passed a group coming out, and one of them was Lorne. He blended in so well with the others, in his rumpled blue serge, I almost overlooked him. To that extent he made a better prisoner than I did, and aroused in me a pang of envy. The guard on my tier of cells, a small, elderly man, with a cap too large for his head, was the image of the one I had seen in the apéritif ads in the Paris Métro. As he pushed my food through the trap he would say, "O-kay, *sì*?" and I would reply, "O-kay."

During the day my sense of personal outrage, seldom exercised, gave way to reflections on the nature of my experience. This in turn, during the long, itchy night, gave way to a rising sense of apprehension. Who knew we were here? It might be weeks or months before anyone we knew would have reason to miss us. Under the name I had scratched on the wall I recorded my captivity.

On the third or fourth morning I was led from the cell to the office of the prison director. A heavy, bald, moon-faced man, he wore the soiled coat of his uniform unbuttoned. He looked at me, from behind his desk, with what I felt to be almost fatherly sorrow. Where had I gone wrong? We did not prove to have much of a language problem. He made faces and gestures. I made drawings on the sketch pad he had found in my rucksack. They were not good, but they were explicit. Was I than an artist? I saw that I was. What else had brought me to Italy, the home and the mother of art? Michelangelo, da Vinci, Raphael, Brunelleschi—not for nothing had I read *Art Through the Ages* and filled notebooks with reproductions mounted on three colors of paper. For him, I made a sketch of my cell, with the occupant huddled in a soiled blanket, a bird perched in the slotted window. He looked at me as Raphael's cherubs looked at the Virgin Mary. He looked, but at the time that seemed to be all. Led back to my cell, I felt that the wheels of justice might be turning but were somewhat creaky with long disuse.

The following morning actual shouts penetrated my cell. Was it a prison riot? A protest for justice? Some time later a guard came for me, and from the walkway on the second tier, I saw a stocky man standing in the lower hall, his arms crossed on his chest, like Mussolini. His clothes were well pressed, and he wore a gray, rolled-rim fedora. As I reached the ground floor, and walked toward him, he threw up his arms, cried out as if wounded, and came on the double toward me. Midway in the great hall we met and embraced, then drew back for a fresh encounter. It was clear that he knew me. His dark eyes flashed. His unshaven face was radiant with recognition. The guard escorted us to the prison office, where my new friend pounded on the desk and shouted. Lorne was brought in, and he was loaned a comb to untangle his hair. He was somewhat befuddled, but not resentful. Our belongings were returned, including our money, minus a deduction for the meals we were served. A pay-as-you-stay prison? Did it mean freedom if you ran out of money? We were both embraced by the prison director, to whom I gave the sketches, and signed them. Our benefactor, whose name still escapes me, led us out of the prison to a horse-drawn two-wheel cab, the one seat tight for the three of us. Slowly we clopped through Grosseto, dismally dreary in the drizzle, to where we were greeted and embraced by two short, substantial women. From among the many photographs on a sideboard our friend selected a snapshot, showed it to me. There I stood, both taller and paler than the dark-skinned boys on each side of me. I knew them well! Sammy and Vito LaMonica. That summer at the Y camp on Lake Hastings, both boys had come down with a bad case of ringworm. These two boys were the grandchildren of the beaming, elated man at my side. Once more we embraced. Then we were seated at the table and encouraged to eat.

Later there were more pictures, but not of me. Sammy LaMonica was married, and stood at the door of a delicatessen. Vito LaMonica drove a pie truck and could be seen in his white uniform, beside it, the plum-colored birthmark dark on his face. I was given his address on Sedgewick Street in Chicago and told to tell him to be sure to write more often. We were then driven back to the Grosseto depot, and put on a train that would stop at Orbetello. Mr. LaMonica trotted along the station platform, waving to us.

On the train to Orbetello, Lorne and I had a chance to discuss all that had recently happened, but we didn't. Not a word about the comedy at the *albergo,* or the three days and nights in prison, or how Mr. LaMonica, of all people, ever got wind of our being there. How do you figure that? I think the problem was that too much had happened, and too fast. First we had the Orbetello business, with the army like one you would see in an opera, then to top it all off, something so unlikely that Lorne didn't know what to make of it. Anywhere else he would have thought it some sort of hoax. How in the world did two Italian kids in Chicago relate to somebody like me in Grosseto? Actually, it did make sense, it was all of a piece, but I knew better than to try to explain it to a person who had just left Orange County for the first time. The Y camp that summer had been a very good one, and Vito LaMonica had had a crush on me. He had forgotten all about the purple birthmark on his face, the envy he usually had for his good-looking brother. Who else would a kid like that write to but his grandfather in Grosseto, which was what he did, telling him what a wonderful person I was. The only strange thing about the whole business was that it had worked.

We found our *biciclettas* right where we had left them, but everything that could be unscrewed had vanished, including the chains. We were so grateful to find our bikes, however, that we didn't make a fuss about it. I did make it a point to ask why, in the first place, we had been arrested. I was dying to know. The proprietor was friendly but nervous. He made the usual jokes about the Italian army being a bit confused as to who they were fighting. His wife, however, a lean,

226

sinewy type of woman, crossed her bony arms on her flat front and assumed the posture of a monument tilted backward. There was no mistaking Il Duce. My professor friend in Trieste would have loved it. The great man himself, we learned from her, had been on the train that passed through at midnight on its way to Rome. And had I not myself been strolling around taking pictures? *Capisce?* she said.

"*Capito,*" I replied.

We could only push our bikes into the wind, or coast on them when we had a downgrade. A peasant with a wagon gave us a lift the last few miles into Civitavecchia. We got chains at a bike shop, but I found out too late, trying to pump up a grade, that the links were not right for the sprocket. The best way to enter Rome is not the way we did it, pushing one bike with a flat tire and one with a slipping chain, but with the road headed to the east, out of the face of the wind, we were able to walk along with sun in our faces or warm on our backs.

Even Lorne had heard that all roads lead to Rome, but we were so long in getting there he was sure we had taken the wrong one. We saw a lot of it trying to find the youth hostel run by the Catholics. In the Forum, green grass was growing among the ruins, and we took our shirts off and had our first sunbath. There was nobody around and we had it all to ourselves. Some of the paths were strewn with chips of marble that might have been left there by the Romans. They were all over the place, like gravel, part of a past that had not entirely vanished. I made a collection of them for my girl friend, but on reflection I put most of them back. I suspected she would think, if she didn't say, that some people were still looting Rome, like the Huns.

The padre who ran the youth hostel would have made a great YMCA secretary. He could not only speak every language you could think of, but he could listen to them all while he was talking. He wore a dark-brown monk's robe, with a cowl, his bare feet in open leather sandals. What struck me was how clean he kept his feet. Because we were Americans he made room for us, moving out a pair of Germans he knew to be loafers. Of the sixty or so *Wandervögel* on hand, about fifty were Germans, with the rest big English fellows, or Swedes. The English fellows had been in Greece over the winter, working on a dig on one of the islands. The Swedes had been to Corfu, Crete, Cairo and all over, but nobody would ever have known it. They didn't talk, but one of them made me a good offer for my bike.

Almost everybody we met had been to Sicily, Sardinia and Capri. Actually, I didn't see as much of Rome as I might have because I liked the life and talk at the hostel. From a Swiss, at a bargain, I bought a watch with a lot of dials on the face, with levers on the side to start and stop them. They told me anything I wanted to know but the right time. Along the Appian Way, between Rome and Naples, my Swiss watch stopped running, but when I gave it a shake and held it to my ear, the ticking I heard was like Antone's, his red lips parted as he gazed, entranced, at the face without hands.

Along the coast of Italy we looked hard for something that would compare with California, but until we came out on the Bay of Naples, neither of us had seen it. A drizzle and blowing mist veiled Capri, shot through with ribbons of rainbows, and trailing off to the south, like the smoke of a steamer, the feathery plume off Vesuvius. Naples itself was something else. Since I had lived in Chicago, I was not unprepared for how things look at a distance and then you saw them close up, but Lorne had seen no more of the slummy side of life than Main Street in Los Angeles.

We started along the waterfront, then just kept rising, pushing our bikes up the alleys with gutters at the center, with flocks of kids yelling and hooting around us, as well as a nanny goat with two young ones, until we came out on a road above the city where there were gardens and walled villas. We could see Pompeii clearly, or where it had been, and several big three-masted ships in the harbor, and on the hazy horizon the isle of Capri the way it would have looked in a Maxfield Parrish painting. Not really; it was more of a purple color, like a cluster of Concord grapes. The full roll of pictures I took at the time, and had developed in Paris (I didn't see them until five weeks later), I didn't think were mine because Capri wasn't even in them. Just the jumble of roofs on the slope below us, some of the boats in the bay, and our two bikes in the foreground. Everything but the bikes was overexposed.

From the pier where we took the boat to Capri the sea was like a big pond, with hardly a ripple on it. I had thought most of the passengers would be *Wandervögel*, but they appeared to be regular tourists or Italians. The boat itself was on the small side, like a lake steamer, with a canvas to cover the open passenger section. Having sailed from New York to Antwerp, and weathered a bad storm in the mid-Atlantic, I was amused to notice how quickly some of the passengers were queasy. It surprised me, as it did Lorne, how soon the open water got rough. We all sat on hard wooden benches, around a clearing where you could walk a few paces, or stand and talk. An elderly Englishman and his tall, thin wife stood up all the way, holding on to each other.

228

I've forgotten how long the trip was supposed to take—it might have been an hour, or less than an hour—but after ten or fifteen minutes both men and women were leaning over the rail, so sick they were gagging, or were sprawled out on the floor with their backs against a wall. There was no letup in the pitch and roll of the boat, or anybody to help the people who seemed to need it. Lorne crouched doubled over, his head in his hands, whooping up on the floor between his knees. I had a worse problem. I was sick but I couldn't whoop up. I tried to sit so I could keep my face in the breeze, where the sea spray would cool it, but the roll was so bad I couldn't. It went on forever. There was puke everywhere. Then it calmed as quickly as it had begun, and we were inside the Capri breakwater. A few of the Italians, as well as the Englishman and his wife, walked right off. Lorne and I just sat there, unable to move, as the sicker people were helped to the pier. Others managed to walk as far as the beach and sprawl in the sand. Which was what we did. It was not a clean beach, there were dead fish on it, and it was strewn with smelly seaweed and buzzing flies. We just lay there like bodies washed up in a wreck. I remember thinking I would live on the island before I would take such a boat back to Naples. If there's a comical side to the nausea of seasickness, it's in how quickly you recover once you're on terra firma. The town of Capri was right there on the cliff above us, and by the time we got there, a pretty good climb, Lorne was ready to eat more than he had whooped up. The last of the sunset was glowing on Naples, so beautiful I could only turn away from it, and we had to make a choice from among the pack of kids shouting their offers at us. We didn't see a *Wandervögel*. They were all back in Rome, living it up.

It had been my intention, since I left California, to present myself at Axel Munthe's villa, with the view of Naples pretty much as he had described it, but once we had found it, all I did was ask Lorne to take a picture of me standing below it. I had also meant to look in on Spengler, and I hadn't, and perhaps Jakob Wassermann, and I hadn't, and it was still my intention, if the occasion offered, to look in on one or two writers in Paris, but the awe and respect in which I held these figures always led me to ask what they would see in me. I was not yet a writer. I was hardly a reader. One of my teachers at college had actually known a writer who had sent him his novel, with his name written in it, and I had felt both privileged and honored to be shown that book, and turn its pages. My interest burned with a gem-like flame, but shed little light.

We spent a week on Capri, the April weather just the way it was in California, warm in the sun but almost frosty in the shade. We saw the cliffs on the backside of the island, where the swallows were as thick as clouds of gnats, and in the early evening, from the south tip of the island, we caught glimpses of Positano and Amalfi. I planned to come back and live here, like Axel Munthe. We both figured it could be done on about forty dollars a month.

We spent our nights in a big high-ceilinged room with about twenty beds, no windows, but just the two of us were usually in it. The woman who ran it said that business picked up later. The burros that pulled the two-wheeled carts up from the beach were hardly larger than dogs, and wore hats trimmed with flowers. On the slope behind Axel Munthe's villa we would sprawl and eat the food we had bought in the market, some bread, cheese and local fruit. I had read in Munthe's book that the Italians trap and eat the birds, which was why we heard so little birdsong.

If Capri lived up to our expectations we planned to go on to Sicily, but the spring-like weather, and a bad case of hives, had got me to thinking about Paris. The only way to get rid of bites and hives was a change of clothes and a change of diet. In the *pensione* where we were staying, the favorite dish was baby octopus. When I gave the soup a stir it moved as if it were alive. My friend Lorne didn't feel about Paris as I did; he had come to Europe to see Italy, and once he had seen it he would get on a boat and sail home.

I think I might have persuaded Lorne to go to Paris with me— my record as a persuader was a good one—but I wasn't sure that was what I wanted. I couldn't have asked for a nicer, more compliant companion, one who seldom took exception to my suggestions, but he was there from the time I woke up in the morning until I closed my eyes at night. He looked to me for what next. If I talked, which I did quite a bit, he moved his beret around on his head, or picked the lint off the sleeves of his coat. He was a real pal, and I would surely miss him, but some of it would be a relief. I would never meet a French girl, let alone a woman, walking around with Lorne like my bodyguard, and the only French I would speak would be to waiters and postal clerks. My girl spoke French, and sometimes put in her letters things I didn't understand.

Cycling back to Rome, we were caught in a downpour and soaked to the skin. The dye ran in the shoes I had bought in Krems and stained my feet the color of maraschino cherries. It changed my mind about cycling all over Europe. The rainy season might be ending in Italy, but it was just beginning in other places.

230

One of the young men I had met in the hostel in Rome was like my friend Karl in Vienna. There was something both aristocratic and military in his manner. He liked to practice his English with me, and talk about my bike. I let him ride it around a bit, to get the feel of it, and when he came up with eighty dollars American, I decided to sacrifice it. It's a relief to be free of something everybody else wants. The big thing was that without the bike I had no choice but to take the train. Lorne would feel a little less than he might have that I was running out on him. His boat sailed from Genoa, the last week in April, so he had a week or so of easy pedaling to get there, and a forty-dollar train ticket would take me up the Rhine as far as Cologne, then back to Paris. I still had, in a zippered pocket of my jacket, sixteen American Express ten-dollar traveler's checks, which would see me through the summer if I lived on about thirty-five dollars a month. I thought it a cinch. If there was one thing I had learned after seven months in Europe, it was how to live cheap—hadn't I?

The day before I left Lorne we sat up half the night talking with two Dutch boys from Amsterdam. They spoke excellent English but they were anxious to learn some American. The smaller, thinner one, who didn't talk so much, made me think of a boy I had tutored in Vienna, the way he read my lips as if to eat the words. He got so much more from language than I did it made me ashamed. They had come to Italy to be in Rome for Easter. The older boy was the first I had met to say to me there would soon be a war. When would that be, I asked him, so I could tell people, and he discussed it for several minutes with the younger one, in their own language, then he said to me, "After the Olympics," which I thought was a strange thing for him to say. That's too bad, I said, since I would miss it. We won't, said the younger one, and gave me his sweet, melancholy smile.

I was up and away early the following morning, Lorne walking with me to the railroad station, where we made plans to meet again in California, in October. I was clear to Milan, where I changed trains, before I noticed my watch was missing. In all the excitement of the night before, I had gone to sleep with it on my wrist, a sure way to lose it. I hated to lose that watch, since I had hoped to pawn it if I ran out of money in Paris, but it gave me a certain satisfaction to know the little thief who had swiped it. He could have done it earlier, but he wanted to be sure I was leaving Rome.

IN THE JUGEND HERBERGE, IN HEIDELBERG, I HAD a room of my own with a dormer window on the park, where blond children were playing. One blond child is not unusual, but a covey of them, blue-eyed, vivacious and sturdy, their chubby legs in half socks, their pink knees scuffed, seem to be a special breed of children. After the black heads and eyes, the gaunt and sallow faces, the blue knees and bony elbows I had seen in Italy, I looked at these *Kinder* with a curious longing. That love of the blond, the Nordic, felt by Tonio Kröger for Hans Hansen and Ingeborg Holm, of the dark for the light, for the outward and the open rather than the inward and the private, was paradoxically felt by the blond themselves in their yearning for the light and sun of Greece and the enchantment of Capri.

When Hans Castorp dozed off in the snow and blizzard in the Magic Mountain, and had his dream of unearthly beauty and serenity where the blue sea lapped the sun-kissed islands, I had cried out as he did, "Lovely! Lovely!" and I was horrified, as he was, at the dream's ghastly conclusion, and that for such a vision of human bliss one must pay in blood. I understood it, but I did not accept it. In California I had experienced such moments myself, and accepted them as part of human expectations. If something whispered to me that for such expectations we must all pay dearly, I was not persuaded. I had not been tutored in seduction by Wagner, and I knew little of subconscious Faustian bargains, and at the edges of a cliff, or a yawning abyss, I simply drew back. I was not lured to grow dizzy with intoxication and jump.

Yet at the open casement window in Heidelberg, along with the keen pleasures of expectation, I registered my first presentiments that something was rotten in this picture of perfection. Behind the light and the shadow, the trilling voices of the children, lurked a danger in which we were all complicit. Was it strange that I should feel this so intensely in Heidelberg?

It was heavenly weather. On the bridge over the Neckar I stood long and long, looking at the castle, my fancy on the Rhine Maidens in the mists behind it. On the posters in the streets of Heidelberg I read that Germany, too, had a depression. The faces of the unemployed stared at me from the billboards. Most of the young I saw in the streets, however, were dressed in some sort of uniform, and seemed buoyant and assured, striding about like *Wandervögel* into the future.

In a tobacco shop, which I entered to look at some pipes, I could see someone spying on me through a curtain. In the shopwoman's smiling, unctuous manner there was something both disturbing and false. I could hear muttered whisperings behind the curtain. My sense of apprehension was unused and rudimentary, since I had felt it so seldom, but in the eyes and furtive manner of this woman I felt, and shared, a nameless disquiet. Back in the sunlight I soon forgot it.

On the Rhine boat to Cologne, American girls crowded the deck, and even those in saddle shoes looked great. It pleased me, however, not to be mistaken for one of their kind. After my winter at Schloss Ranna, in the Wachau, the castles along the Rhine seemed to me like the ruins in romantic paintings. In Cologne, where it rained all day, I saw my first movie since *King Kong,* but I forget what it was.

On the night train to Paris I again shared the compartment with several peasant women, and my own reflection in the grime-smeared window. Once more in the dawn light I saw the greening fields of France with the big two-wheeled carts, drawn by oxen, just as I had seen them the first time, and as the train pulled into the Paris station I felt I was just arriving in Europe. I had the address of a man, known to a classmate, said to be living and writing in a garret, but now that I was actually in Paris this seemed to be remarkably pointless. I walked about the streets, buying food in the markets, since I still felt intimidated by the café waiters and the way they flicked their napkins at the seats of the chairs. In the Luxembourg Gardens I sagged to a bench facing the pond and the cries of the children. I was in Paris. The mauve twilight seemed to bathe me like music. Until I rose to my feet I had been unaware of the holes in my socks, and two broken blisters.

In a hotel near the Sorbonne an exception was made for the guest who would be staying for one night only. Two American girls playing Ping-Pong in the lobby woke me up. To stay clear of the one I could hear hooting, I got away from the Sorbonne, and the student crowd, and found a room behind the Cimetière Montparnasse near where the Rue de la Gaîté joined the Avenue du Maine. My room was on a turn of the stairs, where a lot of the tenants stopped to scratch matches. I had a window on the street, a chair to put my clothes on, a cot about four inches shorter than I was. The lavatory was up one flight of stairs and had the usual crouching arrangement. How do you explain the French coming up with something like that? It was not my idea of *le vie bohème,* but children crowded the street below my

233

window, and directly across the way, a tall, handsome black man lived with a short, dumpy white woman. I often heard them fighting but it was lost on me, since they did it in French.

I had hoped to find a room for four or five dollars a week, but the landlord was not a man to dicker. He wanted his rent in advance, and counted on his fingers to make sure I understood him. A thin, dour little man, he squinted from the smoke of his dangling cigarette. His gobbler's neck stuck out of his collarless shirt like those I had seen in Vienna, but he was the proud father of two enchanting little girls. They played jacks, skipped rope and shrieked like birds until they were bedded down at night. Their dark, gaunt, harrowed mother loved them so much she drove them crazy. At the door, from a window, from an upstairs room, she cried out threats, warnings and cautions. If there was a moment of silence in the street she would swoop down on them like a hawk. She dressed them like little dolls, with big bows in their hair, and seeing me at the window they would scream, "*Me voici! Me voici!*" and run about wildly.

In my boyhood I had often had the time, and the reason, to ponder the big maps on the walls of railroad stations. Maps were the canvas for my imagination. Both those that hung in railroad depots and those on the walls of schoolrooms would provide me with lifelong deceptions. What power is it that makes it possible to confuse a map with the actual, visible world?

I was living in Paris, and I had personal access to the labyrinth that spread and swirled around me, yet I would look for clues to all that escaped me in the big, maddening maps at the Métro stations. What did I hope to perceive? All that I saw was *under* the streets, not above them. As I stood there, daily pondering this puzzle, I was often suffused with the sweetly sorrowful ballads played by the musicians seated at the entrance. The wheezy, gasping accordion, the screechy violin, seemed designed to fully capture what I was feeling but escaped my observation: not the gaiety of Paris, which I found to be lacking, except in the shrill cries of the children, but the bittersweet, haunting melancholy that appealed to me profoundly. How could I explain that my buoyant optimism was so often at its ease in depressing surroundings? Before the palmy days of my years in California, *hard times* were those I understood to be normal. Indeed, what *other* times were there? Nor would I ever question that they were more real than soft times, morally superior, and the proper times for a youth to be raised in. In the spring of 1934, in Paris, I found myself in circumstances that were confining, but in times that suited my nature. Not miserable

234

times, nor pathetic times (they, too, were there, but concealed from me), but the times that pressed from my extravagant expectations a poignant, pensive anticipation of losses. Much of this far exceeded my experience, but it spoke profoundly to my nature. Among these sentiments, if not these people, I was at home.

The city flowed with a life beyond my comprehension, but there were moments, as I stood at an intersection, or peered down a boulevard to a swirling clot of traffic, when I would experience the city as a living body, an organism like myself, cunningly pursuing its own purpose. What provoked these moments of transport? The unavoidable, palpable presence of people. They lived everywhere. That seemed to me the secret of Paris. In the shop where I bought my sour cream in the morning, hardly larger than a closet, the clatter of knives and forks, the smell of food cooking, the squalling of infants, filled the air behind the shabby curtain. A large family, they ate in shifts. A more elegant lifestyle was surely lived elsewhere, by a lot of people, but this was one into which I intruded when I browsed, or shopped, or peered into a doorway. The city was one vast, labyrinthine dwelling, with an inhabitant in every niche of it. Voice shouted or murmured, heaps of rags blocking a doorway might be a body, involving me in the grubby life of the species. No notice was taken of me as a person. No one needed me as a person. I, too, learned to let the coins drop on the counter to reduce the counterfeits my eye was not trained for. The throng seemed and was hostile, but I was also supported by its bustling, indefatigable presence. The great sad city, in the hug of hard times, gave off its sorrow like an odorous exhalation. The seamy side of my life of great expectations found in Paris the matchless example of making do, of getting by, as a way of life. I had gotten by, to the spring of 1934, on the expedient but unexamined principle that the truly deserving would be rewarded. Surely, I was deserving. What else had brought me here, more buoyant than blighted, to this fateful season in the city of light? In every fiber of my optimism I was a deserving fool.

After all, there was nothing between me and Paris but myself. I knew nothing or nobody; nor did I know to what extent this might, or might not, be an advantage. In the presumptions of my optimism Voltaire might have found me an interesting study. I wandered about, loafed in the parks and gardens, sat gawking in cafés or reading newspapers, adding words to my unused vocabulary.

Every morning I bought sour cream, the color and texture of butter, which I spread on a slice of whole wheat bread with my all-purpose Swiss knife. From this food I would look forward to the bowl of borscht

I took at Dominique's in the evening, just off the Boulevard Raspail near the Dôme. I soon learned that the waiters were White Russians, refugees from the Revolution. They were big, jovial, imposing fellows, of the sort I had seen with the touring Cossacks. They had a flair for communications. We had a fluent and clear exchange of signs and mugging. A basket of rolls sat on the counter, into which I freely dipped my hand. I might eat four or five. My waiter, Ivan, usually put me down for two. The bowl of borscht was served with a scoop of sour cream that I would nurse through the meal like ice cream.

After this meal my feeling for Paris—a city the color of smeared newsprint, full of aging, faintly hostile people—changed from one of indignation, occasional resentment, to one of fraternal affection. Twice a week I would top it off with a café au lait at the Dôme.

Just down the street from the Dôme, on the Boulevard Raspail, was the American Club. I had discovered it by chance, seeing a young man seated in the high casement window on the street, reading. He proved to be from Waterloo, in Iowa, in the process of reading all of Balzac's novels in French. A solemn, very earnest young man, burdened with his reading and his future as a writer, he provided me with my first portrait of the artist as a young man. I liked him, but I felt his scorn for such idlers as myself. He earned a dollar a day, plus all the tea he wanted, by opening the club in the morning, serving the tea, and cleaning up after the dances. All bona fide Americans and other aliens, females preferred, were welcome at the club. The large, dark room was attractive, with the windows thrown open, and there was room for ten or twelve couples to dance to the music of a gramophone. Most of the records were battered, but the tunes were great. "Stardust" was there, sung by Bing Crosby, along with "Body and Soul" and "Ain't Misbehavin'," songs I had learned to play on the ukelele. My expertise on the gramophone was welcome, along with my selection of records. I introduced the Balboa, a California dance step the English girls found a bit confusing, but a doe-eyed, slender señorita from Madrid slipped into it like a stocking. There was no learning. She raised her arms and we danced. She favored wide-brimmed hats, long flowing scarves, and cloth gloves with a silken flesh-like texture. When we were better acquainted she would take them off when we held hands at the movies. French being the language we had in common, we both gave it considerable attention. No language is so marvelous to hear from the lips of a girl. Her idol was the dancer Argentina, with whom she had studied, but the shadow I often saw in her eyes was her coming marriage, in the late fall, to a businessman in Buenos Aires. She showed me his picture. He was

236

a nice-looking gray-haired old man, at least fifty. I was not a prospective suitor, but this blighted our hours together.

An English girl from Surrey, hair bobbed, neck shaved, erect, perky, stiff as a board and plainspoken, danced with me in the manner of a sturdy colleague supporting a weaker friend. The space between us we filled with conversation. She did not like to sit, and did most of her talking with her arms folded, while standing. She thought the French politically anemic and as we walked around Paris, we discussed what it would lead to. Her own life was pretty well settled, since she planned to breed and raise fox hounds in Surrey.

If I walked her to her pension, near the Étoile, it might be past midnight before we got there, and I would spend the rest of the night slowly making my way back to Montparnasse. Nothing could be more enchanting than Paris at dawn: absolutely silent, the light in the sky part of an awakening that came by inches, the Eiffel Tower the hub around which it wheeled, the street lamps perceptibly cooling to globes without shadows. The last mile or so I might be so tired I would sit on a bench at the Gare Montparnasse until the first café clattered open, then blow myself to a café noir and a croissant. By sleeping right through until about four o'clock, I saved more money than it had cost me.

Two blond sisters from Holland sometimes came to the club for the dances. One was on the plump side, but very good-looking. She usually referred to her sister as "fatty." This was just one of the many things that made her laugh. When she first set eyes on me, she laughed, and looked around for something to sit down on. Once something started her off, as I seemed to, she couldn't stop. Her big, broad face was usually flushed and perspiring, her frizzly hair stuffed into a hairnet. When she was seated on a bench, her feet were inches short of the walk. I would usually give her a hand to hoist her, and this would set off a fit of laughter. Everything we saw was either mildly funny or hilarious, and if we went to a movie at the Cinéma Montparnasse we might have to leave to avoid a disturbance. Once started, it always ended up with her chewing on her hairnet, her eyes full of tears.

We got along so well together I thought of renting the room on the floor above me, with a double bed and a carpet, but she couldn't bear the idea of my seeing her without her corset. Details of that sort had not crossed my mind. Once it had crossed, and recrossed, several times, it was hard to dislodge. When the humor of it had finally dissipated there was nothing much between us but a bulging figure dimly seen through a screen of curtains. It wasn't funny at all. Perhaps she learned from me that no matter how she looked, it was something she should let a boy judge for himself, especially if he was Dutch.

Tea was poured at the club by Madame Champfleur, a handsome, formidable woman, who preferred to sit back in the room's shadows, as if the light from the windows might fade her. She wore black, except for two long strands of pearls. A wide-brimmed crownless hat, worn low on her forehead, allowed only occasional glimpses of her eyes in the powdered mask of her face. Large bruises of rouge stained her cheeks. Rather than the wide mouth of most Parisian women, painted over the pleats of their lips, Madame Champfleur had no more than a slit through which she sipped her tea. Her voice was husky. Cigarettes had given her a throaty cough. Two or three minutes of real French conversation could be bought with an offer of an American cigarette. She had known Rodin, and could speak personally of his scandalous behavior with his models. To catch the glance of her eyes, as I sometimes did, through the shafts of light from the windows gave me the ponderable sensation of being seen and judged by a woman, rather than being looked at by a girl. Both her chin and her nose were those of an admiral, but my untrained imagination often applied itself to the miracle of her morning toilette. Each day a face to be painted, then the long teetering walk, her cloak held close to her body, as if the eyes of the world were upon her, enduring the gauntlet of the sidewalk cafés to the corner of Montparnasse and Raspail. There, if held by the light, she would pivot slowly to gaze about her at the canaille.

I twice visited her apartment, a room her sister would depart on my arrival so there would be a chair for me to sit on. A mistake. My sympathy for the underdog did not include a woman whose grand illusions were what I admired, and was eager to support. The air reeked of soiled garments, cheap perfume, and canned food heated on hot plates. It shamed me to share this with her. I did learn that her remarkable and singular appearance was of Scottish origin, and when she referred to dastardly events of the past she had in mind the Huguenot wars. Intricate and cunning passages of French culture had made her, to my mind, one of its ornaments.

Before I had ever looked on the ground glass of a camera, the windows of Venice and Paris had framed views that seemed part of my life, before they were part of my experience. They alerted me to the needs of my nature. People about whom I knew nothing, who were strangers to me, like the marching figures in the blind Garten, prefigured what I would look for and find corroborated in what I would come to imagine.

In the street below there is the following group: a small, double wheelbarrow pushed by a woman; lengthwise across the front of it, a hand-organ; across it at the back, a basket in which a quiet young child is standing on firm legs, happy beneath its cap, not wanting to be made to sit. From time to time the woman turns the handle of the organ. Then the child immediately gets up again, stamping in its basket, while a little girl in a green Sunday dress dances and beats a tambourine uplifted towards the windows.

I did not read this passage from Rilke's *The Notebooks of Malte Laurids Brigge* until ten years later. How could another pair of eyes see so clearly what I saw at the back of my own? In the old world I perceived, through the veil of my expectations, realities that predated American experience, but this did not explain my growing preference for the losses. The child happy in its cap, the girl in her Sunday dress, a tambourine uplifted toward the windows.

Twice a week I would take the long walk from the Boulevard Montparnasse to the Avenue de l'Opéra, and ask for my mail at American Express. I usually crossed the Pont Neuf, fronting Notre Dame, loafed my way through the Tuileries, then savored the *haute monde* of the shops along the avenue. My girl was a good writer of letters. They were seldom less than three or four pages, and sometimes thickened to ten or twelve, written on both sides, and not always numbered. Her very personal "hand," a horizontal line like that of ripples on the surface of water, with an occasional loop or splatter, had the fluency of her voice and style, but the gist of the matter escaped me. What *was* she saying? Having the time, and the interest, I gave it much thought.

She was majoring in French, and full of her subject. Did she, when she mentioned Versailles, urge me to go there or not to bother? To be sure and read Saint-Simon, or forget him? I was not a good tourist. I had only twice been to the Louvre. Mona Lisa's enigmatic smile put me very much in mind of Mizi, with her oval eyes and pale, suds-laced arms. In my own, briefer letters I had touched on a new book, recently published, *Les Célibataires,* by Henri de Montherlant. I hadn't bought it, but somehow I had read it. This story of two old men involved me in a way that many stories of young men failed to. In the constrained, monotonous pattern of their lives—which I perceived and sensed in the streets around me—I shared a truth about people, and my own nature, that transcended differences of culture. This painfully obvious observation, in applying to me, personally, seemed a fresh

239

one. My father, my relations, the few older men who had figured, briefly, in my transient life, had left on me impressions that I had hardly been aware of. Was this peculiar to France, to the French language, to the book I happened to be reading? I was aware that a writer had revealed to me much I had overlooked within myself. How was that done? My impressions were blurred, but my inadequate French may have enhanced the images of my imagination. I carried Montherlant's novel about with me. I read certain passages over and over. In the complex craft of writing I sensed that the art of it combined what was new with what was old. What was new would prove to be in the writer, and the writing.

At the club I heard the name of Céline mentioned as the author of *Voyage au bout de la nuit*. I was captivated by the haunting title. I also understood that much of it was an argot impenetrable to foreigners. There were other appealing inducements.

On the Right Bank, on a street of bookstores, I found a mint copy of the novel on one of the tables at the front. The price was the cost of four or five days in Paris. I hovered about the table in a quandary. The uncut pages of the book inflamed my desire for it. Stealthily, with what little cunning I had, I slipped the book into my unbuttoned shirt-front. Before I could button up, before I had moved from the spot, a figure swooped from the interior of the shop to seize me, expertly, by the collar and seat of my pants—as I had so often seen it done in the comics—and projected me, hardly touching the floor, through the shop to an office at the back.

So I had made a mistake.

My twisted arm held firmly at my back, the proprietor emptied my pockets, then put through a call to the police. A short, bullheaded man, his sleeves rolled on powerful arms, a film of perspiration on his fleshy face, he barked questions at me I did not understand. My money was on the table, but what he wanted was the thief. The pleasure that it gave him to catch me competed with his hatred for me. He panted with his excitement when he found and flicked through my passport. An *Américain!* That pleased him. The two gendarmes who appeared also searched me, and my trousers were lowered to look for books in my crotch. They then walked me, my shoulders hoisted to my ears, along the crowded boulevard to an alley, up narrow stairs to an office. A little fellow with bright, darting eyes at behind a large desk. He spoke sharply to the gendarmes, and they left. Courteously, with a smile, he asked me to be seated. We considered each other— or rather he considered me, his face veiled by the smoke of his cigarette.

He seemed amused and delighted. Not every day did they bring him one like me. I remembered the plainclothes pair in Orbetello, who had also been elated by their unusual catch. So what was it I had stolen? A book. And what was the book? I told him. If I had confessed my love for France, for law and order, for the police, I could not have delighted him more. He gazed at me with appreciation. The edge of his scrutiny sharpened. Was I then a student of literature? I was. He paused to offer me a Gauloise, and light it. We smoked for a moment in silence. Did I then—he asked me—plan to be a writer? Oh fateful question! Did I? Had I waited to be asked? Montherlant's novel had aroused in me not merely the heightened pleasure of reading, of self-recognition, but the latent stirrings to be writing, to be that curious conjuror, a writer. Did he perceive in my flushed, perspiring face the lineaments of this recognition?

Briefly, we discussed books. I mentioned Gide and Henri de Montherlant. He made note of *Les Célibataires* on his pad. He then brusquely dropped his role as a man of letters and examined my passport, asked my residence, and inquired into my financial situation, facts I had been keeping from myself. He jotted this information into a ledger while I gazed at the sky through his window. It had begun to drizzle. I did not like rain, but the Paris drizzle seemed to me the most appropriate of its moods. I thought it gave a touch of welcome pathos to my foolish predicament.

He advised me to report back to him, within a month, with evidence that I was self-supporting. Some things that he said I did not understand, but I was reluctant to admit it. I very much appreciated his admiration. But now that he saw me for what I was, for what *we* thought I was, he also lost interest. Another culprit was brought in, with a bruised and bloody face, and I was led to the foot of the alley, and left there. I could have hooted with relief when I walked in the street. The book I had failed to swipe would have instructed me in the risks that are run in small offenses, and in the days left to me in Paris I spent a lot of time glancing behind me. I was on *parole,* one of the words I had clearly understood.

A young man I might have spoken to but had avoided was an English chap from Tangiers. He was about my age, but more experienced. Not one of the big, handsome fellows, pillars of empire, but a short one with a savoir faire I admired. He courted several women. He dressed very smartly in tweeds and sweaters. He played a lot of Ping-Pong with some of his friends, but I was the one he was anxious to beat. He got one of his flunkies to proposition me with a deal I couldn't turn down. He gave me odds of five to one on every point. My big mistake was in settling for a franc a point. If I had had his nerve I would have made forty or fifty francs every time we played. He wasn't a really good player, but he took all the chances, as if he didn't give a damn about winning or losing. Two or three of his flunkies ran around chasing the balls he slammed. We both soon tired of playing Ping-Pong, and spent the evenings in his apartment listening to records. He had American jazz, American novels, and three or four bottles of American whiskey he served with seltzer from a siphon bottle. We had some long, frank talks, especially about women, and what he liked about me was that I was a loner. I didn't live with a woman, mix with a group or run around licking asses. That was what he said. If that was what it was to be a loner, I qualified. Most of his flunky friends were not loners, but a pretty sad bunch of hangers-on, who thought driving around in a Packard with its top down, the horn honking, was really hot stuff. They did a lot of that on Saturday and Sunday nights. Sometimes we all went for a ride out to the Bois de Boulogne, where we played catch with an indoor ball, and batted flies. They really weren't obnoxious, individually, but they acted like fools when they got together. My Tangiers friend said that I should put all of us into a book.

He didn't brag, to speak of. He would just let it drop that he had been on safari. One thing he did tell me about at length was the time he had come down, in the bush, with dysentery. Unable to go to the bathroom, like a normal person, he had to put long hairs in the food he ate so it could be pulled out of him, if necessary. I had never heard of anything like that, nor had he.

One evening my friend, seated back under the awning, yahooed at me as I was passing the Dôme. He was there with two girls, both of them good-looking, one of them the blond sister of my laughing Dutch girl. She was one of those big, handsome types who like to wear a fur piece in the summer. The other one was German, with a dark, creamy complexion, like Mizi. When I arrived they were in a big discussion about the coming war. Both girls believed it would be better if the French didn't fight the Germans, as they did the first time, but just let them run the government since they seemed to be so good at it. Why blow up everything, and kill so many people, if all they wanted to do was have parades and play big shots? My English friend said that it would never work because men loved war, and down deep, women loved warriors. I was startled to be part of such a crazy discussion over something they expected to happen. In their excited, animated faces, I sensed that anything would prove

242

to be acceptable if we knew it would end up as talk. Talk was what it was all about.

When we had the war settled, my friend led me to the men's room, where he groomed his hair with small hairbrushes he carried in his pocket. What he wanted to do was ask me a little favor. You name it, said I. He happened to have a little conflict in his appointments, and found himself with these two great dolls in one evening. Would I be good enough to take the blond off his hands? He could see, he said, that she had high respect for my kind of brains. He peeled off several bills from the wad in his pocket, and mentioned the sort of places where she liked to eat. I said I would do him the favor. We came back to the table, where we sat for twenty minutes while the girls went below and tidied up. I couldn't see this blond, who had ignored me for months, agreeing to take a back seat to this classy brunette, but she seemed to welcome the change. My friend also threw in a pack of Player's cigarettes, since that was what she smoked.

I didn't want to start off blowing money on a taxi, so we strolled down Montparnasse, through the Luxembourg Gardens, then out onto the Boul Mich and the Boulevard St. Germain. We stopped for an apéritif at the Deux Magots, where a different sort of crowd was passing, and after a bit of the usual chitchat she asked me what it was I was writing. I said I was doing more reading than writing, but that I did make a few notes. My friend had let it drop that I was an American writer with connections with the *Atlantic* and some other magazines. She knew a painter or two back in Holland, but she didn't know many American writers. We had another apéritif and she confessed that she had missed the real bohemian side of Paris because her friend always took her to the fancy restaurants. She saw that as a difference between Americans and Englishmen.

At one point I thought we might go to Dominique's, where I had heard violins playing in the basements, but on second thought, liking a change myself, I took her to a café near the Pont Neuf, with a view of Notre Dame. When she excused herself to go to the ladies' room, to be on the safe side I checked to see how much money he had given me. Almost four hundred francs. A big Dutch girl, not as yet corrupted by the idea of a light, nonfat diet, she was still at it late in the evening, one of her real passions being the cheese tray. Early on, the wine had loosened my tongue, and I revealed my life in a Fascist prison. She urged me, she beseeched me—between the distractions of the cheese tray—to write a book. On a piece of paper torn from her list of phone numbers she wrote her name and address in Holland, where I would send the volume the moment it was published. We had been sitting so long it was her idea that we should walk. Her pension was on the Right Bank, near the Étoile, and the summer night was balmy. We crossed the Pont Neuf to the Île de la Cité and headed west, along the river. Although she seemed very different than her sister, and need not worry so much how she looked in a corset, a little wine and a lot of cheese had brought out much that we had in common. She liked to laugh, but she could do it without collapsing. Where there were benches we might sit down while she rested her feet.

We had been walking for quite some time when I was struck by something peculiar. The bench we were on, and the view of the river, as well as what I could see, glancing around me, looked almost identical to where we had been when we started. And so it proved to be. I had forgotten we were on the Île de la Cité, and that following the wall we had walked around it, maybe several times. She had kicked off her shoes to rest her feet, but when she learned what had happened she keeled over with laughter. So did I. We had to lean on the stone wall for support. It then proved impossible to get her shoes back on her swollen feet. In her stocking feet, she leaned on me for support, and we made our way back to the Pont Neuf, where we had started. I managed to flag down a taxi. He was one of those mousy little pop-eyed fellows like the apéritif ads in the Métro, but for all his experience, he said, we had given him something new to consider. I set him up with a big tip. It was something special the way she ran her hands through my hair.

I was so pooped I could hardly stand, but I also had this habit of walking at night, so I didn't take a taxi. On one of the benches along the Seine I fell asleep. For one reason or another the gendarmes didn't find me, and I treated myself to fried eggs, the way the French do them, at the Dôme. What sort of night had my friend had with his brunette? When I saw him he called me "old buddy," and didn't bring up the problem of money. After the whole business I still had almost two hundred francs.

Why didn't I take some of this money and blow it on one of the girls I had seen at the Dôme? I had observed them for weeks. One of them, with slick black bobbed hair, her eyes like Kiki of Montparnasse, stored her gum behind her ear when a customer approached her table. This left a spot white as a Band-Aid. She had once turned her eyes on me, seen nothing of interest, turned away. Sometimes I sat so close to her table I saw the smoked butts stored in her cigarette case. In one of my fantasies I would approach her table, smile and offer her one of my Camels. She had her own lighter. I could hear its click, several tables away, like the key of a typewriter. My scenario provided several witty openings, and went as far as her door, off the Rue de la Gaite, where I had seen her disappear with more confident lovers. The siren song "How could anything that felt so good be all that bad" had been sung to me, and I had listened, but the specter of disease kept me in line. My YMCA experience had been long and explicit, with lectures, sermons and pictures, including an unforgettable visit to the venereal ward of a Chicago hospital. I hesitated to use or pronounce such words as *syphilis* and *gonorrhea*. With the word *clap* I was familiar, and on speaking terms. But if I should catch the clap, what would I do? There were streets in Paris, and open doorways, where the smell of ether led me to seal my lips, and my glimpse into waiting rooms confirmed my worst suspicions. Whatever hell might be elsewhere, this struck me as hell on earth. If these facts slipped my mind for a moment, I also had my girl to think of. On those long walks through the streets at night I would sing to myself "Ain't misbehavin', I'm savin' my love for you," a pact I shared with many of my generation. More than what I had been taught, or read, or pondered, the songs of my adolescence evoked emotions that established profound priorities. It might be regrettable, it was often foolish and pathetic, but that was how it was for Gatsby, and that spring in Paris how it was for me. No misbehavin' to speak of. The Dutch girl had laughed herself out of my reach.

I was seated at the Coupole, having a cognac, reading the headlines of the *Paris-Soir* held by the young man at a table near me. A tall, good-looking fellow, with a clipped moustache, he had draped his summer jacket over the back of his chair and turned the sleeves of his shirt back on his tanned forearms. A packet of Player's cigarettes was beside his lighter, and he had collected four or five saucers under his glass of black coffee.

"You like this paper, matey," he said, "I'm done with it."

I didn't want his paper, but I accepted one of his cigarettes. "Rolled for me by hand," he said, "in the Virgin Islands," which was the first time I had heard that. He flicked his lighter and lit it for me. Back home in Cambridge he mostly smoked a pipe, but when he took his holiday he shifted over to cigarettes. Could I explain that? I said that I had personally found that cigarettes were easier to carry, the pipe requiring the pipe, the pouch and the pocket to be stored in. He looked dumbfounded. "You bloody bugger!" he said. "I think you've got it! It's not just one pipe you need, it's half a dozen. Then there's the bloody matches. You can't light a pipe proper, you know, with a lighter. Ruins the tobacco. What you get in the draw is the bloody fuel!" He took his jacket from the chair and slipped it on the way a lot of girls do, as if his arms were double-jointed. "I've got to run, matey. Why don't I see you tomorrow? This is my table. If you like cheese, try the Welsh rabbit. Very good here, but you've got to like cheese. The frogs are clever when it comes to food." He put his pack of Player's cigarettes on my table and hurried off to flag down a taxi. He waved from the cab. I had never met a fellow just like him before, or heard the French referred to as *frogs*. He had also left a big tip on the table, which the waiter pocketed, rolling his eyes.

Since I didn't have anything very pressing to do I was back under the awning the following evening. The waiter, Louis, seemed pleased to see me. I let him bring me the Welsh rabbit, and a glass of white wine.

My friend arrived so late I first thought he had set me up. He didn't comment on it, just ordered some cognacs, and we sat smoking from his tin of Balkan Sobranies. His name was Harrow. He was married, with three children. He showed me the snapshots of two tall boys, a small girl and a short, long-faced woman. Every year, if he could manage, he took a holiday in Paris. He was a good talker, but like most Britishers he could be heard by the people at the tables around us. He liked to pump his sleeves up and down his arms as he talked. He wanted to know all about me, and I told him. What he envied me was my freedom. With whom was I living? Right at the moment, I said, I was solo. He thought that showed brains, since in his opinion women were expensive and a bloody nuisance. He took an apartment for a month every summer, but he never occupied it for more than three weeks. Would I like to have it for a week, just for a change? It was new and modern, with plenty of hot water. He simply couldn't get enough of a good hot tub himself, and soaked every day.

I said I didn't feel the need to change my apartment now that my stay in Paris was ending, but if the truth were known, I hadn't soaked in a tub, really soaked, that is, since I had left California. Great! he cried. How about this evening? At that moment I couldn't think why not. "While you soak I'll mix the drinks," he said, and walked me up Montparnasse, passing the Dôme, where quite a few people seemed to know him.

He lived in one of the modern apartment buildings on the Boulevard Raspail. Harrow's place was very smartly furnished but it seemed small once the two of us were in it. The bed was one of those that fold against the wall when not in use. The tub was built into the wall of his bathroom, with a place at the end where a person could sit. He sat there as the tub filled with hot water. "You can soak as long as you like, matey," he said, and gave me one of his wooden hangers for my clothes. I was long accustomed, at the Y, to dressing and undressing in front of strangers, but in the confines of the bathroom I was ill at ease. There were holes in my socks, and my shorts were soiled.

"You've got great legs, matey," he said to me. "You know that?" They were good straight legs, and could run, but I had always thought them too much on the lean side. In the mirror on the door I could see where my California tan began and ended. "You like it hot or just normal?" he said. "Just normal," I replied, but when I stepped into the tub it made me gasp. "I'm a good scrubber, matey—how about me scrubbing your back?" He worked up a good lather with the soap, and gave me a scrubbing with a stiff brush. "Sorry about that tan," he said, and slowly massaged the muscles of my neck and shoulders. "How's that feel?" It felt wonderful. I had never experienced anything like it. "You've got the skin of a baby, matey, did you know that?" No, I hadn't known that either. "Sit up," he ordered, and I sat up so he could dip his hands to the small of my back. Suds floated on the water before me like icebergs. I was so relaxed I felt disembodied. A vaporous cloud of steam fogged the doorway, where Harrow stood gazing at me. I sprawled there, floating, till the water had cooled, and I almost dozed off. Music was playing, and I listened. I was surprised to see Harrow, in his pajama bottoms, at the door with a bottle and a large brandy snifter. He poured a little of the brandy into the snifter. "They say they make it out of apples, matey. Take a sniff of it." The scent of apples made me think of Schloss Ranna. What would the Meister think of my Paris adventure, floating in a tub of hot water?

A towel around my waist, I stepped out of the bathroom, to see that the bed had been lowered from the wall, and Harrow was in it. He raised his glass to me, but my sip of brandy burned my tongue and filmed my eyes. "I like Paris in August," he said. "Fewer people. The frogs leave the town, as you probably noticed." Actually, I hadn't noticed anything so obvious. He patted the bed at his side. "Make yourself at home, matey. Room service in the morning. No need for you to get up until you feel like it."

He turned from me to switch off the light, tap a cigarette from the pack, light it. By its glow when he inhaled I could see the narrow gold band on his third finger. In the street below the window, cars were passing. Farther away, on Montparnasse, I could hear horns tooting. Did I have a fever? My body felt hot between the cool sheets. Harrow turned on his side, and in the pause of his breathing I felt the weight of his hand on my thigh. My heart pounded in my throat. My lips and mouth were dry. Harrow raised on his elbow to ask, "You

247

feel okay, matey?" I was unable to speak. "It's the brandy," he said. "You're not used to it. When you add the brandy to a soak in the tub . . . You think you'd like a little fresh air?"

Yes, I thought so. In the dark, seated on the bed, I groped for my shoes. In them I found a pair of his own clean socks, and I pulled them on. Getting into my shirt was not easy, with the film of sweat on my arms and shoulders. As I opened the door he called out, "Don't forget the address, matey. Just push the buzzer."

The perspiration on my body cooled as I walked. On Montparnasse most of the tables and chairs were pushed back under the awnings; a few waiters were hosing down the sidewalks. My steps echoed in the silence. Twice I heard and felt the rumble of the subway, like a sleeper muttering in his sleep. My relief was so great I was buoyant and elated, but it soon passed. Harrow had treated me kindly, and with respect, and I could not honestly say he had deceived me. If there had been any deception, I had deceived myself. The relief I felt to have escaped what I feared cooled to a shamefaced embarrassment. Harrow, too, had had his expectations. Had I led him on?

Two or three days later, as I was passing the Dôme, he stood up to call to me and beckon me to his table. "You had me worried, matey. You know that? You had palpitations. My fault for dosing you with the brandy. Here," he said, giving me one of his cards. "When you come to England be sure to look me up."

"Look me up," I replied, "when you come to California," but I was relieved not to have an address I could give him. As I walked away, feeling his eyes on my back, I sensed that I had overstayed the impulses that had brought me to Europe. My role as an innocent was over. I was now in the shoes of a prodigal son.

My Tangiers friend and his buddies took me with them to a taxi dance near the Bastille. Were my impressions unreal, or surreal? The dance floor had a low wooden fence around it, with gates that opened when a bell clanged. Toughs in tight caps and turtleneck sweaters, the girls with frizzly hair and painted faces, met at the center of the floor and without a word began to dance. When the bell clanged they would uncouple and leave the floor. Nothing was said; you just gave the girl a deadpan stare, and she gave you one. I hopped around in a sort of polka with a girl who never once glanced at my face. A lot of elevator dancing among the regulars (no steps), the man slipping his hands inside the girl's coat, low down on her back, coupled like a pair of stalled wrestlers. We all ended up with a lot of unused dance tickets. How would they behave, I wondered, if they didn't have the bell to break up their smooching? My Tangiers friend warned me, whatever I did, not to slip and make a pass at one of the girls, as if he thought I might.

I was watching a collection of street acrobats, the men in their soiled underwear, lift weights, bend bars and break a few chains while a kid in a clown suit beat on a drum. It took about twenty minutes. When it was over my pockets had been picked.

I don't know how he did it, but he got my billfold, with about twelve dollars in francs and the address of the mystery woman in Mallorca, my ace in the hole. What I had left in traveler's checks was ten dollars less than my freighter passage. I was too depressed to do much more than lie in my room. On the landing above me, in a room like mine, lived a paunchy, balding, middle-aged man who ran some sort of dirty-postcard racket. He was from New Brunswick, New Jersey. Why a man of his age would come to Paris I didn't understand. Now and then I saw him with one of his floozies, but I was careful not to act too friendly. He had once asked me what I did for money, and I had let it drop that I was a writer. He didn't read anything, so far as I could tell, but he had a lot of respect for writers. In one way or another he noticed that I was holed up in my room.

I let him knock two or three times before I let him in. It was one of those godawful, muggy summer nights that most Parisians leave town to get away from. He took the chair at the window, his plump, sallow face glistening with sweat. I wasn't sick, but he could see I was sick at heart. I told him what had happened, but fibbed a bit about the money I had had in the billfold. He offered to lend me five dollars, which I much appreciated but declined. Did I know, he said, that if an American citizen went broke in Paris the consul would ship him home on an American boat? No, I didn't know that. It revived me on the spot. Did he know what he was talking about? He swore that he did. The proof he offered was that the one person who had tried it, known to him personally, was not seen in Paris again. The thing you had to really be, of course, was broke. I could manage that easily enough by just spending the money I had kept for my passage. I could also have checked up on his story by going to the embassy, on the Place de la Concorde, which I had often gazed at with mixed emotions. Why didn't I inquire? I didn't want to hear what I might be told. To leave Paris at that moment, in a depression, and arrive in New York early in August, would pretty well take the bloom off the whole year and leave me stranded in New York. I wasn't expected in Cleveland, where my girl lived, until the first week of September.

On the strength of that hearsay I cashed my checks, all fifty dollars of them, and watched my candle burn at both ends. Back in May I had hinted to my girl that if her Ivy League brother had an extra sweater I just might find a good use for it. In August I was notified that it had arrived. To get it I rode the Métro across Paris into the dismal, dreary torpor of the slums. I had not read Céline, but this day's long journey would prepare me for that experience. I lost my way, wandered about in the heat, and finally faced a clerk so consumed with rage at life in general that his lips frothed white as he talked. His rage was not at me, luckily, but at *them*. Even while speaking to me he would turn away to shake his tight fist at *them*. I thought surely he would take his revenge on me—the only person handy, one who had just been sent an elegant, combed-wool sweater—but his hatred of the system was so great that he took my side, and ignored the duty charges. When I thanked him he embraced me, his two-day beard rough on my cheek.

I put off to the last my visit to the U.S. embassy. A long and broad flight of marble stairs led me up to the consul's office. He was a good-looking man, sweating in his suit coat, like the one from Boston I had met in Vienna, a decent, stuffy sort of cultivated man. As I told him my story about the picked pocket, he sat polishing his pince-nez glasses. One of the many things I had picked up in France was what *pince-nez* meant, and that pleased me. Are the true stories the ones that often sound so false? I should have gone to the police, he said, not to him—it gave me a start to hear him say that—and he advised me to be more careful in the future. Did I read the papers? Had it come to my attention that there was a depression in America? It had come to my attention, and it was on my mind, I said, since I did not have the money for my return passage. Had he heard what I had said? He had heard it so often he felt neither indignation nor amusement. Picking at his sleeve, he asked me why I had brought this very personal matter to his attention. I should write to my family, my friends, or even my enemies if they had any money. The American embassy was not a travel bureau or a charitable organization. Many steamers might be filled with penniless Americans who would return to the States if their passages were free.

We sat in silence. He saw through me so well that I was able to see, with humiliating clarity, just the sort of young panhandler I was.

"What am I to do?" I asked him.

This sober query startled both of us. It had just popped out. He interleaved his fingers for a moment, then said that he could get me, he thought, a second-class passage on an American steamer, but I would be obliged to repay it. I knew about how much such a passage would be, and how unlikely it was that I would be able to pay it back. In this state of depression I left his office, and started down the stairs. I made a better impression when I was not acting. From the top of the stairs his secretary called to me. It embarrassed the consul to say so, but he crisply advised me that if all else failed, he might get me a little money. How little might it be? I said my freighter fare was about sixty dollars, a sum of money small enough to impress him. If I would come back in a few days he would let me know.

During that period of waiting I was offered a job in the porn book racket (my job to paste the illustrations in the paperback books), watched the puppet shows in the Luxembourg Gardens, and made the acquaintance of a man with a pet penguin that toddled along beside him on a leash. When the bird got dirty from the gravel paths the man would dip him in the pond and wash him off. The little fellow liked that, honking excitedly like a baby duck. That was one of the things I hoped to tell people later, but when the time came I seldom did. I'm not even sure that my girl really believed it, but she felt I was entitled to one yarn like that, if it made me happy.

When I had the nerve to go back to the consul, he had gone on his vacation, but he had left a check with his secretary. She felt obliged to tell me, speaking frankly, that in actually giving me money he had departed from a department policy of long standing, and still felt of two minds about it. What sort of example to American youth was I, she asked me, and left me at the top of the stairs to think about it.

How do I explain that all the mirrors and windows of Paris had not returned to me one remembered reflection. What did this young American really look like? He *had* lost weight: the gabardine suit he couldn't get into at Schloss Ranna hung slack on him, and the cuffs were frayed. He still retained the moustache, but who in Paris had cut his hair? On the credit side, my friend the willowy Spanish dancer, on the subway on our way back from the Bois de Boulogne, placed her gloved hand on my tanned one and confided that I was a person of good character.

This comment both pleased and puzzled me, since I had for so long taken it for granted. What reason did I have for such self-esteem?

In the last week of August I took the night train to Antwerp, where I waited for two days for the freighter to New York. I shared a cabin on the *Black Tern* with at least two others, but I have forgotten their names and faces. Most of the time I sprawled in one of the lifeboats, trying to get a tan.

I had anticipated wondering what it would be like to really understand what people were saying around me, but it wasn't much. What I remember is the long row of washbasins in the lavatory of the YMCA, and the toothbrush I bought, with the bent handle and the really stiff bristles. I sometimes felt I hadn't really brushed my teeth since I had left. At a stand on Forty-second Street, from where I could read the news going around the Times Building, I had a Coke without enough crushed ice, then took the night bus for Cleveland, sitting where the breeze off the river blew cool in my face.

Once upon a time—and a very good time it had been—I had begun an adventure that was now over. A time that I had thought I had put far behind me now loomed up around me, at the fringe of the bus lights, where the telephone poles emerged out of the darkness, the wires rising and dipping, rising and dipping, as I had once seen them from a train's diner windows.

I had a seat close behind the driver, watching the insects splatter on the windshield. Back from the winding highway, veiled by the trees, lights glowed at curtained windows, and up ahead, hooded by the night, arcs of light hung over empty corners. I was full of the mystery of the time that had passed, the *Wanderjahr* that was already far behind me, and the time that I could now hear within me, like a clock that had just started. On several occasions at Schloss Ranna I had seemed to see through a crack in the veil of one time into another, but what I had seen through were the cracks in my extravagant expectations. Had I put all that behind me? Or was I doomed to see it wherever I looked, up ahead where the dark fields of the republic rolled on under the night.

A swarming hive of insects blurred the streetlights, pinging at the screens of windows and doorways, and as these lights blinked and receded, the ticking of the clock within me grew louder. Through no fault of my own, the time that had stopped had once more begun.

A CLOAK OF LIGHT

WRITING MY LIFE

For Jo

FOREWORD

The circus posters on the barns and sheds of my boyhood, vivid as flames over the long, hot summer, peeled away over the winter to leave enticing glimpses of the leaping tiger, the girl on the flying trapeze, more enticing than the circus itself.

Filling in what has vanished, filling out what is puzzling, is one of the prerogatives of the writer. Among the gifts reserved for his age, one above all is both welcome and unexampled. He is empowered, if he so wills it, to gift himself with a rerun of the life he has discarded, some of it as fresh as the paint on a park bench. It is the writer's nature and his talent to restore to the present much presumed to be lost. Even those candles he recklessly burned at both ends may prove, on examination, to have cast shadows in which he now sees forms from which he once averted his eyes. The faculty of image-making, of time retrieval, to which he has given the labor of a lifetime, is now at his disposal to evoke his own likeness. In this image there may well be more of a conscience than a resemblance. The emotions generated in this act of repossession may also exceed those he felt at the time, evidence that the past is never so much a part of the present as at this moment of recovery. If there is the risk that something of what he recovers will prove to be more trivia than treasure, it is one he has often run as a writer. He dips into his own life, as into others, at his own peril.

NO WORD IN MY LIFE IS SO CHARGED WITH SENTI-
ment as *dream*. Not the dreams concerned with the phantoms of sleep,
but American dreams, such as mine, concerned with the prevailing
fictions of the wakeful mind. I had lived most of my life in their
presence, and on their energy. For the person under the spell of these
expectations, the time of one's life was the best of times, and that is
how I found them.

In the spring of my sophomore year in college I proposed to a
girl I had known for three days.

She sat at the cool north window of my Chaucer class, the light
frosting her flaxen hair and mouse-colored lashes. I thought her more
beautiful full-face than in profile, but I confess her weak chin troubled
me a little. Not that I wanted a *strong* chin, but I wanted one not
quite so retiring. I liked her best with her gaze slightly averted. I spoke
to her on the creaky hall stairs on Wednesday, and on Friday evening
I proposed. And not in my sleep. This was a dream of my wakeful
mind. On the grid of my memory I see her glowing in the shadow
of a tree that dripped fragrance. As the three-piece band played "Good
Night, Sweetheart," we pledged our troth.

What you have to remember is that the expectations of my
sophomore year lacked a transcendent object. For two years straight
they had been rising. I was ignorant of the past, optimistic about the
future, and took my cues about the present from Hoagy Carmichael's
"Stardust." It was hardly the best tune for my voice, but it was my song.

On the following weekend, in her brother's sporty Ford roadster
—he was a junior at Caltech—she drove me to Redlands to meet
her family. At that time I knew nothing whatsoever about "old"
money, or "new" money. Money was money. I was open to its persuasion, but I lacked experience with it. A chauffeur, in his shirtsleeves,
hosed down the family Pierce-Arrow while chatting with a plump
matronly woman who proved to be her mother. They were discussing flower arrangements. Her father, who came off the porch to greet
me, wore a faded yachting cap and old tennis sneakers. All of the family, including her younger sister and older brother, had assembled at
dinner to see me. I saw, for the first time, a raw oyster served on the
half shell.

256

Her father was a reader of Henri Bergson, and probed me as to what I thought of his writings. I would not read much Bergson for another ten years, but this was not the place for me to admit it. We discussed time and memory. I thought I did pretty good on time. In the questions he began to ask me, however, I was able to see that my remarkable early life and bizarre adventures had not impressed him as much as they had his daughter. What did I plan to do with my life? he asked me. In what manner had I chipped one of my front teeth? This incident had not been narrated to his daughter, so I went into it, fully, while we were having coffee. None of them, it seemed, had ever seen or heard of an Irish Mail.

I'll call this young woman Joan Harwood, since her brief engagement to me was not one of her memorable triumphs. She took a seat on the porch swing beside her mother, who was winding up balls of wool yarn while she gave her daughter tips on the sweater she was knitting for me. I was asked to stand up and be measured for the sleeves. Never before had it been pointed out to me that my right arm was longer than my left. How explain it? Thinking pretty fast, considering the situation, I said that I had recently been playing a lot of tennis, and stretching for the serve had probably lengthened my arm. Her brother took exception to that, but it turned out that he didn't play much tennis. I pointed out that my serve was one of the strong points of my game.

There were no dishes to be washed by the guests in this family, and at an early hour my girl drove us back to college. The sky to the west still flamed with the sunset. The gems of the dashboard light were reflected in the windshield. We drove without any music rather than have an argument as to who was the best female vocalist.

One of the very special aspects of our romance was that my girl, at the time I wooed her, had come down with a pretty bad case of trench mouth. So had most of her dormitory. All of the kissable girls I happened to know seemed to me more upset about it than Joan. My own emotions were so rarefied, however, that this sort of deprivation actually increased my affection for her. All in good time, I said—and what did we have but time? At the door to her dormitory, the air fragrant with the perfume of flowering shrubs, I would gently put my lips to her hair—so much like corn silk, it always struck me—or the nape of her lilac-scented neck. I burned with such a fever of chaste desire it often filmed my eyes.

In June her family moved from Redlands to their summer home in Balboa. To be near her, I accepted a job I wouldn't ordinarily have considered. Some work was being done on the new slip for the Balboa ferry, and I was the one they hired to do the work under the water. I had to wear one of the heavy one-eyed divers' helmets, but not much else. It paid a dollar an hour, more than I'd ever made, and it had simply never occurred to me what things might be like when you saw them under water.

In the evening, if the ferry wasn't running, I would swim the channel to be with my girl. If the tide was strong, as it often was, there were times I wondered if I would make it. I had some close calls with boys in catboats, and old men with outboard motors. Since my girl had spent the day on the beach, playing with her friends, she didn't feel up to much in the evening. Most of the time I played caroms or Parcheesi with her sister, who liked to win.

One evening on the porch, her mother, who liked me, hinted that maybe I had come on too strong for a girl like Joan. There simply weren't many world-beater types among the young men to whom she was accustomed. They were more easygoing, as Joan was herself. I hadn't thought of myself as a world-beater type, and I used some of the time I spent under water to think about it. Some world-beater I was, eyeball to eyeball with a bunch of queer fish! It hadn't even crossed my mind, until her mother pointed it out, that Joan already had most of the things I planned to give her, except myself.

I put off for so long asking Joan about her trench mouth, I found it harder and harder to bring the matter up. Did it ever cross my mind that back in Chicago I had lost a great girl because her mother liked me? It should have, but I don't think it did.

Her brother had gone east for the summer, but he was back in time to darken up his tan and play me his new Mills Brothers records. One day, out in his catboat, we had a long talk. He could see what was happening, he said, but from his own inside, knowledgeable point of view, he felt I should consider myself lucky. Speaking man to man, he thought his sister was a real pain in the ass. Take just one thing— had she finished the sweater she was knitting for me? And I could be thankful she hadn't.

I thanked him for his opinion, but I had never before heard a brother speak that way about his sister, and it shocked me. Whatever her shortcomings—like the small flaw in her profile, and the unusually persistent case of trench mouth—she was not so dumb she failed to perceive I was a bit of a pain in the ass myself. In myself, indeed, I seemed to have found a subject adequate to my expectations. I had been eager to share my life with my girls, but this girl had soon tired of it. I had been so full of myself that that small point had gone unnoticed. I had not yet become an object of my own study (all in due time, as time would reveal), but neither did I prove to be a subject she felt compelled to master. Her nature, as little as I had plumbed it, probably recoiled from the self-made, true-grit, plucky sort of suitor I had unconsciously taken as my model. When I later read that the rich were different from us, I had some personal knowledge of this distinction. My solemn, tireless, relentless wooing, the eagerness with which I would prove myself worthy, the manner of my indifference to her snubs, all of this must have bored her profoundly. If I would only go away! If it disturbed me to learn that she was a pain in the derriere—as attractive as I found it—it did excuse me from my commitment to carry on a losing battle. For a woman like that, should I continue to make a fool of myself?

I had known from the first—a guilty, burdensome knowledge, troubling the surface of my self-esteem—that her family had both class and money, but I felt that in learning what a paragon I was they would make a place for me in the family, and maybe even in the firm. That, too, was pretty dumb on my part, since the trucks they manufactured were all back in Ohio. Once happily married, we would live in La Jolla, or perhaps in Hawaii, where they sometimes vacationed in the winter. As unlikely as it seemed, for a girl of her type, or her attitude to trench mouth, I had once seen her, at one of our dances, do a hula that I couldn't believe. She had all of the great movements really down pat. I think she truly did like to listen to me talk, but when I wasn't talking I could see she was restless. Another thing she didn't like was the sort of young man who was always doing handstands. What it all added up to was that it undermined the pride I took in the way I hung in there, which was pretty much the opposite of what I really was. If I wasn't really crazy about her, would I ever behave like that?

I had already lost a great girl in Chicago because I had been such a hit with her mother—had she wanted me to be unfriendly with her mother? Yes, that was what she wanted—and now I was losing another because I was such a hit with myself, too full of the self in which I was learning to take pride. It seemed to me I had led an interesting life, and I was eager to share it with a good listener. For almost three weeks she had been one—then most of what she heard made her restless. I remember all that. I remember the way she would clasp and unclasp her hands.

At the end of the summer her mother offered me a ride back to Redlands with the rest of the family, but I was too embarrassed to accept when I learned that Joan wouldn't be with them. If there had been anywhere else for me to go, I would have gone there. I felt like a fool going back to college. I thought of going to Chicago, on one of my father's railroad passes, but the mother of the girl I had lost, depending on what else had happened, might no longer want to see me. I had made a real mistake. How do you unmake a real mistake? On the other hand, if I hadn't made it, I would be working in the lobby of the Y or as an usher in one of the North Side movies, until the girl was old enough to get married. She had been fourteen. I still can't believe it, but that's what she had been.

Back in the spring, before I'd met Joan Harwood, and had nothing on my mind but summer vacation, I'd been asked by the mother of one of my classmates to come and live with her son, to serve as a good example. He was having problems with his courses in English, which happened to be my best subject. The two of us would live in a studio apartment at the rear of a house big enough for parties.

What I planned to do, once I got back to Pomona College, was lose myself in work. I would first write up what had happened between me and Joan, in case I might someday actually want to read about it. Parts of it I did read, to this boy I was living with, but he was too inexperienced to appreciate it.

One day I happened to take from a shelf in the college library the two-volume edition of The Decline of the West, I've no idea why. Once I got past the long introduction, I couldn't put it down. The boy's mother, who liked me, gave me a copy of the one-volume edition of Spengler's book for Christmas. On my second close reading, which took me about a month, I underlined what I found of particular interest in red. On my third reading, which took me even longer, I underlined the main points in green. While reading Spengler I was referred to a graduate student who had spent the previous year in a garret, in Paris. Another winter he had spent in Mallorca, as the guest of a woman who liked young people, especially Americans.

I was about to read Spengler one more time, when I made up my mind to take off for Europe. Joan Harwood may have had something to do with this, since she had told me, back when we were talking, that I was one of those people who would end up doing what I said I would do. What I had said was that I was thinking about taking off for Europe.

At the Oxy-Pomona annual football game, I happened to see Joan with a Sigma Tau playboy who drove an Auburn roadster with disk wheels. He wasn't a bad type, really, and better-looking than most girls, with tight curly blond hair and long dark lashes. One thing I remember is how he always dressed for breakfast, and only troubled to attend his afternoon classes. From the way he smiled, some people thought he was tipsy, but that was just how he was.

260

My ex-girl was there at the Oxy game with him, clasping and unclasping her hands the way I remembered. During the whole game she sat with her knees pressed together, but when the fog came in and seemed to tangle in her hair I really couldn't have cared less what a pain in the ass she was.

In late May, just as I had planned, I took off for Europe. Five or six years later, making a sharp right turn in Alexandria, Virginia, I glanced up to see a woman standing on the curb, her hands gripping the handle of a big perambulator. In a clutter of grocery bags and returnable bottles, a very black child was squatted, a clothespin corking its mouth. The woman was hardly black at all, more a golden peanut-brittle color, and about her broad shoulders she wore a ratty fur piece that dangled a grinning shrunken fox head. In her face, like a sunburst, I swear that what I saw was my own salvation. It was all right there in her face, as if the window of the car framed my conversion. In the rearview mirror I caught a glimpse of her figure tilted way back, as if to see me better. She waved first, then I waved. I just drove along with no interest at all in where I was going. This was in the fall of 1939, and may have been the first of my real losses and imaginary gains.

What she saw in my face, and maybe what Joan saw, and others too, that I haven't mentioned, was one of those fools who persists in his folly, never mind what. It seems clear to me now that I was that kind of fool.

In one of the books I happened to read in Paris, the author said: "Scoroncocolo, fetch me my cloak of light!" I've no idea why that seemed so magical to me. Without any idea what the author meant, I knew I was the reader he had in mind. In the best of times, in the worst of times, the writer has within him his own cloak of light, and he travels with it wrapped around him. That lady on the corner in Alexandria, Virginia, recognized in me one of those fools, and the good news is that she both liked and pitied what she saw.

When I came back from Europe I took a bus to Cleveland, where my new girl met me at the station. I had a silky-type moustache she hadn't previously seen, and a more serious demeanor, but she was nervous and flustered to be driving a car on which her brother still owed three payments. Another thing was that the ring with the college seal I had given her when I left for Europe she had left in a washroom.

My new girl and her family lived on a big shaded lot, great for

261

squirrels and birds. A dog named Sox barked and clawed at the screen when we came up the driveway. Her father, a law school professor, was sitting on the steps of the back porch, husking sweet corn. The day was a hot one, the windows of the house were open, the curtains tied back. From the window above the porch, a woman wearing a shower cap put out her head and spoke to all of us in a voice so calm it seemed disembodied. She hadn't expected a houseguest so early, she said, and leaned far out the window to shake a small rug.

My girl led me through the cool, dark house, taking the route that bypassed the kitchen, where the linoleum was covered with newspapers. Just the year before, I had come in through the kitchen, where her mother had been crouched, her backside to me, taking up the old papers and putting down new ones. Her parents had made the Grand Tour in the early twenties, coming back with the Dresden plates stored in the sideboard along with the goblets made in Venice. That day the dog, Sox, was waiting for me on the stairs, making vertical jumps as if he were on springs. He was put into the room on the left, while I was shown the room that had once been my girl's, but was now her brother's. He had put up his tennis racquet, some Dartmouth pennants, and an Arabian sword in a scabbard. We stood facing the rear dormer window, where a big fierce blue jay was hammering at the feed tray. The one thing I remember her saying to me was that she had lived most of her life in her room—could I imagine that? All I could think of at the time was how lucky she had been. That's how dumb I was.

Although I had been away for more than a year, my rucksack bulging with her letters, I had managed to return from Paris without even a bottle of perfume. I had brought her a poem, offering her the gift of myself. She mistook my confusion and embarrassment for a deep understanding of what she had said. What I did happen to have, right there in my pocket, were little chips of marble I had picked up along the grassy paths of the Roman Forum. She was too touched and moved to thank me. Impulsively, I put my arms around her. We were both speechless, and a good thing. Her mother left the bathroom just in time to catch us in this compromising situation, but she had her own problems, flushed from her shower, with her nightgown peeping at the throat of her bathrobe. It was enough to remind us all that from this point on the game was for keeps. I was twenty-four, older than Alexander at the time of his greatest triumphs, and I had seen more of the world than he had, yet I still knew little or nothing of expectations that were not my own.

Two days later, with one of her Scripps school friends, we were headed west by car for California. Her friend dropped us off in

Williams, Arizona, so we could have a few days alone together at the Grand Canyon. I signed the register with a bold but untried hand. I finally read her that poem, and she didn't much like it. She was a reader of "The Waste Land," a poem I had not as yet read.

A few days later we were on the night bus to Claremont, where I carried her bag through the mist of the sprinklers to Browning Hall at Scripps College, where she still had another year. I had another year to go myself, but I had returned determined to be a writer. In one of the comfortable shacks on Hogan's Alley, rented to seniors who were eager to save money, I installed myself with several notebooks of unlined paper and a radio loaned to me by my girl. She had also offered me the use of her typewriter, but first I had to learn to type.

Fifteen months after leaving Claremont, I was back where I had started, with another girl I would soon propose to. What, I had been asked, did I intend to do with my life? Was it sense or folly that led me to feel that this was one of the things I would learn by writing, one of the features of my untried cloak of light. So I was hoping. So, in my ignorance, I told myself.

Although I had gone to Europe for the great adventures writers went in search of, and found them, they did not turn up in what I found myself writing. In their place were scenes and incidents from my boyhood that I had all but forgotten. My Chicago years had proved to be so eventful it had not occurred to me to look behind them. If asked where I was from, I would reply in California. Joan Harwood had heard about my life in Chicago, and my trips to California, but nothing about my boyhood in Nebraska. What had it been like? I had put it all behind me. The year I spent in Europe, especially the long summer in Paris, where I found time to ponder what I was up to, led me to reflect on the separate lives I had lived as a boy. It seemed to me I had had a marvelous childhood, even better than Tom Sawyer's, but what did I know? Something about being an exile, traveling around alone, had aroused in me a curiosity about who I was, and where I was from. Yet my reflections did not reach a conscious level until I found myself seated with a pen and paper, my mind a blank until I began to write.

After a few weeks of rambling, I found a form, even a style, that seemed to come naturally to me. Seldom more than a paragraph, the language simple, compact, the writer straining to evoke an incident from his boyhood. What he wanted above all was a *specific* time, and a *specific* place. One might have reasoned that he described a picture that he saw through a window before him.

*Through the vines was Bickel's General Store and a brown dog drinking
at the fountain. Sparrows dropped from the trees to the wires and then
from the wires to the ditch grass. A pigeon dropped from the belfry
to the roof of the barn. He went along the tin roof to the hole for
pigeons, dropped inside. More sparrows dropped from the wires,
stirred the grass near the road. Mrs. Riddlemosher stopped picking
currants and turned with her pan. Jewel's Tea wagon passed and the
dust came up and went by. Behind the feed store Mr. Cole's mare whinnied and Mr. Bickel smoothed the front of his apron, stopped shooing flies. Tipping her sunbonnet back, Mrs. Riddlemosher looked
toward the square, where the dust came marching down the road with
the rain.* (*The Inhabitants*, 1946)

This writer seems to feel that one word too many would break
the spell that he, and the reader, should be under. Time had not actually stopped, but the movements were slow enough to be photographed. The scene had the characteristics of a still life. The writer
sought a distillation, a decisive moment, that was both visual and ver-
bal. The narration itself introduced a movement he seemed at pains
to minimize. I had a sheaf of such pieces before it crossed my mind
that one might actually "take" the pictures I was describing. On occasion I had seen similar pictures in magazines.

While I was having these reflections, I received a bequest, of almost
five hundred dollars from the will of my Seventh-Day Adventist grandfather, who had just died in Boise, Idaho. With part of this money
I bought a secondhand Rolleiflex camera, and began to take some of
the details I had tried to describe. My instincts led me to artifacts,
rather than people. The people I would conjure up with words (I was
not lacking in assurance), but the power of the photograph to capture the concrete detail, the visible reality, seemed to me even then,
as ignorant as I was, matchless.

In the alleys and backyards of small California towns I found all
that I had left in the Platte Valley of Nebraska, and occasionally more.
Fences and gates, the steps and stoops of back doors, the clutter around
porches, the yards strewn with the ruins and costs of living, the
machinery, the junk, and the haunting presence of wrecked, battered
and abandoned cars. I put the writing aside to concentrate on the pictures. The first few photographs I managed to enlarge astonished me
with their power, their confirmation of what I saw. These were days
of excitement I would continue to feel as my experience with the camera
broadened, but it did not, at the time, occur to me to relate the visual
images to what I had written.

264

Neither did it occur to me that these photographs, appropriate as they were to my intentions, did not displace, for the writer, the image he sought to describe on his mind's eye. They were collaborating, and reassuring, but not at all the same thing. They also proved expensive to enlarge. For the time being I put the photographs aside and went back to work on a novel about a boy, quite a bit like myself, growing up. Like other boys, he started young:

In a room of lampglow, where the shadows waver on a low ceiling, I lie full of longing at the side of a woman whose bosom heaves, but she is faceless. Not knowing the nature of the longing I felt, would it persist and reappear as poignant yearning for what it is in the past that eludes me? (*Will's Boy,* 1981)

It would be years before I read *A Portrait of the Artist as a Young Man,* where these matters are given their due, and brief, recognition.

Once upon a time and a very good time it was there was a moocow coming down along the road and this moocow that was down along the road met a nicens little boy named baby tuckoo.

One thing at a time was more than enough for this young writer, who figured, and rightly, he would get to reading later.

My girl came to visit me on weekends, and I might visit her during the week and sit in the visitors' lounge of her dormitory. On the grand piano in the lounge she would often play for me Cyril Scott's "Lotus Land," a piece to my taste. I had also grown to like the *Symphonic Variations* of César Franck, played on the Victrola. At school in England she had met celebrated pianists, and on one occasion, with Myra Hess, she had played a composition for four hands by Mozart. Even more than the music my girl liked to play, I loved to see her seated at the piano, her body swaying slightly, as she was carried away by the music. At these moments I liked to fancy myself at her side, turning the pages of the music, waiting for that moment when she would turn, gaze into my eyes, and I would embrace her. An embrace was a good deal more than a kiss. I had seen it done properly, in my opinion, in a painting I had seen somewhere in Europe, the man embracing the woman as well as he could while still holding his violin. My girl had her mother's dark, remarkable eyes, one feature being how they went so long without blinking, and it had not escaped my attention, at those Scripps dances where she never wore her glasses, that she had a lot of boyfriends I had not previously met. For a girl, she played a good game of tennis, and when we played catch with an indoor ball she threw it with a zip that sometimes led to an argument. It was never really clear to me where it got the zip.

We were both so busy we didn't often get around to discussing marriage. One of the chief attractions of marriage for me would be that when she visited me on weekends she could spent the night. Another thing would be that her mother would finally understand that I was serious. She was suspicious of would-be writers. Her father didn't want to rush us, but my girl felt that anytime we took the leap he would give us a nest egg to start with, perhaps as much as three hundred dollars. The part-time job I had with the WPA was already paying me about thirty a month.

With the winter rains we had the most beautiful clouds I had ever seen. Great towering cumulus masses backed up against the mountains as they did in the paintings of Maxfield Parrish. I took some pictures of them, and won a second prize in a contest held by Marshall Field, in Chicago. They hung it on its side, as if they didn't know what cumulus clouds looked like. The photograph that won the prize we called *Les Nuages,* after much thought.

Early in the spring, feeling the way we did, an old friend who had loaned us all of his Brahms records drove us to San Bernardino, where we were married by the justice of the peace. My girl was a knockout in her blue knit suit and perky red hat. I had to borrow a suit coat from one of my friends, since the one I'd worn to Europe was no longer fit to be married in.

When the word got around that we had been married—one of the cooks at Scripps read it in the San Berdoo paper—there was hell to pay at Scripps, where married women were not allowed to enroll in the college, or live in the dorms. One of her teachers felt the marriage should be annulled. Another, a very prominent scholar, felt that she had betrayed him personally, and questioned the morals of a society that let young people behave in this manner. Even then I could see that he had a point. My wife's father, however, just as she said he would, wired us a money order for two hundred and fifty dollars, with another hundred dollars in the kitty if we needed it. We found a two-room guesthouse; the rooms weren't so large, but there was space in the kitchen for an upright piano, which we bought from Bekins Storage for thirty-five dollars, including delivery. Our rent was eleven dollars a month. I already had a job with the WPA, and my wife found work teaching the piano at a local private school. We really didn't need the money in the kitty, but we took it. More than two years would pass before Scripps College would allow my wife to take her degree, but that's the way it should be if the place has standards. It just so happened

266

she did it magna cum laude, because once she was married, her mind was free for study.

I thought it strange, as I worked on my novel, that in all my college years I had not once thought of my life prior to Chicago, until I found myself on the top of a freight car rattling downgrade in the Platte Valley of Nebraska. From that elevation, which I had enjoyed as a boy, I had a quick, blurred impression of the town I was born in. I applied myself to this challenge five and six hours a day, sometimes working in the cool of the Pomona library basement. I shared Joyce's sentiments about nicens baby tuckoo and the moocow, but I lacked his crafty example. Several hundred single-spaced pages had accumulated by the time the narrator had reached his ninth year. This volume I titled "So He . . . ," from Robert Browning's "Caliban upon Setebos," and sent off to Saxe Commins of Random House, who published books I liked the looks of. In due time I received it back with a civil, instructive, encouraging letter, suggesting that I send him my next book. This I did. In those confident years it seemed obvious to me that when I wrote a novel that was good enough to publish, it would be published.

I worked a few hours a day giving drawing lessons to some of my wife's music students, and our income rose to ninety dollars a month, more than enough to cover the basics. We bought a record player. We bought our first books. We joined the record rental plan at the college, and our first album of records, *Death and the Maiden,* was one I managed to sit on. On occasion I rode with a friend to Los Angeles and spent the day browsing in secondhand bookstores. The clerk at the Argonaut, on Sixth Street, soon became one of my friends. From him I bought my first Faulkner, *The Sound and the Fury,* which cost me a dollar, being a clean, mint copy. We talked books at lunch. We talked books while I browsed. It interested him to learn that I was a writer. Archer had already begun his Faulkner collection, and he invited me to his home to look it over. His wife, Margot, had a droll and sophisticated humor, and a taste for writers like Carl Van Vechten. She introduced me to *Peter Whiffle,* a wonderful book about Paris before the war, wherein the author pointed out a lot of things I had missed. If there was a sale at Dawson's, around the corner on Wilshire, Archer would tip me off with a postcard. Mr. Dawson's specialty was incunabula, and he would buy a lot of modern stuff just to get the old and rare items. He considered Arthur Machen a modern writer, and was puzzled that so few people read him. I bought my first signed, limited editions from Dawson, for one dollar apiece. He had them all out on tables at the front of his shop and I was out of my mind trying to choose between a thin book of Ezra Pound and a thicker one of Yeats. I borrowed eight dollars from Archer on that occasion, and before lunch I had spent all of it.

Our two-room guesthouse on the alley off Dartmouth was soon crowded with books and records. We hung our clothes on wires across the bathtub. My friend Lorne Ward, whom I had left in Italy when I went to Paris, would bring bags of avocados and oranges when he paid us a visit. We didn't entertain much since we simply didn't have the room. My wife had not had much experience with cooking, but she quickly caught on to casseroles, especially with tuna fish. We could have our milk fresh daily at twenty cents a gallon if I would cycle the four miles out and back for it. The cream was so heavy once it set that we had to spoon it off. I was also good for government handouts, a leg of lamb or a pot roast, but we needed a car to make the pickups, so we usually got along without it. Just a few blocks away we could pick the oranges off the trees. I didn't want to tell my wife I'd seldom had it so good, since she might wonder whom she had married, but except for the three great years in college, and my life with the Mulligans in Omaha, that was a fact. I had arrived back in Clare-mont with about eight of the twenty dollars I had borrowed from my wife's brother, and here we were, just a year later, living about as well as anybody, with the credit to buy an electric refrigerator.

Sometimes we hiked to Johnson's pasture, in the foothills, from where we could see for miles in three directions, and away to the east, at sunset, the snow-capped peak of San Jac made me think of the Alps. The voices of children, the yapping of dogs, seemed to swell like balloons as they rose toward us, just the way it had been at Schloss Ranna. My wife had not seen as much of the world as I had, but most of the time she agreed with me that there was nothing like California. Neither of us would choose to live anywhere else, even if we could.

After the purchase of an electric refrigerator that would not kill us both if a leak occurred in the freezing unit, we moved to more ex-pansive quarters. The green-shingled cottage was actually pretty crum-my, set up on concrete blocks so cats and dogs would fight beneath it, but we had two big bedrooms and a garage at the back we might be able to rent. In the room I used as a study, I kept the cracked green blinds drawn at the window to screen out the light. On the hot days I would begin to perspire about ten o'clock. Our house sat on a cor-ner, under a street light, and one summer evening two high school boys stopped to sit on our curb and have a big discussion. The night was warm and all our windows stood open. This discussion went on until about three o'clock in the morning. I got up to ask them to please

268

move on, but one of them might have been a freshman at the college, since he was wearing a green freshman dink, with the yellow button at the crown I fell to listening to what was being said, and they were having a literary conversation. One had just read *Magnificent Obsession,* a religious-type novel, and he was explaining it all to his friend. On the strength of what I heard, and how he seemed to feel about it, I later read the book.

The need I felt to have a car in our garage was one reason I decided to buy one. On Figueroa Street, in L.A., I found a '29 model A coupe, with yellow wire wheels, for forty-five dollars. It also had a bearing knock in the motor. I got the friend who had driven me to L.A. to follow me all the way back to Claremont in case what what I expected to happen happened. Nothing did, however, but driving more than forty miles with defective oil pump finished off the motor. It locked up so tight the crank wouldn't turn it. The wheels would turn, however, and we were able to coast and push it down the incline to a garage. There it sat for about a month while I figured out what to do next. My wife's father had written, some weeks before, that now we were married we should pay them a visit. To this end, they would pay our railroad fare both ways. When I learned what the fares would come to, I had an idea. The local mechanic, a wizard named Zeke, would swap and install a rebuilt motor for sixty-five dollars, which was less than our one-way passage. We also needed a set of new tires and a top, since the roadster had come without one. Ten months of the year you can do pretty well without a top in California, but not if you're driving to Cleveland in the summer. The motor, the tires, the top, and five quarts of oil came to less than our fare on the Santa Fe *Chief.*

There was one other little problem. One of our neighbors, who taught at Scripps College, had boarded out his dog, Pat, with us for the summer while he went to Europe. Pat was a lapdog-type police dog. He loved us so much he preferred to live with us, so boarding was no problem. There was no one to leave him with, so he had to go to Cleveland with us. He was a big dog and he panted a lot. Around Claremont he liked to ride in our rumble seat, his head thrust up above our new sporty top. If he saw anything coming toward him he loved to bark. Claremont people got accustomed to him, but out on the highway, with the traffic coming toward us, people might get the idea that the dog was driving. My hope was that with the wind in his face, he would soon get tired.

We got away about sunrise, early in June, to get as far as we could before crossing the desert, but going over the pass to Victorville, I noticed that Pat's eyes were red and watering. At every gas station we had to find some shade and try to hose him down with water. It was my idea, in Barstow, to buy him a pair of goggles: racing goggles, with the fur lining, and a piece of elastic to slip behind his ears. He pawed them off unless he was distracted by a passing car. Once the car was in motion, however, in his excitement he failed to notice he had the goggles on. Over in Utah, on the narrow blacktop road approaching St. George, many of the cars coming toward us would pull off the road to watch us go by. Everything went pretty well until my wife noticed that Pat seemed to be missing. We thought we might have lost him on one of the turns, but when we stopped we found him curled up asleep on the floor of the rumble seat. There he stayed. We got him to lap up some water now and then, but he refused to eat. We drove straight through to Cleveland without stopping, and when we pulled into the yard he was still groggy. In the driveway at the back of the yard we hoisted him from the rumble, but he was so dazed and shaky he could hardly stand up. At that moment the family dog, Sox, came out of nowhere and hit him full tilt from the side. The racket was deafening, and I thought it would surely be the end of Sox. My father-in-law came out of the house in his B.V.D.s—it had been a hot day—got a hand on one dog, a firm grip on the other, and held Sox out at his side like a trophy. I got the leash on Pat, and Sox was put in an upstairs bedroom. We hadn't even had the time to greet each other, but when it was over and quiet there was no need to. We all just sat around the yard drinking ice-cold root beer and watching the fireflies rise out of the grass.

The weeks we were in Cleveland we had an airtight system of signals to keep one dog upstairs and one down. It was a big deal for Sox, and he made the most of it. Late in the evening, my father-in-law and I took Pat for a walk to the local drugstore, where we had double-chocolate Cokes. I think Mr. Finfrock liked me well enough, but he regretted the fact that I couldn't play bridge. We saw two Yankee-Cleveland baseball games together, and I met some of the young lawyers who had been his students. They all called him "Fin." He was a big man in Ohio, and since we did the shopping together, I met a lot of influential bird-watching people. "My son-in-law is a writer," he would say as he introduced me, and none of these young lawyers had met a real working writer. I hadn't been published, but they figured, as I did, that I would be in time.

During that summer I had worked my way up from the past to where I was thinking more and more about Schloss Ranna, the castle in Austria where I had spent the winter. Already it seemed farther away than any other part of my life. In a sense of course it was, going back to the Middle Ages, but I was puzzled by the way the nature of time seemed to apportion and dominate my life. It was all in my head, but in such a cunning manner I accepted it as a fact.

My wife's brother, Charles, was doing some law teaching that summer, but he came up for a visit just before we left. I liked the way he would come to the door of our room and stand there, like a dancer, his fingers poised on his hips. His wisecracks were so good I was slow to get them. Some years later, I saw a photograph of T. E. Lawrence standing poised yet casual, his fingers at his hips. I felt a similar concern for them both.

Charles had been a sprinter on the Dartmouth track team, and liked to discuss with me the strategy of sprinting. He saw most things, including the girls he knew, in terms of strategy. It all sounded pretty good to me since I had no strategy whatsoever, except to sit and write. When we played doubles together on the public courts, the time we spent on strategy really riled our opponents. The one occasion we played for money we each won sixty-five cents.

Charles felt his sister was right in settling for me, and that the three of us made a great team. He was smarter than I was, an all-A student in law, but I dimly perceived he had some curious hang-ups. If something impressed him as amusing, it might bring on a fit of chortling glee. When he learned that Robert Taylor had been one of my classmates, a young man from Nebraska named Arlington Brugh, it almost broke him up. When I went on to explain that while he was in college I used to have to arrange his blind dates for him, since the girls were ill at ease with a guy so good-looking, he turned and walked into his room, where I could hear him almost gasping with laughter. It was never anything he would discuss with me later, once he'd had his laugh.

What we had come back for was to reassure his mother that I was a proper son-in-law, and she seemed to accept it. When I spoke to my wife about her mother's feelings, she said to me, "Mother doesn't have feelings." My own impressions of her mother were contradictory. Unless we were going somewhere, she was always in her bathrobe, tidying up. When I came down to breakfast in the morning, I might find her spreading newspapers on the linoleum in the kitchen. That summer her big problem was a new icebox. She was reconciled to the fact that it should be electric, but how could she be sure it was the latest model? Already she had seen the models change twice while she had been weighing their virtues. The old ice chest she had had for twenty-three years was full of jars growing mold on stuff that had rotted. When it began to look as if they might explode, she had taken them out and buried them in the compost pit. Her advice to my wife was that she put her faith in how things smelled, not in how they tasted. At dinner, Mother, wearing her pearl earrings, her beautiful eyes as large and unblinking as an owl's, would solemnly gaze at me while she peeled and sliced an orange. I sometimes wondered if her husband ever wondered, as I did, what it would be like to really kiss her. Would it be at the risk that his sleeping beauty would wake from her sleep?

We drove back to California in August, but not with Pat. He was packed into a crate the size of a playhouse, and shipped back on the *Zephyr*. When the crate finally arrived in Claremont, and we pried the boards loose to let him escape, he ran around and around it, moaning and whimpering, as if he might be mad. Then he stopped to greedily lap up the bucket of water I had brought him. After that he was more or less his same old self, a great lapdog.

IN MY COLLEGE YEARS, THE TOWN OF CLAREMONT
was a green tranquil oasis in a surround of orange groves and desert
wash. Mist from the sprinklers softened the blaze of summer heat and
light. A few miles to the north, the San Gabriel Mountains rose abruptly
from the soft contours of the foothills to the summit of Old Baldy,
capped by snow most of the year. In the crisp shimmering light of
winter, the mountains, framed by my dormitory window, seemed near
enough to touch. This was what I had dreamed about in Chicago,
and to actually be there was the very heaven—a poetic way of putting
it I soon picked up.

Over Christmas vacation, the school cafeteria closed, I would live
pretty well on the oranges my professor Leon Howard and I would
glean from the neighboring groves. We would sneak out at night, with
a couple of pillowcases, and come back with a haul of oranges. Professor Howard was only five or six years my senior, but he proved
to be several decades wiser. He had recently married a very pretty young
woman with an attractive Baltimore accent. His own Southern accent
was very pronounced, and one of the things I liked about him. I was
not his favorite student, however, being one of the serious types he
frowned on. I couldn't seem to get enough of what he was saying,
or whatever it was I was reading. Leon preferred the witty girls at
Scripps who had already read and liked the censored books, and loved
to play charades at the Howards' in the evening. God, how I disliked
charades! In Omaha, as a boy, we had called it "New Orleans," and
played it with the girls under the street light, but to watch a grown-
up Scripps girl crawling around on the floor like a baby was a taste
I had not developed.

Leon was one of the first to encourage me to think I might have
some sort of talent—he was reluctant to say, however, what it might
be for. When my story about my winter at Schloss Ranna began to
take shape, I showed some of it to him. I don't know how he managed
to read it.

It was written in the manner of blank verse and a hundred or
more pages of this cost me a great effort. Was it readable? Leon said
that it was. Not much more than that, really, just that it was. With
this reassurance, I would get up early, before the heat, to sit in the
room where the screened light was green as pond water, and peck away

on a Remington typewriter older than the one used by my father. I was a two-finger typist, and the cuticles of these fingers were usually ragged. But in the fall of that year (1937) I had reached a stage where I thought even a writer like myself should be published. The next book I sent off would be with the understanding that the publisher should not reject it. So I was slow to send it off.

At Scripps College that semester, Magdalene Schindelin, from Vassar, was an exchange teacher in the German Department. My wife had met her in one way or another, and brought her home to meet a real living flesh-and-blood writer. Miss Schindelin was a small, buoyant, assured, radiantly liberated young woman. Her specialties were Thomas Mann and Rainer Maria Rilke. She wore practical shoes, and walked with the stride of a long-practiced grain sower.

"Look here!" she said to me. "What do you write?"

I read her some of my short, compact sketches. I was now smart enough to speak of them as epiphanies, "a showing forth." I showed forth for a good hour or more, and she hailed them as a new art form. I myself accepted that as good. She was not so sure. As a new art form, it would take my readers longer to know what I was up to. And how were readers to do that if I was not published?

"Patience!" she cried, her knitting needles flashing, and she paused to check over the stitches. A woman of profound enthusiasms, she was naturally opinionated. "Look here!" she would cry, often meaning "Look out!" I was quick to return as good as I got. Her eyes would flash, her cheeks puff out, and my wife would say, "It's time to eat!"

Schindy's office at Scripps was just a block away, so we often saw her for lunch. She would arrive with her knitting, and perhaps a sack of apples. Plugged into her energy, my tiring batteries were soon recharged. I was reluctant, however, to send off a book so much in advance of the reading public, in particular the publisher. So I would continue to be patient and try to finish the book in hand. It would be called *The Madmen of Ranna,* and be all about the winter I had spent there. Nothing much had happened, actually, but it had left on me a profound impression. Would it leave a similar one on its readers? I was a bit skeptical.

I did not spring any of this on our Miss Schindelin, fearing she might not get the bloom of it. She adapted to our life style, our diet, our taste in movies, and her place straddling the gearshift in the Ford. At this time a young woman from England, a classmate of my wife's at her progressive prep school (the mixing of boys and girls together) near London, had arrived on a freighter from Australia, and bedded down with her sleeping bag in our front room. She was a lean, intense,

sober-minded young woman with a beautiful complexion and Virginia
Woolf's profile. To walk about our town she wore a pair of soiled
lederhosen, a rucksack and a green beret. During a visit to our friends
the Howards, Leon's wife jokingly said, "Would you like a shower?"
to point up the hot weather we were having.

Crumb replied, "I don't mind if I do," and followed her hostess
to the bathroom. Her name was Brenda, but at school she was known
as Crumb. She proved to play a wicked game of Ping-Pong on one
of the tables in a Scripps dormitory. As a rule, she did not like the
food we were eating, and prepared her own meals out of her rucksack.
She had been away from England, at the time, for a year and a half.
She came close to driving us both crazy the five weeks she spent as
our guest, but when I got around to reading the letters of Gertrude
Bell, I felt I had come to know one of her kind: a British woman of
extreme independence and self-sufficiency. On a trip to the Big Sur
country, which included Schindy and a young English poet, who was
writing a novel, we stopped to have a look at the sea at Point Lobos.

"There's nothing like this anywhere!" I exclaimed, with some
passion.

Everyone agreed to that but Crumb. She was silent until we got
back to the car. From there she had another look, then soberly said,
"Imagine my having been there!"

Was it worth all the trouble she gave us? We decided it was. I
am confident she is now somewhere in England making her way, line
by line, through Doughty's *Arabia Deserta,* which she will justly admire, but not excessively. After all, he was English. And the making
of an Englishman does take time.

My wife had many women friends in Claremont, and with a
husband like me she needed them. The friendship of older women
had come naturally to her, and they appreciated her for both her
qualities and her attention. She welcomed the affectionate concern
she received from housemothers and teachers. One of these was
Mrs. Snyder, a housemother at Scripps, very responsive and attractive, who had recently lost a daughter my wife's age in a car accident.
These women were also very appreciative of a young man who applied himself so seriously to the writing of books it was high time
somebody published.

There were also those, of course, who thought it was more than
high time that I got a job and supported my wife (how long had it
been—almost three years?), but she was not herself unhappy with what
she was doing and rather enjoyed the contribution she was making.
In the meantime, given the continuing Depression, what sort of job

would I find even if I looked? The Great Depression was many writers' ace in the hole.

From our friend Schindelin I heard the startling news that California was not the best place for a writer. There was too much easy living, too much light and heat. There was too much driving to the sea and the mountains, and too much running around on the highways. The life of the mind suffered. The young had no curiosity. They were like young gods in their sunny, open natures, but she felt in them a troubling blandness. They would never write *Death in Venice*. They would probably never read the *Duino Elegies*. The reading of Thomas Mann's *Joseph in Egypt* had led her to reflect about such matters. The life of the mind, of the arts, should experience the nurturing cycle of the seasons! She urged us to consider a new life in the East, where, among other things, I would find my readers. The California people she had met browsed in a book, but they did not read it. Why, indeed, should they? It was hot in the study and the library. Outside, the light sparkled, and the sea washed the beaches. Thomas Mann knew all about it, and saw this life of the body as intoxicating. The sun lulled the mind and the spirit into a languor. If I would forgive her for speaking so frankly, she saw in it the way I was fighting the sunlight. Look how I drew the cracked blinds and sat brooding in the dark! Look how I suffered from eyestrain, a sore back and headaches! This was no place for a truly creative person. It was too much of the outdoors and the outer life, of the desert and the sun.

"But what about the Greeks?" said I, and read her some great lines from Pindar, but a lot of good it did me. What she said was, after needling her brows, "You are not a Greek."

A person like myself, she said (and she had given it some thought), a young person from the new world, not the old world, who felt the forces of the new world rising in him, who should have had better sense than to waste his time on Spengler—such a person should be back where there were seasons like those they had around Poughkeepsie, in Dutchess County. Did I know what it was like around Poughkeepsie? I did not. Therefore I should be quiet until I did. When she herself got back there, next summer, she would invite us for a visit, to see for ourselves.

That was just talk, of course, but I sat there listening. I do a lot of talking myself, and I'm responsive to it.

"What sort of springs are there in Nebraska?" she said.

What sort indeed. Spring came when the winter ended, and we took off our shoes and ran around like crazy. That was spring. By the time we stopped running it was summer, with the asphalt melting, then it was winter and Christmas.

"You've no idea what is spring," she said, reading my mind. "Not just green, but green in all colors. So many greens one didn't need any colors!" How I loved to hear her say that! What a poet she was. With her needles clicking, she said, "You come back to Dutchess County and I show you! You can come back and live in California, when you are old."

My experience of American life had been varied, intense, disorderly, uncritical. I accepted the world as I found it, and as it found me. The serene insularity of college life, a sheltered haven of peace, plenty and promise, I had interrupted with a year of adventure that deprived me of the fruits of my academic labor, the Bachelor of Arts degree that might have provided me a job. With it I might have been part of the future; without it I had thus far been a public burden. A deep frown creased the brow of one of my classmates—secure in his cage at the local bank, trim in his wrinkled summer seersucker—when he cashed my monthly WPA voucher. He flicked the new bills with his rubber-tipped finger, crisp with his contempt. Nevertheless, I envied him the seersucker jacket. What had briefly been my own life, to do with as I pleased (his wife had discussed this with *my* wife), I had immediately complicated in this unacceptable manner. My request for a small loan had been turned down. Nor did I question the wisdom of this judgment, since it was on such hallowed unquestioned principles that I ran boldly at streams too broad for leaping. When my book was finally published, it would be clear (among the other details on the back of the jacket) that my actions were in the interest and spirit of the virtues carved on the stone gates of the college. The one puzzlement to both the college and myself was that I had come back—to our mutual embarrassment. The very least I might have done was go to another country, and marry another girl.

On occasion, some straggling remnant of Okies, in their battered trucks and creaking tin lizzies, might be seen on the east-west highway to the north, or pulled off this highway into the whispering shade of a pepper tree. In Orange County, California, they were like refugees from a foreign country. My country, actually, part of which I had seen from the tilting top of a freight train, but I had not been aroused at the time to ponder consequences. Hard times? When, for me, had it not been hard times? I had not suffered, but I had lived on the rind as well as the bacon. At that very moment, a California writer, John Steinbeck, was giving this problem his full attention, but I would not read *The Grapes of Wrath* until the summer we lived on Cape Cod. I loved most that part about the turtle making his way across the road.

In the summers, as I remember, we sometimes had unexpected visitors. They might come with a friend, or we might have met them at a party, smart Ivy League-type young men and women who liked to sit up half the night and talk, and didn't at all mind sleeping on our car cushions in the front room. The young women might be good at plucking the guitar and singing spirited Russian folk songs. That part I liked. I might even sing along with them, since I had picked up some of the words in my travels. They were all very friendly but committed people, good talkers and eaters, this being the age of the tuna casserole. They preferred to sleep most of the day, and talk and sing most of the night. We had some trouble with our neighbors the Oberholtzers, whose dog might start barking, but after one or two nights our visitors would take off. During the second night I would be asked to join one member of the party in the bathroom for a moment, where I might catch a glimpse, which I was seated on the tub, of the fellow traveler card he was carrying in his wallet. I was usually impressed and a little proud to have had a visit from a real party member. They were smart people. They knew what to say and how to put it on the line. They all saw a great future for me in the party, but I had been born a confirmed nonjoiner—something in my nature told me that the real problem was in the natural order, not in the social. A cardinal rule of my maverick life had been "Don't join anything," and in my ignorance I took comfort in it.

Another one of my wife's English classmates—the first woman I saw wearing blue jeans, with her shirttail hanging out—came to stay with us for two long weeks and taught us songs we sang around the piano. Her family was in the London theater, and she knew everybody I had ever heard of. I greatly admired *The Seven Pillars of Wisdom,* but she had met T. E. Lawrence and didn't like him. Alison was a big handsome girl with broad shoulders that seemed to curve inward, fitting her like a cloak. She was also a writer, and carried along with her a manuscript she worked on when she wasn't sleeping. It was all about her travels and the people she met. She called it *Fellow Travellers,* and read parts of it aloud to us. It astonished me to meet a young woman with that kind of brass and assurance. She had met hundreds of writers and other famous people just by asking around and ringing their doorbells. Some of these people contributed money to her work, and to the party. She wasn't really an official recruiter for the party; she just did it on her own, if the spirit moved her and she thought the person was ready. That's how she felt about me, and half the time

I thought she might be right. But the other half I didn't. We had talked for two weeks about political matters and the war that was coming in Europe, and on the last night I sat with her in her car, parked in our front yard. The door at the front was open, and my wife was playing Bach's Partita in E flat major. Alison didn't really feel my wife was party material, but she knew I was. If I hadn't been married, and pretty confirmed about it, that night I might have become a sort of party member. The advantages were that, come the revolution, you would have a lot of friends. In the meantime I could live a sort of carte blanche life with the inside people in what she referred to as the Jewish Alps. It was just a throwaway line, the way she said it, and I didn't know the Catskills from the Smokies, but I could see the players were all smarter than I was accustomed to play with. I was a pinochle player who played for milk bottle caps; these people were using real silver dollars. My child's soul—the one at issue—took flight at the first ominous creak of harness for the high weeds at the far end of the pasture. Running forward as a joiner, I would just run until I was tripped and tied down. More than forty years would pass before the shape of my fears would emerge from the accumulating clouds of numbers, numbers piled on numbers, ciphers on ciphers, in which I saw revealed the faceless mask of the aggregate, the buzzing hive from which we had once escaped and which we now seemed doomed to rejoin. At some point during my lifetime, the simple, separate person, as celebrated by myself, among others, had so increased in number, in status, in self-awareness, that the result had been a loss of the original substance, single, separate and inviolate. Nobody planned it that way. Nobody actually willed it. It had come to us as a gift of sheer numbers. Quantitative changes that we could measure had led to qualitative changes that continued to elude us. We are accountable, but we no longer know for what it is we account.

I knew nothing of this, seated in Alison's Chevy under the bright arc of the street light. My wife, swaying gently, visible through the doorway, continued to play the Bach Partita. I wanted to slip up behind her, as I sometimes managed, to cup her breasts in my hands as she played and inhale the cologne I had given her for Christmas. I was the captive of other forces, however, and sat low in the seat of the Chevy, astonished by the thickness of my friend's denim-clad knees compared with my own. The red and green gems of the dashboard light spotted her hands. A gleaming eight ball capped the shaft of the gearshift. Clipboards with bundles of notes were tilted on the dashboard, dangled from knobs, bulged the flaps of the door compartments. She knew so damn many people. I felt them gathering to block my exit.

"You've got to make up your mind!" she said, slapping her hand on my thigh, but my ears were full of Bach's Partita, my eyes the sight of my wife, a three-quarter view, leaning back from the piano to accept the advances of the violinist who stooped to gather her into his arms. Without benefit of thought, I got out of the car and walked back to the porch.

Some five or six years later, in an apartment on the backside of Bloomingdale's, my wife and I were with a dozen or so young poets gathered to celebrate Alison's first novel. Copies were piled on the floor before us. Her radiant smiling portrait beamed from the jacket. She could have done a lot for me, she said later, as we stood framed in her doorway, if my fear of guilt by association had not cut me off from what was happening. What did I think I was doing? I was still back where she had left me, up a dry creek paddling my bark canoe.

I was powerfully inclined to let my knees buckle while her strong arms were still around me, holding me up. But she had the maddening habit, while she was talking, of fooling with the temple bars of her glasses; into her mouth, her ears and her nostrils they went while she smoked her corn-tipped Virginia Rounds and let the smoke veil her face. It seemed to me that her broad shoulders had got so round they were like the wings of a hawk who could no longer fly.

In the late spring my wife received an offer to teach at the Westover School, in Middlebury, Connecticut, a polar remove from the world of fellow travelers. This teaching position came with a salary somewhat larger than our combined income, but still small. She would be obliged to live in the school, and I would have to find accommodations elsewhere. All of this greatly pleased our friend Schindelin, in Poughkeepsie, eager to have me freshly dipped in the green of New England. But first we would go to Wellfleet, on Cape Cod, where my wife had spent so many summers at Camp Chequessett. After three winters and summers of California, the light burning at the cracks in the green blinds, the summer silent except for the hiss of the sprinklers, I would only come to know how badly I needed the change after it had occurred. We would load up the Ford, make a stop in Cleveland, then go on for the summer in Wellfleet. Along the way we would visit some of the Indian pueblos near Santa Fe, and make a trip to the cliff house of Mesa Verde in southern Colorado.

At a trading post near Table Rock Mesa, north of Gallup, on the road to Mesa Verde, I saw a turquoise ring, in a setting of six silver raindrops, all of it fashioned from the silver melted down from coins. A Hopi Indian had pawned it for $3.25. It looked great on my third finger. My wife bought it for me, although she knew it would cut into our blanket money. The pawn ticket said the ring dated from about 1885.

There were Navajo squaws in the post, in all their splendor, one of them as tall and fierce as a Japanese warrior, swapping blankets for supplies of flour, sugar and bacon. One had a papoose in the harness at her back; her skin had the shine and color of a new penny. The many things I felt it is impossible for me to describe.

We arrived in Cleveland after midnight, the summer night throbbing with the beat of cicadas, my father-in-law, in his B.V.D.s, asleep in his chair on the screened-in porch. Mother was at the door to the kitchen, spreading papers on the floor as she advanced before us. She was still undecided about which electric refrigerator to buy, and to save the melting ice we drank our root beer without it. I was so tired my head and my eyes ached, but the summer night around me seemed enchanted. Once more we were led through the house, room by room—

. . . so that this room had come as a symbolic climax, as if the house had gathered itself together in the lens of the mirror. Beginning with the kitchen, each room seemed to open on a wider vista, a deeper, more ambitious prospect of American life. A sense of summer leisure, of sweetness and bounty, of innocence and promise without melancholy, seemed to pass through the house, blow in and out of the windows, as if he stood within a grove that Inness might have painted, and gazed out at life. (The Deep Sleep, 1953)

I knew that my wife's impression, as she stood at my side, was of a longing both pleasurable and painful, but I was personally grateful to share an emotion that was part of my expectations. A room of one's own, in a home that seemed both serene and time-defiant. Arcs of haloed light surrounded the street lamps, and some lone, home-bound walker dragged his heels as he whistled tunelessly. Was it possible that any of this might change? Rather than break this trance, I preferred to let it ooze away. I went below to the yard to empty the car, while my father-in-law stood holding a flashlight. In its beam we could see the big night fliers. Trapped in the car's closed rumble seat was the smell of the sage and desert shrubs we had brought back to her mother from Death Valley. Mosquitoes were biting. I heard Fin's hand slap his exposed flesh sharply, scratch at the bite.

"Don't tell Mother," he said, and I was uncertain, at that moment, as to just what he had reference: him in his B.V.D.s, within

281

sight of the neighbors, or the sense we shared of a male conspiracy.

A week later we stopped to see our friend Schindelin, in her hideaway outside Poughkeepsie. I found it far more lavish than she had described it, although her own accommodations were simple enough. On her wall were reproductions of two Munch paintings, at which I stared with interest but not much comprehension. In one, the grass proved to be red, the woman's face yellow, green and purple. I had begun, but did not know it, another adventure. We had come back to Dutchess County and I was being shown the colors of green.

From Schindy we drove through Rip Van Winkle country to the Westover School, the Middlebury village square possessing the chaste perfection of a shrine. The subdued elegance of Westover—a walled enclave, with a touch of the nunnery about it, small dormer windows in a great expanse of the slate roof—led my wife to suggest that I might just drop her off, then go and hide somewhere. That was not a good start, but it was a good suggestion. Some distance down the road, I sat in the car sipping air so lush it filmed my face like syrup. No car disturbed the peace. In the distance I could hear the dampered whine of a grass cutter. In the deep hollow behind the square, where the air seemed to settle, it had the hue of straw-colored wine. Where would I live? There seemed to be no village. A quarter mile to the north, or was it the east, an old house had been converted to a general store. I saw the screen door open and close a measurable instant before I heard it.

My wife was soon back, a handkerchief to her face, which I assumed was an attack of hay fever. When she could speak, her eyes filmed with laugh tears, she explained that she had been met at the door by a handsome Creole maid, who inquired who she was, and if she had an appointment with the mistress. My wife said she did. The maid then declared, "I shell endevah to detuhmin if Mistress Dillingham is ah-vailawbe," which she fortunately proved to be. Both women had greatly enjoyed this performance, for which the maid was locally famous. Mistress Dillingham had also suggested that I might look for a place to live at nearby Quassapaug Pond, where Waterbury people had summer cabins they might rent out for the winter. Never having spent a winter in a summer cabin, I thought that sounded great. We drove by to look at the pond as we left, the shore near the lodge crowded with cabins, but a young man out on the pier, who rented the boats, couldn't get it through his head I wanted to rent a cabin *through* the winter. If I still wanted to, when I got back in the fall he would rent me one.

At the time, Wellfleet was—it still may be—one of those summer places that the lucky visitor may feel he alone had captured the bloom of. Summer after summer had filled my wife with the life and lore of the Cape, seaside and bayside, dunes and freshwater ponds—a pair called "the spectacles" were our favorites—the yearly run of the buried treasure on the island, beach plums for jelly, air like wine, and a mix of natives and summer idlers that kept things sharp. When I needed some change, which was frequently, I would round up returnable bottles and cash them in at the local market.

In a small lunchroom established with the tourists in mind, I saw a portly balding man, with a high-pitched voice, often dining with a female companion. I might pick up fragments of literary gossip. It astonished me to learn that this was Edmund Wilson, author of books difficult to find in the secondhand market. To him I owed my acquaintance with Villiers de L'Isle-Adam, who suggested that his servants should do his living for him.

My wife lived at Camp Chequessett, where she served as one of the cabin leaders. I found a room on the bay side of Wellfleet, in one of the old, handsome and mildewed houses. A block away, where the street forked with the main highway, one of the older renovated houses had just been given a fresh coat of white paint, while the shutters were removed. The sea sun blazed on it daily. It took me several weeks to round up the appropriate camera, one on a tripod with a ground glass, and this marvelous house was my first trophy. Many months would pass before I would see it as a print, but I was confident of the image on my mind's eye. I soon found other matchless subjects, in various shades and intensities of white, but my inexperience with my equipment frequently muffed the performance. I did not at the time have a light meter, an elegant device costing more than twenty dollars. I relied on my instincts and a good run of luck, but my exposures were often bad. An unexpected benefit of my enthusiasm is the way it prepared me for the paintings of Edward Hopper.

One day I took a boat and rowed to Devil's Island to look for pirate treasure and big horseshoe crabs. On the island's beach, the suck of the surf might tip the big crabs to stick up on their spikelike tails, like grave markers. I found a crab big as a breastplate, and black as armor, which I carried into the surf to wash off the sand. As I stood there in the lapping sea froth, I could hear an eerie, rhythmical moaning. It raised the hairs on my neck. There were many weird stories about the island, and parts of it were pitted with holes dug by treasure hunters. The moaning grew worse, and back on the dunes, above the blowing tufted grass, I could see this humped, pumping figure. I thought he might be sick or gagging, and walked to where I saw a big bull-necked man, the muscles in his neck and shoulders corded, crouched on his knees in the soft dune sand between the thighs of an enormous creature. She was so big I wasn't sure it was a woman. Her skirts were thrown back like a collapsed tent, exposing her swollen sowlike belly, white as a squid. One of her soft lobbing breasts spilled out of her blouse, the flesh sugared with sand. What the man seemed to be trying to do was lift the woman's huge bottom so he could penetrate her better. He had his hands and arms beneath her, up to the elbows, but she was simply too heavy for him to lift. His penis was like the neck and head of a great Galápagos turtle, the moist tip of it caked with sand. The harder he thrust at her, the deeper she sank into the dune. I thought his bobbing, pumping head would snap off his neck, like a cork. In the last extremity of his passion, he let out a hoarse bellow and fell forward on her, as if on a sword. The woman had not uttered a sound. I took off and ran, as if I had witnessed a crime, to where I could wade and swim back to the mainland and run to the house. Like Hans Castorp, in his dream in the snow, I had been privileged to see through a chink in the armor that protects the inner temple, where the witchlike old hags, with hanging breasts, dismembered and devoured children. It sickened me to recall it, but I knew—oh, yes, I knew—why it had come to mind. That nature to which we all were captive—in particular the biped who believed himself an exception—turned the very seas into a soup of sperm to make certain of one thing only, the persistence of his ravaging species. In my ears, like the hum of a powerhouse, I could hear the engines of sex at their business, the panting and the groaning, the birds and the bees, the pollen-saturated air.

The next day I saw my wife, in her sailor cap and pinafore blouse with the camp insignia, march by in the weeds at the edge of the highway with a company of her "troops," Raggedy Ann nubiles shuffling along for an ice cream fix in the village. In the voice of a sergeant, my wife was calling, "Left-right, left-right!" as they marched from my sight.

A year later, I would spend most of the summer madly painting watercolors, one of which, a freight car on a siding, was bought by a friend for twenty dollars, my first cash sale in the fine arts. A batch of these sketches, later shown to Lewis Mumford on the chance that I might have an unsuspected talent, earned his appreciative tactful comment that I should continue to work at my writing. At that time I had no Cape photographs to show. Months would pass before my summer pictures would emerge in the darkroom as eight-by-ten enlargements, too many of them pitted with iron from the well water I was using. Occasionally, however, the print reaffirmed what I had seen on the ground glass, the weathered chalk whites and the velvety blacks that I had come to feel I wanted, and had now found.

I'm now vague as to how it happened, but I was persuaded, for part of one summer, to teach the kids of painters, musicians and other idlers how to swim. In a week, some of the young ones were swimming like fish. I was hailed as a magician and, raised to the rank of a paid employee, I soon had more than thirty students, at a dollar a head. With that money I bought a bargain Japanese view camera that looked really great, but proved to be a lemon. On a quick trip to New York, while my wife put up some beach plum jelly, I managed to turn it in on a 4 by 5 Graphic View camera and a Schneider Angulon lens. The wide-angle lens was a revelation. The summer proved to be over before I could really use it, but I had seen my future, and clearly, on the ground glass. A few weeks later I focused this lens on a weathered meeting house in Southbury, Connecticut, the gable like an arrow pointed at the sky. I couldn't wait to see what it would look like in the darkroom, but wait I had to, from late September until the first of March.

That fall reflected my rising spirits, and was wonderful. My cabin on the pond, usually so dark I had to keep a light burning, flamed with the fire and glow of the leaves that piled up on the slopes around it. In my life I had seen nothing like it. I took long wading walks, and sent my father-in-law descriptions of all the birds I had discovered. Then it was suddenly chill. I crawled from the bed to pull on sweat clothes and sit in the kitchen with my feet in the oven, a pad of paper in my lap. I was full of words, but they blurred on the page. The cabin had no ventilation. I would sit for hours in a stupor of oil fumes, waiting to go to bed. I worked hard but badly, burning the crumpled yellow sheets in a coal pail I kept handy. Unable to write, I did manage a bit of reading, and discovered Thoreau. Why not? Was I not in his cabin, marooned on his pond? I freely marked up the copy of the book I was reading, where he so often anticipated my sentiments and my thinking.

What of architectural beauty I now see, I know has gradually grown from within outward, out of the necessities and character of the indweller, who is the only builder . . . it is the life of the inhabitants whose shells they are.

This statement clarified for me my fascination with structures and artifacts. The experience of stumbling on the writer I needed, when he was needed, would prove to be commonplace. The vernacular structures of American life were all, in my opinion, saturated with the character of the indwellers, creating a form that had grown from within outward. From this moment on, the word *Inhabitants* would label and characterize my project. Page after page of Thoreau helped to focus my dispersed enthusiasms. I was also obliged, beginning early in December, to bail my drinking water through a hole in the ice, and adapt myself to lonely weekends. I was often snowed in. My wife sometimes brought me one of the suet puddings that were a Westover speciality, which I would eat while watching her glide about the pond on the skates I had given her for Christmas. A mistake. I saw even less of her than usual. The cabin depressed her, and she seemed to view my accumulating passion with some bafflement. We were dressed for igloos, and on her visits she seldom took off more than her gloves. In her new environment at Westover her needs and challenges had altered; mine had not. I had a great and continuing desire to roll in my mice-infested, hay-filled mattress. Getting out of her clothes—no small task—was something she seemed to have lost the lust for.

To the young woman at the lodge—a Southern girl, from Knoxville, who sometimes cooked for me a chitlin breakfast—I referred to this as my Thoreau period, and I believe she got most of the message. This also proved to be the sort of news that traveled. Word of this bachelor bailing water through a hole in the ice reached the ears of Delia Bronson, a Middlebury widow and retired schoolteacher, who offered to take me into her home, with kitchen and bathroom privileges. I made this move late in February, and just in time. I had not had a bath since the Cape, and my long, uncut hair was matted.

When Delia Bronson saw how I looked with my hair trimmed, my winter duds drying on the line in her basement, I was able to persuade her to let me convert her bathroom into a darkroom, in the interests of art. Neither of us knew where this would lead, but we vibrated to the same high challenge. I set up my machinery (lugged out from Brooklyn, in the rumble seat of the Ford), installed my trays in the tub, my enlarger on the washbowl, and during the long second week of March I managed to print thirty or forty eight-by-ten enlargements, including the meeting house in Southbury. This photograph, happily, awed both of us. I thought it miraculous I was able to print it without the usual pitted surface. Most of the water I used to wash the prints was seeded with tiny particles of rust, pitting the prints like pox. That was the bad news, but the good news outweighed it. Watching these prints emerge in the dark, like objects in a séance, I began to recall, as if I had them before me, some of the prose passages that I had written back in California. I now saw that these passages, like shadow to substance, belonged with the photographs I was now taking, not to illustrate or describe, but to complement the visual image with one of words. My growing excitement was carried to my wife, and to Miss Dillingham, mistress of the Westover School. At her suggestion I agreed to a display of about twenty prints in one of the Westover classrooms. Some of these prints suffered from the pox plague, but they had clarity and brilliance. How had I managed? I feared to dwell on it, and break the spell. The frosty bathroom of Delia Bronson, in Middlebury, had proved to be the scene of this visitation. A few who saw the prints felt that I should be encouraged.

While I had this pressure rising in my boiler, I wrote to James Laughlin, of New Directions, at his home in nearby Norfolk, and hurried over, at his suggestion, to show him what I had wrought. There was also a statement, in the form of a manifesto, in which I clarified the direction I had taken. He asked me to leave some of the prints with him, and a few weeks later he called from New York to suggest I pay a visit to Delmore Schwartz, in Cambridge. After a fairly dismal winter, my expectations were again in full flower. Before leaving for Cambridge, I wrote to Miss Dillingham, who looked with sympathy and favor on my enthusiasm, and told her of my desire to travel the breadth of the country collecting all these marvels before they vanished. This kind and imposing lady, of regal bearing and proportions, agreed to support my proposed enterprise to the extent of five hundred dollars, available through funds contributed by the students. Five hundred dollars! Nothing will measure the effect this expression of confidence had on me.

I was eager to meet Delmore Schwartz, whose essays I had read, and drove to Cambridge at the first opportunity. In an apartment house near Harvard Square, I sounded a buzzer in the hall, and the door opened. Two floors above me, at the railing of the stairwell, a young woman with a broom, a dustcloth about her hair, peered down at me. What was it I wanted? I said I had come from Mr. Laughlin, of New Directions, to see Mr. Schwartz. She considered what I had said, and with some reluctance beckoned me to come up. In a small, sparsely furnished apartment, Mr. Schwartz sat at a desk, smoking a cigar. He turned somewhat abstractedly to look at me, a cloud of smoke hovering between us. I said something or other about what I was doing, as I opened the portfolio and removed the mounted photo-texts.

I passed each photo-text to him, and he looked at it without comment. The woman stood at his shoulder, peering at the photographs, lip-reading lines of the texts. I passed along the material, sometimes with humorous comments, since she read it with such solemn intensity. Mr. Schwartz was silent. His cigar went dead. I realized that he was confronted with a text that required a translation. Nothing he saw or read aroused an echo within himself. With an intensity that I felt faintly hostile, the young woman continued to read, chewing one corner of her lip. I thought her darkly handsome, but overserious. Much that she read I thought to be funny. When they had seen what I had to show them, about twenty photo-texts, I gathered up the materials and put them back in the portfolio. Mr. Schwartz was tactfully speechless. Suddenly, emphatically, the young woman declared, "I like it! I like it!" with the assurance of a judgment, then turned back to her sweeping.

Did Delmore Schwartz comment on that? I've no idea. He sat with his dead cigar, and I felt the burden of his silence. The young woman went on with her sweeping. At the foot of the stairs, my hand on the doorknob, I glanced up, for a last, puzzled impression. The young woman—I thought her gaze almost fierce—stood at the rail, holding her broom.

"I like them!" he said. "Tell him we like them." Then she turned away.

I had the long drive back to Middlebury to reflect on what had happened, and in the fullness of time—it may have been several years—I learned that I had met Mr. and Mrs. Schwartz.

IN LATE MAY WE HEARD FROM OUR FRIEND
Schindy, in Poughkeepsie, suggesting that we go to Mexico with her,
perhaps in July. She would supply the car and the gasoline. We would
provide the travel lore, the tire repairs and the entertainment. Although
I had attended college just a few miles from Mexico, it had never
crossed my mind to *go* there. My dreaming eyes were focused on
Europe. Just before we had left California, however, a book by Stuart
Chase had opened my eyes. The Mexico he had discovered did not
begin at Tia Juana, but lay far to the south, on the high central plateau,
where cities with unpronounceable names revealed a culture that was
older than Europe. Thousands of churches, numberless fabulous ruins,
a native people who wore colorful costumes and lived happily on the
slopes of volcanoes, at the heart of jungles, or walked about the streets
of great cities left over from a decaying colonial empire: it all might
have been on another planet. I was eager to give it a try, but was this
the time? It would take the edge, if nothing more, off the trip I was
planning in the fall. Our friend Schindy agreed that her offer was sudden, but it seemed to be this summer or never. War was spreading
in Europe. She might be called to Germany to visit her family. If we
were going to share this adventure together, it would have to be now,
and as soon as we could arrange it.

On the twenty-eighth of June, three weeks later, we were in the
Blue Ridge Mountains of West Virginia, near the Cumberland Gap,
listening on the radio to the nomination of Wendell Willkie as the
Republican candidate for President. It all seemed a little remote to
a young man whose photographs and texts would soon be published
by the avant-garde New Directions. After a long apprenticeship, was
he finally on his way?

We were up early and drove long and late in the hot, humid days
of July. In New Orleans we melted in the windless swelter, sitting
becalmed in the Vieux Carré, eating slices of un-iced watermelon. I
would return in cooler weather to take some photographs. I was the
one, of course, to consume several paper cups of shaved ice doused
with a purple syrup from a hair tonic bottle, and as my wife assured
me that it might, this delayed our departure for three days. I had never
been so sick with nausea. I lay on wet towels spread on the floor of

the room, and on the third morning I was able to sit up, drink several cups of French coffee, and drive the Ford. We slowly crossed Texas, awash with summer floods, and spent a day in the drugstores of Laredo, drinking Cokes. In the tourist bureau where we acquired our visas, one wall featured a map of Mexico that gave us some indication of what we were in for. Now that we were at the border, the country looked huge. Very loosely speaking, appropriate to the occasion, Mexico City looked as far away as California. Accommodations were minimal. Until we reached the high plateau, the heat was terrible. Our friend Schindy, after a few days of New Orleans, had lost her desire for adventure. Her blouses stuck to her back, her hair to her scalp, and she had settled on a diet of tea and bananas. The smell of the bananas had settled on all of us.

In Laredo we were in a motel with comfortable, shaded rooms, the sounds of children at play in a wading pool, and Schindelin took the liberty of suggesting that we might go on to Mexico City without her, then pick her up as we headed north. She would just sit here in the shade near the pool and *read* about Mexico. There were many good books.

Had I had either the wits or the experience, I would have welcomed her suggestion. She was well, but hardly robust, and none of us understood or spoke the language. To look across the Rio Grande, as I had done, to shacks and mud huts on the south side, was to peer romantically into a world about which I knew nothing. In the shimmering heat it looked as appealing as the Casbah ghettos of Morocco, about which I knew even less. A stream of black-shrouded women filed their way across the bridge to do their shopping in Laredo. A few of these señoras carried sick children, and thrust their hands toward me for coins as they passed. In the Laredo paper I had read with some interest that Mexico was girding for a new revolution. A revolution? I was totally ignorant of Mexican history. I thought their hats and sarapes were romantic. A group of mariachi singers, in the cool of the evening, walked about the courtyard of the motel, singing. Marvelous! I reminded myself, while in Mexico, to be sure and buy some mariachi records. I assured Schindy (and my wife, who had read a bit more of the country's history than I had) that we had come too far to deprive ourselves, in a moment of timidity, of a great adventure. Cars full of tourists crossed the border—sometimes, as I had observed, crossing it very slowly. What was holding things up? Their cars and trailers baked in the sun while they sat on benches gripping sheafs of paper. Uniformed bullies of the type seen in American movies swaggered about maintaining order. But that, of course, was normal.

290

On the first day we hoped to reach Ciudad Victoria—pronounced Bictoria—and start the long drive into the mountains the following morning. Sometime later that day we would be in Mexico City.

In the afternoon, in the foothills of the mountains, the landscape suddenly took on a tropical lushness. In Ciudad Victoria the tourist boom had led to new motels with unshaded light bulbs and high, cell-like windows. Dressing for bed, Schindelin observed an enormous green-and-yellow insect on her pillow. Even larger ones were found on the ceiling and scratching at the slippery tiles in the room's corners. She sat up most of the night reading, armed with a folded newspaper to scare off attackers. What I saw both startled and pleased me. Although I had been exposed to a few Pueblo Indians, their "strangeness" had not impressed me as "exotic." This *exotic* would always prove to be in the eye of the beholder, but with my first glimpse of it, in the dark alleys of Victoria, where the women prepared food over open fires, the spell of Mexico for me was exotic. The ragged urchin in Mexico City, who seized another, slightly smaller urchin, and carried it, instinctively, to the safety of the curb as an American child would scoop up a kitten, profoundly moved and reassured me about a piece of our nature that we seemed able to shed, like a skin. I loved these gentle, infinitely sad-eyed children in proportion to their swelling numbers.

In the early dawn we were awakened by the rattle of drums. Standing on a chair so I could peer out of the high window, I watched a troop of ragged soldiers, as comically disarrayed as those in the streets of Vienna during the Dollfuss period, march up and down a rutted, gutted lane as a bully with a sword cracked out his orders. The revolution was still at its work, and counterwork. In the Hotel Victoria, an Indian waiter, with a Mayan profile, barefooted in his soiled waiter's jacket, took our "orders" while a doomed rooster dangled from a cord at his back. Sometime later, an elderly señora served us a plate of scrambled eggs we did not eat. Little I cared.

The highway over the mountains to San Luis Potosí curled and spiraled endlessly into a cloudland of peaks where wispy rows of corn were planted in tiers. In the clearings we saw thatch-roofed shelters, smoking fires and naked children. At the edge of the highway, sarape-clad Indians plodded along under high piles of fagots, or walked along spinning out strands of wool. If we stopped to recover from car nausea—both Schindelin and my wife were sick—children suddenly appeared with clusters of small, finger-length bananas. A small boy with the bushy eyebrows of a bandit stared at me as if unaware that I was also staring at him. Schindy gave them all coins. Their bare feet slapped along the blacktop beside us. At the summit, where the car started balking, we crawled around a turn that left the tropics behind us, the prospect opening out on a desert mountain landscape. On one side rain fell abundantly. On the other it did not. Early that evening we entered Mexico City and wandered about the unmarked streets of the suburbs, pursued by large packs of *muchachos.* On the Paseo de la Reforma, which seemed empty of traffic, we found accommodations in a Victorian mansion. My wife and I were bedded down in an arboretum, full of uncaged birds. They had us up early (it proved to be a Sunday) and we lay listening to the popping of what I thought must be firecrackers. Cars were racing up and down the Reforma. A fiesta, perhaps? No, that would come later. An election was in process, and the votes were still being taken and counted. It was thought that Camacho had been elected, but there were the usual reservations. When I stepped out to look for a newspaper, the gunfire was still active. Peons riding in a truck, like figures in a Rivera mural, fired their pistols in the air and at anything moving. I ran for the shelter of a tree as they roared past me, grinning and hooting. In the lobby of the new Reforma Hotel, the tourists were huddled out of what was believed to be the line of fire. I purchased a paper and boldly returned to the street. The carnival spirit was so pronounced I waved at the trucks full of peons. They waved back. A passerby who had been hit by the random fire hobbled along with the assistance of a woman, his injured leg dragging. "*Buenos días,*" he greeted me, and smiled as they passed.

Our landlady, a very gracious and patrician señora, her strings of beads rustling as she moved about, apologized for the behavior of people participating in the "disorder." It would soon pass. But she recommended caution until the election was over. During the day we sat at her high curtained windows watching the carriages pass, and hearing occasional distant gunfire. Mexico was not exactly what my companions had expected, but suited me fine. The señora, after a sumptuous tea, showed us photographs of the gardens where she had grown up in Guadalajara. The people of Guadalajara were all like happy children, and loved to sing and dance.

In the summer of 1940, Mexico City was still a frontier metropolis, closer to the turn-of-the-century frontier than it was to Roosevelt, Mussolini and Hitler. The Zócalo was a park in an impressionist painting, the women strolling about with parasols, the empty benches dappled with shadows. Velvety masses of cumulus clouds could be seen above the treetops. In the afternoons it showered. Sometimes we sat in the tiled, sky-flooded rotunda of Sanborns, with a throng of summer students practicing their Spanish. I was eager to see the snow-capped volcano, unpronounceable, visible in the photomural in the lobby.

The coolness of Mexico City in the morning and evening troubled Schindy with fits of chills and sneezes. The señora advised us to go to Cuernavaca, only fifty miles away but with a temperate and sunny climate. It seemed longer than that with the car windows open, to give the ladies plenty of fresh air, and I gave them both my professional opinion that it was quite like Santa Barbara when settled by the Spaniards. A gutted, empty street led us toward the square, past doorways that opened into cool green patios. We were able to park right there on the plaza, in the shade of the trees of India. At the center of the square the sun blazed, the shadows a shimmering purple. A steady stream of men, women, children and burros crossed the plaza in both directions. The men wore loose-fitting trousers and blouses, their faces deep in the shadow of their sombreros. The women were hooded in a black that soaked up the dazzle, the ragged, smiling children were half-naked, but both the men and their burros moved as if in a trance. One man followed along behind a herd of goats, the tip of his long whip trailing behind him. The frieze-like spectacle of this parade of figures simply left me dazzled. To sit there basking in the sun, my eyes resting on the shadows, the frieze unrolling before me like a diorama, seemed to me an earthly consummation of something dreamed. What invisible terror lurked behind it? Hans Castorp's dream in the snow had made me wary of such sun-drenched perfection.

While the women napped, I wandered about in a daze, my camera hanging unused from my neck. Photographs seemed laughable. My thralldom was complete, although I knew nothing of what I was seeing. What had prepared me, in my American experience, for this enchantment with the primitive? I sat on a bench with two small boys, one of whom gripped my hand like the leash of a pet. They seemed to me children of paradise, careless and amoral as puppies.

I was careful to conceal my thralldom from my companions, who found the children dirty and the poverty depressing. We got rooms near the plaza, in a sort of pension run by a black man who had once been a railroad porter. He claimed to have been—and I believed him—the original model for the smiling black man on the Cream of Wheat carton. His smile now had a few gaps, and his curly pelt was white as a barrister's wig. He had worked for Fred Harvey's dining car service, and swore that he had often seen my father loading his day-old leghorn eggs when the train stopped in Central City. What could I say? His memory seemed greener than mine. With the Depression he had come to Cuernavaca, where no one else served American breakfasts and chicken-fried steaks. Was he ever homesick? No, he replied, not much, but he did miss rooting for the White Sox.

On the third or fourth morning, Schindelin did not appear for breakfast, nor did she eat her bananas at lunch. By evening she had the fever and the nausea. The *turista* would soon pass, our host said, but three days later, filmed with perspiration, her face the color of wet bread dough, she wished she would die. Both my wife and I feared that she might. I managed to find a doctor, a sweet, sad man who listened to me with his lips puckered as he fed nuts to a parrot perched on his desk. He gave me a few pills, which she refused to take. On the fourth night, as we sat up with her, her eyes sunken with exhaustion, she fell asleep. By morning the fever had broken and she was able to sip bottled water. I admitted to neither Schindelin nor myself how deathly sick I believed her to be. In a crisis that easily might have killed her, I had proved to be ignorant and helpless, and the nights I had spent putting wet towels on her forehead had also dampened my thralldom. Wasn't it about time we took off for home? I asked. They agreed that it was.

On our way north, at the pyramid of Teotihuacán, we climbed high up the slopes for the view, which included a parking lot where five or six *muchachos* were washing a just washed car. On the long, hot drive to Texas, we were silent, but I knew that my wife was secretly grateful that what she feared had not happened. Having escaped, I was already thinking of my next trip.

We drove from Laredo to Poughkeepsie, with one short stop for sleep. To a close friend Schindelin later confided that she had never— no, never—expected to return alive, and that she would never—no, never—ever again go anywhere in a car. She meant with me. One of those who liked to get started early and seldom stopped.

She kept that vow until almost September, when I offered to drive her to Wellesley, where she planned to teach. I had swapped the Model A roadster for a 1935 Ford V-8 coupe, with a seat wide enough for me to sleep in on my upcoming photo safari. About ninety miles east of Poughkeepsie, it began to heat up, tighten up, smell up, and then it stopped. It had been a swell car for the money—about eighty dollars on the swap—but the pump hadn't pumped any oil. A passing farmer took Schindelin to where she could catch a bus, but I stayed in Easthampton for almost a week while the mechanic installed a rebuilt motor. It ran so well I drove on to Wellesley and took Schindy for a ride as far as Sudbury, where we had lunch. She had loaned me the cash to buy the car and I wanted her to know it was a good investment.

A week later my wife rode with me as far as New York, where we had a parting dinner at Chumley's, in the west Village, a clubby sort of hangout for newspaper people, who liked to sit around and play chess or cards after dining. In frames around the walls were the jackets of the books some of them had written, most of the books already forgotten, a detail lost on me at the time. It was not a festive evening. My wife was nervous and troubled, and I was torn with the Jimmy Durante quandary, eager to be gone but wanting to stay. We tried to cheer things up with our first real cocktails, but the martini I had burned my throat and brought tears to my eyes. I would never prove much of a boozer. My wife liked the maraschino cherries in Manhattans. We had rented a room in one of those dumps that give rates to academic people, the rugs so dirty you dress and undress without getting out of bed.

In the morning, coming out of the Hudson tunnel into New Jersey, I stopped to take the picture of a church as white and pure as Ivory soap. It might have been brought in during the night from a village in Vermont or New Hampshire. I had a long wait for a break in the traffic before I could click the shutter. This beauty lifted my spirits, however, as if I had sighted a hawk in the city. Near Washington, D.C., the narrow highway was lined with used-car lots and fields of wrecked cars, which I was free to pass by since they had been spotted by Walker Evans. Something about it attracted me, but it was not a subject I was eager to salvage.

In the capital, I stopped to see Roy Stryker at the Farm Security Administration. I had seen the photographs taken by members of his staff, and thought I might find a niche in his program. Mr. Stryker looked at my photographs with keen interest, but without enthusiasm. What did I think I was doing? Where, in God's name, were the people? He listened with amusement to my explanation that the absence of the actual people enhanced their presence in the structures, and in the text. He felt this to be a disturbing contradiction, the sort of thing you might get from a young writer. Stryker's compassion for real people, and their enduring hardships, made him suspicious of my word impressions, and he had the plainspoken American's distrust of anything that smacked of arty. I could feel his concern that I might be using this terrible Depression for some trivial, personal artistic ends. He showed me photographs of people—his desk was strewn with them—long-suffering, displaced, disinherited men, women and children, who parked their battered cars and built their lonely campfires

295

along the nation's highways, and I felt the justice of his disapproval. Was I lacking in compassion? I would have time to ponder this question. My sympathies and emotions were profoundly aroused by the socially deprived and defeated person, by the accumulating and irretrievable losses, but the flame that warmed my heart and indeed burned in my soul was not in the government's plans to put an end to hardship. Hardship, indeed, seemed to me indispensable to what I was feeling. There was something in hardship that I valued, and did not want to see the end of. The peace and relative plenty of the house in Cleveland, with its wide shaded lawn and crowded bird feeders, the breeze stirring the curtains at the dormer windows, aroused a deep and sweet sorrow in me because I seemed unable to truly possess them as I was able to savor and possess hardship. Was there then a contradiction in my life, and in the life of my country, that I would not soon, if ever, fathom, between the good and plentiful life we all wanted and the hard times we secretly cherished? Roy Stryker was right in sensing that my inscrutable purpose was not just in social justice. I wanted the *anima* behind both the justice and the abuses, one that would prove to be the same with or without them. Later that afternoon, in the capital's slums, I took pictures of the tilting, box-like houses, so much like a child's crayon drawing, but he would not have approved my reasons. I found them poignantly expressive. For me, they were unmistakable portraits of generations of hard times, of generations of Old Black Joes, and I could look at them with a pleasure that would have distressed Roy Stryker. What could I make of it? One thing I could make was a photograph.

Later that day, across the river in Virginia, I bought leather boots that laced to my knees, and army-style breeches of tough olive corduroy. They would serve me well as I clambered over fences, or waded through fields of weeds and waist-high brush. That night, at the end of the a dark dirt road, I curled up in the seat and tried to sleep as car after car, with dimmed lights, appeared out of the darkness, parked, and then departed. Was it always in the dark we would grope for our pleasure? Shortly after sunrise, I sat up to see I was parked there alone, in the company of birds. I took a walk to stretch my legs, and splashed water on my face from my new canteen.

To be free in this manner, free in my mind and on wheels, yet captive of an abiding and pleasurable enthusiasm that demanded realization—this seemed to me one of the best of possible worlds. It would more than fuel the engine of my purpose on this long trek to California and back, and there was no question in my mind that I would find what was there to be found.

T HE OVERRICH COMPOST OF SOUTHERN LIFE AND
history, which I had sampled in the pages of Faulkner, and visible
wherever I looked. Southern atmosphere, as dense and pungent as leaf
smoke, to be breathed in and savored like pollen, was in such contrast
to my previous experience, I found myself in another country. The
ready hospitality, the inflection of the speech, the suspicion that there
was less just below the surface than on the surface, the provocative sex-
uality that was a matter of custom, of tradition, not intended to incite
more than a flirtation . . . The warm Southern nights, the music and
black voices, seemed as exotic to me as Mexico the previous summer.

But the camera, and the camera eye, is justly looked upon with
suspicion. Soon enough I was seen as an intruding alien. I tramped
about with this machine mounted on its tripod, or set it up to conceal
myself beneath the hood, invariably pointed at some house or doorway judged to be of no pictorial interest. Why would I take *that*, except to reveal what was better concealed? I could only have in mind
the exposure of whoever lived there, a blot on the peeling Southern
escutcheon. Turning from me to note my car, with its out-of-state
license, clarified the picture. I was a Northern snooper out to discredit
the troubled, dilapidated Southern self-image. Black and white both
felt it, the black with less malice but a more profound discomfort.
My presence testified to their worst suspicions about their condition.
The separate yet commingled cultures of black and white that make
of the South a unique and tormented culture were at once unavoidably
visible and subject to instant falsification. The impoverished black,
the debased poor white, had been well exposed in books and
magazines, and such distinctions as might be made were in the eye
of the beholder, not the camera.

At the edge of Culpeper, in Virginia, I found a house and a dead
tree, equally husk-like, both appearing to date from Lee's surrender,
that seemed to speak directly to my troubled state of mind. Was it
a portrait, or a caricature? Did it reveal a state of soul or a state of
abuse? I could see now one, now the other, by merely blinking. What
was there to be seen was in the eye of the beholder. But in the basking
sunshine of a Blue Ridge October, I felt the ripeness and warmth of
survival more than I felt the chill of inhuman custom. The meaning this

structure had to give out was a many-layered, many-voiced passage of history, too dense and complex to do more than acknowledge, but in this surviving husk more life-enhancing than life-defeating.

But that was not all. What I had made, when the shutter clicked, was a photograph. It would be weeks before I saw the negative, and many months would pass before I made a print of what I had seen on the ground glass. Would that image restore my original impressions, or would they be replaced by others? To what extent would this new image, cut off from its surroundings, constitute a new structure? How much of the "reality" had it captured? How much had it ignored? Whether or not it had been my intent, I would end up with something *other* than what was there. It would be a new likeness, a remarkable approximation, a ponderable resemblance, but not a copy. This new image would testify to the photographer's inscrutable presence. I was not appreciative of these distinctions at the time I took the picture, and believed that what I had seen on the ground glass would surely be what I had captured.

I made my way south along the foothills of the Smokies, the blues of the mountains to the west transparent in the hazy light, deepening to purple as the sun set behind them. The warmth of the season, the golden October light, the harmony that prevailed between man and nature (man and man was another matter), seemed to clarify for me, in an instant, the attachment of the Southerner to the place he came from. A ballad-like sense of peace, if not plenty, seemed as palpable to me as strains of music. I was subject, as my experience had proved, to a lyrical euphoria when exposed to new places. I had felt it repeatedly in Europe, and to the point of dazzlement in Mexico. If something unearthly had occurred, I would have been an eager and a willing witness. This mood was both so tangible and so fragile I was reluctant to dispel it. I stayed away from the larger towns, and avoided photographing what might arouse comment or suspicion. I confined myself to farmhouses and outbuildings, and the look of fields and fences in the slanting light. I noted how frequently a coat of whitewash would accent a weathered wall, gate, door or brick chimney. Most of the natives I saw were black, deferential to the white man, and eager to be helpful. I soon found that their answers to my questions, as to where I was and and where I hoped to be going, were concerned less with information than with a desire to be cordial. Was this the right road? Yessuh. Was it a good road? Yessuh. If places were mentioned, I might not understand what was said. This increased my assurance of strangeness. I slept one night in the car—or rather I spent the night awake listening to the movement of cattle, the snuffling of curious

298

dogs. My first night in a hotel, the bed a creaking antique on a floor that tilted toward the window, offered me a curtained view of the street like an illustration of a page of history. A white horse, ghostly in the light of a waning moon, whinnied in a manner I thought to be human. I relished the family-style breakfast in the morning, which I shared with a guest and seven members of the family, having long forgotten what it was like to eat eggs fried in fat and hot slabs of cornbread. The affable garrulousness and easy hospitality charmed me. I liked being huhhh-ney to the woman who served me. I smoked a cigar that crackled like cornflakes when I lit it.

Two days later, a Saturday night in North Carolina, I watched the town fill up with old cars, buggies and wagons that were packed with denim-clad country people and their children, whom I recognized as poor whites. It was new to me to see a real "tribe" of people, the men and women separate, the kids roving about like unleashed pets, the men inclined to hunker down on their hams like Indians, their forearms on their knees, their hands dangling. It amazed me to see that they might crouch like that for an hour or more, silently smoking, or in animated talk. The women were never part of this commingling of the men. I liked the drawling speech, the turns of phrase, and the breeding I saw in the lean faces and work-honed bodies, their postures and gestures acquired from the daily habits of a lifetime. I liked them, but I feared to intrude, spying on them as I would have Gypsies in my home town. They seemed to me more interesting and intense than the people I had known. The women were lean from work and child rearing, the skin of their pale faces tight to the bones as if to emphasize fundamentals, thin-lipped, inclined to uneasy glances that might be quick to take offense. To watch them in the way I cared to, I sat in the car, pretending to read a paper. I wouldn't have dreamed of trying to take a picture. I had always felt the camera eye to be intrusive, but never so profoundly as when I contemplated directing it toward such private people. The barefooted children, in their hand-me-down clothes, ran about beneath the wagons. How was it that I, a native of the plains, should feel that here I was at long last among my own people?

In South Carolina, near the state line, I stopped at the edge of a sun-baked bean field. At its center, raised off the ground so high that a small child might walk beneath it, was a large, one-storied clapboard house with a shingled roof and high windows without glass. They made deep pockets of shadow, and crisp shadows accented the unpainted clapboards. The yard around it was hard and clean as a

299

floor, and between me and the house was a covered well with a pulley to raise and lower the galvanized bucket. Not a soul or a dog in sight. In the high noonday heat I assumed both might be napping.

The patterns of light and shade, the colors of earth and wood, the shimmering flame of light at the edge of the shadows, compelled me to try and get the picture. In all its weathered and man-shaped details it fulfilled my idea of the beautiful. But I would have to intrude on private property. Stealthily, picking my way along the furrows, extending the legs of the tripod as I approached the house, I set up my camera, stooped beneath the cloth, and saw the blurred image on the ground glass. Beads of perspiration burned my eyes. I backed away, shirttailed my face, then once more focused on the ground glass. Just to the left of the house, perhaps ten yards behind it, in colors that appeared designed to conceal him, a black giant stood in a posture of resting, his hands clasping a hoe handle. A narrow-brimmed hat, tilted forward, shaded his eyes. I pretended not to see him. It made my movements more assured and casual. I was deliberate and open in what I was doing. I moved the tripod, I took several pictures. I felt the passing of time would prove to be to my advantage. On the ground glass I watched him approach. Too late to cut and run, I was paralyzed.

"What you see?" he asked me.

Out from under the cloth I peered up, and up, at the ivory smile in his black face. He was curious. "What you see?" he repeated.

"You want to look?" He did. He crouched low, I hooded him with the cloth, and for a long moment he was silent. Backing away, he shook his head, puzzled. "You don't see it?" He did not. I checked to see if the glass was in focus. It was beautiful. Then it occurred to me it was upside down. "It's upside down," I said, apologetic. That was more mystifying. He had another look at it. What he saw led him to stoop, slapping his knees, then straighten up with a bellow of laughter. Why the image was upside down was something I did not want to go into. We moved to the shady side of his well, where we both had a drink from the bucket. He took deep audible swallows, his Adam's apple pumping. When he had finished, he emptied the bucket over his head, the spill of water darkening his shirt. The drops that fell to the ground did not soak in, but rolled into balls of dust. If he had worn a sheet I would have felt in the presence of the Lord in *The Green Pastures*. Near where we stood, a wire-supported pole went up about twenty feet to dangle four or five gourds, the narrow ends chopped off. Small birds, nesting in the gourds, darted in and out. He watched this with such delight and concentration that I walked

300

away, not wanting to disturb him, and when I looked back from the road he was still there, his wet hair gleaming.

A few hours later, in Greenville, I had my dinner in a café, then walked around the streets as the day cooled. There were structures on the main street I planned to take in the morning, when the light would be better. The Southern night was breezeless and humid. It seemed foolish to spend it cooped up in a hotel room. I followed a dusty side road to the edge of town and parked in the shade of a willow. Later I curled up in the seat, and I lay there attentive to the sounds that came from the nearby houses, the voices of children, dogs, radio programs. I had half drowsed off when lights flickered in the rear-view mirror and on the windshield. I heard the throb of an idle motor. A moment later, a cop, with a beefy perspiring face, put his head in the window I had opened. He noted my camera, and the boots I had unlaced to cool my feet. Something about that pleased him. He turned to wag a finger at the cop he had left in the car. Even in my own opinion an intruder like myself had aroused very little suspicion.

"Hi," I said, and smiled.

In 1940 the Second World War had begun, but we were not yet in it. A slight war fever was palpable among those who might be drafted, or felt themselves threatened. In Greenville, South Carolina, I was picked up as a vagrant, and charged with being a possible spy. My camera, at the ready, was there beside me in the seat, and I had obviously been taking pictures. Of what? Of critical installations, surely. The excitement of having captured a spy soon gave rise to a sense of exhilaration. The chief of police, a short, fat man with a nervous, hysterical manner, his leather straps, ammunition belts, and pistol in a holster, might have served Mack Sennett as a model for the comical—as opposed to the beefy and brutal—Southern cop.

I was fingerprinted, questioned, all of my gear was inventoried, then I was taken to the second floor of a jail behind the buildings facing the main street. This was a single large room with bars at the windows, cots placed around the walls, a windowless cell, the door heavily barred, in the room's back corner. A local desperado, by the name of Furman, was kept in this cell.

In the room below—as I found out at sunrise—a chain gang of blacks was incarcerated; the racket they made leaving their quarters woke me up. We had a view through the door, and the glassless windows, over the lower roofs of the town. We could see and hear it come alive in the morning, pause during the heat of the day, become active and noisy approaching the dinner hour, then quiet down in the evening.

I shared the room with a motley crew of bums, ne'er-do-wells and poor whites. They had been drinking and fighting, or merely loafing. Some were loud and bitter for as long as ten minutes. Most were resigned. During part of the day and the long night they were full of talk, tales and wild humor. Having me as a new and interested listener meant more than having me as a talker. I did a lot of listening and scratching. Once or twice a day I gave somber speeches to the chief of police as he stood at the door. He liked my performance. While I talked he chewed on a toothpick, scratched his private parts and gazed reflectively over the roofs of the city, over his domain.

On the strength of the hope that I was a spy, a plainclothes official, a kindly elderly man, with whom I briefly discussed Stark Young and Faulkner, came over from the capital, Columbia. He looked at my papers, heard my story, recommended that I spend at least a week in Charleston, then advised them to release me. I had a long day and night to brood over whether that advice would ever be taken. On the third or fourth morning, shortly after the chain gang rattled its way down the alley, I had a tin cup of coffee with the chief—who had for me, he said, no hard feelings—was given my camera, the keys to my car, and advised to get the hell out of South Carolina. That advice I took. Along with me went a large colony of bugs, some of whom took up fairly permanent residence. I drove without stopping, but with the greatest caution, the eighty miles or so to the Georgia state line, then another fifty miles to Athens. In the Athens YMCA I took a long, long shower and washed myself repeatedly with Lifebuoy soap, scrubbing my scalp and hair. The profound relief I felt—to be free of incarceration, a sense of helplessness that is traumatic—had little or nothing to do with the relatively comical incident. I had also known it in Grosseto, Italy, where I was picked up as a threat to Mussolini, but the jail in Greenville, the character of the law and order, the "outside" world that I could see and share through the windows, left on me a ponderable impression.

While in Georgia—I had heard about Georgia, I had read *Tobacco Road,* I had seen the chain gangs in the movies—I was understandably reluctant to take pictures. I kept a low profile. I had recently read *The Heart Is a Lonely Hunter* and heard that the author had lived in Columbus. I could believe that. The basking Southern heat, the soft golden light, the way structures and people appeared to be saturated with the scent of a past as dense as leaf smoke, smoldering and druglike, in which everybody was a willing compliant victim . . . Walking the dusty streets, I envied the writers fortunate enough to come from such places, still sticky with the pollen that clung to them. It seemed to me they need only close their eyes, open their pores and inhale deeply, to possess their subjects. The sorghum-like richness of Southern life was both on the surface and fermenting beneath it. Through the dusty lace curtains at my hotel room window I spied on passersby whom I secretly envied, as Anderson spied on his neighbors in Winesburg. They were dream-drugged, these people, and I envied the depth of their addiction.

In the nearby countryside, as I was driving around, I saw a glow of lights that I thought might be a fire. It proved to be a small carnival, with a rocking, clanking Ferris wheel, one or two dangerous rides, and sideshows of freaks. It had been set up in a field of trampled grass, the air smoking with the savor of barbecued meat. No carnival or chautauqua of my boyhood generated so much excitement and so many expectations. These country folk, with their throngs of small fry, were the "crackers" I had read about in Erskine Caldwell. I was amazed at the visible kinship ties, the cartoon grotesqueries of Li'l Abner, or the figures in Faulkner's "Spotted Horses," to the people I saw around me. In the context a small occasion provided, larger-than-life figures and sentiments materialized. Given a throng of expectant, deprived rural people, a mythic South might emerge from their shared anticipations. Its sensuality aroused me. I felt the surrounding darkness would soon be cluttered with amorous couples. After the engines had coughed and died, the crowd had dispersed, the tents had collapsed, a cloud of dust so thick I could taste it hung over the field where it had all happened. I spent the night in the car, not far from a banjo that repeated, and repeated, the same chords. Now and then the player cried out in the manner of a flamenco singer. My feeling that hardship, and hard times, if not destructively brutal, if not prolonged to the point of negation, are necessary to a density and richness of emotion that seem noticeably absent in happier situations I largely owe to these few weeks of Southern exposure. I did not say to myself that my life had changed, but with the morning light I felt that it had. Missing from my life had been the emotion that finds its fulfillment and release in the ballad. I had discovered the emotion, but how to cultivate it would prove to be the work of a lifetime. A few years later, when I had read James Agee's *Let Us Now Praise Famous Men* and saw Walker Evans's accompanying photographs of sharecroppers, I would fully appreciate the wide range of impressions I had just experienced.

In Pike County, Alabama, I crossed a field of corn stubble for a better view of several barns and a house, weathered to the color of

303

dead branches. I moved in closer to get the shingled roof of the house, shimmering with heat. Under the hood of the camera, focusing on the ground glass, I heard an angry, bellowing voice. I uncovered my head and looked around. I saw no one. The voice spoke again—it seemed closer—and the corn stubble crackled as if trampled by cattle. The blast that followed was that of a shotgun behind the barns. In the morning stillness the air seemed to tremble like my legs and hands. I ran for the car, dragging the tripod, and some moments later I saw the film of perspiration on the face in the rearview mirror, the wide, staring eyes. Could one smell fear? I thought I could detect it. Inside my clothes I was slippery with perspiration.

A Southern friend had told me that the streets of Montgomery were as fragrant with sex as the smell of magnolia, and I drove about slowly, sniffing the air like a coon dog. The basking, windless heat was stirred only by fans, whirring in the shadows of deep porches. I drank a cold Dr Pepper at a drugstore counter, the mirror vibrating with the throb of a ceiling fan. The postcard I had written and put a stamp on I decided not to mail.

My objective was New Orleans, and I persuaded myself that I should get there a day or so early. I drove south to Mobile, then west along the Gulf Coast, the water as smooth as a pond. Men and boys sat along the shore, fishing, with the lines dangling slack from their long poles. I had not experienced heat that drugged the senses, and had about it a lulling, agreeable torpor. To keep from dozing at the wheel, I parked and took a nap. Animals and people were both becalmed. I understood the necessity of the siesta. Much later I would understand the need for the bourbon and the mint julep.

In New Orleans I had been invited to stay with Otis Lee, who had been one of my teachers at Pomona College. That winter he was on leave from his position at Vassar, to continue his own philosophical writing. The week I spent in New Orleans owed more to Otis and Dorothy Lee, and our long nightly discussions, than the prowling with the camera in the Vieux Carré. There I soaked up atmosphere to the point of saturation, but for reasons that are no longer clear to me I overexposed most of the negatives.

Driving north from New Orleans, I stopped to see my friend Hubert Creekmore, who was then living in Jackson, Mississippi. He took me to meet one of his friends and neighbors, Eudora Welty, and among other things we talked about William Faulkner. Faulkner's town was Oxford, on my route north, but I had no intention of intruding on his privacy. I was encouraged, however, to intrude, if possible, on his old friend Phil Stone. That also seemed unwarranted to me, as a writer who had as yet published nothing, so I spent most of the day in Oxford sitting in the square, waiting for history to strike me. It did not. Late in the afternoon I screwed up enough gall to appear at the door of Stone's law office. He was there. On my admitting my interest in Faulkner, he took me in tow. Phil Stone was a fluent and accomplished talker, and like most talkers craved a fresh and good listener, which I proved to be. I was directed to the house down the street, centered in a large lot, which now looms in my mind like a Faulknerian mansion, but unfortunately the details are blurred. My car was parked in the driveway, approaching the house, where I assumed I would be spending the night. I would meet his wife. I would be modestly feted. I would be gorged with tales beyond the telling, and I would be dimly aware, during the long evening, of the ghostly passage of black figures, and the musical murmur of black voices. Not asked to stay, I inquired if I might spend the night in my car, parked in their drive. I had told them of my adventure in Greenville, South Carolina. I was given permission to sleep in my car.

I lay awake until daylight, seeking a clue to my pleasurable but disordered impressions. In the light of these impressions, Faulkner's fiction seemed both controlled and understated. The soul of the South, as I was privileged to perceive it, seemed to me more complex, and bizarre, than the reports I had read about it. More incredible to me, I found its strangeness wondrous and life-enhancing, rather than merely monstrous and grotesque. I owed these impressions to Phil Stone's remarkable relationship with the Negroes—*his* Negroes, who deliberately chose not to be free. A few were servants in his house, others occupied barns and outbuildings. Something in Phil Stone's nature cultivated and responded to this reversal of historical roles, the master who became the captive of his slaves. I had been greatly impressed by Melville's profound grasp of this dilemma in his novella *Benito Cereno,* which I saw worked out with even greater refinement in the way the blacks dominated the Stone household. A marvelous "mammy," deep and broad as a scow, served the food she had prepared on a schedule of her own making, her eyes rolling, her lips parted in a litany of Yessuhs and Yes ma'ams. With each serving I exchanged knowing glances with the master and the mistress of the house, eager to share their predicament. An old black named Blue, asked to fetch wood for a fire, in an hour's time appeared with a stick, no more than a piece of kindling, on his crossed arms like an offering. Thanked for that, but urged to get more, he almost collapsed with contrition, then appeared, an hour later, with two pieces of the same size. I had been eagerly brought to the Stone house, to share its hospitality, so that

I could bear witness to this drama of the slaves who were now the masters, and seemed even more fawning in their service. The role reversal had been so complete, so lovingly achieved, that Stone felt compelled to share it with someone, even a profoundly ignorant youthful Yankee. He had become captivated by his own captivity. I doubt that was true of his young wife, preoccupied with a squalling infant, but Stone took me off to his study for further comments on his condition. A friend of FDR, and other national figures, he had their signed photographs ornamenting the book-lined room. We smoked stogies imported from Pennsylvania, while he brought me up to date on his pleasurable torments. They were many. Periodically he sent the young men to Memphis, with stakes of money, but separated from the money, they returned to his house. The external world did not appeal to them. Besides, they loved the master and the mistress. The top exhibit—for which I was slowly prepared—was of a satin-lined case full of silver goblets, each goblet twisted on its stem by powerful hands. Who had done it? The loving mammy. It just seemed to happen and she couldn't help it. She was just giving each one of them a polish, and lo and behold, it just seemed to happen. Two dozen goblets. It was clear to both of us that Mammy's twist had made them priceless.

Shortly after midnight, he bid me good night, wished me luck as a writer, and showed me to the door. Before I passed through it I asked him again if I could sleep in my car, parked in his driveway. Yes, that I could do. More than that, if I delayed my departure I might have breakfast with them in the morning. As I made myself comfortable in the seat of the car, I wondered if this, too, was a decision that the slaves had made for the masters. A sleeping guest was a bother. There would be a bed to make, and sheets to be changed. By morning it was drizzling, and just after daylight I opened my eyes to see the aging, half-blind Blue at my window, peering in, muttering to himself. Did he see me? I pretended to sleep. When he shuffled off, in a parody of the gait of Stepin Fetchit, I decided to take off rather than weaken or dispel the incredible events of the evening. I had breakfast in Oxford, grits with my eggs, then drove north to where a bank near the road had eroded to leave a raw gully, red as a bleeding wound. I managed to take a few pictures, in spite of the drizzle, then continued toward Memphis. Perhaps an hour later, as it rained much harder, I passed a field where a harness-patched plow horse, white as Moby Dick, stood luminous in a piece of overgrazed pasture, his heavy head bowed. I should have stopped. That I didn't is why I have forever borne it so vividly in mind.

In Arkansas the rain-washed air dried quickly, like a watercolor. I drove a long day, feeling the need of a change. Late at night, near the Missouri line, I parked off the road to sleep. At sunrise I awoke on the rim of the world. The shadow of the car stretched out before me, the light spreading like a surf, splashing on objects. It may have been the first time I saw the plains as a metaphor for the sea, a place to be possessed by the imagination. I no more than saw it, I did not feel inspired at the sight to possess it, but coming out of the woods, literally and figuratively, where I had been wandering for more than six weeks, I experienced the prodigal son's elation at the sight of the homeland. I think it startled me. My view of the plains had always been dim. My sentiments on the occasional cross-country drives were expressed in my early fiction, where Nebraska was the place you drove all night while your companion slept in the seat. That had been the impression of my friends in the East.

As the sun rose I found much to photograph. Anything that stood up so the light would strike it—an almost audible clamor at sunrise— houses and barns, fences and telephone poles, clusters of trees and dwellings, and like a sail at sea, the occasional gleam of a grain elevator. I saw, but I did not fully sense, that these constructions were pathetically temporary on the vast exposed landscape. In this I found their appeal, their life-enhancing poignancy. My instinct was to celebrate the eloquence of structures so plainly dedicated to human use, and to salvage those that were on the edge of dissolution. The plains provided a scenic prop that was free of obstruction, where the sun was sufficient to delineate the object. I took my subjects on the run, as the light fell on them, frequently not at all to their advantage, since I was eager to see what beckoned down the road, and I was concerned about a change in the weather.

The roll and dip of the plains increased as I drove west, reminding me that my boyhood in the flat Platte Valley of Nebraska had given me a mistaken notion of the high plains. They were remarkably sea-like, the towns sunbaked and windblown, riding the crests of the waves. In western Kansas, near the Colorado border—it might have been Goodland—I found a row of stores, with curtained and blind-drawn windows, slightly tilting false fronts, that would provide me with an inexhaustible image of plains character and experience, mute, implacable and yet expectant. Stubbornly and irrationally optimistic.

Going over Raton Pass, south of Trinidad, Colorado, I recovered the excitement I had felt as a youth on my first car trip to California, the winter of 1926. From the mountains I could see the great blue and rose mesas, like camouflaged ships anchored on the high cloud-dappled New Mexico plateau. The emotions I felt would reassert themselves when I arrived in Los Angeles, in January, and found myself nostalgically pondering my early days and wonderful times on the open road.

In the winter of 1940, Santa Fe was still the town of old adobe houses, warm sun, cool shadows, a bandstand in the square, blankets and silver in the shops, and Pueblo Indians under the awning of the governor's building. Most of the artists and writers had moved on to greener pastures or trickled back to Greenwich Village, but the lobby of the La Fonda Hotel thronged with trend-seeking tourists and self-proclaimed old-timers. I listened to their stories. Mabel Dodge Luhan was at home near Taos, where the natives were reduced to Sears, Roebuck blankets. The air was like wine, the light shimmered like tinsel, and I marveled at how I had dreamed of living anywhere else.

I found a room, a ten-minute walk from the square, for five dollars a week, a detail that is part of the period's aura. I spent the sun-struck days visiting the pueblos, San Ildefonso, Santo Domingo, etc., or following dirt roads wherever they led me. Gas was cheap. My problem was conserving film. I watched Maria Martínez shape and fire her pottery, and bargained with Fred Kabotie for one of his paintings. In the evening I looked for a seat in La Fonda's lobby, fragrant with piñon fires and the smell of Mexican food. I loved the slap and creak of new and old huaraches and felt myself one of the chosen.

The big even of the season was the world premiere of *Santa Fe Trail*, with Errol Flynn and Olivia De Havilland. This trail did not come to Santa Fe, but Hollywood did. The ceremony took place in the floodlit square, white with the first snow, ringed with Christmas lights. The red men and their women viewed the white man's fiesta with their customary resignation. Carols were played. Errol Flynn brushed against me as he made his way into La Fonda's lobby.

In a few weeks I had shot more film than I should have, and suffered from a bad case of pueblo-country enchantment. I had bought some old pottery, some new blankets, and before the fever maimed me, or abated, I managed to take off. I drove through a starry night to Needles, California, where I had a fine breakfast in the Harvey House in the railroad station, one of the first and last sanctuaries of great coffee. As I drove west out of Needles, I knew I was coming down with an old infection. California—before I set eyes on it—had been for me the sanctuary of my great expectations, and my years at Pomona College had fired the clay of these impressions. Once I had crossed the Mojave and from Cajon Pass saw the haze of smudge pots over the valley, through which the tan eucaplytus trees thrust up like

308

feathers, I was hooked. Old Baldy gleamed with a snowcap, and the trees were freighted with oranges and lemons. I stopped to drink my fill of orange juice. In Claremont I drove slowly around the streets and thought the students attractive but extremely youthful. How long had it been? It had not quite been five years. In the post office, with its WPA murals painted by Milford Zornes, a classmate, an old friend was so startled to see me I let myself pass for an imposter. I had received the New Directions volume with the selection of my photographs and texts, along with a brief review from *The New Yorker* in which my name was mentioned. A first on all accounts. At the Sugar Bowl Café I was recognized, and experienced the sensation of being interviewed. Fame, surely. I was treated to a piece of pecan pie. To prolong this occasion I sought out Hal Davis, one of my English teachers, who was very kindly and favorably impressed. Publication—in that far time—was a singular event. Many were called, but few were chosen. I stayed with Hal for two days, smoking his cigarettes and giving him the lowdown on South Carolina hoosegows. The sight of my words in print had stirred banked fires and started other juices flowing. I was eager to write. What? The writing would flow out of my aroused nostalgia, the boy who had arrived, fifteen years before, with his father in the sidecar of a motorcycle.

In Los Angeles I found a light-housekeeping room near Echo Lake Park. I put aside what I had begun in Santa Fe, an effort to recapture my days and nights in Greenville, and started a book that began:

When it was cold we walked around. When it was morning the pigeons came and looked but when nothing happened they walked away. When it was warm we sat in the sun.

That was the way it had been in 1926, and the passage of time had given it vintage. Would it prove to have the bouquet—on the green side—of my own wine? In two months I would write what would prove to be the first hundred and fifty pages of *My Uncle Dudley,* stopping where the car collapsed in Arkansas the morning the Mississippi broke through the levee. With this stint of writing done, I was both free and eager to turn back to photography. I should have waited several weeks, until a touch of spring had softened the weather east of the Rockies, but I was anxious to rejoin my wife, who would meet me in Cleveland, then to set up a darkroom in New York and make my first prints from the negatives.

I headed east in early March, driving northwest from Las Vegas through the mining and ghost towns to Virginia City. Overcast skies, strong winds and freezing cold discouraged much picture taking. I put up in the Comstock Lode Hotel in Virginia City, however, until a day of brilliant sunlight gave me the half-dozen pictures I was determined to get. One was the pair of weathered houses on an incline, every exterior detail of the facade preserved, another the abandoned church and Hudson-bracketed house stark against a landscape of desert and sky, more in the style of the Baroque than American Gothic. With these trophies hopefully in the bag, I headed northwest for Boise, Idaho, to visit my Aunt Winona, one of my mother's Seventh-Day Adventist sisters. A long day with her, and other members of the clan, helped to restore the ties I had with my Nebraska boyhood.

In the morning my Aunt Winona, the only one not to marry, stood in the sunlit kitchen and watched me eat. Her first love had been the Lord, the second her father, and in this world she had found no replacements. It was her father she saw when she gazed at me. She gave to this farmhouse kitchen, the light flaming her hair, the time-stopped dazzle of Vermeer's paintings. She poured milk from a pitcher, threaded a needle, picked up crumbs from the table with her tip-moistened finger. She was at once serene, vulnerable, and unshakable. The appalling facts of this world all existed to be forgiven. In her presence I was subject to fevers of faith, to fits of stark belief. Like the grandfather, she saw me as a preacher in search of a flock. (Will's Boy, 1981)

AT THE END OF MARCH I MET MY WIFE AT HER parents' home in Cleveland Heights, the driveway still packed with the winter ice but spring in early bloom in the compost heap behind the garage. A few days later we drove to New York, from where she went on to her job at the Westover School in Middlebury and I looked for a room on the Heights in Brooklyn, near the Brooklyn Bridge.

I had been introduced to Brooklyn Heights the year before by a young woman who had met Hart Crane and bought him drinks in the bar at the St. George Hotel. On some of my visits to New York I stayed in her apartment, dark as a sleeping car, but with windows at the back that framed a view of the river and lower Manhattan. I had never seen its equal. To have an apartment of my own, on the same street, with or without the view of the river, would actually exceed my expectations.

My new friend was about my age, but I felt that she looked considerably older. She had once gone to Vassar, joined a Communist cell, married one of its leaders, and took a job doing social work in Brooklyn. She wore her hair in a bun, sweaters under her raincoat, no make-up, and chain-smoked cigarettes she rolled herself. I liked Edith, but I did not understand her. The dream of her life was to publish an article in *The Nation*.

While I was looking for a room I slept on her sofa. She kept the blinds drawn on the view of Manhattan because the sun faded the spines on her books. She highly respected some books and authors. She made her own breakfast, and left the dishes in the sink to be washed on Sunday morning. As I say, I liked her, but I looked forward to moving out.

I soon found a one-room unfurnished apartment just a block down the street, at 196 Columbia Heights. The freshly painted room, four steps down from the street level, had a space at the back I could convert into a darkroom. That spring it was thirty-eight dollars a month; one with a view of the river ran about double that. In a nearby storage warehouse I found a set of bedsprings, a table, two overstuffed chairs, a bookcase and an old trunk I could use for storage. From Middlebury I brought all my darkroom clutter, including my big, beautiful Omega enlarger, and several jars of jam from my ex-landlady. On loan from another friend we had pots, dented pans and the bent-tined forks that had opened the holes in many cans of Carnation milk. The prevailing breeze, strong mornings and evenings, smelled of the coffee being roasted under the bridge. I was usually awakened by the spatter of dirt and gravel kicked up by dogs on the front windows. These dogs were usually walked by men, in their bathrobes and pajamas, their bare feet in shoddy scuffs and slippers. All I ever saw of them were their feet, visible at the bottom of my drawn blind. I could see the strumming wires that anchored the small trees, the dented hubcaps on the parked cars, and sometimes the legs and aprons of the boys who pushed the big two-wheeled carts that made local deliveries. It seemed to me like those affluent parts of Paris where I hadn't lived. One of the tenants in the building was French—I could see the French stamps on her mail—and if we happened to enter the building together I would greet her, "*Fait beau aujourd'hui!*" or something like that. "*Vous parlez français très bien!*" she would reply, and pass on the stamps my wife collected for a friend.

Where else, that spring in my life, might I have lived besides Columbia Heights? From the roof of the building I had the same view of the bridge as the son of the man who had designed it, and whose fate was to complete it, watching its progress through a telescope.

And you that shall cross from shore to shore years hence are more to me, and more in my meditations, than you might suppose.

So I quoted to myself Whitman.

Two or three times a week, a matter of the weather, I walked out on the bridge to sit on the promenade, watching the freighters and barges pass below me, or I would cross to City Hall Park and buy my Bock panatelas from the discount cigar stores. Then, seated on a bench, I would smoke one, noting the vein in the wrapper, like Hans Castorp.

Was there anything I lacked? My world was so extravagantly what I had ordered, I lacked only the time to ride off in all directions. Like Fitzgerald, in the streets of summer I would try to walk off my heady euphoria by strolling up Broadway to Washington Square, making a fueling stop for an English muffin at the Schrafft's at the corner of Thirteenth Street and Fifth Avenue. As a walker accustomed to the Paris pissoirs, I plotted my walks with the rest stations in mind, like those on the signs along the big freeways: FOOD AND FUEL.

I had met an editor at Harcourt, Brace and Company who introduced me to the gentlemen's facilities just off the elevator lobby, and as my experience with publishers expanded, so did my access to comfort stations. After such a long trek I would take the subway back to the St. George Hotel, rest a moment in its lobby, allow myself to be thought of as a person of interest, then return to my room.

The days were too short for all that had to be done. Photographs to enlarge, texts to ponder, a fresh draft of the novel I had written in California, the opening pages of which had interested an editor at Harcourt, Brace. With the arrival of summer, and the first blackouts, I was appointed air raid warden to my building and encouraged to spend more time on its roof, watching the lights blink off in Manhattan. Those that persisted were like planets, stalled in their orbits. I did not feel the nearness of the war, but I resented its hovering presence. Would it soon put an end to my little idyll, or would I slip through the net? It has been fashionable, since Vietnam, and the wholesale rejection of all military service, to assume tha the Second World War was one that the young considered worth fighting and dying for. This young man did not, nor did any of the young men he happened to know. My patriotism was intense, but had much of its grounding in Thoreau's Civil Disobedience. I never questioned that what I was doing, and hoped to do, constituted my war effort. The bloody carnage so memorably reported by a generation of gifted writers had left in me nothing but loathing for the war that was emerging. Much of this found its expression in an unpublished manuscript entitled "Journal of the Plague Year."

On alternate weekends, until her summer vacation, my wife came to the city, and we would go to museums, have dinner somewhere, or spend the time with our old and new friends. One of the old ones, Alec Taylor, had worked briefly as a housemother at Scripps College, where she had met my wife. Double-dukes, as I named her, from the way she would double up her small fists and assume a fighter's posture, combined in her tall, willowy person the extravagant promises and ambitions that made her the symbol of the literary hopeful. She had lived a year in France, as part of the Delaware group, and returned to write a long, lyrical report about her early life and times in Wyoming, her polishing at Bryn Mawr, and her creative adventures and anguish. This manuscript had almost won the *Atlantic Monthly* prize of $7,500! It traveled with her, as she enlarged and revised it, and periodically shared segments with us, and those big-time editors who knew the real thing when they saw it (from what they had once read about it) found in Double-dukes what they had been waiting for. Her manuscript clutched to her front, her voice hoarse and throaty, her way of tapping out tobacco from a Bull Durham pouch the envy of the hundreds who had observed it—none of this was soon forgotten, and it could be had for as little as an advance of $250.

Edith was Double-dukes's friend from their college years, but they had had a slight parting of the ways at the fork in the road taken by fellow travelers.

One humid summer evening, Double-dukes escorted me to the apartment of a friend who taught at Columbia, where I would meet James Agee. They were discussing, quietly but intensely, Céline's *Journey to the End of the Night*. Agee admired it extravagantly. His friend's appreciation was qualified. They were so much at ease with this writer and his book, I was reluctant to intrude on their discussion. Agee was very Southern, to my eye and ear, a poet in every vibrant strand of his nature. He was wearing a blue workshirt, khaki pants, and the rough farmwork shoes of a sharecropper. I liked his quiet manner, his fine sad eyes, his well-bred face. *Let Us Now Praise Famous Men* had not as yet been published, but this brief evening with Agee would contribute much to my reading.

Another friend of Double-dukes was Sigmund Bekersky, a giant Russian from the Ukraine who had once been a professional wrestler. He was a master of the basics of communication, but weak on the details. On our first meeting he greeted me by placing his hands on my hips, hoisting me like a child. He liked me. I was one of many people he liked. As a wrestler he had been well known, if not well paid, and in New York he worked as a nightclub bouncer. When Bekersky rumbled, people bounced. I believe that I came to love Bekersky, but my feelings were complex. He visited us often, when he happened to be passing, usually with a loaf of bread and a hunk of ham he sliced with the blade of his jackknife. Our two cats, Sweeney and Agonistes, would crawl into his open shirtfront while he was eating and hungrily lick the perspiration at his armpits. How he would roar! To my knowledge he did not read or speak much English, but his use of fifteen or twenty words was so good he covered all the bases. This gift he had to embrace us all in his fellowship was lavish. I did not question that it was far superior to my limited powers to love a few chosen people. Was this peculiarly Russian? Or was this just Bekersky, an outsized giant of a man doomed to live his life among pygmies? I remember him with both deep affection and the shame that I soon stopped answering his postcards. "How are you? I am fine," they said, mailed to me from a series of army bases. He had joined the army when it was found he understood all those unspeakable languages. My feeling is that the women he knew found him a cross between Zeus and Ulysses.

314

Over the summer we had a few hot and humid nights, the door propped open to catch the draft in the hallway, but life on the Heights seemed to us both like a marvelous resort vacation. We often felt we had the city to ourselves, so many people we knew had left it. Even the subway system (soon to be seen as a monster between Dante's Hell and Purgatory) we thought had been designed for our own convenience, with the medieval Cloisters at one end and Coney Island at the other. It had not yet crossed the minds of either of us that this was one of many feelings that were passing.

My wife had met Howard Devree, an art critic for the *New York Times,* and his personal pleasure seemed to be to introduce attractive young women to the art scene and the galleries. Mr. Devree also liked my photographs—he had reviewed the showing I had had at the New School—and one day he came to visit us in Brooklyn with a carton of Atget photographs, printed by Berenice Abbott. These prints were much superior to those I had previously seen, and appropriated some of the ruins of time that I felt to be my peculiar province. Once more I had found that what I felt to be uniquely my own way of seeing was little more than a measure of my ignorance. If I could see all that existed, it would surely take the bloom off many of my enthusiasms. I was spared that revelation, however, since this humbling knowledge would usually come to me in small doses for the rest of my life.

By midsummer I had printed several hundred of my new photographs, and made a selection for *The Inhabitants.* I had also set up appointments with Clifton Fadiman, at that time the book editor for *The New Yorker,* and Henry Allen Moe of the John Simon Guggenheim Foundation. Mr. Fadiman proved more of a reader than a looker, but he kindly sent me over to Donald Klopfer, of Random House, who was having his shoes shined on my arrival. This impressed me as the height of sensible advantage, like the gas lighters that came with hotel lobby cigar cases. He was both sympathetic and realistic. Such a book, he said, would cost a lot to produce—and who would buy it? I had not diverted myself with that dilemma. I did take reassurance in the fact that the conception itself, photographs and words in a new nonillustrative relationship, had caught the fancy of an observer who did not share my own enthusiasm. Feeling as I did, I knew there were others, somewhere, who might feel the same.

Henry Allen Moe seemed to be one of them. Just the year before, Edward Weston had been the first photographer to receive a Guggenheim Fellowship. Why shouldn't I be the second? This kind of confidence did not dismay Mr. Moe, who seemed to take kindly to my optimism. Through the veil of cigarette smoke that hovered between

315

us, and the butts that cluttered up his ashtray, I observed that what he saw and read brought a twinkle to his eyes which I could appreciate. I liked his succinct comments, his sensible questions, and his no-nonsense brevity. Did he feel I might try for a fellowship? He did. I would write him a statement describing my intentions (which proved to be a long one) and submit it with examples of my work.

It had not yet crossed my mind, as a city dweller, that to get somewhere I could signal a cab. I walked my heavy portfolio back to the Seventh Avenue subway in what proved to be the rush hour. My luck was running good. After a shower, I told my wife all about it in the coffee-fragrant draft that blew through the window. To celebrate our prospects, we walked down to Fulton Street for a dinner at Child's.

By October I had completed a second draft of my novel, and submitted it to Lambert Davis of Harcourt, Brace. His Southern accent put me in mind of my friend Leon Howard. In Lambert's office I had met Edward Dahlberg, a self-possessed man with the detached manner of a diplomat. He was about to publish *Do These Bones Live,* a book very much to my taste, and I felt that much of it took my measure.

Lambert liked the quality of the material I submitted, but felt that my story petered out, rather than concluded, with the kid's return to Chicago and reunion with his Uncle Dudley. The tale of a carful of picaresque loafers and idlers traveling from Los Angeles to Chicago in the mid-twenties needed a more dramatic windup than the one I had supplied. Perhaps, he said, I could think of something. In my highly charged state of mind, that did not take long. On the subway returning to Brooklyn I recalled my adventure in Greenville, and how appropriate that scene and situation might be to a character like Uncle Dudley. During my stay in Santa Fe the previous winter, I had written up a draft of the Greenville experience and recorded the details that I now needed. Within a few weeks, I had a new, long concluding chapter, with my Uncle Dudley, in the Greenville jail, rehearsing the well-known abuses to Yankees at the hands of the fat-assed, perverse and brutal caricatures I had found to be so true to life. There was also Furman Young, a Southern hillbilly sprout of Yankee independence, who would arouse Uncle Dudley to his defiant gesture of spitting in the eye of the cop, Cupid. These sentiments were appropriate to my own, and I felt pretty good about what I had done, not being at that time a writer of fiction with an overview of what he was up to.

That overview would come several months later, on the day the book was published, and a friend came by to share this special occasion with me. She was dying to read it. I sat and smoked my discount panatelas as she read. My happiness was boundless as I observed the gleeful fits of laughing that frequently interrupted her reading. Marvelous! After all, I thought it a pretty funny book.

She broke off her reading a little after midnight, eager to get back to it the following evening. My feeling then, as I sat smoking cigars that had lost their savor, was that she read with continued interest but without further interruptions of laughter. The book finished, she took the occasion to praise my Mexican cigarettes. We discussed Mexico briefly. And *My Uncle Dudley*—had she liked it? Oh, yes, she had liked it. Her feeling was, however—it was just a feeling—that she shouldn't have stopped the night before, at the point that she did, then begin again the next evening. It seemed so different in tone she almost thought it a different book. In the first part she had laughed and laughed—that was what she remembered!—but in the second part, good as she found it, it seemed so damn serious. Was she reading it wrong?

So I learned the hard way that an overview is something you should have before a book is published. Some readers seemed to like the change of "tone" in the novel, once Uncle Dudley ends up in the clinker, but other readers, not so serious, regretted that it stopped being funny. I sympathized with both readers, and sometimes would have liked to have it both ways. I have a boy's affection for the man I would have loved to have had as an uncle, a man who was decent enough, kind enough and on occasion funny enough, but hardly ever really smart enough to win at the game he found himself playing. The old fool who turned to spit the cop Cupid in the eye, to the great pleasure of his nephew, was an extension of the sentiment that had shaped Mark Twain's Colonel Sherburn on the occasion of his potential lynching, and in the course of time, as measured by the drip method, it would prove to have a lasting effect on me.

Persons attempting to find a motive in this narrative will be prosecuted; persons attempting to find a moral in it will be banished; persons attempting to find a plot in it will be shot.

BY ORDER OF THE AUTHOR

On a cold day in December, I learned that my father had died in Chicago. This event was so detached from my expectations, it had, at the time, little effect on me. I seemed to lack the faculties necessary to grasp it. From my early boyhood, my jovial, optimistic father had seemed a genial, neighborly relation, seen by me through the agent's window of the depot or as he passed on the sidewalk across the street from me, wagging his hand. He was no good at all at buttoning and unbuttoning rompers, and I did not like the taste of the kisses flavored by his red-capped indelible pencils. On one occasion, he slipped the belt from his pants to slap it halfheartedly at my well-padded bottom, until I was rescued by Anna. The cause? He had caught me with my pudgy hand in the pocket of his pants, fishing for coins. I bought nut Hershey bars with this money, or soda pop that I learned to drink in concealment, shaking the bottle to work up the fizz. He was the man whose wavy brown hair had been shaved from his head, right before my eyes, when he had erysipelas. Harder to account for, and more lasting, he had brought home from Omaha a red-lipped woman described as my "new mother." Later I would be farmed out, for several years, to an Irish family, then be gifted with the second of my new "mothers" (not a moment of all of this could I have lived without), but it strained our father-son relations. He was a handsome man with an eye for the ladies, who gave me money on the rare occasions that I saw him. The last time I saw him, he studied me with amused perplexity. I was his son, now a young man on his way to Europe. He chewed a match—one of the habits I hated—as a woman took a seat on the arm of his chair, and rested her hand on his shoulder. It pleased me that she was attractive. The idea of going to Europe puzzled him. What was there? Two years later I would write him to say that I was married, and living in California, to which he replied on a sheet of the green lined pulpy paper I remembered from popcorn bags, the periods drilled through the paper after the indelible pencil had been moistened at his lips. What did it say? He would like to make me a partner in his new plan to sell fresh eggs to hotels.

He would be dead for several years before I would be diverted from the story I was writing. I had a landscape in mind, and this man in it. There was not much else that I could say about it. The writing took its tone and texture from the opening lines, and in several hundred pages seldom departed from it.

In the dry places, men begin to dream. Where the rivers run sand there is something in man that begins to flow. West of the 98th Meridian— where it sometimes rains and it sometimes doesn't—towns, like weeds, spring up when it rains, dry up when it stops. But in a dry climate the husk of the plant remains. The stranger might find, as if preserved in amber, something of the green life that was once lived there, and the ghosts of men who have gone on to a better place. The withered towns are empty, but not uninhabited. Faces sometimes peer out from the broken windows, or whisper from the sagging balconies, as if this place—now that it is dead—had come to life. As if empty, it is forever occupied. (*The Works of Love,* 1952)

The narrator of the story, a man named Will Brady, is described as one who neither smoked, drank, gambled, nor swore. Had I ever known such a man? To the extent I knew my father:

A man who headed no cause, fought in no wars, and passed his life unaware of the great public issues . . .

The author of this story, unlikely as it might seem, was unaware both at the time and later of what he was up to. Only when the volume was published, three or four years later, and a few of the sympathetic reviewers spoke of this Will Brady as a man they had known, personally, did it first cross my troubled and haunted imagination that in this way I hoped to get to know my father. It is an old, old story, and not at all unusual that a young man would feel compelled to tell it.

One Sunday, on the crowded train from Grand Central Station to Brooklyn, I stood holding one of the straps. My wife, in the seat before me, wore a small hat with a veil, her gloved hands resting on the purse in her lap. Something about her appearance, her person, attracted the attention of those who could see her. She sat erect but relaxed, compact within herself, proper to the verge of primness, but those who observed her were attracted by her air of good breeding. It gave the women near her, as it did me, the reassurance we get from something of value. Her own attention was held by the blurred glimpses we got of the local stations. At one moment she extended her hand to finger the pocket of my coat. In my constant self-preoccupation, my wife was one of many things that I took for granted. I asked myself, as the train clattered through the stations, what I had done to justify my having such an exceptional and lovely wife. In truth I had done little, one thing had led to another, and at thirty-two years of age I had this companion who accepted the demands my life placed upon her. I felt toward her at that moment such a surge of affection I found it impossible to speak, but by the time we had reached the St. George station this flood of emotion had drained away, and I was thinking of food. In the neighborhood deli we bought a carton of milk and a can of tuna, both of us having learned to eat and like what we could share with the cats.

The bombing of Pearl Harbor took place on the Sunday I signed the contract with Harcourt, Brace to publish *My Uncle Dudley*. This mix of personal elation with national disaster may have been characteristic. In late March, I was once more back in full flight, with the news that I had received a Guggenheim Fellowship. How often had I fantasized, with my wife, what we might do if we received such a windfall. If not all the money in the world, $2,500 seemed a good piece of it. We agreed that we could live the longest, perhaps for two years, if we were back in California. I needed to make the trip west to take more photographs, and the college town of Claremont was stocked with old friends and suited our needs. On the trip west we would make a few stops in Nebraska.

Early in April, *My Uncle Dudley* was published—an attractive volume, bound in buckram, with a paper label on the spine to appease the author—but the event did not make much news. The resident reviewer of the *Herald Tribune* found the story confused. What was going on? He found it hard to determine. It was my first exposure to the problems of a writer addicted to compactness, and economy of statement. One reviewer in San Francisco had no such problem, and spoke of the author as one who might bear watching. In a copy of the book on my shelf I have his review. It gives the plot of the story without a hint of confusion, and in closing he wanted to say that Mr. Wright had made his point. That is what he said.

THE GREAT PLEASURE I TOOK IN NEW YORK, AND
the feeling I continued to have that my future would be tied up with
living on Brooklyn Heights, did not diminish the sense of life-enhancing
escape I always experienced traveling west through the Hudson tunnel. The pull of the West, a convenient illusion for any duffer with
a yen for flight, had become a magnet for me with the discovery of
California. Our friend Schindy was right about the seasons, and the
problem of the chap on whom no snow fell, but the lure of
California was for me like that of the *Wandervögel* for Capri, or Hans
Castorp for Greece. The basking heat, the shimmering light, the matchless tranquility of the California mornings, would take their monotonous toll in time, but how welcome they loomed from the exit of
the tunnel.

One of my real deprivations as a boy had been my inability to
shrilly whistle, using either one or two fingers, but one thing I could
do was give a blast to the horn and slap my hands on the steering
wheel. It had been supplied with a tan suede cover used by the better-
class mechanics, and mounted on the dashboard was a compass that
would keep me headed westward. Except on those occasions when
I insisted on going south.

It pleased my father-in-law, on our stop in Cleveland, to exhibit
me to his colleagues as a Guggenheim fellow. It also pleased me to
be so exhibited, and I comported myself as a fellow in good standing.
This called for my joining my father-in-law on the stoop of the rear
porch, where we pulled the husks off fresh Ohio sweet corn. Mrs.
Finfrock liked the evening meal to be somewhat formal—the exchange
of her bathrobe for a summer print—the four or five of us seated
around the table at the rim of the overhead lamp. Fin was supposed
to be on a diet, and he took only small portions of food on his plate,
but I had often had lunch with him in the city, and observed the bags
of snacks he kept handy in the car seat. His great weaknesses were
peanuts and banana candy. Since I had last seen him, he had taken
to napping on the wicker sofa on the screened-in porch. If the day
was humid, he might spend the night there. After a trip to the john
in the basement, he might be heard wheezing as he came up the stairs.
I accepted this as normal for a man sixty pounds overweight. His great
pleasure and relaxation was cards, especially bridge, at which he was

a modest master, but since I was unable to grasp bridge, we usually played pinochle or rummy. While his wife pondered her next move, he might go to the icebox for a cold root beer, or step out on the porch and smoke a cigarette. Later in the evening we would take the dog, Sox, for his midnight walk. This usually called for a stop at the drugstore on Euclid, where Fin would be served his double-chocolate Coke, then we would stroll under the oaks and elms that had heaved up the neighborhood sidewalks. This was great for Sox, providing him with many places to sniff and scratch. One of the neighbors had a player piano, with some of the rolls I used to pump in Chicago, and the later it got, the more she liked to play "My Blue Heaven" at a fast tempo, "The Sheik of Araby" at a slow one. A girl like that was giving some boy a pretty bad time.

One evening, as the dog tugged at the leash, Fin spoke to me about his son, Charles. He was worried about Charles, who seemed to be having trouble with his law school teaching. Charles had seemed to me exceptionally smart. I could not understand his having trouble with his teaching. His father explained that his nerves were giving him trouble: he seemed to feel he was being followed by people. At the college where he had been teaching, he had been picked up on the street with a pistol in his pocket. My father-in-law turned his back to me as he said this, and I could see that his broad shoulders were trembling. To see so big a man openly weeping stunned me. The dog had circled his legs with the long leash, so that he had to stand there, unable to move. I've no memory of what I said. Perhaps I said nothing. I made a fuss with the dog, untangling the leash, and we stood in the comforting dark together, smoking cigarettes. Fin's white shirt was dark with sweat where it stuck to his back.

"Son," he said to me, "am I crazy?"

"Of course you're not crazy," I replied. "Good God!"

"Then Charles is crazy!" he said. "You hear me? You've got to help me conceal it from Mother."

"I can't believe it," I said.

"Charles believes that I'm a threat to his mother. The last time he was home, he threatened me with his pistol."

He stopped speaking, and let the dog lead us along the street. I couldn't believe what I had heard. My feeling at the time was that Charles *might* be a bit crazy, but not to the point of shooting his father. And why his father? In so many words, he had hinted to me that in his opinion his mother was mighty peculiar. How crazy could normal-seeming people really get? I had from the first noted the strangeness of Mrs. Finfrock, but she had learned to live with it, as had her family.

She was respected and admired by her friends. I had noted in myself a grudging respect for certain qualities in her nature. As we reached the house, my father-in-law spoke to me.

"Not a word of this to Mother," he cautioned me. "Not a word," as if he thought I might actually speak of it. Shortly later, my wife called me upstairs, and I lay sprawled at her side in the airless room. The cicadas sawed away in their ascending lisp. My father-in-law had explained to me how the beat of this sawing accurately registered the temperature, a characteristic piece of his nature lore, which I could never accurately remember. What was I to make of the disclosure about Charles? Was it actually something I should share with my wife, knowing how she felt about her brother? My father-in-law, in his private anguish, had lifted the lid on a loony bin. Dimly I apprehended that Fin, in his eagerness to protect Mother, was concealing from himself the tangle of emotions that had brought on Charles's "nervous breakdown," the label of the time. In this house of leisure and promise, fear had taken root in the water closet in the basement and the compost pit behind the garage, wherever the man of the house went to hide from what he was thinking. Of course, I didn't really believe it. I kept my eyes on the wings of the moths I could see against the street light, as they crawled on the screen. In the morning this touch of nightmare would vanish, and we would all go on with our lives.

I had not returned to my Uncle Harry's farm since my boyhood in Omaha. Why did I now feel that I should? Neither Harry nor Clara had expressed affection for me. My father had "farmed me out" to them part of one summer, as he had farmed me out to the Mulligan family. But my intrusion as a young man, with a city wife, would be far less acceptable to Clara than my visit as a small boy. I knew that, but my father's death had aroused in me a desire to know more about my people. Were they my people? I had no other way of finding out.

My joshing, genial, often blundering father, with a talent for botching his great expectations in butter and eggs, as well as in women, had often spoken with distaste for his dirt-farming brother who didn't seem to have "the brains he was born with." This brother had spoken, if at all, with something like contempt for the ne'er-do-well who ran around with loose women and farmed out his son. I had not warmed to the sullen, scowling, slow-moving man who belched at his meals and sat forever in the privy, the sun on his flour-white knees, while he read the Sears, Roebuck catalogue. I had heard him say frequently to his wife, "That kid ain't worth his feed." That especially hurt, since I didn't find the "feed" all that good, after the Mulligans. One of my unwelcome chores had been to moisten a rag in vinegar and wipe the mold from the pies in the storm cave.

In Omaha I showed my wife the Mulligan house, on Capitol Avenue, still the color of sun-faded chocolate, the porch clapboards warped and peeling where they were thumped and scraped by the swing. It seemed a lot shabbier than I remembered, and the hills less steep. I was able to see, as I knocked at the screen, that gas jets still lit up the hallway that led back to the kitchen, a curtain at the bottom half of the sink window. Nothing had changed. The lady of the house, her untied apron strings dangling, did not herself remember the Mulligans, but she had heard the name. The draft blowing through the house smelled of the drip pan under the icebox. It had been my chore to see that it was emptied. What else had I forgotten?

Over the half curtain at the window I could see the dead tree trunk in the yard, and the battered sheds that lined the steep alley. The summer it had been paved, piles of sand filled the Mulligan yard for weeks. In that sand I had lost a chameleon. I was eager to stoop and peer under the porch to check on other possible losses. There had been a cigar box containing marbles and a piece of gray, grass-stained flannel, a pocket torn from the seat of Babe Ruth's Yankee baseball pants. There had been a Junior Flexible Flyer sled. Learning that I had once lived in the house, as a boy, she peered around me for a better look at my wife. Had she, too, lived here? No, just myself. I felt the shame of this admission. The other half of the duplex stood empty, with a FOR RENT card propped in the window. In my time it had never been rented. Had this been the curse of the large, shouting, Jewish-speaking family who lived in the house next door, the kids known to have head lice? My friend Davy Goodman, with his spindly legs, would peer down to taunt me with his Jewish curses. The wall was crumbling. What had been the meaning of the word *took-us*?

A used-car lot, with wind-whipped banners, had replaced the redbrick schoolhouse at Twenty-ninth and Farnam. Used cars concealed the cinder-covered playground. The success of this "vanishing act" stunned me. Red bricks into thin air? A part of my life had been spelled out in the high ceilinged rooms, in the nurse's annex, in pom-pom pull-away played in the cinders. I wore holes in my knee pants, pulling up my stockings. My legs were fast but thin. Nothing at all remained. I was able to conceal my shock since I lacked the faculty to grasp it. Was I prepared for what might be next? The Blackstone Hotel, where the tall, gentle Max Cohn had worked at the soda fountain, looked to me largely unchanged. What if Max Cohn still worked there? Before eloping with the daughter of my second new

324

mother, he had loaned me his red bathing suit for the summer. That, too, had vanished. Had it been returned?

My Uncle Harry's farm did not prove to be where I thought I had left it, but to the south of Norfolk, toward Battle Creek. Battle Creek itself seemed to be where it should be, along with the spur of the railroad line on which I had ridden up from Columbus. So, too, the catalpa trees still lined the drive leading from the road to the barn. No dog barked, but I saw a scrawny cat slink into the shade. I parked the car in a yard spongy with mounds scratched up by chickens. On the roof of the house, a blue ball tilted on a rusted lightning rod. A single tattered shade tree, dead at the top, with a clump of green foliage like a hula skirt at its middle, still shaded a bit of the porch, but not the house. I had forgotten until I saw the enamel water pail, the dipper floating, that nobody ever used the front door to the house. It was through the rear door, and the kitchen, that one entered the house and left it. Once green and flat as a billiard table, spaced off with the croquet wickets, the stretch of yard between the house and the barn was like a huge, dowdy mattress, sprouting shoots of straw. I saw a few old hens, with their shabby bottoms, scratching in the moist earth near the porch, where Clara emptied her dishpan. Patches of clumped, matted dead grass concealed the last of the wickets and the half-buried balls. Doors tilted on the sheds, fences were down, a few straggly trees stood in the orchard, and every visible object, implement and structure seemed to be at the end of a losing battle. If my wife had not been with me, I might have sneaked off. The old man, surely, would be gone, and my Aunt Clara should be spared the sad memories I would bring her.

The rusted screen door, poked full of holes at the bottom, was latched. In the early afternoon of a hot, humid day, the draft blowing off the kitchen smelled acridly of pickling beets. Why didn't I leave? Nobody seemed aware that we had arrived. The throaty clucking of an old Plymouth Rock hen, bits of dried dung clinging to a few tail feathers, held me like the sound of chords once struck on Clara's player piano. I called out, but nobody answered. I called again, and after several moments I heard the scrape of a pot moved on the stove. The woman who appeared, thin as a lath, wore a faded frock that hung limp from her shoulders. About its waist, the strings dangling, a freshly beet-stained apron. Over her wide, unblinking left eye she placed the fingers of one hand, as if taking an eye test.

"You don't remember me?" I asked. "I'm Will's boy, Wright,"

I said, hardly a recommendation, and it took a moment for her to place me. Her tongue moistened her dry lips.

"You've grown," she said flatly, unlatching the screen. "Come in where it's cool."

We passed through the heat of the kitchen into the front room, where the blinds were drawn. Heat and light, for Clara, were of one compact. In the dim, greenish light she felt cooler. As I introduced my wife, I saw the years twirl on the reel of time between us. The child she had known, now married. She gazed at the young woman who stood beside me. "You folks have children?" We shook our heads. "Well, I suppose there's time for that," she said, "isn't there?" but she expected no answer. The rocker in which she sat herself down creaked as it rocked.

Later we sipped well water from the amber-colored glasses kept high in the cupboard for special occasions. She did not need my help to reach them down. She inquired about my wife's people, and heard with relief that they had settled in Ohio. She knew about Ohio, having crossed it in a wagon on her way west. My wife also had a grandmother, aged ninety-four, still fending for herself in the town she was born in, establishing a kinship that supplanted my own deficient background. When the children did come, they would have at least one foot on the ground.

Some moments before he came into the room, my Uncle Harry stopped on the back porch to skim the drowned flies off the pail of drinking water, and toss them through the hole in the rusted screen. We could hear the gulp of his swallows. He came in without a greeting, his overalls hanging slack from his narrow rounded shoulders. His gray watery eyes, as he faced the light, seemed to have no pupils. He gave little sign of interest or recognition. Clara said, "This is Will's boy, Wright. You remember Wright." It was more of a statement than a question, and he let it pass. "Wright's here with his wife," she added. Hearing that, he perked up. His eyes blinked in preparation for looking at her.

"They see Ed yet?"

"They just got here. Now why'd they see Ed?"

"Well, s'I, how come you ain't up? Well, s'ee, it's in my legs. Can't seem to twitch my toes."

"Why you telling them that?" said Clara, smoothing the wrinkles in her apron.

"Who's Ed?" I inquired.

"Well, s'ee, been lyin' here three or four days, can't use my legs."

This time I puzzled out what he had said the first time. The

326

"s'I"/"s'ee" was dialectic shorthand for *says I/says he,* making it quicker to get on with his story.

"Ed's a Cropper," said Clara. "He farms across the road." It was not a subject she was eager to explore.

My wife said, "Would you have a picture of Wright's father?" I had recently regretted not having a picture, no likeness of this father who was now gone.

"Of Will?" Clara replied. "Now why'd we have picture of him? We didn't see him but once or twice in all those years."

"My father died last fall," I said.

"Will dead?" Harry sat up, spreading his knees. "Why, he's one of the young ones, next to Mae. Now why'd he up and die?"

"I've no pictures," I said. "Not a one."

"I can't think why we'd have pictures of *him*." Clara had little liking for my father, dead or alive. On a trip to the farm before I had come for the summer, he had driven up from Columbus with his new wife, Gertrude, a pretty girl with red lips and a fox fur neckpiece. I had been eight years of age, too young for the scandal.

Harry said, "Come to think . . ." and wheeled slowly as if my father might be standing right behind him. On a table near the front door, family pictures were displayed. All appeared to be young females. Without comment, Clara left the room: I heard her opening a drawer in the bedroom off the kitchen. She reappeared with a shoebox of snapshots and clippings. Harry was using a nail taken from his pocket to loosen the caked tobacco in his corncob pipe. Twice he said, "Dadgummit?" out of respect for the ladies present. I realized that my once dour and sullen Uncle Harry had ripened into an amateur performer. This was one of his acts. He found a kitchen match in one of his pockets, flicked the head with his thumbnail, checked the match to see if it was a good one, then stooped slightly to drag the match up his pants leg, with the sound of a sheet tearing. It burst into a smoking flame he cupped his hands around, held to the bowl of his pipe. A billowing cloud of smoke veiled his head.

"If you can find your glasses," Clara said, "suppose you tell us who's in this picture?" She did not hand it to him until he had found his glasses. The bridge low on his nose, he held the photo at arm's length, moving it toward him, then away, adjusting the focus in the manner of a trombone player adjusting the slide.

"You wearing your glasses?" Clara said, and covered her bad eye to check on him. He had pushed them back on his head to rub his knuckles at his eyes.

327

"Lord, it's fadin'," he said. "Come to think, they never had much as faces."

"Most of them dead and gone, think it would be fadin'," Clara said. "Same as you and me are fadin'."

"Now there," he said, pointing, "that's Mitch." He put a splayed nail on a tall man with a moustache. A row of men and women had gathered in a light snow at the front of a farmhouse. They had either dressed in black for this occasion or it was a Sunday. I counted fourteen of them; five were women. "Mitch was the oldest. Mae was the youngest. That would be Will standin' there with Mae."

Did the last man in the row resemble my father? He had no face, but his wavy hair was parted in the middle.

"If you're not in it, he's not either," said Clara. "The two of you come west to homestead together. You forgotten that?"

"Not him," said Harry. "He never did a day's work in his life."

Even Clara felt that might be going a bit too far, with my wife present. She fidgeted, said, "If it's work that matters, all of you might as well have stayed back in Ohio. What work have you done here?"

He seemed to be wondering. The wet cluck of his pipe was like that of an old hen. "Out in Cozad," he went on, hitching around to face the west, "last time I saw Emerson he was spry as a kid."

"Had pictures on the wall he hand-painted," said Clara.

"One of a dog," said Harry. "Swear he'd come right down and bite you."

"And now he's gone. Same as we'll all soon be gone."

My father had first set eyes on my mother in Chapman, where he had made his start as a Union Pacific station agent. There had been little there at the time, and in the spring of 1942 there was less. She had been born on the bluffs just south of the Platte River, and buried in the cemetery visible from the highway. That was about all I knew about her. My Seventh-Day Adventist grandfather had moved the survivors of his family—the boys had taken off—to the country neighboring Boise, Idaho, where, just twenty years later, I would first see them. My mother's sister, Winona, had tried to keep in touch with me, but I had proved a bad correspondent. My wife had reminded me that I should send her a letter postmarked Chapman.

On a Memorial Day, my father had hitched up the buggy and driven his four- or five-year-old son to put flowers on his mother's grave. I was full of emotion and blankness. Weeds had been scythed from some of the graves, but not others. We sat in the grass and had a picnic. My father worked the handle of the pump, cupping his hand

328

over the nozzle so I could drink. But it proved to be messy. Water spilled on the shiny toes of my Buster Brown shoes. My mother was here, somewhere, and I felt the hollow hallowedness of the occasion. On the long drive back to Central City, the horse's tail flicked on the buckboard, the reins made a lapping sound on his rump.

The town Chapman had planned to be, at the turn of the century, had not materialized. Basements had been dug for stores that were never erected. I saw little evidence that this remarkable windfall had been appreciated by the local small fry. A bicycle lay on its side in front of the general store, blocking the hitch bar. Through the screen at the door I could see a matronly woman wiping the knobs of the syrup dispensers. Harness and lanterns hung on hooks at the back, the horse collars like frames without pictures. A man with heavy web suspenders over oatmeal-colored underwear dipped scoops of creamy flour from a barrel, emptied the scoop into a paper sack. The sleeves of his underwear and the hairy backs of his hands were powdered with the flour.

The building to the left, with a wide, waist-high window, droned with the vibration of a ceiling fan. Over the curtain at the window I could see, as if it were levitated, the horizontal figure of a man being shaved. A mound of lather concealed his face as the barber stropped his razor. A wall mirror reflected the opposite wall of the shop, hung with a display of calendars, but the rear of the shop featured an oak partition with an elaborate grille of wrought iron. Even I knew a bank when I saw one. At the top of the grille a large syrup can held a plant that dangled large shiny leaves and tendrils, well suited to the grille. The barber, Eddie Cahow, a small, gray-haired man, wore the cuffs of his sleeves turned back, and held the long blade of the razor like a bird he had caught in its flight. At that moment he had paused to make a clearing in the lather at the tip of the client's nose. As I opened the screen to his shop, he held up the razor, invoking silence.

"You be quiet a minute," Cahow said, "and I'll tell you who you are." He turned to look at my side-on reflection in the mirror. "You're Grace and Will's boy," he said. "I'd say mostly Grace."

Finger-painted on the mirror was the notice that shaves were fifteen cents, haircuts a quarter.

"When I saw you," said Cahow, "I said, There goes two, three people I know."

Through a puff in the lather the client said, "Whass the genmun's name?"

"Morris," I replied. "Will Morris was my father. Grace Osborn was my mother." He tilted his head for a look at me.

"Mr. Applegate here," said Cahow, "farms on the bluff. About a hunder sixty acres. John," he said, "you remember the Osborns?" John moved his head. "White house with a cupola. See it on your left. Don't think there's anybody in it right now, is there, John?"

On another occasion I would learn that Mr. Applegate had courted Aunt Winona and, mindful of her, he had kept the house in good repair.

A half mile to the south we crossed the Platte River, a wide spread of sandbars and channels of shallow water, then followed the road up the face of the bluff to the flat tableland. A gleaming white house, like a freshly painted signboard, stood at the side of a field of ripening grain. The cupola gave it the look of a small church, the window blazing with the sun's rays. I thought it a small house for the family that had been born and raised in it. My mother had climbed the ladder through the hole in the ceiling, and my maverick Uncle Dwight, for nineteen summers and winters, had learned to hate his god-fearing, Seventh-Day Adventist father. Far to the back, behind the unpainted sheds, a freshly painted white privy sat on the bluff's rim. I tried to picture the girls making that trip in the winter. How was it made by my ill and pregnant grandmother, dead in her late thirties from child bearing and rearing? In addition to his farming, my grandfather had been a bullish land speculator, in Texas and Canada, for the glory of God.

I set up my camera and took pictures of the house, the white surfaces gleaming in the slanting light. On the ground glass, seen against the sky and the field of grain, it bore little resemblance to a farmhouse, and looked new and unused. Without a basement or a foundation, it sat flat on the ground, shoots of grain thrusting up through the boards of the porch. On my mind's eye the whiteness was that of winter, a house of worship, set in a field of drifting snow under a darkening sky, my grandfather a bearded shrouded prophet peering at me from the cupola window.

Down the road a quarter mile, set back in a clump of trees, a low, unpainted structure, with late lean-to additions on both ends, as well as the back side, seemed to be held to the ground by the spread of a huge lilac bush. It screened the porch, and clutched at the shingles of the roof. "That's it!" my wife said. "The house with the lilac bush," and we followed the drive back to a yard cluttered with small sheds and rusting farm implements. It relieved me not to see Mr. Applegate's Chevy pickup. The suppressed emotion I had felt in his manner, at the mention of my mother and Winona, would only be aggravated by the presence of my wife. As we walked toward the house, a figure appeared on the dark porch. A billowing summer frock, with a flower pattern, concealed her enormous bulk: the short, fleshy arm she raised was like a vestigial wing. On her wide, rounded shoulders her head looked small. My wife went forward to meet her; seeing me left her confused and speechless. Her name was Esther, a soft fleshy mound of a woman with a perspiring face, and an extravagantly sweet nature. That I was the child of Grace Osborn she could not believe. She was able to move, wheeling slowly, like an engine in a roundhouse, and make her way to the door of the house, where she called out, "Leah! Leah!" There was a shrill murmuring answer, but no one appeared. Esther turned her figure sidewise to enter the door, rubbing it firmly with her backside, and we followed her into a small, dark room. Leah Applegate—the image of her sister, strands of her long dark hair stuck to her forehead—filled a space that was bolstered with pillows to support her flowing figure. Were they twins? They spoke with the same girlish, murmuring voice. Leah made no movement to rise, and I leaned forward to grip her small, damp, plump hand. A tent-like smock exposed flesh that puddled at her throat. On that round center table, set out for us to examine, were clippings, photo albums and mounted studio portraits. In a large family portrait, of four girls and two boys, I recognized the handsome face of Dwight, and Winona with her large, melting eyes. They were assembled in a row, heads inclined together, but the young woman at the end of the row did not resemble her sisters. Sidewise, she gazed directly into the lens of the camera at who or whatever might be lurking behind it.

"That's her, isn't it?" my wife said.

"Isn't she the prettiest thing?" Esther exclaimed. Grace Osborn was a beauty, but a young man, in line with her gaze, might feel in the curve of her lips a mocking challenge. "Well?" it seemed to ask, and waited for an answer. How had my father fared with this glimpse into liberation? Had he read it, in the fashion of the time, as a young woman who needed taming?

There were other studio portraits, most of them made in Grand Island, of elderly men and women, including one of a young man with clearly defined features, his wavy hair parted in the middle. A good head, set a bit high on the pedestal of a stiff collar, he might have looked inviting to a young woman who needed help from the seat of a buggy. What had she had in mind for the child whose birth would cost her her life?

I asked the two sisters if we could borrow these portraits long enough to make copies of them. Esther declared that we could have the pictures—after all, these were my people—but my wife insisted that we would return them. Leah, the somewhat larger of the two, fanned her perspiring face with a folded newspaper. Lace curtains hung at the closed windows. From my boyhood I could hear the high voice of Clara warning Harry against the night air. Back in the shadows, as my eyes adjusted, I saw plates ornamented with flowers, several Kewpie dolls, calendars with kittens, horses, puppies. A large tabby cat, with clear tiger markings, slept on the seat of a chair I could see in the kitchen. Somewhere in the house a caged bird twittered. Esther gave us a small bag of freshly baked oatmeal cookies to snack on while we were traveling. She had been east to Lincoln, as a girl, and west as far as Kearney, where she attended teachers college. In Central City she had taught in the grade school, but she missed her brother and sister. We last saw her, her fingers wagging, through the lattice of the lilac bushes, a gentle, affectionate, sweet-natured woman one might describe as a cow, meaning no offense to either. She had known my mother, perhaps walked in the road holding her hand, and felt the mocking intensity of her gaze.

IN CLAREMONT WE FOUND AN APARTMENT ON West Sixth Street, over a garage. The house was occupied by Mrs. Ewing, the college librarian, and her housekeeper. The housekeeper, an energetic, plainspoken woman, who walked about with her broom as a trident, had taken a keen interest in my wife, who she felt deserved a better fate. In a novel I would begin a few months later, she has the name Gussie Newcomb. Concern for my wife's welfare brought her to the foot of our stairs every morning, seeking reassurance that she had survived the night. I would see her, her hands shading her eyes, the broom inclined on her shoulder, profiled against the strong backlight. Seeing me, she would inquire if my wife was in. She usually was. A fan placed at one of the windows stirred the warming air. By midmorning, it was usually so hot I would take a walk to the library and sit in the cool but humid air of the basement. Before noon, the perspiration from my hand would smear the pages I was writing.

We had old friends in Claremont, some of whom lived in larger, cooler houses—swimming pools were not as yet mandated—or we might plan a day-long gambol at the beach or at Lake Arrowhead in the mountains. These options were always available, but we soon found it too much trouble. The drive to the beach was hot. We came home too sun- and windburned to sleep. By fall we were at ease with our preoccupations and looked forward eagerly to the rainy season.

In Whittier, about an hour's drive to the southwest, my wife had relations, two sisters of her mother and one husband, Uncle Pete. Uncle Pete worked as a clerk in a Whittier grocery store, and on holidays, or one of the ladies' birthdays, he would drive his Maxwell sedan, with the two ladies, over to Claremont. They usually brought a cut of meat that Uncle Pete considered a bargain, or one of Aunt Alice's masterly cakes and pies. Solidly trained in these matters by her own mother, a woman who made the best crusts in Maumee County, Ohio, Aunt Alice did not spare butter or the use of a fork in blending the shortening. We ate up the cakes in a day or two, but nursed the fruit pies as long as a week.

I was greatly attracted to Uncle Pete, a tall, gentle man with large-knuckled hands and a great fund of experience in groceries. He was only at his ease behind a counter, his hands rolled up in a wad of his apron. He particularly loved to cut slices of "store" cheese, extending toward me, on the blade of the knife, a sliver of the product I could sample. He hand-sliced his bacon with a stroke that went back to seal and whale blubber. He was the first to reassure me that my blind loyalty to the Monarch label on a can of peaches was soundly based on their flavor. In the dim-lighted, high-ceilinged store where he clerked, he used a yardstick to topple the cans from the high shelves, caught them in his apron, then wiped the top lid with a swipe of the cloth. Those gestures were skillful, but chiefly they were expressive of his respect and affection for the product. I noted in him a chronic reluctance to sell cans of hard-to-get Monarch pears, peaches and cherries, or the big dried bulk prunes from Santa Clara. He may have been the first man to arouse in me the suspicion that the good things had had their day, and were on their way out.

"I'd put that on the back of the shelf," he'd say to me with a wink that creased both of his eyes. Every four or five words, his voice tended to crack, and led him to repeat the word in question, as he furtively exchanged a glance with Aunt Alice. She was in no way a tyrant, like her sister in Cleveland, but she had more than a touch of her will and assurance as to what was right. Uncle Pete did not. He quailed like Tom Sawyer under the gaze of Aunt Polly. In some way that defied my imagination, Uncle Pete and Aunt Alice had fathered a son, James, who lived in New York and kept books for a plumber. We had stayed a night with Pete and Alice several days after we were married, lying awake on the daybed in the living room, constrained and heedful to make no sound that might be considered inappropriate. I could hear the ticking of the clock Uncle Pete had been careful to rewind. This day had been festive and somewhat careless, but the morrow, if nothing else, would start on time.

In the morning I parted the curtains at the window to watch him sharpen the blades of the mower. A straw hat shaded his face, the sun was hot on the back of his neck. Later he pushed the mower around the plot of grass as it gave off a different pitch, according to the stroke, the quick thrusts that he made at the end of each row a pleasurable affirmation and a semicolon. There's a proper way to walk when you push a sharp mower, which calls for a flexible bend at the elbow. Both that morning and the others that followed, I was slow to realize that one of the good things on its way out was Uncle Pete.

Aunt Nettie, Alice's older sister, had taught school most of her life in McComb, Ohio, the third grade being her specialty. She didn't like them so much as toddlers, or later when they started to get smart. A small, white-haired woman, with a frosted complexion, she set the table three times a day for meals, and helped wash and put away the

334

dishes. Finding the right get-well cards kept Aunt Nettie busy, and writing them kept her alert and flustered. Nettie's feeling that my wife might have shopped around a little more before succumbing—I had not even completed my college education—had not been eased by my brief brush with fame, not a word of which had been reported in the Whittier papers. Nor had the lending library she sometimes used ever heard of me, or my book. If I was a bit too eager at the Sunday dinner, helping myself to a second slice of angel food cake, Aunt Nettie peered over her glasses to register her disapproval. In what way—she had asked my wife—was I not unemployed?

Under stresses of this sort I had begun a story, "The Vision of Private Reagan," concerned with the rituals of burial in Southern California. My view of these events was that of a young man who had been spared the actual experience. Uncle Pete and Aunt Alice *had* attended a funeral, and Uncle Pete's dry report of his impressions did not conceal from me his dismay. As we sat in the yard with our iced tea glasses, watching a squirrel nibble at a piece of Alice's cake, he made several futile efforts to express this dismay without disturbing the ladies. What he said was that I ought to look in on one myself. This seemed to me very much the sort of challenge that a fiction writer should face up to. I had not as yet heard of the "virus of suggestion," or that the fiction writer was a person on whom little or nothing was lost, but I was open to the thought that a writer might come down with a great infection from a remarkably small exposure, as in love.

I wanted to find in Private Reagan—the GI Joe who had attended the funeral—the Great American Sap who persists in his folly in such a fashion that he becomes wise. From where I had this idea, I don't know. It was true to the nature of much of my varied experience, and might have been my own observation. Over the winter, this short story proved to be a long one as it worked its way to a macabre conclusion, the author blithely unaware that he was engaged in what would prove to be black humor.

My story was too long for magazine publication, too short for a book. I sent it off to Diarmuid Russell, of the new agency Russell & Volkening, who replied that he had been much entertained, but the length of the piece would prove to be a problem. While waiting on this decision, I turned to my impressions of the brief stops we had made in Nebraska, first on the farm near Norfolk, then in Chapman. Recalling and expanding on this experience gave me great satisfaction. It aroused me in a similar way, only more so, as digging for treasure in the dunes of Cape Cod. I felt the unquestioned assurance that if I kept digging I would find something.

335

One day I heard "Gussie Newcomb"—I took the trouble to hear her—gossiping with my wife at the foot of the stairs. A young man she had known, personally, had turned out to be a "missing person." This phrase rang in my head like a chime. What had I been doing, as we crossed Nebraska, but searching for a *missing person,* namely myself? I named this person Agee Ward, a GI who had been reported as missing, with nothing to show for his past existence but a small album of photographs.

I conceived of Agee Ward as one who became more of a presence through his absence, rather than in spite of it: a man who was there. My fresh impressions of the past, acquired on Harry's farm, in Norfolk, and in Cahow's barbershop, in Chapman, would provide me with the background, and Gussie Newcomb, in Claremont, would contribute the foreground. This proved to be more than enough to take my mind off the future of Private Reagan.

As I browsed in the open stacks of the college library, my eye fell on the new books from the Pantheon Press, with their flat spines and European styling. I had not previously read a line of Charles Péguy, and other Catholic writers, outspoken rebels of the beleaguered conscience. Péguy was very much a stylist of my own persuasion, spare, cadenced and uncompromising. I lacked the training and the faith for Léon Bloy, but Georges Bernanos aroused and nourished a deep strain of religious feeling in my own nature. My Aunt Winona would have said I was not my mother's son for nothing.

While I was waiting to be drafted—the dangling man of Saul Bellow's novel—I reached such a stage of impatience that I enlisted in the navy. With my colleagues, about forty of us, I appeared at the induction center in Los Angeles. The examination proved to be a memorable experience for me and is fully and explicitly reported in my novel *The Huge Season.*

I was rejected by the navy for a heart murmur, but a few months later I was back to repeat the performance for the army. My rejection by the navy singled me out as a figure of some interest. I was given a soiled-carpet examination, with special attention from the interns who were curious about heart murmurs. Some heard something (the beat of the heart?), some did not. It took time to reach a consensus. With Uncle Sam's pension system involved, the vote finally went against me. In the early evening I was back on the bus for Claremont, home free.

In our second year in Claremont we made the acquaintance of Morris and Catherine Opler. Morrie was also on a Guggenheim, his specialty being the ethnography of the Plains Indians of the Southwest,

336

but in California he proved to be the resolute champion of the American-Japanese after the panic of Pearl Harbor. This story has been told, and is now familiar, but Opler seemed to be alone at the time in his support of their rights as citizens. In less than a year we established a friendship that survived our mutually provisional, in-transit existences.

My wife had applied for a teaching position at the Baldwin School, in Bryn Mawr, Pennsylvania, and in the late spring she was notified that she had been hired. The pay was good, two thousand dollars a year, and we both liked the idea of living close to New York. Once more we drove across the country, making our usual stop in Cleveland, where we learned that Charles was being treated for his "condition" at a state institution. Since I had last seen him, my father-in-law had changed. A strict diet had enabled him to lose weight, but he looked gaunt. Any exercise resulted in shortness of breath. The dog, Sox, had been given to friends since Fin could no longer walk him in the evening. The lively, clever mutt had filled the house with life, and without him it seemed vacant. Mother moved about in her bathrobe, as usual, indifferent to the mood of dejection. Even playing cards was a strain for Fin, his pale face filmed with perspiration. Mother was heedful of his superficial needs, totally ignorant of the others. In the cool, efficient manner of a nurse, she would dab at his face with a tissue. Even the effort to brush away her hand was too much for him. We left a day early, sparing him as well as ourselves. Fin's mother, ninety-five years of age, and living alone, was having trouble taking care of herself and had finally been persuaded to live with them in Cleveland. Mother did not like her mother-in-law, a woman who had been heedless, for almost a century, of every health rule known to science, as well as being stubborn and stone-deaf to advice. Mother did not look forward to a confrontation she had hoped to be spared, but she would do whatever proved to be necessary.

"She doesn't fool me for a minute," she said to my wife. "Hoping to outlive me has kept her alive." Munching a carrot, she added, "Well, we will see what we will see."

The first week of our arrival in Bryn Mawr, in the high lush humid heat of August, my wife had an attack of hay fever that put her to bed. She had a history of allergies, and had endured all the tests that were then in fashion, but never before had she found it hard to breathe, with fits of continuous sneezing. Was it possible we had moved to a place where she couldn't live? A doctor in Cleveland, who knew my wife's allergic history, sent on a simple drug that brought miraculous relief.

337

Thanks to the favorable impression my wife made on the people in the banking and real estate business, we were able to lease an apartment in Haverford, not far from the Baldwin School. Just a block to the south, on what was called the Pike, and directly across from the Haverford campus, an antique and secondhand store supplied us with the basics for setting up house. Not very practical, but wonderfully ornamental, was a purple velvet platform rocker that neither time, the sun, nor human bottom appeared to have touched. A full leather-bound set of the Eleventh Edition of the *Encyclopaedia Britannica,* in its own mahogany case, proved to be all ours for forty cents a volume. The owner of the store, a figure I would later recognize in the stories of Isaak Babel, put stock in many things, but not in books. The apartment itself, part of a duplex, with a porch of smooth cement level with the yard, was concealed from the street by rhododendron bushes. At the rear we had the remnants of a victory garden left by the previous occupants, and closing off the yard, on a high embankment, the main line of the Pennsylvania Railroad. In addition to the heavy rail traffic of freight, we had the daily commuter trains to Philadelphia. It persuaded us to do most of our sleeping and working in the room at the front.

After two summers in California, I welcomed both the humidity and the lushness. The Philadelphia Main Line had once been the affluent and elegant enclave for Philadelphia money and breeding, neither in short supply. At the turn of the century, mansions had been built and Japanese trees and flowering shrubs had been planted. The spring would bring the miracle of the flowering dogwood. Most of the money and breeding proved to be north of the tracks and the turnpike, but with quick access to the uncrowded electric car commuter service to Philadelphia. The *toot* of these cars, which I could hear from both directions, after stops had been made in Bryn Mawr and Ardmore, would soon displace in my mind the clang of streetcar bells and the sound of iron wheels spinning. That sound would have much to do with my new attachments, and the writing, ten years later, of the Main Line novel *The Deep Sleep.*

The Baldwin School had once been a posh resort hotel, a short carriage ride from the city. Old resort hotels, in my opinion, make marvelous private schools for girls, since the young female is both less rowdy and more ornamental to the setting. I would never tire of the festive hooting and the cardiac apprehension of Parents' Day. Not being a parent, I was spared the risk, but had all the pleasures of the occasion. The college of Bryn Mawr, the alma mater of our Double-dukes, as well as other distinguished nonconformists, was just a few

338

minutes' stroll to the west, one I sometimes took when the leaves were turning.

We had no more than settled in when a professor and his wife rented the apartment upstairs. The ladies met on the morning of the second day at the trash burner at the back of the yard. The ascending pitch of their conversation, with an occasional shriek of laughter, reached me where I was working at the front of the house. Loren and Mabel Eiseley proved to be from Nebraska, by way of Oberlin, where he had been teaching anthropology. For the time being (the summer), he was on loan to the University of Pennsylvania, where he had done his graduate work. Mabel Eiseley was from Hastings, where I had managed to spend one of my boyhood summers. It seemed unusual to both ladies, and remarkably amusing, that they had both married men from Nebraska, a territory not frequently heard from.

We spent that first and most of our other evenings together on the front porch, screened off from the traffic by the rhododendrons. The large dog of a neighbor, making his daily rounds, would appear about the time we were all getting thirsty and leave about the time we were cleaning up. In my opinion, he loved Eiseley's deep voice, pitched to a subterranean rumble. Some years later, however, dozing off as I rambled, Eiseley accounted for it in this manner: "Morris," he generously said, "when I listen to you go on and on, I can relax, knowing the world is in good hands." Good hands or not, we were both from the plains, and when we dipped into the past the same subsoil came up with the roots, and similar artifacts surfaced in our diggings.

My friend's naturally melancholy temperament led me to nickname him Schmerzie—a shortened form of *Weltschmerz*. I think he found it apt. He had a scholar's and a poet's perspective on human affairs, therefore he did not lack reason for pessimism. In our endless and pleasurable discussions, usually several times a week over a period of years, Loren was inclined to provide the perspective, while I proffered the notions of the eager amateur. That we were both the issue of the plains of Nebraska made for much good talk without friction. We had been turned on the same lathe, and were nourished and motivated by the same expectations.

Loren's wife, an Irish woman of the breed James Joyce had married, and bearing her some resemblance, had little patience with our speculations, but she enjoyed my jokes. Her own opinion of bone hunters and their reconstructions was frequently expressed with Irish directness and sarcasm, especially those fictions of Cro-Magnon and Piltdown man based on the molar of a missing jaw. Mabel put me

339

in mind of one of Willa Cather's lost ladies who had found her escape as a professor's wife. Her taste in fiction ran to Henry James, who would have loved both her hats and her style. Loren took pride in her appearance, her independent spirit, and walked at her side with his hand cupped to her elbow, at ease in the role, the suits and the ties, that would have been appropriate to my father.

When we met in the summer of 1943 I was the more published writer. My example may have encouraged Loren to get on with his own unique writing, the essays that expressed the two aspects of his experience and his temperament, the poet and the scientist. On occasion he would read one of the pieces to me, or try out a passage he felt a bit unsure of. His taste at the time was more discriminating than mine, but he welcomed my reassurance. That first summer together we began the long walks through the woods just north of Haverford and Bryn Mawr, escorted by dogs, sometimes a small pack of them, eager for a similar adventure. A big gray-muzzled red setter, with a henna-colored coat, combed the woods on both sides of the road, baying hoarsely when he turned up something. We could hear him thrash off through the brush, the pack howling at his heels. When he eventually returned, winded and slobbering, his coat wet and muddy from the streams he had forded, Eiseley might stoop to take the noble head in his hands, gazing into his eyes for his own dim past. It came easily to him, as it did to D. H. Lawrence, to profoundly empathize with the spirit that animated all living creatures, and might be intuited in the bone fragments of the dead ones. A man of this persuasion, and Eiseley's talents, might come to feel that bones, in an age of raucous babble, spoke clearest for the living. In his silences it was the voices of the dead to which he was attentive.

M Y WIFE HAD NOT SEEN HER COUSIN JAMES SINCE
they had been kids together back in Ohio. He had come east to
New York planning to be an architect, my wife to teach school,
and I to be a writer. We were living in suburban Philadelphia at the
time, and James and his wife were living in Brooklyn, near Coney
Island. I wondered what it was like to be living near the sea, and an
amusement park. James's mother had written to my wife that he was
now married, and a father, and she thought it was time that we all
got together.

We met at the Child's restaurant near Penn Station, where chicken
croquettes was the luncheon special. James was a tall, dark, easygoing
young man, who kept books—for the time being—for a plumber on
East Fifty-third street. When I asked him if he thought it might rain—he
carried an umbrella—he said the weather might be different where
he lived in Brooklyn than it was in the city. To me, that made it sound
interesting. He liked to sit with his hands on the handle of the umbrella, like a diplomat.

James wanted us to come home to Brooklyn with him, and meet
his wife and her family. She was the only girl among five adoring
brothers, none of them married. I liked the way James could tell a
story using the Irish brogue he had picked up from his in-laws. No
matter what it was my wife said, he was able to turn it to her advantage. I can see you haven't changed, my wife said, and he replied that
his wife would be sorry to hear that, flicking me a wink as he said
it. He had worked out a sort of routine, with his talk, so that it flattered the woman in question. He always seemed to take my side, but
in such a way that it pleased my wife. In his marriage, he said, he
had got most of Ireland, but all his wife had got was a husband. Her
father had himself come from Ireland, after the war, and still talked
a brogue strangers found it hard to understand. Nearby, in Brooklyn,
he kept a stable with a carriage and two horses there was no longer
much use for. What it did, though, was keep him out of mischief.

A few weeks later I was back in New York and called James to
say hello. He insisted that I spend the night in Brooklyn with them.
I met him at the subway, and we rode about an hour hanging on to
the straps, then another twenty minutes to where we got off. I hadn't
realized Brooklyn had such depressing neighborhoods. Empty lots were

everywhere, some of them strewn with junk, some of them with piles of smoking rubbish. Sidewalks were torn up, fences pushed over and battered, and some of the shabby frame houses were tilted. The three or four blocks I walked along with James made me think of Céline's slums in Paris, where the aged might be living like rabbits in the warrens at the back of the yards.

James told me that his wife had been born here, and her family had lived here most of their lives. One of the things about the Irish that he had noticed was how little they liked to move. Her brothers got around more, since two of them worked in Queens, but Mary herself had only once been to Times Square. It had frightened her more than it pleased her. She couldn't stand to mingle with so many people she didn't know. One thing that James planned to do, when they were settled, was get a car and drive out in the country. Mary had never seen the country, except in the movies. She didn't know how she would like a place that seemed to have so few people in it.

All her family had assembled to meet me, and sat tight around the kitchen table. There seemed to be about nine, including her handsome older brother, Jerry, and his fiancée, Maria. Jerry had the chiseled features you see in some of the Irish, with the build and natty style of a jockey. He wore a checkered suit, a diamond tiepin. Gold flashed when he smiled, and he had an appealing way of flicking a wink as he sucked air between his teeth. His brothers were more like the father, Paddy-type Irish, with their hair cropped short like the pelts of grass on the clay heads in florists' windows. For almost ten years Jerry had been the catch of the neighborhood. There was some resentment among the brothers that it was an Italian girl who had caught him in a neighborhood where Irish girls were not lacking. They took comfort, however, in Jerry's reluctance to get to the altar. He had now been engaged for just going on twenty-one months.

James's wife, Mary, was at her ease with men, having grown up with so many brothers. Her pale blue Irish eyes were almost as colorless as water, her hair, like her brother Jerry's, prematurely white. She had been the one to bring Maria home, after her first communion, and now she was pushing for an early marriage. Not to imply that she was forward, or felt that much at home, Maria sat the whole evening with her raincoat draped about her shoulders, and her hat on. The real problem was not so much that Maria was Italian but that her brothers were in the numbers racket, and drove fast cars. Going for her was the fact that she came from and looked forward to a big family.

All the while we were talking, Mary's father, Patrick, stood in the door to the hall, his lower lip protruding with a pouch of snuff.

342

At his back he held a can, into which he frequently turned to spit. Patrick did not read or write in any language, but he did it all with his bloodshot twinkling eyes, and the appreciative glances he gave the ladies. When food was served he took his plate and sat in the dark on the stairs, because of the way he smelled of the horses and the stable.

A meal was served and cleared away, beer was poured, and at our backs Mary moved around the table, filling and refilling our coffee cups. To do that, she explained, was why the Lord had made her so short. Sometime after midnight I noticed that James was missing, and found him asleep in the trough of the daybed, since there was not space in the room to open it properly. (On the nights Maria stayed over, she slept with Mary.) When I joined him, in an upright position, my eyes were level with the gap between the sill and the blind, through which I glimpsed a landscape of ruin lit up by moonlight. Unmistakably I felt the vibration of the arriving and departing subway. Something in the room jiggled. It proved to be the subway nickels in a saucer on the mantel. One of Mary's younger brothers had stayed on to discuss a personal matter with his sister, their voices muted like those exchanging confessions.

Sometime later, I awoke to see three of the brothers under the street light, talking. Smoke rose from their nodding, huddled heads like buns under a food warmer.

In December, I called Mary to say how I would miss seeing them all at Christmas, and heard from her that the marriage had now been set for April. Would I be there? I was excused when it was understood that I had never been to the Bronx. In the escort of her family, Mary was driven to the wedding in a limousine with black windows, one of which was lowered so she could see out.

On my visit in March, I learned that Maria's new baby was sickly from the Bronx air and water. Whose eyes and hair it had Mary didn't know, since neither mother nor child had paid her a visit. Mary was now expecting again herself. Did Maria think Mary, in her delicate condition, should now be traveling all the way to the Bronx? It sadly distressed her that Maria's sickly infant would be sorely needing, but not getting, the loving comfort and attention of an Irish family. All that Mary had learned would go wasted like food on the back burner without Maria and her baby there to receive it.

In May, a fire burned the barn where Mary's father kept his horses, and he was terribly burned trying to save them. To escape from this sorrow, James moved his wife and child to a small town in Massachusetts, with a priest known to Father Curran. James clerked,

343

like his father, in a grocery store, and worked as a volunteer in the fire department. At Christmas he sent us a snapshot showing him in his fireman's hat, riding on the truck. Mary had difficulty with her second baby, which she had planned to name Jerry if it was a boy, but it proved to be another girl, allergic to eggs and milk.

One winter day, in Grand Central Station, I recognized the tall, dark man coming toward me with a frail white-haired woman who might have been his mother. Her unseeing gaze looked through and beyond me. I raised my hand to wave, but neither of them saw me. Since I had last seen them, they had both learned to live in a world of people they didn't relate to. In a Christmas letter from James's mother, we learned that Mary had not adjusted well to country living, her health was poor, and at thirty-two years of age she had lost her teeth. Her mother added, however, that the two children seemed to be fine.

After a gap of many years, I sometimes wonder about the splinter in the groove that diverted me to Brooklyn. At that time I had been following a groove of my own, returning home along the tracks I had made going out, and I was not prepared to find myself tangled up with somebody else's family. It led me to spend hours just riding the subway. I came to see the subway as an extension of the nervous system, crucial connections maintained, lines of energy flowing, even while the passengers were in transit. I never felt much in the way of family ties myself. One of my classmates in college, who just might have been Irish, every two weeks would send a fiber carton of his laundry home to his family, whether he really needed it or not. He thought only his mother knew how to iron his shirts.

On a map like those on the walls of railroad stations, I once marked in all the places I had lived, and the places I had been, with chicken-like tracks indicating my travels. I meant to go back, one day, and put in the lines I knew to be missing, adding dense patches of crosshatching to those places important to me. Figuring roughly, for example, I must have crossed the railroad tracks in the town I was born in many thousands of times. Like the chicken in the story, it was the other side of the tracks that attracted me.

The streets in Omaha that I walked the most, especially in the summer when I was barefoot, have all been bulldozed away to make a great cloverleaf freeway intersection. I've often driven out of my way to try and capture the way I feel about it, but it escapes me. Am I compelled to resolve these real losses with imaginary gains?

Where Menomonee Street meets Lincoln Park in Chicago, the streetcar trolleys fill the night with their flashes, and once lit up the room where I should have been sleeping. From that corner, walking west on Menomonee Street, to where it ends at Ogden Avenue, then down Ogden to Larrabee, I suppose I've walked, in both hot and freezing weather, so many times it's a mystery my legs aren't shorter. Just down Menomonee Street, there used to be a sign that glowed warmly at night, advertising a toothbrush. I loved that sign, but somehow it never led me to buy the brush.

People beyond counting walk the streets of New York, wearing away the tracks of all the other walkers. Somehow, it's the wearing in of the tracks I like, the wearing off I don't. The meaning of this, if it has one, has to do with the maintenance of connections. When I turn and look behind me, I like to see where I have been. One of the jobs I once thought I'd wanted as a boy was to push the line marker on a baseball diamond, restoring what the game had obliterated, making again the insignia I see on the TV when the crowd rises to sing the National Anthem. When they sing "Oh, say can you see," this is what I see.

I TOOK MY NEW MANUSCRIPT TO NEW YORK IN
September, and met my agent, Diarmuid Russell. He had formed a
partnership with Henry Volkening at a bad time for fiction, but a very
needy time for young writers. Mr. Russell was a handsome, cultivated
man, both reserved and direct. I had learned that he was the son of
A. E. Russell, the Irish poet and essayist, and I was both impressed
and respectful. He had no good news for me about "The Vision of
Private Reagan," but he wanted to reassure me that I should not lose
heart. I was a good writer. One day, surely, my time would come.
I liked Mr. Russell's direct no-nonsense manner, and stretched my legs
to stay abreast of him after our lunch.

While waiting on what he might think of the new book—and
beginning a habit that would spare me much torment—in my imagination I returned to the plains, where one of its native sons seemed to
obstruct my field of vision. I did not see him as clearly as I *felt* him.
Better access to him, if and when it came, would come through my
feeling that we shared a mutual language. That what he felt, I felt.
Through these feelings I would find the words.

What little I saw was like a dark, featureless figure who stood
before a sod house, set into a barren hillside. The horns of cattle were
strewn about on the sod roof. I had never seen such a thing myself,
but I had glimpsed, from time to time, a few early photographs. I found
these bleak images captivating. In a way I did not understand, the very
lack of detail seemed to my purpose. The tilted windmill, with a few
of the blades missing; the hazy, shadowless blur of the glare that led
me to think of the landscape of China: that I had written down. A
strange conjunction, it seemed to me, the sandhills of Nebraska and
the plains of China. Searching for the voice appropriate to my feelings, I had written:

*In the dry places, men begin to dream. Where the rivers run sand
there is something in man that begins to flow.*

Not all of it was so compactly stated the first time, but that was
the *voice*. From the voice, like a seed, the rest of it would grow. On
another page:

346

Will Brady was born on a river without water, in a sod house, near the town of Indian Bow. In time he grew to be a man who neither smoked, drank, gambled nor swore. What is there left to say of a man with so much of his life left out?

What indeed! And what was that but to my purpose? The one man I knew who neither smoked, drank, nor gambled, and rarely swore, was my father. This fact somewhat bemused me, but I gave it little attention. The past was still the past until I unearthed it. My concern at the time was to establish the *tone* that would make possible all that followed. My preoccupation with *The Works of Love* would continue for some years, and it would not be published until 1952.

I put these pages aside when I heard from Diarmuid Russell that Harcourt, Brace had rejected my new book. Lambert Davis had liked it, personally, but he did not see it as a successful commercial venture. My first novel had done very poorly, and a second book, with a similar response from the public, would seriously diminish my future prospects. I should think hard about this second novel, he said, since for many writers it was their last.

Lambert Davis was right, on every count, but I was not a *smart* writer. How did the writer think of *anything* but writing? The *voice,* for example, that mystifying clue to what was as yet unspoken. How think of anything else? And if that eased off, and you had found this voice, and spoke in it as naturally as your own, there were the words and the characters, and the details to think about, and what, as you sat there, you found yourself reading. For the writer—the true fiction writer—does not write to say what he thinks or feels, but to discover what it is. What I discover I am thinking and feeling takes all the time and thought I am able to muster, and it is seldom enough.

In his accompanying letter, Diarmuid cautioned me not to take this advice too much to heart. That was the way of editors and publishers. Their problem was that they had no way of telling the margarine from the butter. Could I supply him with a copy of *My Uncle Dudley*? He had an editor, Maxwell Perkins, who might like to read it. I did have a copy and sent it on to him, painfully conscious of its shortcomings. What would the editor who had read and published *The Sun Also Rises* and *The Great Gatsby* think of this piece of homespun? I had never seen my writing in this perspective, and it gave me pause.

About this time, my wife brought the principal of her school, Rosamund Cross, to our place for tea. A graduate of Bryn Mawr,

347

self-possessed, attractive, liberated, with a cordial but professional manner, she had a story to tell of her brother's involvement in the naming of a new navy destroyer. Her brother had been lost at sea, and the boat had been named in his memory. The ceremony, which took place at a pier in Brooklyn, had been attended by Miss Cross and her mother. She dramatized the comical aspects of the ceremony so well we were still laughing hours later. And again it was the subject of *missing persons,* and the effort to accommodate these losses.

This incident so intrigued me I applied myself to it. I chose a man and his wife: the man gentle, somewhat passive—on my mind's eye I saw my father-in-law, and felt again his loss and his sorrow—the wife a woman he referred to as Mother. Their son would prove to be missing in a naval engagement, and would be honored with his name on a destroyer. The tone appropriate to this story seemed to be on my tongue, waiting for me to tell it, just as the characters were there in the wings, waiting to play their roles.

The tone of the book wavered between pathos and farce, a mix that seemed appropriate to the subject. Mrs. Ormsby is the object of the author's ridicule, but her role as Mother also gives it substance. I made a good start on the opening Ormsby chapter, before I was distracted by a letter from Diarmuid. Maxwell Perkins had read *My Uncle Dudley,* and expressed an interest in meeting the author. This heady news suspended all work.

Through Schindy we had met Peter and Nanny Sollinger, who lived in a large house in Brooklyn. The Sollingers were Swiss, from near Zurich. Nanny taught German at Brooklyn College, while Peter researched and wrote his book on Sutter, the Swiss explorer of the American West. The son of a peasant, Peter had taught himself to paint, to play the cello, to clean and wax all the floors, to make an apartment in the attic, to add a garage to the house, to hang storm windows, which saved the money to purchase a car, and in the early morning to research and write his scholarly book. I marveled at Peter's self-discipline, his quirky independence, his large gnarled hands that were like the roots of grapevines, but I found it hard to keep abreast of him when we took walks, his instinct to be in front was so persistent. In every detail, his knobby head—the stiff brush of his hair, the roughly hewn, craggy, masculine features—was that of the Swiss wine bottle caps popular at Christmas. It pleased both Nanny and Peter to have American friends who liked Schubert and Mozart, Thomas Mann and Jakob Burckhardt, as well as camomile tea and Jewish Danish. They lived not far from the Avenue J stop of the subway, which was a bit of a ride for us, but we enjoyed their friendship.

The great love of Nanny's life was her violin, which she played with some moaning and great intensity. I could listen to Nanny, but I could not both listen and watch her. If Peter and I began a conversation while the ladies were playing a sonata, Nanny would pause in her playing and come to stand between the folding doors she did not like closed, until we had given her our full attention.

"You understand it is not for me," she would say, and then return to Mozart.

Peter had been the romance of Nanny's life, and she had literally pulled him up by the roots and transplanted him in Brooklyn. In most respects he thrived. I loaned Peter a collapsible, newfangled camp cot the summer he and Nanny visited Yellowstone Park, which he returned to me, a year later, with the comment that it didn't seem to work. The heavy steel supports had been twisted in a manner nobody I knew could straighten out.

The Scribner building and bookstore on Fifth Avenue was directly across the street from a Child's restaurant. I often sat there with a cup of coffee, gazing up to the high windows of Maxwell Perkins's office. He would be the first literary legend I both met and appreciated. The oak-paneled offices on the fifth floor had not been altered since the days of Henry James, whose books were there in the library.

Mr. Perkins had the curtained corner office at the front, with a view of the skyline and Fifth Avenue. He rose from his desk to offer me his hand, then returned it to grip the lapel of his coat. One of the large Western hats given to him by Hemingway was tilted back on his head, framing his shyly smiling face. I liked him on the instant, and began to tell him all, a predictable and regrettable response. Hearing the code word *money*, Max took out his wallet. How much did I need? With some shame, I backed off. He was not given to "loose" talk himself, and he did not expect it from others. We talked about the book I was rewriting, *The Man Who Was There*, and then we talked about writers, *his* writers, Hemingway, Fitzgerald and Thomas Wolfe—on whose unpublished manuscript he was then working— and there I sat in the chair those writers had sat in, discussing them with Max Perkins, a legend. He had read and liked *My Uncle Dudley* but thought it slight. He would feel the same about *Man and Boy*. His complaint about the brevity of my fiction would be the one I heard the most. He liked heft. I would seldom be a writer of heft.

Back in Haverford, I looked again at *The Man Who Was There*, pondering how I might give it more weight. I read again the story of Private Reagan, and it occurred to me that his bizarre vision might be appropriate to the world of Agee Ward. I made some changes, and a few months later heard from Diarmuid Russell that Scribner's planned to publish it.

This occurred in the spring of 1945, and one of my first readers, a teacher at the Baldwin School, a Swiss woman with a profound dislike for speed reading, called me to ask if there was not something peculiar with a line of text on page 219. This line read: "To get her mind off Boulder Dam I took the road up Baldy wanted to know about Boulder Dam." I allowed as how the line did sound a bit strange. A word or phrase had been dropped. I would hasten to check on it. On checking this out—which took some time, since I lacked the original copy of the manuscript—I found that eight or ten pages were missing. I called Max Perkins, who surprised me by saying that the error would be corrected in later printings. How did one get later printings of a book with so many pages missing? It was not a topic in which Max had much interest. Some months later, conducting my own inscrutable investigation, I discovered that the editor in charge of the galleys had been suffering a mid-career crisis, complicated romantically, that had finally revealed itself in pages missing from assorted galleys. They had simply vanished. The prime exhibit, designed to calm small losers like myself, was a mystery novel, written by Marjorie Bonner, the wife of Malcolm Lowry, which was published without its concluding chapter. No question that this book was a mystery that remained unresolved. Only a handful of readers, besides the author, took the pains to point this out.

Vanished also, during that season, had been the prospect for a second printing of *The Man Who Was There,* nor did it again, to my knowledge, receive the close, nonspeed reading that hinted at missing pages.

Thirty-two years later, when the book was reissued by the University of Nebraska, the line that had troubled my Swiss friend had been deleted, the gap skillfully closed. The writer of the novel pondered the gap but he did not recall what he might have written, nor have the missing pages ever surfaced. A truly missing passage from the tale of a missing man.

Diarmuid Russell had thought it ill-advised—in light of what happened to my second novel—to trouble Max Perkins with a book as strange, as expensive and as innovative as *The Inhabitants.* But I was so confident I ignored his advice. On an early fall day, I appeared at the Scribner offices with my portfolio of mounted photographs, and I vividly remember sitting at Max's side as he looked at them one by one, and read the texts. His Hemingway hat was tilted back. He was pleased, but reluctant to say so. What might he be getting into *this* time? I was equally certain that whatever he had seen, and read, had given him no more than the bloom of it. How was the book to speak louder for itself?

The wall of his office was at his back, the high windows on Fifth Avenue to his left. I took several of the prints, a handful of his paper clips, and clipped them to the drapes that concealed the neighboring office. He was amused. I was delighted to see how good they looked. Did he mind? He seemed more pleased than provoked. I took an armful of the mounts and expanded the exhibition to two walls of his office. The light was marvelous. We both agreed it made quite a show. Just for the hell of it, would he let them hang for two weeks? He fussed a bit. What might his visitors think? It would be a good way of finding out, I said, how the public might respond to the book.

The photographs and texts were on his walls when I left, and they were still there two weeks later, when I appeared to take them away. What did he think? He let me wait while he tilted back his chair and took a grip on the lapels of his coat. A few pigeons were pacing the sill of his window. His secretary, as important to Max as his hands, came in with her pad and pencil to tell me how much she had liked looking at the photographs. The Perkins glow gave his smile a cherubic cast. Still faced away from me—he *was* a shy man—he said he felt obliged to publish the book, although it made no sense as a commercial venture. Pete Dymock, from the production department, came in to tell me how much *he* liked it, and he wanted to know which of the photographs had been taken in Georgia, his home state. That was how it came to pass that *The Inhabitants* found a home.

In 1938, before we left California, I had at last found a copy of *The Sleepwalkers*, by Hermann Broch. The author's range had dazzled me, but more to my purpose, I was profoundly moved by his portraits of Mother Hentjen and her lover, Esch. Such people as these, such discards, in a sense, were compacted of the elements that aroused my imagination. Memories of Esch had been at work in my portrait of Private Reagan and his bizarre vision. In my enthusiasm, I had written a letter to Broch in care of his American publisher, Little, Brown. It delighted me to eventually receive his cordial response, with an address in Princeton I might write to.

When we settled in Haverford, I wrote to Broch again, and he suggested we might visit him in Princeton. We managed to do this in the spring of 1945, when I had my just published novel *The Man*

351

Who Was There to show him. Broch was a guest of Erich Kahler, an Austrian writer and scholar, who, like Broch, had recently escaped the Nazis. They lived just a short walk from Albert Einstein, in a large, comfortable house on Evelyn Place. On that first trip to Princeton I also took along my portfolio of photographs and texts, which proved to be of great interest to the émigrés who had gathered for a Sunday dinner. Kahler's very old mother, dressed in black, her eyes sunk deep in their sockets, sat near the fire on our arrival, reading Greek with Broch. I felt she perceived me, if at all, through the veil of another century. Her concern for Broch was that of a grandmother left in charge of a much-loved but somewhat wayward child. At one of the meals, I sat near Broch across from two Viennese women, the refinement of their awareness of each other spun out of the air itself by Rilke's *Malte Laurids Brigge*. Did people of this quality manage to persist in a show of signs that spared them discussion of the unspeakable?

IN 1946 I APPLIED FOR A SECOND GUGGENHEIM Fellowship, and I was fortunate enough to receive it. I exchanged my 3¼ by 4¼ view camera for a 4 by 5. In early May of the following spring, I drove back to the farm near Norfolk. The Depression-ravaged dirt farm of my previous visit was partially concealed and softened by the growth of spring; weeds concealed implements; a gone-to-seed overripeness seemed appropriate. I found my Uncle Harry at his ease, smoking a cob pipe, tinkering with an inner tube. Clara was more resigned than bitter. I found her seated in her rocker, her lap full of eggs, chipping at the dung spots with her thumbnail. To my suggestion that I take pictures they expressed no objection. Did they know what I had in mind? They had seen *The Inhabitants*. Feeling the need to justify, rather than explain, I said I wanted to capture what it was like to have lived on a dirt farm for fifty years, to have lived on this farm for half a century. There was no comment. I recall Clara moving her head from one side to the other, to see and appraise the room she sat in. Her shoes were unlaced. The ties of her apron dangled on the floor. I could hear mice stirring in the kitchen's basket of cobs. "I don't know why," she said, "but if it's what you want to do, you're free to."

It had never crossed my mind that she would give me access to the *inside* of her house. I was about to reassure her: You can trust me, Clara. . . . Trust me to do what? Wasn't I too greedy to be trusted? Didn't I privately feel I had earned this privilege? Just a few weeks before, I had come on a statement that gave me, I felt, unlimited access.

. . . is to be subject to the superstition that objects and places, coherently grouped, disposed for human use and addressed to it, must have a sense of their own, a mystic meaning proper to themselves to give out: to give out, that is, to the participant at once so interested and so detached as to be moved to a report of the matter. (Henry James, *The American Scene*)

I was hardly detached, but otherwise I was qualified. These objects and places spoke to me profoundly, and I was moved to a report of the matter. My Uncle Harry was indifferent to the nuances of exposure. The young man with his camera had come at a time the usual reservations were in abeyance. For Clara, the whole farm was

353

a ruin, an accumulation of losses, a disaster that her Protestant soul must accept, and here comes this youth, a prodigal relation, who saw in these sorry remains something of value. She could not imagine what, but she could believe it was what he saw. The reservations of a lifetime would struggle in her soul with the dim, unlikely hope that the youth might be right.

At the end of the first day, one of a steady drizzle, I had brought my camera on its tripod in from the porch to make sure it was out of the rain. I stood it up in a dark corner of the kitchen, the lens reflecting the lampglow. Clara gazed at it for a moment with her good eye.

"It's not taking pictures now?" she asked me. I assured her it wasn't. "Just so I'm not in them," she said, and glanced down her flat, faded frock. Would anything convince her there was something of value in what she saw?

I was put in the upstairs bedroom I had had as a boy, almost thirty years before. The window frame was just a few inches off the floor, due to some miscalculation, the folds of the gathered lace curtain as dry and crisp as paper. The storm window, put up several years before, had not been taken down. On the doily of the bureau, a satin-lined box that had once contained an ivory-handled comb, mirror and brush set now held several corroded rifle cartridges and the partial handle of the missing mirror. Why had she preserved it? We were alike in that we perceived these objects in the light of our emotions, and judged this the mystic meaning they had to give out.

At the start, my Uncle Harry ignored me. I saw him pass with a hoe, with a pail of water, with another inner tube that needed repairing, indifferent to my presence. I drew him in with questions. Would it rain again? He replied that it usually did. Soon he trailed me around, offered dry suggestions, tested me with his deadpan humor. He still smoked Union Leader, if and when he could find his pipe. When I suggested a picture of himself—the greatest ruin of all—he was compliant. Actually, he had been waiting. In the museum of relics the farm had become, he was one of the few that still almost worked. He pointed that out himself.

I had him walk before me, through the door of the barn he had entered and exited for half a century. He had become, like the denims he wore, an implement of labor, one of the discarded farm tools. A personal pride, however, dormant since the Depression, reasserted itself in the way he accepted my appreciative comments. Why not? Had he not endured and survived it all, like the farm itself? Over several days I had remarked that he changed his hats according to the time of the day and the occasion. A sporty nautical number in the early

354

morning; at high noon and afternoon, one of his wide-brimmed straws. In the dusk of evening, he preferred an old felt, with a narrow brim, the color and texture of tar paper. All hats suited him fine. The only piece of apparel we both found out of fashion was new overalls, blue stripes on white, that in no way adapted to his figure or movements and gave off the rasp of a file. He was quick to sense my disapproval and stopped wearing them.

It was Clara's suggestion that I might look in on Ed's place. Ed was a bachelor, related by marriage, who had died several weeks before my arrival. His small farmhouse was directly across the road. I found the house as a bachelor would have left it. The bric-a-brac of a lifetime—pillboxes, pincushions, shotgun shells, flashlights, a watch and chain, a few snapshots. Although the bed had been made, the imprint of his body remained in the mattress, his feet were visible in the shoes beneath it. What I saw on the ground glass evoked in me a commingling of tenderness, pity and sorrow, to the exclusion of more searing emotions. Was there another American emotion to match pathos? Were not tragic sentiments alien to a free people who were free to choose, and chose more earthly adornments? "Ed passed on last month," Harry had said, as if he had glanced up just a bit too late to catch him. What he seemed to see was a movement of the bushes edging the drive.

One evening, Clara had again shown me a photograph of the Morris family back in Ohio in the late eighties, showing all members except my father and Harry, forming a line in front of a clapboard house in a fresh fall of snow. Their names had been read aloud to me by Harry—Mitchell and Emerson, Ivy and Mae, Martha and Francena—on and on through a dozen. A crack in time had been made by the click of a shutter, through which I could peer into a world that had vanished. This fact exceeded my grasp, but it excited my emotions. The following day I took the photograph into the open air and pinned it to the clapboards on one side of the house. I saw it clearly on the ground glass before the shutter clicked. Was it in this wise I hoped to postpone what was vanishing? A simpler ritual of survival would be hard to imagine. By stopping time, I hoped to suspend mortality.

Since I had taken all of the interior shots without artificial lighting, I was anxious to get the negatives developed, and see what I had done. While they were being processed in Lincoln, I drove around through the neighboring towns, and found many structures of interest. In Central City I woke up the barber, dozing in his chair after lunch. He remembered my father—a railroad man who had turned to raising

355

chickens—but he had no memory of the boy who had sat on the board placed on the chair arms, heard the chirp of the shears, and smelled the tonic water doused on his hair. There had been a lot of boys. Looking at me, front and side, brought none of them to mind.

I stayed on for several days in Lincoln, photographing what I found on the roads around it. Some twenty miles to the south, in beautiful rolling country, lush and green with the spring rains, I came on a house set back from the road in a clump of evergreens. Through the broken windows of the first floor I could see the fields behind it. The tilted, creaking windmill had a mournful look. I carted my camera and tripod up the rain-gutted driveway past a trench piled high with empty cans and trash. Most of the cans looked new, with colorful paper labels. As I approached the house, and set up my tripod, the mournful groaning of the windmill held my attention. The wind wheel itself soared high above the trees into the slanting light. I noted the low fenced-in porch that occupied one corner of the second floor. Farther back I could see a partially opened screen. Tatters of curtains hung at a window. I was focusing on the ground glass, my hands cupped to my face, when I saw this hand, or rather this claw, curl slowly over the fence rail, then grip it. The chill of terror I felt tingled my scalp. I controlled my impulse to run, fooled a bit with my camera, then made my way down the drive to the road. From the seat of the car I dared to peer back, to see the tuft of white hair above a dark forehead. The wind wheel screeched and grated. After two false starts, I managed to make a clammy-handed getaway. The sense that I was pursued led me to crouch over the wheel, press the gas pedal to the floor. I felt I had seen enough to know that this creature might have been one of my abandoned relations, preferring to crumble with the ruins rather than to leave them. Topping a rise, I saw, with relief, the tower of the new capitol building. "You be sure you see it, Wright," my aunt Clara had told me. "It's one of the wonders of the world."

On the ground glass of the negative viewer in the Eastman photographic store, I had my first clear and reassuring impression of several weeks' work. I also wanted a simple, direct narrative that would read, if possible, like a novel, giving uninhibited expression to the sentiments and conflicts of a late-returning native. I had grown to feel such affection for the home place, and its inhabitants, that I was at ease with the sentimental appeal it would have for this urban man and wife, and their snotty kids. That was how I saw it. A young man not unlike myself, a long-departed native son, who had thought

356

he had put all this behind him, caught up in the appeal it proved to have for his city wife and kids, and for himself. At the point he was prepared to "settle down," however, perhaps in the house just vacated by Ed, his wife would bring him to his senses and they would continue down the road, his home town the next in my series of photo-text volumes.

I had these scenarios in mind while I was driving back to Philadelphia, trying out the voice I felt to be appropriate, that of a man who had been born and bred in this landscape, had once, briefly, lived on this farm, and had fortunately never lost his faculty of dramatizing his reflections in the vernacular of his experience. What would better suit my sentiments, and my intention, than the first-person-singular "I" of the very involved author. What reason did I have for concealment? The story of a native's return was an old one, and I would give it a Nebraska accent. As for the dangers of this voice—sentimental, self-indulgent, so appealingly "natural" yet so open to counterfeit and make-believe—I knew about such things in the abstract and I would try to keep the writer under control. There were many precedents, most of them good ones. "I should not talk so much about myself," Thoreau had advised me, "if there were anybody else I knew as well."

How sensible that sounded! And how much to the point of what I had in mind. In my enthusiasm, I was aware of everything about this voice but the pitfalls, the first being the author's evangelical fervor for what he intended to do. How could I miss, since all I had to do was clearly express what I was feeling! These feelings were running so high that I sat down, on arriving in Bryn Mawr, to capture snatches of the dialogue I had been having with the characters, most of them anxious to make this city boy and his family feel right at home.

In mid-July, I stopped writing and went into the darkroom, which also happened to be the coolest part of our new accommodations. On the sale of the property in which we had been living, we had moved over a garage in suburban Bryn Mawr, with "access," as it was called, to the kitchen. We had come by this windfall, in very elegant surroundings, including a museum of antiques, because my wife proved to be the teacher of one of the resident girls. Her older sister had also attended Baldwin, but was currently at Bennington, in Vermont. Our move was actually illegal, in such a restricted area, but the ample and hoarsely baying landlady (I liked her, and arranged an appearance in one of my novels) appreciated both our company and the rent. We had the run of the house, when it was empty, and of the patio most of the summer, the long-gone-to-seed and weedy garden ornamented with concrete statuary. I used the pantry off the kitchen as my darkroom. Over the summer, my friend Eiseley continued his nature studies in the surrounding acreage. After a long day in the darkroom I would show my wife and the Eiseleys the new enlargements I had made. Washing these prints in the tub, then squeegeeing them dry on the ferrotype plates, was back-breaking work. I had to have the glossy prints for the book, however, and I frequently misjudged in the darkroom what I saw later in the full light of day. I wanted both the crisp detail and the bold pattern of light and shadow, velvety blacks and luminous whites. Mabel Eiseley, in particular, was appreciative of the Home Place interiors. With a hundred or more of these prints to choose from, I turned back to the narrative, samples of which I read to the Eiseleys. Early in September, I had a complete, readable draft.

I felt so confident about what I had done—I was so open to my own persuasion—that I again went directly to Max Perkins. He liked it, but he had his reservations about the prospective sales. Charles Scribner, Jr., had just joined the firm, and Max gave him the book for his opinion. To my astonishment (Charles was just out of Princeton), he was enthusiastic about it, and took charge of its production. My idea was, after *The Inhabitants*, to publish the book in the format of a novel, with a photograph facing each page of text. Cropping would mutilate the carefully framed eight-by-ten images, but would focus on a few of the essentials. It seemed imperative to me, at the expense of the photographs, that the text should read like a novel. Young Scribner shared this opinion. Once more Pete Dymock would supervise the press run, and no sensible expense would be spared in the book's production. The jacket would feature the photograph of a piece of burlap, on which, in red, the words THE HOME PLACE would appear to be stenciled.

The first-person voice of *The Home Place* seemed equally effective for the next book, *The World in the Attic*, where Muncy's city-bred boy will prophetically comment, "Is this God's country, Mummy, or is it still Daddy's?"—a question this book would try to answer.

What was I feeling? Something I might call Home Town nausea. I can get it in a lunch room, or at the bend in a road where a telephone pole tips out of a clutter of weeds. Or a track crossing where you lean out to peer into nowhere in both directions. At such times it's hard to tell where the nostalgia stops, the nausea begins. While you're in the grip of one, the other sets in.

After a few weeks of work, it seemed to me that the writing had less of the sentimental "grit" that I could taste in *The Home Place*, but retained the bounce and expectancy crucial to Muncy's experience. But as the plot thickened I was made aware of the hazards of the first-person voice. The ease and flow of the story either concealed, or made light of, the double role of Muncy as a character and as a stand-in for the author. I found it an authorial privilege to exploit this ambivalence. At any moment, just by clearing my throat, I could speak from the wings on matters of morals and taste where I happened to feel strongly. This agreeable afflatus buoyed up the author, and I would soon come to recognize its presence in numerous works of Mark Twain. The ambivalence that is part of the voice itself is subject to both deliberate and unconscious manipulation. The voice that I am now using to describe this occasion, and to comment on it with some detachment, is relatively free of the "self" deception that comes so easily to the "I" as narrator but is inherent in the "I" itself, usually concealed. The impersonal narration that the reader wants, and that is crucial to the craft of fiction, is to some extent qualified or confuted the moment the writer says "I." The nuances of ambiguity in this practice are endless. Years after *The World in the Attic* was published, I would read *The Fall*, by Albert Camus, and have full exposure to the complexities of the voice I had ingenuously adopted. *The Attic* was part of my own emerging world of fiction—not a place on the map, like *The Home Place*—and I was licensed to accommodate or reject as much of the past or the present as I found to my purpose.

The characters of Mr. Purdy and Caddy Hibbard, for example, were imported from my wife's home in Cleveland—Purdy Mother's neighborly handyman, Caddy Hibbard her grandmother—but the unexpected appearance of Tom Scanlon, peripheral to the interests of the novel, would prove to be crucial to much of the fiction I wrote in the fifties, including *Ceremony in Lone Tree*. As I walked along a spur of tracks, in *The World in the Attic*, that proved to lead me nowhere, I was putting down the rails and ties necessary to the novels shaping in my imagination. Joyce's "commodius vicus of recirculation," part of my nature before it was part of my reading, an up-and-downward spiraling of my preoccupations, would prove to lead me away and upward even as it led me back and downward. The role of recurrence is so central to my nature that I sense, in what appears to be new, the other side, the far side, of what appears to be old, and contradicts our sense of time as linear. We plainly lack the faculty to grasp time, in its essence, but the spiral accommodates my own impressions and lends itself to the purposes of fiction. Tom

Scanlon, in *Ceremony*, is preparing to sit at the window with no obstruction but the sky:

Come to the window. The one at the rear of the Lone Tree Hotel. The view is to the west. There is no obstruction but the sky. Although there is no one outside to look in, the yellow blind is drawn at the window, and between it and the pane a fly is trapped. He has stopped buzzing. Only the crawling shadow can be seen. Before the whistle of the train is heard the loose pane rattles like a simmering pot, then stops, as if pressed by a hand, as the train goes past. The blind sucks inward and the dangling cord drags in the dust on the sill.

IN FEBRUARY, AFTER A LONG AND HUMILIATING decline, my father-in-law died. My wife's mother called from Cleveland, and we took the night train from Philadelphia. Flares were burning to keep the track switches from freezing, as I had so often seen them in my boyhood. We were met at the station by the family doctor, the first to tell us that he thought it all for the best. In her kimono with the faded dragons, a recent gift from her daughter, Mother came to the door carrying the clothes she would put on in the bathroom. The house was cold, the heat having been turned off to save fuel. Mother approached me, to pluck a few hairs from the collar of my topcoat. Did I detect in her appraisal of my tie a flicker of approval?

"Do you suppose," she said to my wife, "that one of your father's shirts might fit him?"

"We've already gone into that, Mother. Daddy's shirts are all too long in the sleeves."

In the cold winter light at the bird box window, the Grandmother clattered her cane on the radiator. I could see only the tight topknot of her gray hair, the claw of the hand that gripped the cane. Had anyone troubled to tell her that her son lay dead in the upstairs bedroom? Flecks of light glittered on her steel-rimmed glasses. Her suppressed rage seemed to actually shrink her to a grizzled, wizened fury. On me and my wife, on her daughter-in-law, and on the house itself, she passed a verdict of eternal hellfire.

"We are all going to have to be on our good behavior," said Mother, "and that includes Mrs. You-know-who." Once more the Grandmother raised her cane and brought it down with a whack on the radiator.

"She wants her oatmeal," said Mother, "but I am no longer so sure that Mrs. You-know-who is always going to get just what she wants."

Nevertheless, during the week we were in Cleveland, we were all on our good behavior, including the Grandmother. One of my father-in-law's white shirts (the cuffs doubled back) looked quite acceptable under my coat. One of Charles's black ties pleased both ladies. A steady flow of friends, and a few dignitaries—snow had been cleared so they could use the front entrance—stopped to pay their respects

361

to the dead, but lingered to marvel at the Grandmother, just one year short of her centennial celebration. The front room glowed with their admiration. Where had Mother been *keeping* her? they asked. A grizzled and bearded ninety-nine-year-old lady who told her stories like the comedians on the phonograph records, and who had also, among other things, set her sharp eyes on Abe Lincoln. (Who was to say that she hadn't?) A tall beanstalk of a man, solemn and silent, gripping the lapels of his coat as he rambled. What he had said had not much interested an eight-year-old girl, but she would have voted for him if she could have. She had always voted Republican.

Seldom as low as it had looked that morning, the Grandmother's self-esteem was restored by the praise and attention of the guests. One story followed another, all of them good, many I had not previously heard, their climax followed by a period of silence that some felt to be ominous. Was she, perhaps, a bit overexcited? For a long countdown of twenty or thirty seconds she was silent, her head bowed, as if she had put it all behind her, then her right foot would lift from the floor until her right hand pegged it down, with a slap on the knee. These yarns were told without a pause, through half-clenched false teeth, her mouth spread in what might have been a complicitous smile or a painful grimace. At these moments I saw how closely she resembled her son. He, too, forced his words between half-clenched teeth, and suppressed all but the snort of his laughter. A box of chocolates placed in her lap was found to be half empty before taken from her.

All of these days of mourning, the Grandmother flowered, mumbling to some, croaking hoarsely to others, and sometimes uttering little barks in her sleep, as if playing with children. All the bad birds had the run of the bird box now that her attention was elsewhere, the big fierce jays hammering on the window until Mother came at them with a broom. The social life tired the Grandmother; she might sleep through the early breakfast or fail to appear at lunch, obliging my wife to go to the basement to see if she might be down there ironing. There was no way to tell, except by looking, if she was squatted on the stool, under the dripping water closet.

Wearing blue pumps, with bows, carrying a small blue purse, the veil of her blue straw hat shrouding her remarkable eyes, my mother-in-law, with her sober, dignified manner, would have been highly approved of by her husband. The service attracted a large number of his former students, assorted academic people and numerous local merchants, with their families, all who knew Professor Finfrock as "Fin." The family shopping having been left to him, Mother knew none of these people personally. Mr. Garbanzo, owner of the delicatessen where Fin got his liver sausage and his cheesecake, gripped my hand firmly between his own and looked hard into my eyes. His own were bloodshot from weeping. His wife, too (who helped him on weekends), searched my face for the loss that made it difficult for her to speak. She stared at my wife and me with sorrow and compassion. To have had such a man as a father! Even her children, hovering behind her, knew and loved him. In the men's washroom, bluff and hearty merchants stood about blowing their noses, puffing on cigarettes. Sidelong, I caught their glances. Had I known him well enough to measure my loss?

My wife excused herself, and I later found her seated in the car, red-eyed and tearful. Why was it necessary for us to experience our losses through others? In my measurably less loving sorrow, I remembered I had not wept for my father. Had my too-great self-sufficiency deprived me of the ties that were common to so many? "They really loved him," cried my wife, "they really did!"

I was at once sorrowful, saddened and shamefaced. My family ties had been on the fringe of other families, from where I spied on them from pantries, or concealed by the cloak that draped the dining room table. Later I would be consoled to share this hideaway with Isaak Babel. The losses I had experienced were real enough, but not of the sort that diminished my nature. No man was an island, but I was far from being washed into the sea. I had not felt the shock nor the grief of Miss Lyle, the dead man's secretary, who had been put to bed and sedated to make this loss bearable. What I felt the most intensely was that I had been cut, but proved to be a poor bleeder. I lacked the close, the confining, the indispensable ties that when cut left lacerations. I was a Band-Aid victim, and it was my full knowledge of this deflated loss that filmed my eyes.

We took the train to Covington, in central Ohio, for the burial. Real grass still covered these graves, some of it new, the dark, wet earth piled like coal to one side. A few relations, with their families, stood behind us, and at the edge of the graveyard I could see a few others, reluctant to be counted among the serious mourners. At my side, however, a lean, dapper-looking man, a topcoat over his barber's smock, had found a place for himself. Tufts of white hair grew out of his large ears. He felt it important to explain to me that he had left his shop full of clients, to pay his respects. Fin had been his friend for fifty-three years. Two or three times a year, with the exception of these last years, Professor Finfrock had driven all the way to Covington for a shave, a haircut, a massage, and to be brought up to date on all that had happened, in case anything had. For all of Fin's fame—

that had been the barber's word—he had remained a small-town man at heart. Local Covington people were those he really cared about. As a fairly young man, the barber had recognized that his friend Fin would be an exceptional man. And how was that? His hat size. A full quarter size larger than the average. And this was after his hair had been trimmed at the sides, not when it was full.

It was to him, the barber advised me, that the dean of the law school unburdened himself in both professional and personal matters. It would surprise me to learn, he said, what they had discussed. Speaking frankly to the man who was now head of the family (the barber had been the first to declare it!), he suggested that I should pay him a visit and have a little talk while having my hair cut, since he could see that I shaved myself.

We rode back into town together, the barber seated at the front with the cabdriver, who happened to be one of his clients. His shop proved to be a flight of steps up from the street, overlooking the roofed bench of the shoeshine stand. Through the wide front window, like Eddie Cahow's, I could see that one of the barber chairs was occupied, the client stretched out horizontal, but the second chair sat empty, the cloth folded across the chair arm, facing the street. Did this provide me with the missing context to my own dormant emotions? My eyes filmed over. I put the tip of my tongue to dry lips. I could hear the voice of Eddie Cahow greet me as he tapped his comb on the starched cuff of his sleeve. The barber was aware of my swollen emotions.

"I could tell you some things that would surprise you," he said. "Now you come and see me!"

For the moment we stood there, I was certain that I might. What secret life did my father-in-law share with his barber?

Speaking directly to me (was it as head of the family?), my mother-in-law said, "Do you think that was called for?" It was to me she had spoken, not my wife. I could feel both her concern and her assurance. "Tell him," she said to her daughter, "that if he wants to be surprised, he needn't come all the way to Covington for it."

This would prove to be a simple statement of fact. No one would surprise me, again and again, and again, like my mother-in-law.

Clarence Millard Finfrock, much loved and sorely missed by those who were not members of his intimate family, was the only paterfamilias I had experienced. I had grown accustomed to his solid, reassuring, expansive presence, his easily given affection. "My son-in-law," he would say, introducing me, a statement in which we both took pride. One day a van would arrive from Cleveland with Mother's

Oriental rug, the Chippendale secretary, the Webster's dictionary on the tripod stand, the signed volumes from famous bird lovers, the two framed Audubon prints, and three barrels of unsorted worlds from several attics: Charles's samurai sword, his tennis racquet, and the catcher's glove and mask of "Fin" Finfrock, along with two Louisville Slugger bats.

Max Perkins unexpectedly died before *The Home Place* was published, a shock no one who knew him was prepared for, but it pleased me to think that he would have liked the book's critical reception. Privately I was alerted to my own accumulating losses. It put me back to work on *The World in the Attic*, which I delivered to Scribner's in the fall, at which time I had a long and frank discussion with my new editor, Wally Meyer. Once more, the reception of a book of mine had been good, but not the sales. There was no indication, Wally pointed out to me, that the buying public shared my enthusiasm for the new photo-text format. There was growing indication—which he showed me—that even reviewers were confused as to the purposes of the author. Was he a writer who liked to take photographs, or a photographer who liked to do a little writing? In either case, it played hell with the publisher's intent to establish a new author. The public had never taken well to the ambidextrous talent. Wally Meyer had read, and liked, *The World in the Attic* as a *novel*, without any reference to the photographs. If I would excuse him for speaking frankly, the photographs *distracted* him from the writing. That had also proved to be true of other readers. If I was to hold on to the readers I had (*had?*), I needed their undivided attention. To put it plainly, Scribner's would be glad to publish *The World in the Attic* as a novel, without pictures, but not as another photo-text volume. Why didn't I think about it over the weekend?

I thought long and hard about it even before the weekend, as I rode on a double-decker bus toward the Village, from where I called Wally to reassure him that I, too, was tired of confused readers, and looked forward to my novel being published without photographs.

AT SUMMER CAMP ON CAPE COD, AT SCHOOL IN England and in her years at Scripps College, my wife had written her "Dear Daddy and Mother" letters to her father, and he had written to her. Now, weekly, she heard from Mother, on stationery she had received for Christmas. They were unmistakably the letters of the woman we knew, leader of bird club hikes and salvager of paper towels, but they were also legible and of interest. Like my Aunt Winona, Mother wrote a fine, slanting Spencerian hand.

After the festive excitement of the period of mourning, the Grandmother had suffered a relapse and been put to bed. There she stayed, refusing food, ignoring all calls to the bathroom. She was taken to a rest home, where the attendants gave her, among other things, the first bath she had had in years. The shock had been too much. A few weeks short of her hundredth birthday, she died.

That left Mother alone with the birds at the feed box, most of them bad. They hammered on the windows, in the clogged gutters, and drilled holes in the curling shingles. Her neighbor Mr. Parsons, as he had for years, cut the grass, forked up the compost, took down the storm windows, put up the screens, and shopped for items that were not delivered. Three to four months too late, by Parsons' calculations, she had made up her mind about the new refrigerator. Before a sale was offered in this model, she had been advised to sell the house. Until that was done, the old ice chest would do very well.

In the fall she surprised us with an unexpected visit, calling from the bus depot in Philadelphia. Two of the friends she made on this excursion would prove to be loyal correspondents. The one from Ann Arbor she visited over Christmas. Seeing for herself how we personally lived—two small rooms over a double garage—although frequently described and well illustrated, came to Mother as a great surprise. Why didn't we build a house? We were huddled together at a table without room for our legs. I sat silent while my wife explained that building a house required a large sum of money, even with a mortgage. Mother sat—not to be idle while talking—with a bowl of unshelled almonds. Now and then she ate one. "Your father was the one to do this," she said to us both, having reference to the almonds, not the house. One of the many things her husband had mastered in more

366

than forty years of marriage was the seamless way his wife began and terminated discussions.

"You still can't build a house without a lot," she said. "Have you thought of that?"

Back home in Cleveland, having had several weeks to think it over, she wrote to her daughter suggesting a loan of money, without interest, if that would help. My wife wrote back to say that would help. Several weeks later, Mother wrote to say that her loan was contingent on our having a lot. More time was necessary to clarify this problem, and agree on a sum of five thousand dollars. Five or six weeks of clippings, cut from magazines and newspapers, concerned the pitfalls of building a house. Why didn't we just buy one? She called after midnight to ask this question. Several months later—we had shelved the idea—a cashier's check for five thousand dollars was found among a fresh collection of clippings, on the subject of prefab housing.

We never learned, but the way to deal with Mother was to forget that any deal was pending. One day she would surprise you. Sometimes even favorably. Property was expensive in Bryn Mawr, but a few miles farther west, in Wayne, we found a fine half-acre corner lot, with several great tulip trees and no pressing neighbors. The local real estate agent put us in touch with a young architect from Princeton who had been nurtured on Scott Fitzgerald. The first detail he showed us of our prospective house was a carriage lamp. He would build us a house of his own design, on a concrete slab, for $12,500. One of these houses had actually been built, and we liked it. They were California-style ranch houses, a bit of Hansel and Gretel for the Main Line, with an airy open carport joining the house to a garage. To swing this deal we needed five thousand dollars in cash, and a ten-thousand-dollar mortgage. The cost to us, plus taxes, would be sixty-eight dollars a month.

Pictures were sent to Mother of the architect's drawing, showing the shrubs, the redwood fencing, the children and pets at play, and the surround of park-like woods. That much was true. From Cuyahoga Falls, Ohio, where she had gone bird-watching, Mother sent us more clippings of prefabs, and articles warning us about loan sharks. The lot paid for, we still ended up short. With our dream house and much of our future at stake—as I put it in my letter to Charles Scribner, Sr., I was taking the liberty of asking him for an advance of one thousand dollars on my next two books. I was a productive and up-and-coming writer. He had said so himself, on our visit to the Scribner home in Far Hills, New Jersey, the heart of fox-hunting country. I also thought my appeal was in the tradition much honored by Scribner's in dealing with young and needy writers. With some confidence, I sent the letter off. Very quickly I had Mr. Scribner's reply. Charles Scribner's Sons was a commercial publisher, not a bank. Each year they were obliged to borrow the money from a bank to finance the next year's operation. Of the four books of mine that Scribner's had published, not one had been commercially successful. If they had many authors with this record, no bank would be advised to lend them money. He sent his regards to my wife.

I cite this incident not to reveal the greedy self-interest of the publisher who is insensitive to the plight of the author, but the hold that a few self-serving myths continue to exert on "creative" writers, young and old. Charles Scribner's response to my letter was a bit on the blunt side, but sensible. In the last twenty years, the myth-making has shifted from the charitable, far-seeing editor, to the plush contract for paperback, movie and other subsidiary sources of revenue. A half dozen of these "big" deals, usually headlined in the newspapers, will sustain the largely baseless dreams of the jackpot for several hundred thousand writers.

What do you have, a sensible moneylender asked me, in the way of collateral? The word had for me a historic ring! How often my father had called upon it to gild the towers of his Zenith. "Kid," he would say, chewing up a match, "let's see what we got in the way of collateral." It was never much. To my knowledge, it was never enough.

The only collateral we had was two camera lenses, an enlarger and a quantity of books. Having read and appreciated the O. Henry story, my wife would not hear of my selling my watch to buy a comb for the hair she planned to cut. Over a period of fifteen years, I had assembled with much diligence and some sacrifice an unusual collection of American first editions. A few appreciative dealers had fondled them with lust and admiration. We did a thriving business in creative swapping. But I had to have cash.

In the weeks that buyers pawed over our lovelies, and sprawled on the floor discussing the fine points, I learned the irrelevance of "value" in a market of buying and selling. The value of the books was not questioned. But what I mistakenly wanted was money. I managed to sell them, not to a dealer, whose top offer was fifteen cents on the dollar, but to the library of Haverford College, which recognized them as a windfall. My friend Eiseley bought a few titles—one a fine English edition of Doughty's *Arabia Deserta*—and I had the questionable gratification of knowing that I had taken a step he could not himself have taken. So he told me. We were like Huck Finn and Tom Sawyer pondering, in a cave, our blood ties and steadfast loyalties. I shared

368

his feelings, but I didn't want to be beholden to something that could be bought and sold.

Late in the fall, the house construction began, and two or three times a week we drove by to see what had been done. Three of the big tulip trees had to be uprooted to make room for the foundation. The day the concrete slab was poured, I thought it must be for the garage, not the house. How small it looked! The winter rains soaked the exposed studs and beams, and local hoodlums poked holes in the sheets of insulation. Every night it rained, I lay awake thinking about the house. Why hadn't somebody told us not to start building in the winter? On stormy days it looked vandalized; with the melting of the snow it looked fire-gutted. Small fry built fires in the fireplace. Sometimes I feared to drive by, certain that nothing would be there. Then in March the redwood shakes arrived from California, and on weekends I helped nail them to the exterior. It almost looked like it might prove to be a real *house*. With the bedrooms freshly plastered and papered, I spent the nights in the living room, sleeping on a mattress. The casement windows were in place, but not glazed. They were so low to the yard that passing dogs stopped by to peer in at me. The night noises scared me to death. I kept a battery radio playing. The day the windows were glazed, the asphalt tile, in a black and white mix, was laid on the concrete slab. Looking about me in the early dawn light, I was struck by how the surface gleamed like ice. I thought it beautiful! How explain it? The gloss proved to be a film of water. It splashed when I walked about on it. Broken plumbing? Had the builder struck water? No, it was merely the May humidity, in conjunction with the cold concrete slab. Had we built a house only fish could live in? A half dozen of our friends came to ponder the problem while we picnicked in the carport. The solution proved to be newspapers spread to cover every inch of the floor. My wife's mother would have loved it. Later that same day, we actually moved in.

That night, when we turned out the lights, the Japanese screens at the windows were seductively transparent. People passing in cars honked their horns and hooted. We undressed in the dark. It wasn't just what we had had in mind, but we both agreed, sipping coffee out of a thermos, that if it's what you really want, there's nothing like being in your own place.

In July, to help us with the landscaping, Mother paid us a second visit. She brought packets of seeds from the basement, along with seedlings of ice plant and ivy wrapped in damp paper towels by Mr. Parsons. On this trip she had taken the train to Paoli, a stop a few miles to the west, where I found her on the platform in a deep discussion she was reluctant to interrupt. The gentleman lived in Villanova, where both he and his wife made a specialty of ice plants, and plans were made for us to visit them, before they visited us.

The great view of our place was to be had from the west, and I drove an extra mile to enjoy it. The house did seem to have popped right out of the ground, and looked as natural as a mushroom. There was even smoke in the chimney from the trash burning in the fireplace. I stopped the car to give Mother time to absorb the details. The gravel in the driveway shimmered in the sunlight. Two of the fallen trees had been dragged to make a rustic fence at the rear. My mix of pleasure, pride and relief made it difficult for me to speak. Mother had always surprised us. This time had we surprised Mother?

"Am I to believe you have lilies of the valley?" she said. I had no idea. Everything and nothing seemed to be in profusion at the weedy top of the lot. Mother got out of the car—she wore her low-heeled, sensible pumps for traveling—to zig-zag about in our upper lot, collecting herself a nosegay. Time after time she displayed her backside. Now and then she stood erect to wag her hand at the gnats buzzing her face. She had forgotten about me, and the house, and she was inattentive, in her absorption, to the approach of her daughter. There was no greeting, but a discussion once dropped, somewhere in the past, about nosegays or lilies of the valley, was resumed without comment. They stood together, mother and daughter, in the dapple of morning shadow and sunlight, and I could hear the Latin names of the flowers fall from their lips like liturgical chanting. My wife had been well schooled in these matters, and I noted the eagerness of her collaboration. Her eyes were sharp. She found, in the weeds, specimens that Mother had overlooked. From where I sat in the car, the motor still idling, I loved them both. In being themselves, they were all women who turn from pride-filled young husbands, and idling motors, to consider the lilies of the field, this being one on which we had taken a lease.

I don't recall Mother ever saying what her impressions were of the house. In the tiny kitchen, a dazzle of sunlight off the stainless-steel sink, she removed her attractive bonnet to cool her face with a few dabs of water. Her large eyes were shining as she turned to gaze at me, blankly.

"Where am I to put this?" she said, smoothing out the paper towel she had just dampened. During her three-day visit, mother, daughter and son-in-law worked in the field like peasants.

My study was the bedroom at the back of the house. In the humid heat of summer, I was up and in it early, wearing the swimming trunks I had brought from California. Mother did not approve. She suggested a beady screen at the door to my room. I usually worked till lunch, then picked up again in the midafternoon. If it was going well, I averaged eight to ten hours of work a day.

As I sit here writing, it occurs to me that with the new house I finally had a *desk*. Over the years, in and out of cramped quarters, I had used coffee tables, the seats of chairs, packing boxes, anything that proved to be reasonably solid. I sat on car seats, on cushions, or, if I proved to be lucky, in the low-slung comforts of a Morris chair. All of these accommodations cramped my back, and led to many fruitless discussions.

My first real desk, one with drawers, legs and an actual compartment for the typewriter, had to be dismantled to get it into the study. This proved to be impossible. No way was discovered to get at the screws that cunningly held it together. The solution was to saw off the legs, four inches above the floor, then reattach them once the desk was in the study. It worked well, and I recommend it. I have sometimes wondered if the desk is still there.

This one had a top of dark-green cork-like material in which many names and dates had already been carved, along with three side drawers with adjustable dividers, and a slide shelf at the top on which I could rest my feet. But what good is a desk like that without the appropriate chair?

The secret heart of my long torment was the missing chair. With the purchase of the one on which I am now seated, I brought to an end so many discomforts I prefer not to recall them. But one can see them in the chair's survival. The leather back is split, the cushioned arms are peeling, the padding held in place by strips of black and green adhesive, a cushion now protects me from the springs of the seat, but the great comforts of this chair have not diminished. They are part of my survival; they are the woof of my productive life. The secret of this chair is the back which tilts separately from the seat. That is the touch of genius. That is what I swapped my royalties for, the advance I had received on *Man and Boy*. I went into a store on Chestnut Street in Philadelphia, sat and tilted in the chair, and paid cash for it. It was more money than we had spent for the refrigerator. For weeks I felt both great and guilty. For more than thirty years I have simply felt great.

When Saul Bellow came to see me in my new study, I made him sit in the chair and sang its praises. He had to have one in his house near Bard College. But masterpiece chairs are not so easily come by. Nobody in Poughkeepsie had anything like it. We talked about it a lot, but the last time I saw him in *his* study, he was on one of those things they give to typists. I brought the matter up again, about twenty years later, but I could see it was a sore subject. I thought of it when he won the Nobel Prize. Did he finally get the good chair?

This may seem much ado about not enough, but a great chair is worth whatever it takes, and that is bottom advice.

I still remember the delivery. The rather elegant truck, with the firm's coat of arms, pulled into the driveway and just sat there. The driver checked the address; I understood his problem. Before he went away, I hurried out to reassure him. This was the address. This was where the chair belonged.

Seated in that chair, at my new desk, at my old but reliable typewriter, I was able to release what had been accumulating in me through the distractions and frustrations of house building.

The liquid note of the thrush entered the house through the flowering privet, through the clumps of rhododendron, from where he whistled in the bed of pachysandra, but the Grandmother, eavesdropping on the stairs, wished he would shut up.

The Deep Sleep flowed from this opening line as if I were recording it all as it happened. We had a home of our own, work of our own, I had a desk, a chair and a novel of my own, a ream of rag-content paper, and a lust for work. To save paper, all of my first drafts were single-spaced.

W HEN MY MOTHER-IN-LAW STEPPED FROM THE
car to pluck a nosegay of wildflowers from the weeds of our lot, I
had been brought face to face with my subject. For years I had pondered
her remarkable nature, or her lack of it, since I had entered her home
and found her crouched to spread newspapers on the kitchen linoleum.
The bizarre side of this subject I had written about in a story, "The
Ram in the Thicket," but my caricature lacked all of the elusive essentials. What, indeed, were they? What made Mother tick? Why did
her husband, a man of considerable distinction, admired and loved
by many people, find in her a source of comfort and strength that
justified his many deprivations? I was not merely curious; I felt compelled to try to fathom this woman as a matter of a writer's self-respect.
Mother was a mystery only a novelist might solve.

The occasion was at hand in her husband's death and the
ceremony of mourning. I would see Mother through the eyes of those
who believed they knew her, as well as one pair of eyes that suspended
judgment. Each of these separate witnesses would have a voice. If there
were many sides to her inscrutable nature, this might be one way to
reveal them. I felt a compelling interest to know, but no assurance
whatsoever as to what I would find. I also felt a kinship with the Grandmother and the handyman, Parsons, both outsiders. So, too, was I.

The novel *Man and Boy*, rejected by Scribner's, when published
by Knopf was so well received, critically, that they were persuaded,
largely through the zeal of my friend Harry Ford, to publish *The Works
of Love*, the saga of Will Brady's downward path from the Western
plains to his end in Chicago. I had reduced the bulk of a long and
often incoherent manuscript to the solo recital of a single, monotonous
voice, unvarying in its tone, but true to Brady's muted nature. It was,
in fact, my first plains song, plucked out on one string and mournfully repeated. The brighter touches—and there had surely been a few—
were downpedaled or eliminated: adagio, moderato, lento, all the way.
One strong, vibrant plucking of the plains chord sustained to the end.

As Brady drifted eastward, and grew older—a slight change in
tempo, but not in key—the author increasingly identified with his
nature to the extent of becoming a double agent, speaking in one voice
for both of them. These passages, and there are too many of them,

make an explicit and painful appeal to the reader's sympathies and emotions. Confused as to whose emotions were involved, and the voice appropriate to their control, the writer often lost the distance necessary to distinguish between sentiment and the sentimental. A clear vein of sentiment is crucial to Brady, and constitutes the reedy, windblown music of his nature, but in moments of stress, as he grows older, it frays into the mawkish and pathetic. A more sophisticated writer than I was at the time would have permitted the character some indulgence, but spared both the author and the reader. As a fully committed double agent, I was unaware of this distinction.

My friend Eiseley had read and liked the manuscript—he, too, would identify with the subject—and on the day I signed the contract, in New York, I met Alfred A. Knopf himself, the Grand Panjandrum, an image that well suited his person. In the comparative dimness of his inner sanctum, lit up by his taste in color, we had a brief discussion about Willa Cather, the original plains exile. I gathered he had sampled enough of my novel to know we were both from the same region. I considered it a great honor, I told him, to have the Borzoi insignia on my books. In moments of indecision I had bought Borzoi books on the strength of their design, their colorful boards, their endpapers, their sensible size, their this, their that; it hardly mattered who wrote them. (I am speaking of *secondhand* books; firsthand books were for buyers, not authors.) One of the books I had not sold to Haverford College had been the Knopf edition of Kafka's *The Trial*, with its marvelous jacket, stamped cloth and limp binding. I stop writing at this point to take it from the shelf and admire it.

In the perspective of survival, these were good years. My wife lived in her work, as I did in mine, and these years we lived our lives together. Old friends and new friends came to visit us in our new home, and in these settings I admired and took pride in my wife. Her friends from England and Holland might pay us a visit, an occasion for much tooting on the recorders, and fortissimo playing on the piano, some of it for four hands. The Eiseleys were often part of these occasions, and became friends of our friends. If I went to New York I often stayed with Harry and Elizabeth Ford, and many times a year they came down to see us with good wine and Southern bourbon in their luggage. Wine had not been part of our lives in the past, but it would figure highly in my future. I soon knew the taste and virtues of good bourbon, but a little of it always proved to be enough. Built into me below the level of consideration was the Protestant ethic of moderation, the least sharable of fraternal virtues. Not to have another one, and still another, and the final one for the road is to cast a palpable blight on the good fellowship fermented spirits exist to encourage. Unless tempted with the heavy Italian vermouth Punt e Mes, for which I have a moderate passion (is that a protesting contraction?), I am drier than usual when solo, and might forget to order what I really enjoy.

In the late forties and early fifties, I was able to sell the magazine section of the *New York Times* a few of my photo-text articles, similar in tone and style to my books. I might take off for Michigan, to visit my friend Robert Horton, or on the suggestion of a young woman at Scribner's, who liked *The World in the Attic*, I would head for her home place in southern Indiana. Her mother lived in a forest of great towering trees and flaming leaves. The house had been built during the Civil War, a small frame structure, black with age, but glowing with the light that blazed at its windows. The impression it made on me could not be photographed. In the forest gloom, and the dazzle of light at its fringe, I sensed a mythic, pastoral perfection that no actual person may have experienced but that was there for the taking, a landscape of sweet and intolerable longing. I waded about in the leaves, or sat in a trance, listening to the birds. I saw through the screen of trees, as in a painting by Brueghel, the silvery gleam of the Ohio River as it must have appeared to Daniel Boone and Audubon, the first to intrude into Eden. I took a few pictures. They did not capture my state of soul. When I think of a palpable pastoral bliss, one that is there at the window but subtly eludes us, it is that moment I think of. Quite beyond my actual grasp, but wonderfully present to my sensations. An experience that was surely common to Cézanne. In a nearby motel, where I spent the nights, I found a jukebox that matched this setting in terms of what is luminous, palpable and ineffable. A suitably ineluctable icon.

My wife had made the acquaintance of Catherine Drinker Bowen, who lived in nearby Merion, and in the research for the books she was writing she had the need of an assistant with my wife's talents. They knew each other as friends before I was asked over to tea and a piece of the celebrated Otha pound cake. Otha, more than anyone I would know, had brought to perfection the ceremony of service possible only to a few black men in this century. I do not know what he thought, only the way he entered, answered if spoken to, and departed, every gesture an enhancement of the occasion, and a compliment to those present. In Kitty Bowen he found the mistress he should have found, and I was able to share, briefly, in a vanishing ceremony.

Kitty Bowen herself was equally displaced in time, making it possible for those who knew her to share in the ambience of a better age,

375

and the character of a woman who might well have ruled England. If the first Elizabeth had ever had a second, Kitty Bowen would have been that recurrence. I liked her immensely, and would soon regret seeing less and less of her. She was a jealous ruler, true to her breeding, and she would soon take offense at my reluctance to share what I considered my private life. An Elizabethan in every pore, she loved few things as much as good live gossip.

I have forgotten the name of her aging, marble-eyed Pekingese companion, a creature so fond of me, my smell, my vibrations, she would go into a trance at my feet, free of wheezing and snortling, her unblinking, adoring marble eyes fastened on my face until I left. Changed my feelings about female Pekes, it did, I will say that.

Early one fall evening, on a visit to New York, I stepped into a shop near Thirteenth and Fifth, across from Dauber & Pine, to look at a large table of book remainders. Another browser stood across the table from me. We edged slowly around it, clockwise, then glanced up at same moment, to smile at each other. I had seen his face before—but where?

"You're Wright Morris?" he asked me. How flattering I found that. "I'm Saul Bellow," he said, and offered me his hand. He took from the table a copy of George Borrow's *Lavengro*, and asked if I had read it. I had not. He liked the writer, and I the one I had just met. A splendid nose, to my taste (I'm a believer in noses), the pupils of his large eyes dilating as they took my measure. "Doing anything?" he asked. I was not. "Come along," he said, and we walked south on Fifth to the apartment of his girl friend Sandra. She shared the apartment with a young woman who was about to leave for Mexico. We had all been to Mexico, except Saul's girl, and talked about it. She was thinking of Oaxaca. I suggested Guanajuato, celebrated for its air-dried corpses. Surviving members of a family could go there and talk things over with their relations.

They were all headed uptown, to somebody's party, and Saul asked me to join them, but I said I had to catch a train back to Philadelphia. As they drove off in a cab, I felt like a fool. I did not have to catch a train to Philadelphia, or anywhere else. It was nothing more than my long-ingrained habit of going solo, even at moments when I would have enjoyed the company. This had deprived me of good (and bad) times in the past, and it would do so in the future. I had nothing to do that beautiful fall evening but wander about the streets of the Village, and browse for books I was no longer buying. One thing I could do, however, I did. I saw the George Borrow book in another store and bought it, and as I read it I wondered what my new friend liked about it.

With his *Augie March* money, Bellow had bought property up the Hudson River near Bard College, where he sometimes did some teaching. He suggested I pay him a visit, and give a reading at Bard. The house had once been a Hudson-bracketed mansion, a model for those I had seen in Virginia City. It needed a lot of renovation, but did not lack for room. We took walks in the plowed fields edging the river, or loafed at our ease, a very appropriate posture for the new-model hammock that Saul had installed. There was a small garden that looked forward to carrots, and a few vines that looked forward to tomatoes. An experienced veteran with the new hammock, Saul would sprawl at his bracketed ease while I sagged in one of the sling chairs. At that time Saul favored a long-beaked summer cap that enhanced his resemblance to Buster Keaton. Like all hammocks, new and old models, this one was subject to eccentric behavior. Saul and I happened to find it remarkably amusing. Other guests, hearing our hooting, found it puzzling. We proved to have many things in common, including our early years in Chicago, but the binding mucilage in our friendship was that the same things struck us as funny. Not merely amusing, but matchlessly zany. Once started, we found it hard to stop laughing. A shared glance would set us off, and fraternal vibrations would keep it going.

Friends of Saul's were in and out, over the summer, and I remember with affection a lawyer, with the build of a court jester and a great passion for novels, who would appear with cartons of books stored in the back of his Cadillac Coupe de Ville. He was the first to turn up with some of my own. I later met him at a party in the Village, from where he drove me, timing the lights, the full length of Fifth Avenue seemingly without visible contact with the pedals. He lived with his mother, and it was one of the things he did for kicks.

It flattered me, on some of my visits to Saul, that he would read to me from whatever he was writing. I was mistaken in thinking it favored me—he shrewdly used many friends in this manner—but I would guess only the two of us laughed so hard we would have to break off the reading and wipe the tears from our eyes. *Henderson the Rain King* left us both in stitches. I loved the way Saul enjoyed his own talent, and his sensible acceptance of criticism. Many years later, when he wrote me to say that in the past we had had the best of each other, it was the liberating laughter he had in mind, and he was right. When we were out of our minds with laughter, the ties that bound us were at their strongest, the latest in hammocks creaking and tilting as we guffawed and hooted. Halcyon days!

I had written a story, "A Safe Place," about a colonel and his wife living on the Heights, in Brooklyn, that provided the basis for a macabre novel that would eventually be published as *War Games*. Harry Ford had read it, and it worried him. What was a publisher to think of a writer (one losing him money) who followed *Man and Boy* with *The Works of Love*, and followed that with the tale of a man who turns himself into a woman? This amusing and chilling story was a premature example of what would soon be known as black humor. Was the public ready for it? Not the public of Wright Morris. Harry Ford recommended that I put it aside until my status as a writer had clarified. I liked this book—seeded with so much of my future fiction—but I accepted Ford's suggestion to put it on hold. That would prove to be for more than twenty years, when it would be published by Black Sparrow Press.

In the summer of 1954 I attended a writers' conference in Salt Lake City, directed by the poet Brewster Ghiselin. John Ciardi and Elizabeth Enright were also on hand, with a fine assortment of Utah residents. The sun blazed, we took hikes, went on picnics, ate some Chinese food, and talked books and writing. I attracted some fans from Ogden, who labeled me an interesting but vain person. In the sun on the steps, we discussed my novels.

Ray B. West, who would later be my friend and colleague at San Francisco State, stopped by with his wife, Lu, and recommended a Swiss cheese made by the Mormons. I took a few pounds of it back home to Wayne with me. At the close of the conference I drove north to Missoula, Montana, for a visit with Leslie Fiedler and his family. Fiedler had been appreciative of *Man and Boy*, and I thought him a brilliantly gifted critic, one of the few I read with excitement. He had established his own Western outpost, and gone far to people it with new pioneers. I would have liked to kidnap the youngest Fiedler child. She hugged me madly, however, and I was able to saddle up and gallop off.

I had left Pomona College in 1933, and the span of twenty years seemed to be about right for a period of reflection and reappraisal. Those years had also been umbilically attached to Chicago, so I found I had two infections of nostalgia to deal with. Could I do them up in one package?

I had been rereading, with keen interest, that summer the early novels of Fitzgerald and Hemingway, and I welcomed, more than I

378

feared, the challenge to deal with similar emotions in a different setting. My enthusiasm had once been fired by Lindbergh, and I now wanted to bring the same emotions to focus on a tennis player named Charles Lawrence—a very Gatsby-like romantic. I had no model in mind for Lawrence, but I had played some tennis in college and knew the tension that the game could inspire. At some point in my reading of T. E. Lawrence, which I would have a go at periodically, I had come across a photograph of Lawrence, perhaps in England, standing poised as if to my purpose, at his ease and yet taut, his fingers lightly placed on his trim hips. The photo and the poise embodied, for me, the character and the charm of my tennis player. It spoke of intangibles, and extravagant commitments. I began writing with the name Lawrence, and it stayed. The narrator of the novel would be a classmate, Peter Foley, who had come to California from Chicago, and found that Lawrence was one of his dormitory companions. With the first paragraph, I knew I was off and running.

They tell me that my father, a Latin teacher, would place his silver watch, with the Phi Beta Kappa key dangling, on the right-hand corner of the desk in his Virgil class. When he was not lecturing, the students would hear the loud tick. The watch had been given to him by his father when he became a Cum Laude Latin scholar, and the inscription Incipit Vita Nova *had been engraved on the back. A very punctual man, my father wound the watch when he heard the first bell ring in the morning, then he would place it, with the fob dangling, on the corner of his desk. Time, for my father, seemed to be contained in the watch. It did not skip a beat, fly away, or merely vanish, as it does for me. So long as he remembered to wind the watch, Time would not run out. There was no indication that he found his subject a dead or dying language, or the times, for a man of his temperament, out of joint. He died the winter of the flu epidemic during the First World War.* (The Huge Season, *1954*)

The Huge Season related one story in the present, the life of Peter Foley, a teacher of English, who commuted between Haverford and New York, and an alternate narration concerned with his college years and Charles Lawrence, the tennis player. Our friend Double-dukes appeared as Montana Lou Baker, a portrait intended as a tribute. I felt very good about this novel, but within a few weeks it was rejected by Scribner's. They had made every effort to promote The Deep Sleep, but the sales response had been negligible. My confidence was such that I was more angered than disappointed. I wrote immediately to

379

Granville Hicks, who had long spoken up for my novels, and he quickly replied that I should pay them a visit, in Grafton, New York, and bring along the manuscript.

With my arrival in Grafton, on a fall day of drizzle, I seemed to pick up with a friendship that had been waiting on this occasion. As at the Home Place, I circled the gabled farmhouse, looking for the appropriate entrance. The house and its furnishings—tables, chairs, pillows—its porches, pets and inhabitants, slipped onto me like a glove. The animation and sparkle of Dorothy Hicks not only charmed me, but concealed, on my first visit, the polio affliction she had suffered as a child. She so skillfully accommodated to this handicap, I was unaware of it. Granville was lean, with the build of a jockey, at his ease in the faded shirts and denims of a farmhand. He had the manner and reserve natural to a scholar (he had been a magna cum laude at Harvard), combined with a voice, and an ease of expression, that I found his most distinctive characteristic. I liked to hear him talk— on those occasions when he was offered a chance. I had met few true New Englanders before, and found it uplifting. Some years later, he would tell his own story in a book titled *Part of the Truth*, and the part that I found the truest was the opening line, "I was a good boy." No one who knew him would have questioned that, or have remarked, over the years, any change in his nature. The grain of his mind extended and sustained the American conscience that had its beginnings a few miles to the east, to which he had contributed his own example that the unexamined life is not worth living.

I soon learned that the voices in the kitchen were those of Dorothy and her young neighbors, gossiping. One of these boys, Calvin by name, who fixed me on sight with an unblinking stare, proved to be a man of two words, yes and no. His liking for me was a matter of vibrations, as it was with the cat and the aging beagle. No better environment was possible for a writer seeking both advice and comfort.

Granville spent most of the second day reading my manuscript, as I sat in the kitchen talking with Dorothy. Calvin's younger, and blondly pretty, brother proved to be a budding backwoods aesthete. It startled me to see this flowering in Grafton, and it was no handicap in Dorothy's kitchen. They both loved and elaborated on the latest scuttlebutt. Calvin had other brothers, as well as a sister, whom I might see helping her mother hang out the laundry, but I gathered that she was not pleased to compete with her brother for Dorothy's attention. Calvin liked to hunt, and on arriving might park his gun at the door, or bring it in to dismantle, clean and polish while he listened to others talk. The intactness of his nature was like that of the rural people I had seen in the South, a self-sufficiency that was free of the nagging torments of self-awareness. By another name would I have liked him less?

By late afternoon, Granville confided that he had read my manuscript and thought reasonably well of it. We discussed it briefly, and went over the pages where he had made helpful suggestions. It pleased me greatly to find that we were both reading the same book, and sharing similar responses. The work done, we relaxed with Granville's martinis, a ritual of many years' standing. Just before midnight, with a nightcap of sherry, we toddled off to bed.

This proved to be merely the first of my many pilgrimages to Grafton. On other occasions we might meet in New York, or in the halls of some college, or as far from Grafton as Venice, where, years later, we would have two wonderful weeks together. Both Dorothy and Granville smoked like chimneys, and needed to be near a supply of American cigarettes. A picture cherished is one I snapped of the two of them, huddled in the great door of Santa Maria della Salute, directly beneath a billowing scarlet banner. A holy place, surely, to get out of the wind and light two cigarettes on one flickering match.

Granville had called Marshall Best, of The Viking Press, to recommend that he have a look at *The Huge Season*, and Best had asked me to drop it off at the Viking offices on my way through New York. Not more than two or three days later, in Wayne, I had a call from Mr. Best. He liked the book. I would soon receive their contract. Was I urgently in need of money? I said a little money would be much appreciated. The sum he suggested, fifteen hundred dollars, would be my largest advance up to that time.

I soon went back to the city to meet Mr. Best, Malcolm Cowley, and other editors at Viking. Mr. Cowley, like Max Perkins, had the benefit of the greatest aid ever devised for the publisher's luncheon, a hearing aid that often malfunctioned. On the occasion of our luncheon, I was never long free of the sense that he had the crucial advantage.

Mr. Best made his home near Danbury, Connecticut, but kept an apartment near the Viking offices. As we sat sipping bourbon, he startled me by saying that I didn't look too well. How old was I? Forty-four. I had never given thought to my age, but not to be looking so good disturbed me. Did he not, Marshall asked me, detect in the character of Peter Foley a man in a bit of a mid-life crisis? Was he right or wrong in feeling that Foley sometimes spoke up for the author? I thought that was certainly possible, but I was not sure where. If *The*

Huge Season should happen to be a success, Marshall would like to take the liberty of suggesting that I take a break from work, and go somewhere. Had I been to Spain? Italy? Mexico? It should be somewhere a bit exotic, in his opinion. A real change of scene.

As we talked, I recalled Hemingway's suggestion, in *Death in the Afternoon*, that the place to go if you ever bolted with somebody was Ronda, in Spain. I was not about to bolt—at that moment—but his advice did cross my mind. What I lacked was the appropriate somebody. Nor did I confess—and compromise my luck—that I had just applied for another Guggenheim Fellowship, and if that lightning should once more strike, I was ready for flight to those places pictured in the windows of travel agencies. Before I left the city I picked up a packet of maps from the Mexican Tourist Bureau in Rockefeller Center. I was still landlocked, in my habits of flight, and liked the freedom and convenience of a car. I was one of those who waited, futilely, for the Pan American Highway to Machu Picchu.

The Paseo de la Reforma, the great trees and the throng of Indians in Chapultepec Park, the stream of figures in and out of the dazzle of sunlight in Cuernavaca, the slap of hands and bare feet under my window in Oaxaca, the basking shimmer of heat and light, of *sol* and *sombra*, of the tranquil Mexican morning where the smiling assassin waits in the shadows with his gleaming white teeth: these and other images were still bright as pennies at the back of my mind. They had been newly buffed to brightness by my reading of Malcolm Lowry's *Under the Volcano*, and Lawrence's *Mornings in Mexico*. Was I as ripe and ready as Marshall Best had suggested?

When in March I heard the good news from the Guggenheim Foundation, my sense of release, of buoyancy, was so keen it led me to wonder what I would have done if I had not been one of the chosen. For several years I had been doing most of my living in my writing, and I was feeling the strain on these resources. My experience, as I came up for air, was that of a man who had pushed off the bottom—as Gordon Boyd would soon be doing in *The Field of Vision*. As I recall this moment, I feel again the surge and swell of the emotion I felt at the time, so life-enhancing that I rise from my desk and pace around the room. Was I so much a captive? Or had I, in *The Huge Season*, aroused the fires of old expectations? I felt a compelling need to take off, to hit the road, to be up, up and away, as if I had been reprogrammed by the sentiments of the twenties.

Just west of Wayne, the Pennsylvania Turnpike began to wind and rise into the Alleghenies, and as I passed through the toll gate, early in July, I experienced the sought-for winged sense of liberation, and I was on my way.

One of the gifts of life of this period was my discovery of Henry James's *The American Scene*. It was my practice to find and buy the book I wanted to read, and to find this rare out-of-print volume took me five or six years. I was not a reader of the Master's fiction, where the refinement of his style was a contradiction of what was vital and unique in the American vernacular. As R. P. Blackmur perceived, correctly, in my opinion, James was a *fabulist* with realistic pretensions, but this went gratingly against the grain of my mind and nature. Curiously, and not easily explained, I was able to read *The American Scene* as if its uniquely Jamesian texture was one of the virtues I loved about it. There is no question in my mind that the mind of Henry James is matchless in the many forms in which it is revealed. His effortless power of association, in which one aperçu leads to another, then another, then another—an open-ended series of parenthetical relations—makes it both annoying and exhausting to follow the darts and flashes of his mind, but this experience is simply not to be found elsewhere. I'm sure that readers of his fiction feel the same, but my long apprenticeship to other voices makes it difficult for me to hear his music. In *The American Scene*, mirabile dictu, I am persuaded to give him all that it takes.

I found him both a challenge and an aggravation. Forty years before my time, James had staked out his claim on much I thought to be my property. The keen, sharp edge of my appreciation—like the mind of Thoreau confronting a fact—was that this writer had not merely scooped me, but saw it all more comprehensively than I did.

Here it is then that the world he lives in [the businessman] accepts its doom and becomes, by his default, subject and plastic to his mate; his default having made, all around him, the unexampled opportunity of the woman. . . . She has meanwhile probably her hours of amazement at the size of her windfall; she cannot quite live without wonder at the oddity of her so "sleeping" partner, the strange creature, by her side, with his values and his voids, but who is best known to her as having yielded what she would have clutched to the death.

For the author of *Man and Boy* and *The Deep Sleep*, this was the ultimate stamp of approval, even as it deprived me of my patent. Henry James had been there. My preferred feeling was that I had been prematurely plagiarized. A more sobering reflection, one that I would learn to live with, was that the truth exposed would have as little to do with the manners of the culture as the truth buried: man and woman, mutually deprived, would continue along the way to which they were accustomed.

It also depressed me to realize that the number and complexity of these perceptions, in their effect on the reader, weakened rather than strengthened their impact. There was that stakeout of mine known as the hotel lobby.

. . . It lies there waiting, pleading from all its pores, to be occupied—the lonely waste, the boundless, gaping void of "society"; which is but a name for all the other so numerous relations with the world he lives in that are imputable to a civilized human being.

. . . one is verily tempted to ask if the hotel spirit may not just be the American spirit most seeking and finding itself. . . .

. . . One was in the presence, as never before, of a realized ideal of that childish rush and surrender to it and clutch at it which one was so repeatedly to recognize, in America, as the note of the supremely gregarious state. It made the whole vision unforgettable, and I am now carried back to it, I confess, in musing hours, as to one of my few glimpses of perfect human felicity.

Can it be said that we have finally come abreast of these comments, or have we safely receded from their application, no longer intimately bearing on the affairs of an already altered species?

AFTER A DECADE OF INSISTENT AND INTENSE application, circling and recircling the still points of my fiction, the spirals and helixes of departures and withdrawals, of overlapping associations, of intriguing glimpses of the future, yet seldom if ever issuing in moments of rest, or of satisfactory resolutions, the *open road*—Jack Kerouac would soon publish his book *On the Road*—provided me with a measurable sense of progression, of predictable starts, stops and destinations.

The relief I felt was quite beyond description, and yet it was a sensation to which I was long accustomed. *Taking off* had been one of my father's strategies, and we had often flown the coop together. My emotions were those of an overdue diver who surfaced for air.

I was so eager to get to Mexico, I was up and off early and drove late, sometimes sleeping in the car just out of the glare of the street lights, and this would prove to be the origin of my inflexible mind-set for dawn starts and a minimum number of stops: more than a sufficient cause for friction with my occasional travel companions. The sunrise starts were invariably the high points of the long days. If I was headed east it had its torments, the morning sun burning like a comet on the windshield, but if I headed west, the slow spread of light was like the moment of creation. First the tide of light would splash on objects, or touch with fire the summits of far hills or mountains, then slowly as a tease, or that moment in the darkroom when the first image emerges, preceding the splendor of the visible spectrum. On the occasional farm, splinters of light would be thrown off by the blades of the windmill. Ideally, from my point of view, this magical moment would be capped by the far glimmer of an all-night truck stop, the windows glowing like a train diner. In my experience, the predawn diner breakfast is the one great infallible American meal. Best when you get it in a diner, the bacon sizzling before you, the eggs sunny side up or over easy, the hash browns just to one side, with a crust like a shingle. Proof of the glory of this food is that it survives the predictably ghastly coffee, which brings to mind such things as Postum. The refills seem better, the second or third cigarette having numbed the taste buds.

Back in Pennsylvania, to make sure I would not be caught without them, I had bought two boxes of Marsh-Wheeling stogies, long, slender, black-wrapper cigars of memorable sweetness and mildness, soon to be as essential to Western bad men as their shooting irons and evil looks. I would later be accused, and with some justice, of having spread this weed and its craving to all points west of the Missouri and not a few south of the border. Some years later, about to leave for Europe, I tried to find the precious stogie in New York, and I remember the look of outrage on the face of a "tobacconist" when he finally grasped what I was describing. Where one could find them, in those halcyon days, they were usually six cents.

Predictably, after the sunrise breakfast, I would be half starved by nine o'clock. My second breakfast was usually several rashers of bacon on a field of golden-brown hotcakes. This was not so easily consummated. Tough and leathery flapjacks, with the texture of tire patches, were not unusual on the wide open road. The disaster could be forestalled if I had a seat at the counter, where I could watch them being poured and see their bottom sides pucker before they were flipped, but it is much harder to spot the leathery flapjack than the false meringue on the pie in the pie case. The higher it is piled—to echo an old saw—the worse it will prove to be.

In Indiana, I think it was, the man seated at my side, who had been rolling himself a fresh Bull Durham, when asked if he would like a half cup of coffee, replied, "Bottom half, please, miss," and got it. Nowhere that I have been is there a language so responsive to what is as yet unheard and unspoken as the one I speak.

For my evening meal, I troubled to pick a town that was big enough to offer me a choice. One with a residential area, if possible, with a view through the front screen down the hall into the light of the kitchen. Such a town would usually shut down about six or seven o'clock, except for the gas stations and the drugstore, but if it had been settled before the turn of the century, there would be an old café, perhaps with a ceiling fan, and a smaller new one. The older one would have its menu posted on the window, and while reading the menu I would size the place up. I looked for the big, old-fashioned coffee urns, the steam hissing at the top, rather than the Silex vacuum on the electric hot plate. I looked for pie, still in the pan on the counter, and one of the handsome aluminum milk dispensers, and in Missouri I troubled to look for, and often found, the big trays of fresh berry cobbler or shortcake. On the menu I might look for the chicken-fried steak that had been one of the staples of my boyhood, along with fresh rhubarb pie and tapioca pudding. Most of the small towns along the rural roads of Ohio were so great for homemade pie I hated to leave the state, but they were uniformly terrible for coffee. After eating, I would stroll, with my stogie, around the street doing a little window shopping, check out the movie, and try the rockers in the lobby of the hotel, if they had one. If the lobby was clean, and had a bit of class, I might take a room for the night. These rooms, with the cracked blinds drawn at the windows, and the sound they always made when the clerk let them up, the light bulb dangling on a cord over the chipped iron bed frame, the bent wire hangers in the open door to the closet, were for me time capsules of pathos reduced to an essence. With the window open I could hear the slam of car doors, the town mutts barking, the goon gunning his motor at the street light, and in the silence the far *yoooo-hooo* of an approaching train before it rattled through without stopping. A commingling of the sordid, the lonely, the despondent, scented the stale air, saturated the objects, and distilled a fragrance to which I was incurably subject. On the nightstand I could see, just barely, the faded red stain on the leaves of the Gideon Bible. On the post of the bed I could discern my father's pants, on the chair at the side he had draped his coat, and I would sense the weight of his body in the dipper-like sag of the mattress. One night it occurred to me that as much as we had shared the same bed, I had no idea if he slept well or not, since I was asleep myself.

Other times, I might prefer to find a residential street where a parked car might not arouse much suspicion, and curl up in the seat with sentiments I could sleep with. One night in New York, while staying with a friend, I had been awakened by a cry for *Help!*—as one might get from a person drowning. No other sound. Just that word, with a big balloon around it that left it suspended in the air above me, like the cry Camus would hear on the bridge crossing the Seine. Had my father ever heard it, or cried out himself? It pleased me to believe he had been blessed with the gift of sleep.

On this trip I had left the freeway to go south to Gambier, Ohio, and pay a visit to John Crowe Ransom. He had accepted a story of mine, "A Safe Place," for the *Kenyon Review*, and had suggested I might stop and see him. As with my first meeting with Granville Hicks, we seemed to easily resume a former conversation that had been briefly interrupted. I filled my pipe from his humidor, and we smoked and talked books until it was time for me to leave. What I, and countless other young writers, had missed in not having him as a friend and a neighbor, this brief stop brought home to me.

A flood had washed out the bridge over the Rio Grande at Laredo, and it had been replaced by army pontoons. The movement of people and cars in both directions went at a snail's pace. The long file of Indians, the women shrouded in black, passed so close to my car they brushed against the sides and the fenders. Some of the older men and the children gave it a friendly pat, as if they thought it alive. For a brief moment, as they drew alongside, each face was framed in the open window of my car: the very old, with their great reserve, their lined, somber and dignified faces; the young and frequently striking women, their hair blue-black in the sun's dazzle; the sculpture-like, sad-eyed children, peering at me like the cupidons in the paintings of madonnas. The frieze seemed endless; the dust raised by their feet filled the car and filmed the windshield. It seemed to me that I had become Mexican before entering Mexico. I would never be wholly free of the impression—even when I saw it contradicted—that these people were *the* people tirelessly evoked, on numberless occasions, to reassure all those who were losing their faith in the species. Here they all were— shy, vulnerable, obviously helpless, and profoundly appealing. If I had been stopped while crossing the river, and escorted back to Laredo, I would have felt that Mexico had come to me, and my adventure had not been aborted. But I was not stopped, and just before sundown I was in Monterrey.

The Pan American Highway over the mountains seemed as incredible as I remembered, but there were fewer Indian women walking the road, and their garments were less colorful. Neither did flocks of *muchachos* follow the car and try to sell me melons or midget bananas.

South of Ciudad Victoria, a whitewashed boulder, no larger than a bucket, was all that indicated the road I would take west to Guadalajara. This narrow road followed the contours of a high plateau, with marvelous expansive vistas of the wooded slope to the south and the west. Here and there, I could see the butter-yellow domes of the churches, gleaming like coins. In several hours I passed no other cars in either direction. The matchless serenity of the villages, with a few Indian women on the steps of the churches, or one sweeping the entrance with a broom of faggots, I knew to be a gift of the drug-like inertia and poverty, but I could not resist its appeal. The cries of a few caged birds, a fountain splashing or dripping, the far braying of a burro, gave it a biblical tranquillity.

In the early afternoon, dazed with the heat and the shimmering light, I entered what once had been a substantial city, with a large towering cathedral, but it now appeared to be abandoned. The shadow of the church darkened the steps at its entrance like the shadows in a de Chirico painting. I had to drive in low gear in the broken and gutted street. A Carta Blanca beer sign at a corner indicated a café.

I sat for some time in the drone of flies before a small, shrunken figure, hardly higher than the counter, appeared from the back. One of the eyes she turned to me was like an agate. I used the word *comida*, and after a long delay she brought me a plate of food. A dark sauce of beans, thick as caramel, had been spooned onto an enchilada. I reassured myself that it had been long cooked, and ate a few bites of it, washed down with the warm beer.

Several hours later, approaching Guadalajara through a stream of pedestrian and burro traffic, I stopped at a crowded café with tables along the street. I had some chicken with rice that I thought delicious, and a bottle of ice-cold beer. I smoked a fresh Delicado as I chatted with the waitress, who was pleased with my tip. Just at sunset, I entered Guadalajara and made my way to a motel crowded with Americans. A sallow and sour young woman was not sure if she had a place for me or not. As I leaned on the counter, I had my first flush of nausea and queasiness. Perhaps she saw it in my face. I followed a barefoot boy to a mercifully dark and cool room. Before I could get my shoes off, I had an attack of nausea.

Some time later, the room dark, a clattering roll of thunder approaching, I crawled from the bed into the shower, where I turned on the water and crouched over the drain. The celebrated *turista* is a commonplace but unforgettable experience. I had never before been so sick, for so long a time. The shower rained on me, I whooped and retched, with brief periods of chills and quivers. A dramatic and thundering electric storm, with blinding, incandescent flashes at the windows, penetrated the room like X rays, provided the appropriate backdrop for my inner turmoil. Just at dawn (I could see it at the window), I was able to crawl from the shower back to the bed. Later in the morning, one of the maids, recognizing the symptoms, drew the blinds at the windows and withdrew. I thought surely it would bring me either help or burial, but nothing occurred. In the evening, I was able to lift the phone's receiver and mutter the word *enfermedad*, with many *muys*. This eventually brought me a pot of tea, served up with advice I did not comprehend. The good woman wet a towel and wiped off my face, washed and wrung out my shorts. The musical flow and rising pitch of her comments I took as assurance that I would live. She appeared again in the morning with tea, but I was leery of the toast. In the cool of the evening, my pins shaky, my flesh the color of the light seen in washrooms, I made my way into the courtyard. A young man was there who spoke English, and he was familiar with the problem. I took the capsules he provided, and his advice not to eat. Back in my room, I sprawled on the bed and slept until the maid

389

woke me up. Sunlight blazed at the window, and after I had showered and shaved, I stopped at the lunchroom for two soft-boiled eggs, bacon and four slices of toast. It didn't seem possible, but that's how it was.

I stayed on for several days in Guadalajara, thinking it might be the place for me to settle. Its size and setting, its freedom from urban blight, put me in mind of Santa Barbara, and I spent most of my time in the sun-baked plaza, people-watching. I had heard the *muchachas* were particularly fetching, and so they were. But what I missed—and seemed to feel I wanted—was the bustle and complexity of Mexico City, with its parks, avenues, *futbol*, bullfights and, from my urgent point of view, the Sanborn restaurants, marvelous places to relax, to watch people and to dine. What I wanted was a city, not the leisure world that was already shaped to the lives of the gringos, most of them from California. I had a look at Ajijic, where Lawrence and Frieda had stayed, the luster of the sky and the mountains just as he had described them, but I was critical of the arty atmosphere and the exiles from the colony in Santa Fe, sandaled, bobbed, bored, and cannibalistic. I liked women. I needed a woman. So why was I so reluctant? In the confusion of my motives and my practice, I was not unlike Lawrence: the will to act was not lacking, but I wanted the Protestant props of commitment.

A very attractive young Mexican woman cleaned my room every morning, and I used the occasion to sharpen up my Spanish. She liked me, but I could see she had her scruples. I liked her, and I had my scruples. It would appear, however, that our scruples were more a matter of context than of morals. If the scene could appropriately arrange itself, I sensed that my scruples might vanish—but not hers. The grain of my reluctant nature, on a push-pull arrangement, made a salvaging of morals a question of mutual commitment. If I was committed, if the lady was committed, the morals would be negotiable. I loathed intrigues and art colony affairs, but on the right occasion I would bolt for Ronda. I liked these brown *muchachas*, the crackle of their gossip, and their easy, flirtatious manner, but divined—being one of their kind—that they were scrupulous with their favors. They, too, had listened to a voice that said, "Now there are some things that are right, and some things that are wrong, and *that's* wrong." And *that*, as Stendhal said of sherbet, was all that it lacked.

I made a stop at Uruapan, near the volcano Pátzcuaro. A once bustling colonial city, it had become a decaying theatrical ruin, like something one might find, I imagined, in Malaysia. The folly of capturing my complex impressions kept me from using the camera I had brought along. Coming out of the mountains, east of Morelia, I caught glimpses of the setting that the valley of Mexico had provided for its long bloody history, and just after midnight I was looking for a place to park along the crowded Paseo de la Reforma. A stream of honking traffic flowed in both directions; Indians were curled up like rugs in shop doorways. In the new open-all-night Sanborns, I had my long-awaited *enchiladas de crema*, and sat smoking Delicados and sipping strong coffee until it was time for an early breakfast. The morning was not as sparkling as I remembered, more like the deep summer haze of Paris, but I liked the throb of the waking city. At the stand where I bought more cigarettes and the waxy matches, a young man with a valise, dressed like a mannequin on Olvera Street, said to the cashier as he hurried off, *"Tiempo es dinero!"* For an instant I failed to grasp what he had said. Here in the land time had once forgotten, money had caught up with time. The Indian woman who squatted, less than a block away, Buddha-like as she sliced up papaya for her tribe of little Indians, had not as yet received that message, but it would soon be heard by her offspring. Into the broad palm of her extended hand I dropped a small clinking piece of time's new substance. I would report this in my first letter to my wife, finding it both amusing and exotic, that as slogans were worn out where they began, they could be exported for a new life elsewhere.

I spent several days looking for an apartment. As huge and sprawling as the city had become, there were few accommodations for a not so affluent tourist. I wanted to be near the Paseo de la Reforma, and the Sanborns where I would sometimes have my meals. I found what I needed off Avenida Gutenberg, in a small residential shopping area. There was a bakery on the corner, a delicatessen with freshly barbecued chickens, a *farmacia*, a dry cleaner—his establishment open to the street, his wife doing her mending on a chair on the sidewalk—and just a block away, a new *supermercado* with a meat market. My rooms were large but dark, on the well of a court where water was ceaselessly dripping and splashing. For the first few weeks I thought this was charming. Later I tried plugging my ears. I never clearly understood why my apartment was so quiet. I had the privilege of sunbathing on the roof, but this proved to have its risks. The Mexican system of heating water is a surefire fail-safe arrangement of letting the steam blow through the roof if the tenants happened to forget about it. I forgot on occasion. A familiar practice. I could see geysers shooting off all around me. At one time the view would have been marvelous, but the increasing smog had veiled it off. Of interest, however, were the señoritas who came to the neighboring roofs to wash and dry their hair. They usually did this in pairs, a social arrangement, and sat about in the sun combing and brushing, gossip a welcome music. Each wall of my apartment was painted a different color, but in the dim light this went unnoticed. I had a three-burner gas stove, an electric refrigerator, and the usual infestation of bugs and fleas in the over-stuffed furniture. My landlord, a tall young man with an interest in literature and the arts, liked to sit and discuss with me Mexican paint-ing as he smoked my Delicados. He had picked up his English, as well as his French, from his clients, not a few of them writers. I had often heard of the names he mentioned, but I had not read their books. With understandable pride, he insisted that I would find fewer bugs in his accommodations, but it would be unwise for me to think that I might eliminate them. The key word was control. Frequent spraying would keep them under control. I made the mistake of spreading my Indian blankets on the chairs, so that I took a crop of Mexican bedbugs and fleas home with me, still powerfully active months later in the plush ambience of Mother's Oriental rug.

I was one of the early birds for fresh sweet rolls at the bakery, so inexpensive I recognized my affluent status. By eight o'clock I was at work in the back-aching style to which I was once accustomed, the portable typewriter on the coffee table, the writer squatted on two chair cushions. No time was lost in doodling. I had come to work, and with my second cup of coffee I was at work.

I was intrigued by the appearance of a character that I seemed to have brought along with me, like a hitchhiker, one to whom I was already accustomed to listening. He pretended to be a native of my own "country," and on speaking terms with some of my people. His home town, like mine, had a grain elevator with the name HORD painted at the top of it, visible for miles in both directions. The same name could be seen on the loose boards that fenced in the lumberyard—a few were missing where the small fry made their en-trances and exits—and reappeared in black-and-gold lettering on the window of the bank. He knew all this, reminded me of it, and sarcastically mocked my interest in it. Whose side was he on? I listened to him on the chance that I might find out. We had shared the experience, as boys, of walking past the Hord residence, taking up most of a city block, where a chocolate-colored Franklin with a scooped hood, like a fireman's hat, was often parked in the driveway. An electric car with hard rubber tires was kept in the carriage house at the rear. My friend had experienced, as I had not, the incident that took place at the local bottomless sandpit, where he had attempted to walk on water. I scoffed at that, of course, but I listened to what he said. One of the boys I had known, who couldn't swim, would certainly have tried if I had dared him to do it. It was almost more than he could bear, not to take a dare.

This character was in my mind when I sat down to write. I was troubled by the feeling that I was not really clear just where he began and I ended, and just who, at any moment, might prove to be talking. That ambivalence had surfaced in *The Huge Season*, but I felt I had turned it to the book's advantage. So I was provoked to see where this would lead me, but at the same time I was uneasy. I liked the talk I was having with the character, but I lacked confidence in the voice. It was too much my own. Overhearing what I was saying often led me to wince.

The name Boyd seemed to suit his first appearance on the page. His first name would long be a source of annoyance. He would come from a small plains town, as I had, with shaded streets, comfortable homes, a yearly Hagenbeck-Wallace circus, unseasonable spring blizzards, and early fall Chautauquas. Two or three well-to-do families would set the tone and provide examples of the good life, such as a Pierce-Arrow with lights in the fenders. A small boy in such a town, with his older companions, would walk down a weedy spur of tracks to the sandpit, where the moment of truth would take place. On its glassy surface I would see my own reflection, and wait on events. With his boyhood chum, McKee, Boyd would take that walk, and McKee would forever be his witness.

My feeling was, at the time I began to write, that if the scenes and characters were appropriate to the writer's emotions, as aroused by these scenes and characters, memory and imagination would so commingle in the writing as to produce gratifying fiction. That seemed true of what little I had written, but it astonished me to find that the very clichés I had so often ridiculed were essential to my materials— on occasion they proved to *be* my materials.

Not that McKee didn't sort of like Mexico. In the four days they had been in Mexico City ten or twelve people had asked him for the time, then thanked him kindly no matter what he said. He liked that. He paid a little more attention to the time himself. Having it there in his pocket meant more down here than it did in the States.

It was not possible, it occurred to me, to make such an observation about McKee except in the clichés to which he was accustomed. In his nature, which I found appealing, they acquired the luster of a finer metal. His character, indeed, took the clichés of his life and fleshed them out in a way that made them appealing. Slowly I came to realize that these clichés were my subject, and my problem was how to use them, rather than abuse them. As I sometimes felt ambivalent about the character of Boyd—where he overlapped and where he departed from the character of the writer—so I was sometimes troubled by the ambiguous nature of many clichés. How was it possible, I wondered, that they could be at once the truth of the matter and its parody? But so it was I often found them. Later I would ponder the astonishing fact that the truth of clichés contradicted the truths of more sophisticated language, and that the character of a people had its source in their speech more than in their customs. As so often, I would find this impression confirmed in the comments of writers who were there before me, and in the wondrous, mind-boggling perception of Yeats that "in changing my syntax, I changed my intellect."

In my own experience, the written and spoken "cliché" would often embody the history of the American language and, unavoidably, the history of our people, and speak in one breath from many sources. Gertrude Stein testifies to this in *The Making of Americans*, and I believe my own practice, at its best, confronts this truth in its deep reliance on what is heard and felt when the language is spoken. I speak it to myself, as I write it, in order to better estimate its heft and rightness. In the vernacular it is the cliché that testifies to the burden of meaning that words and phrases from the past bear to us at the moment we speak in the present, where we hear, wherever the language is well spoken, the echoes of the writers who first shaped it. In the vernacular they speak with a familiar accent.

My car was parked in a fenced lot just a block away. There were two others in the lot, one with a California license and two flat tires. At the rear of the lot, in a lean-to open shelter, an Indian woman with the face of the Maya lived with her tribe of children. Not all of them were so authentic. Two were dark as Arabs, their fingers tipped with nails the color of pearls. Were they hers? The question seemed foolish. The movement of her arms, as she slapped out tortillas, revealed the fullness and firmness of her breasts after years of childbearing and rearing. This gave her, surrounded by her tribe, the appearance of a sculpted fertility figure rather than one of flesh and blood. Hemmed in by her little Indians, in the light of the fire and the smoke of the oil that cooked the tortillas, her appeal was to the Ur-mensch that we now feel may be up ahead of us, rather than behind.

The building "superintendent," a dark, powerful young man with long arms, short bowed legs, had recently come to the city from the mountains near Morelia. His black, bristling hair grew directly from his brows: his face had one implacable expression. It amazed him that I could read and speak his language. On the first occasion I tipped him, he dropped to his knees as if at the foot of an idol. Where had he learned *that*? To my questions he merely looked puzzled. When I opened the door to his wife, her huge head seemed to be part of her narrow shoulders, her short, thin, calfless legs those of a beast of burden. She was able to understand and reply to my questions, and spoke of their pleasure in being in Mexico City. Where they had come from there was nothing—*nada. Nada*, she repeated.

Because of my routine, most of my days were like the one that had just preceded, or the one that would follow, but this well suited my state of mind. One morning, as I sat hunched on my cushions, a tiny spider, no larger than a period to which a filigree of hairs had been added, lowered itself from one of the upper floors on an invisible strand of its own making, sometimes drifting in drafts, sometimes jerkily descending, to where a leaf on the plant at the window provided a platform, a space station. There it landed, spent a long moment considering its options, then took off as if it had arrived with maps and directions, crossing the leaf's prominent striations to the woody jungle of the stalk, where I lost it.

Such observations, encouraged by my friend Eiseley, often led me into reflections that had no resolution. I sensed that I shared with the spider a degree of mindless application that went beyond, in my opinion, the call of duty; and as well, we both spun out of our innards the lifelines on which we precariously dangled. So much seemed obvious, but what increasingly held me was the optional perspective in which we were both seen as I saw the spider—one in which the element of scale was of interest—not the two worlds we shared, but the one world where scale was not determined by observation. In this perspective both the spider and I and the vast sprawling city receded as I caught glimpses of it from the tail of a rocket. I nurtured this fantasy, in moments of daydreaming, and when the first photographs were taken from the moon, the blue-and-white marble of the earth seemed to me a product of my own imagination.

In my boyhood I would sometimes sit through the movie to see the rerun of the Pathé news, where I was able to see the planet itself revolving. In this way, I and others were being prepared for space travel and star wars.

When we think of the world, do we not think of a photograph?
Through the rents in the cloud cover, I see the great rolling plains, the

*pattern of fields and highways, the dry bed of a river as it snakes its
way eastward, and where flecks of green and shadow indicate a village
I strain to see who it is that returns my gaze. A child clothed in rompers
sits in the talcum-like dust beneath the porch of a house. Wide-eyed
and entranced, he dreamily gazes through the lattice of side-slats at
the world before him, including myself. Between us there is a cloud
of shimmering dust motes in which time itself is suspended. If I could
peer at this child from far enough in space, where earthly time is in
abeyance, would not the child who sat there, recognizably myself,
return my gaze?* ("The Camera Eye," 1981)

On my afternoon walks I sometimes passed the courts of the Mexican Tennis Club, with their covered bleachers, and heard the slap
of the drives and the sound of the good net rallies. From a banner
hung at its entrance I learned that the U.S.A. and Mexico were playing a Davis Cup match. I could hear the applause as I bought my ticket.

Balls travel a little faster, and a little farther, at the elevation of
Mexico City, and this was giving the American players some trouble. I
yelled encouragement. Not too many months before, in my fiction, I had
identified with the dreams of Charles Lawrence in *The Huge Season*.

A few seats away from me, in moments of tension or excitement,
one of the spectators audibly cracked his knuckles. In time this led
to an exchange of glances. He was a moderately dark, stocky fellow,
with the large, melancholy eyes I had noticed in many of the young
men. Double faults, in particular, deeply pained him, eliciting grimaces
and woeful groans. On a bad shot he might clap both hands to his
face. I grew somewhat reluctant to applaud the winning shots of the
American player. Between the sets, I sidled over to console him with
a cigarette. He did not smoke. To be so unresponsive to my kind offer
also pained him. It seemed to me that the pupils of his eyes dilated.
The whites were bloodshot. He had a very early five o'clock shadow.
A further source of anguish to him was that he did not speak a word
of English. Well, he did speak a word. Twice to me he said "Okay."
Accents were a problem for both of us. Take the word *olé*, for example. I used it often, in my cheering, but usually had it wrong. We sat
and practiced it together. By the time the American, Tony Trabert,
had squeezed out a win, we had made plans to see the next match.
After the final match of doubles, on a Sunday, we walked down the
Reforma together to drink some Dos Equis at Sanborns.

Jaime García, with his sorrowing bloodshot eyes, an expression
that often seemed on the verge of tears, was a man of leisure, in his
fashion, and assistant to his brother Eduardo, who worked for the

light and power company. Both lived with the widow of an older brother, and her four, five, six or more pale children, all of them *muchachas*. Other members of the family were businessmen, sportsmen and taxi drivers. The important detail was the kinship. As one of Jaime's friends, I also shared it, and might be hailed by a stranger in a passing taxi, or embraced in the crowd at the bullring. With his American friend Jaime practiced an infinite maternal patience. My improvement in the language overwhelmed him. Other members of the family were not so impressed, but they were schooled in charity. My effort to teach Jaime English, however, was ill-advised. He intuited, and rightly, that it might interfere with the delicate imbalance that bound us together. We were *camaradas*. He did not want that disturbed.

We saw some bad baseball, a lot of pretty good soccer under clouds of circling *golondrinas*, and for me, and only for me, he sat through one bullfight and walked out on another. That I found this spectacle of interest measurably altered the way he saw me. We went to movies, attended several plays, watched parades, and went to Cuernavaca to buy phonograph records from a member of the family. Two or three times a week we dined together, went to a burlesque, where the jokes were lost on me, then walked for hours around the streets until the only sounds were those we made ourselves.

On those occasions when I tried to speak what was on my mind, or explain to him what I was writing, I might glance up to see, through the muddle of language, the pained and affectionate concern Jaime felt for my handicap. His characteristic melancholy would deepen, his large eyes would grow moist, and his mouth would form an oval as if the breath of life was being forced from him. The profound reluctance of his lips to smile left his cheeks as smooth and wrinkle-free as a child's. A wry pucker was as close as he got to laughter. But when we were together, there was something amusing in most things we set our eyes on. Getting me to laugh was one of his triumphs, one of the things he felt was "good" for me.

On the faces of the children who begged around the bullring I would see the same resigned, irrevocable sadness, a condition to which they seemed born accustomed. How many years of revolution, of discredited expectations, of dreams that proved to be baseless, had Mexicans endured? Already grass was growing and the masonry crumbling between the flagstones of the new University City, the symbol of the Mexican future. It would not prove easy to convert the energy that ground the maize and slapped the tortillas into what burned the lights in Mexico City. And what else was there? There was *nada*. Jaime and others like him had perceived that *tiempo* in Mexico was not *dinero*, and that more than ruins and little Indians would have to come out of the stony fields and mountains. Those sculptured masks that so amazingly resembled the waifs sleeping in the doorway to my apartment seemed to rest their eyeless gaze on neither the past nor the future. Did they dream? Did they intuit one energy replacing another? Jaime García's most characteristic gesture was the shrug.

SINCE MY FRIEND JAIME DID NOT LIKE BULLFIGHTS, I went to them alone. I went because they were there, and the bullring itself fascinated me. From where I preferred to sit, high in the *sol*, the bowl itself seemed to converge on the sandy oval at its center like a bull's eye. This impressed me as a model for my idea of a field of vision. I had been to many of the spectacles before I sat close enough to observe the details. I wrote my wife to the effect that I could take it or leave it— she planned to pay me a visit over the Christmas holidays—but before I mailed that letter I came down with the virus. I saw a great *mano a mano*, I put my tongue to dry lips, and after the hooting I sat around the bonfires of newspapers in the *sombra*. I was hooked. I wrote my wife to prepare herself for a long day at the bullring.

> *He watched the matador, the young magician Da Silva, step from the wings of his imagination, erect but abstract in his pearl gray suit of light. On the column of his spine, like a capital in mourning, the funereal hat. He did not look up to see, nor seem to care about, the bull. The beast stood, a little winded and perplexed, with his rear end to the fence, in his nonexistent corner. Like so many brushes in the palette on his hump were the ribboned darts. Two of them sticking up. But Da Silva? He stood alone with himself. He came to face them, doffing his hat, bending back from his hips like a diver, and with a fine carelessness tossed the hat over his shoulder, like a pinch of salt.* (The Field of Vision, 1956)

Perhaps I was most attracted to the stark ambience of the ring itself, all *sol y sombra*, without intervening stages, a Goya-like spectacle of hooting hucksters, peddlers, and food purveyors with their meat and sliced melons under clouds of flies. Music came from the café, open to the street, with a platform at the front or off to one side, featuring all the members of a large family plucking and strumming guitars and violins, with the zithers placed in the laps of the children. A woman costumed like a Gypsy, her face painted, strings of beads swaying as they dangled, rings of glittering gems on all her fingers, would hoarsely shriek above the strumming clamor. One or two of the smaller children would circulate among the tables, their dirty palms or the crown of a straw hat extended. Never before had

I sought out, Sunday after Sunday, such touching, racking, pitiless heartbreak. They looked fed, some of them even too fed; the maestro of the assembly would have high leather boots, a velvet jacket, and a sombrero that dangled at his back on a noose. But the air of sorrowing supplication was more penetrating than the music. The children had the smooth faces of the clay figurines found in the ruins, but the wide sad eyes of my friend Jaimie. Were they all born knowing? So it seemed.

Music—if that was what it was—led McKee to wheel around and look behind him. A whirring sound. At the front of a café called La Casa de Usted. On a raised platform near the entrance there were ten or twelve people, maybe more, some of them sitting, some standing, but all of them making this whirring noise. Mostly violins.

In mid-December my wife flew down from Philadelphia. A few days later, with a supply of Kaopectate, we drove south to Oaxaca. The American motel was full of the guests who made the Christmas pilgrimage yearly, but we were able to find a room in the suburbs overlooking a very lovelorn burro. In the dawn light his hoarse braying had us in fits of fury and laughter. Midmorning—they came at a loping trot—we heard the slap-slap of the bare feet of the Indian women with their baskets of fresh tortillas, wrapped in towels, balanced on their heads. The central plaza of Oaxaca, a dappling of shadows and dazzling sunlight, featured a bustling market of the Indians who had come from the surrounding villages. Nothing could have been more native and festive. My wife bought pottery and baskets for her friends, and I bought blankets and baskets for the house. The silver jewelry she loved we would buy later in Mexico City and Taxco. Until far into the morning, the mariachi singers serenaded the houses that were near us, the clear hooting of the tenor like the cry of a coyote.

Several times a day we assured each other that Oaxaca would figure in our future. This sentiment was dampened for me, however, by a visit we made to Mitla—the chill of the tombs and the scale of the ruins, low, horizontal masses enclosing a vast empty plaza that seemed to be waiting out the centuries for the appropriate conquering army. These dark-souled people, as Lawrence had intuited, shared the gift of self-fulfilling prophecies of doom. Their expectations were terminal. The lines that defined and delimited Mitla would have profoundly appealed to a modern dictator. The gentle-seeming Indians in the market of Oaxaca, weavers of blankets and baskets, makers

400

of tortillas, were hard to visualize as the descendants of these fate-driven tomb builders. What had turned them on? More puzzling, what had turned them off? The lines of order at Mitla were those of the hive, evoking submission and silence. Were these lines, dormant for centuries, making a comeback in new disguises? The Zapotecs were the creators of Quetzalcoatl, the painted serpent that cast its spell on Lawrence, but what impressed me more was that seven centuries of pitiless sunshine had not penetrated the chill of the tombs. Back in the sun's merciless glare, I was slow to warm up.

On the long drive back to Mexico City we made a stop at a motel in Puebla. At breakfast I thought I recognized the young American giant at a nearby table. His small, pretty blond wife, tight-lipped and harried, spent most of her time sampling the food before she spoon-fed it to her small children. In her pinched, worried face I confronted the Mexico stripped of the adornments of my imagination, a stony, harsh, forbidding landscape of dark alien people, dismaying customs, indigestible food and polluted water. Her out-of-scale husband, who seemed to love what he was eating, had been hailed as the superstar of the future when shipped from Texas to join the Yankees. He could run, occasionally he could hit, but he could seldom judge a flyball in the sun. They had sent him back to Texas, and from there he had gone to Puebla. He was a young man who, if asked, would say that all he wanted to do was play baseball, he didn't care where. The young woman he married, her stringy hair no longer as glossy as pulled taffy, had once smiled when she heard that, and peered up at her giant with a sense of wonder. No more. In her longing for all that she had left behind, she glanced at my wife with envy, and at me with something like loathing, sensing, and correctly, that I had spotted her fallen idol. I spoke to him, briefly, as he packed his car. He still liked baseball, but not the travel. As soon as he learned to hit the curve ball a little better—well, maybe more than a little—he'd be back in the States. That was what he said.

Returning from Cuernavaca, back in November, I had made a wrong turn on a one-way street in Mexico City. Never mind that the street had not been marked where I made my turn. Coming toward me was a battered car packed with what I took to be soldiers. The driver of the car swerved to block the street, got out from behind the wheel, and swaggered toward me, cinema fashion. While his friends hooted, he sized me up. If I would move over in the seat, he told me, he would drive me to the nearest police station. I had heard many stories of this sort, but little advice as to what one should do. I had a loose wad of pesos in my pocket, and I thrust them toward him, a fistful, some of which he dropped in the street. As he stooped to retrieve them, I got the car in reverse, wildly backed away, and made the turn at the nearest corner. From there I raced for the Paseo de la Reforma, which was not far. There I illegally parked, waiting anxiously to be arrested, but the morning traffic flowed smoothly by me. This incident unnerved me for several days. My eyes had taken sharp impressions of the fellow and his companions, the animal that has cunningly learned to survive with a blend of servility, fawning and gratuitous cruelty toward anything that is helpless, and I realized that the aura of infatuation I had maintained for Mexico had lifted. Behind the altar, the old idols gnashed their teeth. I felt something of Jaime's distaste for the exotic contrast. The Indian at his siesta in the midst of the traffic, the tribe of little Indians camped in a clearing, each of them cared for by the one who preceded, a network of links in the long chain of being—for all this my own uncritical ardor had cooled. Where I parked my car, one of the little Indians had learned to lift the hood by crawling through the floorboards, opening the spoils to his companions. One day I found them jam-packed into the seats with their saliva-smeared faces pressed to the windows. Cupidons they once had been, but were no longer. Like the drip of a faucet, they now registered seepage. Seepage had slowly worn away the topsoil of Jaime García, and some of it was now getting to me. The telephone pole on the corner of Avenida Gutenberg, snapped off shortly after my arrival, still lay jutting into the street like a piece of fallen statuary, its shattered base concealed by weeds. I was getting the message. I read it as a sign to head for the border.

IN JANUARY MY WIFE FLEW BACK TO PHILADELPHIA, leaving me in an unaccustomed void, nursing a bad flu. When I had recovered, my depleted batteries would briefly flick my lights, not actually burn them. I would sit at the typewriter, daydreaming, listening to the drip of water in the court. A new infant, on the floor below, found his high decibel range very quickly, and established a predictable howling schedule. I did some reading about the history of the bullfight, but my attention soon wandered.

My landlord could see that I was at loose ends, and suggested a visit to his place in Acapulco. *Acapulco?* The word did not then have the aura it has acquired, but it was destined to have vibrations. His property, he explained, would have five rooms, two with baths, a swimming pool with heated water, a two-car garage—it would have all these things when it was finished. At the moment, it was being constructed. The foundation was poured, and one of the bedrooms, without a bath, had walls and mosquito netting at the window. By now it might even have a door. I was welcome to stay there, if I cared to.

I decided I did care to, for the time being, and suggested to my friend Jaime that he go along with me, but a city without *beisbol* and *futbol* was of limited interest to him. The vibrations to which I responded he did not feel.

On the way down—a steady decline to the edge of the sea—there were numerous detours without signs, or warnings, and one or two that actually lacked an exit. The road, such as it was, simply ended. Unlit lanterns were set about on piles of rocks. The rear of a cow, with the head and glowing eyes just to one side, an apparition in a surreal vision, did not move from the road as I skidded around it, although it was struck by pieces of gravel. Once it was behind me, out of the lights, it disappeared.

On the seaside downgrade of the coastal range the offshore breeze was warm and caressing. The car, however, did not like the sudden change in altitude. The motor misfired, with a series of explosions I thought might blow off the muffler. Coming out of the sierra, I could feel the closeness of the tropical forest. It had not occurred to me that I would come out of the mountains on the west side of the bay, actually facing the east, without the view of the harbor lights I had expected. Widely spaced street lights indicated the coastal highway, and somewhere ahead of my flickering car lights I could hear the wash of the surf. I had been given reasonably explicit directions for a traveler arriving by daylight. In the balmy but black night, the car sputtering, I felt a tingle of terror. How long would it be before anyone missed the American wintering in Mexico? In a month, perhaps, my wife, or my landlord, stopping by for the rent. It did occur to me to pull off the highway and spend the night on the beach, waiting for daylight, but the absence of the racket made by my car would leave an explosive silence. I could see the dim, floating street lights, but nothing of the poles or the street. I had an estimate of how far I should drive to the left, once I reached the coast highway, and I measured it off on the speedometer as I kept the car in second gear. Incredibly, I saw the light bulb, screened off by the trees, and the path that led upward from the highway. I locked the car, and made my way slowly toward the light. Out of the silence, in the gloom to my left, a voice startled me. When I was able to speak, I called out the name of Señor Mendoza, the property's caretaker. A very short man, in a dark sarape—I saw him profiled against the light—took me by the hand, like a child, and led me up the slope to a clearing. In the swing of his lantern I could see the skeletal frame of a structure, like a small cabin on a large raft. White gauze netting hung at one of the windows. Bricks and pails, a shovel in a pile of sand, suggested that the work had stopped at sundown. And Señor Mendoza? He appeared at the rim of the lantern light, at the front of a construction made entirely of netting strung on poles. Invisible through this netting, but audible, I could hear the murmur of voices.

In a hushed voice, I urged the tall, thin man who stood before me to return to his family. To my surprise, without comment, he did. The murmur of the voices inside the netting was like that of a suddenly comforted litter of puppies. I thanked the person with the lantern, man or boy, and pulled back the gauze at the cabin door, to strike a few matches. The flicker of shadowy movement on the walls and ceiling was that of lizards. A cot without bedding occupied one corner. I stood in the faintly luminous darkness and listened to the scurry of creatures. When none attacked me I took courage. With some trembling, I stretched out on the cot, and lay attentive to the voices. Children giggled. A hand slapped a mosquito. In time, a few were buzzing my head, and my perspiring face recorded the fan of their wings as they hovered for a landing. Only then did I become aware of the deafening drone of night music, occasionally pierced by bird-like hoots and cries. I was famished. I was dying of thirst. But what troubled me the most was that I had not brushed my teeth.

404

Just thirty years later, at my desk in Mill Valley, having typed these words on a sheet of yellow paper, I get up to pace the walk at the side of the house, under the laurels and arching live oaks, so displaced and disjointed in time that I know my wife, Jo, feels the strangeness in my smiling but distracted glance.

Where, she asks, am I off to this time, in my disheveled cloak of light? Neither one place nor the other is free of the tremor of recovery, of transformation, yet there is something in both fictions that is profoundly congenial, time being the most adaptable and immaterial of our imaginings. So I accept the nearness, as well as the remoteness, of Señor Mendoza and his family, behind the mesh of the mosquito netting, even as I feel in this retrieval the poignancy of a real loss. Where now is Señor Mendoza, the slender patrician and professional time-killer, proud of his heritage, his Yucatecan breeding and his considerable gift of gab, and where is the señora, huge as a Mayan idol, bronze black and glistening as she slapped out the tortillas, her five penny-colored clones testifying to her fertility?

That first tropical morning, I was awakened by the noise of birds and chickens. Now and then shadows flashed on the netting draped at my door, where the light seemed trapped. Through the gauze I could make out the movement of creatures. When I bolted upright, they disappeared in a fit of hooting and giggling, but they were soon back. Their sizes were staggered. Was I ever really sure of their number? A tall one, so thin she scarcely cast a shadow, brought me a slice of papaya, dressed with a squeeze of lime.

It puzzled me to note, stepping outside, that the sun seemed to be rising where it should be setting. A slender man, with a pointed gray beard, dressed in the manner of the peons, stood wiping his hands in a fastidious manner on the soiled tail of his blouse. It did not startle him to glance up and see me. On a cord at his front dangled glasses that he raised to examine me more closely.

"Señor Mor-rees?" he inquired. I nodded. In carefully enunciated Spanish, he assured me of the pleasure it gave him to meet me. He was Señor Mendoza. Señora Mendoza . . . He wheeled to face her. A massive woman, the color of fired bronze, she sat at the opening to their shelter. Naked brown children, recognizably boys, ran about with their slices of papaya. All had the full-moon faces and saucer eyes of their mother, with the exception of the slender, vine-like señorita, eyeing me with the boldness of a Lolita. Was I to believe that this old bee continued to pollinate his jungle flower?

Of whom did he remind me? In the manner of a maître d', toying with his glasses, he told me that he was not himself Mexican, but Yucatecan—it came from his lips as if I had urgently asked him—and his wife, Carmen, was from Guatemala. He was voluble, but unhurried. Just in passing, he thought it pertinent to tell me that they would return to Yucatán for the education of their children. He had once served as a lecturer at the university, but political unrest had obliged him to flee the country.

Would he happen to know, I asked him, of a reliable automobile mechanic? That was not what he had expected. He studied me for a moment in silence, his left hand supporting his right elbow, one finger of his right hand pressed to his lips. I believe he had waited so long to be asked to be of service that the actual moment left him confused.

The principal mechanic of Acapulco, he said, choosing his words with care, happened to be an old and personal friend. He would escort me. He was at my service. To his wife—who continued to ignore him—he explained the nature of his mission, the time going and the time coming, the time for the unforeseen, and the time it took him to find the dapper black beret that fit him like a skullcap, his hair in tufts at each side. Of whom did he remind me? Don Quixote de la Mancha. I pondered my resemblance to Sancho Panza.

My car was still there, with its spark plugs and its hubcaps, but the glass in the windows was smeared where the curious had pressed their faces. Señor Mendoza was full of praise for the car, an advanced model he had not seen, and he was greatly impressed with my skill as a driver, the way I managed to keep the car on the road. I was able to puzzle out, as we curved around the bay, why the sun had risen where I thought it should set. Several miles up ahead, in whatever direction, the windows of Acapulco flamed with the sun. It was not as yet the jet set mecca it would soon be but the blaze of light off the sea, the long curved avenue that was fringed on both sides by weeds, put me in mind of ruins, both real and imaginary, involving the image of Cleopatra on her barge of painted silken sails. These unreal places of excessive heat and light stimulated in strangers antique fantasies. Thomas Mann had found it so in Los Angeles, where he would finish his book about Joseph in Egypt. The full length of this avenue, the shadow of the car went along beside us, high as a caboose. The high-rise hotels had not yet risen, so that there was not much to see but the oasis of palms at the fishing pier.

On a side street, in a small lot of junked cars, we found Señor Mendoza's old friend the mechanic. He was in a shallow grease pit, shaded by a car. A sallow, sober man, in a soiled T-shirt, he climbed out of the pit to stand wiping his hands on a wad of rags, his arms

406

already greasy to the elbows. The sight of Señor Mendoza did not lift his spirits. Señor Mendoza had begun his oration in praise of my background, my talents as a driver and my interests as a scholar—at which point he was interrupted.

"What's the trouble?" the mechanic asked me, in good Orange County English.

"It misfires," I said. "It might be the plugs."

He tested the plugs with his screwdriver, the smoke of his cigarette creasing one eye. One plug did not fire at all. Another proved weak. He removed the plugs and gave them to his assistant, a boy about eight or nine years of age. Would I like a good *used* plug, he asked me, or a new one? The used one was four, the new one ten pesos. To clean the remaining plugs was five pesos. I paid him twenty pesos even. "Much obliged," he said. After checking the oil, he advised me to add a quart. Did I want the best used, or *neuvo American*? He liked the sound of it.

Señor Mendoza was silent as we drove away. His humiliation at the hands of a *Mexican* mechanic weighed on him. In an American-style drugstore, open on the street, we sat at the counter and had two Carta Blancas. The overhead fluorescent lights and the number of things to buy cheered him up. He accepted, with dignity, one of my cigarettes, but instead of lighting up he stored it, like a pencil, at his ear. His wife, he confessed, was the smoker in the family, and keeping her supplied was something of a problem. Her consumption might run six to ten cigarettes a day. His income as a house caretaker was not large, but on those holidays the Indians came out of the mountains, he set himself up as a scribe in the market, signing documents and writing letters. Was there, perhaps, someone I would like him to write to? There was. I took a postcard from the rack, showing a fish twice the size of the man who had caught it, and Señor Mendoza, with embellishments and curlicues, addressed it to my editor in New York, said I was having a wonderful time and wished he was here. It looked so great I hated to mail it. He, too, liked what he had done, and when I read it aloud he liked the sound of it. While I sat in the shade of the palm trees, facing the pier, he attended to more pressing business.

I should have guessed that he would make a day of it. After my evening meal at a sidewalk café, he appeared in time to join me for a cognac. He had a new string bag stuffed with sliced white bread, a particular passion of the señora. As we followed the curving road around the bay, the sea took fire from the setting sun. With due allowance for the sliced white bread, I thought the life had much to

recommend it. I had bought candy for the kids, cigarettes for the
señora, and for myself an ointment to repel insects. In the dusk, the
sky remained a banked fire, but there was no perceptible cooling with
the evening. Señora Mendoza, considerably deshabille, chain-smoked
her windfall of cigarettes and fanned the smoke with a movie magazine.
The child of a neighbor, a caramel-colored toddler, appeared with
the caps of soft-drink bottles to play a game on the sun-baked surface
of the yard. I spied on the children, but understood little. Periodically
they all ran about screaming.

It had been a long day for me, but I preferred to recline in the
open, swatting and fanning myself with a palm frond, than to take
to the windless calm of my private quarters. The beating of a drum,
like distant sounds of gunfire, rumbled across the bay. What day was
it? Señora Mendoza did not seem to know. She asked her husband,
who seemed sure when asked, but the more he thought about it, the
less he was certain. Would I like him to go and inquire from a neighbor?
No, I thought not. The insect repellent had the suggestion of a fragrance
that I remembered from my camping days in Michigan. What had it
been? *Citronella!* A marvelous word and not a bad repellent.

One morning—it hardly matters which morning—I stopped for
a swim in the misty froth of the sea. I left the car parked off the
highway, where I could see it. A mile of open empty beach stretched
in both directions. A frieze of cruising pelicans, in military formation,
fanning the air in slow motion, sailed by just offshore, low over the
shallow water, their primitive wings flapping like sails. One of them
suddenly dropped like a stone, to reappear with a fish in its scoop-
like gullet. The small button eye of the bird unnerved me. As a youth
of twenty in the Carlsbad Caverns, I had seen time itself drip from
the ceiling, and rise from the floor, as if to finish off time at the point
of their meeting. Hot as it was, watching these birds I felt the tingle
of a primitive chill.

I had left my pants, shoes and T-shirt within a few feet of the
sea and thrashed about for a few moments, then came up for air. On
the white sand of the beach I could see the flashing pelican shadows.
Otherwise nothing. To my surprise, I found I was standing in waist-
deep water. When I glanced back to the beach, my clothes were gone.
Short tracks led down to the beach where a stream passed under the
highway through a metal culvert. The stream was shallow, and a not so
small boy could have easily crawled the length of the culvert. I was out
a pair of pants, about 230 pesos, and a coveted pair of crepe-soled sandals. My traveler's checks, luckily, were in the jacket locked in the car.
One of Señor Mendoza's older boys was able to crawl through

408

the floorboards and open one of the doors. In the car I had a second set of keys, and a pair of old pants wrapped around a jack that rattled. It could have been much worse. The three of us drove into Acapulco together and had a huevos rancheros breakfast. I cashed one of the checks, and bought a pair of huaraches made from an old tire casing, although I knew they would soon give me blisters. On our way back, taking a bit of a ride to that point where the coast road ended, we passed two Indian boys who appeared to be working on a parked car. They were not trying to start it, as I first thought, but had the hood up and were trying to strip the engine. That was not easy, since their tools were limited to a pair of pliers. The car had a shiny new California license. They had managed to remove the seats and the dashboard, but the wheels and the engine confronted them with problems. When we stopped, both boys looked up, ready to run but inwardly triumphant. As an upcoming victim, I was of two minds.

We drove on up the street to where the pavement ended and several goats were grazing. A small boy, wearing a cap with a slowly revolving pinwheel, stood slapping one of the goats with a stick, as if beating a rug. I thought Señor Mendoza left the car to speak to him, but he stooped to gather up handfuls of the bank grass, filling the hamper he had made of the tails of his shirt. The boys working on the car popped up to wave at us as we passed. It occurred to me that the peculiar way I was feeling might be caused by the heat and the shimmering light, but it was also more of an upper than a downer, and in time I might grow to like it.

All four wheels were gone. The rear end of the car was still on the boxes they had used to hoist it. The nose of the car was in the ditch as if trying to hide. We stood there beside it, shading our eyes, but the glare from the paint made it hard to look at.
Mac said, "What'll they do with just the wheels?"
"Sell them back to us," I replied. (Love Among the Cannibals, 1957)

A week or ten days later, it might have been eight, I was still there. In the morning I would stroll along the beach all the way into Acapulco, taking dips when I felt like it. I was soon well known to the beach photographers, most of whom had little to do. They took pictures of me for nothing, just to keep their hand in. Postcard snaps of me, in a variety of poses, were tucked into their hatbands and ornamented their cameras. We all agreed the early morning was the best light. Given time, it seemed to me, I might shape up into a pretty good beach bum. After my usual breakfast, at the drugstore counter, I'd loaf on the beach until the late afternoon, and the first of the fishermen came in with their catch. I could never believe that the people I saw going out would manage to catch anything. I saw these plump-type matrons in baseball hats, wearing Mickey Mouse watches and unlaced tennis sneakers, go out like they'd never before been in a boat, and come back with a marlin weighing four or five hundred pounds. I was asked to stand in some of the pictures, to show the scale of the fish.

In the early evening I would have some food, then walk along the firm sand—the tide being out—all the way back to the Mendozas. At the end of that walk, when I took my dip, I smelled like flint that had just been struck. A mongrel yellow-eyed dog that liked to walk along with me often licked my hands for the taste of the salt.

Later, in the dusky twilight, I would sit with the Mendoza family while the huge señora sprawled on the hammock, waiting for the dance music on her battery radio. It would play loud for five or ten minutes, then begin to fade. The new batteries I had bought her in Acapulco proved to be deader than the old ones. What I wanted to hear about was the romance between the Yucatán scholar, and public scribe, and the massive maiden from Guatemala, who after dining in the evening inclined on her side propped on one flipper, like a sea lion. Between two black fingers, she held one of her treasured Old Gold cigarettes, like a piece of chalk. It had been idle for me to explain that she was not actually smoking old gold. Periodically, and slightly, she coughed. Small as it was, it shook her. It was hardly an attention-getting cough, but it soon got mine. How could something so small create such a tremor in something so large? Not to miss the pleasure of the last few puffs, she used a bit of toothpick to hold the crackling butt to her lips. So nothing would be lost, the pinch of tobacco in the butt was stored in a snuff tin, and rerolled. In the morning, after a night of deprivation, she would light up and inhale with a crackle of tobacco like a miniature brush fire. Her need was so great it made her self-conscious. Now and then she would glance at me, shamefaced. Not Señora Mendoza, nor her budding nymphet, but the impudent gringo from Mexico City had brought to her attention that she was a helpless, vulnerable creature. I was not proud of it. It did us both good when I left.

I was both drawn and repelled by the cult of the primitive, the stripping away of endless inessentials, but the great earth mother Carmen Mendoza, squatted in the shade as she proved for lice on the heads of her children, unswatted flies crawling about on her mounds of flesh, put me in mind of the great sow of Schloss Ranna, with her

410

long fluttering lashes, her squirming litter of mini-piglets, pink and hairless as baby mice. I had loved the way she grunted softly when I spoke to her, like a happy dreamer. I had surely set my eyes on contentment that exceeded expectations, but to what extent could I say the lady was conscious?

Señora Mendoza's pleasure—wherever it was centered in her great mound of flesh—was to look for and find the all but invisible lice in the gleaming, honey-hued hair of her daughter. By the hour, she washed, combed and brushed it to shine like wire. The girl sat before her, facing away, her lips parted and her eyes dreamy, as if being stroked by a lover. A full-blown nymphet at ten. What scent would she give off at twelve? If seated at my side, she would idly play with my fingers; she could not catch my glance without flirting. Her scalp was scoured to shine like a pan, but not her neck. In moments of delight, her long arms would twine around her body and wag the fingers at me from both sides. Was this the knowledge that flew the pelicans in stately formation, to drop like bombs on moving targets, trickling along the nerves that itched to play with my fingers?

Murky thoughts might come to me at night under the ceiling of flickering lizards. Hearing sounds like those of a kitten lapping up something, I beamed my flashlight into the corner. A double apparition, both substance and shadow, thrust its gruesome head toward the light. Rainbow-hued and iridescent, the iguana was a small-scale model for a dragon. I lacked the will to turn away my gaze, or switch off the light. The large head swayed from side to side, to get a bead on me. Under one taloned dragon's claw squirmed whatever he was eating. In her tent of netting, the señora coughed as the creature shuffled off.

All of Mexico, at the moment when my wide eyes stared into the darkness, appeared to me like an appendix that would soon rupture, unaware of its own existence. The nonconscious, the semiconscious, the slowly coming into consciousness, for which D. H. Lawrence had such an unearthly instinct, I accepted as part of the mystique of the "exotic." In the long horizontal structures at Mitla, and in the fermenting juices in the jungles, vegetable and mineral, the orderly and the aimless, achieved a plant-like resignation. At what point did the stripping down to basics strip away the civilized essentials? Piecemeal, the smiling wreckers at work on the highway would make out of the whole a sum of useless parts. The reverse side of the tourist was this dim apprehension that no distinction of importance existed between the diving pelican, cruising the beach, and the smiling scavenger on the highway.

On my last day, we all went for a ride into Acapulco. The señora, her huge feet bare, wore a lime-green shift, flowers braided in her hair. She sat with me in the front, a draped monument. What instinct had led her to choose lime green? Under the fans in the drugstore she gave off vibrations. We sat in two booths, sucking ice cream sodas through straws. Not the pots and pans, the shelves of glasses and dishes, but the smell of wrapped soap held her attention. Eyes lidded as she sniffed the wrappers, she stored away this vital information.

From Acapulco we rode to where the pavement ended and found the abandoned car stripped of its tires, but not its wheels. The windshield, the steering wheel, the generator, the carburetor, the lights, the muffler and the radiator were gone. With a little help, Señor Mendoza suggested, what was left might be carried up the slope and installed in the yard for the children. I saw no reason, at the moment, that the house might not be built around it.

I had come to Acapulco to break ties, but I would leave with troubling attachments. Señor Mendoza had bought, from one of the beach photographers, a snapshot of the gringo as a beachcomber. The child Carmelita studied it soberly, the tip of her pink tongue between her lips. Señor Mendoza rode with me to the turnoff for Mexico City. He had been there. He felt no great desire to return. Months later I would send him the snapshots I had taken of all the Mendozas, in particular the señora, a monument grooming her daughter, which would take its place at the edge of her mirror with that beach shot of myself. In the snapshots Señor Mendoza did not put me in mind of Don Quixote. Perhaps the windmills were missing. But in profile, in his beret, he did look very scholarly.

On my last evening in Mexico City, Jaime García and I took in a movie (I've no idea what it was), then had a late dinner at Sanborns that lasted far into the morning. We both sipped black coffee, and I smoked cigars. Time and time again we said that next time we would go to Veracruz, to Orizaba, to Mérida. With a friend who had a jeep we would go to Guatemala! Why not? All of that was next time. Shortly before dawn, I made room in the front seat (the others were packed with baskets, blankets and numerous pairs of the stirrup-heel boots I could not resist) and drove him to his place. We had an emotional parting. My loss was aggravated by the assurance that for him it would be much worse. It relieved him to savor my freedom. We felt for each other a deep affection. For months he had saved for me his best Mexican jokes.

Out of Toluca, at dawn, a narrow blacktop road took me north through a spectral landscape, but I was too saddened to appreciate it. In the midafternoon heat I pulled off the road in a setting appropriate for Pancho Villa. I spread one of my new blankets out on the sand, and lay with a straw hat shading my face. Even then, lights seemed to flash on the lids of my eyes. Perhaps I dozed. The sound I heard was like a distant crackling fire. In an instant a horse and rider loomed theatrically above me, the blue lips of the horse flecked with blood from the tooth-edge bit. He snorted wildly through dilated nostrils. That horseman who had for so long come riding, riding, over the purple moor and over plain and pampas had finally stumbled on me. Was my number up? The dark horseman was armed like a bandit; a cartridge belt circled his waist and crossed his broad chest. The heavy butt of a pistol thrust out of the holster. Would he shoot me, like a rattler, or simply let the horse trample me? Whatever, whichever it was to be, Mexico had well prepared me for the script. But the horseman himself seemed undecided how to follow up his advantage. I sprawled out on the sand before him. What a windfall for a fearless bandit! How his amigos would admire him! But this occasion had been thrust upon him without adequate preparation. The horse wheeled slowly, pawing up the sand, then the rider, in frustration, suddenly hooted as he dug in the spurs, and off they went. I sat up to dizzily watch the cloud of dust trail along behind them. Far up ahead, a gray smear of smoke indicated the city of Chihuahua, where I would soon take a seat at the bar and study my windburned face in the mirror. Just like in the movies, I took my tequila straight, with a chaser of salt.

On the highway leading west out of El Paso, I stopped for a double cheeseburger and three ice-cold glasses of milk.

"Where you get a tan like that?" the girl asked me.

I replied, "Acapulco."

The word did not ring a bell. A run-of-the-mill Texas-border-type waitress, she had spots on her scalp, scratched with her pencil. I would think of her almost twenty years later, when I saw the movie *Bonnie and Clyde*. On being asked what he planned to do, Clyde replied, "Rob a bank." That was a very good scene. The one with me and the waitress was pretty good too, with the fan whining, the radio squawking, and me lighting up a black-paper cigarette. I forget what brand it was, but it had a sweet taste and a smooth white ash.

Duuring one of our spring vacations at Pomona College, my friend Ed Lundberg and I hitched up the coast to Robinson Jeffers's country, where we slept on the beach at Carmel and made our coffee in a can over a fire of driftwood. The staggering beauty of the coast would leave on me an impression from which Italy would never recover. We saw something of Point Sur, Big Sur and Point Lobos, but it did not cross either of our sun-baked minds to go on to San Francisco or Berkeley, doomed to give birth to the Beat Generation. Nor did I trouble to cross the Bay Bridge when I visited Mark Schorer in Berkeley in March of 1955. I think of that when I feel about on my wrist for the pulse of my time.

Mark Schorer was a scholar, a gifted writer of fiction, and a critic of generous impulses. He had spoken up for books of mine, and I was grateful. Schorer's wife, Ruth, to my astonishment, had been in Vienna the winter I had been there, and at the Studenten Klub we had friends in common. This did not impress her, as it did me, with the inscrutable powers that shape our ends. In the brief time we had together, I felt that Schorer, like D. H. Lawrence, was a man of intuitive judgments. I was not a good reader of my contemporaries—I seemed to like only what I might have written myself—and Schorer's empathy for what he was reading alerted me to the narrowness of my own practice. I had brought with me several unfinished manuscripts, one of them dealing with Gordon Boyd's walk on water, but I was more eager to have his impression of a bizarre piece I called "Babe Ruth's Pocket." This novel-length fiction consisted of characters from my own largely unread novels. It testified to my ongoing preoccupation with fact and fiction, with what is real-seeming in the world I perceive around me, and the fiction we produce to mirror that world. "Babe Ruth's Pocket" perceived the characters of my novels to be more real-seeming, less shadow and more substance, than the actual people with whom they mingled, and on whom they were based. I was perhaps right in thinking that only in Schorer would such an experiment find a sympathetic reader. He not only read it, he liked it. He would later be so rash as to recommend that the University of California Press publish it. Cooler heads prevailed, but I cite this incident as an example of Schorer's ability to read the book the author believed he had written. My novel was not without interest, but it was not an interest shared by the general reader. Schorer quickly grasped the writer's obsession, found it of interest, and enjoyed the performance. It is one of a quantity of my manuscripts that now reside in the Bancroft Library in Berkeley, thanks to James D. Hart's continued advocacy of the author of *My Uncle Dudley*.

Jim Hart had been one of my readers since that book was published, and had persuaded me, just a year or two before, to deposit my accumulating manuscripts in Bancroft. At the home of Jim and Ruth Hart, where I spent several nights, and heard some fine early Bing Crosby recordings, I met a generous sampling of local literary people, including Henry Nash Smith, George Stewart, the visiting celebrity C. S. Forester, and *San Francisco Chronicle* book critic Joseph Henry Jackson, who had spoken up clearly for my first novel. Did it cross my mind that a writer would be fortunate, indeed, to make his home in such surroundings? It did indeed. Some six or seven years, however, would pass before Walter Van Tilburg Clark would ask me to take his place on the faculty of San Francisco State College, just across the bay. In those six years a new generation would stream out of the old American woodwork to make bonfires along North Beach, make trouble, make poems, and make love while putting off war. Of all this the finger on my pulse did not record one beat.

On my way east, at Schorer's suggestion, I stopped to visit with Howard and Dorothy Baker on their orange ranch near Fresno. I thought her novel, *Young Man with a Horn*, masterly. I had not read Howard Baker's poetry, but few Western poets I had heard of were more highly respected. I liked them both immensely, but I felt that Howard Baker especially suffered the torment of those committed, on the one hand, to the good life, and on the other, to great art. I left, soberly swearing I would soon return—a vow that has frequently come back to haunt me. The fault is always mine. I do not take the trouble, in the interests of fraternity, to go out of my way.

From the Bakers' I drove southwest to Death Valley, where I took out my unused Leica and stared about me, like a tourist in Eden who had forgotten his film. Again I made a vow to return that I did not keep. On a cold, clear night I stopped in Santa Fe long enough to warm up in the La Fonda lobby, and splurge on several Navajo blankets. Would the cargo of fleas that I knew I was carrying in the Mexican blankets welcome these new prospects? I think they did.

The great and intricate secret of the open road—but it must be open, not clouded with smog and clotted with traffic—is the way it provokes

415

and sustains image-making, the supreme form of daydreaming. The road should be a blacktop, to escape the whine, the deadening rhythm of the divisions in the concrete, the line down the center reeling in at the front what it reels out, even faster, at the rear, the car in its own inscrutable flight pattern, perfectly scaled to the world we live in, the heart lifting to see the horizon approach, then registering the loss as it vanishes behind us. What dreams seem to do for so many others, a long car trip does for me. I get startling glimpses of what lies ahead, I feel the stretch and pull of what recedes behind me. At unpredictable, miraculous moments, like the sound of blowing music, loose ends of my thinking come together. Most of it is as unreal as fiction, and as permanent.

Somewhere just east of Tucumcari, where the plains begin, a good breakfast under my belt and a following tail wind, the stalled tumblers in my story of Gordon Boyd began to stir and fall into place. I saw that his failure, the quirky and screwball delight he savored in it, was not an old American botchery but a new one, with its own sweetly rancid flavor. This side of his nature needed the special cultivation it would never get from his old friends in Nebraska. He wanted someone to further provoke and challenge him, someone more outrageous than he was. Who else but someone who had managed—in his fashion—to walk on water? Strange to relate, I actually had this person, filed away for this particular occasion.

In the material I had cut from *The Works of Love* was a macabre winter scene in Chicago. I had come upon the news report, in a magazine, of how, in the late spring thaw, an unclaimed body had been found beneath one of the snowdrifts. It was taken to the morgue, and from there to the dissecting room of a medical school. From the pail of severed hands available, one of the students selected one that he recognized as the hand of his missing father. Not long after, this young man also proved to be missing. He would reappear in my fiction as a cleaning woman in a manuscript I had not published, and he was now in the wings waiting to play a key role, as Paula Kahler, companion to Dr. Lehmann, in *The Field of Vision*. Unable to change an impossible world, Paul Kahler had settled for changing himself.

As I rolled eastward across Kansas and Missouri, the white strip down the center luring me onward, it occurred to me that this bizarre assembly of oddballs, dreamers and failures might naturally come together in one place only—the bullring of Mexico City! This least likely of all likelihoods was appropriate to this unlikely gathering: McKee, his wife and their grandson, the boy's great-grandfather Scanlon, the maverick Gordon Boyd with his Viennese companion Dr.

Lehmann, a student of madness, Mozart, and the transcendent Paula Kahler. I saw it all in a quick preview flicker, as I thumped my cold feet on the floorboards. In Missouri an attack of sciatica (I learned the name for it later) compelled me to spend some hours in bed, where I was able to make a few notes. Two days later I honked for my wife, who appeared in the carport with our black cat, Sour Mash.

"Why, you've still got your Acapulco tan!" she said. This I admitted, but I was mum about the imported life in the blankets. Sour Mash loved the smell, but as I recall, he was the first one to scratch.

Before I had settled down to get on with my book, Granville Hicks asked me to do a critical piece on the state of the contemporary novel, for a book he was editing. Eight or ten young novelists had been asked, and agreed to make contributions. I welcomed the encouragement to put in order some of the opinions I had been voicing, and impressions I had been pondering. American writers continued to be both productive and innovative, but our major figures, it seemed to me, were subject to a common and disabling disorder. The past cast its spell over the present. The territory ahead—in the American imagination— proved to be somewhere behind us when we sat down to write.

I was myself a case in point. Was this common affliction seldom, if ever, suffered by writers elsewhere? Were Americans compelled to reconsider their past before they could really deal with the present? How much of this was *self*-recovery—as I recognized it in my own preoccupations? I found the central issue beautifully anticipated by the writer who had first suffered from it. At the close of *Huckleberry Finn*, Mark Twain put it like this:

But I reckon I got to light out for the territory ahead of the rest, because Aunt Sally she's going to adopt me and sivilize me, and I can't stand it. I been there before.

For Twain, this territory would be embalmed in his childhood, a moveable feast to which he could turn again and again. One of its great thralldoms was that this past had no truck with the future. To the window of a childhood friend, Mark Twain wrote:

I should like to call back Will Bowen & John Garth & others, & live the life, and be as we were, & make holiday until 15, then all drown together.

The extraordinary blackness of this judgment is stupefying. Could

417

an American writer of such magnitude, of such world-wide renown and expectations, actually have believed in what he was saying? That it comes in such a context, and at such a moment, gives it the force of a confession. Not merely the past, but the private preserve of a lost boyhood, was defined as the Great Good Place. Out of this compost would sprout the myths that millions of Americans still find congenial, and that Norman Rockwell would sanction with his *Saturday Evening Post* covers. This made it official that these sentiments were a matter of history and policy. On the one hand, the uncorrupt world of sanctified elders, pets and children, and on the other, the mess we were making of the present. Faulkner, too, preferred to locate himself in this semi-savage wilderness and Eden, where David Hogganbeck and Ikkemotubbe eternally pursued Herman Basket's sister, the primal and receding vision of womanly loveliness.

But Mark Twain died before the Great War, and had little precognition of the world that was emerging, to which he had personally contributed not a little cupidity and avarice. Colors that he thought to be of the deepest black—as the century wore on—would prove to be pastel shades of decorator gray.

I saw two deeply rooted native dispositions affecting the direction of the American novel: the first a deep distrust of the "intellectual," the old quarrel between the small-town hick and the urban sophisticate, but with the novel's future at stake; the second a preference for raw material, the less digested and tampered with the better. In each case, what we wanted and what we would get was the writer who was as broad and deep as our rivers, and as high and majestic as our mountains—not a writer in the bookish sense at all, but one of great natural forces. Mark Twain, of course, was such a figure, appropriately identified with the Mississippi River, and Thomas Wolfe, looking homeward, would prove to be another, a writer and a man so out of scale he symbolized our vast resources of both sentiments and raw materials. The large bulk of Wolfe's *Of Time and the River* far outweighed Fitzgerald's *Tender Is the Night*. There was not a lack of craft-conscious writers, who read, criticized and challenged each other, but the public was held in thrall by a writer so singular I overlooked him. Between the two wars, Sinclair Lewis would be the read and world-recognized writer, his energy and his talent mingling the gross and the native, the intellectual and the hick, in just the right proportions. At the summit of his success a Nobel Prize winner, he was on the verge of a long decline, the price of his "success" being both failure and self-destruction.

At that very moment, in *The Field of Vision*, Gordon Boyd was celebrating, with appropriate self-abasement, his long-anticipated failure as a writer. The parallel to Sinclair Lewis was so obvious it had been lost on me. Lewis, indeed, was one of the writers neither mentioned nor discussed in *The Territory Ahead*.

From Hawthorne to Faulkner the mythic past has generated what is memorable in our literature—but what is not so memorable, what is often crippling, we have conspired to overlook. This is the tendency, long prevailing, to start well then peter out. . . . The writer's genius is unique, but in his tendency to fail he shares a common tradition.

For more than a century the territory ahead has been the world that lies somewhere behind us, a world that has become, in the last few decades, a nostalgic myth. . . . It is the myth that now cripples the imagination, rather than the dark and brooding immensity of the continent. It is the territory ahead that defeats our writers of genius, not America. (1958)

Exactly twenty years later, in a preface to the Bison Edition, I had some second thoughts.

. . . The role of nostalgia in our literature has dwindled as our great expectations have diminished. The backward look, the consuming longing, is no longer a crippling preoccupation of the writer. The national purpose, the national conscience, are currently pressured from other quarters. I am now more inclined to a nostalgic view of nostalgia itself. What a passion it was for those possessed by it. Americans did not invent this torment, but surely we have made the most of its follies, a passion that was crippling to Thomas Wolfe but liberating to the mind of Faulkner. Without a mythic and alluring past American writers of genius, with few exceptions, had little to fuel their imaginations. It gave substance to their dreams of national purpose, and faith to sustain their personal visions. On such evidence the virtues of nostalgia more than compensate for its foibles. It would appear to have generated what was essential to a young nation's boundless and soaring expectations, uninhibited by, and often indifferent to, the obvious.

While I was working on these essays I was seeing a lot of Kitty Bowen. She had little time for novel reading—caught up as she was in the research on Sir Edward Coke—but I did what I could to introduce her to a few novels of mine. For those who liked Kitty, and she in turn liked, her vitality was contagious; for others, her assurance

419

and detachment were unmistakably regal and distant. Who did she think she was, Elizabeth the first? I rather hope so. No woman I have known seemed so naturally born to rule.

My new novel, *The Field of Vision*, had progressed to where I knew that *time present*, all of it, would take place on a single afternoon in the bullring, the past materializing in flashback:

What a crazy goddam world, Boyd was thinking—and so made room for himself. Also for Dr. Lehmann, the celebrated quack, with nothing to recommend him but his cures, and Paula Kahler, the only sort of failure he could afford. Also for old man Scanlon, the living fossil, for McKee, the co-inventor of the dust bowl, for his wife, the deep-freeze, and her grandson who would live it all over gain. Here gathered at a bullfight. The sanded navel of the world. Gazing at this fleshy button, each man had the eyes to see only himself. This crisp sabbath afternoon forty thousand pairs of eyes would gaze down on forty thousand separate bullfights, seeing it all very clearly, missing only the one that was said to take place. Forty thousand latent heroes, as many gorings, so many artful dodges it beggared description, two hundred thousand bulls, horses, mules and monsters half man, half beast. In all this zoo, this bloody constellation, only two men and six bulls would be missing. Those in the bullring. Those they would see with their very own eyes.

"So you haf tudge boddom?" Dr. Lehmann had asked, beaming on Boyd with his early-man smile. Then he had added, "Wich boddom?"

For both Gordon Boyd and the author, "the boddom of the boddom" was simply not part of their expectations. It would recede beneath them, and their talent, if they had one, would prove to lie in another direction.

I HAD THOUGHT THE NAME Y̲A̲D̲D̲O̲ SPOKE FOR the flying strands of Far Eastern philosophy in the thinking, or the intent, of the founders, but the facts were not so complicated. A much-loved child, accustomed to play in the groves of trees near the house, the ground dappled and alive with the play of shadows, had sometimes run about crying, "Yaddos! Yaddos!"

I soon came to like almost everything about Yaddo, an artists' retreat near Saratoga Springs, including that story. Perhaps the many-gabled Victorian manse, a cluttered maze of rooms and niches, like the one built in Hartford for Mark Twain, somehow approximated the American dream of each man's house as his castle.

My day started with a crackling wood fire to take the chill off the cabin, and with the far roar of the crowd at the nearby racetrack. I loved the sweeping vista eastward, toward the White Mountains, the excellence of the food, the welcome book talk and gossip, and the presence of the handsome, imposing woman, Elizabeth Ames, who had set the tone for Yaddo from its beginning. The aura of a war-blighted romance did much to enhance the role she played as a Jamesian culture figure. Since I had come to Yaddo primed for work, this tone suited me perfectly.

As I worked, I sometimes wondered if I still had a publisher. Marshall Best had read and rejected the manuscript recommended by Mark Schorer (this did not surprise me), but I was more than reluctant to test him with another commercially suspect novel. An assembly of tourists from the dust bowl gathered in a bullring in Mexico City? What would I think of next? My experience had been—and it was becoming extensive—that a publisher would hustle for the first book, but rest the oars in the locks with the second. With the completed manuscript of *The Field of Vision* I drove east through a landscape beautiful beyond description and twice stopped to wade about in the flaming leaves. Even James had referred to this Arcadia, and the way it resisted human usage, challenging the appreciative outsider to do more *with it* than the natives. But what? It had persisted because it resisted both use and abuse. There it all was, only more so, the cornucopia of riches that defied accounting, and that would be how I found it, and left it. To get beyond appearances was an old American story, but I was fortunate in having Granville and Dorothy Hicks to relate Arcadia to the chronic water shortage in Grafton and to a writer from the Platte Valley of Nebraska. I had come to pay a visit, to talk about Mexico, and to listen to the advice and encouragement of friends who were having a new coat of red paint put on their house. We all thought it looked great.

Granville liked the new manuscript, gave me some helpful criticism, but agreed that it would not be wise to confront Marshall Best with my bullring fable. How was the publisher, or the reader, to get a bead on such a writer? In ten years, no two consecutive novels established or defined my "territory." Some readers had been impressed with my strong sense of "place"; others regretted that this place proved to be where it was. The plains had briefly been the property of Willa Cather, who had soon, and sensibly, turned to other landscapes. Let the writer come from the plains, if he must, but be smart enough to leave them behind him. About that predicament, I was of two minds. *The Field of Vision* displayed a disarray of landscapes, characters and events that mirrored the conscience of the writer, but did not deceive him into thinking that the preoccupations revealed in his writing were shared by his contemporaries: neither what he created, out of reasonably whole cloth, nor the friends and colleagues with whom he shared the status of a writer and a reader. In a really quite tiresome way, he appeared to be a throwback to those "loners" who emerge out of a fabric of fact and fiction, compelled to do what we find them doing, compelled to make a limited model of the world out of an excess of impressions. In this perspective, *The Field of Vision* is coherent, and sometimes successful. The familiar ingredients are present—even the fabled receding past—and the writer's affection for the characters he is also obliged to pillory. A very characteristic performance, in a very unpredictable setting. I went back to my friend Harry Ford, who passed the book on to his friend Jerry Gross, a new editor at Harcourt, Brace, and to my great relief Harcourt, Brace contracted to publish it.

For some time, as part of *The Territory Ahead,* I had been pondering Norman Rockwell's America. His portraits of the presidential candidates Eisenhower and Stevenson, widely displayed in a series of posters, had aroused renewed interest in his work. My own taste and sentiments had been shaped by Rockwell quite beyond my grasp or the telling of it, and this knowledge gave edge and persistence to my reactions. What a bill of goods he had sold me—and I had bought! That barefoot boy with cheek of tan, his feet sticky with roofing tar, his face smeared with the pie still cooling at the pantry window, had also leaped from the bridge into the quicksand, and turned from there to try his hand at walking on water.

422

No cliché has been evaded; every cliché alters the actual image of the past in the interests of the sentiments of the present. To what end? Had the actual past been so bad that the memory of it had been suppressed? To what end would one diminish the truly memorable moment in the interests of a sham sentimentality? Was it a failure of nerve (a fashionable phrase at the time) or of memory itself? Was it feebleness of taste, or intelligence, that would lead us to prefer the spurious to the genuine? Calendar pictures of romantically nuzzling horses (a movie innovation) to the realities of the farmyard? Americans who had searing memories of poverty and hardship, of sickness and death, of real losses without imaginary gains, had put it all behind them with the first calendar pictures of mixed litters of kittens and puppies, steamboats rounding the bend, and amber waving fields of grain. On the graves of what had been both forgotten and suppressed, Rockwell assembled a fiction that was pleasant to remember, and made us all feel good. Including myself. My *Boys' Life* mind had been honed and buffed by the *Saturday Evening Post* covers that celebrated so much I seemed to have forgotten. What access did I have to the real past? Where might it be said to be located? It was my first dim perception that *history* was not a volume of authorized texts, to which, in time of doubt, I would always have access, but rather a landscape of immense and cloudy horizons peopled with figures of my own imagination. The past to which I had access was a film that flickered on my own eyeballs. I might well buff it up, and add to or subtract from it (as I had just done in *The Field of Vision*), but I would never find it on those maps nailed to the walls of railroad stations. Norman Rockwell had his version—the gentle, white-haired old lady (a negotiable image, in the absence of an icon) and the decent small boy, "snapped" at the moment of prayerful silence as they say grace in a "rough" railroad café—and I would eventually prove to have mine if I insisted on writing about it. At the extremities of our lives, youth and age, we had established two durable fictions, but even as I prepared to mock them, I was aware they were receding. I, too, was receding, unobserved by myself, on a belt of time external to my perceptions, about which I sometimes felt quite superior. Hadn't I learned, as a fiction writer, how to run it both forward and reverse? The flashback, that bit of craft cunning, permitted me to conjure up a time of my own, all the while concealing from myself the time in which I was captive. I would get a glimpse of a larger time in those first photographs from space, where planet earth, a sort of timepiece, ticked away like a pocket watch. I would never long to be free, however, of the tricks time would play on such an observer as myself, able to stop time in such a way the blur in the film indicated its passage, a happening to which I bore elaborate witness.

This elusive, ineluctable time had become a commonplace property of fiction. Katherine Anne Porter's story "Old Mortality" closes with Miranda's reflections on her entrapment in time past, but her high hopes for time future.

. . . I can't live in their world any longer, she told herself, listening to the voices back of her. Let them tell their stories to each other. Let them go on explaining how things happened. I don't care. At least I can know the truth about what happens to me, she assured herself silently, making a promise to herself, in her hopefulness, her ignorance.

As a young, and not so young, man, I felt that the conjunction of time and place—in particular, place—that left on me such a memorable impression was a property of the place and the time rather than of an event that took place within me. I also felt that such impressions of time and place were commonplace. Anyone (I felt) with a past would share them. The passage of time, indeed, had given rise to these impressions.

After a lifetime of being time's fool, and observing my own peculiar behavior, I conclude that my response to the time-place syndrome is not as widespread as I had imagined. Ingredients are present in nostalgia, but they are like shavings that have not taken fire. I know these feelings, and I feel such ties, but that is not what I am describing. Many, if not all, writers share it, since it is part of their purpose to recover losses, but the parallel I feel to be more exact is what many feel for "holy" places. That is my feeling, once I allow for a profoundly different orientation. Had I been bred or trained to religious observance, or sentiments, I would have been more than open to religious vibrations, to unearthly perceptions, to "seeing" the appropriate manifestations. Rather than merely open, I would have been eager. Between me and these "places" there is a pact that is earthly enough, in its origins, but with a bit of cultivation gives off its palpable aura. Henry James has captured both its earthly and its unearthly trappings.

To be at all critically, or as we have been fond of calling it, analytically minded—over and beyond an inherent love of the general many-colored picture of things—is to be subject to the superstition that objects and places, coherently grouped, disposed for human use and addressed to it, must have a sense of their own, a mystic meaning proper to themselves to give out: to give out, that is, to the participant at once so interested and so detached as to be moved to a report of the matter.

That remarkably accommodates the sensations I have been evoking, and a lifetime of considering their complexity. I would add to this the exposed but uncritical soul of the child—or any person, such as myself, who accepted the world before he analyzed it, and accumulated a large, ticking store of impressions saturated with their own mystic meaning to give out. I became, as if on a higher order, the participant so interested and so detached that I was moved to a report on the matter.

On such a participant as myself, actual events, casual or dramatic, are of relative unimportance. They might be likened to the blurs in a photograph, indicating time's passage. If my training had been religious, my participation would surely have spoken of "voices," of visitations, of materializations, and called on the resources of the "séance" to give substance to my sensations. The space beneath the porch, or some other concealment, provides the child with his own magical trappings, and I am impressed—as a restless analyst—with how closely they resemble the more orthodox holy places. In Chicago, grown too large for concealment, I attributed qualities to everything at hand, and to routines that emphasized recurrence. The streetcar ride from the Loop: the platform of this car became for me a "place" of ritual observation, with the smell of the track sand as incense, and the view down the streets to the east, the vista over the lake, a prospect of life enhancement. Chicago, indeed, mystically collaborated with a naive but highly conscious young man whose inner voices required a cultivation of more outward forms. I was perhaps overripe for the picking, the quick transplant to Eden, the California oasis that mingled the groves of academe with those of lemons and oranges. In such wise I was approaching that moment, as a participant, when the mystic meanings to which I had been exposed, and it was proper of things to give out, would begin to elicit from me a lifelong response.

This clarified for me why, on my return from Europe, and before I had written a line of fiction, I found myself evoking in words these epiphanal images from my boyhood, those objects and places, coherently grouped, disposed for human use and addressed to it. In terms of what was given, I had been destined to be such a participant.

425

In THE WINTER OF 1956, I APPLIED FOR A STAY AT
the Huntington Hartford Foundation, a colony for writers, painters
and composers, in Santa Monica canyon just north of Bel Air. In the
middle of March I headed west, by car, in my familiar flight pattern.
My expectations as a writer were on the rise, but so was my discontent with my personal life.

Throughout our married life, my wife often felt the need for
the companionship of older women. With such a self-preoccupied
husband, this was perhaps understandable. Her need for such
companionship had its origin in the unusual nature—or denature—
of her mother. Deprived of this affection and nurture, my wife had
learned to find it in the context of her teaching, and a shared love
of music. To keep my mind on my work, I would wangle ways to
be gone. So in the middle of March, I made another of my welcome
escapes.

Somewhere near McCook, Nebraska, in a seasonable blizzard,
I left the car in a rising drift and walked along a fence to a gas station.
A dozen or more stranded travelers were huddled around an electric
heater. There we spent the night, swapping stories, sipping quantities
of instant coffee. By mid-morning, however, it was warming and sunny
and the road to the west had been opened. Just a few miles ahead,
in a defile where cattle had huddled out of the winds, the blowing
snow had covered them over to a depth of fifteen feet. More than three
hundred had suffocated. Following close upon the plow that opened
the road, I could see the white-faced Herefords, still propped upright,
a frieze of bodies in the low relief of the snowbank. Twenty minutes
down the road, there was not enough snow to conceal the grain stubble, and I did not discuss the blizzard, or the snow-buried cattle, with
the travelers from the west in the next diner. This was known to be
a country of remarkable liars and farfetched tales.

Two days later, northwest of Santa Fe, I looked for the adobe
house with the beautiful doorway I had photographed in 1940, for
The Inhabitants. I didn't find it, but I sat for several hours, my back
against a sun-baked wall, in a silence that seemed an inaudible music,
the dazzle of the light penetrating my eyelids. Another time, this moment would have been sufficient, but I wanted other company than
my own. To bear the occasion in mind I bought a small Navajo rug,

of traditional patterns and colors, to be there on the wall in whatever room I might wake up in.

A few days later, on a narrow dirt road winding above a dry firetrap of an arroyo, I got out of the car at a huge iron gate to announce my arrival. This was done by a phone call to the lodge, where a button was pressed and the gate swung open. As I made my windy descent into the canyon, I caught glimpses of the lodge, the skylights of the studios assigned to painters, and in the clearing below me a pattern of tiles in a swimming pool emptied of water. Someone was playing Gershwin's *Rhapsody in Blue,* repeating and repeating the same opening chords.

Among the Hartford residents that season was Edward Hopper, who rose from where he was seated, it seemed to me, in sections, a structure in the process of assemblage, to stand towering solemnly above his petite and pert wife. (He lowered himself to his seat in a similar manner, collapsing behind the posts of his knees.) I would often exchange with Hopper a series of uncoded, inscrutable glances as I listened to the gossip of his wife who was enjoying a holiday among talkers. An original splinter from early Yankee floor planking, Hopper, it was clear, preferred total social deprivation to what passed for social contact. I liked as much of him as I got to know, and often saw that he got his second cup of coffee.

Sam Kaner, an attractive, companionable young artist from New York, who had lived in Paris after the war, among other respectable distinctions had read one of my books. This put him in the class by himself. We began our friendship discussing that book, *Man and Boy,* for which he had a keen and experienced appreciation in his role as a husband and a father. His very pretty Danish wife, with their daughter, made her home with her family in Copenhagen, a topic that inspired the bohemian Sam Kaner to artful passages of self-mockery. We would often begin our talk at the lunch hour, with the sandwiches brought to our cabins, then continue it under the fog that usually veiled the beach where Sunset Boulevard met the sea. This shroud of fog was deceptive since it intensified, rather than diminished, the sun's glare. By mid-afternoon, when it burned away, many of the paler mermaids were already parboiled, iced with gobs of Noxzema. Sam and I would spread our towels just back from the sand edging the water, with a critic's view of the day's offerings.

This chick, with her sun-tan oil, her beach towel, her rubber volleyball, and her radio, came along the beach at the edge of the water where the sand was firm. Soft sand shortens the legs and reduces their

427

charms as you may know. This one pitched her camp where the sand was dry, slipped on one of these caps with the simulated hair, smoked her cigarette, then went in for a dip. Nothing particular, just a run-of-the-mill sort of chick. (Love Among the Cannibals, 1957)

We were usually back at the Foundation for dinner, where the food was good and the company congenial. The mix of personalities was continually changing and restoring the bottomless well of gossip. Max Eastman, vital, handsome, and a source of some apprehension for his plump, blond Russian wife, was instrumental in getting the pool filled with water, and the first to bounce the clanking diving board. One Sunday, Gérard Philippe—as if part of a tour—added real Hollywood luster to our retreat, and I liked him both as a person and an actor. His beautiful French wife seemed to feel the burden of a husband so disarmingly captivating. A few years later, when I learned of his death, I felt a keen personal loss.

On rare occasions, such as a good foreign film, some of us made the long drive into Westwood. As we returned to the Foundation, dipping into and out of the series of canyons along the palisades, the white lights streaming toward us, the red taillights receding, the ineffable sense of adventure that is part of movement, that cunningly enhances romantic expectations, would be so palpable it shamed me to feel it. With the sun's rise these sentiments would burn off, like the fog, but they would return, undiminished, with the evening. If there was appropriate music on the radio, or the appropriate girl in the seat beside you, these moments, however delusive, would prove memorable.

One evening we were invited to a party in the exclusive Bel Air enclave just north of UCLA. There the son of a prominent Midwestern meat packer had bought a mansion. He fancied himself a jazz musician, and had married a Hollywood starlet. In the Hollywood fashion, clusters of partygoers, strangers to each other, milled about for a while and then left. I was captivated by the host's widowed mother, one of the long-suffering agents of mercy and terror I believed I had patented, and she seemed to recognize in me one of her lost prodigal sons. All evening she shared with me her nostalgia for what had been, her anxiety for the future. I sat with several albums of Minnesota photographs, including a leather-bound volume in which her husband was praised as a founder and pillar of the community. I studied his portrait. Toil-worn and thickened hands were placed on his meaty thighs; a chain looped across his wrinkled vest. How many days of his life had he wondered where the time he wound on his watch had gone? Her fingers moved across the photograph for the reassurance

428

her eyes failed to give her. Her hand resting on my arm, she acknowledged that after each party many things were missing. A silver-backed brush from her dresser. Could I explain it? Would guests invited to her home actually steal things? I imagined that in her purse she clutched to her lap she kept her jewels. She was eager for me to read about her husband, born on a farm thirty-one miles north of Oslo, a good, decent, half-conscious man dead at the summit of his career, his name on the best-selling bacon in the supermarkets. I was what she needed, she took the trouble to tell me, not just to advise her son but to be an example to him (I a young man from the same unpopulated landscape, who had come to California and not married a starlet), and I said, yes, yes, of course I would be back, but I knew I would not. One window of her new home offered a view of the cloudland irresistible to starlets, star-makers and such incurable pipe-dreamers as myself, so that the bathos of our mutual pipe dream no longer struck me as amusing. In Joyce's story "The Dead," the character Gabriel, at a moment of deep emotion, catches a glimpse of his reflection in the cheval glass, his face with the expression that always puzzled him when he saw it in a mirror. So I, too, saw myself as a ludicrous, fatuous figure. Only a touch more consciousness was necessary to see that in this tableau I was the most bathetic, since my pretenses were the least defensible. As an observer, I had caught my reflection in the mirror I so often held up to others.

In Brentwood, just a few blocks north of Sunset, Leon Howard lived in a spacious Mediterranean villa happily out of fashion at the time he had bought it. Both Leon and his wife loved parties, and they had found the ideal house to accommodate them. On my frequent visits I would sometimes meet scholars from Europe or Japan who enjoyed, as I did, the Howard hospitality. Leon's book on Melville had just been published, and the Melville scholar Jay Leyda might be on hand.

I had written a short, once-over-lightly piece on Melville, for *The Territory Ahead,* which I was not eager to show to Leon, but I had brought along with me several others, including one on Hemingway, that I wanted his opinion on. To my great relief, he liked it, and thought it said something fresh on a very tired subject. That was high praise from Leon, and on the strength of it I brought over the Faulkner piece. A departmental party was in session, and a young woman introduced herself to me as she brought me a drink. A handsome blond Rhine maiden, with a peeling tan, she had read two of my books, and she wanted to talk. I had to rock back on my heels to keep my eyes on her level. A woman who likes men, and knows herself to be attractive, need have little concern with the usual preliminaries. She wrote her number on a matchbook cover, but cautioned me not to call her during meal hours. She cooked and child-sat for a family of six in Brentwood, out from New York for a California summer. The young man who had brought her, pleased with his role as an escort, took no offense at her expanding interests.

"I paint," she said to me in parting. "I'd like to paint you."

I said something or other about my lack of time, and caught the glance of Leon, across the room from us. His gaze was so absorbed and direct he seemed unaware that I was looking at him. Did he clearly perceive, in this casual encounter, so much more than I did? In his gaze I felt the detachment necessary for appraising the possible results. Later we talked about Faulkner, and about the teaching I might do at USC the following summer, but he did not allude, at that time or later, to my first meeting with the Greek, the name she would bear in *Love Among the Cannibals*.

As willing as she seemed to be, the Greek found it hard to fit me into her schedule. She had several classes at UCLA. On occasion we discussed her reading on the telephone. I usually met her near the Brentwood residence, where she lived in. On occasion she might run late, and I would catch up on a little of my own back reading. She was usually still in her maid's white outfit, which went well with her figure and her tan. We might drive to the beach, near Malibu, or to the deli lunchroom in Brentwood where she liked the pie and I liked iced tea made with mini ice cubes. These were unpredictable encounters. She might be moved to throw her arms around me—a hazard not to be dealt with lightly—or would sit chewing gum and reading Conrad. Her taste in literature I judged to be good, since she liked us both. Another time, we might discuss the young man in Colorado who wanted her to marry him and sent her money. Would she like Colorado? Had I been there? Knowing her as I did, did I *think* she would like it? The thought of horseback riding brought out the Valkyrie in her nature. To please me—only me?—she changed her bra style to one less revealing and uplifting. In due time—which proved to be considerable—I perceived that her features were remarkably common. But little I cared. I was hooked on her vitality, and the desire she could bring to her eyes.

Late one afternoon, she called me to say that she would have the house to herself that evening. Just at dusk, I parked in the street below, and made my way up the driveway to this assignation. I found her sprawled out on her cot in the small maid's room, watching TV and

430

eating a bowl of sliced peaches. Her interest seemed to have drifted to other matters. We sat there watching TV together. I was prepared to be a patient seducer and sipped warm beer until the movie ended. We both needed a shower, and she took one. Somewhere upstairs I could hear the water drumming, and above it the sound of an approaching car. Lights flashed at the window. I heard the shrill, high-pitched squeals of the returning children. One of them ran into the house, shrieking her name. She had told me how the children loved her! I had just time to roll from the bed, and skid beneath it, before the door pushed open. The child ran up to the bed—I saw bobby-socked feet—turned to look around, then ran out. I lay there as the house filled with the inhabitants. There was talk in the kitchen. I heard her chatting with the children. Some time later she entered the room, closed the door. She took a seat on the bed, her broad flat feet on the carpet. I could smell the warmth of her showered body, the fragrance of the soap. The springs began to creak and bounce with her laughter. When she sprawled out wheezing on her back, I gave her a good thump from below with my knees. That set her to gasping hoarsely. Half an hour might have passed while I waited for the first floor to empty of children. She made a place for me on the rim of her cot. My rage was less at her than at the clown, smeared with floor dirt, who sat there watching her set her hair in curlers. The painted nails of her toes were like crushed grapeskins. It did not flatter her figure to be propped up in bed, like a piece of soft chocolate. Quite beyond conception was the fact that I had panted with desire as I came up the driveway.

Finished with her curlers, she smoked my Delicados and seemed to take pains not to intrude on my reflections. On the walls of her room were photographs of boys chasing her into the sea, leaping with her from diving boards, packed with her into the seats of convertibles. At the foot of her bed loomed a poster of the mad King Ludwig's fairy castle in Liechtenstein. That gave me the last smile, if not the last laugh. She was called upstairs to tuck her kiddies in bed, and I was able to make my escape down the driveway. I drove around for quite a while, up the coast as far as the Trancas restaurant, where I stopped for a cup of coffee, and listened to a rehearsal, in the adjoining booth, of the Hollywood and Vine art of seduction. I deserved every word of it. Driving back through Malibu, where the surf was pounding under the cabins, I caught a glimpse, through one of the open doorways, of the high-fishnet style of the interior, just as a Romeo of mature vintage escorted his Rhine maiden to the car. I've no idea why, but she carried her shoes. This would provide me with the image that was true to the Greek and Horter, and to which I owed my quick recovery from the events of the evening. It is the girl who kicked off her shoes that I still bear in mind.

I never saw my Rhine maiden again, not that I didn't try. When I called the residence, a woman's voice said, "You the one who was crazy about her? She just left. You can just be grateful if you don't find her. She's a willful woman. She just takes what she wants."

I had been smitten by a real enough dream girl, with toenails like crushed grapeskins, but the one to seduce me had kicked off her shoes as she entered a Malibu cabin. Losses and gains were equally shared.

It was my good luck that we had in residence, at the Foundation, a flesh-and-blood jazz pianist, a self-described poet of the black keys. One or two of his tunes, played on Broadway, had trickled down to the jukeboxes. One hundred and eighty pounds of heart, he was a wonderful man to watch. For my condition, he was just what the doctor ordered.

"Listen to this one, man," he would say, and play something that sounded familiar. It was always familiar. But that, indeed, was its virtue. Mac—as I chose to call him—saw a great future for both of us. For one of his new tunes I coined these lyrics:

> *What next?*
> *The life of love I knew*
> *No longer loves the things I do.*
> *What next?*

I felt that once I had the appropriate voice, the casting would come easy.

If you have sometimes wondered who really wears the two-tone ensembles that set the new car styling, Mac is your man. That's why I keep him down at the beach. He's quite a sight in his Hawaiian shorts, made of coconut fiber, a cerise jacket with a bunny-fur texture, a sea-green beret, and something like an ascot looped at his throat. . . .

To get away from the raw material—the virus of suggestion threatened to kill me—I left the Foundation and headed for Philadelphia before my period of residence had ended. During the long drive back, I often pulled off the road to make notes on the maps, or anything handy. In my eagerness to hold the wind in my kite, I kept up a flow of two-way dialogue, featuring Mac, Horter and one Billy Harcum, a Southern belle, appropriate to the occasion. On arriving in Wayne, I went to my study before I unpacked the car. The great pleasure of this enterprise was that of a romance without hang-ups. I worked the long, hot days, and got up at night to take dictation from voices that did not sleep. By early October I had the first draft of *Love Among the Cannibals*.

Just as I had hungered for the sea and the sun when I had left in the spring, the dense, lush growth of a Main Line summer now had a soothing effect on me. For the first time in my career, I believed the book I was writing would find me many new readers. A young friend, David Hawke, to whom I read many of the chapters, assured me that *The Cannibals* had the verve, the pace, and above all the *appetite* that would seize the reader and hold him. We spent much of our time wheezing with laughter. The book had also emerged, as if on order, to cut the ties, real and imaginary, that I had developed with the past in my recent fiction. *The Cannibals* explicitly cut such ties, as if with the intention of cutting the author adrift. There are few readers of fiction who trouble to distinguish between the "I" of the narrating voice and the author, a confusion of identities they find too agreeable to either surrender or examine. Even my friend Kitty Bowen, once the book had been published, sometimes glanced at me with Elizabethan misgiving, curious as to what extent she might have misjudged my nature. Kitty had a new book of her own going to press, and my wife was busy with the galleys of *The Lion and the Throne*. Sometimes we stayed on for a buffet supper in the patio, listening to music. These occasions approximated the good life (I repeatedly felt the urge to say so) in so far as I was able to participate in it, or to judge it—good food and good companionship—yet a strand of disease, not quite discontent but a twitching, febrile need to be somewhere *else,* to be someone *else,* to become rather than to merely be, faintly stirred the humid air we all breathed with such satisfaction. *What next?* That chord, tiresomely plucked, drifting in on the breeze, then drifting away, was as present in this civilized, cultivated garden of plenty, within sight and almost sound of similar occasions, as to Nick Carraway at West Egg gazing toward the lights of Gatsby's mansion. What next? Would it be my rendition of "Just One More Chance"?

In November I put aside *The Cannibals* to do a piece for *Holiday* magazine on the plains. I turned to this assignment with the appetite of a man long deprived of his soul food. As a writer who had thought to put all that behind him, this was somewhat puzzling. My editor at *Holiday* liked the piece, and urged me to do others for them. Such as? What about the cars in my life? He had read enough of my fiction to know that cars had played both leading and subordinate roles. One of my childhood memories was of car lights, smoking like torches, crossing the yard as if to enter the house. My father had bought the car in Columbus, a distance of forty miles, and driven it the forty miles in second gear rather than risk the crisis of shifting. That car, an Overland, would soon be followed by a Willys Knight, famed for its sleeve-valve motor and soft blue exhaust. That gave way to a Big Six Studebaker with fold-away seats and flapping side curtains. A Liberty sedan, with plush velour upholstery and a vase for flowers on the doorposts, gave way, briefly, to a Reo Flying Cloud, and for about two hundred miles, an Essex Coach.

The writer who had just symbolically cut his ties with the past spent most of the Christmas season splicing new ties. These cars were links in a chain that led me back to the winter of 1927, when I had arrived in California with my father in the sidecar of a Harley-Davidson motorcycle. The sun shone, pigeons wheeled, and the open cars came down Sunset, with the good-looking women holding on to their hats. A young man had just swum to Catalina Island, winning a lot of William Wrigley's money, and he could be seen, covered with lard, on the front page of the newspapers. In a used-car lot on Sixth Street, a Marmon touring car, with wire wheels and a patented Liberty airplane engine, was waiting to begin its eastward passage with a carload of idlers, a fox terrier, and three passengers on the fold-away seats, one of them my father. Some five weeks later, that car would be abandoned, at high noon, in Lake Village, Arkansas, at the moment the levee broke a few miles to the north, and it had always been my secret, inscrutable intent to one day return and see if it was still there.

How does a boy seventeen years of age, and healthy, having long admitted to such ties, cut them? He eventually writes a tie-cutting book. He writes a tie-splicing book. It's hard to do malice to a great nation where the cutting of ties, the splicing of ties, the staunching, securing and sealing of ties, the rupturing, the breaching, the dissolving of ties, is the passion that binds us, one to the other, the fast and the slow bleeders, shoring up with Band-Aids our accumulating arrears.

Holiday found "The Cars in My Life" amusing, but felt I should turn to something more substantial. In *The Field of Vision* I had written about Mexico. How about a piece on Mexico? This suggestion greatly appealed to me, since it would finance my return, and oblige me to see more of the country. For Christmas, from Acapulco, Señor Mendoza sent a family portrait taken by one of the beach

434

photographers. There sat the massive señora, spread wide as a melting idol, with her tribe assembled about her, and Señor Mendoza, in his beret, holding the hand of the wide-eyed Carmelita. I looked to the side and behind these figures for Mac and Horter, for the Greek and Billy Harcum, who were more real to me than the pile of sand from which the shovel handle still protruded. Having lived for months with the scene I had invented, Mac and Billy Harcum, Horter and the Greek, the day-by-day disassembling of the car on the highway, I had perplexing feelings about the real Acapulco. Was it a tie to reestablish, or to relinquish? In the light of the fiction I had just written, the real seemed unreal. This was disturbing to my sense of facts, my love of things as they were, my respect for memory and the emotion, both of which, in the play of my imagination, had been freely altered and corrupted. I wanted the real world, with its affections, and the adornments of the imagination. Yet I felt that the *real* had been curiously diminished. Was this loss the expense of the imaginary gain? The real had not as yet become the phantom that recedes as we approach it, peeling away like the layers of an onion, but was a commonly perceived state of nature confirmed by observation. I would wait several years for Wittgenstein's comment "My aim is to teach you to pass from a piece of disguised nonsense to something that is patent nonsense" to momentarily locate myself in an orbit subject to predictable corrections, including the train that waited for the arrival of the station.

A writer's life is not entirely lacking in drama. On a mid-winter trip to New York, as I waited, on my publisher's floor, for the arrival of an elevator, I was joined by a graying but vital woman who paced up and down the foyer, pushing the buttons. A handsome woman, with a brisk professional manner, she proved to be unaware that her bloomers had drooped, to hang like a harem costume below her skirt. Here, indeed, was a moment of truth and I met it. We were alone, but as I stepped forward I hoarsely whispered the necessary information.

"Young man," she said to me, "speak up! I can't hear you!"

So I spoke up. I also threw in a few pointed gestures. She tilted forward to check, saw the problem, and walked from me to the limits of the foyer, where she stooped and hoisted the bloomers. We descended to the street in the same elevator. Some weeks later I was able to verify that the lady was Dorothy Canfield Fisher.

That incident may have had something to do with a stop I made in the used-book department of Brentano's, on Fifth Avenue. Waiting there for me, after a search of many years, at a price that was plainly

435

a blunder, was the Oxford edition of John Keats's letters, in the orange buckram with the paper labels on the spine. All but a few pages of the introduction were still uncut. I had coveted these volumes since I had first set eyes on them in the library of Pomona College. I was certain that the clerk would note the mistake in the price, but he was engrossed in expressing his own love of Keats. Two hours later, safely home in Wayne, I called my friend Eiseley to announce my triumph, and point out that the pages were still uncut. A still further refinement, with me in mind, was that the English printer, John Johnson, had bound into each volume an extra paper label for the spine. My excitement about this coup led me to forget, for the moment, my encounter with Mrs. Canfield Fisher, a literary incident calculated to please the ladies.

In mid-February, shortly after midnight, we were awakened by the phone's clatter. My editor, Jerry Gross, was calling from his home. "Prepare yourself," he said to me. I self-prepared. *The Field of Vision* had won the National Book Award for fiction. He explained that there would be no public announcement until the award ceremony, late in March, more than five weeks away.

My wife and I discussed this windfall briefly, then lay awake most of the night with the aftertremors. Surely this would enhance the public reception of *Love Among the Cannibals,* a manuscript I had postponed submitting. I did not want a publisher disappointed by *The Field of Vision* pondering the "problems" of *The Cannibals.* The effects of this on the author were to be seen, and heard, in the buzz given off by the aroused expectations, none of which he was free to discuss. To our friends it perhaps seemed obvious, and to at least one of them it was a pain.

"For heaven's sakes, Wrighty," Kitty Bowen said to me, "I'm sure you deserve it, but stop acting like a ninny."

Once I had been exposed to classical music, I had come to rely on it for both pleasure and relaxation. We loved good jazz, from Dixie to Benny Goodman, but most of the records we bought were of chamber music. Our first extravagant purchase, after the war, had been the London Gramophone record player, the size of a small piano, capable of an unearthly fidelity. With this example in mind, I had become a high-fidelity addict. Recently, to accommodate my wanderings, I wanted a sound system that would travel. I found it in the Ampex tape recorders and amplifiers built into sturdy, compact pieces of luggage. The book award money made it possible for me to own this equipment. Most of March and April, I spent hours of each day transferring our record library to tapes. For several years, the money we had once reserved for books had been channeled to collecting records that would not soon find their way to the new LPs. We were great for Casals, unaccompanied, playing Bach, Landowska on the harpsichord, the Budapest Quartet, and early albums of chamber music with the Victor Red Seal label. Purcell's Trumpet Voluntary, played on our London Gramophone, ceremoniously opened most of our social occasions. I often relied on Ralph Ellison's tips for cigars—the new leaf coming in from the Canaries and from Honduras—and it was Ralph who called to my attention a new album of flamenco music from Spain.

My publishers had an apartment in the East Fifties made available to visiting bigwigs, and for a few days in March I would be one. I went to the city in advance, to bask in the reflection I saw in shop-windows. My friend Sam Kaner was a good man to meet at such a time, with his own private blend of affection and sarcasm. Sam had applied for a fellowship that would take him to Venice for a year, and we talked about that promise as we strolled around the city.

Award ceremonies are seldom moments of drama, but I contrived to make this one a bit unusual. When called to the podium by the master of ceremonies, I made the ascent without trouble, read my acceptance comments, then scooped *all* of the papers from the podium and made my escape. The cries I heard swelling behind me I accepted as part of the applause. I had reached the center aisle before the emcee caught me, sorted his own notes from those that I clutched, then returned to the platform in waves of applause! As my wife said, and a few friends confirmed, the moment was unforgettable.

In interviews with the press the following day, I was frequently asked to what I attributed my memory for details of the past. What details? A few were quickly mentioned. Take, for example, the way the front wheel of a bike will continue to spin when the rider spills it on its side in the yard. Or take the way keys for tightening up skate clamps were invariably bent. It pleased me to be thought so clever, but there was nothing unusual in a bent skate key. Nor would any small, frozen-fingered boy soon forget the battle he had to tighten the clamps. As for that twirling bike wheel, I saw it clearly enough, but I would not say that I remembered it, *then* wrote it. More than memory was at work in what I remembered. The effort and act of memory enabled me to see what I had often both observed, and ignored, until that moment when I actually described it. Thanks to the questions

I was asked, I began to ask myself what I actually *remembered,* and what seemed to appear at the moment of writing—like the voices and actions in a séance.

"Reading your book brought it all back!" one reader said, as if he saw it captured like the fly in amber, embalmed in time until someone's memory brought it back.

One reason I see it all so clearly is that I have so often put it into writing. Perhaps it is the writing I remember, the vibrant image I have made of the memory impression. . . . Image-making is indivisibly a part of remembering.

If I attempt to distinguish between fiction and memory, and press my nose to memory's glass to see more clearly, the remembered image grows more illusive, like the details in a Pointillist painting. I recognize it, more than I see it. The recognition is a fabric of emotion, as immaterial as music. In this defect of memory do we have the emergence of imagination? If we remembered both vibrantly and accurately—a documentary image rather than an impression—the imaginative faculty would be blocked, lacking the stimulus necessary to fill in what is empty or create what is missing. . . . Precisely where memory is frail and emotion is strong, imagination takes fire. (Earthly Delights, Unearthly Adornments, 1978)

I stayed on in the city for several days, breathing air that seemed a bit bubbly with oxygen. One day, I was seated alone in my editor's office, sipping coffee as I peered into an adjoining office. Several Harcourt, Brace executives—I had met them briefly—were crouched about the chair of one of their number, who had lowered his head to read from a manuscript in his lap. He spoke in an excited whisper. Occasionally he glanced up to share his appreciation. As he went on reading, I caught fragments of sentences that sounded familiar.

. . . My room was dark, but the door to the bathroom was open, and this little girl with her glass of ice water stood facing the mirror. I watched her empty the water into the sink, but retain the ice. She put the loose cubes in a face towel, whacked them on the edge of the sink until she had crushed them, then took the crushed ice, a handful of it, and slipped it into the cups of her halter. All the ice she had; then she cupped it to her breasts. I saw her face reflected in the mirror, the eyes closed in a grimace of pain, the teeth clamped down on her lower lip till it turned white. (Love Among the Cannibals)

438

The pleasure shared by the reader and his listeners was interrupted with loud guffaws and thigh slapping. At the appearance of a secretary, the manuscript was slipped into a drawer of his desk. His colleagues made a quick departure. Sometime later, walking the streets, I marveled less at boys being boys than I did at the naiveté of the author. It had been a delight to write that scene, but I would not read it again without the appropriate grimace.

Fortunately for my unsettled state of mind, I had made arrangements to teach a course at the USC summer school. Just before I left, the painter Ynez Johnston, whom I had met at the Hartford Foundation, wrote to tell me I should call her good friend Jo Kantor, an art collector and dealer, in Beverly Hills. I thought it unlikely I would—I had lectures to prepare, but I put the number that would change my future where I could find it if I wanted it.

I left for California in early May, and my wife, to have a visit with her mother, rode along with me as far as Cleveland. Mother had given up the house and moved to an apartment in Shaker Heights. We spent the night in a motel, where, again about midnight, we had our second surprise from my editor. New American Library had bought the paperback rights to *Love Among the Cannibals* for twenty thousand dollars. As part of this agreement they would also publish *The Field of Vision*. This was the largest advance I had ever received. I thought it would surely ruin my sleep, but after a short and practical discussion with my wife, my half share of this vast sum of money did not weigh heavily on me, and I was soon asleep.

In the morning, after one of Mother's calorie-coded, one-egg breakfasts, I drove back to the freeway, dimly aware of tremors in a part of my nature previously unheard from, and conscious that tumblers were falling before I had turned the key in the lock. I liked the sensation. By late afternoon, in Indiana, riding the tailwind of my rising expectations, I decided to drive right through the night to see if I could pick up some music from Mexico on the airwaves. Whatever else might turn up in my future, I also had an agreement with *Holiday* magazine that Mexico would be in it, and soon. And that I liked.

BETWEEN NEEDLES AND LOS ANGELES, EVEN
early in May, I drove with wet towels at the car windows and
cooled my windburned face with swipes of lip ice. In the shade
of gas station awnings, the horizon shimmered like cooling ashes.
The wavering line at the center of the highway seemed to reel me
backward to the safaris of my boyhood: the flapping side curtains,
thumping tires, the ascending hiss of the steam on the inclines, and
the spouting geyser of rust-colored water when I unscrewed the radiator
cap.

Long after sunset, the car interior cooling like an oven, I stopped
at a lunchstand in Claremont, where I had once waited on tables. A
fan droned, stirring the paper napkins. The cook, a heat- and light-
bleached cockney from Liverpool, leaned on his padded elbows at the
food slot window, a cigarette between his lips. I had stopped to have
a milkshake and a cheeseburger before confessing my ties with the
establishment, a vital, freckle-faced bird-eyed woman and her totter-
ing singer of snatches of cockney ballads, who greeted me with "How's
tricks, matey?" My ties with his past had eroded. He cooked my
cheeseburger braced on a crutch. His legs were shot. Even in the dim
past his wife had referred to him as im-*po*-tent. "Besides, he's im-*po*-
tent," she would assure me, a calamity I could judge for myself, if
I had the nerve.

On my return from Europe, in the fall of 1934, I had waited on
tables for Ma and Pa Slade for one "hot meal" a day. When I appeared
with my girl one weekend—pleased to share her radiant bloom and
uncommon beauty—Ma Slade remained in the kitchen while Pa Slade
hobbled about in his carpet slippers. She was there to take my money
at the register, however, and kept me waiting while she checked my
meal ticket. "Don't you trouble to come back," she said to me with
a smile, "if you're going to bring *her*."

Just short of two in the morning, I arrived at the Howard home
in Brentwood. The front door was unlocked, and a desk lamp burned
in the study. On the desk, the floor and the seats of the chairs were
the term papers Leon had been reading. I used the shower in his study,
then cooled my windburned face by lying in the draft from the patio.
In a neighboring house, the white ceiling lit up when the refrigerator

440

door was opened. I heard the clatter when a glass was added to the dishes in the sink.

A letter from Benjamin DeMott, of Amherst, had been forwarded from Wayne. He wanted me to come to Amherst for a week in October, meet with a few classes, give two lectures. For this I would receive fifteen hundred dollars.

I discussed this with Leon while he fried us some eggs and I burned the toast. He thought that I should do what I could to enhance my standing in the academic community. One day I might need it. Speaking for himself, he thought the life of a teacher, with all its maddening frustrations, was still the most civilized and gratifying of vocations. It impressed me to hear this from a teacher and scholar who gave of himself freely, and daily suffered the familiar academic abuses. With a fresh pack of cigarettes and a new pot of coffee, he returned to the papers in his study.

I had worn out the front tires on the trip west, and drove over to Sears in Santa Monica to check on prices. On my way back, driving east on West Pico and passing a large car lot with wind-flapped banners, I glanced up to see a green Jaguar coupe with the price finger-painted on the windshield: $1,795. I proceeded several miles down the street before what I had seen registered, and it dawned on me, after a lifetime of rejecting, that I could now buy some of the things I wanted, if I wanted them badly enough. I wheeled around to drive back to the car lot; I parked where I could get the bloom of the aristocratic profile. Was it a lizard, a leopard, or a green dragon? It was down in the books as an XK-120, well known to Jaguar fanciers. Sensing my vulnerable state of mind, the salesman was charitable about my Studie, a car that I could brake by dragging my feet. After a spin on a side street, the gears gnashing, the pavement as close as in a toboggan, the Jag was almost all mine for $1,095, a good price for such a great folly. As I drove away, my mind would not hold the point of the matter steady. I had taken the step to West Egg. How far up ahead was the green light on Daisy's dock?

Lacking the panache that went along with the car, I spent several days, and long evenings, explaining why it was that I had bought it, I, of all people, when it was apparent to my friends that I had struck it rich, having written a best seller. Why didn't I play the role that was thrust upon me, life- and dream-enhancing as everybody found it? I was an ignoramus. In explaining my folly to others I hoped to explain it to myself.

On a June Sunday morning, a week or two later, the air along Amalfi Drive already misty with sprinklers, I headed for the beach

441

with an attractive poetess of "middle years," who liked to sit on her feet in cars with bucket seats. As we cruised along Sunset toward the sea, she put her hands to her face as if weeping. The problem? The shame she felt that I—this now famous author—tooling westward toward the Malibu cloudland, had in the seat at my side not one of these ravishing starlets, lonely and captive in the houses we were passing, but an almost old woman of thirty-nine!

Were women *actually* crazy, as well as seeming to be? In answer to the question What did they want?: They wanted what they didn't have; they wanted what was missing. This "aging" woman got something of what she was missing in the attention I gave her to ease her sorrow, to compensate for her losses, bringing plates of French fries and deep containers of Coke (fetched from much too far, with the tide sloshing) to where she sat hugging her knees, with her not so pretty feet buried in the sand. Later I drove her to Trancas, and sat at a table near a Hollywood mogul seducing a starlet who (in her opinion) should have been mine.

What is the case but pitiless in its ferocity?

Seeing this starlet in the flesh, exposed as it was, confirmed the fantasy my companion had brought with her from Kansas, and knowing that we shared this knowledge made us good friends.

When the galleys of *The Territory Ahead* arrived, she offered to help me with them. Why did I prove so reluctant? Thanks to her, I had the feeling that *The Cannibals* had picked up from where I had left it, and was still going on. Any day now, surely, as I cruised down Wilshire, or made the seductive curves on Amalfi, I would run into the Greek, with that smile on her lips, or catch a glimpse of Mac and Horter, in their XK-120, paused at Wilshire and Westwood, waiting for the green light.

On the morning after I had bought the car, I called my wife in Wayne, confessing my guilt. On the spur of the occasion I suggested that she might fly out, later in the summer, and drive back with me. In her silence I sensed more than surprise. This would interrupt her summer with Trudy Caspar, the good and loyal companion who I felt meant the most to her, and a few days later she wrote to tell me that Trudy hoped to be flying out with her, to visit old friends in Beverly Hills.

My teaching went so well that I knew there would be more in my future. I welcomed any excuse to talk about writers and writing. I had written to Ben DeMott suggesting that I would like to talk about the works of Morris—a subject in which I had more interest than the public. Could I publicly discuss novels so few people had read? In a few months *The Territory Ahead* would be published—surely marking the end or the beginning of something—and the author of so many unread novels was eager to take a look rearward at his own works. Since 1942 I had published ten novels, two books of phototext, and one volume of criticism. What was it—in the absence of readers and, up until that spring, in the absence of money—that egged me on? Had I made myself into this creature that found both food and pleasure in the act of writing? Was it through writing that I made sense out of the non-sense outside my study window, and perceptibly diminished the quiet desperation common to those who were not writers? I accepted my calling as a form of living necessary to my own nature, requiring no more reason or persuasion than the flowers on bushes, or the leaves on trees. It did take some doing, but what I was doing came naturally. To cease to do it seemed an unnatural, destructive act. In May of 1958 I saw that I was one of those determined to persist in his folly. At the moment, of course, I was feeling the confirmation of a writer who had made ten thousand dollars, and had been repeatedly identified as the debauched author of a coming best seller.

Late in June I made a call to Josephine Kantor, the friend of Ynez Johnston, and she suggested I come by for a drink. She was busy packing several bags for Europe, and partially packed bags occupied the couches and chairs. We talked about where she planned to live—she was thinking she might live in Paris—as I noted the tapered beauty of her hands. Had I never before been captivated by a woman's hands? One held her cigarette, the other toyed—in the way of women—with a lock of her hair, a graceful movement of her fingers as if they played on keys. With each puff of her cigarette, one hand led my gaze back to her oval face. Of whom was I reminded? Could I—on first meeting a woman who now planned to live in Paris—afford to be reminded of more than that? What did I actually know about her? That I did not at all like her hairstyle. It was the hairdo, in fact, that blocked my urgent sense of recognition. The American male, young or old, has a skimpy repertoire of examples to provide him with models of beauty. Fortunate the man who has the image of a mother, a sister, a surpassing fiction, to blot out the image of the starlet, the blond bombshell, the movie siren. This young woman had no kinship with these models, but my sense of recognition was haunting. Where had I met or seen her? This would tantalize and confound me in the months of her absence, to that moment when, as we left the steamer in Dubrovnik (we were on our way to Venice), several young men lounging on the pier cried out, "Gioconda! Gioconda!" and blew her kisses. In such wise did the hands of my love finally sketch in her face.

I had borne the imprint of this classic oval face, painted by two hundred years of Italian masters, since my long afternoons at the magic lantern in Mrs. Josephare's History of Art class in Chicago. And now, at long last, I had found her. In time, I was able to persuade her to wear her dark hair in the classical manner, drawn back to a bun at the base of her neck, a spectacle that intercepted countless forks of spaghetti during our stay in Venice. The European, especially the Southern European, with his tradition of madonnas and icons, has been bred on images of art and responds instinctively. Nor was it only the men. Jo's classic beauty caught the eyes of the women, selling their vegetables, and the eyes of the boys, hawking their strings of beads, in an instinctive act of homage. To hang strings of beads about the neck of my signora was one of the pleasures of the peddlers of Venice. Mamma mia! Kisses blown from the tips of the fingers. The disinterested pleasure taken by the women (not all! not all!) was for me a special enhancement. In time I learned to be at ease with the bold appreciative stares of the men. I will never forget the signal I saw passed from waiter to barman, and from barman to waiter, as Jo entered or left a café. The thumb and first finger form a circle, and the other three stand up like feathers. *Bellissima.* What compared with the gift of beauty as the gift of life?

But I am still in the room with partially packed bags, inquiring about her plans. In ten days she would take a train to New York, and from there she would sail to France. So I had a week? Did that perhaps work to my advantage? It did make me bold. After our third or fourth evening together, in my worst literary manner I asked her to come live with me and be my love—for the remaining five days. At that time Jo Kantor, née Josephine Mary Rossler, was about to escape from the marriage ties that had bound her, and she was not eager for a new involvement. I had so little to offer, it made me reckless. What did she say when I called to ask her? She said yes.

Jo's talents were many, but none was so unexpected, so unex-ampled, as her laughter. An explosive cawing honk, or honking caw, unmistakably bird-like, was still like no bird previously heard from. The release of this blast was so life-enhancing, it was cause for celebration among her friends, of whom I was now one.

I had rented an apartment in Malibu, out near the pier, and we moved in with our toothbrushes. When the tide was out we did a lot of walking. We ate a lot of her scrambled eggs and my cottage cheese salads. Out of the wisdom of almost a week together I concluded she was my kind of woman. Might she, in time, be in the market for my kind of man? I was old, ripe and wise enough not to ask her, but when I stood in her doorway, thinking I might lose her, I said I was coming to Paris. I asked her to write to me, and she said she would.

At the time we met Jo was reading Albert Camus. I had been a fan of Camus since the first line of his novel, *The Stranger*—"Mother died today. Or, maybe, yesterday; I can't be sure."—a matchless summation of modern alienation. One writer I was eager for Jo to read was Wright Morris. Her intelligence, her ear for the voice of the writer in all that he writes, confirmed my feeling that this young woman was my future and the sooner the better.

In July, I found that I took to teaching and, to my relief, that most of the students took to me. In early August, joined by my wife, I drove north to a writers' conference in Portland, Oregon, along the way mashing in the beautiful nose of the Jaguar. Eleven days of the twelve we were in Portland were taken up with the repairs. I remember little, fortunately, of the long, grueling drive east. My wife's relief to arrive home alive was inexpressible. That same day I packed a bag for Europe, and two days later sailed from New York for Le Havre. I wore a natty new corduroy cruising cap, and my face was still windburned from the drive east. In the fall of 1933, twenty-five years in the past, I had sailed on a freighter for Antwerp, and in so far as I could judge them, there was little changed in my expectations. I was now a fool confirmed in the folly that must make him either wise or lucky. In the meager, skimpy annals of my life as a writer, it had been a good year. Waiting for me in Paris (I hoped) was the woman who would give my life safe harbor, as I faced Gordon Boyd's old dilemma of making success out of failure. That would be one book I would give her to read, when we found time for reading, with a marker inserted at the point where Boyd fancies he can walk on water, just as I was doing at this moment.

THE ILE DE FRANCE DOCKED AT LE HAVRE IN
the late afternoon. I stood in line in the salon to have my papers
checked. I glanced up to see a woman, smartly dressed in black, enter
a side door on the left and cross the room to exit through a door on
the right. She clutched a purse. I could hear the sharp clack of her
heels. "Jo?" I called out, but too late. Many doors, in the next fifteen
minutes, closed behind her, to be opened by me. Each time, however,
thanks to the bag I carried, I lost ground. I saw her like a suspect in
a Hitchcock movie, forever receding down corridors, through doorways, never glancing to the right, left or rear. Could I be sure it was
her? I only saw her from the rear. I had written to tell her when the
boat would dock, but it had never crossed my mind she would meet
it. Unmistakably *her,* it seemed to me, was the intent, purposive way
she descended stairs, entered or left rooms, without a pause in the
crisp heel-clacking.

From the deck, where I inhaled the fresh air, I saw her sidewise,
descending the gangplank. *That* would be her. "Jo!" I bellowed. She
paused to glance skyward. Dark glasses gave her the aspect of a movie
star traveling incognito. She waved, then returned up the gangplank.
Moments later she found me, seized my hand, and led me back through
the ship, down to the pier, where the train was about to leave for Paris.
There would always be this apprehension about the departing train.
We found an empty compartment, took seats at the window, and in
its light I saw her face. The exercise had flushed it like that of a
schoolgirl. She removed her sunglasses to powder her nose. My delight
and excitement were so keen I did not speak. Out the window, the
landscape slowly darkened. I gripped the small hand I was holding,
and for once in my life my emotions were in keeping with my extravagant expectations. What did I say? What did she say? I have no
idea.

In the Madison Hotel, just off the Place St. Germain, the young
clerk examined me rather than my passport, with unconcealed distaste.
Could it have been for *me* she had been waiting? He leaned over the
counter to peer at my luggage. Nor could he pronounce my first name.
As he paused to clean the lenses of his glasses, he gazed with sympathy at the young woman beside me. I made the mistake of saying

446

a few words in French. Would I please write it down? He provided a pencil and a pad of paper. My humiliation was brief, however, since I was the one with the girl. The art nouveau cage of the elevator provided a balloonist's view of the lobby. On the top floor, holding a tray of glasses, the *femme du chambre* stepped back to get a less obstructed view of me. Her eyes rolled, but she quickly recovered. What hadn't she seen in her years of service! A bed and a wardrobe crowded the room (one of Jo's partially *un*packed bags occupied the chair), but there was space enough for us to stand, at the doors to the balcony, with our arms around each other. Was I right in feeling that she had filled out a bit? I was right.

The French doors opened out on a view of the city at night. Parts of it glowed with Minister Malraux's new spectacular lighting, with the dazzle of a world's fair, but the city was still scaled to the bustling life of the sidewalks and the hooting horns of the traffic. We were both starved. The clerk was relieved to see us back in the lobby so quickly, and we went off to the Café Royal, close by. In the café, my bad French was much appreciated. Had I acquired it during the war? No, I had been *entre les guerres.* In those days, the waiter, about my age, would have been setting up his first tables. I recall eating fried eggs still sizzling in the pan. All Paris seemed eager for our attention, but we went back to the Madison, where I told the clerk that he need not call us in the morning. We exchanged glances of understanding. His upward-straining gaze, as we rose from the lobby, assured me that I was truly ascending.

At the American Express, I had a letter from Sam Kaner, who was now living in Venice. Why didn't I—why didn't *we*—pay him a visit? He didn't know about Jo, but how often we had discussed bolting to Ronda, or to Paris if that seemed more convenient. As it had. While we went here and there, or sat in taxies, or at a table at Les Deux Magots, or while we lay awake watching the lights on the ceiling, we discussed what we should be doing. I had about three weeks. *Mon dieu,* how long and short that seemed! In October I had lectures to give at Amherst, and in November I would go to Mexico for the *Holiday* piece.

We would make a sort of tour, we decided, our first stop being Venice, full of paintings she must see, then Vienna, from where we would drive out to Schloss Ranna, to reassure myself, after twenty-five years, that it was actually there. From Ranna we would go to Munich, where one of my novels was about to be published, visit with my friends Jack and Leslie Aldridge, then return to Paris.

The man Jo knew at the American Express seemed relieved to note that he and I were about the same age—he may have felt this to be part of *his* problem—but in making out our wagon-lit reservations, and noting our separate passports, his agitation may have led him to reserve accommodations on the right train but for the wrong night. Some hours out of Paris, we were notified that our reservations were not in order, and that we had no sleeping accommodations. We could leave the train at its next stop and spend the night in a hotel, or we could sit it out in the coach compartment.

Jo would have preferred the hotel, in Lyon, but I was for sitting it out. One night in a coach? Were we so feeble? Most of my life, that was how I had traveled. In retrospect it didn't seem to be all that bad. I didn't know, of course, that the train would spend most of the night winding and creaking through the Alps in numerous short and long tunnels, past flashing warning lights and clanging bells, while we rocked and tilted one way, then another.

After the stop at Lyon, several men entered our compartment. One, gripping a string-wrapped parcel, appeared to be a clerk, so weary his head drooped the moment he was seated. At his side, his head so large his features appeared shrunken, a short-legged but powerful man held his huge torso erect by spreading his thighs, like props. He wore an expensive suit, with a silky, iridescent sheen, the material stretched tight across his bulging lap. Fresh food stains spotted his unbuttoned vest. On his small feet, light-tan oxfords with pointed tips had their laces untied. About his small, puckered mouth, beneath the tuft of moustache, smears of grease gleamed like perspiration. Several rings, with large stones, were embedded in the plump fingers that rested on his paunch, just the tips of the fingers touching. The large head, with its close-cropped pelt, tilted from side to side as the coach swayed. In homage to Balzac, I examined him carefully. An archetypical provincial figure, sharpened and honed by centuries of French life and writers, adorned with the fashionable attire of the moment for this night of orgiastic dining. It seemed I could hear his digestive juices percolating. A monumental vision of imperfect, bourgeois felicity.

At first I thought he dozed, but his small piggy eyes peered at us through his brown lashes. We contributed, indeed, to the dessert of his banquet, a strange pair of illicit lovers passing a miserable night in a train seat. To the taste of the peach Melba still on his lips we added the refinement of the flaming cognac, the touch of sin that had been lacking. To enhance his pleasure, I stretched out with my head in Jo's lap.

In Milan, in the late morning, we shared a coach jammed with

Italian families, all of them with their parcels of bread, cheese and salami, slurping from bottles of Chianti in their raffia wrapping. Between choking gulps of food, the children stared at my shoes from Mexico, my tan from California, my turquoise ring from Arizona. In their charmed presence I slowly recovered from a ghastly night. The black-clad women, clutching their string bags, solemnly gazed at my companion. What speculation she would provide them! This madonna traveling with the bleary-eyed stranger.

The coach partially emptied at Verona, and as the train approached Venice I got whiffs of the sea-tanged air. Where was Venice? The glass-hooded railroad station proved to be new. I lowered the window, to see Sam Kaner smiling and waving. How glad I was to see him! Our bags were passed through the window, and Sam went ahead of us after staring, with some disbelief, at my companion. Had I actually *bolted*? The thought pleased and amused him. "Well, Dad," he would say when he could speak, and beam appreciatively.

We pushed through the last doors to step out on a stage that would have tested Shakespeare's imagination. Unreal but fabulous city! On the choppy canal a *vaporetto* tacked about for the pier. Water slapped the stone steps. The peeling walls of Venice, an outdoor museum of art, held Jo's speechless attention. Sam had gone ahead to get our *vaporetto* tickets. I stood there troubled by what seemed to be missing. There were no cars. There were no wheels! The *vaporetto* coughed wetly as we boarded. "Well?" said Sam to me, his eyes gleaming, seeing in our astonished faces something of what he had already forgotten. This city was like nothing. It could only be experienced and compared with itself.

The mind-boggling gift of Venice is that it has escaped the tyranny of wheels. The motor launch coughs, the exhaust pollutes the air, but man walks—he does not run for his life. Only time will accustom us to a fact so profoundly bizarre. Of all unreal cities, this is the one that has its roots deepest in the imagination. Men dreamed it up, and now it is sinking into the ooze that will preserve it. Venice submerged may well prove to be stranger than Venice preserved. The gondolas in the Piazza are merely a reminder that this city was born of illusion, and that what man takes from the sea, the sea will repossess. As if it were sugared, the smog-polluted air crumbles the stones, discolors the marble, and adds the final refinement to our taste for mutilations, our love for man-made ruins. (Love Affair: A Venetian Journal, 1972)

We stayed with Sam Kaner and his wife, but we had most of our meals at the Locanda Montin, just off the Zattere and the Rio San Trovaso. A family establishment (as were most in Venice), with a cat-haunted garden at the rear (a choice between the cats and the rats from the canals), it numbered a group of painters among its clientele, a few of them Americans, most of whom found places to live on Giudecca, some with a view across the water to the piazza of San Marco and the Doge's Palace. What could a modern painter do with this museum of six centuries of masterpieces? Those ignorant of or indifferent to this aesthetic dilemma might do pretty well selling their productions to tourists.

Sam and his blond wife, Ruth, whose almost white hair excited the younger males to hoots and whistling, occupied the top floor, a sort of Venetian penthouse with a view of the Zattere. It was fine October weather, but what would they do in January? Sam had already survived one winter in Venice, and described a world of mist and fog, like that of London, with such apparitions as snow-frosted gondolas. In the cafés, especially the Locanda Montin, with everyone crowded inside, there was much talk and fellowship.

I retained my doubts about January, but October in Venice had us captivated. Would it be possible to find an apartment? The few available were in demand by Venetians. But Sam Kaner happened to know of a choice modern apartment on a walled garden, with steam heat, plumbing and barred windows. The bars were a must if it was on the lower floors. Life was safe enough in Venice, but not easily portable property.

At the moment, this apartment was occupied by Sylvia Brown, a young woman from California, who had lived in Venice for years. We had met Sylvia at Montin's, where her manner, her slow, deliberate way of speaking, was that of someone accustomed to teaching, or to teachers. She was also fluent in Italian and French, and was planning a trip to Spain to improve her Spanish. The apartment she was in, just off the Rio San Trovaso, was very select in every respect, but it was on the first floor and never warmed by sunlight. There was also the problem that the large shuttered windows, with bars but no glass, were terra cognita to the neighborhood cats. People fond of cats might actually like it, but she did not like cats. We did, we thought, like cats, so we made a visit to the garden, from where we had a chat with Sylvia Brown through the closed shutters. She was at that moment about to leave for Paris, and closing up. Discussing this problem through the shutters is one of my very special Venetian impressions (I was never free of the feeling that she was captive, and lying to us

450

at sword point), but we did seem to agree that if she could move to higher and sunnier accommodations, the apartment she occupied would be ours. That was enough for me. (I put little faith in what I was hearing or saying, or what was happening, but I did feel confident about the future.)

On each of our five days in Venice we walked around and around, hoping to get irrevocably lost. Time and again we were mysteriously back where we had started, and paused for an espresso before going on. In the sunny *campos* we watched people, the plump-kneed boys hooting as they played their ball game, and in the dim chill of the Accademia museum we stared at Bellini, Carpaccio and Giorgione. Surely the sense of such abundance would pass, and we would go, like the natives, about our own business, stirring up the pigeons and pausing to stroke or feed an occasional cat. If that were possible, was it a condition to aspire to? We had five days; four of them started with eggs that should not have been boiled, and if boiled never opened. In five days, that was one thing we learned. On the evening of the sixth day, we took the *vaporetto,* with Sam Kaner, up the Grand Canal to the railroad station, where the bottle of champagne he had reserved for the occasion fell from the bag and shattered on the platform. That one was for Venice! He ran back to fetch another one for ourselves.

Would we be back? Sipping the champagne, we made a promise. In the spring, I swore, but I didn't believe it. It was just not possible that the key tumblers in my life would fall again as they fell to bring us to Venice. In our wagon-lit compartment I spelled out for Jo how, twenty-five years in the past, I had been cycling in the reverse direction after my winter at Schloss Ranna. Many people returned to places they had once visited, but I was compelled to return to those where I was still captive. This was at the heart of my agitation. I might indeed find Schloss Ranna, even the Meister, but would I find that young man who had never escaped—who had left part of his life in that bizarre province? Once a place had taken root in my imagination, it had for me an aura of enchantment. I could not explain it, but I knew that it generated the cycle of returns in my writing. A disinterested observer, pondering my behavior, might say of me that the function of the present was to confirm the nature of the past, and by a commodious vicus of recirculation the reality of the present.

Some years back, on a stop in Chicago, I had driven to Menomonee Street, where it began at Clark Street and Lincoln Park. My father and I had lived in rooms over a delicatessen. Bottles of milk had cooled on the windowsill, and in the winter pushed their caps up as the milk froze. I could sometimes hear the ice cracking up on the lake. In the summer I heard the roar of the crowd at Wrigley Field if someone hit a home run. Right beside this delicatessen, on the east, was a ruin that might have survived the Chicago fire. Weeds and crawlers had taken it over. For years, summer and winter, I had walked by it without the memory of having *seen* it. How was that possible? I did not then understand my feelings, but I considered this a loss that had to be salvaged. I sat in the car, the motor idling, staring at it. With certain objects and places I shared both gains and losses. Why had I felt compelled to confirm it as a loss?

One night in Paris, I had awakened Jo to tell her of my strange adventure at Schloss Ranna, and something about the people and the past preserved there. I think she heard it and accepted it as one of my fictions (I seemed to be full of them), but it was not as a fiction that it held me. It was crucial to me that I be able to confirm the reality of my early impressions, since I had failed (in my own opinion) to give them imaginative confirmation. *My* Schloss Ranna was an unacceptable loss—like those that bombs had reduced to rubble—until I had reaffirmed its existence, and given substance to my impressions.

Vienna was still war-scarred. On Florianigasse, the building from which I had peered into the *blind Garten* had vanished. The matronly woman who rented us a car concealed her cracked red hands in the sleeves of her sweater. I was tempted to ask her about Frau Unger, with her flashing eyes and swinging earrings. In the chill garage basement I felt her vibrations. How did the air itself accommodate such losses? Whitman had thought that it bathed the globe, but it was little more than the skin of a bubble. How did it absorb the cries and the shrieks, the deafening, atom-splitting clamor of one unholy, tumultuous day on earth? Was it possible to speak of this congested ether as thin air?

We drove west to Krems, then followed the road along the Danube to Spitz. There we had lunch in the garden behind the hotel, the gravel paths sloping down toward the river. I made it a point to have a carafe of the *neue Wein* I had heard so much about but never tasted. We both thought it sweet as ambrosia. Might the waiter—a black stud at the throat of his collarless shirt, the moist sad eyes of my friend Hermann Unger—have been a child in Spitz when I came down from Ranna to get a haircut? Was the Meister still at Schloss Ranna? I asked him, with the assurance of an escaped inmate. "For certain!" he replied, curious that I might doubt it. And how was he? He temporized, rocking the hand he extended with the palm turned down. He was old. He studied me before saying, "He has remarried." This had the effect

452

he had hoped for. He brought us cups of coffee, then continued. During the war the Meister had been imprisoned. When he returned to Schloss Ranna, it had been with his new wife, a German woman. More than that he was reluctant to say, being a man of discretion. I had thought to ask him if *Ranna* was still there, but lacked the nerve. From the movies, I had gathered that old castles were sometimes used to provide elite quarters for military personnel, but the memorable lack of "civilized" comforts might have spared Ranna.

Where the road turned north to follow the canyon to Muhldorf, we stopped to watch a steamer make the bend in the river, her paddle wheels slapping the water. Travelers standing on the deck waved to us, and we waved in return. I remembered thinking how I had been struck, in the past, with what a remarkable custom that proved to be, even more remarkable after the intervention of the second war. As we approached Muhldorf, I looked for and saw the mill wheel that corked one side of the canyon, but without the ice and snow, the shimmering winter silence, the slanting rays of the sun on the buttressed walls, what I saw on the slope that rose behind the village was a disappointment. How shabby it looked! The field below the walls had not been cultivated, nor had the walls of the inner Schloss been whitewashed.

"Just you wait," I said to Jo, making the turn to Ober Muhldorf, a lane with weeds growing at its center, and we followed it to pass the church, with its onion dome, and the shrine along the trail where we had gathered for the midnight hunt, then passed the vacant, abandoned outbuildings to curve up through the orchard of dead and dying trees. As we approached the gate, I stopped the car and got out. "Come," I said, and led her to the wall that fenced the moat. In my absence it had aged, but not shrunken. Deep in the dry moat, shrubs were growing. At that instant, as I glanced upward, I felt a tremor of the chill that had seized me upon my first hearing the bell rung by that madman, Antone, from the top of the tower. Not this time. The weather vane tilted, ready to fall. Not a sound from the deep moat, the inner Schloss, or the canyon behind it. It relieved me to note that Jo stepped back from the sheer fall, just as I had.

I drove the car through the arch, along the rutted ramp to where it narrowed. There we sat as I reflected on the impulses that had brought me back to Ranna. If the Meister was there, what would he remember? More to the point, what did he care to remember, after the war? Impulsively, I put my hand to the horn. It was not at all the right sound for the silence. We sat there, apprehensive, until one of the small windows opened. I made out the broad face of a woman.

"Herr Deleglise?" I called out. "I have come to see him." She

453

made no comment. "Tell him Herr Morris is here to see him."

"Who?" she inquired. I repeated my name. "Tell him the young American. He will remember!"

She left, but was soon back. "Come in!" she cried, and thrust out her forearm toward the entrance. I led Jo into the corridor, dark as a cave since the door at the far end was shut. The door to the inner court stood ajar, and we crossed it to mount the stairs to the landing. A stout, matronly woman, both broad and deep, the sleeves of her dress turned back on her plump forearms, beckoned to us from a doorway. We saw little but her broad back as she led us down a hallway. Loose floorboards sagged and creaked. Slits of light burned at the base of closed doors. She led us directly to the room I knew to be the Meister's, where we found him propped up in his bunk. The familiar grimacing smile parted his lips; toward me extended his frail claw-like hand. "Not well, not well," he piped, but I thought he looked more the same than altered. The high brow a little higher, the moustache a little grayer, the mother-of-pearl teeth still mother-of-pearl. Also unchanged was his amiable disinterest. Why had I come?

I said that I had long wanted to return to Ranna, and that my friend, Josephine, had been eager to see it. The name Josephine pleased him. He studied her with interest.

"Italian, yes?" he queried. "Madame Deleglise was also Italian."

That I well remembered. Did he see a likeness between my swan and his ugly duckling? He explained to the woman who I was. He described me as an artist from California. This both pleased her and made her bristle. In a fluent German, the text so familiar I could follow where it was leading, she spoke of the barbarous bombing of Dresden. When did we expect to pay reparations? All of her property destroyed. For ten years she had been waiting. Using the cane stretched at his side, the Meister tapped on the wall, like a professor on a blackboard. She fell silent. He spoke to her again, suggesting that we stay for dinner. This caused her the greatest discomfort. In a scene of classic matronly woe, she gathered up and clutched the folds of her skirt. Was she about to weep?

"No! No!" I intervened. "We will take you to dinner. We will go to Krems!"

There were good cafés in Krems, but I felt certain she would decline the invitation. Not so. On the instant, it aroused her. She turned to persuade the Meister, adjusting his position—his left arm clung to his side, the hand deep in the jacket pocket. "*Nein! Nein! Nein!*" he repeated, but she ignored his complaint as if he were a child she was tending. From a hook on the wall she took a long wool scarf, several yards in length, and opened his jacket to wrap it around him. He was soon resigned. His eyes eluded mine, but behind his tantrum I could sense his satisfaction. He was in good hands. She would do with all of us as she would.

We had just finished lunch, but no matter. It would take us an hour or more to get to Krems, and it might be a half hour before we started. A contented, clucking hen, the woman went off with Jo, and I sat with the Meister, smoking. He took deep drags of the Camel cigarette, reluctant to exhale; his eyes were hooded. "And Mizi?" I asked him. She had married. A widower to the west. One of her sons now worked in Spitz. "And Antone?"—the father of his country. A blacksmith in Ottenschlag. Many children. Joseph an *Obermensch* in Krems. I would have heard much the same on a visit to the Home Place. Time marches on. We were silent for a moment, then he asked me:

"Josephine is your wife?"

"Not just yet," I replied. He looked at me with a concern that puzzled me.

"My wife—" he began, stopped.

"We'll stay in Spitz," I said. "There's a *Gasthaus* in Spitz."

He sighed with relief and reached to grip my hand. The good German hausfrau was doing what she could, in a disorderly world, to reestablish order, and reaffirm good, decent German morals. "Frau Deleglise—" he said to me, and we exchanged a reaffirming glance of male understanding.

On the drive back to Schloss Ranna, seeing it emerge dim and ghostly out of the darkness, an ark beached by the receding flood (my impression was that it seemed to be tilting), there revived in me much that I had feared to be lost, having looked in the wrong place for it. A young man from the new world, an older man and a dog of mythic proportions—one could hardly improve on the combination—had slodged through the snow to that point in the canyon where the Schloss appeared to be ascending to heaven, on the froth of a wave, or at the least the cloudland in the glass ball on all sewing machines west of the Missouri. The Meister himself had been the first to come down with the virus, and he had spent his life passing it on to others. Had it taken with any others as it had with me? Had there ever been a canvas better prepared for what was to be painted on it? But even I had failed to imagine the frame that Frau Deleglise had provided: a last stand for *Kultur* in a crumbling ruin pending the arrival of just reparations. She had her plans. Buses of tourists, from Vienna and Salzburg, would stop at Ranna for the night, then proceed elsewhere. Others would come by paddle boat from Budapest and Innsbruck. During the night it had crossed her mind that Americans, too, should come to Schloss Ranna, as I had. Might it not interest me—once she had the reparations—to conduct a tour? I regretted that my work would keep me in California. Frau Deleglise had surprised us with an invitation to spend the night at Ranna. She had made up separate rooms. After a *Butterbrot Frühstück,* and excellent *Schokolade,* we had an almost tearful parting out on the ramp. The Meister wagged his cane from his balcony doorway. I don't know what I was thinking as we drove back to Spitz, and stopped where the road came out on the Danube. A boat, a steamer with big paddle-wheel fenders, was drifting with the current around the curve at Spitz. On the fender, with the hyphen, were the words BUDA-PEST.

In that cold air, veiled with the smoke of our breathing, I seemed to see Richard the Lion-Hearted, on whom I had once written a term paper, cold and clammy in his suit of clanking armor, only his black eyes glinting at the visor of his helmet, weary in mind and aching in body, eaten alive by lice and gnawed with fear and suspicion, uncertain of friend and foe and whether he would ever get back to his homeland, with a large pack of vassals and hangers-on to account for, along with numerous baying dogs, thieves and beggars, pause for a moment right where we were standing to peer down at the black, alien river he would never see again—not a great figure in history, carrying a shield, but a flesh-and-blood bully who was saddle-sore and homesick. Far to the east, where the sun was still shining, the landscape was like a painting on glass through which I could see back to where I had come from. . . . How Richard the Lion-Hearted had felt was not strange to me. (Solo: An American Dreamer in Europe: 1933–34, 1983)

In Munich we met Susi Hofstadt, an editor for Henry Goverts, whom she had persuaded to publish two of my books. Goverts shared my love of Rilke's *Notebooks of Malte Laurids Brigge,* and we talked of little else at dinner. We had some time with Jack and Leslie Aldridge, and an afternoon with Hedda Soellner, who had just translated *The Huge Season* for Goverts. On the train to Strasbourg I was served a bowl of cherries, in a compote, that I have never forgotten. Back at the Hotel Madison, in Paris, the clerk appraised Jo for signs of ennui, of blighted expectations, but reached no reassuring conclusions.

The painter Emerson Woelffer and his wife, Dina, came up from

456

Ischia to see Jo, and meet her new companion. If they were still in Ischia in the spring, Jo said, we would stop and see them on our way to Venice. That unsolicited support, at that moment, did much to solidify my future plans.

Later I took Jo past the Cinema Montparnasse, where I had first seen Disney's *Three Little Pigs,* then I walked her up the Rue de la Gaîté to the Hotel Duguesclin, to point out the front window from which I had leaned to watch the landlord's beautiful daughters cry, "*Me voici! Me voici!*" From there I walked her back to the Boulevard Raspail (she was starving) for a bowl of borscht at Dominique's, served to us at a table with napkins. Monsieur Dominique (he put me in mind of Stravinsky) admired my companion, and claimed to remember the young American who took more rolls from the basket at the counter than he paid for—but all that in the spirit of the times, and meaning no offense.

I was up at six to catch the boat train to Le Havre and send my love a *pneumatique* from the railroad station. "Here's one for my baby, and one for the road."

I was at once elated and deprived, coming off a great high, yet I remember nothing—*nothing*—of my three cabin companions; I know we had a stormy passage. I was in Wayne, packing a bag for Amherst, when I had a letter from Jo telling me that she had fallen ill a few days after my departure, and had been taken to the American Hospital. What distressed me—now that she had recovered—were the comforting fictions I had borne in mind assuring me of her well-being. This discrepancy in time between our infrequent letters would trouble me most in Mexico, where I had little confidence in what I sent off and virtually none in what she mailed from Paris. It would have much to do, once I reached Mexico City, with my heartfelt plea that I needed her with me, right there at my side, no longer at the whims of gaps in our correspondence—I needed the real voice, the glance from real eyes, the warmth and assurance of the real person to be felt and touched. Was it possible something was wrong with me? Yes; I was in love.

I DROVE THE JAGUAR TO AMHERST, LEAVING THE
freeway to get the bloom of the flaming fall colors. I was put up at
the inn, much beloved by the alumni, in a room bringing to mind tradi-
tions of whaling, a cubicle that required caution in getting in and out
of its small berth. At the time of my stay, Robert Frost was making
his yearly visit. The first morning, as I pondered my impressions, he
sat alone along one wall of the dining room, I alone along another.
A bit of tinkle and slurp disturbed the silence. He had his second, and
his third, cup of coffee, waiting for me to pick up the signal. As I passed
by, his mariner's glance caught me directly and I took a seat at his
table. He gave me his splotched farmer's hand, what was left of his
pot of coffee. Frost was eighty-four at that time, a hunkered-down,
bear-like figure with his white icing, and the creaky manner of a valued,
but seldom used, antique. He also wanted company. He told a good
story, and feigned real interest in my own. Former times. How different, we agreed, for both of us.

The week I was at the inn we had breakfast together, and as a
rule I got his bacon. He explained to me that if I sat at his table,
strangers were less likely to intrude on him. That was true enough,
but also something of a problem, since most of these intrusions were
his pleasure. The monument receiving due homage. He liked especially
to hear it from the young. Parents, receiving mutual reinforcement,
after a period of nervous, coffee-cooling indecision, might approach
the great man to speak of his importance to the past, the present, and
of course the future. What a pity they had found so little time for poetry
themselves! Frost played this role with true rustic charm, and just a
touch of humility. He referred to me as his "young friend," and so
I was. That I was headed for Mexico greatly intrigued him. What was
it like? I tried to tell him. In these glimpses up ahead, into the lives
of the young, he hoped to do his living. Would I write to him? he
asked. I said I would. "Dear Bob," I would write, being his friend,
as he had said.

The meetings he had with the students I thought less happy, the
students too much alert to the occasions' importance. One comment
I made drew us together. The waitresses at the inn bore resemblance
to stuffed historical figures, repeating roles that were duly recorded.
They were less matronly than fraternal, a family of kinfolk, male and

458

female, in which the sensual element was totally lacking. I could not imagine a rogue bold enough to pinch or goose one of them. How in God's name did Yankee lust, I asked him, persist in reproducing the species? That he liked. Perhaps only Frost, and only the New England campus, with its swinging birches and unmended fences, would provide on the eve of his canonization a rustic figure still suitable for framing.

I had come to Amherst to meet with the students and lecture on "The Origin of a Species," this being the figures of my own fiction. An ill-advised enterprise, but it had interested me, and I had come prepared to make the best of it. Ben DeMott gave me all the encouragement I needed, and the students were both respectful and responsive. One of them was a young writer named Pete Howe. I met with him occasionally, and I saw and felt in him many of the traits of my better self. One day I found him standing beside my Jaguar, a car he greatly admired. I suggested that we take a spin, but at that moment he lacked the time. I thought Pete Howe a very attractive young man, and a "promising" fiction writer. I suggested he might write to me, if and when he cared to. He was there the morning I drove away, and when I arrived in Mexico City, many weeks later, I would find a letter from Amherst about him. Shortly after my departure, he had been killed in a car accident. In his memory a small volume of his writing would be published, to which I was asked to contribute. To his parents I managed to write a few words, but it shamed me to feel my impotence in this loss. At the head of my list of losses that mocked imaginary gains was the name of Pete Howe.

Did I see myself at the wheel of the Jaguar, cruising along the coast of Mexico to Mazatlán? I did indeed. And there I was. The car purred without knocking. The oil was cheaper. I passed miles of fields under irrigation, and stopped to drink iced beer at the fishing stations. Approaching Mazatlán, I slowed to join a line of traffic made up of trucks, tourists, and carts pulled by donkeys.

An American from Covina, California, had built a new motel just back from the surf. It was so new the beds had not yet been delivered, but the cot in the room seemed acceptable. I stepped from the shower to see a large iguana scooting across the floor like a toy dragon. That his panic was greater than mine calmed me. I stood on the cot, calling for help, until a Mexican youth came to the door. He opened the screen, gave the iguana a boost as it scrambled out. When I asked him if they were dangerous, he shrugged.

The checkered tablecloths had not yet arrived for the tables, but real American T-bone steaks had just been shipped in by air, frozen. I had one, with French fries and a bottle of Dos Equis, and knew that I was among my own people. I learned from the proprietor that the fishing was great. The problem was—and I was listening, what with my piece on Mexico to write—that the plumbing fixtures installed in his new showers twisted off in the hands of the husky American tourists, who didn't know their own strength. The *problem* was, once that had happened, it took time to replace what had been broken. Maybe three, maybe six, maybe eight or nine months. Americans who had been driving for eight or ten hours, or had been fishing for five or six hours, and looked forward to a refreshing shower, were seldom long on understanding. They peered into the showers, looked at the twisted pipes, and took off. His wife, who served as the café hostess, and had designed the menus, the size of newspapers, had never been able to get a really good tan back in Covina, but after seven weeks in Mazatlán he told her some of the tourists thought she was colored, and that settled that.

The second night, I woke up to hear the cries of mariachi singers, and see the lights of a Ferris wheel far down the beach. I walked to where they were having a carnival, with thousands of the Indians in from the country. I loved the way the beautiful children accounted for each other, an older one linked to a younger to where the links gave out. As I mingled with them, sharing their excitement, I was troubled by the suspicion that I was an impostor. I felt that eyes I could not see both saw and judged me. Whose eyes were they? Was I growing wise to myself? At what point did my pleasure in the child carrying a child become a symbol for the situation? If the exotic was stripped away, what would the visitor be left with? Had I fallen into thinking that this many-ringed circus was staged for my fleeting benefit?

It troubled me to have these scruples at the start of my journey, but leaving Mazatlán, I felt better. In the late afternoon, approaching a larger city, I joined a line of trucks and campers moving slowly toward a river. In moments of quiet I could hear the rush of the water. Too late, making the descent toward the river, I saw that the bridge was missing. Parts of the collapsed structure were there, at each end, but the bridge consisted of vehicles, bumper to bumper, moving slowly through water above the hubcaps. In the Jag that would be halfway up the door, and high on the motor. Nor was there any way for me to turn off, or to turn back. It occurred to me—and there proved to be time to reflect on occurrences—that if I should drown here, my love, in Paris, might well *never* learn about it. What would she think? I had no choice but to survive.

460

In my rearview mirror I saw the lights of a truck, looming high behind me, flash me a signal. What did he have in mind? The Jag's motor had stopped the moment I entered the river. Some part of the front end of the truck behind me—the bumper appeared to be as high as my rear window—contacted the rear bumper on the Jag and he pushed me ahead of him like a half-submerged boat. It took some time, but it was not quite long enough to despair. On the far side he pushed me up the slope to the street, clouded with dust, a confusion of vehicles like that of an army fording a stream, and I leaned out of the cab to watch my benefactor, his teeth gleaming in a villain's dark, smiling face, wave at me as he passed. I sat there for some time before I noticed that my feet were ankle deep in water, and I opened the door to let it out.

It seemed idle to trouble to look at the motor, but I wanted to confirm that it was still there. The top of the block, still hot, hissed and steamed like a simmering pot. Water had pooled in the plug sockets, and I used my T-shirt to sop it up. The ignition wiring had been soaked, and I put in my time fussing with it. At my side the traffic clamored as in a scene of wartime panic. I had survived. The woman in Paris would not be puzzled by my disappearance. One day—preferably not in Mazatlán; Venice would be more appropriate—I would attempt to describe my crossing of the Hellespont.

Some of my previous cars had been reluctant to start on those chill mornings when there was mist in the air, so I was not such a fool as to think that this submerged, lifeless mechanical corpse would spring to coughing life when I turned the key. But that was what it did. I sat there too stupefied to believe it. Quickly it choked and died. But it had actually *run*! Was that what it meant to be British? Knowing that the spark of life was there, I went back under the hood, did more sopping and wiping, did more praying, and on the third try it sputtered and ran. One plug was not firing, but I was able to buck along in second gear, like an injured animal at the edge of the pack.

There was still light in the sky, although it was already dark under the trees. One of the features of the city—I had found it in my tour book—was a new and elegant motel, overlooking the sea, approached by a winding, ascending ramp, along which I was escorted by hooting small fry. The car made its bucking entrance without comment from two valets in caps and white jackets. Not being familiar with Jaguars, they accepted what they heard and saw as normal. I let the motor run, fearing that if stopped, it would never start. The high water had left a ring on the sides of the car. The hot motor gave off a fishy odor. I let it continue to run while I had my dinner—I got up frequently to check on it—and after an hour and a half of idling, the firing was almost normal. I stopped the motor, wiped the car with my T-shirt—and discussed with a tourist from Minnesota some of the hazards of Mexican travel. He was glad to get it from a tourist who spoke with authority.

I felt such an adventure augured so well for the future that I spent several days in Guadalajara, drying my wet clothes and making a few notes. I drove out for another look at Ajijic, where Lawrence and Frieda had left their spoor; it was now ornamented with American women with mannish hairdos, peasant blouses, Hopi jewelry and hand-loomed Navajo skirts.

In Mexico City I had a reunion with Jaime García, but after a few hours together I felt his reluctance to repeat the past. Here I was again, full of myself and my plans, and in a few weeks or months I would be gone. On Jaime's lips, when he was silent, I could see the words *Todo pasa*. The burden of our friendship weighed on him. Whatever we had together I would take away with me. We went to a ball game, we walked on the Paseo, we dined and sipped the mild gin at Sanborns, but all we were doing was passing the time, passing the time. . . .

I spent more than a week looking for the right apartment, which I found just down the street from the old one. Described as a "penthouse," it seemed to be on a level with the smog that now veiled the city. It did offer a fine view, however, of the roofs of the houses where the Indian girls came to wash, sun and brush their gleaming black hair. I felt that would please Jo. Waiting for me had been a letter from Paris, for which I was grateful, but of the sort a woman writes with too many other things on her mind. She was seeing friends. She might go to England. She hoped to visit her friends in Ischia. If she went to Italy, should it be Rome or Florence? The thought of her being there *without* me brought me to a decision.

Before leaving for Oaxaca, I wrote Jo a letter with the emphasis on my recent losses. Besides her, what had they been? I cited my new and young friend, Pete Howe. I touched on my loneliness in a strange country. I may have said I did not want to go on without her, an extravagant admission for a lad with my background. I not only said many of these things, but I mailed the letter off. I also managed to mention the new penthouse apartment, the excellent food at Sanborns, the sun and the view from the roof, and the aroma of the broiled chickens on the deli rotisserie on the corner. I overlooked reference to the fleas and the bedbugs in the furniture. I had originally planned that Jo would drive with me to Oaxaca, with side trips to Cuernavaca, Taxco, even Acapulco, but just a few days in my empty penthouse had clarified my priorities.

Early in December I drove south to Acatlán, noting that the Jag purred its smoothest at the lower altitudes. In the dusty patio of the café, one of the resident chickens, light as a feather duster, hopped to my lap and ate out of my soup plate. A small bantam hen with frazzled tail feathers, but with the bold assurance of a street-tough urchin, she had the bald behind of the hens that had scratched up my Aunt Clara's farmyard. With piercing glances at me and at the mongrel yellow-eyed dog who observed her from a safe distance, she plucked the peas, the corn and the gravel from my soup.

In Oaxaca, the California tourists were gathering for the white man's Christmas festival. I spent the cool mornings in the plaza, pondering its enchantment, my evenings at the bar in the motel, sipping the mild Mexican gin. The barman, a handsome young fellow with the hair and the eyes of an Arab, was quick to light my cigarette, to replace my drink, and to see that the dish of olives was at my elbow. Our exchanges were little more than glances and nods. He had the best job in the place, a white shirt, a bow tie, a cummerbund with a sash, and black American patent-leather oxfords. Was he content? He seemed happiest when he was waiting on me. When he learned I was leaving, he spoke to me like a suitor, a short formal speech, not all of which I followed, then he stepped forward to place his hands on my shoulders and gaze into my eyes. Speechless, we confronted each other. The sober formality of his manner testified to the seriousness of this gesture. On my belt I wore a chain of silver, attached to a silver cigar cutter (I had always had a weakness for Mexican silver), and I unhooked it from my belt and gave it to him. In the early morning, as the Jag warmed up, he ran to embrace me in the Mexican manner, then took off. This brief but intense (for him) friendship reminded me how, here in Mexico, old men strolled about the streets holding hands like children.

I may have been thinking of my friend, several hours later, when I rounded a sharp curve north of Acatlán, the road ahead concealed by the cliffside, to find the highway strewn with boulders the size of basketballs. Dodging one, I hit another, then another, and felt the motor shift and rock on the frame as the steering wheel vibrated. Through the window on my side, which was open, I saw an Indian crouched on the cliffside, his head resting on his arms, taking his siesta. A stick with a red warning flag attached to it lay across his lap. He

463

raised his head to gaze at me with sleep-drugged eyes, but he saw nothing. I could hear the car's hot metal pinging, and catch glimpses, in the rearview mirror, of the smear of oil that darkened the street. My hands seemed to be locked to the car's steering wheel. When they loosened, I walked back around the curve to flag my arms at an approaching car. A young man and his girl were crouched behind the wheel of a two-toned Chevy. I pointed ahead to the boulders, the film of oil on the pavement, and it took him a moment to make the connections. His girl eased out of his arms to check on her lipstick, but lucky for me she was there. Without her, he would have had no shortage of excuses—his old car, bad tires, an urgent appointment—but he was a decent fellow, with the sad, knowing eyes of my friend Jaime. He walked with me to look at the Jag. Depressed as he was, he could not suppress the sympathy he felt for the car's owner. Never before had he seen such a car. Two, three times, he circled it slowly. He tracked through the oil smear to admire the dashboard. A pair of miniature huaraches hung by a string from the mirror, showing my Mexican connections. He kneeled on the pavement to see what could be seen from below, and I did the same. A hole bigger than my fist had been poked in the oil pan. My good samaritan had one last ray of hope.

"I have no rope," he said.

How did it happen that I had a rope? After the crash in Oregon, the mechanic had sold me a length of heavy rope in case I might have to be towed to Portland. This coil of rope, still wet from the river, was found in the rear. Neither of us knew much about knots in rope, but with some labor, mostly his, we got it attached. Would it work? Not without some practice. We stopped every ten or twenty miles for water, bringing it back in five-gallon oil cans. I had to buy these cans, then leave them beside the road. Twice the rope broke, sawing through on the frame, and I watched his car leap away to what I assumed would be his freedom—but each time he came back. We did not speak or joke. He had reached that point of no return that asked of me only silence. I was silent. Often I thumped him so hard from the rear I could see both of their heads bob.

The town of Matamoros—I do not know where it is, but I know that it is there, somewhere—we entered late on that Sunday afternoon, the streets empty and in shadow. Barefooted boys ran along beside me, happily beaming. They, too, had not before seen a Jaguar. Some blocks down the street, huge doors stood open on a courtyard crowded with junked cars. Under one of them a youth was working. My companion explained what had happened. Both gazed at me with sympathy. Could they fix it? *Sí, como no?* Of course they could fix it. He spoke at length about how he would fix it. *Muy bueno,* I replied. The Jag was pushed—a platoon of boys had gathered in the courtyard—over an oil pit, from where the young man assured me it was nothing. He would need a few things, but it was nothing. How much oil did it take? He admired its consumption. What a car it must be to take fifteen quarts of oil! One of the others, seated behind the wheel, found that the gears would no longer shift—but that, too, was nothing. How long would it take? All agreed it would take a bit of time.

The good samaritan who had towed me for miles, and surely won the girl with the sallow complexion, rejected my questionable offer of money for gains of a more spiritual nature. I wished him well. We embraced. Not for the first time, I was reassured that I was among my own people, even in Matamoros. Everything is a matter of time and place—boulders in the street, and short lengths of rope—and I have described the gist of the matter that Sunday in Matamoros. Somewhere along the way, I had gained in stature, but lost my French beret.

I asked the young mechanic if he would recommend a place for the night. He led me into the street to point it out. A building with a balcony, just beyond the cantina. To eat also? No; for eating, since it happened to be Sunday, I would have to go to the railroad station. One of the boys led me. It proved to be quite a walk. A station like one seen in movies graphically depicting South American wars of rebellion, it glowed with the rosy light of sunset. A child appeared to ask me if I wanted *la comida?* It was served by an elderly, shrunken woman with one blind eye. Probing with the fork, I saw that I had been served *frijoles* many times *refritos.* In the past I had been fool enough to eat it. Would I repeat this folly? I did—no more than two or three bites—drank the beer to squelch the fire, and left.

Those towns that provide tombs for the living, Matamoros being one of their number, have about them a funereal aura of ruin that is biblical and timeless. No dogs barked or chickens cackled. I thought of Guanajuato, where the dead were available for discussion. Somewhere a Roman writer, and a good one, speaks of entering a city where the corpses of the dead could be seen walking the streets. He puts it better than that, at greater length, and I remembered it at that moment. My room in the hotel featured the balcony, a view of the plaza, and a toilet bowl at the back that lacked a seat. Through the arched doorway to the balcony I could see the stopped hands of the clock on the bell tower. That detail I liked, and it would prove

465

memorable. Some hours later, I awoke in a sweat and the assurance that I had come to Matamoros to die. *Matamoros!* How could a writer of fiction improve on something like that?

> *. . . Two pariah dogs, with unmatched eyes, their bodies like racks for drying skins, cringed at a distance determined by an alert, tailless bantam rooster, their noses pitted with the pecks from his corn-tipped beak. Did not that symbolize something? Too much. Much too much. But in Matamoros everything was a symbol, nothing was its simple, visible self. The square with its tree of India, draped as if with mourning, the fountain that dripped and smelled like an illness, the bright tile benches that managed to be too hot in the sun, too cool in the shade, and the clock in the bell tower that tolled no recognizable hour.*

> *A species of canary, Cowie's first impression had been that it was an object, made of cork and pipe cleaners. Artful, perhaps. No question it was horrible. There were quills, but no feathers, below the neck. The head with its lidded eyes was elevated on the neck like a lampshade. The legs and claws were twisted bits of wire. Cowie took it as an example of the Mexican taste for the macabre: the skull-and-bone cookies eaten by children, the fantastic birds and animals made out of paper. When he glanced up to see it headless, he simply thought the head had dropped off. But no. Nothing lay in the bottom of the cage. The head, with its knife-like beak, had been tucked under the quills of one wing. Fly it could not, lacking the feathers. Sing it would not. But on occasion it hopped. (One Day, 1965)*

I did not die, but my living proved to be like the hands of the clock. The landlady lived in the front apartment, with a window on the street, where she sat and sewed, a plump, matronly, sorrowing woman, surrounded by a large assortment of paintings of saints and religious objects, many lit up at night by the glow of candles. I was struck by how often she made the sign of the cross at what she found herself thinking, or feeling. Her black-haired daughter had her mother's large, moist eyes, but a disfiguring acne that she concealed with a heavy cream paste. At night, if she thought me asleep, she might come to the archway and peer in at me.

> *An Indian girl, Dolores, her broad face pitted like the moon's surface, the mouth wide as a slice of melon, took care of such things as spooning him food and the daily nightmare of the bedpan. That she seemed to feel no disgust herself helped Cowie some, but not much.*

466

She came to him fresh from her own eating, her mouth greasy, her breath scented with chili, and went about her business while loudly sucking air through her teeth.

Every morning, Dolores mopped the upstairs hall, and swabbed down the tile stairs that she was the only one to use. She brought me food without a discernible trace of interest in my condition. I observed in her face an unscrupulous cunning she made no effort to conceal. Her coarse brownish hair was like that of a dog's pelt, the back of her head a smooth slope to her hunched shoulders. I listened to her comments with some amazement that she could speak. Taking my own arm by the wrist, like a handle, she would hold it to her ear to hear my watch tick. She admired the watch so openly—a Swiss chronograph—I acknowledged that she might poison me to get it. Did her boyfriends—she reported on several—feel the quality of her nature as I did? She seemed to me a human to whom it had not occurred that a distinction existed between kindness and indifference. I had seen her lips curl with contempt when her mistress kneeled in prayer.

On what proved to be a Friday, I was able to get up and walk to where I had left the car. A boy with a pail of water swabbed it down with newspapers. Would it run? Would it shift? I looked around the courtyard for the mechanic, found him under one of the wrecked cars. He crawled from beneath to accept one of my cigarettes.

How had I liked Matamoros?

Fine, I replied. He thought that a sensible comment. It led me to add that I had found the food a bit of a problem. Ha! he cried. The tourist problem. I thought he must mean *turista,* but no, he meant tourists. They found the food different than it was where they had come from, wherever that was. If I stayed in Matamoros, I would soon grow accustomed to the food.

And the Jaguar? It was *muy bueno.* He took his place at the wheel and started the motor. He shifted from low to second, and from second to high, but into reverse was a bit of a problem. If it could be avoided, I should not reverse. I might get it there, then not get it out. In Mexico City they could make a finer adjustment. Until Mexico City I should just go forward.

My bill, scrawled on a piece of wrapping paper, was $26 for labor, $4.80 for parts. The fourteen quarts of oil would be extra. Would he accept my traveler's checks? He would. I gave him forty dollars, with my blessings. He walked along beside me as I drove back to the hotel, where he made an adjustment in the gas mixture.

I let the motor run while I collected my razor, and the pajamas

467

that Dolores had just washed. Her broad, grubby palm, like an animal track, clutched the wad of pesos that I gave her. In her grin I saw nothing but greedy pleasure. The landlady urged me (from the balcony) to send her daughter a postcard from El Paso. She collected stamps.

I drove slowly toward Puebla, my lips dry, almost at ease with the folly of it, seeing on the far horizon the snow-capped peak of Ixtacihuatl, the sleeping woman, my sense of having escaped with my life so fragile I knew that I was not yet fully recovered. I drove as Jo had advised me to drive, like an old man. In Puebla I sat in the café on the plaza as it was being hosed down by the waiters, happy as children to be playing with the sparkling water, water being what is green and Go in Mexico.

W HILE WAITING FOR A LETTER FROM JO, I WORKED
on the *Holiday* piece. What did I *know* about Mexico, an immense darkness lit up by fireworks and candles? On several occasions I had passed
through it as a bird flies through a tunnel, coming in at one end and flying out the other. On me Montezuma had taken his revenge in Matamoros, in Acapulco, in Guadalajara and elsewhere. I had had numerous
glimpses through the chinks of time that lured the unwary traveler out
of his depth, and I had dimly felt—not for the first time—the folly of all
such enterprises. A piece on Mexico? A quick reading of the disguises I
had adopted for my travels. *Me voici* in my Jaguar, in a flooding river,
pushed from behind by a villain who smiled like Pancho Villa.

In recording my adventures I somehow assured the reader that
if he just hung in there—in Matamoros, in Acapulco, in a place unmen-
tioned, near Irapuato—it would be all right. On my way south to
Puebla I had driven through a surreal landscape of streetlamps without
streets, thousands of them, streets without houses, without people,
and I had said to myself, *How like Mexico!* What was meant by that?
Perhaps I meant the sudden appearance, and the instant collapse, of
such decent, well-meaning, hard-earned, good intentions. The real-
life fiction of a people who were learning to live with their own arrears, their own prebuilt ruins. But how long would it be before this
affliction appeared in epidemic form north of the border?

On the new escalators in Radio City, from where I caught glimpses
of skaters on the ice rink, I had once felt the prescient chill of crowded
tombs waiting to be plundered. How much, or how little, did it take?
One degree of change in any direction would be enough to set the
tumblers of change in motion. The *keeping up* was what would get
them in Mexico, and it could be seen catching up with us, the inertia
of machinery slowly grinding to a stop.

The more exotic and bizarre the surface of a culture—Mexico,
Brazil, Saudi Arabia—the more fundamental and basic we judged the
mask of life behind it. Was that its charm? The dirt, the squalor, the
women and the children, the animals, and the survival. From my window at night I could see the glow and spit of the fire where an Indian
girl sat on the curbing, slapping out tortillas for her family, her hands
shining like polished brass. She accepted my charity with a glance,
but without a smile.

469

After delays—she had been to England—I heard from Jo. As soon as she could pack, and arrange her affairs, she would fly to Mexico. My relief was so great I saw my situation clearly. If she had not come to me, I would have gone to her. In the airport—I was there at noon, for an 8 P.M. flight from Paris—I watched the plane staffed by Frenchmen who clearly represented a superior order, the big things that came in small packages. I stared at them with admiration as they passed, like gods, through the disorder of the customs office. My girl was there, frantically waving! Once more her brisk, clicking heels reassured me that I was headed in the right direction. What a relief I found it that her first view of the city was at night.

Jo liked Mexico moderately well, but it did not often excite her favorably. After a few weeks, our discussions soon veered back to Venice. A letter was sent off, pronto, to Sam Kaner, inquiring about Sylvia Brown's apartment. Would it be vacant by April? Our plans were to drive to New York—as soon as the weather permitted—and make the arrangements to sail from New York to Venice. This was more of a cruise than a passage, requiring almost three weeks at sea, with stops at all of those places on the walls of the travel bureaus. Mallorca, for example, had haunted me all these years I had failed to make it on my *Wanderjahr* in the mid-thirties. There was also Greece, and Dubrovnik, on the Adriatic, facts I had determined on a quick stop at the Italian tourist office in Manhattan. So what were we doing in Mexico City? We were packing our bags.

I've no idea who it was that first mentioned Rancho Atascadero, in San Miguel Allende. We would make a stop there on our way to the border, and check on the weather they were having in the Midwest. After the inspired repairs made in Matamoros, I had had the Jag checked over by the British Motors shop in Mexico City, but with Jo in the bucket seat beside me, I did feel an occasional tremor of apprehension.

The great roads for Jaguar cruising are those of blacktop, full of dips and curves, but they have to be relatively free of potholes. We had such a road to Querétaro, where an assembly of *muchachos,* in the plaza, washed and polished the car while we were having lunch in the hotel. Querétaro had been designed, it seemed to me, from impressions I had received in the forties, to be discovered by intrepid British females—than whom there are none more intrepid—who had previously exhausted Spain, Morocco, Doughty's Arabia Deserta, but retained their appreciative eye for vanishing colonial empires. We lunched that day with several, refugees from both Santa Fe and Bloomsbury, keenly observant of our illicit romance, as well as of the

470

elderly Indian, with the face of a Chinese sage, who had appeared in the lobby with a brace of turkeys dangling head down from a rope about his neck. While he bartered with the clerk at the desk, the turkeys fastened on me their gimlet eyes. Turkey, alas, was what I was eating, or had been eating up to that moment.

Rancho Atascadero offered no heated swimming pool (at that time), but had extensive resort accommodations, an attractive bar lounge and excellent food. Attractively literate and illiterate vagrants seemed to feel at their ease there, one reason being that ten dollars a day covered all expenses, including a few martinis. San Miguel itself, staggeringly picturesque, created with the tourist and his camera in mind, had an art school, but otherwise had been suitably embalmed by the altitude, like Guanajuato, for the visitors of the future. After our season in Venice, why didn't we return here? The weather seemed perfect. The accommodations were handsome and spacious. We left with the understanding that we would be back in November, just ahead of the Venetian winter. Had we managed to stumble on the best of two worlds? Our only complaint was the number of sand fleas we picked up on our walks.

This firm prospect to return in November did much to lift my spirits on the long drive east. It proved to be a strain for Jo, who was more of a night owl than a meadowlark, and had to adapt to my barbarous on-the-road travel rituals—the worst being my dawn starts, with our first cup of coffee at sunrise.

Incredibly, the Jaguar gave us no trouble until our arrival in suburban Philadelphia, where I had the good sense, and the luck, to turn it in on a new car for my wife. A letter from Sam Kaner was waiting for me in Wayne, and he reported that Sylvia Brown now planned to move from her garden apartment into the one Sam was just leaving. He had found a studio on Giudecca. These moves would be made, he assured me, by the time of our arrival in late April.

Jo found a suite in a hotel off Madison Avenue in New York, and she had already begun our travel arrangements with a clerk at American Express. A tall, handsome and cultivated Britisher, he was greatly appreciative of Jo, and intrigued by the details of our romantic involvement. (How tenderly he handled the passports!) His discovery that I was a *published* writer inflamed his imagination; he saw two of my books in a window! He came to the hotel to discuss steamer accommodations with Jo. Passage on the *Vulcania,* from New York to Venice, making stops at Barcelona, Naples, Palermo, Dubrovnik, a cruise of almost three weeks, cost about $250 each.

My wife's new car did not long distract her from the time I was spending in New York.

I had described Jo as an assistant to my editor. Why did all the details prove to be so threadbare? My wife quickly determined that Jo was not in the publishing business, and she confronted me, in the classic manner, when I came back from New York. There is little that is new in these ancient deceptions. She had not meant to force me to a decision, but in the heat of our spat she could not help it. I had to assure her that I was leaving. With control that I admired, at the time, she used the word *separation,* avoiding the dreaded term *divorce.* For several hours this admission released much of the tension; she asked where we were going, and I told her. We were, as was said, civilized about it. I had hoped to spare her anguish. At that moment it was hell for one of us; but if I compromised, it would be hell for us both.

I packed my bags and took a train for New York. It was apparent to Jo, when she opened the door, that the die had been cast, and that from now on we would be forging ties that would test our affections and our natures. A few days later we sailed on the *Vulcania.* We had the pleasure of stops in Barcelona and Mallorca—Barcelona and the Gaudis we liked so much we thought we might come back, if Venice failed us. A friend wired to say that my wife had not been well, but she was now back at her teaching, and seemed much better.

The turn of events had brought Jo and me closer together, and the ties we were making had been tested. We lived well together. Living together suited us fine. Jo would prove to be a very independent young woman, with absolutely minimal needs for entertainment and distractions. We could sit or stroll for hours, people-watching. I had begun to make some notes for my new work, and it did not occur to her that this was competition. Her observing eyes were often keener than mine, and there was more to be seen than we could absorb. Jo soon became the first reader of my manuscripts, and reader of the proofs.

An old boat, relatively speaking, the *Vulcania* had about it a riper sense of leisure, of elegance and of service than I had experienced. The clatter of plates and cutlery was common, but voices seemed to be subdued. There was also a relaxing ease between the server and the well-served. We loved it.

Perhaps every cruise ship is a ship of fools. Circumstance has selected them from the millions who are still at home, going about their business, and it is not easy to be long out of this world in such an exposed and vulnerable manner. Some dim image of Shangri-la looms far up ahead—it is never the port where you are anchored—

and some haunting image of the past hovers in the darkness behind. A big steamer is a remarkable refuge from both the up ahead and what is behind. Each day there was a new menu to be mastered; each night, the horseplay and the dancing. The dancing could be great! "Arrivederci Roma" was a new and catchy tune.

One of the passengers, a well-curved young woman, traveling with her cat in a large hamper, was in the process of divorcing a husband of fourteen months. "And every one of them was hell," she told us. It was for this hell he was now paying. Having heard that I was a writer, she asked what it was I had written. She was a reader. How was it she had not heard of me, or of my books? This depressed her long day in Barcelona, until the truth of the matter dawned on her. I was an impostor, passing myself off as a writer. This discovery—shared with the passengers—proved to be exhilarating, and preoccupied her as far as Naples, where she disembarked. In a marvelous passage, the Swiss writer Max Frisch speaks of the great things about dogs—you either love them or you needn't have them—and this is also true of cats. Her cat was much loved, and lapped cream from her saucer when she was having tea.

We made a brief stop in Greece, which the movies had prepared us for, the simple village life that seemed to be on hold until the arrival and whir of the cameras. The sense of unreality—I realized later—testified to what was actually real about it. A pause seemed to have occurred, with the boat's arrival, in whatever it was that was going on. The sun shone. We sat at a teetering table waiting for the stopped time to start up.

When, at the pier in Dubrovnik, on seeing Jo, several of the young men cried "Gioconda! Gioconda!" it was a moment in my life that still gives me pleasure. The steamer's approach to Venice—the dawn sea becalmed, abandoned dwellings on islands that seemed to be drifting—was so gradual, with the engines silenced, it seemed to diminish what was actually happening. We had arrived! With Lawrence, I could cry, "Look! We have come through!" I had a glimpse up the Grand Canal before tugs towed us to where we seemed to dock in Lilliputia, a miniature city when seen from the steamer's deck.

I had brought along a stock of Marsh-Wheeling stogies, which I nervously escorted through customs, then found a porter to cart our many bags to the Locanda Montin. There we received the welcome we very much needed, in the absence of Sam Kaner, whose wife was having a baby. Sylvia Brown was actually in the process of moving from her garden apartment the fifty yards to Sam Kaner's penthouse, but there were formalities to be settled before we could take possession.

What sort of occupants were we? How long did we plan to stay? The apartment was hung with many bad Venetian paintings, of the sort the owners get so fond of, was furnished with fragile "antiques"; the bookshelves sagged with mildewed books. An itemized list of these valuables covered more than twenty pages. As tenants, we were responsible for them. We met with one of the owners, an elderly *avvocato* of such reticence, distinction and good breeding that speech of any kind was not in order. He proved to be, once out of his chair, six feet five inches tall; at the table where we assembled in the Locanda Montin, he was compelled to sit with his knees in the aisle. There was not much in the way of communication. We eagerly agreed with everything. Ten days later we were given occupancy. The floor of crushed marble, spotted with throw rugs, seemed designed to conceal the scorpions that came in from the garden, but all of that was in our future. In the immediate and pressing present there was a tub, a shower attachment, hot water, real plumbing, and gas. One of the low tables, and a mound of art books, supported my portable electric typewriter. Would it run on the local current? I had come supplied with a transformer. After all, I was a modern traveler—how would I shave?

I had also come to Venice to work, and I was in a fever to get started. I had brought with me (of all things!) the opening chapter of *Ceremony in Lone Tree,* the driest of enterprises for a city built on islands. Just down the path to the entrance, we could see the canal barges passing, with their cases of Campari and Coca-Cola, the boatman leaning on the tiller as he gave us a few arias from Verdi.

More than ten years later, after Jo and I had returned to Venice, I wrote *Love Affair: A Venetian Journal.*

Accustomed to the bizarre, our friend from California has come to see for himself if we are living in Venice. We assure him that we are. A lease has been signed to ensure our exile. Already my wife Jo has been lost and found. Bells are ringing. The light seems to vibrate with their clamor. Our friend impatiently waits for this unaccustomed racket to stop. Through the gate at the entrance he has left open we watch a barge drift past, we hear the lap of water, we note the cases of Campari, Punt e Mes, and Coca-Cola. The man at the tiller—he leans on it like a fence rail—wears a striped T-shirt, the smile of a happy pirate. To Jo he waves. She is popular with pirates from the way she goes up and down the city's bridges. He is there and gone. There are shouts like a street brawl as he greets his friends.

Right there on both sides of the Rio San Trovaso was everything we needed for housekeeping: a bar with the bottled water, the brandy, the wine (all delivered in a hamper, with a cash discount); a baker with whole-wheat bread (on certain days; on others, a Venetian shrug); several vegetable stands, run by the ladies, with the assistance of a lout who sat on the cartons, reading comic books; a shop with butter, cream to be spooned, and a basket of Russian-roulette eggs (refunds to Jo, a trusted consumer); and just a sprint or a stroll to the south, the promenade of the Zattere, the Montparnasse of Venice, with the decks of tables bobbing on the water as the *vaporettos* skied in for the stop. We soon had our café, and our waiter:

The happy few in Venice have a window on a garden. We are among the happy few, but our happiness is clouded. Venetian cats pad in and out of the window at night, transporting kittens, live bait, and the heads of fish. At the foot of our bed, on which they land with a plop, they launder and dry clean the family pelts, check on gains and losses, practice cat witchery. Their motors hum like refrigerators. There is one with one eye: it winks and flares like the flame of a match. We are cat people, and they seem to know it. The word has spread. By the light of morning we examine saucers tongue-buffed to gleam like enamel. Cat tracks on the table, cat hairs on the chairs, cat smears on my papers, but no visible cats. They are night strollers. During the day they go about masked. A carpenter has come to put a screen at the window, but the idea is novel and will take much reflection. While it is under advisement our new friends pad in and out.

Was there anything like it on the planet? An Italian or a Greek steamer might be docked there, about to depart for Cythera! The Adriatica liners, white and gleaming as yachts, with a crew of villains visible at the portholes, went to such places as Cairo and Istanbul, with travelers long abandoned by Conrad. Week after week we thought about it, but they were not our favorite places. We were holding out for Corfu, Athens and the isles of Greece. There was also—for a month at a time—a battered freighter undergoing repairs that required jackhammers, docked for these repairs on Giudecca, so that each sound carried across the water. But we were, after all, still *on* the planet. For seven cents we could ride, from where we were seated, down the canal and across the bay to the Piazza San Marco, a stage with the world's players on it, the air above it a swirl of color as the local pigeons zoomed in for a landing. What could one do with all this grandeur?

Her name is Dora. She acquired us in an involved transaction concerned with the washing of two bed sheets. The sheets are large, the color and weight of sailcloth, deliberately constructed to outlast the sleeper. But they are not easily washed. To be used as sheets, rather than a shroud, they have to be ironed. The first takes water, which is not in short supply; the second takes electric current that is sold by the drip, like maple syrup. We persuaded a lady in the Campo Santa Margherita (we saw her, Vermeer-like, ironing at an open window) to wash and iron our two sheets for 950 lire. That's a dollar and fifty cents, and it took her a week. This led to a discussion with the baker's wife on the curious scarcity of laundries in Venice. She had not heard about laundries. Anything that gets dirty is washed by a maid. If one had a house, what one had to have next was a maid. Dora Rizzoli, a Rossellini-type woman, long accustomed to making crucial decisions, proved to be willing to wash and iron our sheets, and thereby acquired us.

Jo sleeps. One arm lies at her side, the palm up, as if she floated on the quilt pattern beneath her. Her head is turned to the light, her lips slightly parted, her right hand bent at the wrist like a drooping flower.

Where is she off to, here in Venice?

My breathing is hushed, as if I might hear.

We found we could look at it, and its strolling players, for several hours most days, and another stroll in the evening, when the soft glow of the lamps transformed the real into a surreal canvas. Do you tire of this hyperbole, reader? People are not lacking who *hate* Venice, some of whom have actually been there. When it rains, we are of that number. Or on any one of those hot days of summer, the fetid air smelling of the slued-up garbage, or of a nearby canal that is being cleaned, just a whiff of the stench suffocating. The human folly of having built such a city in the first place, then leaving people to live in a ruin that resists burial but does not resist reminding you of it.

The unsigned murals of Venice, hung in plein air, compete favourably with those displayed at the Biennale. They are old in subject but modern in taste, avant-garde in their harmony of color and texture. The instinct for the ready-made and labeled object comprehends the ready-made and framed abstraction. Walls, doorways and windows, patterns of bricks and mortar, peeling strips of plaster with the gloss of leather, colors blended by time and mixed by the weather, graffiti and collages, the assembly of devices, emblems and symbols in the

476

*gondola, seem to be lacking nothing but the signature of the artist.
If everyone is an artist—a currently fashionable notion—Venice provides everyone with his own ready-made work of art.*

We surely had the best of it, the weather so unseasonable we came
away with a dreamer's notion of summer in Venice—hardly a day of
the stupefying sirocco, the languor that drugs all senses. In its place
we had showers, dramatic blasts of thunder that seemed to roll right
out of the paintings, with crisp, scoured skies, whitecaps on the bay,
and even happy surprises from the butcher. (The beast lies there, but
you have to point out, or divine, what part of it you would like to
be eating.) There is no Gorgonzola anywhere like what we ate that
summer—and that is why: we ate it all. I drank the local Merlot like
water, and reserved the Brolio Chianti for heavy dining. I found and
bought some good pipes, tinned English tobacco, but I did not light
up a smokable cigar, other than my Marsh-Wheeling stogies.

To top it off, even my work went well, and I had a finished
manuscript early in September. I shipped it off—not without some
apprehension—to Hiram Haydn, of the new firm of Atheneum. To
celebrate this occasion, Jo and I took off for Rome, which we found
was not a great place for the walkers we had learned to be in Venice.
The world of wheels and smog soon had us wheezing, so we went
north to Assisi, the landscape one unfolding vibrant painting. We saw
the Pieros in Arezzo, then went on for several good days in Florence
and the memorable confrontation with Botticelli's *Primavera*. Nothing
prepares the viewer for such a marvel but the painting itself. I was
dazzled by its matchless imaginative power, as I would be by Bosch's
Garden of Earthly Delights. How did the modern painter, beholding
such works, make peace with his own shrinking talents? And how
else describe them? I had not been in Florence since Lorne Ward and
I had sat pondering the octopus in our soup, as we exchanged our
less than fearless glances. Jo was able to persuade me to buy for myself
an elegant tobacco pouch, just what I needed, and we bought for her
a very swanky handbag, much admired by the ladies in the second-
class train coach to Bologna.

Every time we saw one of the white, gleaming boats of the
Adriatica Line, at the dock or headed seaward, we spoke of going to
Greece. Occasionally we saw a loose pack of *Wandervögel*, in their
lederhosen and rucksacks, their hair sun-bleached, go clomping by
in their heavy hiking boots. Where were they going? How? We never
actually saw them on one of the boats.

I finally determined, after a week of asking questions, that a Greek boat, the *Philippos*—once said to be a Thames river steamer—sailed from Venice to Piraeus, the port of Athens, and then to Mykonos and other Greek islands. That was for us. But what did this boat look like? I was told I would see that on the day it sailed.

This proved to be in mid-October—a fine time, we were assured, for our sea adventure. The *Philippos* was docked some distance down the Zattere, where the scene was cluttered, an unpainted, peeling hulk less than half the size I had fancied. The cabins proved to be inspired makeshifts for trapping the passengers below deck. I thought of Conrad. I tried, unsuccessfully, to put it out of my mind. I clearly received and recorded the signal that this boat was more than a calculated risk. So what did I do? I calmly began unpacking our bags. On an upper level, there were five or six cabins with teak and mahogany doorways and brass fittings, with an area for dining and lounging, but we were down where the galley slaves were chained between bouts of rowing. I reminded myself that Homer's wine-dark sea was just a big pond.

From the sea, Piraeus, the port of Athens, smoldered like the waste-land of the Jersey marshes, or, more poetically speaking, the gates of hell. Undecided, Soby leaned on the rail rather than risk an early commitment. Behind the sulphurous cloud, on good authority, was Greece. A wind smelling of diesel fuel held the ship flags taut as fraternity pennants, puffing the cheeks of Miss Kollwitz with more than words could express. One sleeve of Soby's promised sweater was looped around her neck . . . A babushka, souvenir of Corfu, flapped about her face.

"Look! Look!" she cried. "We are here!"

(*What a Way to Go,* 1962)

There were no casualties as far as Piraeus, where we were bused to the Acropolis, an experience so out of scale with a schoolboy's impressions I was both staggered and dazzled. It had been true, then? All this time, there had once been giants on the earth. I am also confident that only ruins have this power over the romantic imagination (mine), but I could not people this hallowed ground with real flesh-and-blood figures. Nor can I now. It seemed to have been conceived as a ruin in order to have on me this overwhelming effect. I was awed, and stooped to fondle bits of the shrapnel-like marble that were strewn along the paths.

A Greek schoolboy of such uncommon beauty I simply stared at him, as at a clever restoration, held our attention as he reeled off a litany of names and dates that meant less to him than they did to me. With his dark, bushy brows, his head of thick curly locks, his bronze

478

skin stretched tight over his bursting flesh, he would live to see (in my opinion) this hallowed place sold to the highest bidder. He was a Greek and a realist (a redundancy), not a sentimental schoolboy who had once made a trireme out of nine boxes of Diamond kitchen matches. Both of us were ignorant of the forces once released on this elevation. I bought postcards from him, and touched the skin of his palm when I gave him the coins. He, too, ignorant though he was, had some of this force pulsing in his veins, and it filled me with awe.

A little after midnight, I was awakened by the rolling and pitching of the boat. At the portholes, the blast of the waves made a luminous froth. Everything trembled as if struck by blows of a hammer. I knew, if I knew anything, that the hour had come. Water sloshed under the berths, and to stay in them we had to brace our feet against the frames. Doors flapped in the hall as if loose on their hinges. I futilely rang for the cabin porter. The occasional buoyant inertness of the boat gave me the feeling that it bobbed, like a cork, on the surface, at the mercy of the next wave. Hearing a bell clang, I thought it must be a signal to abandon ship. How did one do it? Ankle-deep water sloshed in the gangway. The lights blinked off, leaving the cabin in a glow that was phosphorescent. My words were not a comfort to Jo. I made a note of this, being a writer.

And then, as if the storm had been turned off with the switch of a button, we were becalmed in a breakwater. I saw a ring of lights, splintered with gusts of rain. Dimly I perceived a few ghostly houses. I heard shouting, the clank of chains, and the *put-put* of an approaching motor. Someone was disembarking. This inspiration came to me too late. I opened the cabin door to see an old man, in his shirttails, calmly urinating into the sloth. He nodded to me, a cigarette dangling at his lip.

"Where are we?" I asked. At the moment, I did not understand his reply. We were at Mykonos, anchored in the small harbor. The gentle rocking of the boat was actually soothing. A sputtering flame of consciousness that fed on my nerves kept me awake for another five or ten minutes, then, seated at the edge of Jo's berth, I lay back with my head in her lap and slept.

What we would do—we were seated at breakfast, our elbows on the soiled tablecloth, a blue-black, white-capped sea sporting like dolphins at the portholes, the light a shimmering dazzle—what we would do would be to go on to Rhodes, and from there *fly* back to Venice. I had never flown, but I could be persuaded to fly for my life.

By noon we were on Rhodes, a picture-postcard fortress lapped

479

by tides of sea and light. We had lunch in the one resort hotel on the beach, the window framing a view of the *Philippos* basking in the sun of the harbor. It looked pretty good. The walled city of Rhodes, thronged with *Wandervögel* (where had they been during the blow?), was as beautiful as the brochure insisted, and only a day's sail from Piraeus. The sea was calm. Had I perhaps exaggerated the crisis? Since the boat was there, and our bags were on it, we sailed peacefully back to Piraeus, from there to Corfu, and from Corfu back to Venice, where it seemed that the dusk came perceptibly sooner, and the shadows on the canals were longer.

These October days we've had barges from Chioggia, painted like banners, moored in the Rio San Trovaso. The men sleep on the decks. We see them plainly at the end of the tunnel that leads to our garden. Lanterns gleam in the hold where they sit eating: they glance at me with the eyes of men sorting booty. These sea dogs are another race from Venetians, they have the air of whalers among city people. Their voices have a deeper register; it pleases me that their speech smacks of faraway places. I think of wandering Greeks, of affluent Phoenicians, of barbarians who raid and loot by water. As the sky cools, the light of dusk enhances the color of their barges. The city before them lies waiting to be ravished, while the leaders discuss the terms of the ransom. The mood is optimistic. A carnival will celebrate the settlement. In the morning, however, I am pleased to find them gone, having sailed at dawn for Byzantium, their holds crowded, their decks jammed with impressions that remain unchallenged. We did not come here to gawk at sea dogs who had lost their bite.

Along the Zattere, most of the tables sat empty; the chairs were being moved back inside. The sound of the water lapping the promenade, slapping the steps of the piazza, gave us a bit of a chill. The light over the city—as one saw it from the crest of the Accademia bridge—was very much as it had been painted by four hundred years of Venetian painters. You could pick your own light, and your own painter, but when we stopped for an espresso we took care to sit in the sun. In the dark, winding alleys we caught the damp whiff and savor of what it would be like in the winter. Snow on the gondolas? We had already seen it in the photographs. How smart we had been to have made the arrangements to be back in San Miguel by December, basking in the Mexican sunshine at Christmas.

Back in the summer, I had received, and accepted, an offer to teach for a year at Los Angeles State College, beginning in the fall

480

of 1960. This would take care of our immediate future, so all we had to deal with was the immediate present. After several days of drizzle, early in November (there is nothing—no, nothing—like a November drizzle in Venice), we made our reservations to sail on the *Columbus* to New York.

Drizzle or no, it proved a painful parting from our friends. Two of our Dora's sons appeared with a barge as wide as a café deck to transport our luggage to the boat. As the drizzle increased, she was encouraged to come up the gangplank for a drink in the bar. She approved of the elegance of the furnishings. It was how, in her opinion, people of Jo's distinction should travel. As we departed, a rising tide lapped the promenade, prophesying, once more, a sea burial for the city. I remember that my sorrow was nicely neutralized by my relief.

Following dinner—our best meal since a marvelous lasagna in Florence—we had our first intimation that the Adriatic also had its surprises. A gale swept the decks. Most of the night, we rolled and tossed. It was somewhat better out of Barcelona—we always meant to get back to Barcelona—but once we had passed through the Strait of Gibraltar, we had an unrelieved winter passage. A dim, mist-filtered light—ideal for paintings of dreams, nightmares, and caverns—veiled whatever might be seen in any direction. I looked with longing at a steamer said to be headed for the Canaries. The Canaries! Why hadn't we thought of them sooner?

We had six days of it, the dining room empty (I had the attention of half a dozen waiters at breakfast), but it proved to be the ideal circumstance for my rediscovery of Thomas Mann's *The Magic Mountain*. The small, dimly lit library, no larger than a cabin, the sea rising and falling at the portholes, restored to me the magical shimmer of Hans Castorp's dream in the snow at Davos. In my mind seascape and snowscape are now of a piece, as if I vividly recalled a darkened theater and a film of Castorp's adventure.

At the bar, I had the time to discuss with the barman, in my fractured Italian, the trials of life at sea. He was from Verona, but seldom saw it. He belonged to this boat, to this life, where he worked a long day, slept in a dormitory, and saw the world, if at all, through a porthole. A handsome fellow, Giuseppe, with a Toscanini moustache, flashing eyes, and a gallant manner with the ladies. But where were they? Bundled up in their berths? What a day it was for him when Jo returned to her place. "Enchoy life!" he cried, as we hoisted our glasses, and he exchanged with me glances of affection and envy. How could I not, with such a girl! There was no revelry or horseplay. Mournfully the orchestra tooted "Arrivederci Roma." A pair of

481

diehards grimly hugged each other. Would it never end? Then one night it did; the ceasing of the battle created an ominous vacuum. What next? I got up early to be prepared for it. Far on the horizon, I saw the telltale hint of land. In the dawn, light birds soared. Over there somewhere, beyond where I was looking, but where I had been born, bred and trained to look, was America.

In New York, I spent some time with my editor, Hiram Haydn, who had some suggestions about my new book, but I was eager to buy a car suitable for our trip to Mexico. I had hoped to find one of the classic Thunderbird coupes, but none were available. In the suburbs of Long Island, driven there by a friend, we found a Studebaker Golden Hawk that appealed to my long history with Studebakers. We loaded up with our luggage, some of which we had left in storage, then drove through a winter landscape that looked like home to me for a reunion with Dorothy and Granville Hicks in Grafton. I reminded myself to make sure, before we left Grafton, to check the antifreeze.

This meeting proved to be our first chance to share with friends the many months of our love affair with Venice. Just ten years later, in May of 1969, Jo and I would persuade Dorothy and Granville to visit us. These happy comminglings of people and places that so often seem to be there for the asking, but will somehow prove to be so elusive, had the bloom of an experience that we may have sensed would not be repeated. The cold drive had given me a touch of arthritis in several fingers, and I was persuaded by Dorothy to apply a remedy she had found in an old almanac—a daily dose of vinegar mixed with honey. I gave it a try. It tasted so god-awful I had the assurance it must be good for me.

Once more, to begin a new life, I was headed west. This time my longed-for companion was there beside me, and I had never felt so confident about the future. First we would have our winter in San Miguel Allende—to which we both looked forward—then in the spring we would drive to Southern California and settle in for a year's teaching. Jo and I were in agreement that the Palisades, just west of Bel Air, would be where we would live. *Ceremony in Lone Tree*— that very dry book written in a wet place—was scheduled to be published in September, and gave us a welcome point of focus. Hovering over us both, however, was the looming divorce that could no longer be ignored or evaded. It had been mercifully suspended during our stay in Venice, and for that I was profoundly grateful. Now that we were back, it was the first fact in our life together.

I was fifty years of age, and that was how I looked. Photographs taken by Jo, at Rancho Atascadero, show a man in what might be called his prime, his face in profile, his hands in the pockets of a coveted field jacket, the sun casting a shadow on the wall of a handball court. This shot will appear on the jacket flap of his new book. It would be hard to say to what extent he felt it, but he is at the threshold of a new life, although still clad in his familiar, self-loomed cloak of light.

Jo tells him, as the shutter clicks, that he looks great.

CODA

I had little or no suspicion that my true feelings were precisely those that I would learn to conceal.

There is a moment in *Will's Boy* where my father and I, headed for California, are driving south from Chicago through the early winter morning. The first light of dawning seems to bathe the world. Up ahead the narrow road swerves to pass between farm buildings, a frame house with the sun blazing on its windows, a red barn that casts a purple shadow on the powdering of snow. The blaze of sunlight and the deep shadow, the sound made by the car as it whooshed between the buildings, left on me an impression that I would feel compelled to recover. Fifty years after this moment I attempt to recapture the spell of that morning.

Near Springfield the road curved between farm buildings that sit so close to its edge I could see in the windows. We crossed a bridge, the water black beneath it, a big tilted barn dark against the snow, with a deep purple shadow beside it. Nothing special. Just something I would never forget.

Something we never forget, something we repeatedly remember, an impression fleeting as a casual gesture or the unprovoked glance of a stranger.

In her face, like a sunburst, I swear that what I saw was my own salvation . . . as if the window of the car framed my conversion.

A solo performer on the flying trapeze, the writer does not know, as he soars through the air, if or not the safety net is stretched beneath him: addicted to flying, he is held aloft by his cloak of light.

484

Printed July 1993 in Santa Barbara & Ann
Arbor for the Black Sparrow Press by Mackintosh
Typography & Edwards Brothers Inc. Text set in
Sabon by Words Worth. Design by Barbara Martin.
This edition is published in paper wrappers;
there are 250 hardcover trade copies;
140 hardcover copies have been numbered & signed
by the author; & 26 copies handbound in boards
by Earle Gray are lettered & signed by the author.

Photo: Barbara Hall

Long regarded as one of the most gifted American writers, Wright Morris received the National Book Award in 1956 for his novel *The Field of Vision*. His most recent novel, *Plains Song,* won the 1981 American Book Award for Fiction. He is the author of seventeen other novels; several collections of short stories; books of criticism and a number of photo-text volumes. He and his wife make their home in Mill Valley, California.